René Girard
and Creative Reconciliation

René Girard

and Creative Reconciliation

Edited by
Vern Neufeld Redekop
and Thomas Ryba

LEXINGTON BOOKS
Lanham • Boulder • New York • Toronto • Plymouth, UK

Published by Lexington Books
A wholly owned subsidiary of Rowman & Littlefield
4501 Forbes Boulevard, Suite 200, Lanham, Maryland 20706
www.rowman.com

10 Thornbury Road, Plymouth PL6 7PP, United Kingdom

British Library Cataloguing in Publication Information Available

Library of Congress Cataloging-in-Publication Data Available

978-0-7391-6900-1 (cloth: alk. paper) -- 978-0-7391-69001-8 (electronic)

∞™ The paper used in this publication meets the minimum requirements of American National Standard for Information Sciences Permanence of Paper for Printed Library Materials, ANSI/NISO Z39.48-1992.

Printed in the United States of America

We dedicate this book to Roel Kaptein, the first to apply Girard's mimetic theory systematically to violent inter-group rivalries, thus deconstructing the dynamics of contemporary identity-based conflicts and furthering the goal of reconciliation without scapegoats.

We also dedicate this book to Rwandan genocide victim/survivor Teteri and Alphonse, a man who killed members of her family (both pictured on the front cover); they represent the many who have offered and received forgiveness as part of reconciliation processes after grievous human atrocities.

Contents

Acknowledgments

In 2006, the Colloquium on Violence and Religion held its annual conference at Saint Paul University in Ottawa, Canada, on the theme Mimesis, Creativity, and Reconciliation. With over 200 participants and over 100 presentations, the Conference proved to be highly generative. That conference was the beginning of two volumes: this volume and the companion, *René Girard and Creative Mimesis.* However, these volumes are far more than a record of proceedings. After the conference, the various authors kept working on their ideas. Indeed, some of the chapters are completely new with some authors interacting with texts and ideas that did not yet exist back in 2006. A few of the chapters were not rooted in the 2006 Conference but were written specifically for this book. Together, these books represent cutting-edge thinking on mimetic theory and reconciliation. While the two books are complementary—some of the chapters could well have been in either book—each is meant to stand alone.

René Girard's work provided the heuristic categories and the launchpad for this effort. As will be noted throughout, all of the authors engage his thought in a respectful way. This engagement has proved to be creative in its own way, with new ideas and insights building on and going beyond the original exposition of Girardian mimetic and scapegoat theory.

For our part as editors, we have benefitted personally from reading and re-reading the various chapters. Our own understandings of positive and creative mimesis and reconciliation have grown through the process.

Eric Wrona and Kathleen Bromelow, our Lexington editors, have been a pleasure to work with as we made final decisions that helped polish the finished text.

Bringing two volumes to publication, during a period in which we have had full-time teaching responsibilities and a number of other research projects, has meant an investment in time beyond normal work hours. This has demanded the understanding of our lifelong partners, Gloria Neufeld Redekop and Christine Ryba, who have in their own way made an indirect contribution to the project.

We would be remiss without thanking Saint Paul University, for graciously hosting the original Conference, and the Social Sciences and Humanities Research Council of Canada, for providing generous funding for the Conference.

We wish to acknowledge the work of *Initiative communautaire pour l'unité et la réconciliation* (ICOPUR), a group of chaplains in Rwanda that facilitates reconcilation encounters between victims and perpetators of the genocide, such as those between Teteri and Alphonse. Teteri offered forgiveness to Alphonse, who had killed her mother, sister, and brother, and treats him now as her son. Alphonse, for his part, is doing what he can for Teteri, including help in her garden plot (the scene of the picture on the front cover). Pierre and Judy Allard of Just.Equipping arranged for Bugenimana Jean d'Amour to take the picture and send it to us.

Introduction

Deep-Rooted Conflict, Reconciliation, and Mimetic Theory

Vern Neufeld Redekop and Thomas Ryba

It is in the context of violent deep-rooted conflict that reconciliation becomes the greatest challenge. Violence can take on many forms. Rape, mass murders, gas chambers, hacking with machetes, suicide bombers, bombs from the sky—these are the dramatic, visible, and unambiguous forms of violence. Other forms are less tangible and visceral: the lateral violence by a colleague who uses innuendo to be sure you don't get a promotion or fraudulent selling of shares, products, or sub-prime mortgages. It can also be indirect and subtle, such as policies of assimilation that not only deprive people of their cultures but are an assault on the human spirit, depriving people of a capacity to take meaningful action. Violence wounds one's spirit, just as it destroys our bodies. It is the covert or overt destruction of one's body, possessions, relationships, and sense of well-being. Violence can be individual or collective. Violent acts may be individual basic actions, chains of actions, on-going practices, or systemic structures that are patterns of hurtful actions that have a cumulative effect.

The effects of violence are physical, emotional, cognitive, and spiritual. Direct physical effects are straightforward, but indirect physical effects include stress-related diseases, reduced physical capacity, and diseases introduced through violent actions (HIV-AIDS introduced through rape, for example). Emotional effects are anger, resentment, shame, and inner pain over profound losses. Secondarily, the effects of emotional trauma could be broken relationships, an inability to cope, and traumatic stress disorders. Distrust and hatred get passed on through generations, leaving a legacy of dehuman-

1

izing enmity. At the cognitive level, there is hermeneutical wounding—an inability to make sense of the situation—coupled with a profound sense of injustice. These effects prepare individuals and groups for another round of violence. Violence can overwhelm one's consciousness. Spiritually, violence wrecks havoc with one's capacity to look hopefully beyond immediate challenges and find the strength to stand up to injustices. It creates an ontological rift (Chanteur 1992) between peoples, making profound human connections well-nigh impossible. Taking away an appreciation for what is good and beautiful, it reduces people to unidimensional, narcissistically wounded individuals.

Reconciliation is meant to constructively and redemptively address the legacy of violence. This is a complex and delicate matter since it is a complex process that cannot be forced or contrived. It is wonderful, almost miraculous, when the barriers between people with deep enmity melt away and people become re-connected. However, when reconciliation is forced, this pressure can re-victimize those already hurt. There are different taxonomies of reconciliation—political, social, and inter-personal to use level of conflict as the organizational structure—as well as a distinction between instrumental and socio-emotional approaches (Nadler et al. 2008). Reconciliation is considered both a process and a goal. We will return to these general observations, later. First, we will examine the dynamics of deep-rooted conflict from the perspective of an integral approach to mimetic theory.

DEEP-ROOTED CONFLICT FROM A MIMETIC PERSPECTIVE

John W. Burton gave definition to deep-rooted conflict in terms of identity-needs (1990a; 1990b; 1996). He recognized that there is something at the nexus of cognition, emotion, and physicality that reacts intensely when threatened. This something he referred to variously as "ontological" needs or "human identity" needs. It is the threat to these ontological needs that drives violent deep-rooted conflict. His insight into this, brought about by his exposure to needs theory, revolutionized his thinking about conflict. However, his work, and that of a constellation of needs theorists in conflict studies, did not address *the dynamic interplay between individuals and groups* that gives rise to both the ontological needs and the desire to see them fulfilled (Burton 1990b). In this regard, Girardian mimetic theory plays a significant role—named after the Greek work *mimēsis* from which we get "mime" and "imitation." Girard speaks of ontological desires—desires to be the Model or become someone like a Model. These are expressed through mimetic desire for an object, but behind this lies the ontological dimension; the self wants all of the satisfaction that the Model apparently enjoys on account of the object. Ontological *needs*, in Burton's sense, are social constructs around what the self deems essential for their sense of being; they are experienced both individually and collectively. Needs, in this sense, are closely associated with desires in the Girardian sense. This being the case, it makes sense to argue that human identity need satisfiers are formed in the context of relationships. They may be shaped benignly as we learn from our role models—often parents or grandparents—what is truly important. (This is the learning through imitation or mimesis made possible through our mirror neurons.[1]) It can also be that we derive our identity need satisfiers through our rivals, through those *other* to us but yet with whom we identify (see Goodhart, chapter 2 for the development of this concept). Both ontological needs and ontological desires can be understood as deriving from relational ontology, a concept developed by Richardson and Frost (chapter 10). This implies that Girard's mimetic theory becomes essential to an understanding of the dynamics of deep-rooted conflict.

What Burton, along with other needs theorists, offers Girard is a taxonomy of the human soul expressed in the language of identity needs. Satisfiers to each of these needs could be the Objects of mimetic desire. What Girard offers Burton are essential insights into how these non-instinctual needs/desires are produced and why they figure so prominently as human motivators. Put in practical terms, using Girard to understand identity needs enables us to de-construct the hermeneutics of justification that drives the perpetrators of genocide and other human atrocities.

Girard makes the case that desire for an Object is mediated through a Model by a Subject. That is, the Subject mimetically takes on the desire of the Model and in doing so wishes to be like the Model. Objects of desire may be physical or they may be intangible, like fame, relationships, or happiness. Even with physical objects, it may be what they represent, what meaning is attached to them, that gives them significance. Inherent in mimetic games, is a sense of justice—if the other person can have a certain Object, then I should have a right to the same thing. In the case of lateral violence directed to one's peers within an oppressed community, it becomes, "If the other person (Model) is getting ahead (Object), and I am not getting ahead (Object deprivation), I will make certain that the other person will be brought down (deprived of Object)."

RWANDA AS AN EXAMPLE OF MIMETIC VIOLENCE

One of the most horrible examples of human atrocity in the latter part of the twentieth century was the Rwandan genocide of Tutsis starting in April 1994. Approaching this from the perspective of mimetic theory in relation to ontological needs/desires will enable us to understand the hermeneutics of justification that drove the Hutu perpetrators.

In the late 1800s, German explorers came upon the Tutsi kingdom of what is now Rwanda and Burundi. (For an analytical account of this history see Redekop and Gasana 2007.) Seeing the efficient organization and administration of the kingdom in which a Tutsi king and elite governed a mixture of Tutsis, Hutus, and Twa peoples, the Germans declared Tutsis to be Aryans with black skins. In the 1900s, Christian religious educators favored the Tutsis, giving only them the education needed to be leaders within society. Proverbs within the culture systematically made the point that Tutsis were superior. Tutsis received satisfiers for their identity needs: *recognition* as historically superior; *connectedness* through solidarity with colonial masters who were now the Belgians; *security* through the resources and status that flowed to them; power to take *action*, lead, and make things happen; and *meaning* through a worldview that legitimated their place in society. All of these satisfiers became Objects of mimetic desire on the part of Hutus. It is easy to see that with this desire for the Objects was an ontological desire to be like the Tutsis—to be Tutsi.

In the 1950s, a Hutu power movement took hold within the country, and when the Belgians left the country, the majority Hutus took political control, which they held onto until 1994. Through the years there were periodic massacres of Tutsis. The education system was used to demonize Tutsis and the elite structure was taken over by Hutus. All of this can be seen as a protracted attempt to acquire the Object—to have the recognition, power, position, superiority, and control that Tutsis had previously had. However, there was always the nagging sense that at an ontological level, Hutus never became Tutsis, that Tutsis just might be superior, might have something more that was unattainable. In other words, the Tutsis were an Obstacle to obtaining full ontological parity.

New factors were introduced in 1994 that threatened the ontological goals of the Hutu. The Rwandan Patriotic Front (RPF) made up of expatriate Tutsis in Uganda had been making incursions into Rwanda. For them, the Object of mimetic desire was control of and status within Rwanda, which had been denied them for nearly fifty years. The Arusha Accords negotiated between the RPF and the Hutu Government of Rwanda had called for power sharing between Hutu and Tutsis. This represented a profound ontological threat to the Hutu. If they believed unconsciously that Tutsis were superior, while explicitly proclaiming their own superiority, then there was a fear that the Tutsis might again become dominant. From a realist perspective, the goods that were in the hands of the Hutu elite, would have to be shared. The solution that emerged for the Hutu was to exterminate all of the Tutsis. If the Tutsis were all gone, they would have overcome their ontological Obstacle. Driven by a Hutu elite who used the radio to call for the elimination of "cockroaches" (code for "Tutsis"), the Hutu population reacted with widespread violence, using the thousands of machetes ordered for the occasion to hack to death their Tutsi neighbors while the international community stood by impotently. Over 800,000 were killed. Eventually the RPF attacked and defeated the Hutu government, establishing a Uganda-Tutsi dominated government led by President Paul Kagame. In the process, Tutsis mimetically engaged in revenge killing, putting 80,000 Hutus to death.

Many identity groups, if not most, have their own bloody histories. The "Chosen Trauma" of one group becomes the basis for "righting the injustice" and mimetically perpetrating violence against former oppressors resulting in a "Chosen Glory," for the first group and a "Chosen Trauma," for the second (Volkan 1998). In each of these stories, elements of the histories of Hutus and Tutsis can be seen, always with a significant role for mimetic desire, rivalries, and violence.

Reconciliation in the Rwandan context is a complex challenge. It involves the personal experiences of violence, the social implications, and political power dynamics. It involves a long history of differentiation made most explicit in the 1930s by the Belgians, who insisted on everyone having an identity card that labeled them Hutu, Tutsi, or Twa. Reconciliation is about the 1994 genocide, for certain, but it is also about the revenge killings and about the hegemonic structures of domination that were kept intact throughout the colonial and post-colonial history, even though there were shifts in who occupied the position of the dominant.

Even in cases where the violence is not as overt as the Rwandan situation, there are situations of ontological mimetic desire involving a desire to not only have what the other has or desires but to obtain the concomitant ontological need satisfiers such as meaning and justice, relationships and connections, power to make a difference, sense of security and confidence, or recognition. People become deeply hurt, sometimes traumatized over the conflict, and there are a multiplicity of passions—anger, resentment, hatred, fear, depression—that drive the thinking, orientation, attitudes, and behaviors of those involved. All this deepens the challenges of reconciliation.

THE CONCEPT OF RECONCILIATION

Within Christian theology, the language of reconciling and reconciliation has been part of the lexicon since the Apostle Paul wrote about it in his epistles (Romans 5:10; 1 Corinthian 7:11; 2 Corinthians 5:18–20). In the Catholic tradition, there has been a sacrament of Reconciliation (Schillebeeckx 1971). This association with Christianity is one of the reasons why there was a reluctance to use the term "reconcilation" in the context of the social sciences—there was a fear of being tainted by religion (Nadler et al. 2008).

Several factors led to the introduction and popularization of this term within the secular academy and popular culture. The first was the recognition of the concept of deep-rooted conflict and the phenomenon of identity-based atrocities. The usual generic phrase for the pacific, mutually agreed upon, end to conflict was "conflict resolution." However, the qualitative difference between what passes for conflict and the magnitude of the violence with its emotional, physical, and collective consequences called for another term that would indicate a profound coming to terms with the relational, ontological rift. Reconciliation emerged as the concept best suited to describe this constructive coming to terms with deep-rooted conflict (Bar-Siman-Tov 2004).

Second, the emergence of Truth and Reconciliation Commissions (TRC), in the 1990s, made the use of the word "reconciliation" commonplace. There was an intuitive sense that reconciliation was what was needed in the wake of violent conflict. Best known of these was the very public South African TRC, which probably did more than anything to make the term reconciliation part of the global vocabulary. (See Praeg's chapter 11 for more on SA; also Battle 1997; de Gruchy 2002.)

Third, since the turn of the millennium, there has been a burgeoning of academic literature that has examined the nature of reconciliation (Bar-Siman-Tov 2004; Bloomfield et al. 2004; du Bois and Du Bois-Pedain; Kim, et al. 2008; Lederach 1997, 1999; Long and Brecke 2003; Nadler et al. 2008; Philpott 2012; Quinn 2009; Rouhana 2004). This has given the term widespread credibility, making it its own field of research with a characteristic set of agreed-upon insights and a host of distinctions.

Fourth, within another new field of practice and theory, reconciliation (as concept and process) gained considerable traction; namely, the field of restorative justice (Zehr 1990). Starting in the 1970s, this approach emphasized bringing together victims and offenders and letting them work through what actions would make things right, constituting a new way of achieving a sense of justice. Included in the programs were Victim-Offender Reconciliation Programs (VORP). Restorative justice principles have also been applied to large group reconciliation processes (Bloomfield et al. 2003; Battle 1997; de Gruchy 2002; Reddy 2006).

Fifth was the exploration of the many psychodynamics of victimization at both the individual and collective level (Julius et al. 1990; Volkan 1998). This included the popularization of the term Post-Traumatic Stress Disorder. Concepts of victim narratives, Chosen Traumas, dehumanization, historic enmity, and demonization became channels to further explore phenomena of deep-rooted conflict. Given the strong relational component of these ideas, something more that victim-centered therapy was needed, something that involved both victims and perpetrators (in some cases both parties shared each role).

Sixth, religious leaders have "escorted" the term into the political realm (Philpott 2012, 7). Notable among these have been Archbishop Desmond Tutu and Pope John Paul II (*ibid.*). Scholars have followed suit, generating a significant amount of transdisciplinary literature that integrates religious and political dimensions of reconciliation (Appleby 2000; Axworthy 2008; Hertog 2010; Gopin 2002; Battle 1999; Helmiuk and Peterson 2001; de Gruchy 2002; earlier, Johnston and Sampson [1994] were some of the first to make the links between religion and political reconciliation).

Besides the generally shared understanding that reconciliation is needed in the wake of deep-rooted violent conflicts and atrocities, it is also generally agreed that it is both a process and a goal. Also clear is that the process needs to address hurts from the past, preferably in a way that involves making amends (Berg 2009; Philpott 2012; Radzik 2009). Concomitant goals to reconciliation in general are the building of relationships, healing from trauma, structural change, and building a shared identity. Process and goals of reconciliation can be combined into a unified framework (for example see Redekop 2007; 2008).

There are some important distinctions being made about different types of reconciliation. When it comes to social reconciliation between identity groups, a key distinction is between instrumental reconciliation and socioemotional reconciliation (Nadler *et al.* 2008). The first focuses on getting groups that have been at enmity with one another to work together on common super-ordinate goals. The second emphasizes a profound transformation of social dynamics and a healing of the deep psychic wounds resulting from violence. Social reconciliation emphasizes "community-building, relationships, social cohesion, and social processes" (Quinn 2009, 7).

Inter-personal reconciliation can take place in two distinctly different contexts. The first is the context of inter-communal violent conflict where the conflict is personalized. For example, Richard Batsinduka, a Tutsi who lost virtually his entire extended family in the Rwandan genocide, heard about the man who killed his brother on the radio, years after the genocide. He went to the prison where the *genocidiare* was being held and personally reconciled with this person (Redekop 2002). Just.Equipping, an NGO dedicated to restorative justice is involved in Rwanda where they are pairing up victims and perpetrators for this kind of interpersonal reconciliation. The second context is one in which the violence or deep-rooted conflict is unrelated to a wider social context. This could either involve criminal acts or non-criminal actions that are experienced as deeply hurtful. Over the last four decades, there have been a number of forms of VORP to deal with the formal type; reconciliation of the non-criminal deep-rooted conflict can involve formal processes like dialogue, mediation, or Indigenous circle processes, in which an Elder introduces some teaching that frames a process that allows everyone to speak, or may happen informally through conciliatory gestures and restoration of communication channels, opening the way to mutual understanding, apology, forgiveness, and new relationships.

Political reconciliation occurs between groups that are formally constituted as states or as significant ethnonationalist entities such as rebel groups
within a country that are vying for political control—either over the country
as a whole, or, over a separate territory. In their research around reconciliation processes, Long and Brecke (2003) have seen a clear distinction between
approaches that work in each context: at the international level, *signaling*
reconciliation events—ceremonies that involve leaders making costly concessions—are important; at the civil level, a *forgiveness* model is more effective. At the political level, there is more emphasis on building and using
institutions that will address issues of redress of past wrongs, public accountability, and eventually effective governance (Bloomfield et al. 2003). In this
regard there are clear links between public reconciliation and transitional
justice (Quinn 2009). Luttwak, in examining the history of France-German
reconciliation, emphasizes how building personal relationships between leaders can expedite the process (1994). Philpott examines the central ethical
issues involved in political reconciliation. These issues include:

• building socially just institutions and relations between states;
• acknowledgement;
• reparations,
• punishment,
• apology, and
• forgiveness. (2012, 4)

As he frames it, "Reconciliation is not so much a solution to evil as it is a
response to evil, a response that in the political realm will always be partially
achieved, compromised by power, challenged by its sheer complexity, and
often delayed in its enactment" (*ibid.*, 5; for an account of the personal
challenges see Lederach 1999). Writing from South Africa, du Bois and du
Bois-Pedain associate reconciliation with citizenship that "comes into view
only once political community is successfully imagined . . . people reconsti-
tute themselves as citizens of a different society, one in which others matter,
and are owed life chances, too" (2008, 292).

DISCURSIVE FIELD OF RECONCILIATION

As the field of reconciliation has grown exponentially over the past three
decades, a number of concepts have emerged that play an integral role. First,
the concept of truth has become central. Note the association of "truth" and
"reconciliation" in the more than twenty commissions that go by that name.
Truth, the telling of truth, the remembering of truth, the exposing of the
truth—all are linked to the concept of injustice. It is the truth about injus-

tices—from unjustified killing, to rape, to character assassination—that needs to be made explicit. This truth-telling is associated with a public record, in part, so the same atrocity does not happen again. It comes out of a primal, visceral passion to address injustices, highlighting justice as a key term in the reconciliation discursive field. Justice as a concept raises many questions, including its relationship to punishment, mercy, and forgiveness (Minow 1998; Murphy and Hampton 1988). Justice making processes—judicial, retributive, and/or restorative—become pivotal and diverse. In Rwanda, for example, the 110,000 prisoners would have taken too long to judge in courts of law so the traditional *gacaca* process was introduced to try many at the community level; meanwhile, the key leaders were tried at the Arusha Tribunal. All of this is linked to healing, another key word. The experience of victims after being violated becomes a matter of increasing significance for reconciliation. Trauma, and the newly popularized notion of Post-Traumatic Stress Disorders (PTSD), have helped to define the challenges of reconciliation (Herman 1997). Adding another wrinkle, new research is starting to move from individual victimization to experiences of collective victimization and how meaning is made of these experiences within different collectivity-oriented cultures (MacDonald-Miner 2013).

This constellation of truth, justice, and trauma highlights the importance of another conceptual constellation—forgiveness, mercy, and pardon. In the search for justice, neither strict justice or even punishment can carry the weight of transforming relationships (Minow 1998; Ricoeur 2000; Volf 1996). Strict justice has many inherent problems as has the mimetically induced vengeance passion that Girard poignantly describes. How to understand and frame forgiveness remains a complex problem in reconciliation studies. How important are apologies, expressions of remorse, and reparations as pre-conditions? As significant as these might seem, are they necessary? What about the observation that forgiveness is a necessary condition for leading a happy, creative, and productive life? (There is now evidence for instance, that it is a pre-condition for producing the measurable alpha-waves and theta-waves in the brain that are associated with creativity; see Hardt 2007.) These concepts then invoke the notion of memory. To what degree must we make memories of past victimization central to our identity narrative? What are the impacts of the different ways of remembering, and, with remembering, interpreting the narrative of what happened. Miroslav Volf, in this regard, develops the concept of remembering rightly (2006) that includes in it some forms of conscious forgetting (see especially Ricoeur 2004).

These more specific concepts feed into broader concepts associated with reconciliation—peace, peace-making, peace-keeping, culture of peace, and peacebuilding (Lederach 1997). The latter calls to consciousness the building of just institutions (Ricoeur 1992) and relational structures that support and contribute to positive relationships. This raises the question: How positive can relationships be in the wake of violent, deep-rooted conflict? This raises the issue of trust, a significant area of inquiry, and the potential that co-existence, living together without hurting one another, may be the best we can hope for (Abu-Nimer 2001; Chayes and Minow 2003).

Finally, recognizing that both deep-rooted conflict and reconciliation are complex phenomena, the whole area of emergent creativity becomes a related area of inquiry. This of course invokes complexity theory, chaos theory, emergent creativity, and new ways of understanding evolution (Kauffman 2008). Cultivating a readiness for emergent creativity could involve such things as hope, vision, inclusiveness, and discursive processes. And these could be motivated, sustained, and enriched by spirituality (Redekop 2012). From an evolutionary perspective, Ismail (2007) argues that for the human species to have survived, they needed a capacity to reconcile and that as complex adaptive systems, and communities will find a way toward reconciliation if outside parties do not interfere.

CONTRIBUTION OF THIS BOOK

The contribution of this book to the field of reconciliation is both theoretical and practical, recognizing that good theory guides effective practice, and practice is the ground for compelling theory. Using a Girardian hermeneutic as a starting point, a new conceptual *Gestalt* emerges in these essays, one not fully integrated in a formal way but showing a clear understanding of some of the challenges and possibilities for dealing with the deep divisions, enmity, hatred, and other effects of violence.

In the volume, *René Girard and Creative Mimesis* (2013), we highlighted what was designated as the Girardian Caution: in any relationship, however positive at the outset, there is always the possibility for mimetic rivalries to enter in, setting in motion feedback loops and mimetic spirals that result in negative emotions, separation, and violence. Likewise, by situating discourse about reconciliation within the context of Girardian thought, it becomes clear that—like Peter who vowed he would never deny Jesus but ended up doing it three times—any of us is susceptible to the siren call of angry resentment and retaliation. It is with a profound awareness of the power of violence that the emergence of mimetic discourse around reconciliation takes on particular urgency.

In the first section of this book, there are some broad theoretical themes that set the context for the remaining chapters. In the first chapter on *aphetic* (from the Greek *aphesis* which means "letting go") mimesis, Cameron Thomson delves into the heart of mimetic theory and its connection to hominization. Arguing that just as infants build their mimetic capacity on joint attention—an awareness that they and another are paying attention to the same thing—so our ancestors started their mimetic capacity building with the joint attentional scene. In this version of the interaction of ontogeny (child development) and phylogeny (evolutionary development), Thomson develops the concept of *aphetic* mimesis. The core argument is that as humans develop their violent tendencies, they, at the same time, develop their capacity for forgiveness and reconciliation (note de Waal's work with primates showing their capacity for empathy and reconciliation, as well as violence [2005; 2009]). In contrast to acquisitive (grasping or holding) mimesis, Thomson argues we should recognize *aphetic* mimesis. *Aphesis* is associated with forgiveness—note, for instance, how young children do not hold grudges. Also working from a primal level of human development, Sandor Goodhart highlights Levinas' philosophy of the pervasiveness of an ethical responsibility for the Other. The links to reconciliation are clear: if the Other is the antagonistic Other, the enemy, the perpetrator of injustice, then to have an infinite sense of responsibility invoked by a face, which is the manifestation of an infinite reality, means that a profound reconciliation is indeed possible. And this possibility is opened up, in Levinas' terms, by communication in the context of hospitality, which is an invitation to the Other to enter the space of the Self. Some of the implications are drawn out in a dialogue, chapter 3, between Goodhart and Redekop. These developments set the stage for Redekop's piece, chapter 4, in which he distinguishes between the violence-based reconciliation, unmasked by Girard's analysis of scapegoating and sacrifice, on the one hand, and blessing-based reconciliation, which proceeds on the basis of an orientation toward mutual well-being. Reconciliation is conceptualized as the transformation of mimetic structures of violence to mimetic structures of blessing. Mimetic structures are reciprocating patterns between Self and Other that go on through time (diachronic). These mimetic structures are characterized by an orientation (of either violence or blessing), attitudes, and behaviors. Reconciliation is motivated and guided by teachings of blessing, which are derived through a hermeneutics of blessing—an examination of texts and experiences with a desire to find what might assist in reconciliation processes. Highlighting five result areas for reconciliation, he shows that both violence-based reconciliation and blessing-based reconciliation can achieve results in all five areas. If, following Thomson, blessing-based reconciliation evolved concomitantly with violence-based sacrificial systems, then there is a hopeful answer to Girard's dark musings that with the discrediting of sacrifice-based conceptual systems, there is a chance of Clausewitzian runaway violence (Girard 2010).

Though the next section is explicitly theological, because of its originality, it has the potential to work heuristically for non-theologians. Nadia Delicata creatively brings together the profound observations of Marshall McLuhan (regarding the implications of an electronic communications revolution) with Girardian theory to develop the challenge of human relationality within a global village. With Internet-based tribalism, Girardian dynamics of collective violence take on a new "virtual" reality. In response she calls for a theology of friendship in which the self-emptying example of Jesus (kenosis) allows us to let go of acquisitive rivalistic tendencies. She speaks of "liking" and "being liked" in the context of generous love and service, marking the potential for human flourishing in the electronic age. Jon Paul, likewise, presents a framework for peace using two important metaphors. Presenting the multi-layered reality of deep-rooted conflict as an iceberg, he goes on to develop the metaphor of a complex garden of peace that draws on a multiplicity of religious sources. He calls for the engagement of the majority within each religious tradition who favor a tolerant, life-giving approach to one another.

The next two chapters, 7 and 8, move the discourse from broad ethical visions to the realities of practice. Sue-Anne Hess takes us into the world of Walter Wink, a dialogue partner of Girard's at the 2006 Conference. She highlights Wink's interpretation of Jesus's Sermon on the Mount in which the teachings of Jesus, to turn the other cheek, for example, are understood to enable victims to creatively expose injustice. This theme is picked up by Peter Smith who develops the concept of 'nonresistance' in line with Wink's work but with the added insights coming from improvisational theatre. Living a way of peace calls for the kind of creativity that sensitively responds to the complex array of factors in a challenging situation, just as improvising actors must constantly be aware of what each of their colleagues is doing and adjust appropriately. The praxis of peace becomes something akin to Bordieu's *habitus* it is indwelling an on-going practice that turns transforming action into an accomplished art form.

With this vision of peace ethic and practice, we turn back to some fundamental questions regarding the nature of human beings in a cultural context of sacrifice and ritual. Seasoned Girardian scholar Eugene Webb uses the New Testament book of Hebrews as a launchpad for rethinking of the concept of sacrifice. Drawing on Hindu and Buddhist traditions, he moves from an analysis of the fire sacrifice to the concept of renouncing one's false self. Jesus's "sacrifice" can then be understood as his renunciation of the desires that could have diverted him from his consecration to God. This is akin to Buddhist enlightenment. It also links Jesus's crucifixion to Jesus's wilderness temptations in which he "sacrifices" fame, power, and recognition (a link not made by Webb but is implied by his argument). Frank Richardson and Kathryn Frost do a trenchant critique of trends in psychology using thinkers, including Charles Taylor and Girard, to highlight the centrality of a relational ontology—meaning that at the core of our humanity we are relational creatures, with meaning, fulfillment, awareness, and consciousness flowing from relationships. Picking up on Girard's concept of reconciliation through violent sacrifice, Praeg uses the experience of South Africa as a foil to deconstruct Girard's analysis of this central concept. He notes that it is not the sacrificial act *per se* that has the long-term irenic consequences but it is this action together with the interpretation and subsequent narrative that has a transforming impact. That is, it is the act of meaning-making associated with scapegoat action that ultimately has the effect of channeling the sense of awe and togetherness into something that contributes to transformed relationships. This observation foregrounds the role of cultural interpreters in moving toward the vision of peace developed in the previous section. Each of the contributors in the next section, "Reconciliation in Context," can be framed as a cultural interpreter.

These cultural interpreters fall into two camps: those who are embedded within a culture, in which they are creatively self-critical of violence and its effects, and those who are third-party observers. In the first group we have Rupa Menon, Duncan Morrow, Cynthia Stirbys, and Nicolas Wandinger. Menon creatively reframes the Hindu concept of *karma* which has been used to shape a mentality that emphasizes "this is how things have to be" to an empowering sense of responsibility, choice, and strategic action. She argues that at any present moment, the concept of *karma* means that we can change the trajectory of our lives. Integrating that understanding with a framework for reconciliation, Menon presents a vision of how the intractable conflict between India and Pakistan might change, if there was a change in thinking. Morrow, who has spent decades working on reconciliation within his native Northern Ireland, eloquently presents the complex challenges of reconciliation. He unmasks the widespread discomfort with victims because their hurt means that someone, sometime, did something to them. Nobody wants to take responsibility for that hurt. However, he uses the image of "a crack that lets the light shine in" to identify the potential for transformative attitudes and actions to change the situation. Stirbys concentrates on the individual and collective trauma resulting from Aboriginal experiences in residential schools, identifying actions that could lead to healing and genuine reconciliation. Wandinger, as a practicing Catholic theologian, offers a sustained critical reflection on the meaning and role of forgiveness in the wake of sexual abuse of children by leaders within his own Church.

Knowledgeable, and partially implicated, third parties to a conflict are Steve Moore, Joel Hodge, Angela Kiraly, and Miguel de Las Casa Roland. Seasoned military chaplain Steve Moore, who was deployed in Bosnia and Herzegovina during the civil wars of the 1990s, points to the role of chaplains in seeding reconciliation among military leaders in a theatre of war. He uses the case study of his colleague Gabriel Legault who brought Serb (Orthodox), Croat (Catholic), and Bosniak (Muslim) religious leaders into a collaborative working relationship. Central to his concept is the mimetic modeling of respectful relations on the part of chaplains. Hodge, an Australian Girardian scholar, draws on extensive field research in East Timor to show how the framing of the deaths of Timorese people (or Catholics) as martyrs during the Indonesian regime was used to motivate resistance to the powerful occupiers leading eventually to independence for Timor Leste. Kiraly tells the heart-rending story of children resulting from command rape during the Bosnian civil war (mainly Serb soldiers raping Bosniak and Croatian women and forcing them to keep their babies). Most of them end up being classical Girardian scapegoats within society, reaping bullying and scorn within their communities. However, there is one such child, who has grown up with a positive self-image and framed herself as a bridge-builder between cultures, who acts as a beacon of blessing-based reconciliation in a conflict-prone environment. Finally, Miguel de Las Casas Rolland works conceptually with Girard's concepts of misrecognition (*mésconnaisance*) and difference to show how reconciliation can occur through a healthy respect for and recognition of difference. He illustrates this through a case study of the Maya Tzotzil Chamula of Chiapas Mexico.

REFERENCES

Abu-Nimer, M., ed. 2001. *Reconciliation, Justice, and Coexistence: Theory and Practice.* Lanham: Lexington Books.

Appleby, R. Scott. 2000. *The Ambivalence of the Sacred: Religion, Violence and Reconciliation.* Lanham: Rowan & Littlefield.

Axworthy, Thomas. 2008. *Bridging the Divide: Religious Dialogue and Universal Ethics.* Montreal & Kingston: McGill-Queens University Press.

Bar-Siman-Tov, Yaacov, ed. 2004. *From Conflict Resolution to Reconciliation.* Oxford: Oxford University Press.

Battle, Michael. 1997. *Reconciliation: The Ubuntu Theology of Desmond Tutu.* Cleveland: The Pilgrim Press.

Baum, Gregory and Harold Wells, eds. 1997. *The Reconciliation of Peoples: Challenge to the Churches.* Maryknoll: Orbis and Geneva: WCC Publications.

Berg, Manfred and Bernd Schaefer, eds. 2009. *Historical Justice in International Perspective: How Societies Are Trying to Right the Wrongs of the Past.* Cambridge: Cambridge University Press.

Bloomfield, David, Teresa Barnes and Luc Huyse, eds. 2004. *Reconciliation After Violent Conflict: A Handbook.* Stockholm: International IDEA.

Booth, Wayne. 2005. "Introduction: The Rhetoric of War and Reconciliation." Pp. 3–13 in *Roads to Reconciliation* edited by Amy Benson and Karen M. Poremski. Armonk and London: M.E. Sharpe.

Bowker, John, ed. 2008. *Conflict and Reconciliation: The Contribution of Religions.* Toronto: The Key Publishing House.

Brown, Amy Benson and Karen M. Poremski, eds. 2005. *Roads to Reconciliation: Conflict and Dialogue in the Twenty-First Century.* Armonk and London: M.E. Sharpe.

Burton, John W. 1990a. *Conflict Resolution and Provention.* New York: St. Martin's Press.

Burton, John W. ed. 1990b. *Conflict: Human Needs Theory.* New York: St. Martin's Press.

Burton, John W. and Frank Dukes, eds. 1990. *Conflict: Readings in Management and Resolution.* London: Macmillan and New York: St. Martin's Press.

Burton, John W. 1996. *Conflict Resolution: Its Language and Process.* London. Scarecrow Press.

Chanteur, Janine. 1992. *From War to Peace.* Translated by Shirley Ann Weisz. Boulder, CO: Westview Press.

Chayes, Antonia and Martha Minow, eds. 2003. *Imagine Coexistence: Restoring Humanity after Violent Ethnic Conflict.* San Francisco: Jossey-Bass.

Daly, Erin and Jeremy Sarkin. 2007. *Reconciliation in Divided Societies: Finding Common Ground.* Philadelphia: University of Pennsylvania Press.

De Gruchy, John. 2002. *Reconciliation: Restoring Justice.* Minneapolis: Fortress.

De Waal, Frans. 2005. "The Law of the Jungle: Conflict Resolution in Primates." Pp. 121–34 in *Roads to Reconciliation: Conflict and Dialogue in the Twenty-First Century* edited by Amy Benson Brown and Karen M. Poremski. Armonk and London: M.E. Sharpe.

———. 2009. *The Age of Empathy: Nature's Lessons for a Kinder Society.* New York: Three Rivers.

Du Bois, Francois and Antje du Bois-Pedain. 2008. Post-Conflict Justice and the Reconciliation Paradigm. Pp. 289–311 in *Justice and Reconciliation in Post-Apartheid South Africa,* edited by Francois du Bois and Antje du Bois-Pedain. Cambridge: Cambridge University Press.

Gopin, Marc. 2002. *Holy War, Holy Peace: How Religion Can Bring Peace to the Middle East.* New York: Oxford University Press.

Hamber, Brandon. 2007. "Forgiveness and Reconciliation: Paradise Lost or Pragmatism?" *Peace and Conflict: Journal of Peace Psychology,* *13*(1), 115–125.

Hamber, Brandon and Gráinne Kelly. 2009. "Beyond Coexistence: Towards a Working Definition of Reconciliation." Pp. 286-310 in *Reconciliation(s): Transitional Justice is Postconflict Societies,* edited by Joanna Quinn. Montreal and Kingston: McGill-Queen's University Press.

Hardt, James. 2007. *The Art of Smart Thinking.* Santa Clara: Biocybernaut Press.

Herman, Judith Lewis. 1997. *Trauma and Recovery.* Rev. ed. New York: Basic Books.

Hertog, Katrien. 2010. *The Complex Realigy of Religious Peacebuilding: Conceptual Contributions and Critical Analysis.* Lanham: Lexington.

Ismael, Jacqueline S. 2007. "Introduction." Pp. 1–18 in *Barriers to Reconciliation: Case Studies on Iraq and the Palestine-Israel Conflict,* edited by Jacqueline S. Ismael and William W. Haddad. Lanham: University Press of America.

Johnston, Douglas and Cynthia Sampson, eds. 1994. *Religion, The Missing Dimension of Statecraft.* Oxford: Oxford University Press.

Julius, Demetrios, Joseph Montville, and Vamik Volkan, eds. 1990. *The Psychodynamics of International Relationships.* Lexington & Toronto: Lexington Books

Kauffman, Stuart A. 2008. *Reinventing the Sacred: A New View of Science, Reason, and Religion.* New York: Basic Books.

Kim, Sebastian, Pauline Kollontai and Greg Hoyland. 2008. *Peace and Reconciliation: In Search of a Shared Identity.* Aldershot: Ashgate.

Lederach, John Paul. 1997. *Building Peace: Sustainable Reconciliation in Divided Societies. Washington:* U.S. Institute of Peace.

———. 1999. *The Journey Toward Reconciliation.* Scottsdale: Herald Press.

Long, William J. and Peter Brecke, (2003). *War and Reconciliation: Reason and Emotion in Conflict Resolution.* Cambridge MA: The MIT Press.

Luttwak, Edward. 1994. "Franco-German Reconciliation: The Overlooked Role of the Moral Re-Armament Movement." Pp. 37–63 in *Religion, The Missing Dimension of Statecraft,* edited by Douglas Johnston and Cynthia Sampson. Oxford: Oxford University Press.

MacDonald-Miner, Melinda. 2013. "The Relationship between Trauma (Including Posttraumatic Stress) and Reconciliation in Transitioning Societies: A Comparative Case Study of Cambodia & Mozambique." PhD Diss. Mahidol University, Thailand.

Moore, S.K. 2013. *Military Chaplains as Agents of Peace: Religious Leader Engagement in Conflict and Post-conflict Environments.* Lanham: Lexington.

Murphy, Jeffrie and Jean Hampton. 1988. *Forgiveness and Mercy.* Cambridge: Cambridge University Press.

Nadler, Arie, Thomas E. Malloy, and Jeffrey Fisher. 2008. "Introduction: Intergroup Reconciliation: Dimensions and Themes" Pp. 3-12 in Nadler et al (eds.) *The Social Psychology of Intergroup Reconciliation.* Oxford: Oxford University Press, 2008.

Newman, Edward and Albrecht Schnable, eds. 2002. *Recovering from Civil Conflict: Reconciliation, Peace and Development.* London and Portland: Frank Cass.

Petersen, Rodney L. and Raymond G. Helmick (eds.). 2001. *Forgiveness and Reconciliation: Religion, Public Policy, and Conflict Transformation.* Philadelphia: Templeton Foundation Press.

Quinn, Joanna, ed. 2009. *Reconciliation(s): Transitional Justice in Postconflict Societies.* Montreal & Kingston: McGill-Queen's University Press.

Radzik, Linda. 2009. *Making Amends: Atonement in Morality, Law, and Politics.* Oxford: Oxford University Press.

Reddy, Peter D. 2006 "Peace Operations and Restorative Justice: Groundwork for Post-Conflict Regeneration." Doctoral dissertation, The Australian National University: http://www.regnet.anu.edu.au/sites/default/files/files/PeterReddy_Thesis.pdf. Accessed August 27, 2013.

Redekop, Vern Neufeld. 2002. *From Violence to Blessing: How an Understanding of Deep-Rooted Conflict Opens Paths to Reconciliation.* Ottawa: Novalis.

———. 2007. "Reconciling Nuers with Dinkas: A Girardian approach to conflict resolution," *Religion—An International Journal.* 37, 64–84.

———. 2008. "A Post-Genocidal Justice of Blessing as an Alternative to a Justice of Violence: The Case of Rwanda." Pp. 205–238 in *Peacebuilding in Traumatized Societies,* edited by Barry Hart. University Press of America.

———. 2011. "Spirituality, Emergent Creativity, and Reconciliation." Pp. 585–600 in *Peacemaking: A Comprehensive Theory and Practice Reference, Volume II ,* edited by Sue Allen Nan, Zachariah Cherian Mampillu, and Andrea Bartoli. Westport: Praeger.

Redekop, V. and O. Gasana. 2007. "Implication of Religious Leaders in Mimetic Structures of Violence: The Case of Rwanda." Pp. 117–37 in *The Contexts of Religion and Violence. Journal of Religion & Society Supplement Series 2,* edited by Ronald A. Simkins. The Kripke Center: http://moses.creighton.edu/jrs/toc/2007SS.html

Ricoeur, Paul. [1990] 1992. *Oneself as Another* (translated by Kathleen Blamey). Chicago: University of Chicago Press.

———. 2000. *The Just.* Translated by David Pellauer. Chicago: University of Chicago Press.

———. 2004. *Memory, History, Forgetting.* Translated by Kathleen Blamey and David Pellauer. Chicago: University of Chicago Press.

Rouhana, Nadin N. 2004. "Group Identity and Power Asymmetry in Reconciliation Processes: The Israeli-Palestinian Case," *Peace and Conflict: Journal of Peace Psychology,* 10(1).

Schillebeeckx, Edward, ed. 1971. *Sacramental Reconciliation.* New York: Herder and Herder.

Volf, Miroslav. 1996. *Exclusion and Embrace: A Theological Exploration of Identity, Otherness, and Reconciliation.* Nashville: Abingdon Press.

———. 2006. *The End of Memory: Remembering Rightly in a Violent World.* Grand Rapids: Eerdmans.

Volkan, Vamik D. 1998. *Bloodlines: From Ethnic Pride to Ethnic Terror.* Boulder: Westview.

Zehr, Howard. 1990. *Changing Lenses: A New Focus for Crime and Justice.* Scottsdale: Herald Press.

NOTE

1. Mirror neurons in the brain have been identified by neuroscientists as providing a capacity for imitation.

I

FORGIVENESS, RESPONSIBILITY, AND BLESSING

Chapter One

Mimetic Desire, Aphetic Mimesis, and Reconciliation as the Nexus of "Letting Go" and "Turning Around"

Conceptual Roots in Tomasello's "Joint Attention" [1]

Cameron M. Thomson

René Girard's fundamental anthropology makes a radical contribution to the human sciences both by its description of the nature and extent of the human being's ineluctable compulsion to imitate her companions and by drawing attention to the potential for apocalyptic violence that inheres in this basic tendency. However, his account of mimetic desire, of the latter's connection to acquisitive mimesis and mimetic rivalry, and his claims concerning the role of violence in hominization and in the evolution of basic human institutions, face the criticism that they concede too much ground to violence and fail to give serious consideration to possible "positive" or "creative" articulations of intersubjective mimesis (so, for example, Adams 2000). A particularly strong form of this criticism is the theologically motivated claim that Girard "ontologizes" violence, that he gives rivalry and violence absolute priority over other modes of human relation and so disavows the priority of grace, or love, or the Good. He seems to deny that violence is merely contingent. He seems to deny that things might have been, and might yet be, otherwise than they are. In this respect, he appears to omit any form of reconciliation that does not have recourse to the scapegoat mechanism (see especially Milbank 1991, 392–8). [2]

Criticism of this kind may be countered by adverting to more recent formulations of Girard's thought and by pointing out that, in any case, his work does not uniformly omit this possibility (see, for example, Girard, de

Castro Rocha, and Antonello 2007, 76). A supplementary approach would be to point out that mimesis, rather than violence, is the fundamental concept in Girard's work. But, while this is so, *mimetic desire*, rather than mimesis *per se*, is Girard's fundamental theme. And we must allow that he does represent mimetic desire as an inevitable and highly volatile human tendency, far more pernicious than it is beneficial.

Girard's approach to these matters has benefited from a number of repairs, which have served to foreground the positive ways in which human beings imitate their conspecific companions. As various scholars (including other contributors to the present work) show, it is possible to represent inter-subjective mimesis without primary and inevitable reference to "the derailments of mimetic desire" (Doran 2007, 35), that is, without conceding the inevitability of resentment, covetousness, rivalry, and collective violence. Doran (2007) offers a good example of the kind of effort that I mean. James Alison's (1998) discussion of "pacific mimesis" also comes to mind, along with Vern Neufeld Redekop's recent (2002, 2008) thinking about reconciliation (see also Adams 2000; Collins 2000; Reineke 2007; Steinmair-Pösel 2007). In this chapter, I offer a complement to such efforts. I argue that the inter-subjective mode of mimesis, whose anthropological centrality Girard sets forth so definitively in his thinking about desire, rivalry, violence, and culture/religion, is a phenomenon whose connection to resentment and violence is not in fact intrinsic.[3] More precisely, I aim at a radical repair that shows that, independently of, and conceptually prior to, its connection to violence, mimesis is not only key for the process of hominization, including especially the possibility of symbolically mediated relations to things and persons, but a condition of the very possibility of the non-violent reconciliation of once and potential rivals.

A key resource in my particular effort will be cultural psychologist Michael Tomasello's notion of "joint attention," coupled with his account of the latter's ground in a unique adaptation that enables human beings to identify with others of their kind. After discussing Tomasello's position, I will argue that mimesis, regarded as an implicit, inter-subjective mode of being oriented to the objects of shared experience, first takes shape in the phylo- and onto-genetic emergence of the uniquely human capacity for sharing attention and that it *is* this (joint) attention. And I will show that this phenomenon is embodied, not only in mimetic desire and acquisitive mimesis and in the conflict that the latter engenders, but also embodied in what I shall term "aphetic mimesis" (from the Greek *aphesis*, which means literally "letting-go") and in the state of reconciliation between potential rivals of which it is an element.

My argument will proceed along two main lines. First, I will identify and explore the links that hold between joint attention, on the one hand, and these two modes of mimesis, on the other. I will do this by way of a discussion of hominization, directing basic insights deriving from Tomasello's research on joint attention[4] to a reading of Girard's account of hominization in *Things Hidden Since the Foundation of the World*—specifically, that is, to his treatment of the origin of what he calls "the first non-instinctual attention." I will argue that what Girard calls "mimetic desire" is a species-unique articulation of human attending-to-things. In other words, I will construe Girardian "desire" as an articulation of specifically human *attention* that is both (1) "joint," or non-instinctual and implicitly mimetic, and (2) acquisitive. I will further argue that this leaves open the possibility of an articulation of attention that is joint, but not acquisitive.

Again, I call this mode of joint attention "aphetic mimesis." By "aphetic mimesis" I intend a mimetism that 1) is profoundly receptive; 2) does not resist the impression that the other makes in the affective and cognitive depths of the self; 3) yields to the pressure by which the "self" is inwardly marked by the other, that is, the "trespasser"; and 4) is a mimetic impulse to surrender to the latter's point of view, to resemble her through the adoption of her perspective on, or orientation to, things—not in a manner that leads to a frenzied attempt to take hold of her things and, finally, her very place in the world, but in a manner that surrenders these things and that place. Mimesis, in this sense, is the profound being-like or mutual resemblance that is effected when one subject yields to, and so enters into, the already extant *attention*-to-things of another subject. By "aphetic mimesis," too, I intend a mode of inter-subjective imitation that bears some of its properties in common with forgiveness. This association, which is not perhaps obvious from the outset, will become clearer as we proceed.

My second main line of inquiry pertains to the several elements of a mimetic-theoretical understanding of non-violent reconciliation. I characterize the latter in terms of what I take to be its two co-informing, mimetic, inter-subjective moments: that is, as the nexus of *aphesis* (a powerless yielding to the other *qua* trespasser), on the one hand, and *metanoia* (the reception of the other's impress, the process of being deeply reoriented in relation to her), on the other. By "*metanoia*" I intend too, however, a reorientation and transformation of perspective that is grounded in aphetic mimesis. *Aphesis* is fundamental, as I will show, while *metanoia* flows from that.

I characterize the power that attracts, draws, and holds the aphetic-metanoic subject as both an inner "gripping" of one subject's attention by another and as a kind of boundary-breaching "trespass." I describe this as a modeling of attention, on the one hand, and as a mimesis of attention, on the other, with the latter, in particular, being no activity of the subject, but rather a passivity to, and reception of, the other's point of view. In its paradigmatic instance, I represent this as the originary, receptive yielding of very young children to adults and older children. I also advert to the far more difficult yielding of older, more powerful subjects to the interests and orientation of children—a receptivity that is hard to endure, given the extent to which the incursion of children disturbs and calls into question pre-established boundaries, routines, habits, and patterns of thought and desire.

Given their shared basis in the capacity for joint attention, I argue, reconciliation as an alternative to rivalry persists within the state of conflict that arises from acquisitive mimesis. Mimetic desire, regarded as a shared attention-to-things that can lead to conflict, always stands in close proximity to a shared attention that takes up the other's interests and needs, and opens onto a yielding of possession for the sake of the other's thriving. The ever-deepening fortification of their respective positions, the self-justification of the parties to some rivalrous conflict, does not eclipse the possibility of a deep transformation of these same subjects' orientation to one another. It is always possible that one or another, or both, of these subjects will move from seeing herself as her rival's victim to seeing herself as the other's victimizer, from a hate-filled fixation on the other that sees her as an alien impediment to the realization of autonomous desires, to a state of likeness, a state of seeing what the other sees, as she sees it. One can always leave off looking obsessively, resentfully at *her* and enter into her looking, especially as she looks back at one.

Thus, I argue, the potential for reconciliation lies within the capacities of our specifically mimetic nature as much does our propensity for violence does. In speaking of reconciliation like this, in connection with mimesis, I do not want to trivialize the concomitant problem of mimetic rivalry and violence, or the significance of early deployments of the scapegoat mechanism for the emergence of "three great pillars of primitive religion," sacrifice, taboo, and myth (Girard 1987, 154). Rather, I am relativizing Girard's necessary, urgent warnings concerning the active power of acquisitive mimesis by adverting to the ongoing presence of the receptivity that grounds mimetic desire itself and returning to the "weakness" and childlikeness of aphetic mimesis. I claim that, given our capacity for the latter, the possibility of reconciliation in both registers (by way of collective violence and by way of mutual *aphesis* and *metanoia*) has existed from the outset. To this extent, our thinking about mimesis is not constrained to focus on its distorted form; rather, such considerations constitute an integral, but subsidiary warning, which attends a more fundamental account. Much remains to be said concerning the fact that the one rather than the other mode of mimesis and reconciliation almost always takes the upper hand. But the philosophical-theological treatment of mimesis that this would entail, a discussion of the receptivity of mimesis in relation to questions of moral accountability and human freedom, is well beyond the scope of this chapter.

Before proceeding, I wish to forestall one possible objection. If there is a normative dimension to what I am setting forth here, it is *not* embodied in the claim that we ought to yield, unconditionally, to dangerous enemies, allowing them to do as they please with impunity, to throw our lives away for nothing, just on principle. Pragmatically speaking, consistent *aphesis* may be an unlivable ideal, although it might also be called for in some exceptional instances. If I am advocating submission to "dangerous" others and calling for passivity and nonresistance in the face of their trespassive action, I am doing so, minimally, with a view to the relationship between adults and children. Moreover, I do not prescribe a yielding to the explicit action of the other but to her implicit attention-to-things, interests, point of view, or to the intentionality of her regard for what matters to her, which is also a matter of entering into her receptivity. The reconciliation of potential rivals ought to be nowhere more practicable than in the case of adults' relation to the children, who come into their lives. In fact, however, this is very difficult to achieve. It seems to me, in any case, that, practically speaking, a call to *aphesis*, here— the *aphesis* that very young children model for us in the earliest expressions of their capacity for joint attention—suffices as a challenge.

I develop the argument of this essay in the course of four sections, as follows. In the first, I offer a sketch of Tomasello's thinking about joint attention. Next, I connect the notions of joint attention and mimetic desire, with particular reference to Girard's thinking about hominization, and show that mimetic desire is a subset of the phenomena associated with joint attention. In the third section, I outline some consequences for Girard's mimetic theory of my prioritization of joint attention. Finally, in the fourth section, I offer an account of inter-subjective mimesis that develops the latter's *aphetic* nature with reference to the collective "grip" to which the originarily aphetic agent is subject and which is best addressed by way of an ongoing practice of mutual *aphesis*, *metanoia*, and so of reconciliation.

JOINT ATTENTION AND THE JOINT ATTENTIONAL SCENE

"Joint attention," writes Tomasello, "has been used to characterize [a] whole complex of triadic social skills and interactions." These interactions are triadic, he explains, "in the sense that they involve a coordination" of the subject's relations "with objects and people" that "result[s] in a referential *triangle*": here, in the fundamental kind of instance discussed by Tomasello, "of child, adult, and the object or event to which they share attention" (1999, 62; my emphasis). These "triadic social skills and interactions" include, in the words of another researcher, such things as "joint visual attention or gaze following, social referencing, and pre-linguistic communicative acts such as pointing" (Moore 1999, 46).

A central argument of Tomasello's seminal work on the topic, *The Cultural Origins of Human Cognition*, is that the capacity for joint attention is grounded in a fundamentally human trait: the human being's unique "social-

cognitive adaptation for identifying with other persons." Human beings differ from other animals, that is, in their capacity for "understanding" conspecific companions "as intentional agents like the self" and by an associated
ability to see the world from others' points of view (Tomasello 1999, 7). As
Tomasello observes, the specific conditions under which this adaptation originally appeared cannot be isolated. In any case, Tomasello argues, it pertains
to a "very small," but anthropologically decisive, "biological difference between humans and their closest primate relatives" (53–54). This difference
"underlies human culture" (90) and enables the "species-unique modes of
cultural transmission" (4) ("imitative learning," "instructed learning," "collaborative learning" [5]) that explain the enormously accelerated advances in
tool-production, symbolic communication, and social organization that characterize the last quarter million years of human evolution.

The human being's identification with other persons and her understanding of them "as intentional agents like the self" is first realized in the life of
the human infant at around nine months of age. Tomasello refers to this
radical change in the neonate's social-cognitive abilities as the "nine-month
revolution" (61).[5] Up to this point, "infants interact dyadically with objects,
grasping and manipulating them, and they interact dyadically with other
people." During the period from nine to twelve months of age, however, a
"new set of behaviors begins to emerge." Interaction with objects and people
is henceforth "triadic" (62). Now, for the first time,

> infants . . . begin to flexibly and reliably look where adults are looking (gaze
> following), to engage with them in relatively extended bouts of social interac-
> tion mediated by an object (joint engagement), to use adults as social reference
> points (social referencing), and to act on objects in the way adults are acting on
> them (imitative learning). In short, it is at this age that infants for the first time
> begin to "tune in" to the attention and behavior of adults toward outside
> entities. (*ibid.*)

In short, the "ontogenetic emergence" of the uniquely human "social-
cognitive adaptation" that Tomasello describes finds expression in the child's
new capacity for joint attention, for "joint-attentional activities," and her
interest in entering into them (7). Joint attentional activities are constitutive
for what Tomasello calls "joint attentional scenes" and the significance of
these "scenes," or the mode of social interaction that constitutes them, can
hardly be overstated: "linguistic reference," in his view, cannot be understood apart from this phenomenon (97). In other words, the instantiation of
this "triadic" structure is a necessary condition for the emergence of language
and of discursive social intentionality and action more generally, as the infant
"also begin[s] to actively direct adult attention and behavior to outside entities using deictic gestures such as pointing or holding up an object to show
it to someone" (62).[6]

Joint attention, or the cognitive entanglement that it entails, constitutes objects as "ours." In other words, it renders individual things instances of determinate kinds relative to the common interests and goals of the participants in joint attentional scenes. Or again, for participants in a joint attentional scene, their shared interests are formally prior to parochial ones. Although Tomasello does not spell it out in these terms, this is an important upshot of his observation that the joint attentional scene does not include anything that is "not part of 'what *we* [i.e., the jointly attentive parties to the scene] are doing'" (98; my emphasis). This "we" expresses the profoundly empathetic attunement that joint attention embodies. Our identification with one another, the mutual attunement of our joint attention to things, narrows and disciplines the idiosyncratic domain of individual perception, while also far exceeding the domain of what can be brought to linguistic expression and subsumed under experience-organizing categories (cf. *ibid*., 97).

ATTENTION, DESIRE, HOMINIZATION

The configuration realized in the joint attentional scene is the minimal, iterable form of specifically human social relations: it is the triadic form instantiated when one subject relates to the world *via* the mediating attention-to-things of another subject, who models this orientation for her. But if the subject's orientation to things *in general* (her attention to them, her interest in them, the intentionality of her consciousness of them) is modeled on the orientation, attention, interest, intentionality of an antecedently present other, then the "jointness" of such attention is precisely a mode of mimesis in Girard's sense. The topic of joint attention connects directly, then, with his work. It connects up, in particular, with his account of hominization in *Things Hidden Since the Foundation of the World* and his description, in that context, of what he refers to as "the first non-instinctual attention."

In *Things Hidden* Girard reflects on "the problem of hominization," which he takes to be the proper point of departure for any theory of culture (Girard 1987, 7; see also Girard, Rocha, and Antonello 2007, 96–8). His account of the role of mimesis in hominization and, above all, of mimesis' role at the hypothetical threshold that marks the origin of the human, may be fruitfully supplemented by subordinating the origin of mimetic desire, in particular, to the appearance of the uniquely human capacity for joint attention, or the "social-cognitive adaptation for identifying with other persons," that Tomasello describes. Girard, in other words, marks the decisive threshold by referring to something rather narrower and more specific than the mimesis of attention in general. "If imitation does indeed play the fundamental role for man," he argues (but without tarrying to offer a general, more neutral characterization of this role), "there must certainly exist an acquisitive imitation . . . a possessive mimesis whose effects and consequences should be carefully studied and considered" (Girard 1987, 9).

Girard marks a fundamental distinction between the psychology of the nonhuman primate, in whose acquisitive or possessive behavior "acquisitive imitation" or "possessive mimesis" is already apparent, and that of human beings. Admittedly, as Girard notes, when a nonhuman primate observes a companion reaching for, grasping, or otherwise manipulating an object "it is immediately tempted to imitate the gesture" (8).[7] The non-human primate's orientation to the object, however, "can be *nearly*," but not yet "defined as desire," (*ibid*.; my emphasis). The human being, by contrast, exhibits something else—"desire" properly so-called. There is some significant ambiguity here. A "fundamental rule," Girard says, which finds expression in the relevant dominance hierarchy, holds the animal in check; the subordinate animal is subject to a natural, irresistible imperative of deferral *vis-à-vis* the object (*ibid*.). The human being, however, is "hyper-mimetic," a being for whom such constraints have no efficacy (Girard 1991, 143). Why does Girard say, however, that the "repressed" orientation of the non-human primate "can be nearly," but not yet "defined as desire"? What does he mean by "desire"? Is his distinction between "desire" and "near-desire" a matter, merely, of the respective force and weakness of a nevertheless common mimetism, relative to the stability and breakdown of the laws governing primate dominance hierarchies? Or does the relevant distinction fall between two radically disparate modes of imitation?

The notion of joint attention helps to focus and clarify what Girard takes to be the decisive difference here. In the case of the non- or not-yet-human primate, the other animal's gesture and even its practical orientation to the object is reproduced, but the two animals are interested in the object *independently* of one another's interest in it. The one animal's gesture reproduces that of the other; the other's intention, aim, goal, or desire is not reproduced. Rather, the latter is simply the same, from the outset (e.g., in the way that the nationality of two persons born in the same country is the same, not due to imitation, but given their shared birthplace). Here, the imitating animal's attention evinces an intrinsic, antecedent fit between the individual and the object of its attention, even if the urge to take hold of this object was occasioned by another's interest in it. In short, the individual animal's attention to the things that interest it is *instinctual*.

Joint attention implies something more: it disrupts the individualism of intention, aim, goal, or desire; it is a reproduction whose object is not the other's gesture but rather the other's attention.[8] Joint attention entails a kind of feedback effect that generates an intentionality, an "aimedness," that is "ours." In the case of the nonhuman primate (in Girard's account, our forebears), the imitator's gesture evinces a parallel goal or intention, but this gesture does so only to the extent that interest in the thing and action aimed at possession of it would be present (*ceteris paribus*) even if there was no model showing an interest in the object. The interest would exist given only the presence of the object. In the case of the nonhuman primate, the model's gesture functions as a mere reminder; it does not *cause* the imitator to take an interest. In other words, the imitator's interest in the object is not constituted by its relation to the other's interest. It is not constitutively "joint"; the two animals are not cognitively entangled with one another or incorporated in what Tomasello calls a "referential triangle."

Girard isolates a specifically human mode of attention and designates it by way of a special name, "mimetic desire," or indeed simply "desire" properly so-called. The key difference that he notices pertains, really, to a phenomenon that is not intrinsically acquisitive or conflictual. Here, the trajectory and intensity of the model's attention, even when this is still only implicit in the inclination of the body, or in the gaze, is reproduced. What interests the imitator is not primarily the thing, but rather the other's attention to the thing. The human being's orientation to an object of interest need not be a function of a dyadic fit between the subject and the thing in question. Her interest might be piqued, not only in the absence of such a fit, but even where the object is entirely superfluous, or when action aiming at its possession is incoherent, or self-defeating, or irrational, provided that a sufficiently compelling *model* evinces an interest in it. And even if a subject does have an idiosyncratic preference for this or that kind of object, this preference, though a feature of her individual psychology, will not be a *necessary* condition for her desiring those objects. Her interest even in such things will be over-determined by the presence of sufficiently compelling models that desire the same things.

Again, the distinction that Girard notices pertains to attention, in general, before it pertains to desire, in particular. The appearance of the human being's capacity for joint attention, the appearance of the trait that grounds her identification with her conspecific companions, the "jointness" of the intentions or interests that she shares with the latter, and the joint attentional activities that serve these interests, are *already* part of what will be required for the phylogenetic appearance of, and ontogenetic entry into, language, mutual understanding, and desire. In other words, the human being's capacity for joint attention and her tendency to identify deeply with others of her kind is antecedent to the violence that generates language and culture in Girard's account in *Things Hidden*.

There, describing this originary collective violence and its aftermath (the archaic community arrayed, ultimately, around the body of their common victim), Girard makes five especially salient claims. First, he characterizes the interdividual psychology that informs the hypothetical scene- (or class of scenes) that is (are) decisive for hominization (i.e., deployment of "the most elementary form of the victimage mechanism" and the latter's aftermath) in quantitative terms as "a new *degree* of attention." Second, he describes this psychology qualitatively as "the first *non-instinctual* attention." Third, Girard describes the unique conditions under which this novel kind and degree of attention appears in terms of a "maximal contrast" between antecedent and consequent states of the social order, between violent "agitation," on the one hand, and awe-filled "tranquility," on the other. Fourth, he describes the body of the community's "common victim" as "the focal point" of this new mode of attention. Fifth, Girard describes how this object of attention is "imbued with the emotions [that are] provoked by the crisis and its resolution" (Girard 99–100; my emphases).

Girard goes on to offer the beginnings of a theory of representation that not only puts the origin of language (and so, too, of "concepts") *after* the chaos that accrues to acquisitive mimesis and the accumulation of rivalries, but that makes this origin supervene on the latter. Other options are open to us. It is also possible to interpolate language, as Gans (1981) does, after the appearance of mimetic desire, but in the position occupied by the threatening eruption of "possessive imitation" in Girard's account, thus making of language a strategy that forestalls open rivalry with all of its deleterious effects. (Of course, I am developing yet another account in the present chapter.) Irrespective of the order of their appearance, in any case, the conditions that support the appearance of language support the appearance of acquisitive rivalry. Again, the human being is "hyper-mimetic" and this trait grounds both language and violence. And yet, Girard does not take either this exacerbated mimetism, the passage of the associated neurophysiological threshold, the realization of conditions favorable to a new and potentially unlimited mode of explicit mimesis, or even the surpassing of what he characterizes as a decisive "threshold of mimetic contagion" to be the decisive endpoint of hominization.

Rather, deployment of the scapegoat mechanism is a condition *sine qua non*, not merely for passing the threshold that opens onto "the process leading toward the sacred" (Girard 1987, 100), toward culture/religion as we have known it and lived it and cannot help but imagine it, but for hominization, which is not distinct from these developments.[9] The decisive break with the (merely) animal realm is not achieved *in advance* of the fundamental problems connected with mimetic desire and acquisitive mimesis, that is, in advance of mimetic rivalry, mimetic contagion, the war of all against all, the polarization of violence, the slaying of the victim. The problems of acquisitive mimesis and desire do not beset an already extant *human* community. Only later, after the individual's temptation to imitate, along with its deleterious consequences, is repressed in a specifically social, externalized register by way of the single-victim mechanism and its civilized *sequelae* and only after it has given rise to such a community, do these problems beset it. In other words, Girard elides the possibility that, insofar as desire is a mode of attention, and insofar as the human being's attention is itself already a mimetic phenomenon, this attention already differs from the instinctual mode of attention that characterizes nonhuman animals' interest in things. He elides the inference that, well in advance of the first appearance of mimetic desire and acquisitive mimesis, this "joint" mode of attention might have sufficed for the emergence of culture, though in a form that we have not yet imagined——culture as a medium for human relations that does not derive from "the process leading toward the sacred." Instead, Girard's emphasis falls on the punctual threshold that corresponds to the origin of "the sacred" (which he equates with the origin of the primitive symbolic order). This is the order that we merely *happen* to inhabit.

Girard leaves us a number of openings that allow us to soften the decisive tone of his description. He does not insist that "non-instinctual" attention could not have emerged otherwise than in this scenario or that it can only have emerged by way of collective violence. He says only that these are "the most favorable conditions possible" for its emergence (1987, 99). Nor does he—or need he—deny that this same kind of attention (non-instinctual attention of precisely this degree of intensity) might have had a different (kind of) focal point under other circumstances. Girard asserts only that this attention happens to have had this focal point in the first instance(s) in which it happens to have been realized. Given the "*common*-victimary" character of the occupant of the centre-of-attention in the scenario that he describes, Girard's description does not exclude the possibility that the community's organization as a people (who are intensely interested in centres-of-attention) might be more fundamental than the specific character of this organization *in this instance*. His description leaves open the possibility that the community's interest in centers-of-their-attention, as such, has features that are more fundamental than the specific affective tenor of their joint attention in the case at hand. To affirm that the centre might have had another character, and the community's attention another tenor, is compatible with the assertion that, in this case, the object of attention happens to have been "imbued with the emotions [that are] provoked by the crisis and its resolution" (Girard 1987, 100). Other provocations and other emotional associations might be possible for beings that are endowed with a capacity for joint attention.

JOINT ATTENTION AS IMPLICIT MIMESIS: SOME CONSEQUENCES FOR MIMETIC THEORY

The notion of implicit mimesis—mimesis that anticipates and rehearses not-yet-executed behavior—which Girard's mimetic desire instantiates in one possible way, allows us to mark a distinction between a receptive, yielding mimesis that surrenders to the model and receives the latter's impression, and one that is scandalizing, aggressive, and forceful.[10] If mimetic desire is a subcutaneous, inner orientation to things that extends outwards into open aggression (passing into primate and then specifically human modes of acquisitive and conflictual mimesis), then a more inclusive notion of implicit mimesis might enable us to imagine modes of social interaction that are not aggressive, but that are *aphetic*, which take the form of a yielding-to and receiving-from the other, a handing-over, a not-contesting, a turning of the (other) cheek, a conversion to the other's perspective, and a "quasi-osmotic"[11] proximity to the other's interests.

Girard's distinction between them aside, mimetic desire is always already, implicitly, acquisitive mimesis. The former rehearses virtually that which the latter openly performs. *Qua* mimetic, however, mimetic desire is a mode of joint attention. And joint attention is a more inclusive category than desire. Where it is realized in desire, then, joint attention can indeed be acquisitive. But there is reason to think that joint attention need not be like this. If (mimetic) desire is regarded as a mode of (joint) attention, and if the notion of attention is more fundamental than the notion of desire, then it might be possible to characterize a uniquely human mode of attention that resembles desire in Girard's sense, one which, though triadic, is not inherently aggressive even in cases of "internal mediation" (see Girard 1965, 9–12). It might be possible to confirm a uniquely human mode of attention that opens onto neither the violent "agitation" and awful "tranquility" of Girard's originary scene, nor the perpetual deferral and resentment of Gans' (see, for example, Gans 1997, 135; Bandera 2013).[12]

If, in general, implicit mimesis begins in the depths of the organism as the incorporation of its attention into the attention of another, as a resonance that reproduces the direction and degree of attention that is implied by the observed behavior of another, then this is also true of the other's acquisitive, or possessive behavior. The mimesis that begins as an inner resonance with the thing-directed attention of another—where this thing is in the possession of this other—is imitation of the other's *desire*. It is a consequence of Girard's rhetorical emphases that he links mimesis too determinately to desire, to covetousness and the open rivalry and aggression of "possessive imitation." The convergence of two or more hands on a single, indivisible object of desire really will lead to rivalry and potentially to violence (Girard 1987, 8). If the relationship between mimesis and desire were intrinsic, then we would be confronted with a scenario in which mimesis would have to be proscribed in all circumstances. And this is what we seem to find in Girard, although he does not abstract from mimetic desire to implicit mimesis, more generally. In *I See Satan Fall Like Lightning,* he makes it clear that the nature of desire, as such, represents a problem of this magnitude: he equates desire with covetousness and adverts to the final imperative of the Decalogue in order to emphasize the seriousness of the menace (Girard 2001, 7–8).[13] By equating mimetic desire with covetousness, Girard associates it with a fundamental orientation to the other that is always already implicitly aggressive, even in advance of its expression in explicitly appropriative and conflictual imitation.

The notion of joint attention enables us to open up an alternative perspective. Girard's account would benefit, then, from three repairs. First, while the attention that Girard describes is indeed noninstinctual, it is not the *first* noninstinctual attention. Rather, this designation ought to be reserved for joint attention *as such*, that is, for the mimetic or triadic attention-to-things of which human beings are uniquely capable. This noninstinctual attention subsumes (mimetic) desire and acquisitive mimesis as subsets of implicit and explicit imitation, but does not simply coincide with them. Moreover, this noninstinctual attention is already sufficient for the organization of a heterogeneous community, the formation of shared interests, and a shared orientation to a common world. It is sufficient for the emergence of a heterogeneous "languaculture"[14] such that none of this had to be, *inevitably*, a derivation of collective homicide, or bought, *without alternative*—as in Gans' version—at the price of an endless deferral of violence and perpetual resentment.

Second, while the attention that Girard describes—the archaic community's joint attention to the intensely interesting body of their "common victim"—may well be construed as a new *degree* of attention, and while this unprecedented intensity may be regarded as an achievement that turns on the maximal contrast that he describes between the "agitation" of the mimetic crisis, on the one hand, and the "tranquility" of its resolution, on the other, the "favorable conditions" for the emergence of the attention that Girard describes do not inhere in the maximal contrast between the "agitation" of the crisis and the "tranquility" of its resolution. Given the antecedently established "social-cognitive adaptation for identifying with other persons" that Tomasello makes the basis for joint attention in the first place, what is decisive, here, is that the victim with whom these poles ("agitation" and "tranquility") and transition are associated is a member of the community, that is, someone with whom the rest of the community's members already identify. This means that empathy—as my affective embodiment of the goals and frustrations of others of my kind—is already in play. Empathy is a phenomenon that depends, just as much as envy and rivalry do, upon the possibility of a mimetic reproduction of the implicit, subjective orientation of one's conspecific companions.[15]

The attention that Girard describes has the new degree that it has, both because it is noninstinctual (i.e., joint) and because it has as its specific "focal point" a victim who is a member of the community, that is, one with whom it is already possible to empathize, even if no one actually does. It is significant that even though this victim is immolated in a manner that implicates the whole community, and even though her death serves interests that are implicitly regarded as universally valid for every member of that community (including the victim herself),[16] this does not eclipse the possibility of the victim's community seeing themselves as active *vis-à-vis* their passive, suffering victim, rather than representing their victim as uniquely active *vis-à-vis* them, the passive, suffering community. This might be construed as an originary receptivity to the revelation that unmasks the scapegoat mechanism, a propensity that is present from the outset, which myth decisively foregoes, but which is sustained in the capacity for empathy.[17]

Third, Girard's "maximal contrast" has value (a) because this contrast is an object of interest for an antecedently established regime of joint attentional activity, for a primary community whose members' inability consistently, always and only, to forgive one another's trespasses led to this crisis in the first place and (b) because the affective consequences of this contrast are intensified by this focal point's being identified with the community and its interests. In other words, the centre-of-attention is "imbued with the emotions provoked by the crisis and its resolution" precisely because this resolution has been achieved in a manner that draws a unique member of the community into an unprecedented mode of relation to the antecedently existing community itself. He or she is absolutely unique, the "single" one (cf. Girard 1987, 100–101), "the one that did it." Or again, he or she is a "god," an agent who is very much like us, who shares our (supposedly non-parochial) interests—including our interest in his or her own death and its beneficial consequences—but who is much more powerful and clever and knowledgeable than we are, altogether active in matters where we are altogether passive and therefore, inevitably, also a rival.

Although the human community's inter-subjective interest in centres-of-attention is more fundamental than the specific affective tenor of their interest *in this case*—an interest that is expressed first as violence and then as awe—the interest that the centre holds will be inflected by this violence and will be renewed by violence henceforth. Although this may be how it *was*, we need not concede that it had to be this way. Something radically other might have made its appearance, instead, in the place where culture/religion was born.

This refusal to concede that culture/religion was inevitable from the outset, even given our mimetic nature, suggests at least the following corrections. First, our social-cognitive capacity "for identifying with other persons" and our capacity for joint attention are not inevitably conflictual—even when activated between proximate social actors as "internal mediation." Second, these propensities promise something else: the possibility of a languaculture hitherto unimagined by us (a way of being human that is not implicated in violence). Third, our mimetic nature is only contingently implicated in the eruption of violence, as a special (and especially distorted) category of human interaction and in the institutionalization of the latter's sublimated effects.

Fourth, violent homicide and the institutions that arise from the deployment of the single-victim mechanism emerge from a crisis that besets an already established, already human order.[18] This allows us to affirm that symbolically mediated human relations (interpersonal relations and relations to non-personal objects) are not necessarily and originally coterminous with "violence and the sacred." Culture need not have been "religion," in Girard's sense, an entombment that systematically conceals collective murder. The conditions for symbolically mediated human relations (the capacity for joint attention, for empathy with other human beings, etc.) might be more fundamental than the conditions that generate religion (the emergence of mimetic desire and its expression as acquisitive mimesis). We might affirm this, even though, because we lack the categorial tools for representing it, we have—and can have—no determinate idea of what human langua culture would be like, if it were not in fact all that it happens to have been thus far: a synthesis of elements deriving from joint attention of an *aphetic* kind, on the one hand, and elements deriving from joint attention that is always already aggressive (i.e., mimetic desire), on the other.

Fifth, and finally, the aporetic character of our predicament calls for opening moves in a soteriology that articulates the hope that, in spite of what Gans (1993, 2) characterizes as our "chief problem" (the danger that we pose to ourselves as a species, given our mimetism), we are always already safe. This is a soteriology whose lineaments have been made visible in the midst of culture/religion, but which can only point away from the latter, insofar as the latter is a complex of forms of life that are simply inimical to this very disclosure. Let us affirm, then, that the aporia of our predicament is an obstacle on "our" side, but that there is no aporia from the side of this other possibility, which is "outside" religion. In this picture, mimesis, as the ground of loving cooperation, of our flourishing through participation in one another's lives, would be fundamental. Aggression and violence would not be.

APHESIS, "MAINMISE," METANOIA

As *aphetic*, mimesis does not resist the impression that the other, the model of attention, the trespasser, makes in the affective and cognitive depths of the self. The *aphetic* imitator radically adapts to this call by internally resembling the one that calls. She does not go on to strive with the one that she so profoundly resembles. As *aphetic*, mimesis' receptivity is linked instead with an attitude of welcome and forgiveness.

It may not be surprising that I associate the practice of forgiveness (the gospels' "*aphesis*") with the political and theological teachings of Jesus of Nazareth. By "*aphesis*" I intend what I take to be the term's main, but overlooked, sense. In the New Testament the many nuances of "to forgive" (*aphienai*) include: *to dismiss, to yield, to let alone, to relax*. In Matthew 18:21–35, for example, Jesus tells the story of a servant who owes an enormous debt to his master. Unable to pay, the servant and his wife and children are about to be sold into slavery. He begs for mercy, asking for more time to settle the debt. In response, quite unexpectedly, the master cancels his entire debt and he is allowed to go free. The evangelist writes that "[the] slave's lord pardoned (*apelusen* [freed, released, let go]) him and forgave (*apheken* [cancelled]) him the debt" (18:27). Now, this same man meets a fellow servant who owes him a paltry sum. He takes hold of him violently, gets his hands around the man's neck and begins to choke him, demanding immediate repayment. The second servant begs patience of the first, but the latter refuses and has his debtor thrown in prison.

This representation of the refusal to forgive vividly displays, by way of stark contrast, the main aspect of *aphesis* that I wish to emphasize. To refuse to forgive is to bind and to hold fast to one who can only thrive by being released. It is to obstruct, to block and to trip up the one that seeks to be allowed to pass, to proceed on her way. It is to strive with this other, to enter into a state of rivalry with her, rather than to yield and to let her pass. The unforgiving agent sets up—or *is*—the *skandalon* (the *trap* or *obstacle*) of Matthew 18:6–9 and elsewhere.[19] In contrast to scandal, *aphesis* is a matter of foregoing rivalry, foregoing recovery of a debt owed, and foregoing justice when one's debtor fails to pay. The *aphetic* agent yields to the other's intention to pass on her way, endorses it, intends it along with her, and takes on herself whatever consequences accrue to this forward movement.[20]

Given the significance that I attribute to this notion of yielding, the Greek "*aphesis*" is preferable in the present context, then, to "forgiveness" or "pardon." My use of "*aphesis*" foregrounds as far as possible the receptive position of the forgiving subject: she yields to the other's immediate attention to things, an attention that precludes attention to the first subject's immediate interest in being "repaid." She lets the other go, releases her, allows her to pass and continue on her way. "*Aphesis*" captures a yielding, malleable, adaptive, non-resistant relation to the other and contrasts with anything that might be conceived of as an autonomous undertaking on the initiative of an unassisted, independent subject. In short, by its receptivity, *aphesis* is clearly distinguished from the grasping, taking, and impeding that are embodied in acquisitive mimesis and its literally scandalous *sequelae*.

Another key advantage of my use of "*aphesis*" is that, unlike "forgiveness," it does not have the immediate ethical connotation of a social configuration in which an injured party stands before an autonomous, responsible, mature victimizer. It subsumes this configuration, naturally, but also allows for the idea of an *aphetic* relation and ongoing state of reconciliation between innocent children, on the one hand, and older more powerful subjects, on the other. In their mundane and (ethically speaking) innocent transgressions, little children, more clearly than any others, "know not what they do" and are, to that extent, prototypical trespassers. Similarly, *aphesis* allows us to speak in theological terms of an ongoing state of reconciliation to the *Para-kletos*, to the defender of those that we accuse (and of ourselves *qua* subject to accusation), whose unexpected, unpredictable, boundary-transgressing presence may be resisted or welcomed. And it allows us to speak of Jesus's relation to those whose expectations he shattered, those would-be rivals whose lives he put into disarray. Indeed, it allows us to speak of the relation of anyone who transgresses any boundaries whatsoever to those who hold dearly to those boundaries (whatever their moral quality).

Drawing on the foregoing, then, a paradigm for *aphesis* would be the very young child's passage from the "autism" of her first months into the world that is opened up by joint attention, the world as an order of things that antedates her arrival and demands that she surrender her autonomy (an illusion in any case) to a heteronomous regime. At the outset of her life, to an astonishing degree, the human being "forgives" those whose interests and attention-to-things she finds embodied within the lineaments of her independent frame. She yields to them and allows them to "be" her very self. This position is an entirely natural one. Her "internalization of the perspectives of other persons," of the attention and interests of the "many"—the implicit, inward, mimetic reproduction of other persons' own "internal" orientation to things—enables "infants to virtually mediate their understanding of the world through other persons" (Tomasello 1999, 93).

But when her surrender is not met by an equally *aphetic* stance by those who greet her entrance into the social order this leaves the "little one" vulnerable to scandal. With reference specifically to desire, Girard describes this in terms of Bateson's "double-bind," a predicament that arises when the model that mediates desire becomes an obstacle and a rival (Girard 1987, 91). Implicitly, just by attending to things in the world, the model says: *Look at the thing that I am looking at! Attend to it as though you were me!* But then— explicitly: *Do not relate to this thing as I do! Do not take hold of it, as though you were me!*[21] Jean-François Lyotard (1993, 148) offers a powerful supplement to Girard's description of this scenario, one that can be applied broadly, not only to desire, but to attention more generally. He illuminates the human being's possession-by-others in terms of a *"mainmise,"* or "grip," that is applied ontogenetically to the subject but which is maintained throughout her life. Since we begin life as *infants*—and not, after all, as already walking, talking, independent beings—we can never "enter into full possession of ourselves." We never get to be the subjects of desire, or interest, or attention, *selon soi* (to borrow Girard's term) that we nevertheless take ourselves to be. As Lyotard writes "we are held by the grasp of others since childhood [and] our childhood does not cease to exercise its *mancipium* even when we imagine ourselves to be emancipated" (1993, 149). This notion of childhood references a predicament that always leaves us entangled with those who inhabit the world (which they cannot help but regard as *theirs*) before we do. Thus, Lyotard writes:

> [b]y childhood, I do not mean, as the rationalists have it, an age deprived of reason. I mean this condition of being *affected* at a time when we do not have the means—linguistic and representational—to name, identify, reproduce, and recognize what it is that is affecting us. By childhood, I mean the fact that we are born before we are born to ourselves. And thus we are born of others, but also born to others, delivered into the hands of others without any defenses. We are subjected to their *mancipium*, which they themselves do not comprehend. For they are themselves children in their turn, whether fathers or mothers. (*ibid.*)

At the *origin* of individuality and subjectivity then, or, more precisely, of interdividuality and inter-subjectivity, the subject does not need to "*try,*" as Tomasello claims, "to understand things from [others'] point of view" (1999, 14).[22] She is simply unable to resist the compulsion to enter into her caregivers', older siblings', teachers', or other more powerful persons' inter-subjective perspectives on her and other objects. She is radically, irreversibly compelled (in advance of self-possession, in advance of every *option*) to exemplify a complex of motivational structures, of incentives and loves that is not "hers." Her perspective, desires, interests, general ends, and aims—in short, the point of departure for her whole practical life—are radically grounded in "the perspectives of other persons."

Given these inter-subjective entanglements, the idea of an unequivocally *proprietary* perspective (interest, attention, orientation, desire) is manifestly spurious. Girard is correct to refer to the ideology that promotes the notion of desire *"selon soi"* as a *lie* ("*le mensonge romantique*") (Girard 1965, 16–17). Let us extend this to the notion of attention. The position from which one openly and explicitly *acts* is always already grounded in others' own orientation to things, their attention, interest, desire, which is not, however, theirs in an individualistic sense either. *I* act, but the determinateness of the "thing" that I do (the fact that this deed is an instance of a *kind* of action, a member of the class of deeds, say, that are motivated in such-and-such a manner) is "ours." Analogously, when I speak, my utterances are mine, *I* say them, but I do not exercise independent jurisdiction over what I *mean*. The nature of the subject's "own" deeds is a common one; she has no independent ownership of it. She is, in the language of St. Paul, "in Adam" and "in Christ." *She* acts; but she has a "nature" that she did not choose. Her perspective on the world is always internalized and yet never, strictly speaking, *absolutely* "internal," never essentially "hers." Rather, it is originarily ingested or absorbed like an aroma (I owe a debt, here, to Horkheimer and Adorno [2002, 151]).

By "*metanoia*" (often translated as "conversion" or "repentance") I intend, among other things, the transformative recognition of other persons' radical proximity to oneself and/or others. More specifically, my use of the term references a radical awakening of mind and affect to the originary entanglement of "the one" and "the many" that we have been discussing. This entanglement is achieved behind the backs of all involved, in the collective, mimetically mediated "grip" by which her community first takes hold of the child. It is extended then, too, in the grip by which this subject, as she matures, takes hold of others. It is perpetuated in the grip by which she joins in taking hold of other neonatal trespassers that intrude into—and *disorder*—the community to which she has come to belong. *Aphesis*, in its most fundamental manifestation, is the new human being's yielding to models of attention and her surrendering to the entanglement that this entails. *Metanoia*, then, entails the recognition that our description of human action must have constant reference to this entanglement. In other words, "*metanoia*" refers to a changed understanding, evidenced in one's practice, of moral accountability and of the imputability of deeds. It is rightly characterized as a decisive "turning-around." It is instantiated, to a significant extent, in Girard's notion of "novelistic conversion," which is, among other things, the recognition that human beings are heteronomous, rather than autonomous agents.

This recognition is an acknowledgment that we are entangled with "the one that did it," the one that we accuse, in such a way that her defenders—if indeed she has any—might begin by pointing to this entanglement, by pointing out that she is one of *us*, that she is truly a member of the same community to which we, her accusers, also belong. Her defenders might insist that what she does, she does without knowing *what* she does. When she acts, her defenders might say, she does not adequately know what her actions "are"; she does not know, and cannot know, what *kind* of thing her actions are instances of. Indeed, Jesus says even of the people that are publicly humiliating him and torturing him to death that "they know not what they do" (Luke 23:34). I take him to be pointing, among other things, to two absolutely fundamental features of human agency.

The first is that it is in the nature of human agency that saying "what" one does means adverting to reasons for acting that are neither "hers," nor "mine," nor "yours," but rather constitutively, irreducibly "ours." "The one that did it" pursues "our" ends, which are shrouded in an obscurity that no human being can adequately penetrate. She, like you and me, is caught up in what the human race, taken together, is always already doing; but to say what *that* is lies beyond the conceptual resources of the historically situated subject. The second is that, when we act, we transgress boundaries that we, the people acting, cannot have seen, whose nature and significance it is beyond our capacity to understand. Whatever action I take, the one thing that cannot be *known* concerning it, neither by me, nor by any spectator, is that it does not transgress boundaries whose presence and significance I am in no position to assess. I cannot know that it is not "*hamartia*," that there is not a good "mark" that it misses. I cannot know, on the other hand, that the boundaries that it *does* transgress are boundaries whose antecedent instauration may not be questioned. This is not to say that we know nothing whatsoever about what we do, or that we cannot judge deeds to be good or evil, but only that such judgments are not absolute, that they serve the specific interests of the beings that we happen to be, here and now, and that our judgments themselves stand, perhaps, under another more universal judgment that we are in no position to render.

Metanoia feels and responds, then, to the blind spot in the motivational structure of individual agency that is created by the situated "jointness" of the human being's attention-to-things, the collective, historical dimension of the intentionality of her cognition, the deep sharedness of her interests, the mimetic ground of the character in accordance with which she acts. Identifying this blind spot and communicating its significance is a task for Christian ethics. Specifically, this task pertains to our reorientation to "the knowledge of good and evil." As Deitrich Bonhoeffer (1995, 27) observes, while "[t]he knowledge of good and evil seems to be the aim of all ethical reflection . . . the first task of Christian ethics is to invalidate this knowledge." The Pharisee who announces his charity with trumpets, or who prays loudly on the street corner, "knows" the good that he does (and that he announces). He takes his wicked neighbors to know what they do as well. He is, as Bonhoeffer sardonically observes, "[t]hat extremely admirable man who subordinates his entire life to his knowledge of good and evil and is as severe a judge of himself as of his neighbor to the honour of God, whom he humbly thanks for this knowledge (*ibid.*)." But this knowledge is spurious; in *metanoia* the subject is set free from the bonds that it sustains.

Metanoia is a turning away from what Doxtader (2003, 290n58) describes (paraphrasing Desmond Tutu) as "Western philosophical views about identity, particularly as they work in political contexts to delineate the substance of the individual subject." As Tutu puts it, "people are people through other people." *Metanoia* supervenes, in other words, upon a changed understanding of others' and one's own past actions and of the desires that these express. *Metanoia* entails a profound empathy with others, including one's enemies—empathy being, as I suggested earlier, itself a mode of implicit mimesis, of *aphesis*. It sees their trespasses from *their* point of view and so, too, our trespasses against them. It relativizes "the knowledge of good and evil" and enables the subject to claim for the other what she wants for herself, that is, for her deeds to be regarded as the actions of an agent that "knows not what she does." *Metanoia* pertains to the individual alone. Certainly, it involves a changed orientation to one's rivals and potential rivals or, indeed, a changed orientation to these others' orientation to things. But it does not entail a reciprocal change in one's rival. Where *metanoia* is mutual, however, where rivals, or potential rivals, yield to one another, where their mutual adaptation means that each is deeply altered by the other, where *aphetic* mimesis, in other words, moves in both directions, one encounters reconciliation and, too, a mode of reconciliation that has nothing to do with the scapegoat mechanism.

Contrast this with the state of affairs that is sustained by what Redekop (2008) calls the "hermeneutics of [the] justification" of violence, which, as he points out, is a natural concomitant of mimetic desire, acquisitive mimesis, and mimetic rivalry. This way of understanding the deliverances of one's own and others' agency depends upon the occlusion of any insight into the blind spot that I have described. It refuses to qualify the notion of "trespass" by relativizing the boundaries upon which the former depends. It will not take seriously the mimetically mediated entanglement of human agents with one another. It serves "my" or "our" violence by justifying and so sustaining it. It presupposes "knowledge" of so-called "facts" concerning the unambiguous good and evil of other persons. It also takes for granted—as if it were a matter of *a priori* certainty—the intrinsic, necessary relationship that is supposed to hold between evil and suffering where the latter is regarded in strictly retributivist terms. This "knowledge" then funds unambiguous judgments of blame and praise concerning these others and the approbation, if not the production, of their suffering.

Reconciliation, however, as Doxtader puts it, "opposes the way in which we establish the essence (the exclusivity) of things, challenges the ways that we justify the value of such distinctions, and endeavors to dismantle those modes of definition that legitimize identitarian violence" (Doxtader 2003, 267). In the present context, I would specify this "dismantling" as one that operates upon "modes of definition" which, in enlightened modernity (especially in and after Kant), remain integral for the theoretical coherence and ongoing practical possibility of punishment (more generally, of the archaic, collective approbation of the suffering of "evildoers"), to the extent, specifically, that punishment is regarded in retributivist terms.[23] More precisely, reconciliation demands a dismantling of the radically individualistic understanding of human agency that retributivism presupposes, with distinctions between actor and patient, speaker and hearer, guilty and innocent, that ascribe too lucid an accountability, too transparent a "knowledge" of "what she does," to even the most immature subject (cf. Redekop 2008, 211–12).

In a sense, *metanoia* is best regarded as a consequence of *aphesis*, rather than as a condition for one agent's being forgiven by another. The receptivity of *aphesis* is conceptually and ontologically fundamental, while *metanoia*, the latter's other moment, flows from this antecedent yielding. The subject that yields to the trespasser is inwardly changed; her transformation is shown in this yielding. By contrast with the *metanoia* that flows from *aphetic* mimesis and which is, as Girard has argued, a direct consequence of sustained exposure to the Hebrew and Christian scriptures, our persistent, archaic unwillingness to yield to those who trespass against us widens the scope of the "unforgivable" in a manner that serves our rather limited sense of what can be expected of human beings. *Aphesis*, which yields and allows this passage to unfold, opens a space for new action; it opens a space too for the trespasser's own *metanoic* transformation.

Who, however, trespasses? Who is called upon to yield? Whose vision stands in need of inflection by its incorporation into the vision of another? To the extent that human beings are always on the verge of rivalry with those nearest to them and given that, as rivalries develop, rivals are always less and less distinguishable "doubles" of each other, there can be no unambiguous distinction between the class of human agents that are called, in general, to conversion, to "turn around," and those that are called upon to "let go," to forgive. Each may yield to the many others who conjointly live "her" life; each mind may be transformed by a welcoming receptivity to unexpected points of view. And the reconciliation that this mutuality entails is no merely *ex post facto* alternative to rivalry and violence. Rather, it is a state of affairs that, in principle, might have taken precedence over rivalry from the outset. Had trespassers always been forgiven and set free to go on their way, had forgiven trespassers always been reciprocally transformed in relation to those against whom they had trespassed, our history of rivalry would never have arisen in the first place.

CONCLUSION

In this chapter, I have argued that mimetic desire, acquisitive mimesis, and mimetic rivalry entail a contingent orientation to things and other persons that is grounded in joint attention. Mimetic desire is a function of our profound, antecedent identification with one another. The problematic of mimetic desire is not, however, an inevitable concomitant of this deep mutuality. The same capacity that grounds scandal and rivalrous animosity grounds empathy and love and friendship. Our capacity for joint attention is a necessary (but not a sufficient) condition on both sides. Thus the human capacity for joint attention and the "social-cognitive adaptation for identifying with other persons" are ambivalent. Indeed, Tomasello's account of joint attention elides the potential for rivalry and violence that inheres in mimetic desire. He does not notice that the capacity for joint attention, good in itself, might nevertheless ground problems of intraspecific relating that threaten the survival of the human species. This oversight needs correction.

I have argued that we are bound by our roots, by means of our shared mimetic faculty, to those that we love, but that we are also bound to those that we accuse and hate, to those, especially, that we impede, block, and trip-up. We are bound to those to whom we will not yield, to those who will not yield to us. Our hands are locked around their throats and theirs are locked around ours. I have adverted to non-violent reconciliation as one way out of this predicament. In the scapegoating that Girard describes, scandalous mimesis achieves a result that is analogous to non-violent reconciliation. But the two modes of reconciliation are utterly opposed. As the decisive, focused negation of the indecisive, antecedent violence of all against all, scapegoating shows that authentic reconciliation is in fact lacking, that no one repents and no one forgives.

These considerations suggest a direction for mimetic theory *vis-à-vis* the theme of reconciliation and in connection with what Gans (1993, 1) characterizes as the fundamental problem of ethics, the urgent necessity attaching to the human being's reflexive self-knowledge (in short, the urgent necessity of anthropology itself). Suppose that we answer the question, *What ought we to do?* by affirming that we ought to enter into and remain in a state of non-violent reconciliation with one another. Our understanding of this answer must be inflected by the fact that non-violent reconciliation (the nexus of mutual *aphesis* and *metanoia*) is not a simple alternative to violence. The two are not simply alien to one another. They are not entirely and mutually exclusive. Instead, the human being's capacity for creative, peaceful, life-giving relations with others of her kind supervenes on the same features of her deep make-up that open onto violence. Anthropology is urgently important, here, precisely because human beings are animals who, in relating to one another, pose a problem that is unique to them, a problem that is more pressing than any threat that they face from external, non-human nature. This problem arises independently of their intentions, no matter how good these may be. Ethics pertains to the identification, description, and normativity of the practical strategies by which the human community manages attention to the things that interest them conjointly and which achieve and maintain the community's stability (cf. *ibid.*, 2–3). But practical strategies aimed at a common life that has no recourse to violence must contend with the fact that the alternative to violence grows, like violence itself, from our capacity and propensity for joint attention.

If we could forgive the "little one," radically and perpetually, in the ontogenetic context of her origin, yield to her, let her pass, receive her impress unresistingly, bear the weight of the effects that emerge from her living presence—perhaps here, in this forgiveness, we would find a sense of "religion" and "ethics" that is not entangled with the Girardian "sacred," with the *sequelae* of collective violence. This can only take place, however, in the context of actual, concrete instances of childhood, in the actual, contingently organized relations of particular children and adults.

It is worth noting, here, that both *baptism* (infant baptism, especially, but also baptism more generally, and also anointing with *chrism*, etc.) and *child sacrifice* instantiate a similar structure: on the one hand, again, the "cadaver [that] constitutes the first object . . . of [noninstinctual] attention" (Girard 1987, 99) and, on the other, the living body of the "little one," the intruder, welcomed rather than scandalized. This scene, no matter how imperfectly lived-out in subsequent practice, suggests the possibility of a mode of attention that does not take hold of trespassers in order to block their passage, but yields to them. It is a mode of attention that does not merely defer possession of a potentially divisive object, but surrenders it to the other, generously. (It is significant that in the joint attentional scenes that Tomasello describes, roles are interchangeable: the child can model attentiveness for the adult or direct the adult's attention and the adult can *acquiesce* in this in a way that is nourishing for the child.)

But if our shared history—our shared "history of violence," with its endless piling up of insurmountable debt—has rendered us *incapable* of what is required here, then the hope that pertains to this "abundant life," yet to be lived by us, must at the same time be a hope that we will be healed, transformed, rendered agents who are capable, really, of yielding to one another. For this, evidently, we are not.

REFERENCES

Adams, Rebecca. 2000. "Loving Mimesis and Girard's 'Scapegoat of the Text': A Creative Reassessment of Mimetic Desire." Pp. 277–307 in *Violence Renounced: René Girard, Biblical Studies, and Peacemaking*, edited by Willard M. Swartley. Telford, PA: Pandora Press.

Adorno, Theodor. 1974. *Minima Moralia: Reflections from Damaged Life*. Translated by E. F. N. Jephcott. New York: Verso.

Agar, Michael. 1994. *Language Shock: Understanding the Culture of Conversation*. New York: William Morrow.

Alison, James. 1998. *The Joy of Being Wrong: Original Sin through Easter Eyes*. New York: Crossroads.

Augsburger, David W. 1988. *The Freedom of Forgiveness*. Chicago: Moody Press.

Balthasar, Hans Urs von. 1988. *Theo-Drama: Theological Dramatic Theory*. 5 vols. Vol. 4 (The Action). San Francisco: Ignatius Press.

Bandara, Pablo. 2013. "Love vs. Resentment: The Absence of Positive Mimesis in Generative Anthropology." Pp. 277-290 in *René Girard and Creative Mimesis*. Edited by Vern Neufeld Redekop and Tom Ryba. Lanham, MD: Lexington Books.

Baron-Cohen, Simon. 1995. *Mindblindness: An Essay on Autism and Theory of Mind*. Cambridge, MA: MIT Press.

Baron-Cohen, Simon, Donald J. Cohen, and Helen Tager-Flusberg. 2000. *Understanding Other Minds: Perspectives from Developmental Cognitive Neuroscience*. 2nd ed. Oxford: Oxford University Press.

Bonhoeffer, Dietrich. 1995. *Ethics*. Translated by Neville H. Smith. New York: Simon & Schuster Books.

Cavanaugh, William T. 2009. *The Myth of Religious Violence: Secular Ideology and the Roots of Modern Conflict*. Oxford: Oxford University Press.

Collins, Robin. 2000. "Girard and Atonement: An Incarnational Theory of Mimetic Participation." Pp. 132–56 in *Violence Renounced: René Girard, Biblical Studies, and Peacemaking*, edited by Willard M. Swartley. Telford, PA: Pandora Press.

Doran, Robert M. 2007. "Summarizing 'Imitating the Divine Relations: A Theological Contribution to Mimetic Theory'." *Contagion* no. 14: 27–38.

Doxtader, Erik. 2003. "Reconciliation: a Rhetorical Concept/ion." *Quarterly Journal of Speech* no. 89 (4): 267–292.

Fleming, Chris. 2004. *René Girard: Violence and Mimesis*. Cambridge, MA: Polity.

Friedrich, Paul. 1989. "Language, Ideology, and Political Economy." *American Anthropologist* no. 91 (2): 295–312.

Gans, Eric Lawrence. 1981. *The Origin of Language: A Formal Theory of Representation*. Berkeley, CA: University of California Press.

———.1993. *Originary Thinking: Elements of Generative Anthropology*. Stanford, CA: Stanford University Press.

———. 1997. *Signs of Paradox: Irony, Resentment, and Other Mimetic Structures*. Stanford, Calif.: Stanford University Press.

Garrels, Scott R. 2006. "Imitation, Mirror Neurons, and Mimetic Desire: Convergence between the Mimetic Theory of René Girard and Empirical Research on Imitation." *Contagion* no. 12–13: 47–86.

Girard, René. 1965. *Deceit, Desire, and the Novel: Self and Other in Literary Structure*. Translated by Yvonne Freccero. Baltimore: John Hopkins Press.

———. 1978. *'To Double Business Bound': Essays on Literature, Mimesis, and Anthropology*. Baltimore, MD: Johns Hopkins University Press.

———. 1991. *A Theater of Envy: William Shakespeare*. South Bend, IN: St. Augustine's Press.

———. 2001. *I See Satan Fall Like Lightning*. Translated by James Williams. Maryknoll, NY: Orbis Books.

———. 1987. *Things Hidden Since the Foundation of the World: Research Undertaken in Collaboration with Jean-Michel Oughourlian and Guy Lefort*. Translated by Stephen Bann and Michae Metter. Stanford, CA: Stanford University Press.

Girard, René, João Cezar de Castro Rocha, and Pierpaolo Antonello. 2007. *Evolution and Conversion: Dialogues on the Origins of Culture*. London: T & T Clark.

Gruzinski, Serge. 1993. *The Conquest of Mexico: The Incorporation of Indian Societies into the Western World, 16th–18th Centuries*. Cambridge, MA: Polity Press.

Hart, David Bentley. 2003. *The Beauty of the Infinite: The Aesthetics of Christian Truth*. Grand Rapids, MI: W.B. Eerdmans.

Horkheimer, Max, and Theodor Adorno. 2002. *Dialectic of Enlightenment: Philosophical Fragments*. Translated by Edmund Jephcott. Stanford, CA: Stanford University Press.

Lyotard, Jean François. 1993. "The Grip (*Mainmise*)." Pp. 148–58 in *Political Writings*, edited by Bill Readings and Kevin Paul Geiman. Minneapolis: University of Minnesota Press.

Milbank, John. 1991. *Theology and Social Theory: Beyond Secular Reason*. Cambridge, Mass., USA: Blackwell.

Moore, C. 1999. "Intentional Relations and Triadic Interactions." Pp. 43-62 in *Developing Theories of Intention: Social Understanding and Self-control*, edited by Janet W. Astington, David R. Olson and Philip David Zelazo. Mahwah, NJ: Lawrence Erlbaum Associates.

Redekop, Vern Neufeld. 2002. "Mimetic Structures of Violence and of Blessing: Creating a Discursive Framework for Reconciliation." *Theoforum* no. 33 (3): 311–335.

———. 2008. "A Post-Genocidal Justice of Blessing as an Alternative to a Justice of Violence: The Case of Rwanda." Pp. 205–41 in *Peacebuilding in Traumatized Societies*, edited by Barry Hart. Lanham: University Press of America.

Reineke, Martha. 2007. "Transforming Space: Creativity, Destruction, and Mimesis in Winnicott and Girard." *Contagion* no. 14: 79–95.

Rizzolatti, Giacomo. 2005. "The Mirror Neuron System and Imitation." Pp. 55–76 in *Perspectives on Imitation: From Neuroscience to Social Science: Vol. 1: Mechanisms of Imitation and Imitation in Animals*, edited by Susan Hurley and Nick Chater. Cambridge, MA: MIT Press.

Rizzolatti, Giacomo, and Michael Arbib. 1998. "Language within Our Grasp." *Trends in Neuroscience* no. 21: 188–194.

Steinmair-Pösel, Petra. 2007. "Original Sin, Grace, and Positive Mimesis." *Contagion* no. 14: 1–12.

Thomson, Cameron M. 2006. "Mimesis, Trauma, and the Linguistification of the Sacred: Habermas between Adorno and Girard." MA thesis, University of St. Michael's College.

———. 2009. "The Transformation of Blame: 'Religious Thought' and the Genealogy of Scientific Explanation." *Religious Studies and Theology* no. 28 (2): 207–40.

Thomson, Gregory. 2006. "The Sociocultural Dimension of Second Language Acquisition." Unpublished manuscript.

Tomasello, Michael. 1999. *The Cultural Origins of Human Cognition*. Cambridge, MA.: Harvard University Press.

Van Oort, Richard. 2007. "Imitation and Human Ontogeny: Michael Tomasello and the Scene of Joint Attention." *Anthropoetics* no. 13 (1): http://www.anthropoetics.ucla.edu/ap1301/1301vano.htm.

Vygotsky, L. 1978. *Mind in Society: The Development of Higher Psychological Processes*. Edited by M. Cole. Cambridge, MA: Harvard University Press.

———. 1986. *Thought and Language*. London: The MIT Press.

Williams, J. H., A. Whiten, T. Suddendorf, and D. I. Perrett. 2001. "Imitation, Mirror Neurons and Autism." *Neuroscience and Biobehavioral Reviews* no. 25 (4): 287–295.

NOTES

1. This chapter is based on a paper ("Acquisitive Mimesis and the Joint Attentional Scene") presented in June 2006 at COV&R's annual meeting at Saint Paul University in Ottawa. Many thanks are due to Vern Neufeld Redekop and Thomas Ryba for their detailed comments and suggestions, which have greatly focused and improved this piece.

2. Milbank's argument is a classic and influential example of this kind of critique, but others have offered negative assessments of the theological upshot of Girard's thinking as well. Balthasar (1988, 297–310) is much more nuanced and appreciative than Milbank, but still critical (the Swiss theologian's discussion of Raymund Schwager is pertinent too [see *ibid.*, 310–13]). David Bentley Hart's (2003, 345–9) soteriological retrieval of the notion of sacrifice also addresses Girard's thinking directly and critically.

3. "Culture/religion" is an awkward construction, to be sure, but ought to be retained if we take Girard seriously. Cavanaugh (2009) reminds us why: "In traditional societies, Girard is clear, religion does not pick out something distinct from culture in general" (40) and "Girard . . . den[ies] that religion picks out any distinct cultural activity in traditional societies and . . . blur[s] the distinction between religious and secular in modern societies" (41).

4. Since the time of the 2006 conference presentation upon which this chapter is based, the relevance of joint attention and related topics—of Tomasello's work in particular—has been acknowledged in another context (Van Oort 2007). Van Oort's essay offers a detailed, but succinct overview of Tomasello's work with direct application to mimetic theory and generative anthropology. I also deploy Tomasello's and Girard's thinking together in another connection (C. Thomson 2009).

5. Prior to this time, the human infant resembles nonhuman primates and many autists: she is *unable* to "understand others as intentional agents." Because she lacks this ability, the very young infant is not yet equipped "to take advantage of the cognitive skills and knowledge of conspecifics that is manifest in [her] cultural milieu" (78). Work on the connection between joint attention (or rather a deficit in the capacity for it) and autism is particularly illustrative of the former's immense significance. (See, for example, Baron-Cohen 1995; Baron-Cohen, Cohen, and Tager-Flusberg 2000; Williams et al 2001.)

6. It is preferable to avoid saying that the neonate "acquires" language—any more than the first human beings did. The neonate does not acquire language, but, as psycholinguist Greg

Thomson (2006) puts it, is drawn into a life of ongoing, ever "growing participation" in the life of a people. In the first instance, the people in question would be the subject's own, but this is hardly the end of the story: Thomson's discussion pertains to second language acquisition (his reference to "growing participation" is inspired by Vygotsky's notion of the "proximal zone of development" [cf. Vygotsky 1978, 86–91] and it is worth noting that, like Tomasello's work, Vygotsky's has significance for the further refinement of Girard's mimetic theory; see, for example, his [1986, 188–9] contrasting descriptions of the role of imitation in the intellectual development of apes and human children, respectively; Vygotsky offers an assessment of the theoretical importance of imitation in connection with his notion of the zone of proximal development [1978, 87–8]). As Gans (1993, 1–2) points out, in any case, language is not an institution that is ontologically prior to the human being, which then puts "its" stamp upon us. The language by means of whose "use" the "prehuman creature becom[es] human" develops from the interactions of these creatures and is identical to them. This is so, insofar as no other animals relate to one in the medium of joint attention and insofar as this mode of relation, along with the neurobiological conditions of its possibility (the trait that grounds our identification with our conspecific companions), is the "criterion" (or criteria) of the human.

7. There is much recent evidence suggesting a strong physiological basis for this "temptation." In a now classic paper, Giacomo Rizzolatti and Michael Arbib (1998, 188) describe a peculiar class of neurons ("mirror neurons") that are located "in the rostral part of . . . inferior area 6 (area F5)" of their subjects' (here, monkeys) brains (probable homologue of Broca's area, which is closely associated with language production in human beings). These neurons "discharge, both when the monkey grasps or manipulates objects and when it observes the experimenter making similar actions." They are especially remarkable for the fact that they do not discharge upon "object presentation," but only in response to "specific observed action." Some of these actions must be highly specific in order to evoke a response and "code," not merely "the action aim, but also how that action is executed." For example, there are particular neurons that fire only "during the observation of grasping movement," but then "only when the object is grasped with the index finger and the thumb." According to the authors, "[t]he actions most represented are: grasp, manipulate, tear, and put an object on a plate." Also worth noting is the apparent fact that these neurons also "have motor properties that are indistinguishable from those of F5 neurons that do not respond to action observation." More (and ever more sophisticated) research results continue to explore the role that these neurons play in the functioning of the human brain and chart their relevance for human social psychology, for phenomena such as empathy, and for language and other cultural behaviours (see, for example, Rizzolatti 2005). Garrels (2006) offers an excellent treatment of these matters from a mimetic-theoretical point of view.

8. As Girard (1965, 10) says, "[t]he impulse toward the object is ultimately an impulse toward the mediator."

9. Girard remains strongly committed to this perspective. In *Evolution and Conversion* he avers that "[Religion] is . . . the source of hominization, of the differentiation between animals and human beings, because, as I explained in *Things Hidden*, through sacrifice it creates culture and institutions." He goes on to affirm that "the creation of culture is engendered by religion through the victimary mechanism, which is in fact contingent and mechanistic" (2007, 98).

10. Horkheimer and Adorno offer fruitful resources for thinking about this. In their treatment of mimesis, just as in Girard's, the mimetic impulse does not fasten, in the first instance, on the superficial form of the *actions* of the other. Rather, they describe a receptive, epistemic mimesis in which what is not original to the self is encountered only by being allowed to take place in the depths of the subject. Mimesis is a "mirroring" that occurs within the sensing and socially embedded subject, whose "inner depth . . . consists in nothing other than the delicacy and richness of the outer perceptual world" (2002, 156), and all of whose "content comes from society" (Adorno 1974, 154). This "inward" character of mimesis is ambiguous, however, for it also funds shared interests that inform human inter-subjectivity. In any case, the "intermeshing" and ambiguity of "inner" and "outer" *topoi* is so constitutive of subjectivity that if it is fractured "the self petrifies" (Horkheimer and Adorno 2002, 156). For a detailed discussion of Horkheimer's and Adorno's work with reference to mimetic theory see C. Thomson (2006).

11. Obviously, I am alluding to (Girard 1978, 89): "This mode of imitation operates with a quasi-osmotic immediacy necessarily betrayed and lost in all the dualities of the modern problematic of desire."

12. Gans avers that "[r]esentment at others' real or fancied proximity to the center provides the fuel for the motor of history, a motor that does most of its work in crises, when the accumulated resentment of a social group is released in sparagmatic rage against its object" (1997, 135 Bandera 2003).

13. Girard expresses this point quite forcefully: "The notion that the Decalogue devotes its supreme commandment, the longest of all, to the prohibition of a marginal desire reserved for a minority is hardly likely. The desire prohibited by the tenth commandment must be the desire of all human beings—in other words, simply desire as such" (2001, 8).

14. This useful term is Michael Agar's (1994) emendation of Paul Friedrich's (1989) "languaculture." Both authors affirm a radical entanglement of language and culture. Friederich, in particular, refers to "a domain of experience that fuses and intermingles the vocabulary, many semantic aspects of grammar, and the verbal aspects of culture; both grammar and culture have underlying structure while they are constantly being used and constructed by actual people on the ground" (307). I am not using the term in a technical sense, but as a tool for preventing too strong a distinction between language (roughly, grammar and vocabulary) and culture (background knowledge, lifeworld, pre-reflective forms of life, etc.).

15. This suggests a link between aphetic mimesis and our sense of responsibility to, and for, others. Sandor Goodhart's contribution to this volume is highly suggestive in this regard. Goodhart argues, with reference to Levinas, that there is a connection here with the process of hominization. Our capacity for recognizing other human agents as beings like ourselves is entailed by our fundamentally mimetic capacity for recognizing, specifically, that others of our kind have a point of view on the world. Goodhart suggests that hominization was marked by the early emergence of a profound capacity for mutual care and empathy. He also affirms that Girard's account of hominization is not inimical to other accounts. Indeed, he adverts to a basic complementarity between Girard's account and the Levinasian one. Similarly, I suggest that aphetic mimesis and acquisitive mimetic desire emerged concomitantly; that these phenomena are grounded in the same human capacity for joint attention and, neurologically, in the same properties of mirror neurons.

16. In this regard Chris Fleming (2004, 48) observes that "contrary to acquisitive mimesis . . . this second, *accusatory* mimesis draws together those who are implicated in it, with the moral certitude of the accusation itself standing in almost exact proportion to the extent of the *esprit de corps* that it is able to produce."

17. I discuss the relationship between the human being's originary and persistent capacity for empathy and the transition from mythological to "non-agentic" modes of explanation in C. Thomson (2009).

18. This need not be regarded as a historical claim; I am not adverting to some lost, golden age. The order in question is an incipient one, always on the verge of actualization—always possible and always (thus far) refused.

19. The limitations of the present essay do not allow me to more adequately justify my claim that the canonical gospels depict an integral conceptual relationship between *un*forgiveness, the refusal (or perhaps the inability) to forgive, and what these texts refer to as "scandal." For the moment, I merely suggest that this is a connection that bears making from a mimetic-theoretical point of view: the relation between *scandal* (the obstacle or stumbling-block) and *satan* (the accuser) is an important theme for Girard (see Girard 2001, especially chapter 3: "Satan" [32–46]) and it is a short step from Girard's understanding of accusation to my present discussion of *aphesis*.

20. For this representation of forgiveness in terms of the forgiving agent's bearing a burden that, from the point of view of "justice," belongs to another, I owe a debt to Augsburger and his little (1988) book on forgiveness.

21. The first visible expression of attention is the *gaze*. This is attested to anthropologically in the prevalence of worries about the evil eye (see, for example, Gruzinski 1993, 168). It is as a mode of *attention* that the universality of the problem of covetousness seems most plausible.

22. Tomasello claims that "she . . . *tries* to understand things from their point of view" (1999, 14; my emphasis).

23. I cannot make a case for this claim here. I am not suggesting, in any case, that the changed understanding of moral accountability and of the imputability of deeds that *metanoia* entails is incompatible with the notion of punishment, across the board. Rather, my claim would be that, if we are indeed heteronomous and not autonomous agents, then punishment must have reference to the malefactor in a manner which, at the same time, addresses the community with (at least some of) whose other members the malefactor is radically entangled. In other words, the justification of punishment must take a consequentialist form. All forms of retributivism turn on—or express—a radical individualism about crime and punishment that is incompatible with the features of human agency to which Girard and Tomasello draw our attention.

Chapter Two

The Self and Other People

*Reading Conflict Resolution and Reconciliation with
René Girard and Emmanuel Levinas*

Sandor Goodhart

Here is a quote from Ruel Kaptein (to whom this chapter is dedicated) with which I would like to start: "Emmanuel Levinas . . . talks of the defenseless face of the other which shows itself to us in a way we can't avoid. When we recognize this face, it makes us a captive. This face is the face of the scapegoat, the victim, helpless and without possibility of escape." One of the hot topics in conflict resolution studies over the past thirty years or so has been the introduction of the idea of reconciliation.[1] The idea behind it is that the resolution of conflict remains temporary as long as we focus exclusively upon the symptomatic issues at hand and that only if we step back and look more broadly at the people involved and the larger contexts in which they live and work can it be made permanent—and thus something like reconciliation becomes possible. In this expanding contextual understanding, the work of René Girard has assumed special importance.

Why? Girard posits that all culture operates in effect as a management system for mimetic desire, a system sustained by what he calls the scapegoat mechanism, a system in which a victim arbitrarily chosen and sacrificially removed from the community in a veritable lynching is understood to be at the origin of all social distinction, founded as such distinction is upon the difference between the sacred and violence. The sacred and violence for Girard are one and the same. The sacred is violence effectively removed from the community, and violence is the sacred deviated from its segregated transcendent status and come down into the city to wreak havoc among its citizenry. If the system is effectively maintained, the originating violence is reenacted each year in the form of commemorative ritual, and the result is the regeneration of the sacred. If the system is not maintained, the result is violence, which is to say, difference gone wrong, distinction gone awry, asserted in the extreme in its inefficacy. Untouched by the outside world, archaic communities, as Girard tells the story, sustained their existence for thousands of years within this cycle of difference, difference gone wrong (or sacrificial crisis), paroxysmal exclusionary behavior (or surrogate victim-age), and new differentiation (and commemorative reenactment). With the advent of the "modern" world some twenty-five hundred years ago (and for whatever reason), these sacrificial systems were threatened and the ones that survived were the ones that effectively developed a means of living more or less without sacrificial victims in the traditional sense.

CONFLICT RESOLUTION, GIRARD, AND LEVINAS

It is not hard to imagine how or why conflict resolution theorists would be interested in these ideas and identify in this account of sacrificial violence and its mechanism a useful model.

Here for example is how Roel Kaptein[2] explains Girard:

> Our culture increasingly gives us the impression that we are atomized individuals, responsible for and to ourselves and free to do what we want. Inevitably in this situation, everybody and everything else become tools, which we can use to reach our own goals. Others get in the way between us and our goals.
>
> When we see other people scapegoating and blaming others, we despise it. However, in despising and loathing it we actually prove that we are not free of it ourselves. Instead we show that we know all about it. Nevertheless, we continue to scapegoat and blame others, over and over again, without ever acknowledging what we are doing. Even while we are doing it, we remain absolutely certain that we ourselves are not scapegoating. We are sure that we are simply right!
>
> Given this situation, everything which is in this enchiridion, indeed even everything which we learn from the gospel can be used to play the game of scapegoating, the game of culture, better. We can become even cleverer hypocrites, thinking ourselves superior. There is only one possibility of escape from this cycle; to recognize the scapegoating mechanism operating through us. We know that time and again we are made scapegoats ourselves. We fight to escape this predicament by scapegoating others. The alternative, a wholly different possibility, is to find the freedom to let it be. We can stop the fighting and so be free at last.
>
> How do we go about this? How can we find a way to this possibility? Emmanuel Levinas, the great Jewish thinker, talks of the defenseless face of the other, which shows itself to us in a way we can't avoid. When we recognize this face, it makes us a captive. This face is the face of the scapegoat, the

victim, helpless and without possibility of escape. When we see this face, it shows us ourselves and our helplessness. We can only bow and serve.

In this way, the gospels ask us to look at Jesus, who shows us who we are, bringing us to the place we must find in order to find new life, freedom. It is the place we fear most, that of the scapegoat. (1993, 12)

Using Girard's ideas as a basis for his analysis, Kaptein asks the inevitable question: How do we go about finding a way out of this sacrificial crisis? This is an important move on Kaptein's part, and it highlights a very important feature of Girard's ideas, a feature often missed by a good many of the individuals who currently use Girard's ideas: namely, that there is no implied remedy. There is no ethical consequence to be gleaned from Girard's analysis, other than to end the violence, to *refuser la violence*.

Why do so many researchers think there is a "Girardian" solution to sacrificial violence? For two reasons, I would suggest. First, because Girard gives great weight to the exposé of sacrificial violence offered in the Jewish and Christian scriptural texts. The Christian Gospel is not the only place for Girard that it shows up (it shows up first in Hebrew scripture—and especially the prophetic texts—and somewhat later in Greek tragedy hundreds of years before it does in the Gospel) but it is one of key places, and, in any event, the place where, in his view, its analysis is "completed." If Girard gives so much weight to Christian reading of these matters, it must be, these researchers reason, because Girard finds the Christian reading an acceptable one *in toto* and endorses its fundamental postulates.

But there is a second reason researchers easily move from a descriptive account to a prescriptive one. Girard himself has declared publicly that he is a practicing Christian, a member in good standing of the Roman Catholic Church, and Girardianism, therefore, these researchers argue, must be a Christian intellectual phenomenon. It is not unreasonable that fellow Christians (especially fellow Catholics) should surmise that Girard's view is specifically a Catholic one.

In fact, however, it is not. It is not a Christian view—Catholic or Protestant. It is not a Jewish view. It is not the view of ancient Greek tragedy (in the hands of Aeschylus, Sophocles, or Euripides), any more than it is the view of the ancient writers of the Hindu, Buddhist, or Islamic scriptures. And yet at the same time it is undoubtedly related to all of these orientations (and perhaps others we have not mentioned). It may even be the province of all of the so-called "revealed" religions—if we understand these orientations in a broad enough historical context. Girardianism as an intellectual movement—wherever Girard himself found it and to whatever moral consequences it leads him personally—is an understanding shared in part or as a whole by all of the above interpretative structures whether these structures have been used as the basis for systems of religious practice or not.

How is Girardianism not one of these orientations, and yet how does it nonetheless participate within the domain in which they constitute interpretative structures? It is not these views because it is not an ethical system. Girard has spared no pains to assert that he is not writing theology—of any kind—although his work has indeed been profitably compared with that of anthropologically oriented theologians, like Karl Rahner and Bernard Lonergan.[3] He is not attempting to derive knowledge about the divine from within any one of these systems with an eye toward discerning what to do about it, what code of behavior to adopt on its basis. Girardianism is not a version of preaching, although, again, the knowledge of the sacrificial mechanism he offers has been usefully incorporated into the orientation of readers whose avowed aim is preaching.[4]

On the other hand, like each of these orientations, Girardian thinking is an interpretative system. As Girard understands the process, what he is doing is offering a reading, specifically, the reading that he feels first Judaism, and later Christianity, offers of archaic cultures. Part of the limitation of our own customary perspective on these matters may be our thinking that traditional scriptural texts are only (or even primarily) scripts for religious practice. It may be that in order to understand a thinker like René Girard we need to expand our conception of both "the religious" and of "religious scripture" and to recognize the extent to which scriptural writing, like the writing we have identified for the past two hundred years in European culture as the "literary," participates in the deepest and most thorough-going questioning available to us.[5]

Does that mean that in order to participate in a Girardian perspective one needs of necessity to share his reverence for Jewish and Christian interpretative readings? Again, not necessarily. Girard has asserted that his reading is a "scientific hypothesis," and his claim has, indeed, been taken very seriously by a number of researchers interested for example in the phenomena of mirror neurons.[6] We may identify a Girardian reading of archaic cultures, even one he identifies with Judaism and Christianity, or as rigorously scientific, without subscribing to any of the currently reigning religious or scientific views, views that may in fact only extend the representational understanding of these matters we have inherited from Platonic and Aristotelian philosophy. In my own work, I have tried to identify Girard's perspective as a species of prophetic thinking, as aligned with the "the prophetic" following the intuition of Martin Buber and Franz Rosenzweig in this endeavor—who see in it the interpretative structure "behind" the great prophetic writers of the ancient sixth century in Hebrew-speaking communities (Mabee, 2000, shares this perspective). But my identification (or, more precisely, my use of Buber and Rosenzweig's identification) is no more sacrosanct than any of the others.

Roel Kaptein is keenly aware of this state of affairs. Girardianism, like Greek tragedy, leads us to the door of the ethical by providing the critique of the sacrificial on which it is necessarily to be based but does not—by constitution cannot—take us through that door. To do that, we need another orientation. Kaptein finds that additional orientation in Emmanuel Levinas:

> Emmanuel Levinas, the great Jewish thinker, talks of the defenseless face of the other which shows itself to us in a way we can't avoid. When we recognize this face, it makes us a captive. This face is the face of the scapegoat, the victim, helpless and without possibility of escape. When we see this face, it shows us ourselves and our helplessness. We can only bow and serve. (1993, 12)

The face of the other individual, to which we are bound as a captive or hostage to a hostage taker, is the face of the victim, the face of the scapegoat, the face of the one we have blamed unjustly for the violence we ourselves have committed, whether the individual who bears that face has committed any violence or not. The face of the other individual is the face of the figure in Isaiah 53 who, "although he had done no violence," is counted among the evil-doers, and whose punishment (or "stripes") "heals us" and leads us to proclaim in complete misunderstanding (and denial of our own responsibility) that "God or the Lord has caused this to happen to him."

Roel Kaptein is a Christian so, like Girard, he interprets Girard's ideas about imitative desire and scapegoating in preeminently Christian terms: "In this way, the gospels ask us to look at Jesus, who shows us who we are, bringing us to the place we must find in order to find new life, freedom. It is the place we fear most, that of the scapegoat" (*ibid.*). Jesus for him, we may say, is a "knowing Levinasian," bringing us to the place where we may find escape from these sacrificial trials, the place which is also at the origin of our fear, and thus for Kaptein of conflict. For Roel Kaptein, these remarks (as prefatory to the book that follows) offer a way of opening the door, not just to the temporary resolutions of conflicting agendas, but to more enduring reconciliatory ones.

Other conflict resolution theorists, within the Girardian fold, have made similar moves. Vern Neufeld Redekop, for example, similarly picks up on the importance of the work of Levinas for a Girardian approach to conflict resolution. Here is Redekop on Levinas:

> Emmanuel Levinas contrasts the concepts of totality and infinity. Totality is an approach to life in which the core of one's being—one's inner life, one's identity—can be grasped and controlled. Within each of us, however, is a vast, infinite universe of thought, feeling, spirit, memory, aspiration, and a host of other factors. The human face is the exterior manifestation of this infinite *interiority*, but it is in the *exteriority* of the face of the Other through which the

fullness of humanity is encountered. Communication—using language in face-to-face interaction—is the bridge between Self and Other. (2002, 148)[7]

Redekop takes things a bit farther than Kaptein. He situates Levinas within the phenomenological setting in which Levinas's work specifically arises. Levinas's postulation occurs in the course of his meditation on tradition, on understandings of self and other, a reevaluation of traditional understandings of the constitution of identity in context of subjects and objects and in particular the role of the ethical. In *Totality and Infinity*, for example, Levinas's first major publication (written the same year—as Benoît Chantre astutely points out—as *Mensonge romantique et vérité romanèsque [Romantic Lie and Novelistic Truth]*), Levinas argues that traditional subjectivity has curiously excluded the category of the moral, and that if we are not to be "duped" by the morality we are offered in the wake of Kantian analysis—a consciousness that is distinguishable from conscience—we will need to rethink subjectivity accordingly. In phenomenology, as in Jewish understanding, Levinas will argue, "ethics is an optics."[8] There is no non-ethical realm. The ethical is already in place once the sensory is activated. The ethical is built in to our very encounter with the other individual, although our traditional renderings of that ontological encounter have failed to observe that ethical conditioning. And the "human face" for Levinas (as Redekop notes) is the place where in customary encounters this obligation originates, the gateway or opening through which the infinite passes, so to speak. To the extent that we can take stock of this occurrence of the "infinite within the finite," and give up the veritable warfare to which the ontological totalizing analyses constructed in the wake of Hegel and Kant commit us, we may be able to move beyond the conflicts seeking resolutions in which we most commonly find ourselves. More specifically, to the extent that we can shift our familiar understanding of self and others, and use language in a way that owns what Levinas calls the *dire* before the *dit*, the "to say" before the "said," we may gain some headway in face-to-face interactions and move toward constructing a "bridge" over troubled ontological waters.

It is toward a clarification of the four ideas coming from Levinas, and dominating the above passage, that I would like to move in the chapter that follows. The ideas of 1) totality (and concomitantly of the infinite), of 2) the face as an opening of gateway, of 3) the Other (or the neighbor or the other individual), and of 4) language or communication, as a distinction between the *dire* and the *dit*, are central to Levinas's conception of things. Levinas uses these ideas with great precision within the analysis he undertakes, and it behooves us to do the same in using them as intellectual tools. In looking more closely at Levinas's work in this way, we may provide a complement to a Girardian understanding of these matters and advance conflict resolution theorizing a bit, edging it a little closer to an ethical account of human behavior and thereby to its stated goal of reconciliation.

TOTALITY, THE FACE, THE OTHER, AND LANGUAGE

"Totality," as Levinas uses the word, is a reference to Hegel, and, in particular, what Franz Rosenzweig calls Hegel's "philosophy of the all" or "philosophy of the whole" (2005, Chapter 1). In *The Phenomenology of Spirit*, for example, Hegel set out to trace the history of the absolute in Western culture, a history beginning in ancient Greece and concluding, literally, in Hegel's time amidst the sounds of the French revolution that he heard outside his window as he was writing its final passages.[9] Its content, in his view, was consciousness and its burgeoning awareness of both itself (and thus the subject or "self-consciousness") and its objects. Dissatisfied with this account as just one more treatment of God, the world, or humankind for its exclusivity (one that in Hegel's case simply emphasizes the last), Rosenzweig sets out to do something different: to trace the relations between these three philosophic nodes in terms he labels creation, revelation, and redemption as three modalities of the "infinite within the finite."[10]

The idea is decisive for Levinas who finds in it a new non-representation understanding of temporality and combines Rosenzweig's insight with an account of the infinite he finds in Descartes (e.g., 1992). Levinas's project is nothing less than a reconstruction of subjectivity itself. We traditionally define subjectivity in terms of self and other. We start out in the domain of the familiar and the same. We venture out through sensory experience (and the enjoyment it confers upon us) until we bump up against the other, at which point we begin our return journey to our point of origin. Upon reaching home, we recount our round-trip journey as a narrative of self-formation, confident that we have fully elaborated the self, the other, and the identity they construct for us.

Levinas's account introduces important conceptual changes. The self that feels satisfactorily defined by the journey's conclusion differs in the first place from the agency who began in the realm of the familiar, an agency Levinas names the "self-same." Secondly, what this earlier agency encounters as a limit and names the "other" (to distinguish it from itself) is more complicated than suspected. The other hides another foreigner to the self-same, another or second other, the real other individual also making the same journey and yet radically separated from our metaphysical protagonist by an exteriority or alterity that is non-traversable.

Finally, when the traveler returns to the "home" he thought he left, he finds himself in effect in a "no-man's land." Far from "round-trip," the journey has proved singularly "one-way," and he now identifies for himself, in context of a new internal experience of the Other, an unlimited responsibility he can no more shirk than he can shirk his own death. For all its pretense, the ego, and its account of this egoic journey, has been shattered, and far from free or in control of its experience and its encounters, the ego finds itself hostage to the other individual and to a responsibility that had been conferred upon it before the journey began, a responsibility from which in fact its real freedom turns out to be delimited.

The key to this breach of totality and our conceptualization of the movement beyond is the infinite and its accessibility through the face. The infinite for Levinas is the "more within the less," the "container within the contained." And Levinas often refers to "the infinite" borrowing Rosenzweig's conceptualization of the "infinite within the finite": not the finite within the infinite, nor the finite plus the infinite, but, more precisely, the infinite *within* the finite.[11]

Why is this definition important? Because this is where traditionally we have located the divine. The divine in Levinas has traditionally been presented to us at a remove of radical externality, radical alterity, unlimited separation—for example, in the medieval definition of God as "a circle whose center is everywhere and whose circumference is nowhere" (Poulet 1967). And yet what our traveler encounters, first in the other that is not an other, then in the same that is not the same, is that the infinite separation is to be found "closer to home."

Where? In the face. The face, *le visage*, is in Levinas's conception the gateway through which the infinite passes. What allows us to escape totality, to pass beyond and open onto the infinite, is the face. The face for Levinas is a passageway, an opening. It is not an object, or a manifestation, or a form of any kind. If we had to delimit the face, Levinas, says, we would have to say that the face is nakedness itself, defenselessness itself, utter vulnerability, a "passivity more passive than the opposite of active." It is the speaking of the commandments, or, more precisely, of all the commandments as one commandment in particular, the speaking of the "Thou shalt not kill." The face is the *dire*, the "to say" (or "saying") as opposed to the said (which is that from which systems of signs are derived). It is "signifyingness itself," Levinas tells us.

And in its wake, we are held captive. We are its hostages, no more free to walk away from it than we are free to have the other individual die in our place. Why? Because to walk away from the other individual, to reject the face of the Other, is to walk away from consciousness itself, and from everything consciousness entails.

There are thus finally for Levinas two others in phenomenological discussion: the non-self which stands in contrast to everything I identify as mine, and the other individual who is also doing that. French has two different words for these two very different conceptions. *L'autre* refers to the other pure and simple, whatever falls into that category, whatever is not mine. *L'autrui* on the other hand refers to the neighbor, the other individual standing next to me or in front of me who is doing roughly the same that I am doing—for example, making self-other distinctions. It is customary in writing about Levinas to render the first as simply "the other" and to say in the case of the second "the other individual," "the neighbor," or to write is as "the Other" with a capital "o".

And mention of the other individual leads us to language or communication. Language as communication is decidedly not for Levinas a system of signs. Rather it is welcome, hospitality, an openness to the orphan, the widow, the poor, in short the disenfranchised of all species. As in the case of the face, Levinas distinguishes in language what has already been said from what is in the process of being said, what is still open—infinitely so—to what transpires before us.

* * *

How does this discussion impact the discussion we have been having vis-à-vis conflict resolution read in connection with Girard and Levinas? René Girard's thinking offers us the best account available of the sacrificial and its mechanism. It is an account that has long been available to us, Girard insists, long before he expressed it: in Greek tragedy, for example; in Hebrew scripture; and especially in Christian scripture. But his account does not tell us what to do about it. There is no morality attached to Girard's ideas, however Christian his references turn out to be, and however Christian he himself is personally.

For an account of the ethical dimensions of the crisis, we must turn elsewhere—in this case to the thought of Emmanuel Levinas. And Levinas does not disappoint on that score. If conflict resolution theory seeks ways of describing a shift in orientation that allows for a redefinition of self, ways of reconstructing our conceptualization of identity so that what currently generates conflict finds a less conflictual home within it, Levinas would appear to fill the bill. His entire project is a new account of subjectivity, a movement away from one grounded in consciousness (and which posits a moral faculty as distinguishable from other non-moral faculties as we have learned from Kant and Hegel) to one grounded in our infinite obligation to the other individual (accessible in this instance via the face and language) in which the entire fabric of consciousness is moral and in which ethics is an optics, a way of seeing, a vision that focuses upon the other individual before me in my face-to-face encounter without limiting that gaze to formal manifestations.

There is one hitch, however, and this point is as important for Levinas studies as the non-theological nature of Girard's ideas is for Girardian studies. What Levinas offers is a descriptive ethical orientation, not a prescriptive one. His account of ethical consciousness is no more of a "remedy" to the sacrificial crisis than Girard's account is. What he offers that Girardian theory does not offer is an account, in full, of ethical dimensions of our dilemma: namely, our infinite responsibility for others, the fact that our relation to others passes already through the ethical not as an add-on or supplementary feature but as its very fabric. How we instrumentalize that responsibility, how we enact justice, for example, in the context in which a third person appears and my infinite responsibility to the other is doubled (since it remains in effect for each of the others facing me) is still open to discussion. Indeed, it may be that from both a Girardian and a Levinasian perspective that is what our scriptural texts are all about, how we enact these sacrificial mechanisms and these ethical obligations in this or that situation in which we happen to find ourselves, situations in which the customary way of doing things would lead to disaster.

* * *

An anecdote might help to amplify these distinctions. When I met Levinas for the first (and only) time in summer of 1994, the woman who lived in the apartment down the hall from his on rue Michelange (I was later to learn) came to the door from within his apartment to greet me. After introducing herself, she introduced Emmanuel and Raissa Levinas. "Permit me to introduce Monsieur and Madame Levinas," she said to me (in French), "I am the neighbor." "Indeed," I reflected to myself. "I have heard a great deal about you!" And as I entered his home after the introductions, and we were walking to the area of the room where our discussions would take place, Levinas said to me (in French) "I have been thinking that hospitality, the welcome, politeness, is everything."

The welcome—of the orphan, the widow, the poor, the disenfranchised of all stripes—is the key to all of it. The face of the victim in Girard's understanding and Levinas's. Do we not have in that welcoming gesture—as the ancient prophetic texts teach us—the pathway to all conflict resolution?

CONCLUSIONS FOR CONFLICT RESOLUTION

The story goes that King Solomon was brought in to adjudicate between two women with rival claims to a human life—a young baby who was also in the room. The two women have been part of the profession of prostitutes and have each had babies. The woman first to speak claims that the other woman had a baby (as she herself did), that the baby (of the other woman) died during the night, and that the other woman then switched the living child with the deceased one and now claims that the living child (born in fact of the first woman) is her own and has been stolen from her. The second speaker—the second woman—tells a similar story. Yes, they both had babies. Yes, one of the babies died during the night. But, in fact, the baby who died during the night was the child of the first woman who now blames the mishap upon her colleague and would steal her own rightful living child whom she has placed before the king.

Solomon is faced with a dilemma. If he credits the first woman's story, then justice may or may not be served. If the living baby (placed before them) is the child of the first woman, and he awards the child to the first speaker, then indeed the rightful mother has reclaimed her child. Whatever grief has inspired the second woman to steal the child of the first is separable from the fact that the living child is born from the body of the first woman. But what if the woman is lying? What if indeed what the second woman says is true, and the child before them is truly the child of the second speaker, the first woman having lost a child during the night to death? Then in awarding the child to the first speaker he will have given the child to the mother whose child has died and participated in the theft of the living child from its rightful living mother.

Consideration in this instance of the truth, in short, of the empirical truth, would not seem a judicious path to justice. It may yield justice. But it may as well participate in its opposite. If ever there was a situation in which conflict resolution theory would be of assistance, this would seem to be one.

What does Solomon do? He redefines what counts as the "mother." The "mother"—whether empirically accurate or not—is the one who would sacrifice herself for the life of the child. The mother is the individual who would assume infinite responsibility for the other individual, for the other's responsibility, for the other's death. How is that determined? The king orders that the child be cut in half, that the child be treated as property, as an object. One woman is satisfied with that solution. The other is not. And Solomon now has his answer. He awards the child to the one who relinquishes her claim to the child for fear that it would cost the child its life.

What has taken place? Solomon has read the situation prophetically. The child could come indeed from either woman. And barring the introduction of testimony of witnesses there is no way of knowing, which one is speaking accurately. The best candidate for the child's future well-being—which is all that is really of concern here given the ambiguity of all other considerations—will have to be decided on another basis. And Solomon makes a decision: it is the woman who can think prophetically, who can see where the road is leading—in this case to the death of the living child—and can act on that basis. If laying claim to the child results in the child's death, in insisting either upon my right or the empirical truth of the matter results in the death of the child, then my right and the empirical truth must be themselves be abandoned for the sake of the child's life. A new theory of sacrifice must be adopted. Only in such a way can justice be served, a justice based not upon the empirical truth exclusively (although that truth is considered), or even upon the juridical rights of one individual over another exclusively (although those rights are also to be considered) but upon human life itself and my infinite responsibility for it, my responsibility, that is to say, to shoulder on earth the responsibilities of God, to shoulder the "otherwise than being," the otherwise than the ontological warfare in which since the nineteenth century our subjectivity conditions us to be embroiled.

It is to such responsibility that both the work of René Girard and Emmanuel Levinas lead us, a responsibility to which Girard points us in his book on Dostoyevsky (1963) written shortly after the publication of *Romantic Lie*, and to which Levinas will point us in the second major volume of his phenomenological enterprise ([1974] 2004). It is a responsibility to which neither Girard nor Levinas lay originary claim since in their view both Jewish and Christian traditions (among other traditions) already refer us to such responsibility throughout, and to which I would like to suggest in the present essay that conflict resolution theorists, following the examples of Roel Kaptein and Vern Neufeld Redekop, would be well-advised to pay significant heed.

REFERENCES

Bar-Siman-Tov, Yaacov, ed. 2004. *From Conflict Resolution to Reconciliation.* Oxford and New York: Oxford University Press.
Burton, John W. 1987. *Resolving Deep-Rooted Conflicts.* Lanham: University Press of America.
———. 1990a. *Conflict Resolution and Provention.* New York: St. Martin's Press.
———. (ed.) 1990b. *Conflict: Human Needs Theory.* New York: St. Martin's Press.
Derrida, Jacques. 2007. *The Gift of Death, Second Edition, and Literature in Secret.* Translated by David Wills. Chicago: University of Chicago Press.
Dupuy, Jean-Pierre. 2011. "Naturalizing Mimetic Theory." Pp. 194–214 in *Mimesis and Science*, edited by Scott Garrels. East Lansing: Michigan State University Press.
Garrels, Scott. 2006. "Imitation, Mirror Neurons, and Mimetic Desire: Convergence between the Mimetic Theory of René Girard and Empirical Research on Imitation." *Contagion* 12–13 (2005–2006): 47–86.
Girard, René. 1961. *Mensonge romantique et vérité romanèsque.* Paris: Grasset. Published in English as *Deceit, Desire, and the Novel.* Translated by Yvonne Freccero. Baltimore: Johns Hopkins University Press, 1965.
———. 1963. *Du double à l'unité.* Paris: Plon. Translated by James G. Williams as *Resurrection from the Underground: Feodor Dostoyesky.* New York: Crossroad, 1997.
———. 2011. *Achever Clausewitz: Entretiens avec Benoît Chantre.* Paris: Flammarion.
Kaptein, Roel. 1993. *On the Way of Freedom.* Dublin, Ireland: The Columbia Press.
Levinas, Immanuel. 1990. "A Religion of Adults." Pp. 11–23 in *Difficult Freedom: Essays on Judaism*, translated by Seán Hand. Baltimore: Johns Hopkins University Press.
———. 1992. "Foreword." Pp. 13–22 in *System and Revelation: The Philosophy of Franz Rosenzweig* by Stéphane Mosès. Translated by Catherine Tihanyi. Detroit: Wayne State University Press.
———. [1974] 2004. *Autrement qu'être: ou, au délà de l'essence.* Paris: Livre de Poche. Translated by Alphonso Lingis as *Otherwise Than Being: Or, Beyond Essence.* Pittsburgh, PA: Duquesne University Press, 1998.

Mabee, Charles. 2000. "A New Approach to the Christian- Jewish Dialogue." Pp. 321–327 in *Reading the Hebrew Bible for a New Millennium: Form, Concept, and Theological Perspective, Volume 1* edited by Deborah Ellens, Marvin Sweeney, Michael Floyd, and Wonil Kim. Harrisburg, PA: Trinity Press International.

Poulet, Georges. 1967. *The Metamorphoses of the Circle.* Baltimore: The Johns Hopkins University Press.

Sherwood, Yvonne and Kevin Hart, eds. 2004. *Derrida and Religion: Other Testaments.* New York: Routledge.

Redekop, Vern Neufeld. 2002. *From Violence to Blessing: How an Understanding of Deep-Rooted Conflict Opens Paths to Reconciliation.* Ottawa: Novalis.

Rosenzweig, Franz. 2005. *The Star of Redemption.* Translated by Barbara Galli. Madison: The University of Wisconsin Press.

NOTES

1. See, for example, the volume of Yaacov Bar-Siman-Tov (2004) on this idea. "In its simplest form," Bar-Siman-Tov writes, "reconciliation means restoring friendship and harmony between the rival sides after conflict resolution, or transforming relations of hostility and resentment to friendly and harmonious ones" (4).

2. Nearly thirty years ago, at a conference held in Cerisy–la Salle in 1983 in honor of René Girard, I first met Roel Kaptein. We took to each other immediately and I spent a wonderful afternoon wandering the French countryside with him and another member of his religious community. We continued to meet at COV&R conferences and to share insights about scapegoating and mimetic desire. His untimely death in 1996 of brain cancer cut short the life of an extraordinary human being whose work in peace-making and conflict resolution in the broadest terms was only beginning to be more widely known. I dedicate this chapter to his memory.

3. See, for example, Robert Daly's volume on the COV&R conference of 2000 in *Contagion* 9 (Spring 2002) which took place at Boston College in which the relation of the five "revealed" religions to Girardian thinking were addressed.

4. See, for example, Paul Nuechterlein's "Girard lectionary" (http://www.girardianlectionary.net/) or the website on "preaching peace" developed by Michael Hardin and Anthony Bartlett (http://www.preachingpeace.org/).

5. Jacques Derrida (2007) offers this insight in an essay translated recently (although obscured to some extent from public view previously) entitled "La littérature au secrêt" (which would have to be translated, if taken literally, as something like "Literature Put into Solitary Confinement"); the theme of his essay is his analysis of Biblical scripture.

6. The work of Jean Pierre Dupuy (2011) should be cited in this context, as should the work of Scott R. Garrels (2006), on "mirror neurons."

7. Vern Neufeld Redekop, *From Violence to Blessing* (2002, 148). The subtitle of Redekop's book, "How an understanding of deep-rooted conflict can open paths to reconciliation," echoes John W. Burton's work (1987), and Redekop credits Burton with the theoretical underpinnings of this idea. See, also, for example, Burton 1990a and 1990b. Redekop's volume contains a very useful bibliography of conflict resolution theory.

8. *Mensonge romantique et vérité romanèsque* (1961) is the original title of Girard's book, published in English as *Deceit, Desire, and the Novel* (1965). Benoît Chantre (2011) makes that point in his conversation with Girard in *Achever Clauswitz* and again in the "postface" to the second edition. Levinas's sentence has appeared in numerous essays (see 1990, for example).

9. It was Alexander Kojève (1980) who first pointed out how literally Hegel thought he was nearing the end of history.

10. Rosenzweig speaks about his ideas in the opening chapter of *The Star of Redemption* (2005), a work, Levinas famously says, is too omnipresent in his own book to cite.

11. In a public interview at the AAR, Jacques Derrida was asked directly about this idea and responded that he could not accept it. An account of that exchange was published in Sherwood and Hart (2004, 27–52).

Chapter Three

Dialogue

Sandor Goodhart and Vern Neufeld Redekop

Vern: What you have just described is significant because it places an infinite ethical responsibility for the other human being at the core of our humanity. This means that it is something that can always be appealed to. It functions as a counterpoint, an alternate theme, running parallel to the mimetic violence theme developed by Girard. When it comes to reconciliation, some form of ethical impulse is important in order to have a desire and vision for reconciliation, along with the will to proceed. Another point of resonance is with the concept of "breaking the trance" of dehumanization in the reconciliation process. Frequently, this happens in face to face (literally) encounters.

Sandor: Yes, I think it is at the core of our humanity, as Levinas understands it. In fact, he says as much in an essay at the end of *Entre Nous*, in one of his last interviews (1998). He feels, he says, that what is at stake is a new understanding of the human. What he means by that no doubt is a rejection of the Hegelian and Kantian sense of the human in which the ethical is separable from other realms of consciousness (in which, for example consciousness and conscience are two different ideas), as if in any case there could be a part of consciousness not ruled by conscience. For Levinas, that is not a possibility. And, in fact, I would suggest that it may not have been a possibility since the ancients, and that that may be, among other things, what they are trying to tell us. We haven't seen it because we are led around by the blinders of Platonic representation, in which something stands for something, for somebody, which is to say, a structure of analogy with a gap in the middle. The human is not a structure of analogy but of diachronic extension for Levinas. I am an extension of the other individual in the same way that a mother is the extension of her child. In fact, in chapter 4 of *Otherwise Than Being*, where

Levinas talks about our infinite responsibility, he first defines that responsibility under the aegis of the maternal, and maternity. The fact that we are responsible for the other individual before all else, or that I am an extension of the other individual in some way, does not deny the distance between us. He is still radically external to me and it is his alterity, in fact, that precisely conditions my relation to him. But by owning that responsibility, perhaps I move "closer"; I gain some proximity to the other, which is after all one of the major themes of the Psalms: "nearer my God to thee." Paradoxically, it is my owning of my very alterity to the other individual and gains for me some proximity to him. Perhaps, that is a part of the famous "mystery" of the human.

So, yes, I think this form of thinking gives us the missing step between Girard and reconciliation. Reconciliation only becomes possible on the basis of our owning our infinite responsibility for others, before all else.

Vern: If what you and Levinas are saying is correct, then this ethical responsibility emerged through the very process of hominization. If, for our collective survival as a species, reconciliation was critical, then it makes sense that a capacity for reconciliation emerged in the process of the development of our humanity. This then draws upon the theory of emergent creativity as developed by Stuart Kauffman. According to his theory, the creatively emergent comes out of a complex system at the edge of chaos. The whole Girardian scenario of the emergence of scapegoating and sacrificial mechanisms can be thought of as emergent creativity and can be one track for the development of reconciliation in the midst of runaway violence. However, as Frances de Waal points out, mammals have a capacity for empathy; they also have a well-developed sense of maternal caring for young. Levinas's argument suggests that this sense of ethical responsibility and the possibility of reconciliation, already apparent among primates, emerged out of the care associated with it. Another interesting link is Hurlbut's observation that humans have over "30 finely tuned muscles of facial expressions and vocal control" (2011, 179), enabling highly nuanced emotional expressions. We know that facial expressions induce, mimetically, certain emotions in others. Hence the emergence of the ethical as a core component of our humanity was concomitant with the capacity of the face to express interior dynamics.

Sandor: Yes, I think that is right. Reconciliation may be as old as hominization itself. And yes, scapegoating is itself already a form of reconciliation, although not perhaps one that has staying power, today. The shift may have taken place in the ancient world, from reconciliation as scapegoating to reconciliation as infinite respect for the neighbor. I think that is what the prophetic writers of the ancient Sixth Century were already thinking about.

What good are all your sacrifices, if that for which the whole machinery takes place—namely, human life—is not served by that gesture.

Vern: With Levinas, we are left with a core ethical impulse of infinite responsibility. As you point out, this responsibility is without content. That is, there is no inherent definition for how one is to act on this responsibility. It is primal—like the sense that "somebody needs to do something about . . ." without defining the somebody or the something. Paul Ricoeur takes this a step further by developing the notion of an ethical vision—something still very broad. One version he puts forward is that of "living a good life, with and for others, in just institutions" (1992). Out of this vision can flow moral principles and eventual law, customs, and norms. Girard envisioned taboos and laws being defensive measures to avoid mimetic violence. Again, this is not one versus the other, but rather the recognition that out of an impulse of responsibility or care *and* a fear of mimetic violence, grew principles that would both enable the living out and the definition of what this responsibility might entail.

Sandor: It is without content. It is not as if we are responsible in this way but not that way. We are responsible precisely without limitation. We are hard wired to be responsible, Levinas thinks. Our very capacity for conceptualizing ourselves as subjects depends upon that idea. We are always the "subjects of responsibility," to use a phrase Andrew McKenna used a few years ago as the title for a conference on Girard.

Vern: I appreciated your drawing out of Levinas the distinction between "saying" and the "said." Saying is a process, and what is said is an object that can be analyzed. By placing the primary emphasis of communication on the process, rather than the signifier and the signified a number of things happen. First, the relationship and the mutuality of communication become foregrounded. Second, there are many intangibles that enter into this complex process. Some of these, like gestures and body language, are subject to observation, but at the heart of it is the change of heart—orientation and perspective—that happens through communication. Third, the process then points to relationship, which has everything to do with how the communication process works. Fourth, from the perspective of integral theory, which recognizes both the exterior and interior aspects of phenomena, it allows for an examination of the interior dynamics involved in the journey from the Self to the Other and back again.

Sandor: Levinas is very much upset by sign theory since it misses language. If we speak of the "signified," then we speak of what has already happened. And if we speak of the signifier (*signifiant* in French), we speak either of something that will happen or has already happened (in order for us to know that it has the capacity to signify). In all cases, in other words, we miss the "signifyingness" itself, if we can speak that way. The face, Levinas says somewhere, is that signifyingness; it is "signifyingness itself." I never understood what that phrase meant for Levinas, until I thought about it in these terms. Irving Massey once said to me, when I was a graduate student at the University of Buffalo, during the heyday of interest in Sassurean thinking, that we still have very little idea what language is. Although, at the time, I thought he was being somewhat disingenuous, given the plethora of studies on language as a system of signs. I now think the opposite, that, in fact, he may have been right, and that I may have had it entirely wrong, and that he may have been more generous than I was, that, in fact, the moment we "know" what language is, we have lost the game, since we have turned language into the foundation for an idol. That is what Levinas is trying to get at with the *dire* (saying) and the *dit* (said), I think.

REFERENCES

Hurlbut, William. 2011. "Desire, Mimesis, and the Phylogeny of Freedom." Pp. 175–192 in *Mimesis and Science*, edited by Scott Garrels. East Lansing: State University of Michigan Press.

Levinas, Immanuel. 1998a. "The Other, Utopia and Justice." *Entre Nous: Thinking of the Other*. Translated by Michael B. Smith and Barbara Harshav. New York: Columbia University Press, 223–34.

———. 1998b. *Otherwise Than Being: Or, Beyond Essence.* Translated by Alphonso Lingis. Pittsburgh, PA: Duquesne University Press, 1998.

Ricoeur, Paul. 1992. *Oneself as Another.* Translated by Kathleen Blamey. Chicago: University of Chicago Press.

Chapter Four

Blessing-Based Reconciliation in the Face of Violence

Vern Neufeld Redekop

René Girard's collective corpus has left us with some profound challenges, regarding the potential for reconciliation without the use of violence. First, he traces the links between acquisitive mimetic desire, mimetic rivalry, mimetic doubling, and mimetic violence, showing how there is a tendency for passions to increase, to the point of violence and for violence to increase since it is always returned with interest. Second, though allowing for the possibility of positive reciprocity, he argues that negative, violence-based reciprocity trumps the positive. Third, he posits that the basis of reconciliation lies in the scapegoat mechanism, which involves a limited use of violence to diffuse rampant escalating violence. Fourth, he argues that the scapegoat mechanism can morph into sacrificial systems with their own mythologies and taboos; when people believe in them they rein in violence but when they do not there is a crisis. Fifth, he argues that the process of hominization is rooted in scapegoating as a response to the mimetic violence that grew out of the increased mimetic capabilities of proto-humans; hence our phylogeny as humans has violent origins that translate into a natural propensity toward violence. Sixth, he suggests that with a breakdown of beliefs in sacrificially based thought systems there is a very real possibility for ever-increasing runaway violence (2010). These challenges then add up to the question the Innsbruck Girardian group first articulated: "Can there be reconciliation without scapegoats?" For reasons that will become clear, I am reframing the challenges raised by this question through articulation of a second one: "Can there be a theoretical basis, consistent with the insights of mimetic theory, for blessing-based reconciliation?" This is not meant as a negation of Girard's profound insights; rather, it is an argument that they can be supplemented with complementary understandings.[1]

To address the Girardian challenges raised initially by the Innsbruck group, my argument will unfold as follows. First, I will introduce the concept of justice as a mimetic phenomenon that has deep roots in our human psyche. Second will be a description of blessing, along with related concepts of empathy, compassion, and responsibility, showing how these can be understood mimetically. Third, I will develop the concepts of mimetic structures and fields, arguing that mimetic phenomena can have a longitudinal and pervasive effect. This will lead to a fourth point: reconciliation can be understood as a transformation of mimetic structures of violence to mimetic structures of blessing. The five key result areas of reconciliation will then be presented as a fifth step; they are transcendence, new relationships, healing from trauma, a change of structures, and a sense of justice. I will show how these help us to understand the effects of scapegoat-based reconciliation; this is the name I give to the concept of reconciliation Girard has identified with the peace in the community following scapegoat or sacrificial action. Sixth will be the presentation of a framework for reconciliation. Seventh, I will then present reconciliation as emergent creativity. Eighth, I will use the conceptual base developed in steps one to seven to engage the question of whether and under what conditions there can be a blessing-based reconciliation.

JUSTICE AS A MIMETIC PHENOMENON

Recent studies show that between the ages of three and eight, children develop a sense of fairness in relation to distribution of goods (Fehr et al. 2008). Before this development, they are only interested in what they can get for themselves. Ethological studies show that primates have a sense of justice: monkeys who get a relatively small reward for performing a task, compared with others, will stop performing for what they regard as a pittance (de Waal 2009). Also monkeys who get extra food will share it with those lacking food, as opposed to those with ample food, in an experimental situation. These and many other studies suggest that early on in the hominization process there was a sense of justice. But what really is justice?

Early writings that develop the concept of justice were those of the Eighth Century (BCE) Greek writers and the Hebrew prophets. For the Greeks, the roots of justice were balance and rightness (Kolbert 1979). In fact, around the same period, coined by Karl Jaspers as the Axial Age, several major religious traditions came to a deeper understanding about the notion of justice: e.g., Jainism, Buddhism, etc. The prophets, likewise, used similar concepts but put greater emphasis on that which contributes to healthy relationships (Martens 2009). They spoke up against fraud, economic oppression, and unfair trading practices. Ancient Rome built upon Greek concepts as it established a sophisticated legal system emphasizing procedural justice. Roman law, later, became the foundation for Western judicial systems.

Not only is a sense of justice understood in formal terms, it seems to be woven into our everyday encounters, as is demonstrated in a research game called Ultimatum. In this game, party A is given money (say $20) and asked to share it with party B. If party B accepts the offer, they both keep the money; if not, neither get any. At a certain point, when the split is too unbalanced, Party B would rather not get anything than see the other party get a disproportionately higher amount (Gospic et al. 2011).

We can nuance the understanding of justice as balance and rightness by distinguishing among the principles of equality, equity, and need as principles (Deutsch 1975, 147). "Equality" means that everyone gets the same amount of goods; "equity" means that people get what they deserve based on what they contribute; "need" means that each gets what they need. (Indigenous peoples of the Americas have old traditions of justice based on need.) Any one of these can establish a normative sense of rightness. Within contemporary societies, there is generally a balance found among these principles.

When it comes to harmful actions, Murphy and Jeffrey point to three dimensions of victimization: 1) a decrease in dignity, 2) the actual hurt, and 3) a moral woundedness in that there is an injustice involved (1988). The decrease in dignity comes from the perpetrator having put him/herself in a superior position by presupposing they have a right to inflict injury—the relative importance shows an imbalance. The actual crime results in an imbalance—if something is stolen, the perpetrator has more goods, and if someone is hurt, there is an imbalance in capability. In ancient times, murder was thought of removing a member from a community creating a relative imbalance. The moral dimension of the woundedness means that the sense of rightness concerning acceptable conduct has been offended.

That we developed a sense of rightness and balance early on in the hominization process is consistent with mimetic theory. One dimension of mimesis is that of comparison. Mimetic desire operates most potently between people who identify with one another. This involves a comparison among various potential mimetic models and a determination that a given model is one with which the desiring self can identify. Another aspect of comparison is that the Model has something more than the Self and that this something more can justly be sought by the Self. Why justly? It may be perceived that there is an imbalance—the Model has something more than the Self—and according to the rules of rightness it is not right that this supposedly equal being has more. These operations take place at the tacit level, but it becomes evident that there is operative within the structure of mimetic desire a sense of justice that justifies acquisitive action.

Isn't it curious how the rallying cry of victims is "We want justice! We want justice!" Invariably, what is meant is that they want perpetrators punished. Girard has done a marvelous job of showing how this instinct toward a violent form of justice has its roots in vengeance, which is a highly mimetic phenomenon (1977). This idea of cloaking vengeance in some form of justice is manifest in stories, movies, films, newscasts, and public demonstrations (cf. Wink's myth of Redemptive Violence discussed in chapter 7). There is a mentality that suffering brought upon the perpetrator of violence is legitimate. It is easy to see how, given the profundity of the power of vengeance, that Girard would cheer for a rule of law in which retributive justice would be administered by a third party in accordance with procedures to limit unwarranted punishment of the innocent (1977).[2]

Given the profundity of the craving for a justice that tries to balance harm done through punishment, reparations, payment, or some form of duress for perpetrators, that is, a profundity that is linked to a mimetic drive to replicate the initial harm, it seems important to take this into consideration in any attempt to move toward reconciliation in the wake of atrocity at a collective level or individual violent act (normally constituted as a crime). Punishment of any kind involves violence. The need for punishment is woven into many cultures; indeed, violent punishment of children has been a cultural norm in European-based traditions. As Martha Minow argues, justice as vengeance cannot be the only consideration, however (1998). Complexifying factors include the following points:

- Many atrocities are themselves justified in the minds of perpetrators by past injustices on the part of the victims.
- Justifying worldviews of violence go back a long way.
- Often targeted victim groups are not totally innocent themselves.
- There are many mimetic models of violent leaders who triumph and become heroes.
- There is an unwarranted assumption that one party is clearly guilty and unequivocally responsible for the harm done (Ricoeur 2000).
- The consequences of violence-oriented justice making actions could be either impossible to implement consistently or would have devastating human consequences, if they were (that is why, for instance, the Allies after WW II decided to try only the top Nazi leaders).
- A violent way of achieving balance (justice) may not produce the long-term positive results that would be regarded as optimum, particularly, if the punishment would not be accepted by perpetrators as being justified.

We are left with a profound aporia that is characteristic of complex systems. On the one hand, we crave justice as a way of balancing out a situation that has become unbalanced by violence and demand justice as rightness in the face of an affront to moral codes, norms, and laws. We also call for justice as order in the face of injustice that has brought chaos. On the other hand, we need to stop runaway contagious violence that could result from our justice-making actions and we need to find a way to live well with one another in a post-conflict situation. Girard's way through this aporia is through the scapegoat/sacrificial mechanism in which limited "good" violence is directed toward the scapegoat (sacrificial victim), venting the pent up vengeance feelings and uniting the people and creating a new sense of order. The ethical and practical problems are the following:

- Are we willing to continue to sacrifice innocent victims, if we know how the system operates?
- This system is predicated on the tacit belief that scapegoat/sacrificial actions are justified and that they will solve the problem. What happens when this belief is discredited? (Girard 2009)

These problems with retributive justice and scapegoat/sacrificial approaches to dealing with violence raise the question of whether or not there is another way.

BLESSING AND ITS DISCURSIVE FIELD

In many cultures, the concept of curse has been very real. This has operated in two ways: first, curse can function as a spell or a powerful word that has the power to negatively affect an Other,[3] and second, when some force of nature, accident, or unexplained event negatively affects an individual or group, it is framed as some form of curse. Curse then is conceptually linked to primal justice. In the first instance, it is a way of getting back at someone who is the cause of an imbalance, functioning as an indirect way of inflicting punishment. In the second instance, the hardship caused by an event (pestilence or getting sick) or accident is thought of as a result of the victim having done something wrong; hence, the curse-event achieves justice. Girard has pointed out that, when there is a calamity, a person responsible is sought out and this person becomes a scapegoat; the scapegoat can be framed as a cursed individual or group. Cursing involves an orientation toward the other that is directed toward causing the suffering of that person. Generally, it is justified on the basis of some injustice, real or perceived.

Historically, in the Hebrew tradition, *berakhah* or blessing was set as the opposite to a curse. Blessing implied an orientation of wishing the well-being of the other. Blessings were a way of introducing an ethical vision of flourishing that would extend well into the future. Like curses, words of blessing were expected to have the power to affect change. The root metaphor of blessing was the verb *barakh*, which was the word for kneeling: the link was that people would kneel down to formally receive a blessing. This kneeling action put them in a position of vulnerability and receptivity. As the concept developed, it was associated with living the teachings (Torah) given to the ancient Israelites, culminating with sustained life on a land, which would provide the means of living well. Particular blessings were given to particular people; e.g., Abraham and Sarah were told that they would have many descendants and that these descendants would be a blessing (provide the means of living a fuller life) to the world. Blessing functioned as a gift, exemplifying generosity.

A mimetic structure of violence is something bigger than any one individual. It can infuse a relational system, putting pressure on those caught up in it to orient themselves toward actions meant to harm or disempower the other. When I had this insight, I thought to myself, "What could designate another orientation?" "Blessing" was the word that best brought together the range of concepts associated with an orientation that desired the well-being of the other. The choice of this word was controversial since for some it has a decidedly religious connotation, and my desire is to create an inclusive discursive field. I subsequently developed a full argument for its inclusion in the field of conflict studies by way of a hermeneutical circle in which I presented its Hebrew origins, presented all the reasons why it was scandalous to use the term, showed what new opportunities were opened up by its use, and finally developed a new definition:

> Blessing is used to connote a life-oriented, creative impulse oriented toward the mutual well-being of Self and Other. Within a mimetic structure of blessing Self and Other feed one another at many different levels of reality. If blessing becomes mimetic, both parties are at the same time receptive and generous. Symptoms of blessing are joy, confidence, self-esteem, peace, dignity and respect. (Redekop 2007b, 135–36)

We are now in a better position to open up the discursive field of blessing by systematically introducing a vocabulary of related concepts. These include empathy, responsibility, love, generosity, hospitality, hope, faithfulness, trust, aphesis (letting go, see Thompson, chapter 1), *Paraclete*, creative mimesis, and spirituality. Some of these have etymological roots in the Judaic and Christian biblical traditions. However, they have been augmented by new realizations coming from the biological and human sciences. We will establish links among these concepts, mimetic theory and blessing. Note, at this point, that we acknowledge the power of mimetic structures of violence in all their complex manifestations; we will return to these, later.

There is a growing trend in the field of ethology to recognize the capacity for empathy on the part of mammals, generally, and among primates, more particularly (de Waal 2009). Empathy may be thought of as a capacity to enter into the emotional space of the other, replicating in ourselves some measure of what they are feeling. In this regard, it is highly mimetic. Among humans, empathy is related to the face (Haliburton 1996, 2011). It is clear that, across cultures, faces have universal codes for conveying emotion (Goleman 2003). An empathetic person looking into the face of another will mimetically generate the same emotions as the model. Watching a person cry, for instance, can induce tears. This tendency is intensified with the knowledge of the narrative of the sorrowful—knowing the context and reasons for the tears intensifies the emotion, particularly when one can identify with the same loss or suffering causing the tears. If one is oriented toward blessing in relation to the other, empathy turns into sympathy, marked by a desire to address the suffering of others. Altruistic empathy, in the words of Haliburton, "is a genuine communion in the shared identity of life, an alignment with the spirit of love" (1996, 7). Empathy may also include celebrating with those who celebrate, reinforcing a sense of well-being.[4]

Sandor Goodhart argues that Levinas' concept of an infinite responsibility for the other, prompted by the confrontation with the face of the other, can be projected into the hominization process (Goodhart, chapter 2). That is, the emergence of humanity was prompted by a sense of responsibility one for another. It is interesting that responsibility is linked to the face, which is also the ground for empathy. This suggests that a sense of responsibility, that is, a profound other-orientation, is linked to a capacity to enter into the world of the other. This links to the notion of the emergence of self-consciousness and with it the sense that the self of the other is akin to that of the self of oneself (Reineke 2013). This sense of oneself being like that of an other self emerges in babies at the moment of joint attention (Thompson, chapter 1). Our capacity for mimesis, biologically enabled by mirror neurons, leads through empathy to this sense of responsibility. Blessing can be framed as mutual responsibility for each other, for the relationship, and for the common good, including Nature (Collins 2013). Empathy and responsibility can also be framed as constituents of what Collins develops as interbeing—a recognition of the interconnectedness of Self and Other.

The ancient Greeks had three words for love: '*eros*" connoted an emotional rapturous feeling around attraction to someone that had its religious correlates in the passion of the gods and the practice of sacred prostitution; '*philos*' connoted a sense of connection with family and friends; and '*agapē*' had the sense of volitional choice to care about someone in particular (Redekop 2013). Ancient Hebrews used the word "*ahav*' most extensively—it combined the sense of attraction with that of volition. The Septuagint (ancient Greek approximation of the Hebrew Bible) translated '*ahav*' as '*agapē*.' A related Hebrew word was '*chesed*,' which means to go beyond the call of custom or duty to look out for the well-being of an other; sometimes it is translated "loving-kindness." One of the most significant Hebrew texts related to love comes at the textual center of the Torah in Leviticus 19 (reinforced in later by Jesus), where, in the contexts both of a perceived injustice and of ethnic others, Hebrews were told to "love (*ahav*) their neighbors as themselves." In the Christian Bible, the concept of *agapē* love is developed further to denote a profound self-giving commitment to the well-being of the Other. What is interesting, is that the formulation to love the Other as oneself can be understood mimetically, expressed as "imitate the love you have for your self, including your own self-interest, in the love you have for your Other." For Jesus, and for many subsequently, the epitome of love is to give one's life for someone else; this resonates with Levinas's sense of infinite responsibility for the Other. The Johannine Jesus calls for his disciples to imitate his love for them in the love they show to one another.

Rebecca Adams has developed the concept of loving mimesis, which can be formulated as follows. If a mimetic Model desires the full subjectivity of a wounded Subject, as the Subject then imitates the desire of the Model she desires her own full subjectivity (Adams 2000).

Mercy takes on meaning in the context of retributive justice. It basically means that when punishment is deserved, according to the laws and customs of society, a decision is made not to mete out the punishment to the perpetrator. In Jewish, Christian, and Muslim traditions, God is seen as essentially merciful. The ideal of mercy as presented in narratives about the Divine becomes a model to be imitated in human relationships. Mercy, though related, is different from forgiveness, which we will touch on below. Mercy relates to blessing in that, in the case of a harm done, mercy may be the means by which a perpetrator moves on to a full life, and it opens the possibility of new relationships within the community. Longitudinally, mercy may be subject to imitation as the merciful person, in one instance, becomes the recipient of mercy in another; conversely, the one who receives mercy becomes mimetically merciful in another instance. Where this does not happen, every instinct about injustice is ignited, and we demand that the merciless person be punished. This impulse is revealed by Jesus in the story of the man who was forgiven a huge debt, then showed no mercy to the one who owed him a pittance (Matthew 18:23–35).

Generosity is a tendency to give to another freely. Most often, generosity is extended to someone with a particular need. In terms of cognates, it is akin to grace, which really means a gift freely given. Reciprocated generosity is at the heart of mimetic structures of blessing. Mercy can be seen as a gift and is thus linked to generosity. The tendency to share with others, or to look out for the well-being of others, is already apparent among primates.

Hospitality is a particular form of generosity in which guests are invited into the private space of the Self, where they are given what they need in terms of shelter and food. In some cultures, hospitality is a primary value, and a family will give its very best to guests. Metaphorically, listening attentively with an open mind and spirit is a form of hospitality—inviting the other into one's psychic space. Mutually reciprocated hospitality is an important process in cultivating friendship and building trust. Steve Moore develops the links between hospitality extended to religious leaders from both sides of a conflict and "seeding reconciliation" in a theatre of war (Moore 2009 and chapter 12).

Hope is an orientation of blessing directed toward the future. In includes waiting for, watching for, trusting, openness toward, and actively working toward that which will contribute to well-being. Hope may be projected onto another—"I hope that you will . . ."—besides being addressed to oneself or one's community. The basis of hope is mimetic in that it is derived from instances, where people faced bitter challenges and were able to turn things around. Throughout the history of the United States and Canada, there have been instances of hope being mimetically inspired from one immigrant group to another—each came to the country with the hope of starting a new life. Mutually expressed hope, within a relational system, may be the basis for transformation and mimetic structures of blessing.

Like hope, faithfulness is a diachronic term. It derives from commitments. To be faithful is to continue on a trajectory established by a commitment to an ethical vision—a view of the future. This is most often thought of in terms of relationship, particularly where there is a ritual, symbolic, or articulated commitment to do something or to simply keep up the relationship. The concept of such a relationship has roots in the ancient Hittite concept of covenant, which implied a complete sense of solidarity with one with another. Lasting relationships can be seen in terms of mutual mimetic faithfulness in which the faithfulness of one party inspires the other to remain faithful. Betrayal, in this context, is often interpreted as a form of violence, calling for some form of reconciliation which may or may not involve the reestablishment of trust, which is basically the confident hope that the other will be faithful to commitments undertaken, including an understanding that in challenging new circumstances the other will act in a way that contributes to the sustained well-being of the self.

Cameron Thompson (chapter 1) makes a compelling case for the emergence of aphetic mimesis, early in the hominization process. At this point, I need only point out that *aphēsis* is the Greek root of forgiveness, which can be understood as letting go of a right to seek retribution and a letting go of resentment and hatred that can attend victimization. Whereas mercy is extended by those who have a right to exact punishment, forgiveness is extended by victims. In the case of interpersonal situations where wrong-doing is not of a criminal nature, mercy and forgiveness may be extended by the same party. In a criminal situation, it is some party within the criminal justice system who grants mercy. The reciprocal dimension of *aphēsis* is summed up in "forgive me for wrongdoing as I have forgiven those who have wronged me" (cf. Matthew 6:12; 18:23–35) Aphetic mimesis can be a lifestyle as one habitually lets go of resentful feelings. It is mimetic in that it may be reciprocal; it may also be a matter of imitating those who have lived such a life. It is an essential element in the maintenance of mimetic structures of blessing; it is akin to a generosity of spirit. Related to this is Miroslav Volf's concept of remembering rightly, a remembering in which the memory of victimization is in effect stored in a safe place in the attic of one's mind, where it is not given the power to determine identity (2006).

Girard contrasts Paraclete with Satan. "Satan" has etymological roots in the Hebrew word for persecutor; Girard sees Satan as personifying the impulse behind scapegoating. It is pointing the finger of judgment in a way that legitimizes the collective murder of the innocent victim. The Paraclete (*paraklētos*) he takes to be the advocate for the victim. (In Christian terms, the Paraclete refers to the Holy Spirit but here we are not limited to this designation.) In the establishment of blessing in the face of violence, advocates for and supporters of victims are frequently needed. The calling to take on such a role is directly related to a capacity for empathy described above. Within mimetic structures of blessing, there is mutual support.

Creative Mimesis

Creative mimesis plays a key role within mimetic structures of blessing. It is an umbrella term that includes loving mimesis, aphetic mimesis, emergent mimesis, transcendent mimesis, competitive mimesis, and a mimesis of blessing. "Loving mimesis," can be defined as "a model desiring the full subjectivity and flourishing of a self that is wounded or otherwise limited" (Adams 2000). In this case, as the self imitates the desire of the model, desire works reflexively to enhance the self-esteem and capacity of the self. This is a tricky concept since paternalism/maternalism can easily be framed as being for the well-being of the wounded subject but may, in fact, squelch self-esteem and capacity.

Aphetic mimesis means to welcome the other into one's own psychic space. Empathy is one manifestation (Thomson, chapter 1). Receptivity is another. This openness to the perspective of the other entails a willingness to let go of one's own hurts, resentments, and hatreds. It involves a transformation of attitude and relationship.

Emergent mimesis can be linked analogically to emergent creativity (Kauffman 2009) in which a complex set of factors interact to produce something new that cannot be reduced to its parts. With emergent mimesis, a self can have a multiplicity of Models, each contributing ideas, insights, and actions that could be subject to mimesis. In this case, the self mimetically draws on this multiplicity of ideas, allowing a new combination to emerge (Martin 2009).

Transcendent mimesis can be understood as imitating that which is transcendent. This involves indwelling a bigger world than one's own. Seeing the profound interconnections within the universe and, *mutatis mutandis*, then seeing one's own world, being, and relationships as having an infinite quality. In Levinas's terms, it is seeing the exteriority of the face as a reflection of transcendence (1969) and reflexively realizing that one's own face, likewise, reflects a transcendent quality (Goodhart, chapter 2). In theological terms transcendent mimesis is imitating the ways of the Divine as these can be discerned from clues that point to the Infinite.

Competitive mimesis can be understood as "the pursuit of excellence where standards of excellence are derived mimetically from one's peers" (Ryba 2013).

A mimesis of blessing is to enter into a vision of and commitment to the generation and maintenance of mimetic structures of blessing (see below). This means that to imitate the qualities of such structures as they find expression in other relational systems, to imitate that which adds to the wellbeing of the Other in one's own relational system, and to appropriate a sense of one's own well-being mimetically through relationship and receptivity to the positive reciprocity that comes from the Other.

Spirituality may be thought of as the animating energy behind reconciliation. It has an interesting relationship with religion in that it transcends religion yet it draws its root metaphors and many of its practices from religious traditions (King 2008). It may be thought of as the source of inner strength, the basis of transpersonal connection (interbeing, cf. Collins 2013), the link with that which is transcendent, and the source of empowerment to act on an ethics of care (Redekop 2011). Spirituality can be seen as connecting the flow of empathy, generosity, hope, aphesis, and creative mimesis.[5]

MIMETIC STRUCTURES AND FIELDS

Within *Things Hidden Since the Foundation of the World*, Girard uses the word "structure" with two different semic valences. It is used critically and negatively in relation to structuralism and positively when talking about mimetic desire and scapegoating in structural terms.[6] My own understanding of the term is derived from an exhaustive analysis of this positive use; that use can be synthesized as follows. Structures are diachronic relational patterns that can take on lives of their own. Mimetic structures, then, are mutually reciprocated patterns of orientation, attitudes, and actions. A mimetic

structure of violence is present within a relational system, when the antagonists' orientation, attitudes and actions are directed at either doing harm to
one another or getting ahead at the expense of the other. Seen this way,
colonialism, war (international and civil), slavery, and exploitation can be
seen as mimetic structures of violence. Variations are power asymmetry and
latent violence, as compared to overt actions of violence. All of the Girardian
concepts of acquisitive mimetic desire, rivalry, reciprocated violence, and
scapegoating figure in mimetic structures of violence. For example, the conflict in the Western Balkans that flared up in the 1990s, with its most violent
manifestation in Bosnia and Herzegovina, can be understood as a mimetic
structure of violence with a long complex history, a key part of which included actions taken by Serbs and Croats during World War II. The defensive side of mimetic structures of violence are mimetic structures of entrenchment (a term suggested to me by Rebecca Adams), which are expressed in Manichean-like fundamentalism: you are either friends or enemies; perspective and ideas are either absolutely right or wrong; in these
there is a militant defense of community and perspectives (Redekop 2002).

Mimetic structures of blessing are characterized by mutual empowerment. There may be competition (or even conflict) that occurs within them
but these are channeled toward creativity and resolution. As I did a careful
reading of Adam Smith's *Wealth of Nations*, it became clear that his vision of
a market had many characteristics of a mimetic structure of blessing. His
vision was that by each doing what they enjoyed and did best, people could
more efficiently produce more and better goods. By exchanging them
through the market system everyone would be better off.[7] Associated with
mimetic structures of blessing are mimetic structures of transcendence in
which the well-being of the Self is integrally tied to the well-being of the
Other. Expressed in dialogue fashion, this means, "I will not have a sense of
thriving unless you thrive."

Pierre Bourdieu has developed the concept of social field in a way that
resembles the concept of mimetic structure. A social field is a differentiated
social space (e.g., politics) that includes people and institutions in different
places with a network of interconnections. Each individual has a range of
developed competencies at the sub-conscious level, which he calls "habitus."
Resources are thought of as capital; the exercise of habitus with capital in a
social field becomes a practice. Paula Du Hamel Yellowhorn used Bourdieu's concept of social field to analyze internal violence and resiliency
among within a First Nations community in Canada (2009). She argued that
the social field was permeated with violence and that this violence had its
genesis with colonial practices of cultural genocide, paternalism, and residential schools but that it morphed into lateral violence among Aboriginal
people. A similar analysis could have been made using mimetic structures of
violence.

Rupert Shelldrake takes the concept of field to another level of abstraction with some interesting heuristic possibilities (2003). He speaks of morphogenic fields, which are information fields by which information is communicated across time and place, among those who have morphic resonance with a particular information field. Animal studies show that animals in one part of the world seem to pick up knowledge generated by those of their species living elsewhere. Among humans, Shelldrake has examined the phenomenon of people being aware of someone staring at them from behind even without seeing the person staring at them. Just as Du Hamel Yellowhorn argues that social fields can become permeated with debilitating violence, it is arguable that morphogenic fields can be affected by both violence and blessing. This suggests that Shelldrake's morphogenic fields could be oriented toward violence or blessing. Those who resonate with these fields could then be influenced by them—either to be more violent or more empathetic. This would mean that concentrated passion for either could have a wider general influence. One corroborating study to this effect involves an experiment in Washington, D.C. in which several hundred meditators consciously meditated in the city during the summer of 1993 (Hagelin 1993). That summer, the crime rate went down considerably, by 23%—enough to be a strong statistical difference. Analysts were not able to find any variable that could have explained the anomaly that summer. What this suggests is that our orientation, attitudes, and actions could have broader implications in an interconnected world than we even dreamed of. In mimetic terms, within the context of morphogenic fields, one mimetic structure in one relational system could have a mimetic impact on mimetic structures in other relational systems.

RECONCILIATION: FROM MIMETIC STRUCTURES OF VIOLENCE TO MIMETIC STRUCTURES OF BLESSING

One way of understanding reconciliation is the transformation of mimetic structures of violence into mimetic structures of blessing (Redekop 2002). That is, people with anger and resentment directed toward their Other and, doing what they can to harm the interests of each Other, are transformed such that they are oriented toward the well-being of the Other and the actions of each are mutually empowering. Manifest in this transformation are empathy, remorse, generosity of spirit, mercy, and forgiveness. The transformation is from closed relational systems (in which options are limited and freedom is curtailed) to open systems, where new options and possibilities are generated. The transformation involves diminishing the scope, depth, and power of mimetic structures of violence and augmenting mimetic structures of blessing.[8]

Girard distinguishes between a violence of indifferentiation and a violence of differentiation. The former is exemplified in mimetic doubling, where the differences between rivals diminish such that they are almost the same to an outside observer. All the while, they make the most of the smallest differences. Violence of differentiation is seen in scapegoating where the other becomes a dehumanized, demonized Other, whom it is legitimate to kill. From this, we can postulate a blessing of differentiation and a blessing of indifferentiation. The blessing of differentiation takes place in the context of mimetic doubling (violence of indifferentiation in which case parties are locked in an intense rivalry). The structure of blessing takes the form of the parties giving themselves additional space, creating psychic, temporal, or physical distance from one another. One example from the book of Genesis (chapter 13) is the story of Lot and Abraham, whose servants were fighting over grass for their large flocks. Abraham suggested that they part company and offered Lot the choice of where he wanted to be. The blessing of indifferentiation takes place in the context of scapegoating and involves seeing the humanity and possible similarities between parties in conflict.

Mimetic structures of violence and of blessing are both complex, making their transformation extremely complex. Hence, they bear all the marks of complex adaptive systems. Within complex adaptive systems, things proceed in a non-linear fashion. There are bifurcation points (critical junctures) at which a small change generates cascading effects that have far-reaching consequences (cf the butterfly effect). We will return to the implications of complexity in the discussion of reconciliation as emergent creativity below. Before getting to that, I will introduce the key result areas of reconciliation and provide a framework for understanding reconciliation as a process and a goal (Bar-Siman-Tov 2004).

Key Result Areas of Reconciliation

If reconciliation truly occurs, without getting into the question of how or why it occurs, what is clear is that there will be certain results that can be observed. It is important that there be results in all five categories: personal healing, new relationships, change of structures, sense of justice, and transcendence.

Violent actions result in severe wounding—physical, emotional, spiritual, and hermeneutic. The latter constitutes a breakdown of worldview in which it becomes impossible to make sense of the victimization. Wounding can be traumatic, at an extreme, expressed in Post-Traumatic Stress Disorder, which can be severely debilitating. As parties go through a reconciliation process, they should develop a new understanding of the perspective of the other and reasons for the violence, or at least factors that played a role, a sense of security, and (with it) some hope. All of this should contribute to healing.

Evidence can be seen in a movement from a rhetoric of victimization to a rhetoric of constructive action and a celebration of life with all its possibilities.

New relationships can be understood in two ways. First, relationships are formed with new people from the other side of the conflict with whom one has not had relationships before. This is evident in the breaking down of silos that isolate people. The second sense is that new relationships develop with those previously thought of as demonized monsters. The sense of enmity dissipates. There can be a whole range of possibilities, from a willingness to tolerate the existence of the others, to finding a way to co-exist without further violence, to the rebuilding of trust, to actually becoming friends. Time also plays a role. On the one hand, one could anticipate that it might take a long time to rebuild trust and establish friendships. This is, in fact, the case in some instances, and intuitively it is the most compelling. However, given that reconciliation functions as a complex adaptive system, anything is possible. There are instances of relational transformation, after just a few encounters.

There are four senses of the word "structure" that apply. First are the mimetic structures, which, by definition, change. Second, if the conflict involves hegemonic structures, which entrench dominance and exploitation, these hegemonic structures need to change. One example was the Apartheid system in South Africa in which there was a clear hegemonic structure with whites in the dominant position. The first aspect of the hegemonic structure to change was political in that full democracy granted voting rights to blacks, resulting in the election of the African National Congress. Still to come are economic changes that transform economic structures, especially land tenure, such that blacks have a proportionate stake in and benefit from the economy. Another aspect has to do with discursive hegemonic structures that entrench feelings of inferiority. Third, "structure" can refer to the constellation of laws and customs that constitute a political and social culture. Included in this is a tacit ethical vision and sets of values by which people live. In a violent context, there may be values that legitimate corruption, extortion, deceit, fraud, and other practices that could be framed as violent. These must be changed so that violence and the potential for violence are diminished. Fourth, structure can be thought of as institutions. In some instances, there need to be new institutions of governance to hold leaders accountable and conflict resolution (from court systems to tribunals to mediation centers).

As reconciliation occurs, there should be a sense of justice, such that there is a perception of fairness, balance and rightness. This can be achieved in a number of ways. Forgiveness, mercy, and restitution may play a role. Reparations and victim support enter into it. A sense of justice, for some, is achieved through retributive approaches to justice, though the limits of this must be understood. For most, constructive actions to make reparation or amends (Radzic 2009) have long-lasting effects.

One must consider legal justice, moral justice, rights-based justice, and distributive justice in the overall assessment. One example of injustice in Rwanda had to do with women who were raped by men who were known to have HIV–AIDS. Perpetrators who were sent to Arusha for trial were given AIDS medication while their victims were not. This highlights the need to be sensitive to issues of fairness, balance, and rightness in every aspect of the process.

Transcendence can be understood in a number of ways. At a first level, it is transcending the feelings, circumstances, and structures that can lead to debilitation, dysfunction, and paralysis. In the words of Rwandan Oscar Gasana, it is like "getting out of the ditch onto the road again." In tragically violent situation, there are so many hurts and wrongs that can never be addressed properly that at a certain point people need to let go of them and transcend the situation. At a second level, transcendence means to get beyond one's own perspective and see things in a way that integrates the experience and perspective of the other. A transcendent narrative of the violence is one that includes, and goes beyond, all perspectives. At a third level, and related to the second level, is the development of a more complex level of consciousness (McGuigan and Popp 2013). At a fourth level, transcendence allows one to feel connected with a transcendent reality, whether expressed in religious terms or in a sense of being connected to the bigger interconnected web of the universe. In this sense, transcendence is linked both with spirituality and emergent creativity.

Scapegoat-based Reconciliation

We will now explore how scapegoat-based reconciliation contributes to these five result areas. First, with the catharsis of violently having killed or banished the scapegoat, the mimetic rivalries are dissipated. The sense of personal relief and self-vindication can, in the short run, result in a sense of *healing*—the sense that problems have been dealt with. Second, mutual antagonisms are projected onto the scapegoat who has been eliminated; hence it is possible for *relationships* among former mimetic rivals to be renewed. Third, as Girard points out, a new order is introduced, which can be understood as a *change of structures*. Fourth, there clearly is a *sense of justice* in that the scapegoat is seen to be the blame for problems within the relational system so the violence directed toward the scapegoat is justified. Finally, according to Girard, there is a sense of awe associated with the scapegoat phenomenon, connecting this to the Sacred. This sense of awe that something bigger than the community being at play resonates with the concept of *transcendence*.

From this first glance at scapegoat-based reconciliation, we can see that it seems to work. Problems arise, however, when it is revealed that the scapegoat is innocent; the sense of justice starts to dissipate. Furthermore, the reconciliation cannot be sustained. New rivalries develop and sacrificial systems are invented to institutionalize this type of reconciliation. When these break down, there is a crisis. What this analysis suggests is that some kind of "powerful medicine" is needed to affect the kinds of transformation that long-term reconciliation calls for. This medicine has to touch people profoundly at physical, emotional, cognitive, and spiritual levels so that the woundedness of violence can be transformed into wholeness, peace, and blessing. If the scapegoat/sacrificial route seems to work to a degree, what does that say about who we are as humans and what we need? We will return to this at the end, but first we need to look at what has been discovered about reconciliation and about emergent creativity.

FRAMEWORK FOR RECONCILIATION

Reconciliation is all about transformation; as such it is both a process and a goal. While there are no techniques that will guarantee that it will happen, there are elements of the process that expedite its occurrence. These I have organized into the following framework.[9]

At the heart of reconciliation are discursive and symbolic processes of transformation that produce results in the five areas already discussed. For these processes to occur and occur effectively there are pre-requisites and meta-requisites that contribute to the overall effectiveness. Reconciliation processes may be relatively short or may extend for a long time—over a period of years. They may be simple or they may be complex with many sub-processes. They may be straightforward or they may be iterative and cyclical in that parties may make progress and then go back to cover in a new way points that were dealt with earlier. Reconciliation may occur through clear, direct, interactive, processes or may occur indirectly through cooperation in joint activities that are not focused on reconciliation per se. This is known in the literature as instrumental reconciliation (Nadler et al. 2008). It may be psycho-emotional—focusing on healing and deeper relationships—or it may concentrate on political, social group, or interpersonal levels. Political reconciliation can be differentiated on the basis of inter-state or intra-state reconciliation (Long and Brecke 2003).

Foremost among the pre-requisites are a vision and mandate for reconciliation, followed by the resources to work on it. Someone needs to have a sense that reconciliation is desirable and possible. The mandate may be granted formally, or it may be given tacitly as people respond to preliminary initiatives. Developing a vision means to identify the parties (primary, secon-

Reconciliation

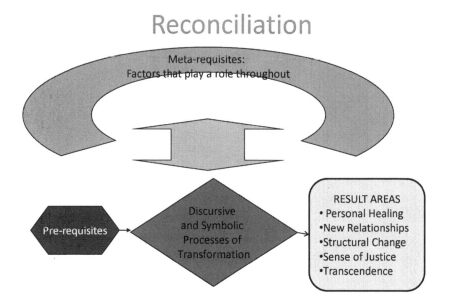

Figure 4.1.

dary, and tertiary) that need to be reconciled, along with the different levels. In the case of large-group or international situations, the mandate and resources could be significant. Other pre-requisites have to do with safety of individuals involved if the situation is still volatile and logistical arrangements. The symbolic significance of the venue needs to be considered, too (Schirch 2005).

Reconciliation processes can include mediation, facilitation, and dialogue, or even formal adjudication processes (tribunals and commissions). During these processes, there are expressions of remorse and apology, particularly after parties tell their stories of loss, suffering, and woundedness (for an example see Redekop 2007a). There may be responses of openness to forgiveness and explorations of what life together could continue to be. As part of a larger process, sub-groups of mixed identity might choose to live together in the same village or community to demonstrate a reconciliation lifestyle. (There are examples in both Rwanda and Israel.) There may be a process of reframing the narrative of the violence to include the experience of all. Symbolic processes are designed to have an impact at the emotional and spiritual levels—gift giving, symbolically letting go of grievances, symbolic reparations, eating together, music, and a symbolic change of structures. For example, in a village in Kenya there were two tribally based markets and the challenge was to combine them into one market (Ashafa and

Wuye 2010). In relatively simple processes, the complexity of the situation and of the various experiences can come out.

Meta-requisites include teachings of blessing, GRIT—Gradual Reciprocated Initiatives in Tension-Reduction, institution building, process skills, and support of the Third Side—bystanders, donors, human resources (Ury 2000). Teachings of blessing can be stories and examples that function as mimetic models for reconciliation (Redekop 2007b; 2010b). GRIT is a mimetic phenomenon in which small trust-building steps are taken; as they are mimetically reciprocated, they can be built upon (Osgoode 1962). Process skills are important; a gifted and sensitive process leader, who mimetically models respect of all the parties, can start a positive contagion of mutual respect. Bystander communities can support the process by reinforcing positive steps and providing necessary resources—human, intellectual, physical, and financial—to keep the processes going in a good direction. Ervin Staub has effectively demonstrated that bystanders can play a tremendous role in influencing the behavior of protagonists (1989); though he doesn't use the concept, in effect, he argues that they are mimetic models—those in conflict pick up clues on how they should act from bystanders.

As part of the reconciliation process, I have proposed a justice of blessing by which an assessment is made of where victims and perpetrators stand in terms of the five key result areas (Redekop 2008). If former perpetrators would like to work toward the balancing of the harm done by contributing to the well-being of victims, they could work toward goals based on result areas for reconciliation such as healing and a change of structures. Periodically these goals would be revisited and revised.

Having all of the necessary elements of reconciliation in place does not guarantee that reconciliation will take place. It is a complex human process, in fact, each instance of reconciliation can be seen as a creative process. The human capacity for empathy, love, fairness, and spirituality plays a significant role in allowing this to happen. These can be encouraged through teachings of blessing and mimetic modeling.

RECONCILIATION AS EMERGENT CREATIVITY

Stuart Kauffman has argued that the universe functions on the basis of emergent creativity and that this realization fills in a major gap in evolutionary theory. Emergent creativity works on the basis of several principles. It is non-reductionistic. That means that when something new emerges it is a truly new entity that cannot be reduced to what was before. For example, the emergence of life cannot be reduced to nor be derived from the principles of physics. Emergent creativity occurs within complex adaptive systems. This means that both complexity and a potential for chaos exist within a context favorable to emergent creativity. The potential for emergent creativity is optimum along a line of criticality, which is a function of the number of elements that could potentially be combined in a new way and the number of possible combinations that could be made. As can be seen in the following figure, if there is little diversity and few ways of making new connections (bottom left of the graph), the system will be static—there will be little change. If there are many different resources with many ways of making new connections (upper right), there will be chaos with little chance of anything new emerging. However along the line of criticality, which can also be understood as the edge of chaos, chances are optimum for new things to emerge.

For every new entity that emerges there are adjacent possibilities that open up. These adjacent possibilities include secondary and tertiary uses for the new entity. For instance, the emergence of the Internet opened up adjacent possibilities for social networking, like Facebook. There are also new substitutions and complements such that for every instance of emergent creativity there are creative spin-offs that could not have been anticipated. Emergent creativity is manifest with the emergence of life and the generation of increasingly complex life-forms. It is also apparent within human cultures; Kauffman cites the emergence and development of both legal systems and economic systems as examples.

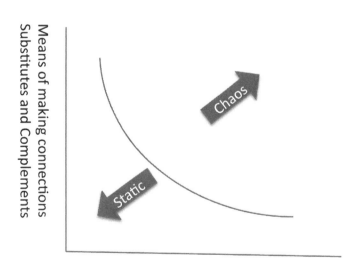

Diversity of Resources

Figure 4.2.

Some evolutionary thinkers now argue that reconciliation was an essential element for the survival of the human species (Ismael 2007). This is evident because human beings were reliant on communities to survive (Clark 1990). Without reconciliation, there was the potential for reciprocal violence to reduce communities to the point of not being viable. With this line of thinking, the emergence of the scapegoat mechanism as one solution to the problem was entirely consistent with the framework of emergent creativity: it comes out of a situation of chaos. The community dynamics are complex with all against all. Reconciliation's emergence cannot be reduced to nor predicted from what was the case before. It opened up adjacent possibilities: in this case cultural taboos, myth, and sacrificial rituals.

I would like to argue that concomitantly there was the emergence of empathy, aphetic mimesis, love, mercy, generosity, and fairness that constituted the possibility for a blessing-based reconciliation that did not rely on scapegoats. Already, many of these elements are evident in a primitive form among primates. What this means is that either scapegoat/sacrificial reconciliation supplied a category/need for reconciliation (and that other means were found to make this possible) or that there was an earlier or concomitant development of blessing-based reconciliation processes. In the latter case, the sense of awe at the scapegoat event may have been that reconciliation, normally achieved without violence, was achieved in this manner. This brings us to the contemporary situation.

Girard observes that the literature of the West and the human psyche imagine a violent catastrophic end to human society. The genre is apocalyptic. It has its roots in extreme oppression and victimization and is tied to a deeply held passion that there be justice (Hanson 1975). In other words, given the gross injustices manifest by the powerful in this world, the apocalyptic vision is one of judgment that ends and may transcend history. Building on the Clauswitzian observation that violence could potentially spin out of control in ever intensifying rounds of mimetic conflict, Girard suggests that with the breakdown of belief in sacrificial systems, which limit violence through a safe outlet, there is every possibility that an apocalyptic vision might become a reality.

I would like to address this challenge, which is a real possibility, with a vision for how blessing-based reconciliation is a plausible antidote.

First, based on the principles of emergent creativity, it becomes evident that given the complexity of conflict situations, new patterns of reconciliation might also emerge.

Second, in fact, the number of large-scale violent conflicts has been decreasing over the last few decades; however, there are many geographically smaller (yet equally complex) conflicts. With globalization the interconnectedness of conflict (and hence the number of people affected) has grown, adding to this complexity.

Third, all of the conceptual elements in the discursive field of blessing can now be framed as having been the result of emergent creativity. As such, they have an ontological basis that is not reducible to what may have existed, previously. That many of them are now evident, in primitive form, among primates indicates that they have a long history. If we can transcend the materialist and reductionist assumptions that characterized the post-enlightenment modern world, these concepts might be re-valued and find their way into the public and political domains.

Fourth, the emergence of restorative justice in the 1970s (and its growth to global proportions) exemplifies how a blessing-based manner of addressing the primal need for justice has a capacity to grow rapidly. The current explosion of social media means that the potential for new and productive approaches is only increasing.

Fifth, the emergence of reconciliation as a *bona fide* field of academic studies means that in the coming years insights will multiply around its meaning and what might make it more effective. There is, for example, now widespread consensus that reconciliation is now a process and goal (Bar-Siman-tov 2004). Likewise, the links between reconciliation and trauma healing, relationships, and structural change are becoming well established. Empirical research is now helping to identify actions that have the potential of contributing to sustained reconciliation processes.

Sixth, the emergence of spirituality as a category that inclusively goes beyond particular religious traditions (King 2008) (and as a field of academic studies with its own methodologies), means that the chances improve of finding an animating generator of blessing-based reconciliation (Beauregard and O'Leary 2007). Notwithstanding this development, there is a growing realization that religion and religious leaders can be engaged constructively in the service of peace and reconciliation (Appleby *et al.* 2010; Appleby 2001; Bowker 2008; Hertog 2010; Moore chapter 12).

Seventh, complexity studies, generally, and emergent creativity (as part of that field) show promise of identifying more clearly the kinds of adjustments that would need to be made to a complex relational system dominated by mimetic structures of violence, such that the chances of transformation would be improved. This would involve doing a criticality assessment and either expanding the relational system to allow for more possibilities in some cases, or contracting it for the same reason in others.

Eighth and finally, many of the chapters in this volume either make a compelling argument for some of the points I have only alluded to or explore examples of reconciliation that exemplify principles and ideas introduced here.

REFERENCES

Abu-Nimer, M, ed. 2001. *Reconciliation, Justice, and Coexistence: Theory and Practice.* Lanham: Lexington Books.

Abu-Nimer, Mohammed. 1999. *Dialogue, Conflict Resolution, and Change: Arab-Jewish Encounters in Israel.* New York: State University of New York Press.

Adams, Rebecca. 2000. "'Loving Mimesis and Girard's 'Scapegoat of the Text' : A Creative Reassessment of Mimetic Desire." Pp. 277–307 in Willard Swartley (ed.). *Violence Renounced : René Girard, Biblical Studies and Peacemaking.* Telford: Pandora.

Aertsen, Ivo, Jane Arsovska, Holger-C. Rohne, Marta Valiñas, and Kris Vanspauwen, eds. 2008. *Restoring Justice after Large-scale Violent Conflicts: Kosovo, DR Congo and the Israeli-Palestinian Case.* Cullompton: Willan.

Appleby, R. Scott. 2000. *The Ambivalence of the Sacred: Religion, Violence and Reconciliation.* Lanham: Rowan & Littlefield.

———. 2001. "Religion as an Agent of Conflict Resolution and Peacebuilding." Pp. 821–840 in *Turbulent Peace: The Challenges of Managing International Conflict,* edited by C. Crocker, F. Hampson, and P. Aall. Washington: United States Institute of Peace.

Appleby R. Scott & Richard Cizik, eds. 2010. *Engaging Religious Communities Abroad: A New Imperative for U.S. Foreign Policy, Report of the Task Force on Religion and the Making of U.S. Foreign Policy co-chaired by R. Scott Appleby and Richard Cizik.* Chicago: The Chicago Council on Global Affairs.

Ashafa, Imam Mohammad and Pastor James Wuye. 2010. *An African Answer*, DVD. Edited and Produced by Amad Karam. London: FTLfilms.

Bar-Siman-Tov, Yaacov, ed. 2004. *From Conflict Resolution to Reconciliation.* Oxford: Oxford University Press.

Baum, Gregory and Harold Wells, eds. 1997. *The Reconciliation of Peoples: Challenge to the Churches.* Maryknoll: Orbis and Geneva: WCC Publications.

Beauregard, M. & D. O'Leary. 2007. *The Spiritual Brain.* New York: HarperCollins.

Beck, D., and C. Cowan. 1996. *Spiral dynamics: Mastering Values, Leadership and Change.* Cambridge, MA: Blackwell.

Bloomfield, David, Teresa Barnes, and Luc Huyse, eds. 2004. *Reconciliation After Violent Conflict: A Handbook.* Stockholm: International IDEA.

Booth, Wayne. 2005. "Introduction: The Rhetoric of War and Reconciliation." Pp. 3–13 in *Roads to Reconciliation* edited by Amy Benson and Karen M. Poremski. Armonk and London: M.E. Sharpe.

Bourdieu, Pierre. 2005. *The Social Structures of the Economy.* Cambridge: Polity Press.

Bowker, John, ed. 2008. *Conflict and Reconciliation: The Contribution of Religions.* Toronto: The Key Publishing House.

Burton, John W. 1990. *Conflict Resolution and Provention.* New York: St. Martin's Press.

———. 1993. *Conflict: Human Needs Theory.* London: Palgrave Macmillan.

———. 1996. *Conflict Resolution: Its Language and Process.* London. Scarecrow Press,

———. 2010. *Systems, States, Diplomacy and Rules.* Cambridge: Cambridge University Press.

Burton, John W. & Frank Dukes. 1990. *Conflict: Readings in Management and Resolution.* London: Macmillan and New York: St. Martin's Press.

Clark, Mary. 1990. "Meaningful Social Bonding as a Universal Human Need." Pp. 34–59 in *Conflict: Human Needs Theory,* edited by John W. Burton. New York: St. Martin's Press.

Collins, Robin. 2013. "Nature as a Source of Non-Conflictual Desire." Pp. 291–314 in *René Girard and Creative Mimesis,* edited by Vern Neufeld Redekop and Thomas Ryba. Lanham: Lexington.

Daly, Erin and Jeremy Sarkin. 2007. *Reconciliation in Divided Societies: Finding Common Ground.* Philadelphia: University of Pennsylvania Press.

Deutsch, Morton. 1975. "Equity, equality, and need: What determines which value will be used as the basis of distributive justice?" *Journal of Social Issues,* 31–3, 137–149.

De Waal, Frans. 1989. *Peacemaking among Primates.* Cambridge MA: Harvard University Press.

———. 2005. "The Law of the Jungle: Conflict Resolution in Primates." Pp. 121–134 in *Roads to Reconciliation: Conflict and Dialogue in the Twenty-First Century* edited by Amy Benson Brown and Karen M. Poremski. Armonk and London: M.E. Sharpe.

———. 2009. *The Age of Empathy: Nature's Lessons for a Kinder Society.* New York: Three Rivers.

Du Bois, Francois, and Antje du Bois-Pedain. 2008. "Post-Conflict Justice and the Reconciliation Paradigm." Pp. 289–311 in *Justice and Reconciliation in Post-Apartheid South Africa,* edited by Francois du Bois and Antje du Bois-Pedain. Cambridge: Cambridge University Press.

Du Hamel Yellow Horn, Paula. 2009. "Education For Resiliency: An Examination Of Risks In A Native American Youth Environment." Doctoral dissertation, Charles Sturt University.

Epp, Edgar. 1982. *Law Breaking and Peacemaking.* Sunderland P. Gardner Lecture, Memramcook Institute, Saint Joseph, New Brunswick, August 19, 1982. Canadian Quaker Pamphlet Number 15.

Fehr, E., H. Bernard, and B. Rochenbach. 2008. "Egalitarianism in Young Children." *Nature.* 454 (7208): 1079–83.

Flanagan, K., & P.C. Jupp, eds. 2007. *A Sociology of Spirituality.* Aldershot: Ashgate.

Foerster. [1964] 1980. "The Greek Concept of *eirene.*" P. 401 in Gerhard Kittel, ed. *Theological Dictionary of the New Testament,* vol. 2. Grand Rapids: Eerdmans.

Folger, Robert, Blair Sheppard, and Robert Buttram. 1995. "Equity, Equality, and Need: Three Faces of Social Justice." Pp. 261–90 in *Conflict, Cooperation and Justice: Essays Inspired by the Work of Morton Deutsch,* edited by Barbara Bunker and Jeffrey Rubin. San Francisco: Jossey-Bass.

Fry, Douglas P. 2007. *The Human Potential for Peace.* Oxford: Oxford University Press.

Fukuyama, Francis. 1992. *The End of History and the Last Man.* New York: Avon.

Galtung, Johan. 1971. "A Structural Theory of Imperialism." *Journal of Peace Research* 8 (2), 81–117.

———. 1992. "The Emerging Conflict Formations." Pp. 23–24 in *Restructuring for World Peace: on the Threshold of the Twenty-First Century,* edited by Katharine Tehranian & Majid Tehranian. Cresskill (NJ): Hampton Press,.

———. 2009. *The Fall of the US Empire - And Then What?* Basel:Transcend University Press.

Girard, René. 1976. *Deceit, Desire, and the Novel: Self and Other in Literary Structure.* Translated by Y. Freccero. Baltimore: Johns Hopkins University Press.

———. 1977. *Violence and the Sacred.* Translated by P. Gregory. Baltimore: Johns Hopkins University Press.

———. 1978. *To Double Business Bound: Essays on Literature, Mimesis, and Anthropology.* Baltimore: Johns Hopkins University Press.

———. 1987. *Things Hidden Since the Foundation of the World.* Translated by S. Bann. Stanford: Stanford University Press.

———. 1989. *The Scapegoat.* Translated by Y. Freccero. Baltimore: Johns Hopkins University Press.

———. 2010. *Battling to the End: Conversations with Benoît Chantre.* Translated by M. Baker. East Lansing (MI): Michigan University Press.

Gobod-Madikizela, Pumla and Chris Van Der Merwe, eds. 2009. *Memory, Narrative, and Forgiveness: Perspectives on the Unfinished Journeys of the Past.* Newcastle upon Tyne: Cambridge Scholars Publishing.

Goleman, D. 2003. *Destructive emotions: A Scientific Dialogue with the Dalai Lama.* New York, NY: Bantam Books.

Goodhart, Sandor. 2009. "'A land that devours its inhabitants': Midrashic Reading, Levinas and Literary Medieval Exegesis." Pp. 227–253 in *Levinas and Medieval Literature: The "Difficult Reading"of English and Rabbinic Texts,* edited by Ann Astell and J.A. Jackson. Pittsburgh: Duquesne University Press.

Gospic, K., E. Mohlin, P. Frensson, P. Petrovic, M. Johannesson, and M. Ingvar. 2011. "Limbic Justice—Amygdala Involvement in Immediate Rejection in the Ultimatum Game." *PLoS Biology,* May 20aa, Vol. 9, Issue 5, e1001054. www.plosbiology.org

Gould, Stephen Jay. 1978. "Sociobiology: The Art of Storytelling." *New Scientist* 80, 530–533.

Gramsci, Antonio. 1971. *Selections from the Prison Notebooks.* New York: International Publishers.

Grimsrud, Ted. 1999. "Healing Justice: The Prophet Amos and a 'New' Theology of Justice." Pp. 64–85 in *Peace and Justice Shall Embrace: Power and Theopolitics in the Bible,* edited by Ted Grimsrud and Loren Johns. Telford, PA: Pandora Press.

Griswold, Charles. 2007. *Forgiveness: A Philosophical Exploration.* Cambridge: Cambridge University Press.

John S. Hagelin, Maxwell V. Rainforth, David W. Orme-Johnson, Kenneth L. Cavanaugh, Charles N. Alexander, Susan F. Shatkin, John L. Davies, Anne O. Hughes, and Emanuel Ross. 1993. Effects of Group Practice of the Transcendental Meditation Program on Preventing Violent Crime in Washington, DC: Results of the National Demonstration Project, June-July 1993. Fairfield, IA : Institute of Science, Technology and Public Policy. http://www.istpp.org/crime_prevention/ Accessed October 28, 2011

Hamber, Brandon. 2007. "Forgiveness and Reconciliation: Paradise Lost or Pragmatism?" *Peace and Conflict: Journal of Peace Psychology, 13*(1), 115–125.

Hamber, Brandon and Gráinne Kelly. 2009. "Beyond Coexistence: Toward a Working Definition of Reconciliation." Pp. 286–310 in *Reconciliation(s): Transitional Justice is Postconflict Societies,* edited by Joanna Quinn. Montreal and Kingston: McGill-Queen's University Press.

Hammerich, Beata, Johannes Pfäfflin, Peter Pogany-Wnend, Erda Siebert, and Bernd Sonntag. 2009. "Handing Down the Holocaust in Germany: A Reflection on the Dialogue between second-Generation Descendants of Perpetrators and Survivors." Pp. 27–46 in *Memory, Narrative and Forgiveness: Perspectives on the Unfinished Journeys of the Past,* edited by Pumla Gobod-Madikizela and Chris Van Der Merwe. Newcastle upon Tyne: Cambridge Scholars Publishing.

Hanh, Thich Nhat. 1987. *Being Peace.* Berkeley: Parallax Press.

———. 2003. *Joyfully Together: The Art of Building a Harmonious Community.* Berkeley: Parallax Press.

Hanson, Paul. 1975. *The Dawn of Apocalyptic: The Historical and Sociological Roots of Jewish Apocalyptic Eschatology.* Minneapolis: Fortress.

Hardin, Garrett. 1968. "The Tragedy of the Commons." *Science* 162, pp.1243–1248.

Harper, Charles. 2005. *Spiritual Information: 100 Perspectives on Science and Religion.* Philadelphia: Templeton.

Hauser, Marc D. 2006. *Moral Minds: How Nature Designed Our Universal Sense of Right and Wrong.* San Francisco: Ecco/HarperCollins.

Herman, Judith Lewis. 1997. *Trauma and Recovery.* Rev. ed. New York: Basic Books.

Hertog, Katrien. 2010. *The Complex Reality of Religious Peacebuilding: Conceptual Contributions and Critical Analysis.* Lanham: Lexington.

Hoffman, Aaron. 2006. *Building Trust: Overcoming Suspicion in International Conflicts.* Albany: State University of New York Press.

Howell, Signe & Roy Willis, eds. 1989. *Societies at Peace: Anthropological Perspectives.* London: Routledge.

Ismael, Jacqueline S. 2007. "Introduction." Pp. 1–18 in *Barriers to Reconciliation: Case Studies on Iraq and the Palestine-Israel Conflict,* edited by Jacqueline S. Ismael and William W. Haddad. Lanham: University Press of America

Ismael, Jacqueline S. and William W. Haddad, eds. 2007. *Barriers to Reconciliation: Case Studies on Iraq and the Palestine-Israel Conflict.* Lanham: University Press of America.

Kauffman, Stuart. 1995. *At Home in the Universe: The Search for Laws of Self-Organization and Complexity.* Oxford: Oxford University Press.

———. 2008. *Reinventing the Sacred: A New View of Science, Reason, and Religion.* New York: Basic Books.

Kegan, R. G. 2001. "Competencies as Working Epistemologies: Ways We Want Adults to Know." In *Defining and Selecting Key Competencies,* edited by D. S. Rychen and L. H. Salganik. Kirkland, WA: Hogrefe & Huber.

Keller, Alexis. 2006. "Justice, Peace, and History: A Reappraisal." Pp. 19–51 in *What is a Just Peace?,* edited by Pierre Allan and Alexis Keller. Oxford: Oxford University Press.

Kemp, Graham & Douglas P. Fry, eds. 2004. *Keeping the Peace: Conflict Resolution and Peaceful Societies Around the World.* New York: Routledge.

Kim, Sebastian, Pauline Kollontai and Greg Hoyland. 2008. *Peace and Reconciliation: In Search of a Shared Identity.* Aldershot: Ashgate.

King, Ursula. 2008. The *Search for Spirituality: Our Global Quest for a Spiritual Life.* New York: Bluebridge.

Kolbert, C. F. 1979. "The Legal Background." Pp. 48–63 in *Justinian: The Digest of Roman Law—Theft, Rapine, Damage and Insult.* Translated by C.F. Kolbert. New York: Penguin.

Levinas, Emmanuel. [1961] 1969. *Totality and Infinity: An Essay on Exteriority.* Translated by Alphonso Lingis. Pittsburgh: Duquesne University Press.

———. 1978. Otherwise than Being or Beyond Essence. Translated by Alphonso Lingis. Dordrecht and Boston, MA: Kluwer Academic Publishers.

Lewis, Thomas, Fari Amini, and Robert Lannon. 2000. *A General Theory of Love.* New York: Random House.

Lewontin, R. C. Lewontin, S. Rose & L. J. Kamin. 1984. *Not in Our Genes.* New York: Random House.

Long, William J. and Peter Brecke. 2003. *War and Reconciliation: Reason and Emotion in Conflict Resolution.* Cambridge MA: The MIT Press.

Lopreato, J. & P. Green. 1990. "The Evolutionary Foundations of Revolution." Pp. 107–122 in *Sociobiology and Conflict,* edited by J.Van Der Dennen & V. Falger. New York: Springer.

Lorenz, Konrad. 2002. *On Aggression.* New York: Routledge.

Luttwak, Edward. 1994. "Franco-German Reconciliation: The Overlooked Role of the Moral Re-Armament Movement." Pp. 37–63 in Douglas Johnston and Cynthia Sampson (eds.) *Religion, The Missing Dimension of Statecraft.* Oxford: Oxford University Press.

Martens, Elmer. 2009. "Yahweh, Justice and Religious Pluralism in the Old Testament." Pp. 123–42 in *The Old Testament in the Life of God's People,* edited by Jon Isaac. Winona Lake: Eisenbrauns.

Martin, Roger. 2007. *The Opposable Mind.* Boston: Harvard Business School Press.

McGuigan, Richard. 2006. "How Do Evolving Deep Structures of Consciousness Impact the Disputant's Creation of Meaning in a Conflict?" PhD Dissertation. Cincinnati: Union Institute & University.

McGuigan, Richard and Nancy Popp. 2013. "The Good, the True, and the Beautiful and Rene Girard's Mimetic Theory." Pp. 67–70 in *René Girard and Creative Mimesis* edited by Vern Neufeld Redekop and Thomas Ryba. Lanham: Lexington.

Mead, Margaret, ed. 1961. *Cooperation and Competition among Primitive People.* Boston: Beacon Press.

Minow, Martha. 1998. *Between Vengeance and Forgiveness: Facing History after Genocide and Mass Violence.* Boston: Beacon Press.

Mitchell, Christopher. 2000. *Gestures of Conciliation: Factors Contributing to Successful Olive Branches.* London: MacMillan and New York: St. Martin's.

Murphy, Jeffrie and Jean Hampton. 1988. *Forgiveness and Mercy.* Cambridge: Cambridge University Press.

Nadler, Arie, Thomas E. Malloy, and Jeffrey Fisher. 2008. "Introduction: Intergroup Reconciliation: Dimensions and Themes." Pp. 3–12 in *The Social Psychology of Intergroup Reconciliation,* edited by Arie Nadler, Thomas Malloy, and Jeffrey Fisher. Oxford: Oxford University Press.

Niehoff, Debra. 1999. *The Biology of Violence.* New York: The Free Press.

Osgoode, Charles. 1962. *An Alternative to War or Surrender.* Urbana, Il: University of Illinois Press.

Radzik, Linda. 2009. *Making Amends: Atonement in Morality, Law, and Politics.* Oxford: Oxford University Press.

Redekop, Vern Neufeld. 1995. "The Centrality of Torah as Ethical Projection for the Exodus." *Contagion: Journal of Violence, Mimesis, and Culture* 2, Spring, 1995.

———. 2002. *From Violence to Blessing: How an Understanding of Deep-Rooted Conflict Opens Paths to Reconciliation.* Ottawa: Novalis.

————. 2007a. "Reconciling Nuers with Dinkas: A Girardian approach to conflict resolution," *Religion—An International Journal.* 37, 64–84.

————. 2007b. "Teachings of Blessing as Elements of Reconciliation: Intra- and Inter-Religious Hermeneutical Challenges and Opportunities in the Face of Violent Deep-Rooted Conflict." Pp. 129–46 in *The Next Step in Studying Religion: A Graduate's Guide*, edited by Mathieu E. Courville. London: Continuum.

————. 2008. "A Post-Genocidal Justice of Blessing as an Alternative to a Justice of Violence: The Case of Rwanda." Pp. 205–38 in *Peacebuilding in Traumatized Societies,* edited by Barry Hart. University Press of America.

————. 2010a. "Healing, Justice, and Reconciliation" and "Reconciliation." *The Oxford International Encyclopedia of Peace,* Oxford: Oxford University Press.

————. 2010b. "A Hermeneutics of Blessing as a Meta-Requisite for Reconciliation: John E. Toews' Romans Paradigm as a Case Study." *Journal of Peace and Conflict Studies.*

————. 2011. "Spirituality, Emergent Creativity, and Reconciliation." Pp. 585–600 in *Peacemaking: A Comprehensive Theory and Practice Reference, Volume II,* edited by Sue Allen Nan, Zachariah Cherian Mampilly and Andrea Bartoli. Westport: Praeger.

————. 2013. "Blessing-Based Love (*agapē*) as a Heuristic Key to Understanding Effective Reconciliation Practices: A Reading of I Corinthians 13 in a Peacebuilding Context." In *Peace on Earth: The Role of Religion in Peace and Conflict Studies*, edited by Tom Matyok. Lanham: Rowman and Littlefield.

Reineke, Martha. 2013. "Transforming Intersubjective Space: From Ruthlessness to Primary Creativity and Loving Mimesis." Pp. 37–50 in *René Girard and Creative Mimesis* edited by Vern Neufeld Redekop and Thomas Ryba. Lanham: Lexington.

Ricoeur, Paul [1990] 1992. *Oneself as Another.* Translated by Kathleen Blamey. Chicago: University of Chicago Press.

Ricoeur, Paul. 2000. *The Just.* Translated by David Pellauer. Chicago: University of Chicago Press.

Ryba, Thomas. 2013. "Mimesis and Immortal Glory: How Creativity is Spurred by the Desire for One's Ideas to Dominate the *Meme* Pool." Pp. 123–140 in *René Girard and Creative Mimesis* edited by Vern Neufeld Redekop and Thomas Ryba. Lanham: Lexington.

Schirch, Lisa. 2005. *Ritual and Symbol in Peacebuilding.* Bloomfield, CT: Kumarian Press.

Sheldrake, Rupert. 2003. *The Sense of Being Stared At: And Other Aspects of the Extended Mind.* New York: Crown.

Staub, Ervin. 1989. *The Roots of Evil: The Origins of Genocide and other Group Violence.* Cambridge, United Kingdom: Cambridge University Press.

Ury, William. 2000. *The Third Side: Why We Fight and How We Can Stop.* New York, NY: Penguin.

Volf, Miroslav 2006. *The End of Memory: Remembering Rightly in a Violent World.* Grand Rapids: Eerdmans.

NOTES

1. Throughout this chapter, I will include autobiographical notes to show the personal side of the exploration. These will be in endnotes. I was first introduced to the work of Girard in the 1980s when Dave Worth, then head of Victim-Offender Ministries for the Mennonite Central Committee, asked me to write a short monograph which would make Girard's ideas accessible to victims and offenders and those working on criminal justice issues. The result was *Scapegoats, the Bible, and Criminal Justice: Interacting with René Girard,* a text to which he responded positively. In 1984, during the Ethiopian famine, it was pointed out that behind such famines were conflicts such that food was used as weapon resulting in thousands of deaths. I determined that, if I ever had the chance, I would like to understand in depth the phenomenon of atrocities, like mass murder and genocide. Hence, when I started my PhD program in 1991 this became my focus and Girardian theory was to play a major heuristic role in this endeavor. The understanding of atrocities was meant as a basis for prevention and reconciliation. This chapter encapsulates the results of over a quarter of a century of focus on these questions.

2. I first met Girard at a COV&R gathering at Stanford in 1992. I had studied *Violence and the Sacred*, after more than a decade of being immersed in restorative justice and after seeing first hand the violence operative in the criminal justice system (CJS). In my *Scapegoats* monograph, I had already made an argument that the CJS functions as a sacrificial system within society with most of those incarcerated meeting all the criteria Girard had laid out for scapegoat victims. While taking Girard's point that the CJS functioning under the rule of law is a big improvement over blood feuds and visceral vengeance, my experience of CJS led to a realization that we could do better.

3. Perhaps some of the appeal of the Harry Potter series is that it appeals to this primal worldview that included powerful magic as a means of achieving justice. Objectively it can be seen that there is a mimetic rivalry between opposing frames of justice. The Harry Potter narrative makes it clear which is the "good" side, appealing to our primal need to identify with an in-group that is ours, is good, is justified in its actions, and is powerful enough to either defend against attacks or inflict vengeful pain on the other side.

4. (cf. laugh with those who laugh)

5. The impulse to bring spirituality into the orb of conflict studies came from an event in which I had to facilitate a gathering of 85 angry protesters and 14 police officers, who were the object of their wrath. For a number of hours, I kept a clear sense of focus and a capacity not only to contain the hostility but eventually to re-channel it into making constructive recommendations. As I reflected on this, I asked myself how I could do this. The answer was framed for me in terms of a spirituality that gave me the inner strength. This led to including a course on Spirituality and Conflict Resolution within the Masters program that I developed. Teaching the course was the occasion for generating the insights summarized above.

6. I remember walking with Girard in Stanford on the way back from a special COV&R event; I pointed out his different uses of the word structure in *Things Hidden*. He immediately agreed with my observation and said he should have had a footnote to that effect. The concept of mimetic structure of blessing came to me as an epiphany after immersing myself in an analysis of the Canadian 1990 Oka/Kanesata:ke Crisis. I recognized that individuals, who might otherwise have been living peaceful lives got drawn into a violent conflict in a way that changed their orientation, attitudes, and actions. It became clear that there was something bigger than any one person that put enormous pressure on people to support the violence. This "something bigger" I called a mimetic structure of violence. I then thought about what an alternative might be and concluded that mimetic structure of blessing would be the best designation. Mimetic structures of entrenchment and transcendence I worked out with Rebecca Adams.

7. How Smith's vision for a free market deteriorated into a market system often exemplifying mimetic structures of violence demands its own analysis.

8. I came to the realization that reconciliation involved a transformation out of violence into blessing, through a structural analysis of the Exodus of the ancient Israelites from slavery in Egypt to the freedom to enter what for them was a land of promise and blessing. A meta-theoretical framework was Isaiah Berlin's conceptualization of freedom in both positive and negative terms: freedom *to* and freedom *from*. My study was oriented around the question, how can those who were oppressed at one time and place avoid mimetically oppressing other when they get into positions of power? My insight was that within the story of the Exodus was a period of wandering in the desert during which time they got the Torah, understood as transformative teachings. From that, I developed the concept of teachings of blessing (1995).

9. In the 1990s when I was with the Canadian Institute for Conflict Resolution, I introduced a two-day interactive seminar on reconciliation. I started by saying that reconciliation is complex, and we don't know much about it but it is worth exploring. Each iteration of the seminar was an uplifting experience for all participants. First thing in the morning of the second day, I would facilitate an open brainstorming session on the elements of reconciliation. I gathered hundreds of suggestions, which I eventually synthesized into 14 key elements. Subsequently, these came together in the framework I present below. Since 2000, there has been enormous growth in the literature dealing with reconciliation. New insights from this literature have contributed to the growth and nuancing of the framework, which for me is an open system.

II

THEOLOGY OF FRIENDSHIP, PEACE, AND NON-VIOLENCE

Chapter Five

Towards a Theology of Friendship in the "Global Village"

Nadia Delicata

Before *Facebook* and *Twitter* became our *de facto* channels for all news items, information, and trivia, in a TV series ominously entitled *The End*,[1] the Canadian Broadcasting Corporation (CBC) aired three shows that prophesied in succession *The End of Radio*, *The End of TV* and *The End of Print*. The timing was perfect: just as *Twitter* was being launched and *Facebook* was opening its doors to all global users, rather than be limited to American students, the 2006 documentary series signalled the demise of three of the most powerful news and entertainment media to shape the world from the Renaissance until the death of modernity, witnessed in our own times. Three media that (in a radically metamorphosized form) still accompany us in our living rooms and cars, in our classrooms, and public libraries but are fast approaching the cultic state of artefacts. Radio, television, newspapers, magazines, books, and the like no longer exist as necessary extensions of our thoughts, of our memories, of our stories, of our creativity, of our desire to reach out to others in space and time, but have become "obsolesced"—*objets d'art*, sophisticated and beautiful relics of a world that was, but that is fast slipping through our fingers (McLuhan and McLuhan 1988, 99).[2] Today our world is different, and in its playful way, *The End* sought to explore this novelty in order to understand who we are becoming in a post-modern, post-mass media, digital world.

INTERIM TIMES

As early as the 1950s, the Canadian, Marshall McLuhan, father of media ecology,[3] and one of the first to take mediation seriously in fashioning our human becoming in the global household, postulated that we were living in interim times: between the "literate age" and the "electric age," between modernity as culmination of the visual Gutenberg legacy and the new acoustic and tactile era of the "global village"; between the world of print and the new world symbolized by the Internet[4] :

> We are today as far into the electric age as the Elizabethans [16th century] had advanced into the typographical and mechanical age. And we are living the same confusion and indecisions which they had felt when living simultaneously in two contrasted forms of society and experience. Whereas the Elizabethans were poised between medieval corporate experience and modern individualism, we reverse their pattern by confronting an electric technology which would seem to render individualism obsolete and the corporate interdependence mandatory (McLuhan 1962, 1).

This becomes McLuhan's key to interpreting the confusion of our "age of anxiety" (McLuhan and Fiore 1967, 9): our seeing and understanding ourselves "through the rear-view mirror" (McLuhan and Fiore 1967, 75), that is, through the ashes of a modern culture of individualism, linearity, and structured fragmentation as institutionalism, rather than observing, understanding, and recognizing the effects of contemporary technologies to mould a radically novel culture. Because our senses are over-stimulated, we are entranced and paradoxically numbed by the effects of electricity and digitality (McLuhan 2003, 63).[5] To compensate, we fill our perceptual and conceptual darkness through what we knew—the biases of the past—as we are held captive by these new "extensions" (McLuhan 2003) of ourselves that are fast morphing our very human becoming.[6] Electricity is the defining medium of the new age and it is also the perfect medium, because it replicates globally what goes on in every human body, in every nervous system. The Internet is the obvious progeny of electricity, an extension and externalization of our nervous system creating a communal consciousness. The ubiquitous and simultaneous transfer of stimuli, or of data, through neurones is extended and externalized in a global nervous system: an electric connectivity, whose very message is not merely "information" but mediation (McLuhan and McLuhan 1988, 86).[7] It is a cultural becoming as an intricate web, as one whole body that grows organically, amorphously, and exponentially. "The medium is the message" and electricity, the defining medium of our age, communicates that we are connected. Indeed it makes us connected, because the medium also "messages" us into itself, since it is the very extension of ourselves.[8] Yet, paradoxically, we continue to misunderstand the medium and ourselves. We continue to act through the delusion of the past, of individualism, hierarchy, and bureaucracy, because like Narcissus we are also narcotized by extensions of ourselves who are the very image of ourselves. We become numb in being split as our idea of self, and our reality of self conceived as another.[9]

The first obvious signs of narcosis in the electric age emerged with the birthing of such culturally-defining media as radio and television. In the 1930s and throughout the Second World War, Germany was hypnotized by the voice of Hitler, echoing through the radio waves, only to become transformed into the one *Reich*, the one German empire. The modern sense of self, the sense of being an individual solely responsible for one's thoughts and actions, dissipated into the communal experience of hearing one voice, of becoming one people. Like the drum in a tribal culture, radio had become the means to control a people, to fire their fury, to determine their commitment, to make them belong to something greater than themselves.[10]

Radio marked the formidable return of the ear after five hundred years of relative deafness under the predominance of the eye, extended through the printing press. In the past five hundred years, as the mechanization of writing, of the linear alphabet, became ubiquitous, so the person morphed into the mirror of the medium, and hence became the extension of fragmented letters, of serial thoughts, of logical order. The world that was born after the printing press was an age of reason (the Enlightenment), of production (the Industrial Revolution) and of self-actualization (the rise of capitalism and private ownership). It marked the birth of the nation state, of individual or human rights, of the triumph of the "I" over and above the "we." The singularity of this accomplishment cannot be over-stated: never had the human being, who for millennia had existed primarily as a corporate member of a village, of a tribe, of an extended family, become so clearly defined as a self, as possessing an individual identity, as detached from the world, and hence as its "observer."[11] The reversal of this process, the return to the "village," with its preliminary re-initiation through the birth of electric "mass media"— through the radio as extension of the ear and, particularly in North America, through TV as extension of our skin—is an equally traumatic and confusing event in our recent history.

Confusion is evident, for instance, in the ambivalent reception of TV in American households in the 1950s, where it was simultaneously hailed as friend and foe of the "American" way of life. Early TV sets were involving, compelling, urging the "viewer" to fill in the poor resolution of the tube, to color its gray picture. As TV filled American living rooms with guests, entertainment, news, the American dream itself, it symbolically awakened tactility in a culture of heightened visual detachment.[12] American families were far from being TV "spectators": they became hypnotized by a medium that pulled them out of themselves to be magnetically absorbed into mass stories, mass dramas, mass fantasies. Metaphorically speaking, people felt the urge to reach out, to welcome, to share in the life of people on television—yet insofar as all households remained detached, separate from each other, they reached out to a frustrating nothingness. As individualism was collapsing, so were people becoming a replicated herd.

Radio and TV, however, remain primitive media of the electric age, whose *raison d'être*, whose *modus operandi* is antithetical to the spirit of electricity itself. Electricity creates webs of interaction, where there is no center but only participation. Radio and TV are interim media of the electric age because they reflect the model of print inherited from the literate age where one story, one song, one content, is spread to the masses from the one centralized power, be it the writer, the artist, the government, the corporation.[13] For this reason, as Noam Chomsky has astutely pointed out, "mass media" are also lethal weapons of political control, of propaganda, "manufacturing consent," and alienating the public (Chomsky 2002). For this reason, parasites that feed on "mass media" (like corporate branding, marketing, and even the entertainment industry) produce images, advertising, and media "content" as commodities to be sold to "consumers," who, quite literally, morph into "fans," buying into a "lifestyle" and replicating its image, its corporate herd (Klein 2000). "Mass media," with their one-way communication, epitomize the fusion of contemporary technology with the contradiction of individualism as passive compositeness. Even so, the very act of mutual mediation (implicit through electricity as medium) has been forcefully pushing its ethos. As the CBC series *The End* ominously (or triumphantly) noted, "mass media" are becoming obsolete (or vacuous artefacts) as the electric age has resolutely moved to its second phase: the "web."

Quite tellingly, the World Wide Web started by incorporating primitive forms of other mass and private media. It became a ubiquitous and simultaneous medium for all media: a faster, more efficient way of sending and receiving mail, of advertising, of accessing libraries of information, of doing business transactions, of receiving the news, even of watching "TV," and of listening to the "radio." Yet after the 2001 burst of the dot.com bubble, the web re-invented itself and through Web 2.0 technologies, it became easier than ever to not only "surf" the web, but become the web (O'Reilly 2002). The real power of the electric age was starting to emerge, as fragile voices could be heard from all people, irrespective of gender, geographical location, or culture. Media "content" was not being primarily dispersed to the masses, but was being created by the masses. People across the globe were taking ownership of their extended selves in the global village and were actively mediating themselves through blogs, podcasts, and video blogs. At the pinnacle of this era, *Facebook* and *Twitter* became the quintessential "village squares," accessed continually through mobile technologies, as their aim to create small groups of men and women who work together, play together, and exchange their daily trivia reveals the true power and *raison d'être* of the web.

We are now entering the next phase of connectivity, driven mostly through mobile and wearable technologies. In Web 3.0, or the so-called "semantic web," the web itself becomes "intelligent," interpreting and streamlining massive data to suit (and create) individual needs (Shadbolt, Berners-Lee, and Hall 2006; Agarwal 2009). Web 2.0's excessively wide-spread, large, and even random followings become obsolesced, as tribes become smaller and more tightly knit through bonds of common interest (Stibel 2013). In our new, virtual global village, we are no longer in the stage of merely reaching out haphazardly to seek community and "friending." Rather, we are becoming true dwellers, carving a network of associates (or *niche*) we can call "home." In these new liquid, constantly morphing, relational configurations we are attempting to redefine our personal identity, as we seek to go beyond detached individualism without being completely amalgamated into a global undifferentiated herd. At the birth of this new digital culture, the same hope for sociality and friendship continues to be grounded in the human desire to reach out to the other.

THE CHALLENGE OF HUMAN RELATIONALITY

Desire, or rather amorphous desire, is the heart of René Girard's anthropology. From his study of literature and the classics, especially the works of Sophocles (2004), Shakespeare (1991), Cervantes, Proust, Freud, Dostoevsky, (1966, 1978), and the Bible (1986, 1987, and 2001), Girard recognizes how human beings are essentially mimetic, because we are consumed by a desire that needs to take form: the desire to become a "being," a unique person. Thus, we not only overtly imitate each other's mannerisms, clothing, language, or ideas, we also become human through imitating our parents, our teachers, through all "models" who socialize us into a culture. We become like them, we actually become extensions of our mediators, by replicating and appropriating our "models" as our very pre-selves. However, while the self-created, totally-distinct automaton, is unquestionably a myth, chaos also ensues through the breakdown of *all* personal distinctions characteristic of the herd. Thus, the project of culture is to maintain a tight balance between similarity and dissimilarity, between commonality and absolute mirroring. Girard describes this mean as "interdividuals": clusters of human relationality, where we paradoxically narrate and embrace unique identities through the imitation of others (Girard 1987, 283–431). Through language, we become both separate from the other, as well as forever interwoven with them. We are unique selves as well as a herd.

Fascinatingly, however, these two poles of identity configuration emerge very strongly in McLuhan's understanding of our cultural interim times. We are caught up between the modern ideal of individualism and self-creation and the postmodern temptation to go with the flow and become clones by imitating the same models and desiring the same objects in our global theatre of ubiquitous mass mediation. As a "rear-view" defense mechanism against the anxiety of our amorphous cultural transition, we desperately seek to have a sharply defined identity: to be unique—or at least to belong to clearly differentiated tribal or institutional structures that provide us a sense of self. Yet, precisely because electricity and its children morph us into a connected whole, a "global village," simultaneously we cannot but share the same culture, the same socialization, indeed, even the same networks of "friends," as we become a collective of replicated identities, or—in Baudrillard's term—"fractal" selves (Baudrillard 1988, 40). As the modern division between public and private is giving way to the techno-tribal fusion of "publicy," Girard's insights are more crucial than ever not only with respect to dynamics that make us social beings, but especially to guide us in our struggles accentuated by a fast escalating "village" and agonistic mentality (Federman 2003, 8).

Girard's anthropology of interdividuality starts, unremarkably enough, with explicit imitation or "pacific *mimesis*," that is, the creative process of learning and enculturation, from cradle to tomb.[14] From birth, the child mimics the gestures, sounds, emotions, attitudes, and behaviors of the adult, to acquire language, values, performance, and communication skills in order to be formed as a socialized human being, apt at belonging and functioning adequately within a group bound together by a common culture. Pacific *mimesis* is thus the "civilizing" process through which we undergo the dual challenge of becoming a group (that is, the inculcation of the *ethos* and *mores*) through consolidating personal freedom and identity (that is, delineating boundaries between my unique self and the imitated other).

The erection of psychological boundaries, a trend that increases through literacy, is a process of individuation, of asserting a self in relation (possibly even, in opposition) to the other. However, individuality is a profound and dangerous paradox: to actualize the deep desire to become a unique "I," I desperately need the other, but the more egocentric I become, the more I shun the other. I not only choose the hubris of denying my need for the other, but also the indulgence of accentuating separation from the other through superficial differentiation.[15] Self-aggrandizement and the concomitant belittling of the other, suppress *mimesis* to the unconscious.

Yet, the denial of my need for the other contorts human desire for personhood to the mere longing to have an object. Girard repeatedly notes how acquisitive *mimesis*, where I imitate the perceived desire of the model (by desiring the object they possess or regard highly), is the most common form of *mimesis*. Desire becomes "triangular," with an overt focus on the object, even if the real, but unconscious, pull remains toward the model. All is well, if model and imitator are removed by insuperable distance, but if mediation shifts to the internal sphere, that is, "when the mediator moves within the same 'sphere of possibilities' of the imitator" (Anspach 2004, xxxiv), it becomes highly probable that trapped in this triangular dynamic, the covert "model-mediator" is perceived as the overt "rival-stumbling block" to the fulfilment of my newly fashioned desire trapped in the form of the object (Girard 1966, 9).[16] Depending on the response of the model *vis-à-vis* attachment to the object, and the model's awareness of the dynamic of *mimesis*, in all likelihood (Girard often seems to suggest, inevitably) a cycle of decline is sustained, as model and disciple, rival and imitator, become clones of each other, feeding off each other's desire for the same object—their very mutual desire. Indeed, as the object is forgotten, desire becomes even more solidly intertwined in an unconscious lust for each other[17]—a loathsome yearning for the being of the other, even if both clones recognise each other's inherent emptiness and insufficiency for the mutual fulfilment of their desire. The worst nightmare of the imitator of the model, becomes terrifying reality: I am no longer unique because the other is exactly like me, and I have lost all hope of satisfying my desire for being. Murder, the total annihilation of the clone, is conceived as solution, both to restore identity and placate frustration, as well as out of vengeance for being robbed of the hope of fulfilling the emptiness of desire.

If annihilation is tragic between model and mediator, how much more appalling it is when triangular desire replicates virally, creating the plague of an entire horde inextricably bound in mutual conflictual *mimesis*. The traditional relationality of tribalism is founded on an endemic herd mentality that teaches conformity and despises all dissimilarity—except that it is imposed through a rigid social ladder ("to each their own place") and taboos of intransgressible difference. Notwithstanding these protective measures of enforced "difference," even more than modern individualism, tribalism is susceptible to the maddening drive to slaughter each other that can only be controlled through finding a common enemy, a new common "other" who restores differentiation among the clones. The murder of a "scapegoat" (the one who in being superficially marked as different restores difference) loosens the ties of the slavery of cloning and frustrated desire (Girard 1986 and 1996, 118–141). The scapegoat is lynched as a sacrifice of expiation from the plague of sameness, and a "peaceful" society is restored out of the blood of the victim. The transformation is so awesome and palpable that the victim itself is made sacred (Girard 1977, 39–67, 89–118). Thus, the way out of the double bind, of the inevitability of *mimesis* yet the inherent violent danger of *mimesis* gone wild, is the irenic (and ironic) solution of violence in controlled doses. Controlled, ritualized violence becomes the inoculation that offers resistance and hope for survival amidst inevitable cycles of murderous hostility. This dynamic is witnessed in different eras of cultural unrest when the king, the witch, or the infidel have been elevated as radical "other," as the *pharmakos* that purges the plague of violence.

The paradox of our own cultural interim times is that the pendulum is swinging from extreme individualism (replicated through typography) to intense tribalism (configured through digital technologies). Thus, in the period of transition, we schizophrenically embrace (and shun) sameness and difference at the same time. Through our "rear-view" perception, we desperately seek to have a sharply defined identity, to be unique and original, even if we are more the same than ever. Through the urge of the tribe, we seek to belong to the "in" crowd, sect, or ideology that gives us a social "place" and a sense of self, even if our "polite" liberal democratic creed claims that we despise all social stratification. "Friending" as ethos of social networking tools captures this conflictual dynamic as it is both a mode of tribalizing and of parading self-importance, just as techno-tribalism itself is the paradox of the narcissism (overt self-absorption) of the fractal "I" (overt clones).

Yet, as modern individualism loses its grip on our consciousness through the herding pressure of the global village—which we witness, for instance, through the collapse of privacy—we put on more tribalistic defenses to contain violence and protect the herded group from collective murder/suicide. For the digital tribe as it was for the tribes of old, "hominization" through the "scapegoat mechanism" is the means through which humanity is caught up in a cycle of violence and shielded against its own aggression. In the native tribe, it is the process of controlled violence replicated as ritual, that is, the recognition of the victim as possessing the sacred power over life and death and thus the birth of religion. In the digital tribe, it is the rebirth of ritual and "religion" (widely construed)—whether through the overt rise of religious fundamentalism, or through rituals of movies and video games that enact violence as purification, or through the many sects, ideologies, and obsessions that rise in the digital age. Most paradigmatically, religion as the primordial cultural defence mechanism becomes the pivotal symbol of the "clash of civilizations" (Huntington 1996), where members of a global herd mutually seek to expel each "other" as scapegoat. Still, the cataclysmic danger of global herding remains global destruction. It is perhaps not surprising that the beginning of the twentieth century perfected electricity as medium and established more sophisticated means of communication, but was also threatened by two World Wars that birthed almost half a century of superpowers' rivalry, or the Cold War. Just as worth pondering are the symbolic implications of the War on Terror that marked the first decade of the Third Millennium: a war against fear that has been fuelled by extreme fear itself, the fear of the phantasm "other" who is just like me.

Interim times are thus potentially dangerous times. In these times of ours, it becomes essential to seek ethical paths that not only protect us from ourselves, but that urge us to transcend our propensity for blindness, become wise and thus more fully human. Even if human civilizations have never been perfect, they are ample proof that the mark of *Homo sapiens* is "reason" as the freedom to transcend animal instinct and even hominization itself to mould culture. Accordingly, if Girard appears to offer a dark portrayal of human nature, the human *qua* human can never be irrevocably determined and, as McLuhan notes, "There is absolutely no inevitability as long as there is a willingness to contemplate what is happening" (McLuhan and Fiore 1967, 25).

Nevertheless, the tragic mistakes of human history are also a definitive proof that, on its own, reason to act freely is not sufficient. Just as freedom without responsibility is tyranny, reason without humility is blind and even delusional. And our blindness is collective in at least two senses: (1) blindness to the effects of media that form us and our cultures (and through which we desperately seek to imitate each other in reaching out to the other); but also (2) blindness to *mimesis* itself. McLuhan has noted that the former requires attentiveness to the tetradic effects of each medium (what it enhances, reverses into, retrieves from the past, and obsolesces in the present) (McLuhan and McLuhan 1988, 93–128). This involves "reading" and interpreting the effects of each medium as a language with its particular grammar and rhetoric. But the latter necessitates not only an awareness of how we ourselves act as media, as mentors to others, but also discernment in choosing whom to imitate, in whose image we desire to become. The former requires an education of the senses, a profound awakening to our bodies and to balance in the ecosystem, and the critical pondering of collective memories to discern their true meaning for the present. But the latter necessitates what, at face value, would appear to be impossible or sheer madness: the imitation of an Other untainted by hominization, by human violence, the imitation of a human who is "divine."[18]

Thus, it becomes evident that the wisdom that humanity seeks in order to live together harmoniously is both human and more-than-human. Human wisdom demands a long, arduous process of *askesis* or discipline to pay attention, interpret the signs of the times, acknowledge their truth, and act responsibly (Lonergan 1992 and 1996). Yet, if Girard is to be taken seriously, human wisdom must also be supplemented and perfected by the radically novel and supra-human: the imitation of a supernatural dynamic of *caritas* that has the power to transform weapons to ploughshares, and human mutual expulsion to friendship. To become wise, to become fully human in a mutual *mimesis* of "blessing" (Redekop 2002), is to empty oneself in the transcending imitation of the One who offers their Self first as the Scapegoat of human violence.

Just as the self-offering *pharmakos* dies to expose the violence of hominization and rises up again to lay bare its deceptiveness, so the human path to flourishing as *askesis* and *caritas* demands the purging of self to become whole. *Askesis* is the purging of the "false self" trapped in bias. *Caritas* is the free offering of one's purified desire to the other in order to become one with them through their gift of self: to become a person in a mutual loving relationship. Thus, an ethical model of *askesis* and *caritas* can be described as an act of "emptying" or *kenosis*[19] that is paradoxically also a "fulfilling." In other words, the path to subvert the threat of violence in the global village, to reverse its ethos of tribalism to life-giving personhood and thus to embrace the vision of human flourishing as the *communio* of friendship, is an ethic of *kenosis* in imitation of a supernatural dynamic of exchanged love that is inherently fullness, completeness, *pleroma*.

TOWARD A THEOLOGY OF FRIENDSHIP

So far, we have seen how the birth pangs of a new culture of digitality include widespread anxiety and confusion as the effects of new media re-shape our collective sensorium and local modes of interaction—whether they are cultures still rooted in an oral, acoustic and therefore holistic sensitivity (like most of the south and east), to the western typographical, visual ethos of individualism, reductionism and instrumentalism, or a novel "global village" characterized by (virtual) tactility and the terror of tribalism.[20] In turn, we have analysed the danger of tribalism, or herding as a pattern of relationality through Girard's mimetic theory. If, according to Girard, individualism is a myth that contradicts our mimetic nature, the dark side of *mimesis* is precise-ly to eliminate all difference—a condition of frustration to the human desire to become unique persons-in-relationship that inevitably collapses to vio-lence. In our age, where tribes are amorphous entities that span the entire globe, the carnage of mutual scapegoating could lead to global annihilation.

Yet, it is a profound paradox of our times that, if the rise of violence is often due to religious extremism, so the promise at the heart of world relig-ions remains the flourishing to personhood: the ascetical quest to enlighten-ment and the imitation of a supra-human ideal who transforms our very humanity. If our contemporary "global village" is the tempestuous ground where neighbours are caught up in worldwide rivalry, so the hope of univer-sal concord as symbolized by the Golden Rule (of world religions) and exemplified by Jesus Christ's kenotic ethic in particular, could signify the conversion from the prospect of global destructiveness to the expectation of human thriving. The key dynamic necessary for this age of anxiety is the ordering of desire—re-orienting our desire for being toward the source of true Being—a transformation of our mimetic potential to reach out to the other without annihilating their otherness. And the essence of the Christian project of becoming, that is, to be a "disciple" or follower of Christ, is precisely this conversion of human rivalristic desire to a non-naïve form of unobstacled desire (Alison 1998, 13–14)—indeed to take the form of a "divi-nized" desire, through an ascetic imitation of the "holy."

As literary scholar, Girard has shown how the novel interpretation of classic texts can reveal the profound wisdom buried in treasured myths and reconfigure them as important narratives to illumine us today. Likewise, in the following pages, a brief and thematic hermeneutic of the Fourth Gospel will offer a Christian theo-anthropology that speaks to our times. If, as Girard notes, a key universal significance of the Christian Gospels as *muthos* is to narrate how Christ as human-and-divine *pharmakos* reveals the violent dynamic of hominization in order to save humanity from its trappings, this reconfigured narrative of human flourishing will show how a kenotic ethic that is surprisingly transcendent can be gleaned through Christ's ordering of his desire in his absolute self-offering to the Father. The *pharmakos* teaches through apocalypse-revelation but also reveals through his final teachings to the Twelve—the Gospel of John's famous last supper discourses (chapters 13 to 17)—how the "glory" of Love, the *Parakletos* or empowering Holy Spirit, is the supernatural gift flowing from the Father through the *pharmakos'* act of self-offering. Moreover, the gift of "glory" or *caritas* is for humanity's flourishing to "oneness" as a communion of friendship in imitation of the Trinitarian dynamism of mutual self-emptying. Thus, the Fourth Gospel presents its kenotic ethos as a theology of friendship that is a corrective to the contemporary digital ethos of "Friending," just as its ideal of personhood in imitation of Christ contrasts with the techno-tribalism of the age.

> I ask not only on behalf of these, but also on behalf of those who will believe in me through their word, that they may all be one. As you, Father, are in me and I am in you, may they also be in us, so that the world may believe that you have sent me. The glory that you have given me I have given them, so that they may be one, as we are one, I in them and you in me, that they may become completely one, so that the world may know that you have sent me and have loved them even as you have loved me. (Jn 17:20–23)

HUMAN FLOURISHING AS IMITATION OF THE DIVINE

The imitation of a Model, who is outside of the human trappings of violence, yet close enough to be one of us, offers the freedom to revert the collective foundation of hominization to the hope of a new human community bound in friendship. Christianity, as the religion of the radical Other who exposes once and for all the scapegoat mechanism as original sin (Girard 2001, 103–193), offers Christ, human and divine, for the human *mimesis* to holiness. As Irenaeus, bishop of Lyon, taught the Christian churches as early as the second century, "God became flesh that humanity may become divine."

In Girard's scriptural hermeneutics, this mentoring is revealed to be the hope of non-violent personhood, the freedom from mimetic violence. Girard and the Christian tradition note that Jesus is the new Adam because he is the Scapegoat, the Lamb of God, who chooses to be victimized in order to expose the face of mimetic rivalry and end all violence and death. Even more compellingly, Christ is the new human not only through destroying death through offering new "life" as "children of God" (Jn 1:12). This life is both the orientation of desire to the Father, who in being *archē*, the fullness of Being, is the ground in whom humanity finds its being, but also the conversion to a radically pacific *mimesis*—a *mimesis* that has the power to transform the "teacher" and "disciple" into "friends":

> This is my commandment, that you love one another as I have loved you. No one has greater love than this, to lay down one's life for one's friends. You are my friends if you do what I command you. I do not call you servants any longer, because the servant does not know what the master is doing; but I have called you friends, because I have made known to you everything that I have heard from my Father (Jn 15:12–15).

These verses pack a new anthropology of the divinized human being, of men and women freed of mimetic rivalry. They present "a commandment"—and hence, a freely chosen action decided in perfect awareness, understanding and judgment—that fully respects the integrity of the person as a responsible agent. Yet the foundation of the action remains *mimesis* itself. Girard notes that, "Without mimetic desire there would be neither freedom nor humanity. Mimetic desire is intrinsically good" (Girard 2001, 15) and its goodness is manifested in our imitation for *theosis*, the imitation of God's perfect love revealed in the Christ. Thus, human mimetic desire reaches its fulfilment in imitating the Christ as new human, in becoming his disciples. The Johannine tradition, like the Synoptics or the Epistles of Paul, emphasizes the vocation of the disciple, of the one who imitates the Teacher, over and above that of the "apostle", of the one who is sent by the Lord. It is the "Beloved Disciple," the *mathetes* who is chosen as the model *par excellence* of the Johannine community. It is Mary, Mother of God and "servant (or imitator) of the Lord" (Lk 1:38), who is the first to be filled by the Spirit, and, accordingly, raised as "mother" for all humanity (Jn 19:26–27) and as model of the Christian life.

The imitation of Christ presented by John 15:12–15 also reveals two very distinct elements that distinguish divinized humanity. First, the *mimesis* demanded is of the love of the master who chooses to become scapegoat. It is only in loving selflessly (or kenotically) that humanity is freed of the compulsion to accentuate individuality or succumb to being mere copies of each other. It is only in love, given freely and wholly, that men and women become unique persons in relationship to embrace the human vocation of communion. One becomes a "Christian," a friend of Christ, through imitating the divine ethos of mutual self-emptying in daily life. As Karl Rahner has emphasized, the love of God can only be manifested in the love of neighbor (Rahner 1969, 231–249).

However, the Johannine community also teaches how the love of neighbor demanded by Jesus is the mutual personal offering in the particularity of friendship. It is in "being liked" and in "liking" the other (Alison 2003) that we can truly love the other with the generosity of Christ's love. Sandra M. Schneiders notes that this Johannine preferential love for one's inner circle is even more radical than the universality (but relative anonymity) of *agapē* preached by the other gospels. This is because the very self-offering of service can often be perverted, limiting and twisting that very love it is supposed to embody. Only in relationships of true equality, that is "in perfect friendship, which is indeed rare," can service be an authentic expression of generous self-offering for the love of the other (Schneiders 2003, 192–193). The greatest love emphasized by Christ is not the freedom to become victim or of offering the self indiscriminately or impersonally, but rather to love selflessly and preferentially: to love one's friends. Friends know the other and recognize the other's gifts, without seeking to possess the other or to become the other. Friendship in imitation of Christ's love celebrates the mutual relationship of becoming, a relationship of reciprocal delight.

THE HOLY SPIRIT

For human beings caught up in the sinfulness of mimetic rivalry, it is not enough to be simply exposed to Christ as the radically new Model of human becoming. We also need a special divine power to receive Christ's teaching, to be slowly transformed into his image. Thus, while the Christ event culminates on the cross and in the resurrection, its fruits begin to be accomplished through the descent of the Holy Spirit. Though Christ as Mentor is the Absolute Image of the Father whose Being we desire, we can only recognize the Christ, choose to imitate his love, and be transformed in his image in the power of the Holy Spirit. The Son and the Spirit are the two hands of God who invite humanity to our recreation as glorification and together they educate us to an *imitatio Dei*; they invite us to participate in the life of the Trinity of self-emptying love, by becoming a human community in imitation of God's own *koinonia*.

Through "Easter eyes" enlightened by the Paraclete, the cross is precisely a revelation of this absolute self-offering love. Jesus chooses to be victim, and in being victim he empties himself in his love for his disciples and for the world. The Scapegoat not only annihilates violence by taking it upon himself. In his last breath, he redeems it by accepting the abandonment of the Father and by giving up his Spirit (Jn 19:30), thus revealing to humanity the kenotic love that is the very life, the very essence of the Triune God. In the immanent Trinity, this life is the mutual self-emptying love of the Father and Son, and the triumph of their *kenosis* in the self-emptying of the Holy Spirit, who in being the hypostasis of Love, Love Himself, empties his personality to become—to quote Sergius Bulgakov—the "copula between the subject and the predicate," "the 'and' of the Father AND the Son" (Bulgakov 2004, 64). The Holy Spirit is thus revealed as the beauty, the triumph, the glory of Triune love. He is the Joy that fulfills divine *kenosis*.

In the economy, this joy and triumph of love (in the Spirit) is the event of Pentecost. In Pentecost, the fragmentation of Babel is obliterated, as all languages become a common mediation to create community. Community is born when the "object" of our triangular desire, the "third" that binds mediator and imitator, becomes the Spirit himself. He becomes the "copula," the "and" that binds master and disciple, lover and beloved, the two friends, in the imitation of Christ's desire for the Father. He recreates a humanity fragmented by violence into our ultimate splendour of becoming in "the image and likeness of God." It is the "male and female" together, as multiplicity forming one community, that are created in God's image to become in divine likeness, and it is in the complementarity of friendship, in the becoming one human family, that God becomes perfectly revealed in human nature.

The Spirit does not force himself upon us. Just like the "object" of the "other," He must be truly desired by the imitator. Hence, He must be witnessed as joy and beauty in the life of the mediator. The mediators of the Spirit in the world are the "saints": the holy ones who in their life of self-offering love are perfecting their imitation of Christ to become the "christs," the anointed ones of God and mentors for our human becoming in space and time. They are the community of saints, the holy *ecclesia*, for as Irenaeus teaches: "Where the Holy Spirit is, there is the Church," the fellowship in the Spirit of the friends of Christ who reveal him to the world by being his disciples and apostles for the world. As the famous story of St. Seraphim of Sarov and his disciple Motovilov teaches, the mark of their interdividuality being transformed to holiness, and of their personal becoming as friends being reborn in the "light" of the Spirit, is simultaneously their becoming reflections of Christ, the "light of the world" (Mt 5:14; Jn 8:12; 9:5). St. Seraphim witnesses:

> "We are both now, my dear fellow, in the Holy Spirit." It was as if Motovilov's eyes had been opened, for he saw that the face of the elder was brighter than the sun. In his heart Motovilov felt joy and peace, in his body a warmth as if it were summer, and a fragrance began to spread around them. Motovilov was terrified by the unusual change, but especially by the fact that the face of the Teacher shone like the sun.
>
> But St. Seraphim said to him, "Do not fear, dear fellow. You would not even be able to see me if you yourself were not in the fullness of the Holy Spirit. Thank the Lord for His mercy toward us." Thus Motovilov understood, in mind and heart, what the descent of the Holy Spirit and his transfiguration of a person meant. (Mileant 2001)

WITNESS

If friendship in the Spirit radically reconfigures our mimetic rivalry to the imitation of God's holiness, it follows that the commandment to be friends is fundamentally a new way of being human that is extended to all people in order to transform all relationships irrespective of color, creed, or culture. As a universal invitation to human divinization, to mutual "abiding" in the Spirit in imitation of God's triune *perichoresis*, particular friendship is also a school of human becoming that transforms all patterns of desire and human relationality.

In this journey to human finality, it also follows that the specific role of the Christian and the *ecclesia* in the digital age is to be ambassadors of a new human becoming, through being witnesses of the Good News of friendship. In this role, the baptized have the responsibility of living friendship on at least four distinct levels. The fundamental level is that of friendship in and with the Lord, and consequently, of the intimate local community. Christian families come together to break the bread, contemplate the Christian narratives and share brotherly and sisterly love. In this exchange that is so intimate that men, women, and children can truly pray together and become an abiding community in the Spirit, there is a mutual understanding of the significance of intimate friendship and the friends unite to be nourished, in order to have the strength to spread a spirit of collaboration in all the other circles of interaction in their daily life.

Thus, another crucial expression of friendship for the Christian is that within the local neighborhood with the religious or secular other. This mode of friendship is essential to witness the gospel and a Christian lifestyle—to evangelize through deeds more than words. Through attentiveness to the needs of the local neighbour and community, and the generosity to share one's gifts unconditionally, neighbors (who are friends) allow for the development of mutual concern and understanding, as well as a grounding in the flesh that renews a shared respect for the immediate local ecology of the community.

The new technologies of the digital age, however, allow for—and even demand—expressions of friendship that transcend distinct localities and embrace the entire globe. This creates the opportunity for new concrete experiences of friendship among the churches, as well as among different peoples, political groups, and nations. As far as the church is concerned, today's Christian communities can truly experience the beauty and value of the universal church through active communication, collaboration, and gift exchange (O'Gara 1998) among local churches, even those of different denominations. New technologies allow for regular interaction among the churches and encourage more frequent gatherings of church leaders and communities. The robust formation of each member of the Christian community, as well as the collegiality among bishops and leaders, allows for an ecclesial culture of collaboration and solidarity for the good of the universal church. In such a "catholic" church characterized by friendship and communal discernment, the ministry of the Pontiff as teacher and interpreter of the faith can be particularly enriching, if the ancient model of the Roman church being first among equals is retrieved. This indeed seems to be the stance of Pope Francis who, from the moment of his election has preferred to style himself as the Bishop of Rome.

If the universal church succeeds in being a model of friendship and collaboration among different peoples, traditions, and histories in the digital age, then it will also be a more credible model for global political and economic cooperation and solidarity among governments and nations. Indeed, as friendship depends on the dignity of all persons, it can be understood as a global ethic of personhood, a personhood born of mutual self-offering in relationship that would be the foundation for a more equitable and just sharing of the Earth's resources and responsibilities. The awareness and sensitivity that grows with personal flourishing in friendship allows for a deepening of personal freedom and responsibility that plays out not merely with one's fellow human neighbor but also with other creatures and the entire ecosystem. It is only through developing a sense of self, of one's profound and unique role in the universe, that one becomes truly attuned to the dynamics of the environment, including the footprint and influence one leaves on the Earth.

CONCLUSION

In his final discourses, Jesus promised to send the Paraclete from the Father, to reveal to us our human becoming not as individuals, not as a herd, but in the harmony that celebrates the human freedom of personhood by being oriented towards the other in perfect love: the joy of friendship. The Paraclete comforts us by calling us to become like Christ, to share in his divinity. As the ideal of the Christ-like life to which we are all called to participate, friendship bound in the power of the Spirit is an invitation for the conversion of all human relationships. It is the way to holiness that frees us from fear, from violence, even from the double oppression of individualism and herding. It is our authentic human becoming, especially in our age of anxiety, where our vocation is to become a global community, mutually mediating the gifts of our local cultures, customs and stories. In an age of terror and confusion, where our very selves reach out to embrace the entire globe, hope lies in every "heart of flesh" (Ez 36:26) empowered by the Spirit that loves in friendship—as Christ has loved us first.

REFERENCES

Agarwal, Amit. May 30, 2009. "Web 3.0 Concepts Explained in Plain English." Digital Inspiration: Tech à la carte. http://www.labnol.org/internet/web-3–concepts-explained/8908/.

Alison, James. 1998. *The Joy of Being Wrong: Original Sin Through Easter Eyes*. New York: Crossroad.

Alison, James. 2003. *On Being Liked*. New York: Crossroad.

Anspach, Mark R. 2004. "Editor's Introduction: Imitating Oedipus." In *Oedipus Unbound: Selected Writings on Rivalry and Desire*, by René Girard, edited by Mark R. Anspach, vii-liv. Stanford: Stanford University Press.

Baudrillard, Jean. 1988. *The Ecstasy of Communication*. Translated by Bernard and Caroline Schutze. New York: Semiotext(e).

Bulgakov, Sergius. 2004. *The Comforter*. Translated by Boris Jakim. Grand Rapids, MI: Eerdmans.

Chomsky, Noam. 2002. *Media Control: the Spectacular Achievements of Propaganda*, 2nd ed. New York: Seven Stories Press.

Federman, Mark. February 10, 2003. "McLuhan Thinking: Integral Awareness in the Connected Society." McLuhan Program in Culture and Technology. http://individual.utoronto.ca/markfederman/IntegralAwarenessintheConnectedSociety.pdf

Girard, René. 1966. *Deceit, Desire and the Novel*. Translated by Yvonne Freccero. Baltimore, MD: Johns Hopkins University Press.

———. 1977. *Violence and the Sacred*. Translated by Patrick Gregory. Baltimore, MD: Johns Hopkins University Press.

———. 1978. *To double business bound: Essays on Literature, Mimesis, and Anthropology*. Baltimore, MD: Johns Hopkins University Press.

———. 1986. *The Scapegoat*. Baltimore, MD: The Johns Hopkins University Press.

———. 1987. *Things Hidden Since the Foundation of the World*. With J.-M. Oughourlian and G. Lefort. Translated by Stephen Bann and Michael Metteer. Stanford, CA: Stanford University Press.

———. 1991. *A Theater of Envy: William Shakespeare*. New York: Oxford University Press.

———. 1996. *The Girard Reader*. Edited by James G. Williams. New York: Crossroad.

———. 2001. *I See Satan Fall Like Lightning*. Translated by James G. Williams. Maryknoll, NY: Orbis.

———. 2004. *Oedipus Unbound: Selected Writings on Rivalry and Desire*. Edited by Mark R. Anspach. Stanford, CA: Stanford University Press.

Havelock, Eric A. 1963. *Preface to Plato*. Cambridge, MA: Harvard University Press.

———. 1986. *The Muse Learns to Write: Reflections on Orality and Literacy from Antiquity to the Present*. New Haven: Yale University Press.

Huntington, Samuel P. 1996. *The Clash of Civilizations and the Remaking of World Order*. New York, Simon & Schuster.

Innis, Harold A. 1951. *The Bias of Communication*. Toronto: University of Toronto Press.

———. 2007. *Empire and Communications*. Toronto: Dundurn Press.

Klein, Naomi. 2000. *No Logo: Taking Aim at the Brand Bullies*. Toronto, Vintage.

Lonergan, Bernard. 1992. *Insight: A Study of Human Understanding*. Toronto: University of Toronto Press.

———. 1996. *Method in Theology*. Toronto: University of Toronto Press.

McLuhan, Marshall. 1962. *The Gutenberg Galaxy*. University of Toronto Press.

———. 2003. *Understanding Media: The Extensions of Man*. critical ed. Edited by W. Terrence Gordon. Corte Madera, CA: Gingko Press.

McLuhan, Marshall, and Quentin Fiore. 1967. *The Medium is the Massage: An Inventory of Effects*. Toronto: Bantam Books.

McLuhan, Marshall and Eric McLuhan. 1988. *Laws of Media: The New Science*. Toronto: University of Toronto Press.

Mileant, Alexander. 2001. *Life of St. Seraphim of Sarov*. Translated by Nicholas Semyanko and Natalia Semyanko. http://www.fatheralexander.org/booklets/english/seraphim_e.htm.

O'Gara, Margaret. 1998. *The Ecumenical Gift Exchange*. Liturgical Press.

Ong, Walter J. 1988. *Orality and Literacy: The Technologizing of the Word*. London: Routledge.

O'Reilly, Tim. September 30, 2005. "What is Web 2.0: Design patterns and business models
for the next generation of software," O'Reilly. http://www.oreillynet.com/pub/a/oreilly/tim/
news/2005/09/30/what-is-web-20.html.

Rahner, Karl. 1969. "Reflections on the Unity of the Love of Neighbour and the Love of God."
Theological Investigations Vol. 6, 231–249. London: Darton, Longman & Todd.

Redekop, Vern Neufeld. 2002. "Mimetic Structures of Violence and of Blessing: Creating a
Discursive Framework for Reconciliation." *Theoforum*, 33(3): 311–335.

Schneiders, Sandra. 2003. *Written that You May Believe: Encountering Jesus in the Fourth
Gospel*. New York: Crossroad.

Shadbolt, Nigel, Tim Berners-Lee and Wendy Hall. 2006. "The Semantic Web Revisited."
IEEE Intelligent Systems, 21(3): 96–101.

Shannon, Claude E. and Warren Weaver. 1949. *The Mathematical Theory of Communication*.
University of Illinois Press.

Stibel, Jeff. 2013. *Breakpoint: Why the Web will Implode, Search will be Obsolete, and Everything Else you Need to Know about Technology is in Your Brain*. Palgrave Macmillan.

NOTES

1. Hosted by Jian Ghomeshi, *The End* aired on Saturdays May 6, 13 and 20 (at 12:00pm
ET and 9:30pm ET/PT) and on Sundays May 7, 14 and 21 at 5:00 pm ET, 2006. More
information about the three-part documentary series is available at http://films.com/id/15140/
The_End_Media_at_the_Tipping_Point.htm

2. Obsolescence—the second effect or "law" of media together with the other laws of
enhancement, reversal and retrieval—is different from obsoleteness. While with obsoleteness
the medium virtually disappears, through obsolescence its presence can remain prevalent but its
function as formator of culture is in demise.

3. "Media ecology," which studies how human artifacts or "media" create culture through
changing patterns of perception, understanding and behaviour, includes the Toronto School of
Communications as one of its pillars. McLuhan is the primary exponent of the Toronto School,
but other seminal media ecologists associated with the University of Toronto include classicist
Eric A. Havelock, economist Harold A. Innis, and McLuhan's close collaborators and students.

4. As an Aristotelian and a Thomist, McLuhan believed that knowledge and wisdom depend on the *sensus communis*, that is, the balance among the senses, which in turn, takes its
distinct form in a culture through the effects of its dominant media on the sensorium. Thus,
McLuhan noted that in the age of literacy, the primary effect of the alphabet accentuated by
typography was to emphasize the sense of sight over and above the other senses creating a
visual bias. On the other hand, in the age of orality, it was the sense of hearing that was
dominant. The electric age retrieves orality and all other senses. Most dominant is the sense of
touch paradoxically disconnected from the flesh.

5. What McLuhan dubs the Narcissus effect or narcosis follows his Thomistic epistemology of critical realism. In the electric age, the senses are over-stimulated so we find it harder to
pay attention and perceive accurately. Moreover, as the senses have previously been biased
through the effects of literacy, we continue to attempt to make sense of the new with the "eyes"
of the old. This is the rear-view mirror effect.

6. McLuhan's critical realism is also evident in his famous metaphor that media are "extensions of man" (sub-title of *Understanding Media*). Our senses get acclimatized to sounds,
sights, tastes, smells, and feelings, to the extent that the media that cause the sensations become
part of who we are. A writer is nothing without his pen—laptop or tablet—just as a violinist is
nothing without her instrument.

7. McLuhan notes that in our digital times, the root of our bias of perception is the Shannon-Weaver model of communication. First formulated by mathematician Claude E. Shannon,
father of information theory, the idea was popularized by Warren Weaver in their co-authored
book containing the original scientific article and its explanation for the non-specialist. The

Shannon-Weaver model relies on such notions as "information source," "message," "receiver," "code," "decode," and "noise" to postulate that communication is the linear transmission of a message from a sender to a receiver, where context is merely "noise." The model is so widely known that today, we take its veracity for granted.

8. Thus McLuhan's famous dictum "the medium is the message" becomes "the medium is the massage" in the famous book of the same title created by McLuhan with Quentin Fiore.

9. Girard's insight that through mimetic rivalry "clones" are narcotized because they do not realize they are the images of one another can also be interpreted through McLuhan's language: the model becomes the "extension" of the imitator. Yet, like all extensions, it remains unrecognized as part of the self.

10. Influenced by his colleague anthropologist Edmund Carpenter, McLuhan used the term "tribalism" to describe the mode of relationality under electric conditions that retrieves village-like dynamics.

11. Havelock was the first to note that the effect of the alphabet was to accentuate individuality. In an oral culture, the singer or utterer necessarily assumes the presence of the audience, and thus a communal, tribal or "village-like" sensitivity, over and above the sense of self. Writing, however, encourages individual thoughts, just as, after the advent of typography, silent reading enhances individualism, even if all books and readers are copies of each other. The definitive work on orality and literacy remains Walter Ong's, where the author ponders the psychology of the communal oral mind in contrast to the individual literate mind.

12. By "tactility" I mean, first and foremost, the urge to reach out and to grasp the other. This is in sharp contrast to the dominant action that accompanies reading, that is, keeping a distance from the artifact. McLuhan notes that it is only the sense of sight that requires distance from the object. The other senses are more involving, in particular, touch, which obliterates the very dichotomy of subject and object.

13. This is the ethos of typography, since its power is precisely to break down to individual parts (letters), while making many exact copies of the whole. This ethos is replicated in the Industrial Revolution through the advent of machinery and in the birth of nation states, where individual citizens are contractually bound to contribute to the whole.

14. Since Girard has studied mostly modern authors, his mimetic theory usually traces the rise and then collapse of individualism to the dreaded clone. However, his work on Greek mythology and his exegesis of biblical passages enable us to trace the dynamic of tribal cultures that creates rigid hierarchies to protect against excessive similarity. While individualism and tribalism can be seen as two modes of human sociality, the former becomes a cultural mark only with the onset of typography as a more impersonal and, therefore, efficient way of controlling violence. Yet the dynamics of differentiating and cloning are in fact present in the primordial desire of every human to be a self-in-relationship.

15. As Girard pinpoints a number of times, this psychological mechanism is more prevalent in a modernist culture that mistakenly believes in the self-creation of the individual. In tribal cultures, every member would have gladly endorsed the identity of the group, precisely because there existed no identity outside of the one shared through enculturating *mimesis*.

16. Mediation happens in two kinds of relational dynamics: "external mediation," where the difference between model and imitator, master and disciple, parent and child is vast enough that the imitator can desire to become like the model, without threatening the superiority of (and thus difference from) the former, and "internal mediation", where imitator and imitated are on an equal footing and subsume their inevitable mutual *mimesis*—and eventually total similarity—to the unconscious, allowing resentment and fear to erupt to violence.

17. Girard's most powerful examples of acquisitive *mimesis* are related to sexuality. See in particular *Violence and the Sacred*, 219–222 and the essays "Masochism and Sadism" in *Deceit, Desire and the Novel*, 176–192; and "*Mimesis* and Sexuality" in *Things Hidden Since the Foundation of the World*, 326–351.

18. The same tendency to violence is also evident in the way acquisitive *mimesis* has, today, taken global proportions and become a desirable lifestyle. Capitalism and consumerism have ravaged the Earth and, directly or indirectly, threaten all its life forms.

19. Theologically, the Greek term *kenosis* derives from Philippians 2:7 where the verb form is used in relation to Jesus who is held up as mimetic model to those tempted to get carried

away by mimetic rivalries. In this case, Jesus was entitled to divine privilege but emptied himself of such entitlement by taking on the "form" of a servant or slave.

20. Even though the primary effect of electricity as medium is to connect, as digital media reveal, this tactility is (paradoxically) divorced from the flesh. We reach out to the other, but mostly in a virtual rather than physical environment. These dual effects also have a profound effect on how we see ourselves as humans and, therefore, on the way we relate to one another. However, in this paper I am limiting myself to the effect of tribalism. If the laws of media are applied to electricity as medium, acceleration, and reversal are marked by a virtual *oikos* and disembodied humanity respectively, while what is retrieved is a tribal mode of interacting. Individualism as mark of literacy, of course, is obsolesced.

Chapter Six

Clashing Minorities, Converging Majorities

Toward a Coming Religious Peace

Jon Pahl

For scholars of religion and violence, the recent past poses a conundrum. Are civilizations clashing—as Samuel Huntington has provocatively posed in a now famous (or infamous) article, "The Clash of Civilizations?" (1993; in the 1996 book of the same title the question mark was gone). Or are they cooperating, as Steven Pinker has recently contended in *The Better Angels of Our Nature: Why Violence Has Declined*? (2011). Pinker recognizes the apparently quixotic character of his argument on behalf of cooperation and acknowledges that the 20th Century (and first decade of the 21st) were notable in a notorious way for World Wars, genocides, and the rise of terrorism. But Pinker also marshals impressive data on behalf of his claim that, over the centuries but especially in the past fifty years, developments in political organization, literacy, scientific and technological mastery, and social and economic cooperation have significantly improved the duration and quality of life for many human beings.

And yet, where Pinker meets Huntington is on religion. Huntington, obviously, sees the global resurgence of religion, and particularly Islam, as a problem. Huntington quotes Bernard Lewis to make the point:

> We are facing a . . . movement far transcending the level of issues and policies and the governments that pursue them. This is no less than a clash of civilizations—the perhaps irrational but surely historic reaction of an ancient rival [Islam] against our Judeo-Christian heritage, our secular present, and the worldwide expansion of both. (1990, 60)

Pinker, more generally, sees religion as a problem in any of its manifestations. He writes, dismissing in one breath Jews and Christians: "The Bible is
one long celebration of violence" (2011, 6). Islam fares no better. "The
Muslim world, to all appearances," Pinker contends, "is sitting out the decline of violence" (*ibid.*, 362).

In what follows, I will side with Pinker's argument that violence has
declined on the global scale, against Huntington's clash hypothesis. But I
will also argue against Pinker and Huntington to contend that religion, far
from being only a source of conflict and violence, in fact provides the most
durable and secure foundation for lasting peace between peoples.[1] The global
resurgence of religion is, perhaps, the most significant social trend of late
modernity; that this resurgence of religion coincides with Pinker's data that
documents a dramatic decline in violence may not be a mere coincidence.
Because he draws on an ignorance of lived religion typical of cultured de-
spisers of faith, such as Richard Dawkins (2008) or Sam Harris (2006), and
because he thereby depends on stereotypes rather than empirical data when it
comes to the roles religious actors play in cultural systems, Pinker fails to
recognize what peacemakers, like Mohandis Gandhi (Brown and Parel 2011;
Iyer 191), Rosa Parks (1996), Thich Nhat Hanh (Hahn 1992; O'Brien and
O'Brien 2009), Badshah Khan (Easwaran 1985), Rabbi Jonathan Sacks
(2003), Fethullah Gülen (2006), and Leymah Gbowee (2011), share in common: a deep and critical grounding in a spiritual tradition.

To develop my argument, I will make three points. First, I will sketch
how Huntington's famous "clash of civilizations" hypothesis does point to an
empirical truth, but not exactly the one he imagined. A clash does exist
between contending religious minorities within (and across) traditions. But at
the core of their practices, in their teachings, in institutional arrangements,
and increasingly in everyday life, the vast majority of religiously motivated
actors on the global stage are not clashing but converging. This is not to say
that religions are, or will ever be, all in agreement in some happy utopia. It is
to suggest that the growing awareness of the details of religious diversity
(really only available to average believers in any depth in the past several
decades), mixed with the proximity created by globalization and technology,
is promoting tolerance and respect for what Rabbi Jonathan Sacks has called
the "dignity of difference" (2003).

Secondly, then, I'll show how Pinker's "better angels of our nature" that
reduce violence quite clearly must, and do, include religions. I will briefly
introduce what I call "the peace-building garden" as a way to clarify what I
mean when I say that religions increasingly are promoting a more just, peaceful world. Based on an emerging science of conflict resolution, we can identify some clear marks of how and when religions contribute to cultivating
peace.[2] And to be sure: peace takes cultivation—hence the image of a garden. Just as a garden takes careful planning, hard work, and imagination—so

does cultivating peace. Yet, such efforts are not in vain; religious peace making is empirically evident, and can be empirically tested, although peace always remains, as anyone who has tried to lead a congregation or community torn by violence knows, fragile and contingent.

Finally, for my third point, I will exemplify how the cultivation of peace engages religious actors and resources through two historical cases. The first case, treated briefly, is an account of the recent Nobel Peace Laureate from Liberia, Leymah Gbowee. The second case, treated in more detail, is the *Hizmet* (service) movement associated with M. Fethullah Gülen. In each case, we see how religions can cultivate habits of mind, heart, and body in people to promote peace. That such a prospect is fragile should, once again, go without saying. But when we recognize our mutual fragility, ironically, we find collective power beyond force (Arendt 1970), because we know we need to cooperate. And when we cooperate, when we work together to accomplish some necessary goal, we learn to trust (Marty 2010). In that simple process is found the evolutionary, historical, and (ultimately) the religious ground in which peace grows: a coming religious peace.[3]

CLASHING MINORITIES

Huntington's hypothesis holds true for a minority. There are groups across spiritual traditions that continue to cling to reactive or parochial forms of performative violence, or what has been called "terrorism." I am persuaded by the arguments of Robert Pape (2006; 2010) that these acts (notably suicide bombings) are largely reactions to occupation, and that (following Mark Juergensmeyer 2003) they are acts of performative violence designed to maximize symbolic impact in situations of political asymmetry.[4] And—as should be obvious (but isn't)—the number of people who participate in, and even who are impacted by, such attacks is on the global scale minute. Pinker puts it well: "In every year but 1995 and 2001, more Americans were killed by lightning, deer, peanut allergies, bee stings, and 'ignition or melting of nightwear' than by terrorist attacks" (2006, 345). Terrorists, simply put, are minorities across religious traditions. Even Pinker admits as much. In a backhanded compliment, he allows that "the overwhelming majority of observant Jews and Christians [and Muslims, I must add] are, needless to say, thoroughly decent people who do not sanction genocide" (*ibid.*, 11). As an observant Christian, I also must admit to being under-whelmed by being welcomed into this moral elite of non-genocide sanctioners.

More damaging to Pinker's thesis, confirming of Huntington's, and troubling (in many senses) on the global scene are those religious minorities devoted to what I call, in my book *Empire of Sacrifice*, American "innocent domination" (2011). These devotees of what used to be called "manifest destiny" imagine a God-given mission for America that absolves the nation, in a spasm of innocent exceptionalism, of any moral responsibility for any atrocities. These are the believers who might sanction atrocities, from the scapegoating of gay and lesbian youth in DOMA laws, to the justification of torture under the euphemism of "enhanced interrogation," to the justification of war on Iraq for the mere suspicion of a weapon of mass destruction, when the U.S. holds an entire arsenal of them.[5] Often, devotees of innocent domination resort to discourses of "sacrifice." For example, Presidents George W. Bush and Barack Obama have repeatedly invoked "sacrifice" to explain and justify sending youth to die in Afghanistan and Iraq (Denton-Borhaug 2011). Such language, of course, has become almost conventional in warfare, but we must not thereby miss its significance. Calling a death from policy in warfare a "sacrifice" associates a religious practice with killing and dying, and therefore cloaks violence in a religious aura. This invokes Girard's profound analysis of the realtionship between religion and sacrifice (1977). The state symbolically hijacks the power of transcendence, traditionally identified with religion in the service of warfare or some other social policy.

These examples of how religion can be mobilized on behalf of violence—in suicide bombing and in state policies—are troubling, and yet they represent perversions of the ethics at the core of the world's deep traditions, and they are always justified as exceptional enactments that violate what ought to be the normal course of things. Or as I put it in *Empire of Sacrifice*: religions exist to end violence, insofar as possible.[6] It is because this is true that we see religious violence as a particularly egregious form of hypocrisy. Religions use symbolic means to resolve conflicts and seek power through cultural means ("how many divisions has the Pope?" as Stalin famously asked). Religions substitute language, rituals, communal solidarity, and institutional mobilization for the "war of all against all" that threatens any social order. And religious teachings, while undoubtedly at points reflective of archaic cultural patterns dedicated to "might makes right," ultimately propose (through their very structures) a "higher ethic" or third way beyond fight or flight that engages people on behalf of civilization and the common good (see especially Wink 2003; for more on this see chapters 7 and 8).

It is, then, true that there is a clash of civilizations underway but not exactly the one that Samuel Huntington imagined. The clash is not, as Huntington supposed, the "West" against "the rest." Instead, the clash is *within* the West *and* the rest—between those minorities of religious believers who compromise with force against those majorities committed to the principles and practices of their traditions that promote peace.[7] The clash, to reiterate, is *not* the West against "the rest." Instead, the clash is *within* the West and *within* the rest—between those minorities of people of faith who have sanctioned atrocities versus those majorities committed to the patient work of diplomacy that stems from the deep trust fostered by commitments to transcendent values. The clash, one last time, is not the West against "the rest," but is *within* the West and the rest between those minorities of believers who are committed to blessed brutalities of utopian sacrifice against those majorities who are spiritually grounded in a community and in the contingencies of history, so as to recognize our mutual fragility and the need to cooperate. In this clash, representatives of historic religious traditions are, as even Steven Pinker candidly admits, in the "overwhelming majority" on the side of the peaceful, the diplomatic, and the grounded. Those committed to violence are increasingly in the minority and on the defensive across historic traditions, with the possible exception of those blinded by US military and economic might, devotees of what might be called the American "civil religion" (for the classic formulation see Bellah 1967; see also Kao and Coulsky 2007).

THE PEACE-BUILDING GARDEN

If I am going to persuade you to see a coming religious peace on the horizon, I will first have to show that I have some idea of what "peace" looks like. To do so, it will be helpful to draw a contrast, namely, with violence. Violence is simply harm to or destruction of life. But this simple definition hides extraordinary complexity. For violence operates on many levels, in many ways. In my teaching, I often visualize how violence works in terms of an iceberg, with four levels.[8] At the top of the iceberg—visible to the eye—is what everyone recognizes as violence—intentional physical force: for example, rape, murder, street crime, and vandalism. Here, harm to or destruction of life is overt and obvious. But underneath this layer of activity, under the surface of the water, is another layer—what we might call legitimized violence. Police, prisons, the legal system, and just wars all intentionally produce harm to or destruction of life, but in the interest of some greater cause or through a process of legal justification that renders the violence necessary, if not "good." But harm to or destruction of life operates beyond even these two forms of illegitimate and legitimate physical force. What we might call a third level of "social violence" also exists.[9] Inequitable or unjust policies connected to education, housing, and healthcare (for just a few examples), kill people just as surely as a gunshot, only more slowly and with greater suffering over time. Yet, the consequences of these policies are not always recognized as violence, primarily because it is difficult to assign moral responsibility for systems as opposed to individual actions. But that policies can be violent is obvious to anyone who has ever had to live under economic and political systems that are unjust: Communism in Eastern Europe, Apartheid in South Africa, Jim Crow America.

Finally, at the base of the violence iceberg—deep under the surface of the water—is what I call "cultural violence." Simply put: words can kill. Systems of domination, revenge, and aggression—including wars—are crystallized in discrete formulations of discourse that do profound harm, often while appearing innocent and even noble. Racist or sexist stereotypes, myths of ethnocentric superiority, rituals that stoke hatred of an enemy are examples of cultural formations that produce harm to or destruction of life. At the base of the violence iceberg, in sum, are the manifold ways that human beings *articulate* (whether in word, image, symbol, or other cultural product) the terms that make harm to or destruction of life plausible—against the world, another, or one's self. Any act of aggression, especially if it is collectively enacted, must involve some signs or symbols that motivate or at least initiate the action. And most troublingly, these signs and symbols can often be used to hide or to obscure the violence, to cloak something heinous and vicious in something "good," "true," or even "beautiful." To locate the origin of violence, in this way, is to include within the scope of its study such phenomena as myth and ritual, religious doctrines and practices, but also other aspects of culture—art, literature, music, and manifold forms of communication. Anything human, in short, can be (and probably has been) used to produce harm to or destruction of life. Ultimately, the most troubling sources of violence are those linguistic-cultural systems of discourse, practices, communities, and institutions we call "religions." Religions have been among the most effective ways humans have persuaded themselves, in the name of lofty and even "sacred" ideals, to harm one another.

If the "violence iceberg" can help us to recognize the vast scope of the problem peacemakers must contend with, the "peace-building garden" is intended to identify practically and (for empirical verification and falsification) some ways that have been found historically to promote more just, peaceful, societies. "Peace" can for now simply be described as the capacity of people to live in security, with access to resources, to meet basic needs and with the potential to flourish.[10] As with our definition of violence, of course, this simplicity hides complex relationships. Peace, when real and not just an ideal, engages all of the domains of human society and the natural world. If violence operates across different levels (physical, social, and cultural), so too does peace. For the purposes of comparison, we shall isolate three levels of peace, comparable to the dynamics in the violence iceberg: "basic peace," "policy peace," and "deep peace."

Basic peace, which is often taken to be fundamental in peace studies, I locate at the "top" of the garden. We can think of it as the fruit of the labor done at deeper levels of cultivation: basic peace is the plant that grows or the fruit that is produced through cultivation (e.g., pruning, harvesting, etc.). Basic peace, more prosaically, is the condition where people are not threatened by any extrinsic threat to their existence or capacity to flourish and where people have a voice in the decisions that affect their lives. Ordinarily, this basic peace depends upon the existence of a government (e.g., democracy, republic, monarchy), what Pinker calls (drawing on Thomas Hobbes) "Leviathan."[11] Such a collective ensures the security of people by establishing something like the rule of law, by providing for the common relief in face of natural or other disasters, by placing limits (if not establishing a monopoly) on the exercise of force, and by perpetuating itself according to some recognized legitimating structures. Basic peace, secured by "Leviathan," is most succinctly the absence of war, and the functioning of some system of collective power to provide for basic human needs and to promote human flourishing. "Basic peace" in the peace-building garden corresponds, then, to the top two layers of the violence iceberg; basic peace is the relative absence of, or successful responses to, illegitimate physical aggression. Tangentially, then, we can see how force among peaceful people is always a last resort in a *response* to primary aggression, an attempt to protect the innocent. And we can see how any disruption in basic peace, within this way of understanding matters, must be enacted by legitimate entities, with carefully controlled checks and balances, to *limit* the employment of violence and to produce or restore the conditions where basic human needs are met and where people have potential to flourish.

As these latter comments suggest, "basic peace" blurs into (or depends upon) "policy peace"(which we can think of as the quality of the soil in which peace grows, or fails). Peaceful societies do not only require the existence of systems to restrain violence and give people a voice in the decisions that affect their lives; peaceful societies also require the cultivation of *policies*: ways to implement the voice of people to prevent violence and to promote human flourishing. "Policy peace," then, has two dimensions: the absence of gross inequity and the presence of opportunity. Together, Pinker calls these dynamics "gentle commerce."[12] Policy peace is cultivated when a society allocates resources and organizes power in practices designed to promote relative equity and opportunities for fulfillment among its people. Here are included laws and procedures, not directly connected to security and force, that promote coexistence and collaboration. When a society, through its laws, equitably distributes food, water, shelter, energy, education, and healthcare, peace emerges as the expressed consent of people to live together or as the articulation of people's capacity to act in concert in support of their own needs and interests, in ways that also take into account the needs and interests of others. Crucial at this level of operation is what has come to be called environmental sustainability—or care for those basic resources that people must share in common and over which conflict often occurs. Crucial also is what Muhammad Yunus has taken to called "social business" or "social enterprise."[13] Social entrepreneurs use market economics and business practices not only to promote short-term profits but also to promote the common good by solving social problems. This level of cultivation, like the one above it, is again often taken to be the chief criterion for peace: if everyone just had "enough" there would be peace. Alternatively, economic and social policies are often seen to be the chief obstacle to peace; wars are supposed to be fought "over" this or that resource, or the way some policy prevents some from access to it. Yet, I contend that even this layer of cultivating peace is less crucial than some matters that are both slipperier to assess and yet closer to the lived experience of people in their everyday interactions and, therefore, more volatile and more fertile at one and the same time.

We return once again, then, to culture, the domain of what I call "deep peace." That is, finally, I am persuaded that peace among humans is at its deepest level constituted of cultural causes, including (of course) religions (deep peace we might think of as the "seeds" from which everything grows, *and* the interactions between seeds and soil and water and climate and cultivator, in short, the entire ecosystem of the garden). At their best, and for the billions of people around the globe who choose to participate in them, religions are the fundamental "ecosystems" that promote trust (Marty 2010). Peace exists when people engage the most powerful and distinctive of all human behaviors—symbol-making—to resolve conflict, ameliorate suffering, set terms for cooperation, and imagine new futures. Religions do all of these. They promote trust, not merely as an individual or private phenomenon, but as the fiber of lived relationships woven through quotidian social interactions, from the local to the international, through face-to-face dialogue, and through social media.

Here is where Pinker fails to recognize the potential of religions to build peace. Pinker contends that peace follows when people participate in democratic governments, when they engage in "gentle commerce," and when they participate in international cooperation. This three-fold foundation for peace is also called "the Kantian triad," since it was first proposed by Immanuel Kant's essay entitled "Perpetual Peace" (1795). Nations that are democratic, that trade together, and that participate in international cooperatives would not be inclined to go to war with each other, Kant accurately foresaw. What Pinker fails to recognize, along with many other theorists, is that *by far* the most effective international institutions are not governments but religions. Judaism, Christianity, and Islam—to mention only the three monotheisms—are truly *international movements* that engage well more than half of the people on the planet. Even more, the reason these international mass movements exist, I contend, the reason they have grown to persuade billions over millennia, outliving countless nations and empires, is because they exist to eliminate violence, insofar as possible. They cultivate deep peace.

More specifically, religions (along with other cultural sources such as art, literature, music, and even sports) cultivate peace in five broad ways, through five "seeds of peace" that I will, very briefly, summarize. The first is *literacy* but not in the narrow sense of epistemological conformity to Western scientific (or any other) knowing. Plenty of damage has been done in the name of that ideal. Rather, literacy as symbolic facility—oral as well as textual, practical as well as scientific, ethical as well as material—is what promotes peace (see Appleby 2000). Second, is what I call *practiced means*.[14] Deep peace is cultivated through repeated practices that use non-violent means. (See chapters 7 and 8.) Religions, of course, share with other cultural practices in depending upon disciplined, learned behavior that also acquaints persons with joy and that opens to them paths to fulfillment. Rituals, to put it succinctly, cultivate embodied habits of non-violence in people, engaging symbolic means in communal interactions marked (again) by trust. A third way to cultivate peace is through *empathy*, or (less elegantly) through "interdependent sociability" (see Boulding 2000; Lederach 2010). Peace is learned in social interactions. Peace is learned from observing and abhorring suffering, from identifying with the pain of another and committing to working together with others to alleviate that pain. A fourth aspect of deep peace is *grounded pluralism* (Appleby 2000; Diana Eck's Pluralism Project at Harvard). That is, the kind of robust arguments and debates necessary to forge policy peace and basic peace requires people to recognize unity-in-diversity. There may be a shared ground or horizon to cultural activity, but that activity is also premised on working together across differences. Finally, deep peace depends upon *organizing*. Nothing happens without institutional capacity, without leaders, followers, and structures to implement the ways a culture promotes human flourishing (Putnam 2010).

Seen in light of the violence iceberg and the peace-building garden, then, it becomes apparent how human religious traditions are both the greatest obstacles to peace and the greatest potential sources of peace. It is time to turn to a couple examples of the latter, a couple harbingers of a coming religious peace.

CONVERGING MAJORITIES: A COMING RELIGIOUS PEACE

Once again, to reiterate my thesis: the vast majority of spiritually grounded people and communities around the globe are converging. They are doing so by engaging in public life so as to prevent illegitimate violence and to claim a voice (democratic participation). Religious folk are also converging on ways to promote policy peace, notably through social enterprise, but also through a range of programs and policies that hold governments accountable and that mobilize people on behalf of relative equity and opportunity. Finally, religiously motivated men and women are taking the organizing capacity of their communities—the trust that religion fosters as the deepest source of peace—

and applying the international movements in which they participate to programs in literacy, practiced means, empathy, and grounded pluralism. From
among many possible cases, we shall study briefly two.

Leymah Gbowee (1972–) received the Nobel Peace Prize in 2011 for her
work in ending the fourteen-year civil war in Liberia in 2003.[15] Gbowee was
trained as a social worker, and employed at St. Peter Lutheran Church in
Monrovia, to do post-trauma counseling with former child soldiers. She studied non-violent organizing through a program of Eastern Mennonite University, and as she records in her memoirs, *Mighty Be Our Powers: How Sisterhood, Sex, and Prayer Changed a Nation at War*, how one night in 2002 she
dreamed that God told her to "gather the women and pray for peace" (2011,
122). Along with a Muslim sister, Asatu Bah Kenneth (who just happened to
be on the police force), Gbowee began organizing groups of women from
Christian congregations and Muslim mosques to gather in public places to
sing, pray, and (eventually) threaten a "sex strike," if the war did not stop.
Gbowee's message to recruit women was clear: "We are tired! We are tired
of our children being killed! We are tired of being raped! Women, wake up—
you have a voice in the peace process!" (*ibid.*, 127). As the campaign continued for weeks, the women eventually forced a meeting between the dictator
Charles Taylor and representatives of various warring tribal groups at a
"peace conference" held in Ghana, which eventually produced an agreement
for Taylor to go into exile and for a new constitution to be drafted and
eventually led to the democratic election of Ellen Johnson Sirleaf (another
2011 Nobel laureate) as the first female president of an African nation.

Now, such a compressed summary of dramatic events (vividly portrayed
in Abigail Disney's documentary, *Pray the Devil Back to Hell* (2008)), might
lead us to miss how this case demonstrates the viability of the peace-building
garden. Nevertheless it shows how if peace is to come it must come from
religions and culture. There was no security in Liberia when Gbowee began
her women's campaign; there was no Leviathan—no basic peace. Similarly,
policy peace was absent: housing, education, healthcare were non-existent—
many Liberians had fled cities for tent encampments in forests or desert.
Commerce was conducted at the barrel of a Kalashnikov. Yet a congregation—St. Peter's Lutheran Church in Monrovia—existed, and networks of
women in similar congregations and mosques across Liberia provided the
social capital—the symbolic facility, practiced means of non-violent engagement, empathy, and grounded pluralism (Muslim and Christian)—for a
movement that changed a nation. Gbowee translated the trust of her religious
convictions (God spoke to her in a dream) into a social movement that
brought greater justice and peace to Liberia. As she put it in a lecture at
Eastern Mennonite University in 2009:

I didn't get there by myself . . . or anything I did as an individual, but it was by the grace and mercy of God. . . . In the most difficult of times, [God] has been there. They have this song, "Order my steps in your ways, dear Lord," and every day as I wake up, that is my prayer, because there's no way that anyone can take this journey as a peacebuilder, as an agent of change in your community, without having a sense of faith. . . . As I continue this journey in this life, I remind myself: All that I am, all that I hope to be, is because of God. [16]

To deny the religious origins of her engagement would be to deny the source of her personal, and political, power.

If the case of Leymah Gbowee can serve as an example of how a coming religious peace appears on the local and national scale, internationally an example can be seen in the *Hizmet* (service) movement associated with M. Fethullah Gülen. (For a blog connected to the movement, go to: http://www.gulenmovement.us/blog, as accessed 7/9/12. For an overview, see 2010.)

First, then, *Hizmet* welcomes democratic participation, and joins in the demands of people around the world for basic peace. In his book, *Toward a Global Civilization of Love and Tolerance*, that directly answers to Huntington's "clash" hypothesis, Gülen offers six fundamental principles at the intersection of Islam and politics:

1. Power lies in truth, a repudiation of the common idea that truth relies upon power.
2. Justice and the rule of law are essential.
3. Freedom of belief and rights to life, personal property, reproduction, and health . . . cannot be violated.
4. The privacy and immunity of individual life must be maintained.
5. No one can be convicted of a crime without evidence, or accused and punished for someone else's crime.
6. An advisory system of administration [checks and balances] is essential. (2006, 221)

Any actual government, of course, will more or less effectively and in actuality promote these principles—as has historically been the case both in the United States and in the Republic of Turkey, to take just two examples. Individuals of *Hizmet*, however, have consistently been committed to working within the systems of government wherever they reside, while also working to transform those governments and hold them accountable to democratic, participatory principles—to basic peace (Esposito and Yilmaz 2010).

Second, *Hizmet* supports social enterprise and policy peace. Sociologists Helen Rose Ebaugh and Muhammad Çetin have independently profiled the contours of *Hizmet* as a "civil society" movement "rooted in moderate Islam" (Çetin 2010). More specifically, however, the movement engages a model of business and trade called "social enterprise," which according to Temple University Professor of Business T. L. Hill is "the *disciplined, innovative, risk-tolerant entrepreneurial process of opportunity recognition and resource assembly directed toward creating social value by changing underlying social and economic structures*" (Hill and Pahl, forthcoming). Social ventures associated with *Hizmet* mobilize the considerable resources of entrepreneurial activity and organize it on behalf of a healthier commons through engaging stake-holders (not just shareholders) in operations. What the category of a "spiritually grounded" social enterprise like *Hizmet* adds to this understanding of social entrepreneurship is the capacity to articulate the deep symbolic motives and discourses, ritual processes, communal and ethical horizons, and institutional or system-wide organizing principles that the leaders of these agencies engage (Lincoln 2006). That is, social entrepreneurship is a catalyst for fundamental social change, a process of transforming opportunities and resources into going concerns that support good jobs through *social* efforts, involving in meaningful ways a wide variety of stakeholders in the design, management and governance of ventures. Within *Hizmet*, the range of social enterprises includes media, banks, construction companies, think tanks, and, especially, schools (Ebaugh 2010).

An increasing body of scholarly literature is identifying and describing these processes across spiritually grounded social ventures, including *Hizmet*. Robert Putnam's conception of the way religious communities create "social capital" is only one notable recent foray, but perhaps the best example of the work of social enterprise within *Hizmet*, and its contribution toward peace-building, is the work of the *Hizmet* schools around the globe, which can (happily) clarify the third aspect of how *Hizmet* contributes to strengthening "the better angels of our nature" and fosters "deep peace" (Putnam and Campbell 2010; Esposito and Yilmaz 2010). I have visited schools associated with the *Hizmet* movement on every continent except South America, including in some of the poorest places on Earth, and have been impressed by the quality and quantity of the efforts to develop sustainable and participatory institutions that promote literacy in the sciences and humanities. I have often compared these efforts to the far-better known attempts by Greg Mortenson (2007), in *Three Cups of Tea,* and have tried to point out that these schools flourish despite the lack of publicity associated with a large publishing contract, on the one hand, and without the apparent administrative incompetence (at best) that has eroded Mortensen's reputation in recent years, on the other (Krakauer 2011). Other scholars, such as Harun Akyol, Greg Barton, Philipp Bruckmayer, Mehmet Kalyoncu, Martha Ann Kirk, Jonathan Lacey, and Mohamed Nawab bin Mohamed Osman (to name only a few), are analyzing in discrete case studies the contours of these social enterprises and their effectiveness in promoting more just, peaceful societies (Esposito and Yilmaz 2010; Kirk 2012). As Gülen puts it: "Now that we live in a global village, education is the best way to serve humanity and to establish a dialogue with other civilizations" (2006, 198). Literacy, the first seed of deep peace, is a core commitment of the *Hizmet* movement, and is being activated through institutional organizing in schools around the globe.

Finally, the same is true of grounded pluralism, another of the seeds of peace. The commitment of *Hizmet* members to inter-religious dialogue and organizing is evident in the building of agencies such as the Peace Islands Institute, the Gülen Institute in Houston, Dialogue Forum in Philadelphia, and similar centers around the globe.[17] It is easy to forget that inter-religious understanding and cooperation is, in contrast to the advances in other scientific disciplines, a relatively recent phenomenon. (There are, of course, historical exceptions among some particularly generous missionary types.) We have only had the opportunity to read widely in translations of each others' most profound spiritual texts translations of for the past century or so, and the critical study of religions in the academy is an even more recent phenomenon (dating, in the U.S., basically to the 1960s). Inter-religious agencies on behalf of peace and justice date (by and large) from the founding of the Fellowship of Reconciliation in 1914 but have produced (again) notable successes on the global stage: the Tolstoy-inspired non-violent revolution of Gandhi, the Gandhian-inspired Civil Rights Movement that was organized in church basements across the United States, the inter-religious Kairos theologians and their anti-Apartheid activism in South Africa, the Catholic (and Protestant and secular) Solidarity Movement in Poland, and (most recently, as we noted earlier) the Muslim-Christian Women's Movement for Peace in Liberia—to name only a few (Ackerman and Duvall 2000).

Gülen is no expert in the history of religions, but he does assert clearly that "no divine religion has ever been based on conflict, whether it be the religions represented by Moses and Jesus or the religion represented by Muhammad, upon them be peace. On the contrary, these religions, especially Islam, are strictly against disorder, treachery, conflict, and oppression" (2006, 256). To recognize the foundational mutual accountability of Jews, Christians, and Muslims to peace is, of course, only a necessary first step toward the difficult work of negotiating the terms of any such peace. But as the theologian Hans Küng has famously put it: "No peace among the nations without peace among the religions. No peace among the religions without dialogue between the religions. No dialogue between the religions without investigation of the foundation of the religions."[18] Huntington is right, unmistakably so, about a minority of religious believers around the globe. But the historical evidence is growing, with considerable track record over the past decades in ways that extends and deepens what Steven Pinker has observed, namely that the majority of people of faith around the globe are not only not perpetrators of genocide but can be enlisted in movements, such as *Hizmet*, that promote participatory politics, social enterprise, literacy, and dialogue, in a word, that promote peace. Through such efforts to "compete in goodness," as the Holy Qu'ran puts it (2:148), we hold each other accountable to the high standards of truth, goodness, and beauty shared across our traditions and contribute to a more just and joyful world—to a coming religious peace.

REFERENCES

Ackerman, Peter and Jack Duvall. 2000. *A Force More Powerful: A Century of Non-Violent Conflict.* NY: Diane Publishing.

Arendt, Hannah. 1970. *On Violence.* NY: Harcourt, Brace, and World.

Appleby, R. Scott. 2000. *The Ambivalence of the Sacred: Religion, Violence, and Reconciliation* London: Rowman and Littlefield.

Bellah, Robert N. 1967. "Civil Religion in America." *Daedalus: Journal of the American Academy of Arts and Sciences* 96 (Winter): 1–21.

Boulding, Elise. 2000. *Cultures of Peace: The Hidden Side of History.* Syracuse, NY: Syracuse University Press.

Brown, Judith M. and Anthony Parel, eds. 2011. *The Cambridge Companion to Gandhi.* NY: Cambridge University Press.

Cortright, David. 2008. *Peace: A History of Movements and Ideas.* NY: Columbia University Press.

Çetin, Muhammed. 2010. *The Gulen Movement: Civic Service without Borders.* NY: Blue Dome Press.

Dawkins, Richard. 2008. *The God Delusion.* NY: Houghton-Mifflin.

Denton-Borhaug, Kelly. 2011. *U.S. War-Culture, Sacrifice and Salvation.* Sheffield: Equinox.

Disney, Abigail. 2008. *Pray the Devil Back to Hell* (DVD). Online at: http://www.praythedevilbacktohell.com/

Easwaran, Eknath. 1985. *A Man to Match His Mountains: Badshah Khan, Nonviolent Soldier of Islam.* NY: Random House.

Ebaugh, Helen Rose. 2010. *The Gülen Movement: A Sociological Examination of a Civic Movement Rooted in Moderate Islam.* NY: Springer.

Esposito, John L. and Ihsan Yilmaz. 2010. *Islam and Peacebuilding; Gülen Movement Initiatives.* NY: Blue Dome Press.

Galtung, Johan. 1969. "Violence, Peace, and Peace Research." *Journal of Peace Research* 6: 167–91.

Gan , Barry L. and Robert L. Holmes, eds. 2004. *Nonviolence in Theory and Practice,* 2nd ed. NY: Waveland Press.

Gbowee, Leymah. 2011. *Mighty Be Our Powers: How Sisterhood, Sex, and Prayer Changed a Nation at War.* NY: Beast Books.

Girard, René. 1977. *Violence and the Sacred.* Translated by Patrick Gregory. Baltimore/London: Johns Hopkins University Press.

———. 1978. *Things Hidden Since the Foundation of the World.* Translated by Stephen Bann and Michael Metteer. Palo Alto, CA: Stanford University Press.

Gülen, M. Fethullah. 2006. *Toward a Global Civilization of Love and Tolerance.* Somerset, NJ: The Light.

Hanh, Thich Nhat.1992. *Peace Is Every Step: The Path of Mindfulness in Everyday Life.* NY: Bantam.

Harris, Sam. 2006. *Letter to a Christian Nation.* NY: Knopf.

Hill, T. L. and Jon Pahl. (forthcoming). "Social Entrepreneurship as a Catalyst for Practical Social Justice." In *The Gülen Movement and Social Justice*, edited by Heon Kim.

Huntington,Samuel. 1993. "The Clash of Civilizations?" *Foreign Affairs* 72 (Summer): 22–49.

———. 1996. *The Clash of Civilizations and the Remaking of World Order.* NY: Simon and Schuster.

Iyer, Raghavan, ed. 1991. *The Essential Writings of Mahatma Gandhi.* Delhi: Oxford University Press.

Juergensmeyer, Mark. 2003. *Terror in the Mind of God: The Global Rise of Religious Violence, 3rd ed.* Berkeley: The University of California Press.

Kant, Immanual. 1795. "Perpetual Peace: A Philosophical Sketch." Translated by Kevin Paul Geiman. Online at https://www.mtholyoke.edu/acad/intrel/kant/kant1.htm, as accessed 7/9/12.

Kao, Grace Y. and Jerome E. Copulsky. 2007. "The Pledge of Allegiance and the Meanings and Limits of Civil Religion." *Journal of the American Academy of Religion,* 75 (March): 121–49.

Kirk, Martha Ann. 2012. *Growing Seeds of Peace: Stories and Images of Service of the Gülen Movement in Southeastern Turkey.* Houston: Gülen Institute.

Krakauer, Jon. 2011. *Three Cups of Deceit: How Greg Mortenson, Humanitarian Hero, Lost His Way.* NY: Anchor.

Lewis, Bernard. 1990. "The Roots of Muslim Rage." *The Atlantic Monthly,* vol. 266, September, 60.

Lincoln, Bruce. 2006. *Holy Terrors: Thinking about Religion after September 11.* Chicago: The University of Chicago Press.

Marsh, Charles. 2005. *The Beloved Community: How Faith Shapes Social Justice, from the Civil Rights Movement to Today.* NY: Basic Books.

Marty, Martin E. 2010. *Building Cultures of Trust.* Emory University Studies in Law and Religion. Grand Rapids, MI: Eerdmans.

Mortenson, Greg. 2007. *Three Cups of Tea: One Man's Mission to Promote Peace . . . One School at a Time.* NY: Penguin.

O'Brien, Anne Sibley and Perry Edmond O'Brien. 2009. *After Gandhi: One Hundred Years of Nonviolent Resistance.* Watertown, MA: Charlesbridge.

Pahl, Jon. 2010. *Empire of Sacrifice: The Religious Origins of American Violence.* NY: New York University Press.

Pape, Robert. 2006. *Dying to Win: The Strategic Logic of Suicide Terrorism.* NY: Random House.

———. 2010. "It's the Occupation, Stupid," *Foreign Policy,* October 18, 2010, online at: http://www.foreignpolicy.com/articles/2010/10/18/it_s_the_occupation_stupid, as accessed 7/9/2012.

Parks, Rosa. 1996. *Rosa Parks: My Story.* With James Haskins. NY: Dial.

Pinker, Steven. 2011. *The Better Angels of Our Nature: Why Violence Has Declined.* NY: Viking.

Putnam, Robert D. and David E. Campbell. 2010. *American Grace: How Religion Divides and Unites Us.* NY: Simon and Schuster.

Sacks, Jonathan. 2003. *The Dignity of Difference: How to Avoid the Clash of Civilizations.* NY: Continuum.

van der Linden, Harry. 2012. "On the Violence of 'Systemic Violence'': A Critique of Slavoj Zizek," *Digital Commons @ Butler University,* 1/1/2012, online at http://digitalcommons.butler.edu/facsch_papers/248/, as accessed 11/18/2012.

White, Vera. 1997. *A Call to Hope: Living as Christians in a Violent Society.* Washington, DC: Friendship Press.

Wink, Walter. 2003. *Jesus and Nonviolence: A Third Way.* Minneapolis: Fortress Press.

Yaple, Ted. 1997. *Christian Faith in a Violent World: Study Guide.* Cincinnati: Friendship Press.

Yunus, Muhammad. 2009. *Creating a World without Poverty: Social Business and the Future of Capitalism.* NY: Public Affairs.

NOTES

1. I begin to develop this argument in *Empire of Sacrifice: The Religious Origins of American* (2010). See also David Cortright (2008).

2. The growth of peace and justice studies around the globe is truly extraordinary in recent decades. See, most notably, the Kroc Institute for International Peace Studies at the University of Notre Dame, online at http://kroc.nd.edu/, as accessed 11/18/2012. See also the Peace and Collaborative Development Network, at http://www.internationalpeaceandconflict.org/, as accessed 11/18/2012.

3. The role of cooperation in science (especially biological evolution) is one of the most important developments in the past several decades of research. See, for one example, the research project on Evolution and Theology of Cooperation, at Harvard University, here: http://www.fas.harvard.edu/~etc/, as accessed 11/18/2012.

4. See for a succinct version of his research, Pape "It's the Occupation, Stupid," in *Foreign Policy*, October 18, 2010, online at: http://www.foreignpolicy.com/articles/2010/10/18/it_s_the_occupation_stupid, as accessed 7/9/2012; for more extensive comments, see *Dying to Win: The Strategic Logic of Suicide Terrorism* (NY: Random House, 2006). On Juergensmeyer, see *Terror in the Mind of God: The Global Rise of Religious Violence, 3rd ed.* (Berkeley: The University of California Press, 2003).

5. DOMA is the term for the many "defense of marriage acts" that have arisen around the United States to define legally marriage as the relationship between one man and one woman, to the exclusion (by intent) of lesbian and gay partnerships. These laws are violent because they prevent gays and lesbians from enjoying the rights and privileges (economic and cultural) enjoyed by the heterosexual majority. See again *Empire of Sacrifice.*

6. I here follow René Girard, to a point. Girard argues similarly that religions exist to end violence, but contends that they invariably fail to do so. While this is accurate, ultimately, it also misses the importance of proximate and pragmatic gains in justice and peace that can be fostered through the engagement of religious discourses and communities. There is no pure "religion" apart from the messy contingencies of history, and this surely includes the Christianities that Girard sometimes, and Girardians more often, exempt from critique. See most notably, for what might be called "Christian exceptionalism," Rene Girard, *Things Hidden Since the Foundation of the World* (1978).

7. Here, again, Girard is helpful. The structures that incline religions to violence—notably mimetic rivalry—are not unique to Islam, or to archaic religions, but challenge each and every cultural construction, including some that are not obviously apparent as "religious." See again my argument in *Empire of Sacrifice* about the emergence of "hybrid" religions, such as civil and cultural religions, and see Girard's most original statement of his argument, in *Violence and the Sacred* (1977).

8. I adapted this metaphor from a video and study guide produced by Ted Yaple (1997, 5); he credits Vera White (1997) for the metaphor.

9. There is a lively, and necessary, debate about defining "violence." Among the first to extend the term to what he called "structural" systems was Johan Galtung (1969). For a well-reasoned critique, see Harry van der Linden (2012). Suffice it to say I side with Galtung. Van der Linden's point is not that "structural violence" isn't truly violent, but he contends that "structural violence" cannot (or should not) be used to legitimize "revolutionary violence" against unjust structures—a point I clearly support, given that reacting to systemic violence with physical violence against structures (e.g., governments) fails to address the roots of violence in cultural sources.

10. "Peace," like "violence," is not as simple as it seems. In focusing on the cultural side of peace-building, I follow among others Elise Boulding (2000).

11. In addition to the massive argument in *The Better Angels of Our Nature*, see an interview with Pinker by John Naughton, in *The Observer*, October 15, 2012, online at http://www.guardian.co.uk/science/2011/oct/15/steven-pinker-better-angels-violence-interview,   as accessed 11/18/2012.

12. On this point, see another interview with Pinker by Ronald Bailey in *Reason.com,* February 2012, online at http://reason.com/archives/2012/01/11/the-decline-of-violence, as accessed 11/18/2012.

13. See among many resources, Muhammad Yunus (2009). The broadest agency studying and encouraging social enterprise is Ashoka, online at https://www.ashoka.org/, as accessed 11/18/2012.

14. Satyagraha, "truth-force," is perhaps the best example, but the entire range of non-violent engagement associated with Gandhi and many movements since, is what I have in mind here. See Gan and Holmes 2004.

15. Nobel Prize 2011, online at http://www.nobelprize.org/nobel_prizes/peace/laureates/2011/gbowee.html#, as accessed 11/19/2012.

16. Leymah Gbowee, "The Faith of a Peacebuilder," online at http://emu.edu/now/podcast/2009/10/23/the-faith-of-a-peacebuilder-leymah-gbowee/.

17. *Peace Islands Institute (NJ) Homepage*, at http://www.peaceislands.org/, as accessed 11/19/12; *The Gülen Institute Homepage*, at http://www.guleninstitute.org/, as accessed 11/19/12; *Philadelphia Dialogue Forum Homepage*, at http://dialogueforum.us/, as accessed 11/19/12.

18. There are many variants on this quote. See Global Ethic Foundation Homepage, at http://www.weltethos.org/index-en.php, as accessed 7/10/12.

Chapter Seven

The Creative Non-Violent Approach of Walter Wink

Sue-Anne Hess

The world in which we live evidences a spirit of discouragement about the human capacity for living peacefully. Conflict between persons, genders, communities, religions, races, and nations seems to be unceasing. We might be tempted to believe that forgiveness, reconciliation, and peaceful conflict resolution are out-dated concepts inherited from our more simplistic and romanticized past. Immersed in a context of competition, retribution, and gratuitous violence, we might wonder whether it makes sense to hope for a more harmonious world. Is it realistic to imagine that circumstances of oppression and abuses of power can be transformed without bloodshed? It is not from a sense of naïve hopefulness that Walter Wink offers his affirmative reply, but from an impressive career of study, insight, and experience.

This chapter synthesizes Walter Wink's key ideas and shows how they complement and build on those of René Girard. While there are clear differences between their theoretical premises, this chapter is intended to illustrate the rich field of conceptual and practical conversations stimulated, when the ideas of these theorists are combined.

Wink's "Myth of Redemptive Violence" is presented as a starting point. This leads into a consideration of René Girard's theories of mimetic violence and scapegoating. We then return to Wink, whose exploration of power (or "The Powers") deepens our understanding of these patterns of human behavior. Wink offers a politically contextualized interpretation of the words and actions of Jesus Christ, which reveals the perfect human embodiment of these ideas. Through this framework, Wink presents Jesus as the best mentor and example of non-violence as an expression of the "Reign of God" present among us and yet to come.

THE MYTH OF REDEMPTIVE VIOLENCE

> The Myth of Redemptive Violence is the simplest, laziest, most exciting, uncomplicated, irrational, and primitive depiction of evil the world has even known (Wink 1992, 22).

Wink initially presents to us what he believes is the dominant narrative or "myth" of the modern world. This is not (as many might expect) a story born from the religious accounts of Christianity, Judaism, or Islam, but rather from the ancient Babylonian creation myth entitled *Enuma Elish* (Wink 2012). This myth reveals that our world has its origins in a culture of violent competition between the gods. In fact, the earth and skies have been fashioned from the ripped corpse of the defeated god, Tiamat. Humankind, created for the purpose of "doing work for the gods," is made from the blood spilled by the murder of Tiamat's husband, Kingu (Wink 1992). This myth communicates the fundamental need for violence to achieve order. In this story, violence is an essential precursor to our creation. And we, though originating from a divine source, are created to be a dominated breed. We learn that the strong survive at the expense of the weak and that violent conflict remains a natural and inevitable element in human interaction. Those who are identified as "enemy" are beyond redemption and must be destroyed without mercy.

Wink shows us how this "myth" surfaces in entertainment media, using the example of Maxwell Smart, the comical protagonist in the 1960's television series, *Get Smart* (Wink 1992). His bumbling character represents the forces of good, working for the organization "CONTROL" to destroy the work of the evil enemy organization "KAOS." Wink shows how the Myth of Redemptive Violence is made explicit in a moment of introspection by Max's assistant, Agent 99. She comments,

> "You know, Max, sometimes I think we're no better than they are, the way we murder and kill and destroy people." To which Smart retorts, "Why, 99, you know we have to murder and kill and destroy in order to preserve everything that's good in the world." (Wink 1992, 21)

We find humor in the irony of this exchange and may be tempted to dismiss it as ridiculous. Yet, the Myth of Redemptive Violence reveals reasoning of this type. To further illustrate the point, we might reflect on the underlying messages of any action/adventure story. Examples such as films from the *Wild West*, *Superman*, and those about vigilante heroes—even *The Wizard of Oz*—present the message that the total destruction of the enemy is essential to a "happy" ending.

Wink also invites us to consider the message communicated by children's cartoons. Before they are able to reason, children are exposed to this myth and taught (by repetition) the message that violence is the most natural means of bringing order out of chaos. The characters are uncomplicated. Their motives, we are shown, are never mixed or confused, but rather all good and noble (as in the case of our hero) or all evil and unchanging (as is our villain) (Wink 2012). Using the classic example of Popeye and Bluto as representative, he explains how the same "story" is presented time and again, always with the same result. Popeye destroys Bluto.

> In a typical segment, Bluto abducts a screaming and kicking Olive Oyl, Popeye's girlfriend. When Popeye attempts to rescue her, the massive Bluto beats his diminutive opponent to a pulp, while Olive Oyl helplessly wrings her hands. At the last moment, as our hero oozes to the floor, and Bluto is trying, in effect, to rape Olive Oyl, a can of spinach pops from Popeye's pocket and spills into his mouth. Transformed by this gracious infusion of power, he easily demolishes the villain and rescues his beloved. (Wink 1992, 18)

Wink observes that much of the episode characterizes Popeye as a "good guy" who is likeable, accessible, and (at least for the first three-quarters of the story) resilient against harm (Wink 2012). He is someone with whom the audience can identify. It is not until he is faced with the disproportionate and indestructible power of the villain that we see, first, his vulnerability and, then, his subsequent transcendent ability to overcome the enemy. We sympathize with his motives and celebrate his violent triumph. Olive Oyl (the woman) is presented as helpless and ineffective. She is unable to initiate any response of her own, but, rather, looks on passively.

Wink challenges us to reflect on the possibility that our attraction to this recurring plot goes beyond the satisfaction of seeing "right" win out in the end. While our hero is usually presented as appealing and wholesome, there is also something seductive about our villain. Wink suggests that the villain provides a symbol upon whom to project our "inner anger, violence, rebelliousness, or lust" (Wink 1998, 49) and to privately enjoy their expressions of power and dominance. These emotions, which we find uncomfortable and are often unwilling to face, are then put to death, as the villain is destroyed. We can be satisfied that the evil has been dealt with, but more importantly, our goodness, despite these emotions, has been reaffirmed.

This myth is re-enacted almost unceasingly in various forms of literature, art, and media (Wink 2012). Video and Internet games, action films, and television shows, which depict this formula of an evil so abhorrent that it can only be overcome by a climax of violence, destruction, and death, are becoming increasingly explicit by the day (Wink 2012). Good wins out in the end but only by desperate and bloody means.

Sadly, this Myth of Redemptive Violence is not merely the stuff of stories and games. Wink submits that we see this rationale present elsewhere, in "media, in sports, in nationalism, in militarism, in foreign policy, in televangelism, in the religious right, and in self-styled militia groups" (Wink 1998, 49). We don't need to look far to find examples of vigilante action, where the appropriate system of law is rejected in preference of emotionally loaded and reactive retaliation. We might consider the disturbing examples of an abused wife who kills her husband, or the bombing of abortion clinics, or even anti-Muslim hate-crimes following the 9/11 attacks. The enemy is dehumanized, magnified, and "justifiably" condemned to a violent end. These ideas refer to our inner chaos as it is projected onto the external world and are echoed in the work of French philosopher René Girard and his reflections on mimetic violence.

WINK AND GIRARD: THE SCAPEGOATING MODEL

René Girard's work offers powerful insight into our understanding of the nature of violence in human relationships. By revealing the unspoken workings of these interactions, Girard provides a necessary elaboration of Martin Luther King Jr.'s assertion: "The choice is no longer between violence and non-violence. It's non-violence or non-existence" (Wink 2000, xi). Unlike Wink, yet reminiscent of The Myth of Redemptive Violence, Girard regards violence as inherent in human behavior, stimulated by the competitive and mimetic nature of our interactions (Girard 1996).

In brief, he argues that, from our earliest socialization, we learn via imitation, or mimesis (Girard 1996). Overall, this mimetic learning is beneficial in that we are socialized to understand what is productive in our interactions with others (Girard 1996). At a 2006 conference in Ottawa, Girard used the example of a handshake, showing how, once person A puts a hand out, person B reciprocates this behavior and the interaction is mutually satisfying. However, if person B chooses not to imitate the gesture of person A, the relationship is damaged and a negative reciprocity, or mimesis, is initiated. There is then a potential for this interaction to deteriorate as each party pays back to the other "with some extra." An unreciprocated handshake may be met with a closing of body language, crossed arms, or a backward step. The closed body language may then be imitated with an unwelcoming facial expression or words of insult as a response. Neither party regards themselves as the aggressor, rather the victim responds to the actions of a hostile "other."

Mimetic rivalries are revealed in a similar fashion. Girard explains how an object is not considered desirable until a subject observes and imitates another's attachment to it (Girard 1996). In turn, the model's attachment to the object increases as they observe the subject's desire for the object and subsequently imitates this. A rivalry evolves as the subject and the model begin to perceive one another simultaneously as an obstacle to the object and also as a "Model" (Girard, cited in Redekop 2002, 66). As the parties become more intensely focused on one another, they become more alike in their mimesis, intensifying the hostility between the two. The situation is then vulnerable to a "loss of distinction" where the mimetic violence takes on its own identity and the initial object is forgotten (Girard, 1977, 49).

While this competitive behavior can also be observed in the animal kingdom, Girard tells us that, at the critical point, the weaker animal will offer his throat to the stronger animal in a gesture of surrender. In turn, the stronger animal releases the defeated enemy and thus establishes a relationship of dominance (Redekop, 1993). Human rivalries by contrast, will continue to escalate until one or both of the parties is killed. In animals, the conflict is resolved by the mutually recognized defeat of one over the other. For humans, a third party is required to bring about an end to the violence, the scapegoat.

Four characteristics qualify the scapegoat for bringing about a resolution to hostilities. The scapegoat must be acknowledged as an "other": illegitimate, terrifyingly powerful, irredeemably evil and yet curiously incapable of retribution (Girard 1996). At the height of the crisis, both parties join forces to destroy the scapegoat (usually by death), which immediately results in a diffusion of hostility and a sense of peaceful well-being (Girard 1996). The "source" of the violence is identified, punished, and removed, reinforcing the belief that violence is external to the self and can be done away with (Girard 1996). The collective sense of well-being justifies the preceding brutality and, for the time being, helps to re-establish a sense of order. The scapegoat, in death, takes on an elevated identity. To it is attributed a transcendent and yet tragic nature that forms the basis for sacrificial religious myths and practices (Girard 1977).

Girard makes clear that the resulting sense of calm is a false peace. In fact, these scapegoat sacrifices fail to resolve the crisis at its deepest level because they enable parties to avoid recognizing and taking ownership of the violence that is rooted within themselves (Girard 1996). At the same time, it raises this group brutality to a spiritual level, where the murder of the scapegoat acquires symbolic significance. Religious practice and ritual, therefore, is a human creation, designed to justify the cruelty and violence that exists within each person, who, in his or her humanity, is unwilling and unable to own it (Girard 1977).

We can observe considerable common ground between Wink and Girard's perspectives. Fundamentally, they both draw to light processes and justifications that are unseen, allowing our recognition of these forces to be the first step to confronting them. They highlight the danger in failing to own our inner violence, and they highlight how this failure can have cataclysmic results. Both also highlight the evil of reciprocal violence and its inherent inability to bring about peaceful outcomes.

While Wink is largely in agreement with Girard and commends his ability to uncover the processes of our mimetic behaviors, he disagrees on a few points that may have implications for future reflections. First, Wink reminds us that scapegoating is not the only human behavior that diffuses conflict. He reminds us that there are also inhibitive structures such as legal processes, police, cultural taboos, and conciliatory processes to reduce tensions without the need for a scapegoat (Wink 1992; cf. Redekop chapter 4). He also questions the assertion that human sacrifice and scapegoating can be evidenced throughout history. On the contrary, Wink offers us examples of non-violent cultures in our early history, which show little or no evidence of this competitive behavior. Instead, Wink aligns the rise of scapegoating behavior with the rise of city-states that necessitated military defense (Wink 1992). He is critical of Girard's assumption that all peoples participate in this behavior and offers evidence of communities today that have a non-violent culture.

As we build on Girard's theory of structural violence, and incorporate the notion of the Myth of Redemptive Violence that gives these actions credibility, Wink draws us into a deeper level of insight. He introduces us to his theory of "The Powers," which adds a critical spiritual dimension to the conversation.

THE POWERS

> How can we oppose evil without creating new evils and being made evil ourselves? (Wink 1992, 3)

Having established that we are immersed in these systems of violence, Wink raises a question: Is there a way to not only overcome these circumstances, but be liberated from the structures that create them? Is the establishment of the "Reign of God" something that can only be transformational at the individual level, or is there also a political implication to it? (Wink 1998, 2). So often, we see a regime of oppression overthrown, only to be replaced by one that is equally repressive or worse. Both the Myth of Redemptive Violence and mimetic theory make clear to us that violence has a spiraling nature. Violence escalates and increases into further violence and destruction, not peace. Wink asserts, "Violence is simply not radical enough [to end oppression], since it generally changes only the rulers, but not the rules" (Wink 2003, 72). We need a model that revolutionizes our current patterns and presents an entirely new frame of reference. Wink invites us to consider that God has already given us this life-giving alternative in a non-violent response to abuses of power.

The discussion continues with a moment of necessary reflection. Wink reminds us that it is not fashionable in today's world to speak of spiritual matters (Wink 1986, 1). In our reductionist and scientific age, reference to

God, Satan, and spiritual realities can automatically discredit our position as either superstitious or old-fashioned. In a world where the pursuit of wealth and materialism is the dominating faith, talk of an unseen world is relegated to fiction and the realm of the fantastic (Wink 1992). And yet, Wink assures us that the myth of materialism is also unsatisfying, that there is something beyond the "matter" of things which is irreducible and for which we have no words. We have a sense of a spiritual dimension but have little time for cartoon-like caricatures of angels and demons flying about in the sky. Still, we long for a way to identify (and therefore comprehend) the spiritual forces around us (Wink 1992, 9).

Wink encourages us to turn our attention to ancient scripture (Old and New Testament, canonical and non-canonical), and the Gospels in particular, as our guides (Wink 1986, 8). He challenges us to wager that scripture "has the power, in each new age, to evoke life, to strike fire, to convey the stark reality of God's Hunger to be known" and subsequently endeavors to prove this claim by highlighting references to power in these texts (Wink 1986, 1).

While the concept of Principalities and Powers is a common idea in Pauline writings, allusions to power relations are dispersed throughout the New Testament (Wink 1984). Previous interpretations have argued that these "forces" can be understood simply as the socially constructed order of things, such as institutions, political forces, and unwritten cultural laws (Wink 1992). In this way, we might be excused from attempting to reconcile our reductionist world-view with the spirituality of the time. Yet, Wink observes how these writers spoke of "spiritual" and "earthly" powers simultaneously, concurrently and interchangeably (Wink 1986). Rather than dismissing this observation as a reflection of these earlier "unsophisticated" cultures, Wink compels us to set aside our current perceptions so that we might capture the insights that are being offered.

These ancient writers, he states, were correct in identifying the dual essence of an outer manifestation and an inner invisible spirit of structures of power (Wink 1992). They are inseparable, indistinguishable, and interdependent. A structure of power may be established by human effort, yet it takes on a nature that exceeds the will or imagination of any given individual.

Wink assures us that the "Powers," just like us, are good, fallen, and must be redeemed. This is not a sequential formula; rather, all three realities exist concurrently (Wink 1992, 71). We might consider an institution such as a hospital, school, or government. For humans to live peacefully, there must be some sense of order and boundary, which these structures are able to provide. However, we also recognize that in their fallen nature, the powers have the potential to become controlling and oppressive, insensitive to human integrity. In this state, Wink argues that the powers must be brought back under the authority of God, by exposing their abdication and recalling them to their initial purpose (Wink 1984).

> For example, a factory is polluting the water and air of our city, and we want it cleaned up. We can engage in that struggle knowing that its employees need jobs, and that their families also are at risk from the pollution, just as ours are. We can talk without hatred to the hard-nosed representatives of the plant, because we know that they and we and this factory are encompassed by the Love of God, and exist to serve the One in and through and for whom we were all created. We do not have to struggle to bring this plant into the orbit of God's created. It is already there. We have only to remind its managers that it exists to serve values beyond itself (though this 'reminding' may require a protracted boycott or strike) (Wink 1992, 68).

If we accept that the true nature of these spiritual forces represents the unseen portion of physical phenomena (rather than independent creatures), then we are given an opportunity to explore and expose their effects, as the above example shows.

In summary, we find ourselves captured by a "Domination System" (Wink 1992, 33). Described by Wink as "what happens when an entire network of Powers becomes integrated around idolatrous values" (Wink 1992, 9). We may conceptualize this as the inevitable result of a society built on the foundations of violence. Paradoxically, control of others by force becomes the most effective means of self-defense and protection against being dominated.

Wink identifies Satan as the "world-encompassing spirit of the Domination System" (Wink 1992, 9). As an enemy of the Gospel and as a Power, Satan is characterized by "self-assertion, self-protection and self-expansion: the formation of separations, isolation, and alienation: the repression of thought, feeling and impulse" (Bakan, cited in Wink, 57). In this system, we perceive others defensively, dehumanizing and devaluing them in the never-ending pursuit of invulnerability. Power over others is our objective at an individual and corporate level, and we become defensive against working cooperatively. This System of Domination could not be further from God's plan for humanity. "The Reign of God," described as a "Domination-free Order" is described below:

> Where is God's reign? Wherever domination is overcome, people freed, the soul fed, God's reality known. When is God's reign? Whenever people turn from the idols of power and wealth and fame to the governance of God in a society of equals. What is God's reign? It is the transformation of the Domination System into a nonviolent, humane, ecologically sustainable, livable environment fashioned to enable people to grow and grow well (Wink 1998, 10).

JESUS'S THIRD WAY

Returning to scapegoating theory, Girard directs our attention toward Christianity, which offers an inverted understanding of the scapegoat. He argues that the religious myth is usually presented from the perspective of the crowd who, innocent, must destroy the evil of the scapegoat. When we consider Jesus, we see the story presented from the perspective of the victim (Girard 1989). Scripture reveals the mob as the wrongdoers and the scapegoat, not as the villain, but as the innocent character. The crucifixion narrative shows us the hidden mechanisms of the scapegoating pattern. Because of this change of perspective, the horror of this behavior is laid bare and Jesus, as the victim, models for us perfect, non-violent response (Wink 2003). By His refusal to enter into a mimetic exchange of violence for violence, he reveals that our ideas of a dominant and oppressive God are nothing more than a projection, based on our experience of a violent culture. The God that Jesus reveals desires the freedom of His people. Jesus's actions serve to expose and dis-empower this dynamic to offer a free and loving alternative.

Building on the above insights, Wink challenges us to consider the example of Jesus as a third option that transcends the fight/flight responses of mimetic rivalries and Redemptive Violence. Referring to the Gospel of Matthew, he describes a teaching (which is generally misunderstood) and offers us an interpretation based on the re-contextualization of the scriptural passage:

> [38]You have heard that it was said, "An eye for an eye and a tooth for a tooth." [39]But I say to you, Do not resist an evildoer. But if anyone strikes you on the right cheek, turn the other also; [40]and if anyone wants to sue you and take your coat, give your cloak as well; [41]and if anyone forces you to go one mile, go also the second mile. [42]Give to everyone who begs from you, and do not refuse anyone who wants to borrow from you. (Mt 5: 38–42 NRSV)

Sadly, he says, this passage of scripture has either been ignored by the Christian audience; discarded as "too difficult," or worse, it has been used as a justification for Christian passivity and inaction in the face of injustice. And yet, we know that Jesus was anything but passive. The Gospels reveal, and Wink affirms, that "Jesus in short, abhors both passivity and violence" (Wink 1998, 109). Herein we see an important contradiction. In the absence of fleeing or reacting in violence, what kind of response was Jesus inviting from His followers?

To begin, Wink invites us to re-discover the instruction "Do not resist an evildoer" and, in particular, the term "resist." In the English translation, it would be easy to interpret this term in the passive sense, that is, in "not resisting" we are permissive of evil actions. However, if we consider that this term "resist" incorporates the idea of retaliation or reciprocation, it becomes clear that Jesus is not calling us to mute helplessness in the face of domination. Instead, He is condemning the escalation of conflict and the emergence of those reactive behaviors that place us in danger of "becoming what we hate" (Wink 1992, 159).

Dividing the remainder of the passage into three separate teachings, Wink shows how each part is calling for a creative, non-violent response from the victim that sustains the human integrity, not only of the victim, but also of the aggressor. This type of response spares the victim from entering into an escalating and mimetic relationship of violence and simultaneously exposes the system of domination.

In the first example, we are commanded to "turn the other cheek." Rather than an act of submission, as it is popularly understood, Wink explains that by doing this, the victim forces the aggressor to choose between two equally unattractive options. He must either use his left (culturally unclean) hand to strike, or use his fist, a gesture that would symbolically implicate the victim as his equal. Wink reminds us to consider that a backhanded slap was (and is) a gesture of humiliation, given by the aggressor to reassert a relationship of dominance such as a master to slave, husband to wife, or Roman to Jew. Imagine how this gesture loses its intended meaning when the power balance is challenged and the aggressor is met with a response that implies "You can hit me, but cannot humiliate or demean me"?

In a similar way, the second example instructs those who are taken to court in debt to "offer the inner garment." Wink reveals how this instruction is commonly misunderstood to mean that Jesus required his followers to extend themselves beyond their capabilities for others. Instead, this is a strategy intended to expose and shame not the debtor, but the creditor (Wink 2012). Upon removing the outer and inner garments, the victim stands publicly naked where (culturally) shame was also attributed to those, who looked at the nakedness (Wink 2012). Here, we are presented with a creative and comical response to circumstances of dominance. Again, Jesus offers to those who are familiar with cruel systems of "justice," a tactic that refuses to concede to humiliation and be degraded by it.

In the third example, Wink offers a new reflection on the Jesus's instruction to "go the extra mile" (Wink 2003). While it was legally permissible for a Roman officer to command a civilian to carry his pack, this was restricted to a distance of no more than one mile. If a civilian were to carry the pack any further distance, this would leave the officer vulnerable to reprimand by his superiors. We can, therefore, appreciate how confusing (and perhaps embarrassing) it might be for an officer who, having forced a civilian to carry his pack for the required mile, must now request the return of the pack from this inferior or be punished himself for failing to uphold the law.

In each of these examples we are invited to look again at Jesus's instruction and to understand it in light of the context in which He was speaking.

Those who were present at the time, says Wink, would have had no need for this kind of clarification, as they experienced daily the struggles of an occupied people (Wink 1986). Generations later, we are the ones who must carefully consider the implications of Jesus's instruction in the context of His other teachings and the mission of His life.

These insights allow us to see that we find ourselves in a world that has been deceived. Mistakenly, we've learned that violence is to be anticipated as a necessary means of maintaining control, that we must kill or be killed and that a consideration of spiritual influence in our world may be regarded as an embarrassment. Recognizing this erroneous foundation, we are able to reflect on scripture by an entirely new framework. We are able to see how, so many years ago, we were given a revelation of God's plan for us to live peacefully and instructions as to how we might live this out. These will be discussed in the following section.

OUR RESPONSE

Ultimately, Wink shows us how the "domination-free order" (also known as the "Reign of God") is not only possible at a conceptual level but is occurring in our midst. Reflecting deeply and insightfully on the words and actions of Jesus, he presents a vision of a world where structural injustices, such as racism, homophobia, gender, and economic inequality are challenged and undermined. This is not achieved by a confrontation of violence to overcome violence (a self-perpetuating system of the exchange of power and dominance), but by a Third Way. This Third Way is a non-violent response to domination which, retaining the affirmation of humanity for all parties, seeks creative, intentional, and even comical methods to identify and diffuse power abuses. He contextualizes the conduct of Jesus within the political environment of his time, allowing us to see Jesus as a person of exceptional social insight and awareness, a direct challenge to the notion that religion and politics must not coincide. As a result, Wink presents Jesus as the perfect example of non-violent, courageous, and conscious activism.

Our role then, first, is to be aware. Wink reminds us that Powers are most destructive, while unnamed (Wink, 1992). By recognizing and making them known, we automatically reduce their force. We are neither capable nor required to overcome them (matching force with force) but, rather, become sensitive to their presence and influence. We might, with humility, own those mimetic patterns of interacting that cause us to devalue others. If we accept that the fallen powers seek to control and dominate us, we might ask, in moments of powerlessness, "what Principality or Power has me in its spell?" (Wink 1992, 103) We are empowered to recognize and repent of our subconscious complicity with these forces and the delusion that they feed us. Most disturbingly, we must confront the violence within ourselves (Wink 2003). Knowing that we will never perfectly attain our hopes, we diffuse the power of these forces by claiming an integrity as God's creation that has an intrinsic value beyond our given context. And, following the example of Jesus, we submit to the inevitable suffering of the Cross that requires us to absorb these injustices into ourselves, rather than retaliating in kind.

Second, we must acknowledge that Christianity has repeatedly fallen short of the mission to realize the domination-free order that Jesus pioneered (Wink 1998). Throughout history, we see how the Christian family has, sometimes, supported these structures of dominance; in others, it has turned a blind eye to them or worse, docilely submitted to them, quieting those who suffer with promises of future heavenly reward. Christians must courageously own their passivity and unwillingness to step into the non-violent struggle. We must resolve, again, to imitate Jesus in his concern for the weak, the broken and the poor, despite the personal cost. We begin to understand that our current struggle against the "Principalities and Powers" is made evident to us in "the really mammoth and crushing evils of our day—racism, sexism, political oppression, ecological degradation, militarism, patriarchy, homelessness, economic greed," rather than the dramatic representations we are fed from the horror film genre (Wink 1992, 9).

Thirdly, we must respond. Once we are able to identify the systems and structures at work in our world (both interpersonally and at a broader political level), we are empowered to become agents of peace and reconciliation. When we remain firm in our identification of the humanity of all parties in a conflict, we are set free to offer true forgiveness and offer a challenge to the injustices that we encounter.

Wink offers no agenda, but invites us to look to the example of those non-violent greats who have gone before us, whose determination and humility might inspire our own creative action. We might reflect on the work and writings of A. J. Muste, Martin Luther King Jr., Mahatma Gandhi, and Dorothy Day, whose personal reflections offer an intimate viewpoint into the reality of the non-violent Third Way and the inner change that it demands (Wink 2000).

Fortunately, examples of this type of action are endless and increasing: from the story of Lysistrata, an ancient Greek play depicting women withholding sexual favors from their husbands unless they interact peacefully with one another, to the life of St. Francis of Assisi, who abandoned a wealthy, military lifestyle for the sake of discipleship. We might also consider the anti-slavery movement in the United States, as well as Gandhi's struggle for Indian independence in the early 20th century. Further instances of this Third Way of non-violence include boycotts, strikes, mass mobilizations, marches, political activism, petitions, protests, demonstrations, educational campaigns, prayer meetings, dialogues, and debates. Wink assures us that there is no limit to the style, strategy, or scope for own action, yet these illustrations help to energize and inspire us.

However, Wink also reminds us that non-violent change will not come easily or quickly. He warns, reminiscent of the words of Gandhi and imitative of the actions of Jesus, that before a dialogue of non-violence can begin, one must be prepared to die for one's cause (Wink 2003). Beyond particular actions or events, we are reminded that non-violence is a process, a skill to be learned, a passion, and a calling. It is born out of a desire to see injustice confronted in a way that honors the humanity of all persons and sees no person beyond redemption.

CONCLUSION

By careful examination of the forces at work in our human family, Wink brings us to a place of new hope. His "Third Way" rejects submissive inactivity, posing as peaceful non-resistance, and compels us to a new kind of action. This Third Way demands that we denounce of the Myth of Redemptive Violence and recognize the mimetic Rivalries and Scapegoating behaviors which reveal our inner darkness and feed off this mentality. Yet, beyond mere insights, Wink offers us an entirely new framework based on the example of Jesus. We develop the ability to uncover and challenge the might of the Powers in those instances, where they are burdensome and oppressive. In this new way, we refuse to match violence for violence but are empowered to recognize and reverence the humanity of all people (regardless of the evil of their actions).

We are armed with the valuable tools of insight, hope, and a sense of purpose, grounded in a painfully real awareness of the disordered state of the world. By delineating the spiritual and social dimensions of conflict today, Wink creates a space for both prayerful intercession and social action. Most importantly, he calls us away from our inner violence and back to our original purpose, to love and serve God and neighbor. Paradoxically, this vision owns the impossibility of its mandate in our fallen world, yet advocates for our wholehearted commitment to its goals. He shows us how this vision is the only coherent choice for those, who are working for true justice and peace.

In sum, Wink encourages us to commit to make present the Reign of God as Jesus described it. Rather than vague idealism, he unpacks a vision for the re-alliance of the Powers with their original mission, in the service of God. This vision incorporates practical implications such as economic equality, equal status of persons (regardless of gender, nationality, religious belief or sexuality), non-violent responses to injustice and authentic reconciliation between peoples (Wink 1992; 2003; 1998; 1987). A domination-free order is not a society devoid of justice or accountability, but one that proactively commits to the empowerment of the oppressed so that integrity may be restored.

In this brief exploration of his ideas, we see how Wink presents a coherent, spiritual understanding of our reality, a way of seeing the real and invisible forces we struggle against, and a new vision for a non-violent, humane world. Through these reflections, we begin to see, like Wink, that it is still reasonable to believe in our capacity for transformation. Taking the example of Jesus as a role model, we are drawn into a paradigm shift that is "making all things new" (Rv 21:5 NRSV).

REFERENCES

Girard, Rene. 1977. *Violence and the Sacred*. Baltimore: Johns Hopkins University Press.

——. 1987. *Things Hidden since the Foundation of the World*. With Jean-Michel Oughourlian and Guy Lefort; translated by Stephen Bann and Michael Metteer. Stanford, Calif.: Stanford University Press.

——. 1989. *The Scapegoat*. Baltimore: Johns Hopkins University Press.

——. 1996. T*he Girard Reader*. Edited by James G. Williams. New York: Crossroad.

Holy Bible: NRSV, New Revised Standard Version. 2007. New York: Harper Bibles.

Redekop, Vern Neufeld. 2002. *From Violence to Blessing: How an Understanding of Deep-Rooted Conflict Can Open Paths to Reconciliation*. Ottawa, Ontario: Novalis.

——. 1993. *Scapegoats, the Bible, and Criminal Justice: Interacting with René Girard*. Akron, PA: MCC U.S. Office of Criminal Justice.

Wink, Walter. n.d."Walter Wink on Jesus." *CRES Multifaith Resources - Community Resources for Exploring Spirituality - Center for Religious Experience and Study*. N.p., n.d. Web. 16 Aug. 2013. http://www.cres.org/star/_wink.htm.

——. 1984. *Naming the Powers: The Language of Power in the New Testament*. Philadelphia: Fortress Press.

——. 1986. *Unmasking the Powers: The Invisible Forces that Determine Human Existence*. Philadelphia: Fortress Press.

——. 1987. *Violence and Nonviolence in South Africa: Jesus' Third Way*. Philadelphia, PA: New Society Publishers.

——. 1992. *Engaging the Powers: Discernment and Resistance in a World of Domination*. Minneapolis: Fortress Press.

——. 1998. *When the Powers Fall: Reconciliation in the Healing of Nations*. Minneapolis, MN: Fortress Press.

——. 1998. *The Powers That Be: Theology for a New Millennium*. New York: Doubleday.

——. 2000. *Peace is the Way: Writings on Nonviolence from the Fellowship of Reconciliation*. Maryknoll, N.Y.: Orbis Books.

——. 2003. *Jesus and Nonviolence: A Third Way*. Minneapolis, MN: Fortress,.

——. 2012. "Facing the Myth of Redemptive Violence | Ekklesia." *Welcome to Ekklesia | Ekklesia*. N.p., 21 May 2012. Web. 16 Aug. 2013. http://www.ekklesia.co.uk/content/cpt/article_060823wink.shtml.

Chapter Eight

Improvising the Practice of Nonresistance as Creative Mimesis

Peter Smith

In light of mimetic theory, I propose to explore how we can more fully realize ways of life *not* organized around violence and scapegoats. My point of departure begins with an insight sometimes attributed to William Stafford (2003): "Violence is a failure of the imagination." This is a powerful indictment by Stafford, an American poet and anti-war activist of the twentieth century, and its truth is something I want to explore further in this essay. A second quote providing a point of departure is a teaching of Jesus as recorded in Matthew's gospel:

> You have heard that it was said, "An eye for an eye and a tooth for a tooth." But I say to you, Do not resist an evildoer. But if anyone strikes you on the right cheek, turn the other also; and if anyone wants to sue you and take your coat, give your cloak as well; and if anyone forces you to go one mile, go also the second mile. Give to everyone who begs from you, and do not refuse anyone who wants to borrow from you. (Mt. 5:38–42 NRSV)

This teaching holds a truth that suggests, I will argue, an understanding of "Do not resist . . ." (nonresistance) as an invitation to creative rather than destructive *mimesis*.

If we were to translate Stafford's statement into the terms of mimetic theory, we might say, "Violence is an outcome of distorted *mimesis*." That is, when imagination becomes locked into the narrow and addictive confines of distorted, rivalrous mimetic behavior, it breeds violence. Similarly, Jesus, in commending creative nonresistance, seems to be putting his finger on human imagination and action as keys to unleashing life-giving practices—or "structures of blessing" (Redekop, chapter 4)—among humanity. That is, instead of becoming locked in to the logic of retaliation and revenge, Jesus encourages the intentional attempt at opening up of a new relational space through the practice of nonresistance.

Some explanation regarding my use of the term "practice" is in order here. The word has rich meaning, and I use it in a two-fold sense. In the first, simplest sense, "practice" refers to the intentional performance, usually in a repetitive manner: praxis. Thus, it is used when speaking of "practicing piano" or "practicing basketball." Neither activity can be done while lying in one's bed and just thinking about the activity. Movement is required for praxis; purposeful movement of enacting and polishing skills constitutes practice. To practice Christian nonresistance is to engage habitually in actions that offer/foster benign relations with the other rather than mirroring hostile provocations.

In the second, more technical sense, "practice" refers to a larger set of activities and assumptions that lead to and embody the flourishing of human communities. Said another way, practices are ongoing activities engaged in for their own sakes as well as for the good goals that they pursue. They are stable, yet flexible, endeavors that combine reflection, doing, refining and excelling. Practices have ends and means, allow for the formulation of rules to govern proper praxis and require good faith participation. They cultivate character and, at their best, lead to the embodiment of virtues (MacIntyre 1984). We frequently use this terminology when we speak of practicing law or medicine, but "practices" refers to other contexts as well. In this case, the practice of Christian nonresistance points to not just occasional acts of isolated nonresistance but an ongoing way of life governed by a goal and intrinsically valuable, as well.

Further, and crucially, practices exist and make sense in the light of narratives connected to communities. The Christian narrative exemplified in Scripture is key for understanding the practices that make up the life of Christian communities (McClendon 2000, 173–4). Dunking people in water can be a game in the pool, until it is narratively connected to the Hebrew-Christian tradition of ritual cleansing and symbolic transformation that comes to be called "baptism." Likewise, to understand the practice of nonresistance requires attending to the narrative that gives shape to this language and practice, particularly in the Gospels. I am suggesting that this robust understanding of the flexible, ongoing, narrative-embedded practice of nonresistance will aid in understanding the role of improvisation and positive *mimesis*.

The practice of nonresistance, far from being passive, entails the active, improvisational embodiment of life-giving relations. Again, though nonresistance is a negative word, it does not denote doing nothing. Indeed, Jesus provides instruction regarding creative responses that move beyond simple fight or flight reactions. This is one reason that I stress nonresistance as praxis and a (flexible, ongoing) practice of the church (and those committed to a just peace). It is performed and a course of action, not something abstained from or a non-action. Nonresistance might be best understood by defining it as "not-resisting-in-kind" or "not-resisting-in-like-manner." The counsel of Jesus is to respond to provocations with something other than "payback." Better to respond in a creative way that will introduce new relational possibilities. I will explore nonresistance further below.

In this essay, I will suggest that the practice of nonresistance viewed through the lens of improvisational performance serves to create opportunities for pacific *mimesis*. To show this, I will reflect on each of the parts of this argument: *mimesis*, nonresistance, and improvisation, and then draw them altogether at the end.

MIMESIS: THE INTERPLAY OF IMAGINATION AND ACTION

There are two key aspects to human *mimesis* that I want to bring to the fore in these considerations. The first is imagination, the second, action. These two capacities make *mimesis* possible. If *mimesis* had only to do with action, it would be reduced to the child's game of "copycat" behavior. But, Girard (1977) has demonstrated that human *mimesis*—with its basis in metaphysical desire—is more than wooden imitation of another's action. On the other hand, if *mimesis* only had to do with imagination, it would be reduced to rather innocuous mental games played in one's head, detached from concrete behavior. But the interplay of imagination and action makes human *mimesis* reality.

A brief word on how I understand imagination in this chapter. Often, we think of imagination in relation to children and the world of play that they can construct for themselves. This association tends to lump imagination with fantasy and unreality. However, the use of imagination does not cease in adulthood, it merely takes on different forms and still plays a significant role in shaping/constructing reality. Indeed, imagination and epistemology could be usefully explored in greater detail but that will have to wait for another chapter. I am assuming, at minimum, a significantly corresponding relationship between truth and imagination. That is, what we imagine to be reality (in some sense) corresponds to what we hold to be true, and we act accordingly. However, it does not follow that just because we imagine something to be true that it is, in fact, or will become, true. Self-deception remains a recurring problem for humankind. Nonetheless, the human capacity for imagination is central to what makes human communities possible.

There is no *mimesis* without imagination, because it is imagination that allows humans to observe and imitate a model. It is through imagination that people perceive and interpret another as a model. It is imagination that leads us to perceive rivalry and threat found in the transformation of a model into an obstacle. Thus, imagination shapes how we act.

At the same time, it is also the case that action shapes imagination. To illustrate this relationship, consider a particular species of human action: habits. Habits shape our ways of thinking, and our ways of thinking shape our habits (Duhigg 2012; Margolis 1993). That is, there is not a one-way, causal relationship that can be specified in regard to habits but a dynamic reciprocity with change possible on both counts. In its most straightforward sense, we give the name "habit" to actions—healthy or unhealthy—that are performed consistently over time. Habits have a critical relationship to imagination and to human mimetic capacities. Just as a shift in imagination can issue in changing habits, so a change in habits can issue in a shift in imagination. For example, affluent North Americans, who never travel beyond First World borders, typically adopt habits of consumption that make it very difficult to imagine the possibility of life lived any other way. Or, in ascetic traditions, the habit of fasting can move the imagination from concern with bodily appetites to contemplation of higher values.

These brief reflections on *mimesis*, imagination, and habits are meant to set the stage for consideration of a way of life marked by nonresistance. My contention is that the action and imagination involved in nonresistance display creative mimetic possibilities, when seen in light of improvisation. It also has the potential to induce creative *mimesis* in others. But to make this argument requires more clarity regarding nonresistance and improvisation.

NONRESISTANCE: TERMINOLOGY AND USE

"Nonresistance" is not a particularly common word and its meaning can be somewhat elusive (Hershberger 1944; Toews 1986). Thus, I will try to set out further how I am employing the term in this chapter. I have already alluded to its root in the words of Jesus recorded in Matthew. Further, I take the life of Jesus as paradigmatic of what nonresistance looks like, giving narrative shape to what creative nonresistance is all about.

I am choosing to use the term "nonresistance" rather than "non-violence" (or even "non-violent resistance") due to an assumption that accompanies the terminology of non-violence. This assumption holds that humans are morally bound to resist certain things such that resistance is not only justified, but it is glorified. Thus, the debate shifts to one of locating one's resistance on a spectrum of action classed closer to "violent" or "non-violent" options. But if we are morally bound in this way, are we not still operating in the cycle of reciprocity initiated by violent action? And is not resistance, therefore, ultimately beholden to violence because it allows the parameters of our thinking and acting—indeed our morality—to be defined by violence? (Milbank

1997, chapter 9). Resisting evil and violence seems inevitably to mean adopting evil's terms and becoming locked in its logic or accepting its framework. Further, and ironically, resistance to something can be integral to sustaining the very thing one intends to oppose. Thus, it is instructive that the gospels do not portray Jesus resisting evil, injustice, and his own persecution unto death—contrary to the common expectations of what Messiah would do. He went toward his death in a way that did not fatalistically accept it, nor violently resist it, but nonresistantly improvised a creative engagement that unleashed powerful possibilities.

Using the more archaic term "nonresistance" critically questions the assumption of the morality of resistance named above. (As the logic of improvisational drama informs us—discussed below—resistance is not the only or best option for opening up alternative relationship possibilities.) The term "nonresistance" acknowledges both initial violence and potential resistance but does not assign either a higher moral value. Indeed, by intentionally opposing retaliatory resistance that would otherwise be assumed as justified, nonresistance simultaneously indicts the preceding violence as well, putting violence and counter-violence on the same level, as actions that march to the beat of the same drum. That drumbeat is one that creates victims/scapegoats so as to renew group cohesion (Girard 1977). But the point of creative nonresistance (and all Christ-like action) is not to indict actions and actors so much as to unleash alternatives and creative engagement for all those trapped in the spiral of violence. This requires a different way of imagining or perceiving which derives from narratives and practices integral to Christian discipleship that will be discussed below.

At first glance, it appears cruel to cut the feet out from under the "moral claims" of revenge and resistance typically granted to the attacked party. However, upon closer inspection, the victim's position, as the narrative of Jesus demonstrates, affords the best (only?) chance to break out of the cycle of violence. If a way beyond the parameters of violence is to be had only via the victim, this is because it is through suffering that human transformation becomes possible. The recurrent falsehood—Wink's "myth of redemptive violence"—is that resistance and revenge will effect transformation in human relations (Wink 1992; see also Hess, chapter 7 of this volume). But revenge never yields transformation, only further destruction and the capacity for resistance to yield transformation is mixed, at best. Nonresistance points in the direction of suffering, not as a destination or end-point, but as that which must be risked in the process of creating alternatives in human relations. In this way, nonresistance is not delimited by the parameters of violence but opens up new horizons of possibility. It has been suggested that Christian love, what I am calling "creative nonresistance," consists in giving unselfishly to those bent on harming you (Kaufman 1979, 65). Admittedly, this seems like a most unlikely stance unless one's imagination has been habitually trained to perceive situations differently than conventional wisdom would dictate.

Having set out these parameters for my terminology and having made some perhaps stark claims regarding how we approach issues of violence and nonresistance, let me offer a few other thoughts. The concern over terminology is appropriate but can come across overstated. For it is the case that we must use the language we have before us, living in the here and now, and working with the tools at hand. This is rather obvious but, happily, follows the model of Jesus, who incarnated a God who dwells among humanity, living in human time, and experiencing the depths of our realities. This Jesus can be seen constantly using the language of his tradition and milieu but often in different ways than might be expected. Language must not be taken as absolute and unchanging but rather as the frail means that it is. Some terms associated with weakness and low-esteem like "servant," Jesus filled with new meaning and dignity according to the purposes of God. Other terms, like "Messiah," carried their own weighty baggage of pomp and assumption that Jesus would subvert so as to redefine the terms in more life-giving forms. To follow in this path entails being careful about the language that is used and how it is used but not allowing the terminology itself to dictate all possibilities.

To summarize thus far, the understanding of creative nonresistance I am proposing assumes that it is a narrative-embedded practice, an enduring activity that is performed in many flexible forms by communities and persons-in-community in continuity with their narratively shaped imagination. Space does not permit me to spell all of this out in detail but merely to point to the centrality of the Jesus narrative as that which gives most concrete shape to the meaning of nonresistance. The point I am developing is that, rather than reciprocal resisting, creative nonresistance looks for alternative engagements with others, seeking relational connections that might transcend and deliver from the cycle of violence (Stassen and Gushee 2003). Turning to the language of theatrical improvisation can enlighten what this looks like.

IMPROVISATION AND NONRESISTANCE

The argument I have been making so far (in regard to nonresistance as active and imaginative) finds compelling display through the theatrical concept of improvisation. In what follows, I will provide an outline of several key facets of improvisation and show how these relate to the practice of nonresistance (Wells 2004). I call these improvisational facets disposition, position, and modes of action. These three facets provide a kind of flexible framework for improvisation and point in the direction of guidelines or "rules" that can foster the practice of nonresistance.

Disposition: Trust and Doing the Obvious

Improvisation does not depend on the originality or the wittiness of the actors. In fact, when actors attempt to be clever or original they often doom the improvisational action (Wells 2004, 66–70). Instead, what is key for improvisational actors is an atmosphere of trust and the willingness to do the obvious based on cues from each other. From this stance, the actors can relax and let the story unfold, enjoying its telling as much as the audience does. The actors must trust one another enough to do the obvious and not seek to be original. They must have a disposition to trust.

Likewise, nonresistance requires a disposition to trust. This may prove difficult when one has any number of suspicions about the trustworthiness of other (hostile) actors, but there are two things to keep in mind here. First, basic human relations remind us that, when one acts as if the other is trustworthy, the other will often respond in kind and reciprocate trust, thus building relationship. Not many years ago, I read a newspaper story that recounted how offering trust in the face of dubious circumstances changed the course of an initially hostile encounter. An armed burglar entered the back yard of a home. He found the family and some friends enjoying a bottle of wine while the grill was heating up and proceeded to "hold them up," demanding money at gunpoint. Unexpectedly, in a disposition of trust, the hosts offered him a glass of wine and asked him to join them in their little gathering. The burglar, undoubtedly taken aback by this departure from his intended script, put away his gun, accepted the offer of wine and stayed for a while in the circle of friends in the back yard. At some point, he decided it was time to depart, so he left the group and went his way. Thus, an offer of trust in the face of hostility led to a reciprocation of trusting relations and transformed a threatening situation and the lives of those involved.

Secondly, from a Christian perspective, one must also keep in mind God as an engaged actor, pre-eminently worthy of trust, regardless of how others may perform. The performance of nonresistance—particularly when thought of as a risky response to a perceived threat—is centrally a function of having one's imagination trained on the God who can be trusted. This was the disposition Jesus exhibited and serves as the model for Christian nonresistance (cf. Phil. 2:5–8; Heb. 12:2; 1 Pet. 2:21–23). Further, trusting in God while acting nonresistantly, also allows for the potential of initiating trust and seeing it potentially reciprocated in creative *mimesis* by the other.

Living in the pattern of creative nonresistance does not mean striving for originality. Rather, the habits of this way of life issue forth in nonresistant acts that involve doing the obvious. Granted, nonresistant actions may (in some sense) appear original to those whose imaginations are constrained by the cycle of revenge. However, to those who have cultivated habits of nonresistance nurtured by the practices of a community oriented to a God who can be trusted unreservedly, the performance of nonresistance will seem natural and obvious. This sense of what is obvious is cultivated in the habits and imagination formed in the Christian form of life we call "discipleship." To the group gathered in the back yard, it seemed obvious (or at least possible) to invite the intruder to join them for a glass of wine. And that is what they did, extending an invitation, showing trust and risking the outcome.

So, this first aspect of improvisation has to do with trusting, a disposition that can be recognized as differing markedly from the common envy and rivalry associated with mimetic desire. The modeling of trust also unleashes the potential for others to imitate it, enlarging space for enriching human interactions.

Position or Status

A second aspect of improvisation has to do with position or status. The dialogue of improvisation involves negotiating status by taking a low or high position. Everyday human interaction is a series of these very status negotiations, but something about which we are not always conscious. Other times, we are quite aware of seeking particular positions or status in particular relationships or situations.

In mimetic light, these status-negotiating strategies can be seen as often manipulative and generative of envy and rivalry. The perception (or imagining) of someone else's high status often becomes reason to adopt that person as a model and to acquire their desires and grasp after their being. But status negotiation need not be rivalistic and destructive. This is where nonresistance comes to bear. Those inhabiting the practice of nonresistance have the capacity to see status roles as just that—functional roles to be used creatively to bring about new relational possibilities. Nonresistance does not mean always adopting a low-status approach but, rather, entails discerning which approach or combination of approaches, might serve to introduce change into a destructive script.

To resist violently (in-kind) to an attack is to seek to obtain a higher status—to come out on top, as the saying goes. Yet to become passive in the face of some kind of attack appears to be accepting of a lower, submissive position that entails domination and defeat for the one in the lower position. Nonresistance seeks a kind of third (and flexible) way of responding and, therefore, is not fixated upon either higher or lower status positions.

Modes of Action

In modes of action, we come to a third facet of improvisation, to what I consider the heart of how the practice of nonresistance works itself out in this framework. Wells (2004) proposes that within this facet there are three modes of response for improvisational actors: blocking, accepting, and super-accepting. These modes represent three basic options in human relations.

Blocking. To block is to seek to stop the action, to resist where the story seems to be leading. We might see this exemplified in children playing where one points a finger at another and says "Bang! You're dead!" To which the other child responds (blockingly), "I am not!" Blocking is resistance to where a script appears to be leading. However, it rarely works in changing the direction of the action or in effecting real change in other actors. For our immediate purposes, we can equate the words "resist" and "block" and understand Jesus's counsel in Matthew 5 as: "Block not the evil doer." Jesus recognized that standard blocking (or resisting) would not lead to a transformative outcome. Thus, alternatives must be explored.

Accepting. Another ethical/improvisational option is to accept. This is opposite of blocking and the only seeming alternative, if blocking is forbidden or futile. Accepting offers from other actors is an important skill that provides a basis for positive interaction and keeping the story going. We might not always like what is being offered but, in learning to accept, we develop creative ways of working with others so as to produce something workable out of the bits and fragments of available material.

Of course, the pressing ethical issue that arises, when accepting is advocated as better than blocking, is what to do in the case of evil offers. In the face of violence, if we are not to block, are we then to passively accept and allow human violence to run free, doing whatever damage it may? This is a typical charge against nonresistance, in general, and leads to doubting its effectiveness altogether. Nonresistance, however, as a biblically-based practice, is not entirely about acceptance. It is sometimes this, but, more often, it partakes of the third mode of action: over-accepting or super-accepting.

Super-accepting. Super-accepting is the ability to take an offer, even a hostile or destructive offer, and provide it with a larger frame of reference, weaving it into a larger narrative so that what appeared terminal or life-threatening becomes a departure point for creative, life-giving action. Super-acceptance recognizes the frequent folly of blocking and the sometime folly of accepting. Then, using imagination cultivated in habits oriented toward a different way of seeing things, it seeks to reframe a hostile offer so as to give it new meaning in relation to another narrative. Thus, nonresistance often resembles super-accepting, the practice of taking the violence and rivalry offered by others and seeking to re-frame them as opportunities for fresh engagement in constructive human relations.

The examples that Jesus provided in the initial Matthew 5 quote above provide an excellent starting point for understanding this coalescence between super-accepting and creative nonresistance. As Walter Wink has helped us to understand, the scenarios that Jesus traces in regard to "turning the other cheek," "giving the cloak, too," and "going the extra mile," are all drawn from daily, peasant life in ancient Palestine (Wink 1992, 175–85). In the first scenario, the striking of the cheek was a slap of insult and humiliation to someone in a lower social status. It was done with the back of the right hand to the right cheek of one's inferiors: slaves, women, children, etc. To hit someone on the left cheek (again, with the right hand, since the left hand was for unclean tasks) would signal a relationship of more equality. The option of blocking/resisting an insulting blow by a superior would only lead to greater punishment for someone in an inferior position, like a slave. The option of accepting such a blow would be to heap humiliation upon humiliation, typically the only viable option available for survival in one's low-status position. The option of super-accepting such an insulting slap would be to "turn the other cheek" so as to communicate to the slapper: If you want to relate to me, then hit me like I am your equal. Such creative super-acceptance would provide a glimmer of possibility for a transformation of the human relationship in question.

In like manner, "giving the cloak, too" depicts a scenario in which the peasant farmer had become indebted. Jewish law allowed for debtors to give their cloak as collateral for a loan, but the lender could not keep the cloak overnight, since the cloak was also the peasant's blanket. To get around this obstacle, some lenders had taken to suing for the peasant's undergarment (the tunic) since the law did not forbid that. Again, Jesus counsels super-acceptance as creative nonresistance because, in giving up the cloak after losing one's tunic, the peasant would be standing naked in the court. In the ancient world, the shame of nakedness fell on the one who caused the nakedness more than on the one found naked. Thus, the lender would be presented with an awkward situation in which there would be a glimmer of opportunity for change, for repentance, and transformation of relationship.

Finally, the last scenario that Jesus alludes to is one in which Roman soldiers were restricted in how much forced labor they could extract from civilians during military marches. Typically, soldiers would force a peasant on the road to carry their heavy equipment pack. However, Roman law stated that this could only be done for one mile. Imagine the discomfort that a peasant would cause to a soldier, if the civilian super-accepted the carrying of the pack beyond the mile marker. The soldier could get in serious trouble with his commanding officer for this violation. And his status position as "superior-oppressor" would have been undermined by the low-status peasant, who had introduced uncertainty and opportunity for change in relations on the way to mile marker number two. These provocative acts of nonresistance, suggested by Jesus, illustrate the power of the option of super-acceptance for creating conditions and opportunities for transformed relationships.

But, again, for nonresistance to be practiced creatively requires actors to be steeped in a narrative capable of reframing even the most outrageous offers. The unfolding story of Jesus's death, as recorded in the Gospels, has to be one of the most destructive offers ever made. But the power in that story is that death was not the final word. The death and resurrection of Jesus paradigmatically represents the divine lifestyle of super-acceptance. Whereby, instead of violently blocking or fatalistically accepting death, Jesus super-accepted his death and found it incorporated as a part of the story of the life-giving God. In this sense, nonresistance can be seen as imitation of the super-accepting pattern of God in Jesus Christ. In the way of life called Christian discipleship, Christ-followers learn to reframe offers of rivalry and violence into a larger frame of reference that opens up possibilities for transformed human relationships. And it is in these various forms of the embodiment of nonresistance that it becomes possible for seemingly hostile others to creatively imitate and reciprocate the life-giving offers being made by the nonresistant such that structures of rivalry become transformed into structures of blessing.

IMPROVISING NONRESISTANCE AS CREATIVE *MIMESIS*

Nonresistance is a powerful mimetic engagement with others, because it does not enter into retaliatory rivalry with them but, rather, engages relationship on a different basis. It introduces creative *mimesis* into situations through the modes of improvisation. For instance, by adopting an unexpected status or reframing adversarial relations in new terms via super-acceptance, creativity is unleashed. While it can appear that such action is hugely original and creative, the real creativity being sought in nonresistance is the creation of cooperative rather than rivalrous relations. And this creativity is not so much about the performance of one actor but about the synergistic interaction that is possible between persons by introducing a larger frame of reference.

But must one wait for conflict and rivalry to blossom in order to practice nonresistance? Not necessarily. Nonresistance is best conceived of as a way of life (a manner of living and a habit of relating) that is not merely pragmatic or calculated technique. Indeed, it becomes something less than what I am talking about, when it is reduced to the status of technique. To employ nonresistance in the mode of technique means that one sees it as merely one option among many possible responses. The kind of creative nonresistance, I am suggesting, emerges as a seamless, whole way of life wherein the possibilities for nonresistant action in times of particular crisis are predicated upon the ongoing formation of character through habitual training. To say it more simply, nonresistance cannot be turned on or turned off in an instant, as if it is a light switch. To adopt it as a mode of action requires training, commitment, and learning to perceive people and situations in different light—in the light of biblical narrative. The biblical narrative is precisely what Jesus drew upon to formulate his counsel on nonresistance in the Sermon on the Mount. He was able to make the claims that he did and hold out the vision that he saw because his imagination was suffused with the in-breaking of the Reign of God. If the Reign of God was available to humans, then all kinds of new possibilities began to open up. The dominating frame of violence need not set the human agenda any longer, and the spiral of destructive violence can be overcome through the practice of creative nonresistance.

Like all modes of action and ways of life, nonresistance invites imitation by all who experience it. Admittedly, it is not a magic talisman or a guarantor of successful outcomes. Indeed, the greatest model of nonresistance that this essay has drawn upon met his cruel death on a cross, executed by the reigning imperial power and betrayed by his own people. Nonetheless, the power of nonresistance is seen in outcomes beyond immediate cause and effect calculations. Death, that most terminal of offers, was not the end of Jesus's story. Resurrection life was God's super-accepting response and it is this resurrection, finally, that makes the improvising of nonresistance possible and powerful for creative *mimesis*.

However, we need to be clear that nonresistance does not mean the exact same, wooden response in every circumstance. This is one reason that the realm of improvisation is illuminating in relation to understanding nonresistance. Nonresistance and improvisation are both open-ended and, though they rely upon habits of training and guidelines, when it comes to particular performances they will almost always be non-identical repetitions, though family resemblances will be discernable. Imagination is crucial to carry out both nonresistance and improvisation. Thus, there is implicit creativity in nonresistance, but such recognized creativity or originality is not an end in itself. It is employed with hopes that a true co-creation might take place between the human actors involved in any given drama, such that opportunities for life can be realized rather than seeing the action run toward death.

Improvisation and nonresistance are both activities that draw heavily upon trust to be judged successful. But any time trust is involved, it means that there is also risk, the potential that trust will not be reciprocated and the performance will fail. This element of trust applies on the human level but, in the practice of nonresistance I am arguing for, trust has much to do with a relationship with God as trustworthy participant. Drawing on the narrative framework of Scripture, practicing nonresistance comes to be judged by criteria different than immediate outcomes. What appears as failure and betrayal of trust has the potential to be super-accepted and, thereby, reframed into another life-giving departure point. The risk is still real and suffering, violence, and, even death are possible but they are never the final word in the Christian story. Nonresistance means not fighting against these things but accepting and super-accepting them as factors in a larger story in which an improvising, vulnerable God, a God of love and mercy, participates.

Adopting nonresistant ways of life will entail adopting habits that can shape character in appropriate ways. The practices of Christian discipleship provide a framework for developing nonresistant habits. Such habits include things like forgiving others, receiving others' forgiveness, serving neighbors in need, worshipping God, and seeking relational wholeness with others. Becoming steeped in these practices and schooled in these habits, we will find ourselves less inclined to destructive rivalries and the fratricidal striving after "being" so characteristic of much of human life. Instead, the new patterns of nonresistance can issue in invitations for creative and positive *mimesis* to take place. Or, said another way, the drama of improvisation can take the risks of super-accepting the seemingly hostile offers endemic to human relations. And, in helping to enlarge the framework by appeal to a greater script, the improvisers of nonresistance may well help other actors to find their way into creative, nonresistant life as well.

CONCLUSION

I have argued that the practice of improvisational nonresistance provides an avenue for creative *mimesis* as an alternative to the cycle of revenge that spawns from a failure of imagination. The imagination and action necessary for *mimesis* find positive and creative outworking in the disposition, positions, and modes of action necessary for improvisation. And the skills of improvisation, particularly super-accepting, correspond strongly to the practice of creative nonresistance by enabling actors to change the terms of engagement in the face of violent offers. This issues in a bid to recast seemingly negative human relations by reframing them in terms of the creative, life-giving story of God, thereby, enabling mimetic relations that need no longer be trapped in rivalry and destruction. The transforming of such relationships can give birth to creative mimesis, the flourishing of imagination and the actualization of reconciliation that is based in blessing rather than in scapegoats.

REFERENCES

Duhigg, C. 2012. *The Power of Habit: Why We Do What We Do in Life and Business*. New York: Random House.

Hershberger, G. F. 1944. *War, Peace, and Nonresistance. A Christian Peace Shelf Selection* (3rd ed.). Scottdale, Pa.: Herald Press.

Kaufman, G. D. 1979. *Nonresistance and Responsibility, and Other Mennonite Essays*. Institute of Mennonite Studies Series. Newton, Kan.: Faith and Life Press.

MacIntyre, A. 1984. *After Virtue: A Study in Moral Theory* (Vol. 2nd). Notre Dame: University of Notre Dame Press.

Margolis, H. 1993. *Paradigms & Barriers: How Habits of Mind Govern Scientific Beliefs*. Chicago: University of Chicago Press.

McClendon, J. W. 2000. *Ethics. Systematic Theology* (Rev. and enl.). Nashville: Abingdon Press.

Milbank, J. 1997. *The Word Made Strange: Theology, Language, Culture.* Oxford: Blackwell.

Stafford, W. 2003. *Every War has Two Losers: William Stafford on Peace and War* (1st ed.). Minneapolis, Minn: Milkweed Editions.

Stassen, G. H., & Gushee, D. P. 2003. *Kingdom Ethics: Following Jesus in Contemporary Context.* Downers Grove: InterVarsity Press.

Toews, P. 1986. "The Long Weekend or the Short Week: Mennonite Peace Theology, 1925–1944." *Mennonite Quarterly Review,* 60, 38–57.

Wells, S. 2004. *Improvisation: The Drama of Christian Ethics.* London: SPCK.

Wink, W. 1992. *Engaging the Powers: Discernment and Resistance in a World of Domination. The Powers.* Minneapolis: Fortress Press.

III

RETHINKING GIRARDIAN CONCEPTS

Chapter Nine

René Girard and the Symbolism of Religious Sacrifice

Eugene Webb

René Girard is well known for his critique of the imagery of sacrifice. As he reads religious symbolism and the rituals that present and enact it, these constitute ways of simultaneously commemorating and masking the real collective violence and victimization that gave rise to human society. His *Violence and the Sacred* argued forcefully for the universality of this fundamental cultural force: "All religious rituals spring from the surrogate victim, and all the great institutions of mankind, both secular and religious, spring from ritual. . . . It could hardly be otherwise, for the working basis of human thought, the process of 'symbolization,' is rooted in the surrogate victim" (1977, 306). As a counterforce to the general pattern of religion, Girard went on to argue in later studies that the prophetic tradition in Israel, culminating in the story of Jesus of Nazareth, gradually disclosed these secrets "hidden since the foundation of the world" (Matt. 13:35, the epigraph of Girard's *Things Hidden Since the Foundation of the World*). This revelation, however, was more than its recipients could bear, and they soon buried it again under a "sacrificial reading" that interpreted Jesus' death not as the unmasking and exploding of the victimizing mechanism but as itself the ultimate satisfaction (and confirmation) of its exigency. In *Things Hidden*, Girard identifies the Epistle to the Hebrews, in particular, as the fountainhead of this sacrificial misreading of Christianity.

In this chapter, from the point of view of the comparative study of religious symbolism, I would like to explore the theme of sacrifice in the Epistle to the Hebrews and to suggest some ways in which Girard's analysis of that theme might benefit from the broader perspective that the history of religions can provide. In particular, I will try to show that the epistle's symbolism (and the experience of spiritual transformation it represents) may be understood more deeply and more favorably than Girard may have realized, through a comparison with Hinduism and Buddhism. I realize, of course, that this comparison may in itself look problematic from a Girardian point of view, since Girard has spoken critically of those religions, too. Near the end of *Things Hidden*, Girard makes the important observation that no merely intellectual process of thinking can win victory over mimetic desire and the urge to victimize; rather that requires a kind of "conversion experience," which "always retains the form of the great religious experiences"; then he adds that "[t]his kind of experience can be found in the great oriental religions. But there the aim is to allow the individual to escape completely from the world and its cycles of violence by an absolute renunciation of all worldly concerns, a kind of living death" (1987, 400). Hinduism and Buddhism are most probably the "great oriental religions" he had in mind. I hope to show, however, that it may be possible to discover in these something greater, and also more congenial to Girard's own thought, than the cultivation of "a kind of living death." I will argue, that is, that both the Epistle to the Hebrews and these Asian traditions may share more with, and offer more to, Girard than he has realized.[1]

For the sake of brevity, and because I have already done so at length elsewhere, I will not try to present a full exposition of Girard's theory of mimetic desire, mimetic rivalry, and the sacrificial crisis with its trajectory toward identifying, and sacrificing, some victim as a scapegoat. (A reader wanting a full exposition of those theories might look at Webb 1993, 87–119 and 175–193.) I will simply summarize a few points pertinent to my initial focus on Girard's critique of sacrifice and of Hebrews.

In Girard's interpretation, the secret "hidden since the foundation of the world" referred to in Matt. 13:35 (and Luke 11:50–51)—and alluded to, of course, in his book's title—was the founding role played in all human enterprises by the *mécanisme victimaire* (victimizing mechanism) of scapegoating, which is itself an outgrowth of mimetic desire. Mimetic desire is a deeply rooted tendency in human beings to imitate the desires of others. This eventually leads to mimetic rivalry and mimetic conflict—not only because to desire what another desires, in a world of finite resources, will inevitably lead to conflict over the same objects of desire, but also because even in a world of unlimited fungibility it would still be precisely our rival's object we would desire and not even a perfect equivalent would satisfy us. The victimizing mechanism is both a further development in this process and also, in most societies that have developed historically, the solution to the crises it generates. To explain the logic of Girard's idea very simply:

- Since mimetic desire is a fundamental trait of human beings, people will inevitably fall into mimetic rivalries and these will spread like wildfire, especially where no system of traditional restraints and boundaries has been developed or where such a system has broken down.

- When these circumstances (lack of an effective system of restraints) prevail, the mimetic conflict will multiply until it threatens to destroy the entire society in a paroxysm of violence.

- At this point, the victimizing mechanism will be triggered by the same mechanism that started the trouble to begin with, namely mimesis. Some individual (perhaps someone with a limp, or with noticeable racial differences, or with non-conformist ideas) may attract the attention of several others, who will gang up on him, and others will also be drawn to join them by the mimesis of their violence.

- Those drawn by mimesis into such shared hostility to a common victim will experience among themselves, in place of their earlier rivalry, a new unanimity and fellowship.

- But the peace that proceeds from this is inherently fragile: new rivalries may develop and threaten the group—until once again they seek a new common scapegoat.

- Or, as the ancient Israelites did, they may forswear intra-group violence and restrain themselves from mimetic rivalry by adherence to a Law deemed transcendent. And they may reinforce their loyalty to that system of restraint by instituting ritualized commemorations of the original collective victimization, i.e., ritual sacrifices, to remind them of its originating, life-giving effects while protecting themselves from having actually to repeat it in all its dangerous reality.

- But such a system of the control of violence is far from perfectly effective, especially because it masks the reality of the whole complex of mimetic desire, rivalry, and victimization. New crises therefore continue to arise and call for new victims.

This, says Girard, is the reality behind all the imagery of sacrifice in primitive religions and in the Hebrew Bible, except where the prophets gradually moved toward the realization that the God of Israel did not want "the blood of bulls, or of lambs, or of he-goats" (Isaiah 1:12). (Cf. the important theological study of Girard's thought by Schwager 1987, 88.) In the imagery of the gospels, the Satan that Jesus resisted, and finally conquered, is a personification of the victimizing mechanism and the symbol of the insidious force with which it sneaks up on us from behind and insinuates itself into all our endeavors.[2] The principal act of Jesus and of the gospel writers was their exposing of this hidden force. This, for Girard, is the truth that makes us free—or that *can* do so, if we relive in the conversion of our own hearts, the realization the gospels try to share with us.

The power of the victimizing mechanism to resist being exposed and disarmed is exemplified with supreme irony in the development Girard calls "historical Christianity"—the religion that took shape around a sacrificial reading of what had been the anti-sacrificial revelation in the gospels. (See Girard 1987, 225–227.) In this distorted tradition, Jesus came to be interpreted as having cooperated voluntarily with his victimizers in order to offer himself in his crucifixion as a sacrificial victim for the purpose of appeasing an angry God. This conception, says Girard in *Things Hidden*,

> was most completely formulated by the medieval theologians, and it amounted to the statement that the Father himself insisted upon the sacrifice. Efforts to explain this sacrificial pact only result in absurdities: God feels the need to revenge his honour, which has been tainted by the sins of humanity, and so on. Not only does God require a new victim, but he requires the victim who is most precious and most dear to him, his very son. (1987, 182)

Girard identifies the Epistle to the Hebrews as the chief New Testament source of this misreading: "The author of the Epistle to the Hebrews interprets Christ's death on the basis of the sacrifices under the Old Law. The new bond with God, like the old one, is inaugurated in blood. But as it is perfect, it is no longer the blood of animals[,] which is 'powerless to remove sins,' but the blood of Christ" (1987, 228). The author, Girard says, "may well say that Christ's sacrifice is, by contrast with the others, unique, perfect, and definitive. But in reality he can see only continuity with previous sacrifices, if he takes no account of the scapegoat mechanism." Hebrews, one might say, is to Girard what the Epistle of James was to Luther: the one book of the New Testament that really missed the point.

I think Girard is correct that much traditional reading of Hebrews has fostered a way of reading Christian symbols that has obscured the very important truth Girard has himself done such admirable work in bringing to light. I hope, then, that it will not seem merely retrograde, if I suggest that there may be more to this text, and to the theme of sacrifice in Christianity and in other religions, than Girard's immensely valuable, but rather narrowly focused, anti-sacrificial critique has yet managed to take into account.

Girard's interpretation of Hebrews attributes to it two key ideas that might be analyzed logically as:

- The true, fully effective sacrifice = Jesus' crucifixion.
- The function of the crucifixion = appeasement of God.

I will try to show, however, that on a more careful reading Hebrews can be seen to be saying something quite different:

- The true, fully effective sacrifice is not Jesus' crucifixion but something else that I will try to clarify below (although his willingness to face death on the cross was an expression and sign of that something else).

- The crucifixion did have a redemptive function, but that function was not sacrificial in the sense Girard focuses on and had nothing to do with appeasing God.

Girard is correct that Hebrews is not especially concerned with exposing the scapegoat mechanism in the manner Girard himself does, but neither is it concerned with affirming or hiding it; in fact, its explicit critique of the sacrifices of the Temple system as ineffective constitute an explicit repudiation of the idea that the slaying of victims can be in any way salvific.

Let me begin my own analysis by looking at a few passages from Hebrews that I think an interpretation of the theme of sacrifice needs to consider. I will not attempt an interpretation of Hebrews as a whole, and I will ignore the final 13th chapter entirely, since it does not appear to have been a part of the original document, which was something more like a sermon or "homiletical midrash" than a letter, according to George Wesley Buchanan in the Anchor Bible edition, *To the Hebrews* (1972, 246).

Buchanan's commentary on Hebrews also presupposes, by the way, the sort of sacrificial reading Girard criticizes, as do the editors of the *New Oxford Annotated Bible* (Revised Standard Version). This way of reading Hebrews has become pervasively conventional, and Girard is quite right to criticize it. My own reading presupposes Girard's critique of sacrifice; far from wanting to oppose or correct it, I wish to complement it with a recovery of what I think is a deeper, genuinely "anti-sacrificial" (in Girard's sense) reading intended by the epistle's author—or at least implied in what his epistle says. I hope also, through some comparison of this early[3] Christian text with Hindu and Buddhist themes, to show that there can be further meanings in religious images of sacrifice than only those that mask and act out the *mécanisme victimaire.*

I use purposely the phrases "there *can* be further meanings" and "at least implied," because there is no way to prove with certainty what some ancient author meant or "had in mind," especially one so lost in anonymity as the author of Hebrews. But a good way to approach the question of what this text might have meant for its author, or at least to an intelligent Jewish-Christian reader of the mid-first century, is to separate out and set aside meanings that would seem incoherent or that are based on later ways of thinking that have lost touch with the original milieu of meaning.

One example of what has to be set aside as an anachronistic reading is the now conventional notion of what it means to speak of Jesus as "son of God" or "Christ": that he was some kind of divine figure. For first-century Jews like the author of this text and his readers,[4] references to someone as "son of God" or as "the anointed one" (the precise meaning of "messiah" or "Christ") would not, in themselves, have involved the idea that the person referred to was divine. The term "son of God" had a long Biblical history. Its most important use was to refer to the calling of Israel as a people, as when God tells Moses to say to Pharaoh, "Thus says the Lord, Israel is my first-born son, and I say to you, 'Let my son go that he may serve me'" (Exodus 4:22), or when God says in Hosea 11:1: "Out of Egypt I called my son." (Passages from the Bible will be quoted in the Revised Standard Version translation.) To say in the first-century Jewish milieu that Jesus was "son of God" was to say that he truly fulfilled the calling of Israel to live in sonship to God. When Hebrews speaks of him as a "pioneer . . . leading many sons to glory" (2:10),[5] it is clear that the focus is on the idea of the first true Israelite leading others to fulfill the same calling, i.e., the calling of Israel to divine sonship.

"Anointing" was an image used to refer to the idea that God called and empowered some individual for an important work. In so far as it might refer to one called and empowered to fulfill the calling of Israel as a whole, to heed God's will in a filial manner, and, to help others to fulfill it, the titles "son of God" and "messiah" or "christ" could even overlap in meaning. In first-century Palestine, "anointed" was most commonly used to refer to someone called to drive out the Romans and restore an Israelite state, like the one attributed to David and Solomon. But, like "son of God," the symbolism of being "anointed" had a long history of more diverse use behind it. In the Hebrew Bible, it was used to refer to a wide range of figures, mainly kings—including Saul, David, Zerubbabel, and even Cyrus of Persia (Isaiah 45:1)—and important priests, such as Aaron (Exodus 29:7). We know it was used in the first century B.C.E. community that left the Dead Sea scrolls to refer to expected leaders of both the kingly and the priestly type, spoken of in the scrolls as messiahs "of Israel" and "of Aaron," respectively. In most New Testament documents, "anointed" was used mainly to identify Jesus as a kingly figure fulfilling the prophecy that someday Yahweh would rule in Zion, but in Hebrews it is Jesus' role as high priest that is emphasized, a role that is underscored by associating him with Melchizedek, whose superior priesthood even Abraham recognized and deferred to (Hebrews 7:4).

Although he says Jesus "reflects the glory of God and bears the very stamp of his nature" (Hebrews 1:3; literally: "being the radiance of his glory and the stamp [representation, mark] of his substantial reality" [*charaktér tés hypostaseos autou*]) the author of the epistle emphasizes that he was fully human: "Since therefore the children share in flesh and blood, he himself likewise partook of the same nature [literally: "shared in what is theirs" (*meteschen ton auton*)], that through death he might destroy him who has the power of death, that is, the devil, and deliver all those who through fear of death were subject to lifelong bondage" (2:14–15). Only a human being could die a human death, but also, only a human being "who in every respect has been tempted as we are, yet without sin" (4:15) could conquer, as the representative of all humanity, the power of sin and death.

This is the central idea of Hebrews: that Jesus, fulfilling the calling of Israel to divine sonship, raised humanity into that sonship, in his own person, by conquering sin and breaking the power of Satan over all human beings. Satan's power was, in Biblical tradition, the power to tempt and lead astray. But it was also the power of death. Hebrews is quite explicit in linking the tendency of humans to sin (i.e., to fail to fulfill their calling to sonship) to their fear of death. They have been enslaved by the fear of death, and Jesus' death has delivered them from that slavery so that now they are free to respond to the calling to sonship as he did. [6]

How did Jesus free them from these tendencies? How did he break the power of Satan over them, once and for all? This is the crux of the text. Hebrews does not spell out the answer to this obvious question, probably because the author expected the answer would be obvious to his readers. But it is no longer so obvious as it once was. To a Western Christian reader today, as to Girard himself, there is one obvious but misleading answer: Jesus did it by dying on the cross as a propitiatory sacrifice, i.e., by offering his "blood" to appease the God who inflicts death as a punishment. The reason this seems so obvious now is that Anselm of Canterbury answered the question in this way in the eleventh century in his *Cur Deus Homo?* (Why Did God Become Man?).[7] But would this have been obvious (or even credible) to the epistle's first-century audience, a millennium before Anselm and three centuries before Augustine developed the ideas of Original Sin and inherited guilt that Anselm could interpret as an offense against God's honor? This propitiatory-sacrificial reading is clearly incoherent with numerous elements of the text. For example, the one who is described in Hebrews 2:14–15 as having "the power of death" is not an offended God but "the devil" (*ton diabolon*). And God is described repeatedly in the text as not wanting the kinds of sacrifice that involved killing victims. Girard says in the quotation above from *Things Hidden* (1987, 182), that "[e]fforts to explain this sacrificial pact only result in absurdities." Might it not be possible that this Western medieval reading of Hebrews would have seemed just as absurd to its author and first-century audience as it rightly does to Girard?

To an early Christian there would have been a different obvious way to interpret the idea that Jesus' death freed human beings from enslavement by the fear of death, a way that is clearly attested as current in the first-century Christian milieu: that Jesus' death was the prelude to his resurrection. To someone who believed in Jesus' resurrection, it would have shown, in the most dramatic and convincing way, that God's victory over death was no longer merely a dream or hope for the future but had actually become, in the life of one concrete human being, a reality. And as such, it was also a token of future resurrection for others. Paul alludes to this idea again and again in his own epistles, so it should not be surprising to find it in Hebrews as well.

That Hebrews does not represent Jesus as seeking crucifixion in order to make his own death a propitiatory sacrifice should be evident from 5:7: "In the days of his flesh, Jesus offered up prayers and supplications with loud cries and tears, to him who was able to save him from death, and he was heard for his godly fear [literally, devoutness (*eulabeias*)]." This is hardly coherent with the idea of a conscious pact with God to die as a propitiation, but it is perfectly coherent with the idea that, in fulfillment of his prayers, he was delivered by God from death and that belief in this could be interpreted as also delivering the epistle's author and audience from enslavement by the fear of their own deaths.

But what then *was* Jesus' sacrifice, if it was not his death on the cross? For Hebrews *does* represent Jesus as offering a sacrifice: "he has appeared once for all at the end of the age to put away sin by the sacrifice of himself" (9:26). And this new covenant with God is even said to be inaugurated in blood: "But when Christ appeared as a high priest of the good things that have come, then through the greater and more perfect tent . . . he entered once for all into the Holy Place, taking not the blood of goats and calves but his own blood, thus securing an eternal redemption" (9:11–12).

Is this physical blood, like that of the goats and calves, or metaphorical blood? If it is physical blood, then certainly Girard is right to say that the author of the epistle "can see only continuity with previous sacrifices." But if Jesus' blood here is a metaphor for some other sort of sacrifice, then the picture is quite different. Which kind of meaning does the text suggest, and what sort of sacrifice?

It will help to clarify the question further, if we consider where the sacrifice is supposed to take place. It is certainly not in the Temple in Jerusalem, like the Levitical sacrifices, but is it on Golgotha? Several passages in Hebrews make clear that its locus is not there, either. The passage just quoted from 9:11–12 says that passing "through the greater and more perfect tent" he "entered once for all into the Holy Place. . . ." Where might that be?

The "tent" is clearly a reference to the structure of the Jerusalem Temple, which was spoken of as divided into two "tents": "the Holy" and "the Holy of Holies." (See Buchanan 1972, 140–142.) The "Holy Place" of 9:12 would correspond to the part of the Temple called "the Holy," where the sacrificial offerings were prepared for the altar which stood in front of that tent. The Levitical priests who prepared offerings there, Hebrews tells us, "serve a copy and shadow of the heavenly sanctuary" (8:5). Jesus, on the other hand, offered his "blood" in the true, heavenly "Holy Place," and having done that, has now passed in his resurrection life into the true Holy of Holies, "into the inner shrine behind the curtain" (6:19), "not into a sanctuary made with hands, a copy of the true one, but into heaven itself, now to appear in the presence of God on our behalf" (9:24).

So Jesus' sacrifice took place not in a physical place but a metaphorical place. The "blood" he offered in this metaphorical place, was perforce metaphorical blood. But what "heavenly" (spiritual or psychological) reality might that metaphor represent?

To get an initial sense of what Jesus' sacrifice might have involved, let us consider further the way the text contrasts it with those of the Temple tradition: "When Christ came into the world, he said 'Sacrifices and offerings thou hast not desired . . . in burnt offerings and sin offerings thou hast taken no pleasure'. Then I said, 'Lo, I have come to do thy will, O God', as it is written of me in the roll of the book" (10:5; the quotation within the quotation is Psalm 40:6–8). Hebrews then goes on to say that God, ". . . abolishes the first in order to establish the second. And by that will we have been sanctified through the offering of the body of Jesus Christ once for all" (10:9–10) "The first" clearly refers to the traditional animal sacrifices; "the second," just as clearly, is "to do thy will."

These passages make it abundantly clear that the "blood" of Jesus' sacrifice, like the Holy Place where it is offered, is a metaphor: the sacrifices that involved physical blood have been abolished; the new, fully adequate sacrifice ("the offering of the body of Jesus Christ once for all") is the perfect fulfillment of God's will. What, then, might that mean, and why might "blood" be an appropriate metaphor for it? The text does not spell it out, but again the answer was probably sufficiently evident to the original author and his intended audience not to require that. Perhaps the author was referring to what was probably already Jesus' well-known dictum about the two great commandments cited, for example, in Matthew 22:37–39: "You shall love the Lord your God with all your heart and with all your soul, and with all your mind," and "You shall love your neighbor as yourself."[8] This certainly describes the calling of Israel, the calling to sonship to God, that was fulfilled, from the early Christian point of view, for the first time in a fully adequate way by Jesus.

As fine a formulation of God's will as these two commandments are, however, they remain by themselves a bit abstract, and it may not be immediately clear just how fulfilling them could appropriately be imaged as a kind of sacrifice, even if one demanding only metaphorical blood. To get a better sense of how the imagery of sacrifice operates here it may help to turn to a consideration of some parallel ideas and images in "the great oriental religions" to which we saw Girard refer.

In this connection, it is noteworthy that Bede Griffiths, a Benedictine monk who spent more than two decades in India practicing a life of contemplative prayer and writing about it in a way that draws on both Christian and Hindu symbols, opens his book, *The Cosmic Revelation: The Hindu Way to God*, with an allusion to the Epistle to the Hebrews:

> We are going to reflect on what I call the Vedic Revelation; and I use the word
> revelation intentionally because I think we have to recognize today that God
> has revealed Himself in other ways than through the Bible. God has been
> speaking to humanity, 'in many and various ways,' as it says in the Letter to
> the Hebrews, from the beginning of time. (1983, 7)

Griffiths develops further this idea of a "cosmic revelation" beyond the confines of Israel and Christianity by invoking the same imagery of Melchizedek as does Hebrews: ". . . the Messiah is said to be 'a priest forever of the order of Melchizedek'—not the order of Aaron, of the Jewish priesthood, but of Melchizedek, this 'pagan' priesthood. . . . That is why, when I enter a Hindu temple, I feel that I am entering a holy place . . ." (1983, 30).

Griffiths' point of departure for understanding "the Hindu way to God" is the Vedic fire sacrifice. He explains its symbolism as representing a circulation of gifts: gifts from the divine to humans and the return of those gifts to the divine. The fire symbolizes the transcendent source of life and spirit: ". . . the whole Vedic religion is centered on the fire sacrifice. The god of fire is *Agni*, and worship was paid to the sun as the source of fire. But the sun is the source of light to the mind as well as to the body" (p. 22). The symbolism of fire in this rite compresses a large range of meanings: the fire is vitality; it is consciousness; it is energy; it is not only the divine energy descending into incarnate life, but it is also the energy of the liturgical offering, and as such it is simultaneously worldly and divine, immanent and transcendent:

> Agni, as we have said, is the god of fire. The fire is centred in the sun. . . . The
> fire comes down from heaven and is buried in the earth and when you take
> twigs or a flint and rub them together, the fire, Agni, leaps up. This is the god
> of fire who has come down from heaven to consume the sacrifice. But this fire
> is also a spiritual fire. . . . Agni, the fire, is the All-knowing One. It is a
> physical fire, yet they call it the fire of knowledge, of wisdom, and he is the
> All-knowing One. He is the mediator between God and man. He takes the
> sacrifice, consumes the sacrifice, and carries it back to heaven, and you ask
> him to direct your sacrifice. (1983, 23)

What sacrifice in this interpretation symbolizes is the recognition that all life comes from a transcendent source and ultimately belongs to that transcendent source. The failure to: recognize that concretely; relinquish one's claim to possession; and to thankfully allow all gifts to belong to the one source is the essence of sin.

> In the Vedas it is very clear that everything comes down from above, from
> heaven. We receive everything from above and everything must be returned. A
> sacrifice is the return to God, and sin is the opposite, the appropriation of
> something to one's self. . . . I am not my own possession; I am a gift—my

being is a gift from God. I have got to return that gift. Sacrifice is this return. (1983, 49)

Likening the Vedic sacrifice to the Christian eucharist, Griffiths says:

> So it reads: "Who in all his work, sees Brahman, he in truth goes to Brahman; Brahman is his worship, Brahman is his offering, offered by Brahman, in the fire of Brahman." Now that really is a Eucharistic action. In the Eucharist God is worshipped. You offer what you are doing to God. At the same time it is God Himself who makes the offering and who is being offered. God is both priest and victim. And it is offered in the fire of God. . . . So every action should be a Eucharistic action, that is the goal, to be united with Christ in His offering, so that one's total life is offered to God. The offering is God Himself, He is offering Himself in us, in the fire of His own love, that is by the power of His own grace, resulting in a totally transformed human life. That is to make one's whole life a sacrifice. (1983, 99)

To get a more concrete sense of the particular sacrifice and transformation indicated in Hebrews, it may help to consider some of the symbols of the Vedic religion and then compare them with those of Buddhism. There are many deities in Hindu religion, but in the tradition of the Vedas, Upanishads, and Bhagavad Gita, they are all symbols and embodiments of what Griffiths terms "the One Being," which the Rig-Veda says "the wise called by many names" (1983, 18). In Hinduism, there are three major symbols that encompass all of the divine in its various forms: Brahman, Atman, and Purusha. Brahman is the One Being, considered as the radically transcendent source of all that is, but also as that which can become immanent in the forms of Atman and Purusha. Atman is usually translated as "self." It is the spirit of the One Being, present within consciousness and animating consciousness. Purusha is usually translated as "person." To the extent that the presence of Brahman becomes embodied as true Atman, one might say, the result is a true person or "*purusha.*" Whether one says Atman is the center or animating principle of one person or of many persons will depend on the angle from which one considers it; as Griffiths puts it, "Each of us is a little Purusha, and there is one great Purusha who embraces us all" (1983, 74).

The symbolism of the possible unity or multiplicity of Purusha also connects with the symbolism of sacrifice: ". . . creation comes from the sacrifice of Purusha. At the beginning of time Purusha is sacrificed and his limbs are scattered all over the world. In the ritual sacrifice Purusha is gathered together and becomes one again" (1983, 75).

"Aha!" one might hear a strict Girardian say, "Here is an obvious instance of the imagery of sacrifice masking a primordial collective murder." Well, that may be true—but it does not imply that there can be no more meaning to the symbol than that alone, as I hope will be clear from the comparison Griffiths proceeds to with some similar Christian symbols:

> This has a profound relationship to the conception of Adam and the Son of Man. As St. Augustine said, "Adam at his fall, was scattered over all the earth." Man was once one, one with nature, one with himself, one with God. And then when he fell he was scattered and divided. The atonement means that God comes into this divided universe and gathers those scattered pieces together and in his sacrifice reunites mankind. He brings all these persons together in his Person. Another wonderful text of St. Augustine says, "In the end there will be *unus Christus amans seipsum*—One Christ, loving himself in all his members." (1983, 75)

The Hindu symbolism is complicated by the fact that the symbols Brahman, Atman, and Purusha can have levels of meaning. For example, there is "the Atman in man which is the Spirit of God in man; but Atman can also be the 'spirit of man'" (1983, 105). Similarly, Purusha can refer to the "Supreme Person," but each one of us can also be said to be "a purusha." (The ambiguity is similar to that with which St. Paul uses the word "Christ" to refer sometimes to Jesus as an individual and sometimes to what sounds more like a cosmic person embracing all of the redeemed humans who live "in Christ.")

It is this ambiguity in the Indian tradition—the idea of Purusha and Atman as also human and individual—that seems to have given rise to the core Buddhist teaching of *anatman*, or "no-self." In Buddhism (very much as in Girard and Oughourlian, as will be explained below), the human self is not an enduring, substantial reality but an accidental configuration of memory and desire. If, from the Buddhist point of view, one believes that one has an individual, substantial *atman* or "self," then that belief is an illusion that enslaves one to illusory desires—desires that seek to preserve and augment that illusory, insubstantial self. The whole purpose of Buddhism is to assist the individual held in this bondage to discover, through meditative practice leading to inward realization and transformation, the truth of *anatman*: that there is no such "self." Although Buddhists, having dropped the theistic language of Hindu religion, do not use the symbolism of sacrifice, the Buddhist radical relinquishing of the individual *atman* through realization of *anatman* could also be called a kind of sacrifice of the self.

There have been patterns of thought in Indian tradition (especially in Jain) that have emphasized the idea of *atman* as individual in a way to which the Buddhist critique is appropriate, but the two traditions are not inherently in conflict over this point; rather, the Vedic tradition, like the Buddhist tradition, can also be interpreted as advocating a transcendence of what in the West we might now call the individual ego. This can be seen from a Vedic verse Griffiths quotes: "When by the real nature of the Atman he sees as by a lamp the real nature of Brahman, then having known the one eternal God, who is beyond all natures, he is freed from bondage" (1983, 82). Griffiths says that the insight this verse expresses is "not merely a speculative theory but a fact of experience." The same is certainly true for the Buddhist realization of *anatman*. Both refer to psychological reality that must be known experientially.

If the symbols of Hinduism and Buddhism regarding self-transcendence are expressions of potentially universal human experience, then they may also serve as analogies for the experience the author of Hebrews refers to as Jesus' sacrifice. Sin, the force within us that causes us to center our life in the false self of our [acquisitive] mimetic desires, rather than in the love of God and of our neighbors, is the ultimate obstacle to the sonship to which Israel understood itself to be called. In psychological terms, sin may be described as equivalent to what Buddhism calls the "craving" that binds us to the false *atman* or illusory self. It was by his conquest of sin and the shift of the center of his being from the false self to its true center in God that Jesus fulfilled, for Israel and for mankind, God's call to sonship. In psychological terms, this shift of the center of personhood may be considered equivalent to putting to death, or "sacrificing," the false self.

It is appropriate, in this connection, to mention also a pertinent Girardian symbol, the *moi-du-désir* or "desire-self" that Jean-Michel Oughourlian explores extensively in his *The Puppet of Desire*. This, like the Buddhist idea of the *atman*, is an accidental configuration of memory and desire—of memories, that is, that collect around and give an illusory sense of permanence to constantly shifting patterns of desire. As Oughourlian explains his specifically psychological development of Girardian theory:

> I have always thought that what one customarily calls the *I* or *self* in psychology is an unstable, constantly changing, and ultimately evanescent structure. I think . . . that only *desire* brings this self into existence. Because desire is the only psychological motion, it alone, it seems to me, is capable of producing the self and breathing life into it. The first hypothesis that I would like to formulate in this regard is this: *desire gives rise to the self and, by its movement, animates it.* The second hypothesis . . . is that *desire is mimetic.* This postulate, which was advanced by René Girard as early as 1961, seems to me capable of serving as the foundation for a new, pure psychology—that is, one unencumbered by any sort of biologism. . . . These two hypotheses make it necessary to revise earlier psychologies, since these are psychologies either of the subject or of the object. They demand that one renounce the mythical claim to a self that would be a permanent structure in a monadic subject. (1993, 11–12)

The idea of the *atman* that the Buddhist doctrine of *anatman* opposes is precisely such a "mythical claim to a self that would be a permanent structure in a monadic subject." The very valuable Girardian addition to the Buddhist insight is the idea of the force of unconscious mimesis and the role of the mediator of desire as a model for the patterns of desire that spring up and grip us.

Perhaps, it may be helpful, if I explain this idea a little further. Initially, Girard developed his concept of mimetic desire and the role of the mediator of desire in a study of the novel, *Mensonge romantique et vérité Romanesque* (*Deceit, Desire, and The Novel*), the 1961 work that Oughourlian refers to. It has frequently been observed by literary scholars that a (if not *the*) principal focus of the novel as a genre has been the conflict between appearance and reality, both in society and in the life of the individual. What Girard found in this study of the novel from Cervantes to Dostoyevsky and Proust was that the great novelists examined showed that most of what appear to us to be "our" desires are really imitated from what we perceive to be the desires of others in our milieu. More particularly, we seek out models of desire (what Girard calls "mediators") in order to learn what is worth desiring.

Why do we do this? The reality Girard thinks the great novelists discovered and disclose to us is that each person who comes into the world begins with a feeling of radical lack or emptiness, of weakness and vulnerability. Beginning as helpless infants, utterly dependent on powerful others, we feel acutely our lack of power. We also have a strong inner drive to seek to become like those powerful others so as to acquire their power for ourselves. We think of the mediator as free from the lack of power we feel. When we notice that the mediator has desires, we assume that these must be for things the mediator perceives as having the potential to augment his or her "being" (i.e., power). That is why we want them for ourselves: we want to "be." This is why Girard also calls mimetic desire "metaphysical desire": mimetic desire is only superficially a desire to have what the other has or wants; on a deeper level, it is a desire to possess not the other's objects but his "being," to *be* what he is and wield his power.

All of this normally takes place below the threshold of our awareness—though it is not exactly unconscious either. Rather, our consciousness is virtually "possessed" by our fascination with the mediator, the prestigious other we strive to imitate.[9] The great novelists, however, raise this into awareness and give us the opportunity to reflect on it and, ideally, to break free from it. This is the "novelistic truth" Girard's title refers to, and the "romantic lying" is our tendency in our ordinary lives to avoid noticing that truth.

"A basic contention of this essay," Girard said at the beginning of that work, "is that the great writers apprehend intuitively and concretely, through the medium of their art, if not formally, the system in which they were first imprisoned together with their contemporaries" (1965, 3). Something else they can be said to have apprehended intuitively and concretely, to put the matter in Buddhist language, is that life in that self-generated prison is characterized by *dukkha*, the Buddhist term often translated as "suffering" but more accurately translated as "unsatisfactoriness." Mimetic desire is unsatisfactory for some very fundamental reasons:

- As desire, it is really illusory. That is, we do not really want what we think we want or for the reasons we think we want it. We want it because we think (mistakenly) that the reason our mediator of desire wants it is that he actually knows what will enhance his being and make it invulnerable. (This is the "romantic lie.")
- Even if we could acquire the object of desire, it would not bring us satisfaction, because the "being," the power and invulnerability, we really long for and of which the object is only a symbol, will always remain out of reach. We are finite and can never achieve the divine super-sufficiency or plenitude of being that we attribute to our mediators. (This is the "novelistic truth.")

To win freedom from self-imprisonment in this system of illusion requires that one both understand its real structure and be willing to relinquish its illusory comforts—in particular, the comforting belief that if only one could make just a little more progress in acquiring the mediator's objects or becoming what the mediator is, or if only one could defeat the rival (which is really only a negative version of the mediator), or kill the scapegoat (another negative version of the mediator), then one would enjoy the plenitude of being one longs for.

The core of the Girardian idea, as of the Buddhist, is that the desire-self, though a tenaciously powerful force in one's psychic life, is ultimately insubstantial and that seeing through it can lead to liberation from the power of the illusions it generates. Jesus' breaking free, in this way, from the whole complex of mimetic desire and its conflictual and victimizing mechanisms is the heart of Girard's own christology. Although the word might surprise a strict Girardian, Jesus' seeing through and letting go of the desire-self could also appropriately be described as a kind of sacrifice. The excursus into "the great oriental religions," then, has not been a mere detour. One might even say that Girard is closer to the deepest insights of these religions than he seems to have noticed.

If the imagery of sacrifice in Hebrews is interpreted in the light of these considerations, the sacrifice talked about there shows two aspects: (1) it refers to something that might be imaged as the "bloody" sacrifice or putting to death of what Buddhism calls the *atman* and Girardian psychology the desire-self; and (2) it refers to the consecration of the true person, the "body" of 10:5, to a life that finds its true center in God: "Sacrifices and offerings thou hast not desired, but a body hast thou prepared for me." The image of Jesus' "own blood" (9:12), that is, represents what dies in the sacrifice; the image of his "body" represents the person who is consecrated. It also refers to the continuing life of that consecrated person, which Hebrews speaks of in 8:2 as that of "a minister in the sanctuary and the true tent, which is set up not by man but by the Lord." Jesus' willingness to undergo crucifixion rather than abandon his prophetic calling was an expression and sign of his complete consecration of his life to God's service. His sacrifice in its full meaning was not his crucifixion alone but his self-emptying (cf. the concept of *kenosis* developed by Delicata in chapter 5) throughout his life: both his sacrifice of all false selfhood, of the desire-self, and his self-giving to God. The "offering of the body of Jesus Christ once for all" (10:10) was the total consecration of his living personhood, of his whole life, to heeding and fulfilling God's calling of Israel to sonship. This was a ministry which constituted Jesus' life in this world before his crucifixion and continues still, from the point of view of the author of Hebrews, in his resurrection life in the heavenly sanctuary.

Of course, if one were to approach this idea from the point of view of the sort of mythifying later christology that sometimes interpreted Jesus as a preexistent divine individual who took on a human body and walked around in it omnipotent and omniscient but without a really human mind and psychology, then it would be inconceivable that Jesus could actually experience the pull of a desire-self, the gravitational force of a false center.[10] After all, he would just be God, and how could the infinite source of all that is experience temptation or be deceived by a false self-understanding? From this point of view, Jesus' fidelity would simply be an expression of his divine nature, not the kind of costly, even painful, self-conquest and self-sacrifice to which the image of shedding blood would be appropriate. With no desire-self, there would be nothing to sacrifice or blood to shed except the physical blood of his physical body on the cross.

If one were to view the whole picture in this way, it would seem natural and virtually inevitable to interpret Jesus' sacrifice in the conventional way that Girard rightly finds absurd. But this is not the vision expressed in Hebrews, with its emphasis that Jesus was truly human and was "in every respect . . . tempted as we are, yet without sin" (4:15). Nor is it what eventually came to be defined in the councils of the fourth and fifth centuries as orthodoxy: the Council of Chalcedon echoed the epistle's phrasing when it described the second hypostasis as "complete in manhood" and "in every way like us, except for sin."[11]

This leaves only the question of what light this analysis of Jesus' sacrifice in "the Holy Place" might throw on what it could mean to speak of him as also a manifestation of God, one who "reflects the glory of God and bears the very stamp of his nature" (Hebrews 1:3). Any modern New Testament scholar would object to the anachronism of reading back into this very early document the doctrine of the Trinity, which was not formulated until the fourth century. But it is not anachronistic to recognize that the seeds that developed into the Trinitarian idea are in the New Testament, already in references to Jesus as in some manner manifesting divine presence and to the Holy Spirit as indwelling both him and those who faithfully follow him. The symbol "son of God," as was mentioned earlier, carried no connotations of divinity for the Jews of the first century and earlier, but "spirit of God" did. How might the idea of the Holy Spirit relate to the picture developed so far of Jesus' sacrifice as a self-emptying and self-dedication? In particular, how might it relate to the psychological and spiritual structure of the person, the true self, who is left after the death of the desire-self?

In Buddhism, too, the question arises as to what remains when the illusory *atman* is seen through and transcended. The answer there is *Bodhi*, enlightenment. One who has actually realized *anatman*, "no self," does not cease to exist but becomes an enlightened one, a Buddha. Sometimes Buddhists also speak of what is left in the state of enlightenment as Buddha-mind or Buddha-nature, and they speak of the compassion or love for all living things that characterizes the Bodhisattva life or nirvana. Contrary to conventional western misunderstandings, it is not the case that in nirvana there is simply nothing left. The word *nirvana* or *nibbana* means literally to be "blown out" or to be "cooled by blowing." What is cooled is the fire of craving, and what is extinguished is the desire-self, the *atman*—but that was never real anyway. What is left is *Bodhi*, Buddha-nature, Buddha-mind. Buddhism is not therefore a nihilism or annihilationism; it does not cultivate "a kind of living death." One who becomes enlightened is freed from the power of karma (cf. Menon's chapter 13) and the wheel of rebirth, symbols that refer to the power of the illusory *atman*, the desire-self, to endlessly regenerate itself in the psychology of the person who succumbs to its lure. Freedom from that cycle is true life, the freedom to live with a clear mind and a compassionate heart.

Buddhism is explicit about this new life or animating principle that would be left after the realization of *anatman*. The Epistle to the Hebrews may spell it out less explicitly, but it does seem, in its symbolism of the Holy Spirit, to have a parallel to Buddha-mind or Buddha-nature. In many places in the New Testament, the Holy Spirit is spoken of as indwelling Jesus and guiding and impelling him in his work, and also as giving new life to his followers in fulfillment of the prophecy that the Law that was formerly written on tablets of stone would one day be written on the hearts of God's people (Jeremiah 31:33). In Hebrews, the Holy Spirit is mentioned explicitly only once, but in that one verse it is indicated as the animating principle of Jesus' sacrifice and of the new life that sacrifice opens to his followers: ". . . how much more shall the blood of Christ, who through the eternal Spirit offered himself without blemish to God, purify your conscience . . ." (9:14).

This may be the only reference in Hebrews to the Holy Spirit, but it has implications that gradually unfold as the author goes on to describe the consequences of Jesus' sacrifice for his readers: He exhorts them to hold fast in faith to the new life Jesus' sacrifice has won for them by freeing them from slavery to the fear of death and by renewing their consciences. "Now faith is the assurance of things hoped for, the conviction of things not seen" (11:1). Freedom from the fear of death comes from their faith in Jesus' resurrection and the hope for their own to come. The renewal of their consciences comes from the breaking of that fear's power to make them cling to the life of the illusory desire-self that must be given up. This means they are called to undergo their own metaphorical, but very real, deaths by imitating him in his sacrifice: "In your struggle against sin you have not yet resisted to the point of shedding your blood" (12:4). In the last line of what Buchanan thinks is the original "homiletical midrash," we can even hear a distant echo of the image of the Vedic Agni as the fire that comes down from heaven, is buried in the earth, and leaps up again to consume the sacrifice: "Therefore let us be grateful for receiving a kingdom that cannot be shaken, and thus let us offer to God acceptable worship, with reverence and awe; for our God is a consuming fire" (12:28–29).

REFERENCES

Anselm of Canterbury. 1962. *Basic Writings: Proslogium; Monologium; Gaunilon's on Behalf of the Fool; Cur Deus Homo*. Translated by S. N. Deane. La Salle, Ill: Open Court Pub. Co.
Becker, Ernest. 1973. *The Denial of Death*. New York: The Free Press.
Buchoul, Samuel. 2013. "The Nonself of Girard." *Contagion: Journal of Violence, Mimesis, and Culture*, 20: 101–116.
Buchanan, George Wesley. 1972. *To the Hebrews*. Translation, Comment, and Conclusions by George Wesley Buchanan. Garden City, NY: Doubleday.
Davies, J. H. 1967. *A Letter to the Hebrews: Commentary by J. H. Davies*. Cambridge: Cambridge University Press.
Girard, René. 1965. *Deceit, Desire, and the Novel: Self and Other in Literary Structure*. Translated by Yvonne Freccero. Baltimore: Johns Hopkins University Press. Translation of *Mensonge romantique et vérité Romanesque* (1961).
———. 1977. *Violence and the Sacred*. Trans. Patrick Gregory. Baltimore: John Hopkins University Press. Translation of *La Violence et le sacré* (1972).
———. 1986. *The Scapegoat*. Trans. Yvonne Freccero . Baltimore and London: Johns Hopkins University Press. Translation of *Le bouc émissaire* (1982).
———. 1987. *Things Hidden since the Foundation of the World*. With Jean-Michel Oughourlian and Guy Lefort. Translated by Stephen Bann and Michael Metteer. Stanford: Stanford University Press. Translation of *Des Choses cachées depuis la fondation du monde* (1978).
———. 2011. *Sacrifice*. East Lansing : Michigan State University Press, 2011.
Griffiths, Bede. 1983. *The Cosmic Revelation: The Hindu Way to God*. Springfield, Ill.: Templegate Publishers.
Oughourlian, Jean-Michel. 1993. *The Puppet of Desire: The Psychology of Hysteria, Possession, and Hypnosis*. Translated with an introduction by Eugene Webb. Stanford: Stanford University Press. Translation of *Un Mime nommé désir* (1982).

Schwager, Raymund, S. J. 1987. *Must There Be Scapegoats?: Violence and Redemption in the Bible*. Translated by Maria L. Assad. San Francisco: Harper and Row, 1987. Translation of *Brauchen Wir Einen Sündenbock?* (1978).
Webb, Eugene. 1993. *The Self Between: From Freud to the New Social Psychology of France*. Seattle and London: University of Washington Press.

NOTES

1. Girard has recently spoken more favorably of these Asian religions because he has come to see "an anti-sacrificial and even nonsacrificial inspiration in the most advanced parts of the Vedic tradition, those which announce the great Indian mysticism of the Upanishads, as well as those which, leaving India, ultimately give rise to Buddhism," *Sacrifice* (2011), 87–88. One point of the present chapter, however, will be that the imagery of religious sacrifice can also be used to refer to the sort of radical self-transcendence that Buddhism uses the term *anatman* ("no-self") to speak of. Cf. Buchoul (2013) on the topic of *anatman* (Sanskrit) or *anatta* (Pali) in relation to the thought of Girard.

2. Cf. Girard (1986, 187): "But the kingdom of Satan is not one among others. The Gospels state explicitly that Satan is the principle of every kingdom."

3. Buchanan (1972, 257), thinks Hebrews, because it refers to Temple sacrifices that are still going on, dates from before the destruction of the Temple in 70 CE. This would make it, along with the epistles of Paul, one of the earliest documents in the New Testament. J.H. Davies (1967, 8) agrees with Buchanan on this early date of the document.

4. If this text really does date from the mid-first century, it would be anachronistic to interpret the author and his audience as "Christians" (as opposed to "Jews") in the sense that word later took on. There is every reason to suppose that it would have been a very rare Christian of the first century who might have thought that Christianity was a new religion separate from the Jewish tradition; for all of its earliest adherents, the Christian movement was understood as a development within the Jewish tradition, not something radically different from it.

5. Material in brackets will be my own comments and occasional more literal translations. A more literal translation of *archegon* than "pioneer" might be something like "original leader." Arndt and Gingrich's *Greek-English Lexicon of the New Testament* spells it out as "one who begins someth[ing] as first in a series and thus supplies the impetus."

6. For a psychological discussion of the idea of enslavement by the fear of death, see Becker (1973).

7. Written ca. 1094–1098. Anselm is clearly the major figure among "the medieval theologians" Girard refers to in the quote above from *Things Hidden*, 182. The reason I speak of this as obvious to specifically Western Christians is that Anselm was a Westerner working out of a tradition deriving from Augustine of Hippo, who developed the idea of Original Sin, which for Anselm is the offense the propitiatory sacrifice was needed to compensate for. The Eastern Christian tradition did not read either of these Latin writers, had no doctrine of Original Sin as heritable guilt (although it did believe humanity had "fallen," in the sense of going astray from the path God intended for it), and had an entirely different idea of atonement; for the Christian East, atonement (at-one-ment) was effected by the Incarnation as such, which in and of itself united humanity and divinity, rather than by propitiation of divine wrath.

8. This interpretation of the essence of Torah was not an invention of Jesus but was already familiar to his Jewish audience, as can be seen from the fact that in the parallel passage in Luke 10:25–28 it is stated not by Jesus but by the "lawyer" whom Jesus challenges to tell him what in his view the principal commandments are. For the traditions behind this summation, see, for example, Deut. 6:5 and Lev. 19:18.

9. The psychology of possession is a major theme of Oughourlian's *Puppet of Desire*. He considers it, in fact, the key to understanding the other phenomena he analyzes: hysteria and hypnosis.

10. I am referring here not only to Docetism (which held that Jesus's humanity was only an appearance) but specifically to the christology of Apollinaris of Laodicea (d. 390) who held

that in Jesus the rational soul or mind (*nous*) was replaced by the divine Logos. This position was condemned as heretical by the Council of Constantinople (381 CE) and specifically ruled out by the Council of Chalcedon (451 CE) when it declared that Jesus was "of a rational soul and a body" (*ek psychés logikés et somatos*). The still fairly common picture of Jesus as omniscient divine person seems to be a mixture of several of the positions the Council of Chalcedon explicitly rejected in its definition of the hypostatic union: docetism, monophysitism (the position that in Jesus the human nature was extinguished at the moment of conception, leaving only the divine nature), and apollinarianism.

  11. "*teleion . . . en anthropotéti*" and "*kata panta homoion hémin choris hamartias.*"

Chapter Ten

Psychology, Hermeneutic Philosophy, and Girardian Thought

Toward a Creative Mimesis

Frank C. Richardson and Kathryn M. Frost

René Girard (1977; 1978) has pursued a rich dialogue with Freudian thought that both uncovers insights in Freud's writings consonant with mimetic theory and affords a number of telling critiques of the psychoanalytic enterprise. Oughourlian (1991) has analyzed hysteria, possession, and hypnosis, showing that Girard's mimetic theory may be required to make full sense of such extraordinary phenomena. Also, a handful of articles over the last few decades have sought to blend Girardian ideas with insights from one or another psychological theory or theorist, usually from the broad psychoanalytic tradition (e.g., Reineke 2007). But much of the burgeoning field of academic and professional psychology in the twentieth and twenty-first centuries has either explicitly rejected or largely ignored Freud and psychoanalysis as it goes about its business. One cannot help wondering what might be said about this vast, diverse plethora of theories and findings from the standpoint of mimetic theory, even though very little has been written on the topic. Are there insights buried in this mass of purported data that might confirm or complement mimetic theory? Or does much of it consist of "wordy elaborations of the obvious" that at their best only "recapture the insights of ordinary life in their manifestly reductive explanatory languages" (Taylor 1985a, 1).

Things get interesting when philosophically equipped or critically minded social scientists take up this last question. Many of them doubt the lasting significance of many or most of the findings of contemporary social science, including psychology, however plentiful they may have been. Part of the problem, they feel, is just the reductionism and effacement of human relationships that Girard refers to the following: "The greatest weakness in modern thought consists in the false identification that is constantly made between scientific thought and the effacement of all human relationships, their reduction to the simple objectiveity of things" (1978, 124). Another issue for many is that theory and the interpretation of research findings in these disciplines seem to be suffused with unacknowledged modern ideologies—masked by pretensions to "value-neutrality"—that celebrate the free-standing individual and his or her unfettered autonomy and prerogatives. This last critique closely parallels Girard's analysis of the "romantic lie" that exaggerates and valorizes the originality and spontaneity of the modern subject and obscures the "interdividual" nature of human life.

In the view of many commentators, one of the most remarkable features of the burgeoning field of psychology in the last half of the 20th century is a striking failure to realize its defining aspiration to achieve a genuine science of human behavior on the model of the successful natural sciences. Many hundreds of disparate little islands of theory and research are pursued independently, with no apparent prospect of their being linked up in any coherent, overall picture of human activity, and no agreement whatsoever about what sorts of methods or approach to inquiry, from positivism to postmodernism, would remedy this situation. Indeed, the philosopher David Hoy remarks: "Unlike a natural scientist's explanation, which relies on the pragmatic criterion of predictive success, a social scientist's evaluation of the data in terms of a commitment to a social theory would be more like taking a political stand" (1986, 124). This confusing situation may begin to clear up as one consults the work of philosophers, social theorists, and cultural critics (Bellah, Madsen, Sullivan, Swidler, and Tipton 1985; Bernstein 1976; Bishop 2007; Fancher 1995; Habermas 1973; Gadamer 1989; Richardson, Fowers, and Guignon 1999; Taylor, 1985b, to mention just a few) who have tried to identify a few key "hidden assumptions" (Slife and Williams 1995) and concealed values that in their view motivate and shape much of this would-be social "science."

Richardson (2005) suggests three broad kinds of such assumptions and ideals. One is a confusing and paradoxical ideal of sheer objectivity or value-neutrality (Thou shalt be value neutral!) that serves to mask the influence of the cultural and moral values of the investigators and their community. Another is a narrow instrumentalism that collapses the cultural and moral dimensions of human action into merely technical and instrumental considerations (Habermas, 1973; 1991). A third is a one-sided individualism, often termed "liberal individualism" (Sandel 1996; Sullivan 1986), a moral outlook and ethical program that many critics from de Tocqueville (1969/1835) to the present have felt affords us invaluable liberties but at the price of much debilitating alienation and social fragmentation. We would argue that this individualistic outlook (in our view, what Hoy's "political stand" turns out to involve) shapes the findings and supplies much of the cultural force of the modern psychology enterprise, in spite of or perhaps just because of its all too convenient blind spots (Bishop 2007).

In this chapter, we suggest that hermeneutic philosophy (Bishop 2007; Gadamer 1989; Taylor 1985b; Richardson, Fowers, and Guignon 1999) can make the best sense of these deep confusions about social inquiry and its moral underpinnings can point the way to a relational ontology (Slife, 2004) of the human realm and human agency. We find that this hermeneutic view is congruent with Girardian theory in a number of ways. However, we argue, the hermeneutic account needs to be deepened and extended by mimetic theory, especially as regards to human violence and conflict. In turn, hermeneutic thought, we believe, can assist in clearing up some apparent problems with mimetic theory's account of human agency. Also, it underscores the need (some Girardian thinkers have stressed) to develop the idea of a "creative" mimesis, a fundamental human appetite or orientation toward reconciliation and love.

EARLY CRITIQUES

Erich Fromm: The Ambiguity of Modern Freedom. A number of years ago, Erich Fromm (1965/1941, 53) complained that much psychology and social thought—the situation is not much changed today—uncritically perpetuate and rationalize what he terms the fatally "ambiguous" modern notion of freedom. In his view, we tend to make "freedom an unbearable burden" because our understanding of it creates a "lag between 'freedom from' and 'freedom to.'" As a result, we unthinkingly exalt "freedom from" most meaningful social ties, thus creating a devastating "lack of possibilities for the positive realization of freedom and individuality."[1]

In this situation, Fromm felt that most of us were afflicted with some degree of what he termed a quasi-pathological "marketing orientation." According to Fromm (1975/47, 75 ff.), the "modern market is no longer a meeting place," imbued with the shared standards of a community, but "a mechanism characterized by abstract and impersonal demand. "The value of commodities is determined by impersonal market demand and often quite shallow or transient desires. This pervasive modern market has a profound effect on social character and emotional well-being over time. In the economic sphere, spilling over into social life, a wide-spread "personality market" develops in which both professionals and laborers greatly depend for their material survival and success on a capricious kind of personal acceptance rather than on lasting social ties or ethical qualities. More and more one experiences oneself as a "commodity." More precisely, one experiences oneself simultaneously as the *seller* and the *commodity* to be sold. Increasingly, one's "self-esteem depends on conditions beyond [one's] control." In this exchange, "success" makes one valuable, otherwise one is "worthless." The result is "shaky self-esteem," a constant "need of confirmation by others," and feelings of "helplessness, insecurity, and inferiority." Also, of course, one comes to experience others as commodities in a similar fashion. Thus, equality no longer means the basic right of humans "to be considered as ends in themselves and not as mere means" but signifies "interchangeability," the very negation of individuality.

Fromm notes that in this kind of world, relationships among people become "superficial" because it is not really they themselves but themselves, viewed as interchangeable commodities that are related. Many hope that they can find a cure for this superficiality and alienation in the "depth and intensity of individual love." Unfortunately, he points out, "love for one person and love for one's neighbor are indivisible; in any given culture, love relationships are only a more intense expression of the relatedness to [others] prevalent in that culture" (1975/47, 80). In the marketing orientation, one's self-esteem is never secure. One cannot ever get enough acceptance from others. As a result, lasting, satisfying ties of love and friendship become enormously difficult. The consequences include significant degrees of "depersonalization, emptiness, and meaninglessness" (p. 82). Thus, Fromm astutely anticipates more contemporary discussions of our "culture of narcissism" (Cushman 1990; Lasch 1978).

Fromm's answer to this predicament is a refurbished humanism, a doctrine of sturdy "self-realization." First of all, "man, indeed, is the measure of all things" (1975/47, 23). Individuals should courageously embrace their freedom to be themselves and reject both "hedonism," which is really an escape from facing the challenge, and any sort of authoritarian solution that derives moral authority from "something *transcending* man" (1975/47, 24). Neat trick if you can pull it off. But Fromm's solution only seems to reinscribe the situation of the morally isolated and confused individual who is guided mainly by aspirations to be "free from" assorted injustices and impediments, leading to the very problems Fromm documents!

As if he were aware of this lack, Fromm proposes another more positive solution, a would-be kind of "freedom to," namely our joining together in "active solidarity" as "free and independent individuals" in a program of "productive work contributing to the general welfare" (1975/47, 53). But it is unclear how this could effectively counter a one-sided individualism, tending toward emptiness. What shared ends should we cultivate *after* breaking the bonds of paternalism and oppression? What sorts of convictions plausibly could stem the tide of the "marketing orientation" in this brave new world, where it is not clear what there would be left to do besides just enjoy ourselves and go shopping (Richardson et al. 1999, 64–66)?

It seems to us that much of Fromm's characterization of the interpersonal tensions, inauthenticity, and mutual manipulation in our kind of society could be folded into a Girardian account of human dynamics. Fromm exposes some of the shortcomings of a confused individualism but fails to envision a genuinely relational or *interdividual* alternative. At bottom, he continues sharply to dichotomize (1) a sturdy, individually anchored kind of "self-esteem" and (2) fickle, irresolute, or slavish dependence on the approval or direction of others. Mimetic theory considerably extends and deepens his critique by revealing the underlying dynamic or double bind, to which Fromm is largely oblivious, whereby others are necessarily models for our desires and yet often become implacable rivals in trying to satisfy them, the conflict being intensified by modern ideologies that put the highest premium on "autonomy." Fromm can't explain the great extent to which we would not join a club that would have us for members. In the Girardian view, in Webb's crisp formulation of it, one can meet the "universal need to find models to imitate . . . either well or poorly." One does well "when one acknowledges this need in a more or less conscious manner, chooses appropriate models, and accepts in an appropriate spirit the relationship of modeling or *apprentissage*." One does poorly "when one drifts unwittingly toward models," typically others who also deny their need for the same, "who become sources of conflict and objects of rivalry" (1993, 89–90).

Cushman and the "Empty Self." The writings of Philip Cushman (1990; 1995) update and improve on Fromm's critique. Cushman argues that our society and much psychological theory defines the mature or ideal individual as a "bounded, masterful self" that is expected to "function in a highly autonomous, isolated way" and "to be self-soothing, self-loving, and self-sufficient" (1990, 604 ff.). Unfortunately, Cushman thinks, there is evidence that this inflated, would-be autonomous self almost inevitably collapses into an "empty self," whose characteristics of fragility, sense of emptiness, and proneness to fluctuation between feelings of worthlessness and grandiosity are often said to be the hallmarks of neurotic psychopathology in our day (Kohut 1977).

Cushman defines emptiness as, "in part, an absence of communal forms and beliefs" which leaves individuals quite vulnerable to influence from cultural forms such as advertising and psychology, both professional and "pop," which emanate authority and certainty (1990, 604). In other words, the field tends to perpetuate many problems in living in the cures that are offered for them. Academic and professional psychology may reinforce a one-sided "preoccupation with the inner self" which "causes the social world to be devalued or ignored except to the degree that it mirrors and thus becomes appropriated by the self." As a result, the social and cultural milieu "loses its impact as a material force, and social problems lose their relation to political action" (1990, 605).

This powerful analysis of psychology's predicament seems illuminating but only of limited help in effectively re-envisioning psychology as a less individualistic and more ethically substantive enterprise. Cushman is more aware than Fromm of the extent to which both our problems and remedies are "social artifacts," thoroughly contextualized in history and culture, and he calls for a more "situated psychology" that will speak to our way of life, not just entertain therapeutic and political nostrums. But he casts about not altogether convincingly for a way to do this. In one place, Cushman tries out a "social constructionist" approach with the suggestion, "Perhaps then we could develop social practices that could construct a terrain in which the obsessive preoccupations of a hypertrophied self, such as self-acceptance, would not show up" (1991, 543). But this tends to reduce the ethical struggle to social tinkering and doesn't explain why these new practices would have any authority or staying power for us. If we are right, it is striking how mimetic entanglement and rivalry are a blind spot for Fromm, Cushman, and most social theory and research. Cushman evidences a real feel for traditional communal and religious ideals that have lost force in our time, but he doesn't speak to the issue of how we might recapture some version of them in a post-traditional world.

A number of other critical psychologists, as well, have spoken wistfully about lost traditional ideals. For example, Fancher argues forcefully that all modern therapy systems, from psychoanalysis to behavior therapy, hide behind a facade of objective theory, a value system, a view of the good life, or a "culture." These "cultures of healing," whatever their virtues, have many questionable features. He writes,

> There is no inherent reason why internal dynamics, rather than one's place in society, must be the principal source of health or illness. For most of history, in most civilized cultures, the kind of internal fulfillment that psychoanalysis values has been suspect, and fidelity to 'one's station and its duties' has generally been a higher value. (1995, 124–125)

That older vision of the good life has been replaced by one centered on self-preoccupation and self-management or self-realization.[2] The trouble is, these "theories" rarely defend their guiding values on moral or social grounds, despite their having weighty personal and social consequences. Rather, Fancher contends, they are justified deceptively by presenting their bias concerning the best or most decent kind of life as simply "what 'health' is," as a kind of objective, quasi-scientific fact that can't be morally challenged. Does anyone want to oppose health?

Similarly, Jerome Frank, the distinguished interpreter of psychology as a cultural phenomenon, observes that as "institutions of American society, all psychotherapies . . . share a value system that accords primacy to individual self-fulfillment," including "maximum self-awareness, unlimited access to one's own feelings, increased autonomy and creativity" (1978, 6–7). The individual is seen as "the center of his moral universe, and concern for others is believed [automatically] to follow from his own self-realization" (*ibid.*) These ideals may be admirable to an extent, but in the end they seem morally quite ambiguous. Thus, Frank notes, the implicit value system of modern psychotherapy "can easily become a source of misery in itself" because of its unrealistic expectations for personal happiness and the burden of resentment it imposes when inevitable disappointments occur. In his opinion, the literature of psychotherapy gives little attention to such traditional, possibly worthwhile values or virtues as "the redemptive power of suffering, acceptance of one's lot in life, adherence to tradition, self-restraint and moderation" (*ibid.*)

Unfortunately, these thoughtful critiques also illustrate how difficult it is to get around the impasse they identify. They afford few clues concerning how we might envision a cultural universe in which it might make sense to practice "fidelity to one's station and duties" or synthesize, let us say, self-restraint or finding meaning in suffering with the aggressive modern pursuit of health, success, and individual self-actualization. The heavily anti-authoritarian bent of modern ideologies makes us uncomfortable in advocating anything more than a "negative liberty," even if we sense its shortcomings. These critics and many others remain torn between nostalgia and a sense of emptiness. Below, we suggest some ways we think mimetic theory can help break this impasse.

DISGUISED IDEOLOGY

We get to the bottom of many of modern psychology's problems and gain some real leverage for change, we feel, with the notion that "disguised ideology" (Bernstein 1976; Bishop 2007; Richardson & Fowers 1998) appears to animate much social theory and research at its core. A plausible account of this situation, it seems to us, is provided by philosophers of social science with a hermeneutic or interpretive bent (Bishop 2007; Gadamer, 1989; Root 1993; Taylor 1989). In their view, psychology and the social sciences generally rely excessively on a kind of *objectifying* stance toward human experience and social life, one that ignores or abstracts away from most of the meanings of things, events, and relationships among them that show up in ordinary human experience, concerned with our shifting passions, values, and aims. Obviously, this objectifying approach has proved its mettle in the natural sciences, making possible the formulation of causal laws and models of the natural world that have universal applicability and immense pragmatic utility. But it may greatly distort our understanding of lived experience and cultural life.

Taylor (1995, 7) analyzes how this kind of objectifying stance toward the world, which decontextualizes the knowing subject from the ongoing flow of practical life and human relationships, fits hand in glove with the widespread modern picture of the self as disengaged, disembodied, and atomistic or "punctual." This self is "distinguished . . . from [the] natural and social worlds, so that [its] identity is no longer to be defined in terms of what lies outside... in these worlds." When mature, this modern self is ready to freely and rationally treat both itself and the outside world instrumentally, in order to advance some conception of individual and social well-being.

Put this way, the objectifying outlook adopted by so much social science inquiry begins to look like a central strand of the way of life in modern culture, one often thought to purchase valuable freedoms at the price of much alienation. Indeed, Taylor (1995, 7) suggests that the modern notion of a "punctual self" confronting a natural and social world to which it has no essential ties is as much a *moral* as a scientific ideal. It "connects with . . . central moral and spiritual ideas of the modern age," especially the modern ideal of "freedom as self-autonomy . . . to be self-responsible, to rely on one's [own] judgment, to find one's purpose in oneself."

It now seems possible to spell out much of the content of this moral outlook, centered on a disengaged, "punctual self." First formulated by Kant, this approach centers on *formal* principles of *procedural* justice or fairness (Neal 1990; Rawls 1971). Such principles "constitute a fair framework within which individuals and groups can choose their own values and ends, consistent with a similar liberty for others" (Sandel 1996, 11). The purpose of this scheme is to avoid designating any particular ends in living or ways of life as superior, while still assuring respect for individuals and their choices. In the mental health arena, we adopt this approach by talking about more or less "effective" therapeutic means to reaching ends that we often label "health" or "well-being," as if these ends were purely given by nature or chosen by clients without any outside influence. We maintain *both* our neutrality about others' choices *and* our dedication to the their welfare by obscuring how much "health" is always, in part, defined by cultural and moral norms and by obscuring how much we authoritatively influence clients in adopting or reworking the meanings they live by (Christopher 1999; Fancher 1995; Richardson and Zeddies 1999).

Liberal individualism enshrines and promotes values of moral equality and respect for human rights and dignity that are precious and indispensable to most of us. It represents a sincere effort to affirm freedom without dissolving responsibility or to eliminate dogmatism without abandoning our moral duties to others. But it may be one sided and ultimately inadequate, reflecting modern culture's revulsion against what it sees as tyrannical abuses of power and their rationalization in earlier times, while remaining bewildered concerning what might best be put in their place. This moral outlook is embroiled in the paradox of advocating a thoroughgoing *neutrality* toward all values as a way of *promoting* certain basic values of liberty, tolerance, and human rights. However, if we can't reason together about the worth of ends, then we are prevented from rationally defending liberal individualism's own vision of a way of life characterized by dignity and respect (Sullivan 1986, 39), a way of life that it plainly takes as morally superior or good *in itself*. In practice, this may make individualism's insistent characterization of human action and motivation (as deeply self-interested) a self-fulfilling prophecy. It may erode our capacity for devotion, not just to more traditional virtues of self-restraint and concern for the common good, but to the best modern ideals of freedom and justice, as well. Thus, Michael Sandel suggests that the individualistic public philosophy by which we live "cannot secure the liberty it promises, because it cannot inspire the sense of community and civic engagement that liberty requires" (1996, 6).

Bellah et al. identify two main forms of individualism, "utilitarian individualism," portraying human action as mainly instrumental in nature and "expressive individualism," stemming from Romanticism, that views human life in terms of the fullest possible expression of an individual's "unique core of feeling and intuition" (1985, 334). There is, of course, a close parallel between expressive individualism and what Girard (1965) famously calls the "romantic lie." A third, quite prevalent form of individualism is one we might term "existential" (Richardson et al., 1999). Born of twentieth century existentialism's protest against scientific materialism, determinism, and social conformism, it debunks even the idea of such a given, unique, personal core of personality and celebrates a radically free and unconstrained *choice* of one's own values and meanings, which then somehow mysteriously acquire personal authority and meaning-giving power for the individual. All three show up in various forms and mixtures at the base of diverse psychological theories and therapies. They are, we would contend, the lifeblood of those theories and therapies. Their different emphases notwithstanding, in all three varieties of individualism, one's purposes and meanings have been arrived at in an inward, self-dependent, sometimes termed "authentic" way, their implementation in everyday life takes place in a largely *instrumental* manner, promoting mainly individual protection and enhancement rather than qualities of character, co-operation, or relationship that are deemed worthwhile for their own sake. Fleshing out the picture of liberal individualism in this way might be of assistance to Girardian thinkers in clarifying the "romantic lie" and how theory in the human sciences and elsewhere obscures mimetic desire and entanglement.

OVERCOMING INDIVIDUALISM

Gaining a grip on key hidden assumptions of the 20th century psychology enterprise puts theory and research in the field in a position to participate in what Jonathan Sacks, the Chief Rabbi of Great Britain and a leading public intellectual, identifies as a profound shift in the "governing presuppositions of modern thought." In Sacks's (2002) view, we are discovering that the "concept of the isolated or atomic self, the 'I' with which thought and action supposedly began," the "lonely self," assured of "nothing [but] its own existence" that is the "hero of almost all the great Enlightenment drama's," is a "fiction, or at least an abstraction." Early breakthroughs came with Wittgenstein's demonstration that "the idea of a 'private language' is incoherent" and that we "learn language only by communicating, by engaging, that is to say, in relationship with others," and with Mead's beginning to show "that we develop a sense of personal identity only through close and continuous conversation with 'significant others'" (2002, 150–151.).

According to Sacks (2002), this change goes hand in glove with another epic shift in Western thought away from the view of mature human relationships as fundamentally "contractual" to one in which the most basic human ties are what he terms "covenantal," giving a "richer sense of the importance of culture and community . . . in sustaining social life." The question arises as to what happens when "the sense of sin and the deeply internalized constraints of a religious age . . . begin to weaken" (2002, 143). The answer typically comes in the form of an assumption that the only workable alternative to conformity and stagnation are fundamentally competitive schemes of human interaction. In these arrangements, altruism is limited to giving individuals the right to participate in the game and it is felt that indelible self-interest and even enmity between people need not be destructive but often will generate outcomes beneficial to all. "Private vice would become public virtue when society was so organized as to turn passions into interests. Thus was economics born" (2002, 144).

Sacks (2002) describes how on many fronts a new paradigm is emerging, according to which the "most fundamental forms of association" tend to be "open-ended and enduring." They consist in bonds "not of interest or advantage, but belonging," and operate on the basis of an "unconscious choreography of mutuality" in which individuals commonly help one another spontaneously, "without calculations of relative advantage." He argues that we are beginning to discern how the unique benefits of competition not only are compatible with such mutuality but cannot be sustained without the kind of "trust" it affords (2002, 151). Sacks summarizes the results of Fukuyama's (1995) extensive and influential study of the role of trust in economic and social affairs with the statement that "markets depend on virtues not produced by the market, just as states depend on virtues not created by the state" (2002, 152).

Sacks (2002) illumines just how much this responsibility entails in a globalized, postmodern society. It requires a great deal more than liberal tolerance or finding common ground, namely appreciation of the "dignity of difference." Like Girard, to an extent, Sacks finds a stress on sameness suspect because it is often masks a violently maintained uniformity. In his view, "difference is the source of value, and indeed society itself" (2002, 14). Greater understanding, knowledge of who one really is, and insight into one's shortcomings or blind spots requires nonviolent encounter with and a sincere effort to appreciate the goodness or wisdom of particular human others or communities that can be disturbingly different. For Sacks, this applies even or especially in the realm of religion. In the "sheer variety of the imaginative expressions of the human spirit . . . if we listen carefully, we will hear the voice of God telling us something we need to know" (2002, 21). Also, "We will make peace only when we learn that God loves difference" (2002, 23).

This turn away from social atomism to a fundamentally relational ontology seems to resonate with mimetic theory in a number of ways. First of all, we suggest that mimetic scapegoat theory has the potential to deepen and extend the account of social science's disguised ideology (outlined above) and Sacks's complementary analysis of our entrapment in an either/or dichotomy between traditional values and purely contractual relationships.

From the standpoint of mimetic theory, we suggest, it appears that valuable as these insights are, we have not yet fully dismantled liberal individualism's master narrative of the human struggle as moving from oppression to liberty, a story that greatly obscures the profound interdependence of humans, including as models for one another, in fashioning fundamental desires and aims in living. In Bailie's (1999) words, "Ultimately there are only two alternatives to apocalyptic violence: the sacred violence and scapegoating of conventional culture and religion, on the one hand, and forgiveness and the renunciation of violence, on the other" (1999, 25). In this Girardian view, invaluable moral achievements of modern times such as a greater respect for the dignity and rights of individuals could not have developed without an extensive seeing through of the misapprehensions of the surrogate victimage process, insights that represent a different and more demanding spiritual accomplishment than just seizing one's natural autonomy and rolling back oppression.[3] This unveiling of violence involves a letting go of projections of comforting blame onto and the provision of security by scapegoats and also a forsaking of a kind of solidarity with others that seems like the only alternative to a truly frightening breakdown of one's world. These require an ability to tolerate great uncertainty and vulnerability—not the absence of fear, as is often said, but courage and steadfastness in spite of it—supported mainly by membership in the company of those who share a similar empathy for victims and refuse to refocus their anger in any fashion on new enemies, even the enemies of reform as we conceive of it.

It takes at least a measure of this kind of empathy and restraint for individuals to follow the rules of a capitalist economy and democratic politics and, as a result, enjoy the cultural and material benefits that kind of managed rivalry affords.[4] But our situation is a precarious one, which Girard keenly describes as generating "considerable material benefits" but leading to "even more considerable spiritual suffering" (1978, 137). Sacks (2002) comments on this same phenomenon. He reminds us, "For life to have personal meaning, there must be people that matter to us, and for whom we matter, unconditionally and non-substitutability." But in a hyperactive and turbocharged global economy we tend to "lose this . . . concept of happiness, of a life well-lived, of dedication to something larger than ourselves." Indeed, he feels, there is "measurable evidence" that in "a single generation, despite economic progress and technological advance, the incidence of depressive illness, stress-related syndromes, suicide attempts and alcohol and drug abuse have all risen" (2002, 157).[5]

The Girardian analysis, however, gives us tools for digging deeper into the sources and underlying dynamics of these regrettable trends. In this view, problematic mimetic and victimizing mechanisms have been unmasked and disarmed in modern times to such an extent that we have great difficulty, and then only fitfully, indulging in scapegoating violence in order to reinforce social ties and psychic stability. Mimetic rivalry is attenuated, allowing for increased flexibility, creativity, and enjoyment in social life. However, "fighting over prestige," which Girard (1978, 305) reminds us is "fighting over nothing," remains a considerable force in our lives. Fundamental tensions are far from fully eased. These include tensions in relationships between modeling and rivalry—using other language we might say between profound dependency and ingrained antagonism—and tension within individuals. This is really the same thing described differently as tension between a deep desire for harmonious bonds or genuine friendship with others and a will to surpass or supersede them, or between simply appreciating them in their uniqueness[6] and urgently wanting them to play a particular role in one's life, a homely illustration of which might be the condition of being able only to temper or suppress one's chronic irritation with a child or an intimate. Another simple illustration might be the kind of persistent self-blame or self-criticism in which we commonly engage. It does seem to be rooted in metaphysical desire. It makes no sense except as an invidious comparison of oneself with a superior model, the only cure for which would be to possess that model's splendid qualities. Any progress in that rivalry will only bring us face to face with their illusory nature, or their irrelevance to a meaningful life, at which point we either gain significantly in wisdom or cast about for another misperceived model.

Mimetic theory suggests that liberal individualism and the modern ideologies that animate most psychological theory represent significant gain along the path from violence to peace, but hardly a secure resting place, even temporarily. Unfortunately, however, precisely the kind of gain that modern psychology and psychotherapy, at their best, represent also serves to mask their inadequacies. Our theories and methods oversimplify the devilish intricacies of the violence from which we have partly escaped and underestimate the challenges we still face. The "bounded, masterful self" (Cushman 1990) of modern imagination and theory itself represents a kind of delusion that we cling to compulsively, like a child to its mother in a time of threat. It certainly represents an improvement on the self-deceiving "double projection" of full-blown sacred violence (Girard 1977). But further diminution of that "spiritual suffering" of which Girard speaks would seem to require not just correction or reform of social and personal goals but a more spiritually exacting effort to achieve a transformed perspective on self, relationships, and aims in living.

Webb (1993) gives us an image of such a transformed perspective. He reminds us that the tendency of so much modern psychological theory to decontextualize the self, in order to both exalt and protect it, turns it into a problematic kind of object. He suggests that in the Girardian view this results, at bottom, from a "misguided will to be . . . an object-subject" that "lures us to seek psychological fusion with figures of power, individual and collective" and to "try to find in the desires of rivals the secrets of ontological sufficiency" (1993, 243). The alternative

> . . . requires courage—the courage to endure the tensions of genuinely human existence and to accept our inherently contingent lives precisely as the gift of that tension. Above all, it requires radically self-transcending love—love of the unrealized possibilities of subjective actuality both in oneself and in others, the love that makes one willing not only to exist subjectively oneself but also to bless and let go of every other so that he or she may do so as well. (*ibid.*)

If a more mature, self-aware, and realistic kind of psychological inquiry wanted to make a fresh start, it might begin here.

This Girardian view eliminates the tension and vacillation between poles of nostalgia and a gnawing sense of emptiness to which so many modern people are prone. Earlier times are not marked by authoritarian elements that can be easily separated from a desirable sense of community or meaningful social bonds to which we might aspire with a whole heart. The inherent quality of those bonds consists, in part, in the kind of solidarity achieved only through more or less attenuated scapegoating violence. Any enduring goods they reflect can be recaptured only through transformation in the direction of the sort of radically self-transcending love of which Webb speaks. Moreover, even if we could, in the way Cushman (1990) describes, fill up our present-day empty selves with more traditional practices and ideals, it wouldn't work. First of all, we are bound to reject the residue of sacred violence in traditional forms, upon which we actually have made some improvement. Secondly, our fundamental need is not to salve the wounds of our somewhat empty freedom, but to transform the significant degree of rivalrous desire that still animates our way of life further in the direction of forgiving love (cf. Thompson's chapter 1). Looking ahead in that way would seem to be entirely possible for anyone, in any place or time, who is fortunate enough to have models of that love and the receptivity and courage to be guided by them.

TOWARD A RELATIONAL ONTOLOGY

It seems to us that the most promising developments in social theory involve a turn to a deeply relational ontology. Only on the basis of such a profound ontological shift is it possible to demythologize and begin to remediate the one-sided individualism and instrumentalism that have dominated the field. For example, what is termed the "practice turn in contemporary theory" (Shatzki, Cetina, and Savigny 2001) heralds a "distinct social ontology" (Schatzki 2001, 3) according to which basic human reality is neither (1) objectified social structures and systems that override or obliterate personal responsibility or (2) an amalgamation of separate individuals and their qualities (sometimes called methodological individualism). Rather, knowledge, meaning, human activity, power, language, and social institutions occur within and are aspects of *fields of practices* (cf. Redekop's concept of mimetic structures infusing relational systems, chapter 4). Co-operative social practices, whether carried out poorly or well, are ontological bedrock. We just *are* such shared practices and their results are a thoroughly joint achievement.[7]

Philosophical Hermeneutics. In the search for a more profoundly relational approach, a number of psychological theorists in recent years (Fowers 2005; Flyvbjerg 2001; Martin, Sugarman, and Thompson 2003; Richardson et al. 1999; Slife, Reber, and Richardson [Eds.] 2005) have turned to the hermeneutic philosophy or ontological hermeneutics of Gadamer (1989) and Taylor (1985; 1989) for a scrupulous and thoroughgoing alternative to naturalism and individualism. In the hermeneutic view, humans are "self-interpreting beings" (Taylor 1989) who are "always 'thrown' into a familiar life-world from which they draw their possibilities of self-interpretation. Their life-stories only make sense against the backdrop of possible story-lines opened by our historical culture" (Guignon 1989, 109). These lives are woven into the fabric of a holistic life-world where there are no sharp divisions between the person or mind and the world, body, or others. The meanings we live by permeate and shape the practices and institutions of the "outer" world much as they belong to our "inner" life. There is certainly a place for scientific knowing and an instrumental stance toward the world. But in this view there is a more fundamental, ultimately practical or moral kind of understanding that humans always and everywhere hammer out together, as they seek to understand the meaning for them of events, the past, texts, works of art, social reality, and the actions of others, so that they can relate to them appropriately along the story-lines of their living.

On this account, a basic fact about humans, in Heidegger's (1962, 228) words, is that they "care" about whether their lives make sense and what they are amounting to. Taylor (1985b) develops this notion of care with the idea that humans do *not* simply desire particular outcomes or satisfactions in living. Rather, they always or inherently make "strong evaluations," even if only tacitly or unconsciously, about the *quality* of their desires and motivations and the *worth* of the ends they seek in terms of how they fit in with their overall sense of a decent or worthwhile life.[8]

The kind of understanding pursued in this way is above all *dialogical*. In Taylor's words, in both everyday life and human science inquiry, "understanding of a text or an event . . . has to be construed, not on the model of the 'scientific' grasp of an object, but rather on the model of speech-partners coming to an understanding" (2002, 126). In other words, understanding is the result of a process of mutual communication, influence, negotiation, accommodation, and struggle, as in a conversation or a relationship. This process involves an exquisite, quintessentially human, sometimes almost unbearable, tension. On the one hand, we harbor self-defining beliefs and values concerning things we truly care about, in which we have a "deep identity investment," sometimes an investment in "distorted images we cherish of others" (Taylor 2002, 141.) On the other hand, since our ideals and our images of others and events are always partial or distorted in some way, we need to not just compromise and get along with others but to *learn from* the past, others, or other cultures. Thus, in matters closest to our hearts, we *depend* upon these others, their insights, and their beneficent influence greatly. It is striking to us how this account of dialogical understanding, in which we depend upon just those others concerning whom we often have a distorted picture, begins to inch into the territory of mimetic theory.

Weak and Strong Relationality. Some theoretical psychologists (Richardson and Frost 2006; Slife 2004), propose, based on hermeneutic philosophy, adopting a fully "relational ontology." This might be a very general and useful way to conceive of the shift underway described by Sacks, sociological practice theorists, and hermeneutic thinkers. Slife argues that most theory and research in psychology are built around a conception of "weak relationality," according to which events, situations, persons, and practices "begin and end as self-contained individualities that often take in information from the outside" (2004, 2). The term "interaction" or synonyms of it often connote weak relationality because "members of the interaction 'act on' each other from the outside." There is great interest in psychology in the "internalization of 'outside' influences of all types." We commonly think of the identity of entities or persons as something that "stems from what is ultimately 'inside' and within, even if some of what is inside might have originated from without." The liberal individualist picture of things, with which much psychology falls right in line, is very much a "weak relational" one. Somewhat paradoxically, in this view, people are causally shaped by environmental forces, ideally, to become self-dependent, self-directing individuals who then mysteriously can resist such causes or influences in order to function autonomously or "do their own thing." By contrast, what Slife calls "strong relationality" is an "ontological relationality." Relationships are not just the interactions of what was originally nonrelational; they are relational "all the way down." Things and persons are not first self-contained entities and then interactive, but each is "first and always a nexus of relations." They have a "shared being and mutual constitution" (*ibid.*).

The work of the maverick and brilliant sociologist Thomas Scheff (1997; 2004) is notable for the way it clarifies strong relational ties as basic human reality. Scheff offers an original, penetrating reinterpretation of rage, shame, and depression in much less individualistic terms than usual. He suggests the prevalence of depression and other ills in our society may stem from the fact that "human interdependency" and experiences of shame are routinely denied by us, reflected in the fact that our public discourse is in the language of individuals, rather than relationships. In his view, some kind of hurt or insult produces feelings of rejection or inadequacy that are not acknowledged to others or even oneself. An essential part of this injury is that it threatens or severs a social bond. It is followed by a continuing spiral of "intense emotions of shame and anger," which is "experienced as hate and rage." This spiral of hatred and rage, rather than "expressing and discharging one's shame," masks it with rage and aggression. A "loop of unlimited duration and intensity," in which one may be angry that one is ashamed and ashamed that one is angry, can serve as the "emotional basis of lengthy episodes or even life-long hatred and rage" (2004, 25–29).

Scheff (2004) suggests the way we typically obscure interdependency in our kind of society makes it difficult to effect what is often the best, sometimes the only, cure for estrangement or hostility between individuals or groups, namely an "apology/forgiveness transaction." Healing through apology begins with acknowledgment of human interdependency. When the bond is threatened, both parties are in "a state of shame," one for injuring, one for being injured. A successful apology allows both parties to acknowledge and discharge the shame evoked by the injury. The apology "makes things right" between the parties, both emotionally and cognitively. It repairs the breach in the bond. "The success of the action of repair is felt and signaled by both parties; they both feel and display the emotion of pride" (2004, 36). Pride is another emotion Scheff wants to reinterpret, as the experience, at its best, of a mutually indebted accomplishment of something worthwhile, rather than merely an individualistic sense of achievement or sheer superiority.

From a Girardian perspective, it is obvious that Scheff's description largely lacks any theory of desire or basic human motivation, let alone an explicit, full account of mimetic desire and entanglement. But it does represent the sort of paradigm shift toward a covenantal or strong relational view of human ties of the sort that Sacks (2004) outlines. Moreover, he makes rage and violence central to his theoretical story and glimpses the fact that there is no safe middle ground between apocalyptic violence, on the one hand, and forgiveness and the renunciation of violence on the other.

A particularly compelling illustration of strong relationality can be found in the life of Iulia de Beausobre (Allen 2006), a Russian peasant woman who was tortured and made the subject of medical experimentation in one of Stalin's prisons in the early 1930s. She eventually wrote two books, *The Woman Who Could Not Die* and *Creative Suffering*, describing her redemptive suffering in the face of such cruelty and sadism. She states that one way to survive in this situation is to cause the torturer to lose interest by becoming completely passive and indifferent ("clod-like," she puts it), but the cost of doing so is losing a humanity one will never recover. However, there is an alternative kind of "invulnerability" (her word for it) that involves intense, creative engagement with the actual situation (cf. Hess's chapter 7 and Smith's concept of nonresistance in chapter 8). It requires close attention to one's surroundings and the examiner, trying to gain insight into his mind, even cultivating a kind of sympathy that has nothing to do with sentimentality or excusing responsibility. Passions like "self-pity, fear, and despair must be controlled because they severely upset clarity of perception" (Allen 2006, 63) and interfere with the job or purpose at hand of relating as honestly and kindly as possible to one's tormentor. One has to let go of any protection those passions might provide as well as the illusion of most ordinary possibilities for influence or control.

Strong relationality comes into the picture for de Beausobre in two main ways. First, there forms a "bond between the tortured and the torturer; they do not remain isolated from on another, but become a part of each other's lives. Together they are part of one event" (Allen 1981, 64). Second, de Beausobre feels that her self at its core has no separate identity of its own but lives in union with a divine love that "goes forth from her to others" (*ibid.*, 66). One thing de Beausobre's account illustrates is the way in which a condition of intimately overlapping and interdependent lives, human or divine, need not undermine personal responsibility and independence of mind but can exemplify them to the fullest. This account seems to presuppose, even if it does not articulate, a philosophical anthropology like Girard's. Perhaps it should be read as a compelling and instructive example of the kind of "loving mimesis" (Adams 2000) that can be described only after we have gained the ability to "'unthink' the necessity of violence" (Colborne 2008).

HERMENEUTICS AND MIMETIC THEORY

Finally, we would like tentatively to suggest a few additional ways in which mimetic theory, on the one hand, and critical psychology and hermeneutic philosophy, on the other, might complement or cross-fertilize one another. First, it appears that Sacks's notion of covenantal relationships, sociological practice theory, Scheff's discussion of social bonds, the portrayal of mutual influence and dialogue by hermeneutic thinkers, and Girard's (1978) "interdividual psychology" have a great deal in common. They all seek, often explicitly, to "steer a course between Enlightenment foundationalism and postmodern relativism" (Browning 2004, 266). In Bernstein's (1983) terms, they all seek a way "beyond objectivism and relativism." Specifically, they outline a view of the human agency and social processes that represents a distinct alternative to both (1) the modern bounded, masterful self and (2) postmodern viewpoints that decenter human agency entirely and portray it as a mere byproduct of the play of social forces. Such postmodern approaches actually seem surreptitiously to *preserve* the modern picture of a lonely, isolated self (at the very least the one that formulates postmodern theory!) lost in a world of objects or forces with which it has no meaningful ties. Thus, Selznick characterizes much postmodern thought as the "wayward child of modernism, carrying its logic to extremes rather than presenting a clear alternative" (1992, 8). For Sacks, hermeneutic thought, and Girard, the self, is partially decentered into relationships with others and the cultural past, where it lacks absolute sovereignty or autonomy, its very identity is shaped at the core through meaningful dealings with others, and it must work out its destiny for good or ill in close concert with others from cradle to grave (cf. Goodhart, chapter 2).

Reciprocity and the Hermeneutic Circle. In the Girardian view, "[W]hat one customarily calls the *I* or *self* in psychology is an unstable, constantly changing, and ultimately evanescent structure . . . only *desire* brings this self into existence, [and] *desire is mimetic*" (Oughourlian 1991, 11–12). Analogously, for hermeneutic thought, the self is irreducibly "dialogical" (Richardson, Rogers, and McCarroll 1998; Taylor 1991). It *consists in* an ongoing interplay between "voices" (Bakhtin, 1981), commitments, and identifications within and between persons. The philosopher Joseph Dunne summarizes this common ground with the observation that the self "lacks the substantiality and discreteness of an object which is amenable to direct description or explanation. Nor can it be captured privately by an internal act of introspection or self-perception. Its reality is peculiarly dispersed. It is always partly outside and beyond itself . . . implicated in and formed by relationships, permeated by otherness" (1996, 143).

Because of this common ground, we would respectfully disagree with one of Girard's (2002, 8) assertions that "the idea of the hermeneutic circle" prevents investigating the origins of religion, of the sacrificial system, in actual human struggles with one another and violence. Girard feels this idea implies, quoting Lévi-Strauss, that "you cannot find any origin because you only get into a vicious circle." Thus, you end up not challenging or even rationalizing the struggle with violence that is disguised in myths and texts of persecution. "You cannot have any origin of the Oedipus myth if you accept the guilt of Oedipus. . . . If you say that Oedipus was innocent, then everything changes. You can have a genesis that is beyond the hermeneutic circle."

This critique may apply to structuralist and many postmodern viewpoints, which may be the sort of theory Girard has in mind. In the hermeneutic view, however, the interpretations or understandings that are hammered out in everyday life are ultimately *practical*, concerned with matters of meaning and morality that shape the trajectory of human lives in a concrete way. It very much tries, in its own way, to do what Doran (2008) says is Girard's central aim, namely to elucidate "actual human comportment as a function of the concrete relations between Self and Other" (2008, xvii). It seems to us that the processes of mutual influence and dialogue set out in Gadamer's (1989) and Taylor's (1989) hermeneutics closely parallel Girard's (1977) notion of "reciprocity" and the idea of a thoroughly interdividual psychology. Both exhibit the character of "strong relationality." Both claim to describe ontologically basic human relations, just how things work on the open and often messy plain of life, that are commonly obscured or distorted for ideological or inauthentic reasons. Mimetic theory is concerned with diagnosing and unveiling our need to disguise the machinations of violence. Hermeneutics is concerned with diagnosing and unveiling the kind of scientific abstractionism that abets somewhat utopian modern ideologies in obscuring the full measure of human interdependence, and with our need to take full responsibility for how we constitute one another and our way of life by the manner in which we interpret events, the past, and the actions and intentions of others.

Thus, we would say that hermeneutics aims to refocus on concrete human struggles rather than selectively abstracting away from and obscuring parts of that struggle, consciously or unconsciously, for questionable reasons. In support of that view, we would contend that hermeneutics, even though hermeneutic thinkers do not always make this point explicit, accepts the idea that communication is always already imbued with power (Richardson, 2003). In other words, there is no form of communication concerned with meanings that matter to us that is not permeated with or carried along by efforts on our part to influence one another or the course of events. This may take place in either a deceptive or coercive manner, as in intimidation, seduction, or scape-goating activities, or in a more constructive or benign manner, as when we seek to inculcate children in our best values, which cannot avoid causing some resentment and doing some harm, or when we seek to influence one another in friendly or civic dialogue, which cannot avoid disturbing or threat-ening others to a degree at times. A defining characteristic of more construc-tive influence may be that whenever possible it exemplifies the principles of hermeneutic dialogue discussed above. According to Warnke (1987, 167), one of the key principles of Gadamer's (1989) philosophy is genuine open-ness to any meaning or claim, which means actually granting it "provisional authority" to challenge one's current beliefs or biases. The reciprocal inter-play of sincere conviction and such openness lies at the heart of this kind of dialogue (Richardson, Rogers, and McCarroll 1998). To engage in this pro-cess requires a vulnerability and a willingness to dissolve or desist from defensive, retaliatory, or blaming reactions to uncertainty or threat that seem in important ways to parallel or overlap with the ability to see through mys-tifications and rationalizations of scapegoating violence. Characterizations of such vulnerability and non-defensiveness may shed some additional light on both the destructive and self-defeating features of mimetic entanglement and on the kind of life that becomes available after conversion to a thoroughly non-violent path of living.

Nevertheless, even assuming such commonality, it is plain that mimetic theory adds a great deal of detail and dynamism to our picture of human action. Hermeneutics, practice theory, and Scheff's account of our "interde-pendency" all seem to be missing much of a certain "existential" dimension. By "existential," we mean not the classic kind of Sartrean (1995) existential-ism according to which one responds to the perceived groundlessness of human existence with a highly individuated, ultimately arbitrary, choice of meaning and purpose. Rather we have in mind the sense in which Webb uses the term to refer to "living creatively and joyfully with the tension that is the animating principle of our lives" (1993, 242). That means, for Webb, partici-pating in a thoroughly intersubjective or interdividual process in which one is brought to conclusions about what is worth being committed or devoted to in the face of much uncertainty and enduring human limitations. It means cop-ing with the mimetic entanglement that affords no safe ground between sa-cred violence, and forgiving love. Perhaps even the best kinds of contempo-rary social theory share in the reluctance of modern liberal thought to risk dogmatism or undue political partiality by plunging into the realities of rage, envy, violence, and hate that are all around us, preferring to rely on liberal democracy, legislating against discriminatory or prejudicial practices, and surrounding the self with a phalanx of rights to keep them at bay. However, we suggest that a hermeneutic view, as we have outlined it, sets the stage for and invites something like mimetic theory to take this plunge and, moreover, contains powerful resources for helping to unmask the distortions of expressive individualism and the romantic lie.

In a famous passage, Gadamer wrote that "history does not belong to us, but we belong to it," and that the "self-awareness of the individual is only a flickering in the closed circuits of historical life" (1989, 245). Similarly, Taylor asserts that "we are aware of the world through a 'we' before we are through an 'I,'" so that "we always find ourselves as a we-consciousness before we can be an I-consciousness" (1985, 40). A sense of "throwness" of this sort highlights the mystery and radical contingency of human life in a way that parallels the Girardian account of the situation in which culture is embarked upon by deeply unfinished creatures who start out with very little idea about what to do or be, or why, and remain exquisitely dependent upon one another in the adventure that ensues. In both cases, it would seem quite natural or inevitable that the basic teleological thrust of life would be "constitutionally imitative" (Fleming 2004, 10) and involve the imitation of both acts and *intentions* toward whatever we come to desire, even though hermeneutic thought does not make that kind of mimesis fully explicit. But a hermeneutic ontology does effectively overcome social atomism, we suggest, by clarifying how fully responsible human agency—including the practices of social theory and research—transpires only in a thoroughly strong relational context, even though this achievement may be at risk or its impact diluted without mimetic theory's further unveiling of the ways we cling to the semi-delusion of a separate self to ward off the effects (within and without) of enmity and envy.

Contributions of Hermeneutics. It seems to us, though, that some benefits might run from hermeneutics to mimetic scapegoat theory. In this chapter, we can only hint at some of the possibilities, hoping to interest others in the topic. For both hermeneutics and mimetic theory, the source of dynamism and direction in life does not lie within delimited subjects but in a wider current of existence that carries persons along even as they must play some part in it, responsibly or otherwise. Gadamer's (1989) term for this temporal current is "effective history." It refers to the way our current horizon of understanding is historically embedded and a product of what has come before, the past—the "variety of voices in which the echo of the past is heard" (Gadamer 1989, 284)—which constantly influences "what seems to us worth inquiring about and what will appear as an object of investigation" (*ibid.*, 300). It also refers to how our current ways of appropriating the past determine how those traditions can *count* for us, or how the horizon of the present first gives the past the voice in which it can speak to us, in an ongoing reciprocal interaction or circular relation between the past and the present.

Oughourlian calls this wider current of human affairs "universal mimesis," elucidating it with an analogy to universal gravitation. He writes,

> Universal mimesis, considered as a principle of gravitation, binds people together and constitutes the human being as a "social" animal essentially through its spatial dimension . . . But . . . by its temporal dimension mimesis holds a person together and constitutes him as "psychological" man . . . These two absolutely inseparable dimensions . . . together cause our ontogenesis. (1991, 6)

This analogy helps to bring out how mimesis in some sense, as Oughourlian puts it, is a fundamental force that "precedes consciousness and creates it by its action." However, the analogy is not apt for the reason that universal mimesis is not a natural law governed field of events but a cultural and historical life world, a scene of purposeful human action (however unconscious or perverse). It does seem important to explicate the kind of basic social ontology entailed by mimetic theory. But the analogy to physical forces tends to discourage any further investigation, should it become an issue, of the ontology of these processes and how they unfold, because they are qualitatively different in kind from the dynamics of historical, temporal events. It tends to freeze one's current, preferred understanding of mimetic desire and seal it off from continuing critical analysis and elaboration. It will remind critical psychologists of the way many psychoanalytic theorists over the years elaborate an essentially interpretive account of psychological life for which they then abruptly claim the status of "science." The claim to "science" can be intimidating. However, it is plain that psychoanalytic theories are not based on experimental findings, and cannot decisively be confirmed or disconfirmed by them (Bishop 2007; Root 1993).

More recently, Oughourlian further develops the analogy to universal gravitation: "Just as the force of attraction between two physical objects . . . is directly proportional to their mass and inversely proportional to the distance that separates them from one another, so also is the force of attraction between two psychological subjects" (2010, 85). This leads Oughourlian to portray what he terms including the "back-and-forth movement of the interdividual relation" (*ibid.*, 97), including the interplay of suggestion and imitation between individuals, in what seems like a highly deterministic fashion. He writes about a subject's desire resulting from "mimetic necessity" or being "copied" in what seems like an automatic or helpless manner from others.

However, Oughourlian is too wise as a thinker and clinician really to advocate a thoroughgoing determinism. In one place, he abruptly asserts that even though mimesis is a "universal mechanism" that "none of us can escape," we can still "resist" a desire that may clash with one of our "convictions," even "reject" it, and "retain the ability . . . to choose another model" (2010, 27). Well, one can only wonder where that power to reject or choose came from, and on what *basis* we would reject or choose? Perhaps the power to choose itself? It is entirely unclear. In order not to banish freedom and responsibility entirely, the author seems to lapse back into a facsimile of the kind of ungrounded, autonomous choice we very much want to avoid. Hermeneutic thought might contain valuable resources for clarifying some of the key ontological claims of mimetic theory. "Universal hermeneutics" (Gadamer 1989, 431) seems closer to the mark than the metaphor of gravitational forces and efficient causality.

Here is another example of a way in which hermeneutics might contribute to elaborating mimetic theory. In one of the few writings that tries to interrelate Girardian theory and other contributions to the philosophy of human action in a detailed way, Livingston (1992) argues that a Girardian approach certainly does not wish to portray mimesis as a largely passive response to exposure to models. Livingston reminds us that "individual agency is the effective locus of a spontaneous, and in some sense selective process, even if this process is not a matter of fully reflective and effective deliberation," and that "mimetic desire may in fact involve a selective transformation of the model's desire" (1992, 3). He indicates that Girardian theory essentially tries to (1) capture the active and creative (even if often misguided) kinds of interpreting, evaluating, reflecting, learning, forgetting, taking responsibility, and the like that belong to human agency without (2) relapsing back, in Girard's words, into a "psychology of the subject" (Girard 1978, 303).

Livingston (1992) and others (O'Shea, 2007) suggest, however, that some characterizations of mimetic processes may be somewhat obscure and potentially misleading. Girard writes, for example, that ". . . [Desire,] far from being unconscious in Freud's sense and only appearing in its true form in our dreams . . . not only observes but never stops thinking about the meaning of its observations. *Desire is always reflection on desire*" (1978, 328). Livingston (1992) feels this almost sounds like "desire . . . were what pulled the strings of the human marionette . . . a kind of homunculus equipped with whatever cognitive faculties" might be involved (1992, 25). To correct this possible overreaction against individualism or psychologism, Livingston recommends that we import some of the terms of an "intentionalist psychology" (*ibid.*, 28) in order to portray a kind of human agency that steers a middle path between subjectivism and reifying desire.

However, Livingston says little about what sort of ontology of the human realm we might rely on to interrelate human agency and social forces or influences in a realistic, undistorted manner. Without that ontology, we are likely to continue to vacillate between two quite unsatisfying viewpoints on this essential question, between a one-sided individualism on the one hand

and, on the other hand, dissolving personal agency and responsibility into some other kind of reality or process. It seems to us that a hermeneutic ontology and the idea of strong relationality speak directly to this need and contribute to a more credible picture of the interdividual human being. On this account, humans are self-interpreting agents. In terms of mimetic theory, this means that every imitation of another's desire is an active, creative interpretation on the part of that agent. But this notion in no way means reverting to subjectivism in order to capture agency, because it is the interpretation of partly decentered selves, whose fundamental reality in the human life world is co-constituted by self and other, present and past, individual and cultural context.

Positive or Creative Mimesis. In recent years, a number of writers in Girardian circles (e.g., Colborne 2008; Redekop 2002; Swartley 2000) have recommended extending mimetic theory to be able to characterize a more positive or what Adams (2000) calls a "loving mimesis" that focuses as much on transformed living as on destructive mimetic entanglement. Anyone who has hung around the water cooler, so to speak, at COV&R meetings knows that this thesis is complicated and controversial. It seems to us to have merit. In Swartley's (2000) words, "Girard's theory works well through Good Friday but does not connect adequately—and perhaps by definition cannot— with post-Easter potential for human reality" (2000, 23). Swartley summarizes Adam's seminal article concisely. She wants to expand the "dimension of shalom-love *desire* among humans" in the Girardian model. She questions the "split between subject and object" that she feels still somewhat colors that model. Also, she "seeks to reconceptualize a primal, ultimate reality based on intersubjectivity in human relations, so that rivalry is not an inevitable outcome of social relations." In this way, "she seeks a nondualistic conceptualization of the nature of the human, a model she holds to be primal, and congruent with feminist critique generally" (2000, 23–24). If what we have said about the hermeneutic viewpoint makes sense, its possible contribution to reconceptualizing basic human reality along these lines should be evident.

Webb writes about the need to expand the Girardian view in a similar way. He argues that Girard "conceives of desire *by definition* as inherently oriented toward objects" that are perceived to be "defended with invincible forces," in other words, metaphysical desire. However, there is "no necessary reason why mediated aspirations must be bound to the pursuit of objects" of this sort, why "an aspiration bearing on the 'being' of the other might not lead to death but life" (1993, 228). New terminology and indeed a "new theory of desire" (*ibid.*) will be needed to explicate this possibility, Webb argues. He points out that Girard distinguishes between "appetite and need on the one hand and desire . . . on the other . . . as an artificial craving learned by imitation of the desires, or supposed desires, of others" (227). But if we are going to develop a positive "conception of what constitutes the best possibilities of human love" (226), we will need a new term for a fundamental kind of "beneficent motivation" (229), perhaps an "existential appetite" that "seeks to enjoy a mode of existence" that "would contrast both with the strictly animal appetites . . . and with mimetic 'desires.'" (230). In his view, such a notion would supply the "only possible foundation for a theory of value adequate to the needs of a psychology concerned with helping people to discover and attain a true human good" (227).

This notion of an "existential appetite" oriented toward a true human good, easily thwarted, certainly resonates with the hermeneutic conception of an inherent teleology of life, easily distorted, toward greater understanding of a practical or ethical sort, within the limits of human finitude. Webb borrows terms from Voegelin, Ricoeur, Kierkegaard, and Lonergan to give a sense of what such a "single underlying energy of appetite" might involve. For example, he favors Voeglin's idea of a "questioning unrest" (1978, 101) because

> questioning, the appetite for understanding and knowledge, is the fundamental form in which this energy manifests itself in human consciousness. Even the slightest experience can give rise to wonder . . . Any thwarting of that energy in an attempt to close off from questioning some area of experience, some possible interpretation, some grasp of reality or sense of what is worthy of love, can be expected to result in various forms of psychological and spiritual disturbance. (Webb 1993, 239–240)

This formulation seems almost designed to serve as a way to link up mimetic theory, this new construct of an existential energy or appetite, and hermeneutic ontology, or at least point in that direction. Hermeneutic thought, with its careful clarification of the strong relational or interdividual character of human agency and the role of interpretation in social inquiry and everyday life, it seems to us, might make valuable contributions to this conversation, while hermeneutics, for its part, needs to take much fuller account of what Webb calls "the undertow of mimeticism" (1993, 239).

REFERENCES

Adams, R. 2000. "Loving Mimesis and Girard's 'scapegoat of the text': A Creative Reassessment of Mimetic Desire." Pp., 278–307 in *Violence Renounced: Réne Girard, Biblical Studies, and Peacemaking* edited by W. Swartley. Telford, PA: Pandora Press US.

Allen, D. 2006. *Traces of God*. New York: Seabury Books.

Bailie, G. 1995. *Violence Unveiled: Humanity at the Crossroads*. New York: Crossroad Publishing Co.

Bakhtin M. 1981. *The Dialogical Imagination: Four Essays by M. M. Bakhtin.* Michael Holquist, Ed. Austin: University of Texas Press.

Baxter, L. 2004. "Relationships as Dialogues." *Personal Relationships*, 11, 1–22.

Bellah, R., R. Madsen, W. Sullivan, A. Swindler, & S. Tipton. 1985. *Habits of the Heart: Individualism and Community in American Life*. Berkeley: University of California Press.

Bernstein, R. J. 1976. *The Restructuring of Social and Political Theory.* Philadelphia: University of Pennsylvania Press.

Bernstein, R. 1983. *Beyond Objectivism and Relativism.* Philadelphia: University of Pennsylvania Press.

Bishop, R. 2007. *The Philosophy of the Social Sciences.* New York: Continuum.

Browning, D. & T. Cooper. 2004. *Religious Thought and the Modern Psychologies,* 2nd ed. Minneapolis: Fortress press.

Christopher, J. 1999. "Situating Psychological Well-being: Exploring the Cultural Roots of Its Theory and Research." *Journal of Counseling and Development,* 77, 141–152.

Colborne, N. 2008. "Resentment and Transcendence." Paper delivered at the annual meeting of the Colloquium on Religion and Violence, Riverside, CA.

Cushman, P. 1990. "Why the Self Is Empty." *American Psychologist,* 45, 599–611.

———. 1991. "No Empty Fixes: A Rejoinder to Rostafinski, Ellis, and Col." *American Psychologist,* 46, 542–54.

———. 1995. *Constructing the Self, Constructing America.* Menlo Park, CA: Addison-Wesley Publishing Company.

de Tocqueville, A. 1969. *Democracy in America.* New York: Doubleday Anchor Books. (Original work published in 1835.)

Doran, R. 2008. "Editor's Introduction: Literature as Theory." Pp. xi–xvii in R. Girard, *Mimesis & Theory.* Stanford: Stanford University Press.

Dunne, J. 1996. "Beyond Sovereignty and Deconstruction: The Storied Self." *Philosophy and Social Criticism,* 21, 137–157.

Etzioni, A. 1993. *The Spirit of Community.* New York: Crown.

———. 1996. *The New Golden Rule: Community and Morality in a Democratic Society.* New York: BasicBooks.

Fancher, R. 1995. *Cultures of Healing: Correcting the mage of American Mental Health Care. Image.* New York: W. H. Freeman and Company.

Flyvbjerg, B. 2001. *Making Social Science Matter: Why Social Inquiry Fails and How It Can Succeed Again.* Cambridge: Cambridge University Press.

Fleming, C. 2004. *René Girard: Violence and Mimesis.* Malden, MA: Polity Press

Fowers, B. J. 2005. *Virtue and Psychology: Pursuing Excellence in Ordinary Practices.* Washington, DC: APA Press.

Frank, J. 1978. *Psychotherapy and the Human Predicament.* New York: Schocken.

Fromm, E. 1969. *Escape from Freedom.* New York: Avon (Original work published in 1941).

———. 1975. *Man for Himself.* New York: Fawcett Premier (Original work published in 1947.)

Frost, K., & F. Richardson. 2004. "Hate, Individualism, and the Social Bond." *Humanity & Society,* 28, 102–118.

Fukuyama, F. 1995. *Trust.* London: Hamish Hamilton.

Gadamer, H-G. 1989. *Truth and Method,* second revised edition. Translated by J Weinsheimer and D. Marshall. New York: Crossroad.

Girard, R. 1965. *Deceit, Desire, and the Novel: Self and Other in Literary Structure.* Baltimore: The Johns Hopkins University Press.

———. 1977. *Violence and the Sacred.* Baltimore: Johns Hopkins Univ. Press.

———. 1978. *Things hidden since the foundation of the world.* Stanford: Stanford University Press.

———. 2002. "Psychoanalysis and Sacrifice: Difference and Identity between Psychoanalysis and Mimetic Theory." *Journal of European Psychoanalysis,* 14.

Guignon, C. 1989. "Truth as Disclosure: Art, Language, History." *The Southern Journal of Philosophy,* 28, 105–121.

———. 2004. *On Being Authentic.* New York: Routledge.

Habermas, J. 1973. *Theory and Practice.* Boston: Beacon Press.

———. 1977. "A Review of Gadamer's *Truth and Method.*" Pp. 335–363 in *Understanding and Social Inquiry,* edited by F. Dallmayr and T. McCarthy. University of Notre Dame Press, Notre Dame, IN.

Heidegger, M. 1962. *Being and Time.* New York: Harper & Row.

Hoy D. 1986. "Power, Repression, Progress." Pp. 123–47 in *Foucault: A Critical Reader,* edited by D. Hoy. New York: Basil Blackwell.

Kohut, H. 1977. *The Restoration of the Self.* New York: International Universities Press, Inc.

Lasch, C. 1978. *The Culture of Narcissism.* New York: Norton.

Livingston, P. 1992. *Models of Desire.* Baltimore: Johns Hopkins Press.

Martin, J., J. Sugarman, & J. Thompson. 2003. *Psychology and the Question of Agency.* Albany, NY: SUNY Press.

Neal, P. 1990. "Justice as Fairness." *Political Theory,* 18, 24–50.

O'Shea, A. 2006. "Modern Freedom and Creativity: '. . . truth stripped of its cloak of time.'" Paper delivered at the annual meeting of the Colloquium on Religion and Violence, Ottawa, Canada, June, 2006.

Oughourlian, J.-M. 1991. *The Puppet of Desire.* Stanford: Stanford University Press.

Rawls, J. 1971. *A Theory of Justice.* Cambridge, MA: Harvard University Press.

Redekop, V. 2002. *From Violence to Blessing: How an Understanding of Deep-rooted Conflict Can Open Paths to Reconciliation.* Ottawa, Canada: Novalis.

Reineke, M. 2007. "Transforming Space: Creativity, Destruction, and Mimesis in Winnicott and Girard." *Contagion,* 14, 79–96.

Richardson, F. 2003. "Current Dilemmas, Hermeneutics, and Power." *Journal of Theoretical and Philosophical Psychology, 22,* 113–132.

———. (2005). "Psychotherapy and Modern Dilemmas." Pp. 17–38 in *Critical Thinking about Psychology: Hidden Assumptions and Plausible Alternatives,* edited by B. Slife, J. Reber, & F. Richardson. Washington, D. C.: APA Books.

Richardson, F., & Fowers, B. 1998. "Interpretive Social Science: An Overview." *American Behavioral Scientist,* 41, 465–495.

Richardson, F. & R. Bishop. 2002. "Rethinking Determinism in Social Science." Pp. 425–45 in *Interdisciplinary Perspectives on Determinism,* edited by R. Bishop and H. Atmanspacher. Thorverton, UK and Charlottesville, VA: Imprint Academic.

Richardson, F., & K. Frost. 2006. "Girard & Psychology: Furthering the Dialogue." Paper delivered at the annual meeting of Colloquium on Violence & Religion, Ottawa, Canada, June.

Richardson, F., B. Fowers, & C. Guignon. 1999. *Re-envisioning Psychology: Moral Dimensions of Theory and Practice.* San Francisco, CA: Jossey-Bass.

Richardson, F., A. Rogers, & J. McCarroll. 1998. Toward a Dialogical Self. *American Behavioral Scientist, 41,* 496–515.

Root, M. 1993. *Philosophy of Social Science.* Oxford, UK: Blackwell.

Sacks, J. 2002. *The Dignity of Difference: How to Avoid the Clash of Civilizations.* London: Continuum.

Sandel, M. 1996. *Democracy's Discontent: America in Search of a Public Philosophy.* Cambridge, MA: Harvard University Press.

Sartre, J-P. 1995. "The Humanism of Existentialism." Pp. 268–86 in *Existentialism: Basic Writings,* edited by C. Guignon and D. Pereboom. Indianapolis, IN: Hackett

Schatzki, T. 2001. "Introduction: Practice Theory." Pp. 1–14 in *The Practice Turn in Contemporary Theory,* edited by T. Schatzki, K. Cetina, & E. von Savigny. London: Routledge.

Schatzki, T., K. Cetina, & E. von Savigny. (Eds.). 2001. *The Practice Turn in Contemporary Theory.* London: Routledge.

Scheff, T. 1997. *Emotions, The Social Bond, and Human Reality: Part/Whole Analysis.* Cambridge: Cambridge University Press

———. 2000. "Shame and Community: Social Components in Depression." Available at: http://www.soc.ucsb.edu/faculty/scheff/ .

———. 2004. "Is Hatred Formed by Hidden Shame and Rage?" *Humanity & Society,* 28, 25–39.

Schumaker, J. 2001. *The Age of Insanity: Modernity and Mental Health.* Westport, CT: Praeger.

Selznick, P. 1992. *The Moral Commonwealth.* Berkeley: University of California Press.

Slife, B. 2004. "Taking Practice Seriously: Toward a Relational Ontology." *Journal of Theoretical and Philosophical Psychology,* 24, 157–178.

Slife, B., A. Smith, & C. Burchfield. 2003. "Psychotherapists as Crypto-Missionaries: An Exemplar on the Crossroads of History, Theory, and Philosophy." Pp. 55–72 in *About Psychology: at the Crossroads of History, Theory, and Philosophy*, edited by D. Hill & M. Kral. Albany, New York: State University of New York Press.

Slife, B., J. Reber, & F. Richardson. (Eds.). 2005. *Critical Thinking about Psychology: Hidden Assumptions and Plausible Alternatives.* Washington, DC: APA Books.

Sullivan, W. 1986. *Reconstructing Public Philosophy.* Berkeley: University of California Press.

Swartly, W. 2000. *Violence Renounced: Réne Girard, Biblical Studies, and Peacemaking.* Telford, PA: Pandora Press US.

Taylor, C. 1979. *Hegel and Modern Society.* Cambridge: Cambridge University Press.

———. 1985a. *Human Agency and Language: Philosophical Papers* (Vol. 1). Cambridge: Cambridge University Press.

———. 1985b. *Philosophy and the Human Sciences: Philosophical papers* (Vol. 2). Cambridge: Cambridge University Press.

———. 1985c. "What Is Human Agency." Pp. 15–44 in C. Taylor, *Human Agency and Language: Philosophical Papers* (Vol. 1). Cambridge: Cambridge University Press.

———. 1989. *Sources of the self.* Cambridge, MA: Harvard University Press.

———. 1991. "The Dialogical Self." Pp. 304–314 in *The Interpretive Turn*, edited by J. Bohman, D. Hiley, & R. Schusterman. Ithaca, NY: Cornell University Press

———. 1995. *Philosophical Arguments.* Cambridge, MA: Harvard University Press

———. 2002. "Gadamer and the Human Sciences." Pp. 126–42 in *The Cambridge Companion to Gadamer* edited by R. Dostal. Cambridge: Cambridge University Press.

Voegelin, E. 1978. *Anamnesis.* Translated and edited by Gerhart Niemeyer. Notre Dame & London: University of Notre Dame Press.

Warnke, G. 1987. *Gadamer: Hermeneutics, Tradition, and Reason.* Stanford: Stanford university Press.

Webb, E. 1993. *The Self Between: From Freud to the New Social Psychology of France.* Seattle: University of Washington Press.

Zeddies, T., & F. Richardson. 1999. "Analytic Authority in Historical and Critical Perspective: Beyond Objectivism and Relativism." *Contemporary Psychoanalysis*, 35, 581–601.

NOTES

1. In response to a similar perception of this dilemma, Taylor (1979, 155) advocates that we develop a notion of "situated freedom." He contends that the modern understanding of freedom as "negative liberty," as largely a matter of "freedom from" constraints, can lead to a destructive, "anything-goes" attitude of "doing whatever feels good." Instead, he recommends that we develop a conception of "positive liberty" or the freedom to do things deemed worthwhile by one's community and oneself. On his account of freedom, the agent is always situated in a cultural and historical context which provides meaningful objectives and guidelines in terms of which people can deliberate meaningfully about possible courses of action. To a much greater extent than Fromm, Taylor is aware that these objectives and guidelines concern deeply social as well and individual goods and that we need to clarify philosophically how the fact that they are tied to particular cultural contexts does not entail moral relativism.

2. Kierkegaard's idea, "The door to happiness opens outward," we might say, has been discarded.

3. That is, decreasing the exercise of arbitrary authority in the political sphere and softening of the tyranny of the superego and "guilt trips" in the realm of the psyche.

4. These include not only cultural diversity and richness of various kinds, but as part of or a result of that richness, greater individuation, and a wider variety of individual tastes, sensibilities, and "personality."

5. See Schumaker (2001), *The Age of Insanity: Modernity and Mental Health*, for a compelling documentation and interesting interpretation of these trends.

6. Such appreciation was one of H. Richard, Neibuhr's definitions of "love."

7. Another example of this turn is the work of Leslie Baxter (2004), a researcher in the field of communication studies, who draws on the ideas of Mikhail Bakhtin to argue that we should not talk about "communication in relationships" but of "relationships as dialogues." Also, Bakhtin (1981) and Taylor (1991) have carefully delineated a view of humans as essentially "dialogical selves." A growing handful of research programs in developmental, social, and personality psychology have begun to take these ideas seriously as a theoretical backdrop for their work.

8. In a similar vein, Guignon (2003) distinguishes between "constituent/whole" and "means/ends" styles of living. The former involves acting "*for the sake of being* a person of a particular sort, and you experience your actions as constituents of a complete life that you are realizing in all you do." The latter centers on acting "in order to achieve social approval or to attain the awards that come from having acted [effectively or] properly."

Chapter Eleven

Rethinking Girardian Reconciliation

South Africa and the Myth of the Exception

Leonhard Praeg

There is a general perception that South Africa's transition from Apartheid to democracy was exceptional, because the country avoided the kind of bloodshed we have come to associate with such transitions. Transitions to new political orders are routinely accompanied by extreme massacres, genocides, and prolonged civil war. In fact, much of the sustained violence we have come to associate with post-colonial Africa can be interpreted from such a perspective, that is, as sustained transitional violence, the kind of violence that should, at some point, culminate in the state's monopoly on the means of violence in order to institute a lasting distinction between legitimate and illegitimate violence.

Of course, in the case of post-colonial Africa, the reasons for this failure are "super-complex" in the sense that they pertain both to the legacy of colonialism as well as to the difficulty of violence to succeed in a time of human rights and globalization. In such a context, violence is anticipated and pre-judged, as it must be, before and while it is expected to fulfill its generative function. This creates a profound aporia between the need for violence to execute its generative function and the in-execution of that function through a human rights-based critique, a condemnation of that violence (Praeg 2008).

How can violence fulfill its generative function in a globalizing context that tolerates no violation of human dignity? This aporia is generated by the fact that we generally subscribe to two mutually exclusive, yet equally imperative beliefs: first, that the transition to new politico-juridical orders are always necessarily violent; second, that in an era of human rights we will no longer tolerate human rights violations regardless of how "generative" some would argue such violations may be. In fact, it is fair to say that the West, by and large, expects of all new, emerging nation-states to somehow resolve this aporia and to come into existence without recourse to the very generative violence that brought into existence, the same nation-states that will judge them for failing to do so. All of this, perhaps, accounts for the impression that the history of post-colonial Africa is really the story of one failed state after another, when, in fact, it is a story of failed violence. It probably also accounts for much of the fascination with South Africa's so-called miraculously peaceful transition, the fact that the country seems to have been an exception to the rule of violent transitions. In the literature on South Africa, this transition is considered so exceptional that it often seems as if only a political theology can do justice to it, one in which the peaceful transition appears "miraculous" and the leaders who conducted South Africans through it, notably Nelson Mandela and Desmond Tutu, are referred to as contemporary "saints."

Of course, there are many ways to explain the possibility of this exception. Political realists remind us that South Africa was dominated, not by an externally imposed colonialism, but by Afrikaners who were then, as they are now, an internal, Africanized minority. By the time their government had started serious negotiations with the major representative of the armed struggle against apartheid (the now ruling African National Congress or ANC), two things were abundantly clear: first, that the historical tide had turned against the very possibility of continued Afrikaner domination and, second, that being a form of internal or, as some preferred to call it, "special colonialism," no act of collective violence could have expelled them or forced them to return to their colonial motherland. In some sense, then, what appears as an exceptional negotiated settlement was really just an impasse, one in which it was just as impossible to continue the oppression of black South Africans as it was to expel the white minority responsible for that oppression. This *political* explanation is closely related to a second, *juridical*, explanation.

One of the main reasons the white minority did not resort to violence on a massive scale around the time of the first democratic elections, and the five years immediately following, was because the negotiated settlement made provision for a juridical process that fundamentally prioritized reconciliation and forgiveness—that is, restorative justice—over Nürenberg-style retributive justice, which, it was argued, would amount to little more than juridical revenge. This is not so much an alternative as a supplementary explanation to the political explanation, because even this decision was to some extent informed by the pragmatic realization that, if the perpetrators of Apartheid violence were to continue living among the liberated, reconciliation would be a more sensible strategy than retribution. But as quasi-strategic as all this may have been, neither the political nor the juridical explanations would have been possible in the absence of a specific factor peculiar to the (South) African context. This compels us to consider a third, *ethical,* explanation for the peaceful transition. The choice to prioritize reconciliation and forgiveness, over truth and justice, would not have been possible, or perhaps even conceivable, in the absence of an African communitarian praxis generally known as African humanism or, in the South African context, as *uBuntu*. An ethical praxis more than an abstract philosophy, *uBuntu* does not subscribe to the kind of individualism presupposed by political liberalism and its various models of retributive justice (Praeg 2000, 246–281). I will say a little bit more about *uBuntu* toward the end of this chapter but it is not my main focus. In fact, I have no intention of exploring these three separate, but intimately related, causes of the peaceful transition at all. I briefly mentioned them only to provide a context for my real concern, which is with the narrative of South Africa's peaceful transition *as a very specific mythology*, one that, because of the implicit and often explicit claim to exceptionalism, compels us to consider the rule from which it is considered an exception.

THE RULE

What is this rule? Simply stated it is the claim that politico-juridical orders are (re-)generated through violence. This is not simply an *historical* claim ("states are routinely founded on violence") but something closer to a *constitutive* claim ("founding moments are per definition violent"). The historical claim is an empirical claim while the constitutive claim is a rationalist, *a priori* claim. Regarding the latter, René Girard is probably the most explicit, although, as I shall argue here, he really offers us quite a complex and, I would say, uncomfortable combination of the historical and constitutive claims.

The difference between these two kinds of claim is perhaps best illustrated by contract theory, a theory that has a notoriously complicated relationship with the truth. It is probably no exaggeration to say that, bar a couple of historical aberrations, contract theory was only ever thought of as an analytical device, a methodological fiction devised to answer a seemingly simple question: Given the way civil society works, what do we have to assume about the process that people went through in order to create such a thing? Note here how the historical ("the way things *seem to work*") is taken as point of departure for an explanation of the constitutive ("the way things *came to work*").

That the logic according to which something seems to work can be transformed into an explanation of how that thing came into being is not per definition a terrible conjecture. In fact, it probably contains some element of truth, but it does make for a very complex relationship between the historical and the constitutive, that is, between what we know as empirical, verifiable fact (always falsifiable) and what we postulate at rationalist *a priori* (per definition always the case). This troubled relationship between historical fact and constitutive cause haunts all modernist accounts of the origin; that is, it haunts all accounts that seek to postulate or describe the logic of the origin with Euclidian certainty. Such accounts routinely depart from the empirical in order to posit the constitutive as explanation for the existence of the empirical.[1] In the case of contract theory, this circularity manifests in a curious paradox that assumes that a number of individuals who live in a state of nature because they cannot honor a contract will leave the state of nature by honoring a contract (see Hampton 1986).

Less abstractly, we get a sense of the paradox when we ask: "In order to have entered a social contract, must we not assume that the individuals verbally agreed to do so and that they must have shared certain ideas about the undesirability of the state of nature and the desirability of civil society?" And do we not understand, under the former, a community of symbolic exchange and, under the latter, shared values? If so, is it not obvious then that civil society must have existed prior to the social contract? Formulated less stridently, would communication and shared values be possible in a world where individuals recognized merely the need for promises but not the need to keep them? Either way, it is clear that contract, contract theory must presuppose the kind of individuals who can no longer in any meaningful sense of the word be said to inhabit a "state of nature."

My suspicion is that, when it comes to his account of the origin, Girard's theory, too, is haunted by this circularity or tension between the historical and the constitutive. Girard seems to recognize a limit to the kind of constitutive causality we can posit on the back of empirical data. In "Generative Scapegoating," for instance, he comments:

> None of the clues I have discussed will ever enable us to reconstitute the real events behind the myth but, I repeat, it does not matter. The only thing that these clues permit us to ascertain is that some real violence must have taken place. This is insignificant from a historical viewpoint but of considerable significance in regard to the nature of mythology. The goal of this research is a generative principle, not a historical reconstitution. Anthropologists are right to regard the second goal as unattainable. (1987, 89)

The purpose of this chapter is not to trace the fine line between "generative principle" and "historical reconstitution." Rather, I am interested in trying to square the constitutive nature of this "generative principle" with the myth of South Africa's exceptionalism. To put it simply, if sacrificial violence *qua* generative principle explains the constitutive role that violence plays in the generation and regeneration of politico-juridical orders, how can peaceful transitions like that of South Africa be possible at all? Do exceptions like this—and there are others, besides South Africa—take us to the limits of Girard's theory? Or are they just that—exceptions that confirm the rule?

Here, I want to explore a third option that does not require us to either abandon Girard or simply accept that there may be exceptions to his theory. I want to save what I can of his rather strong claim that "some real violence" lurks behind every mythological account of the (re)generation of the social. To do that I will explore the possibility that what the South African case problematizes is not Girard's claim that violence *qua* generative principle is constitutive of all (re)generated orders, but rather, the relationship he posits between violence and mythology. My suspicion is that it problematizes if we want to understand the foundational nature of South Africa's discourse on reconciliation and forgiveness, we need to firstly deconstruct the model in relation to which that transition appears as an exception. In short, what I want to explore is the possibility that a deconstructed re-appropriation of Girard's claim will render that transition a very good example *of*, and not an exception *to*, his theory. This, then, is also an exercise in theory-making that seeks to address two related questions: How do we expand a theory in order to explain what appears to be an exception to that theory?

RETURN TO THE ORIGIN

So, where do we start? Perhaps with the commonplace belief that South Africa miraculously managed to avoid the kind of collective violence we have come to associate with transitions to democracy. Anybody who makes this claim recognizes an analytical or constitutive principle to the effect that "as a rule such transitions are violent." In other words, any allusion to "exceptionalism" implicitly or explicitly affirms a rule. What this rule is can be articulated quite precisely in Girardian terms as follows: any politico-juridical order exists as a system of difference that makes our lives as individuals and our existence as particular kinds of subjects meaningful. When, for a variety of socioeconomic reasons, that system de-differentiates, the most fundamental distinction upon which the system is premised, a distinction between legitimate and illegitimate violence, is eroded, exposing us in the process to what Hobbes would call the constitutive causes of social existence. This, for Girard, is mimetic rivalry. For the system to regenerate itself, the violent trajectory of this mimetic rivalry has to be directed towards a victim who will stand accused of having caused the de-differentiation in the first instance. The sacrificial exclusion of the victim will redirect the destructive trajectory of violence and either reinstate (regenerate) the historical system of difference or found (generate) a new politico-juridical order. Either way, this re-differentiation will be realized and legitimized, only when it successfully reinstates and institutionalizes the difference between legitimate

and illegitimate violence through a mythology that retrospectively commemorates the founding act of violence as legitimate sacrifice as opposed to
illegitimate murder. For Girard, this structure of collective violence is originary in the sense that it founded human culture and is repeated with every
crisis of de-differentiation, irrespective of time and place. One of the clearest
articulations of this claim can be found in "Generative Scapegoating." In that
essay, Girard writes that following a founding act of scapegoating, the primal
"community" immediately mythologizes the event. The myth will become
their recollection—"typically distorted, yet reliable on some crucially specific points—of a scapegoat process so powerful that it turns its victim . . . into
a transcendental symbol" (1987, 92). It is the detail of this account that we
need to look at for a deconstruction of the claims that result from it:

> The agitation and fear that preceded the selection of the scapegoat and the
> violence against him are followed, after his death, by a new mood of harmony
> and peace. To what, or, rather, to whom will the change be attributed? Obvi-
> ously, to *the all-powerful cause that dominates the entire community*: the
> scapegoat himself. Thus the scapegoat is *credited* with the *reconciliation and
> the peace, after being credited with the earlier disruption*. The absorption of
> all causality by the victim is so complete that he becomes a dynamic symbol of
> *supreme benevolence* as well as *supreme malevolence, of social order as well
> as disorder* . . . The change in the mood of the community, the change from
> panic to serenity, must be so swift and radical that it does not appear *"natu-
> ral."* It must therefore be *"supernatural,"* manipulated *from outside*; and since
> the scapegoat has subsumed all active causality unto himself, he cannot fail to
> be the grand manipulator, must be the *sole and all-powerful agent* in this affair
> (1987, 91–92; emphasis added).

In this story, we are presented with a simple, and, I would argue, unwork-
able opposition between violence and mythology. It is maintained that violence founds, but mythology "merely" legitimizes, that founding through an
act of retrospective interpretation. Now, we can only claim (as Girard does)
that violence is foundational, if we accord sole originary status to the brute
fact of violence, while considering the interpretation of that violence as,
perhaps, crucial and necessary in terms of that retrospective legitimation but
supplementary in terms of the origin. I find this problematic, and perhaps the
best way to illustrate why we need to surface the circularity between the
historical and constitutive at work here.

The story tells of a primordial act of sacrifice that unifies a hitherto
disparate collection of individuals as a community. Following the sacrifice of
the original victim the primal community experiences a profound sense of
"harmony and peace" or, as Girard also puts it, "reconciliation and peace."
(The idea that the primal community could have experienced a profound
sense of "reconciliation" is problematic, and I return to this, below). The

community explains this profound sense of calm and harmony to itself by crediting the scapegoat with the capacity to both destroy it and, through his death, being able to restore peace and calm. The original victim is the cause of "supreme benevolence" as well as "supreme malevolence, of social order as well as disorder." So far so good, but it is the originary experience of this ambivalence, the manner in which the original community interprets their own experience as a result of which they emerge unified, that I want to draw attention to. We are told that "[t]he change in the mood of the community, the change from panic to serenity, must be so swift and radical that it does not appear 'natural.' It must therefore be 'supernatural', manipulated from outside." It is important to note that Girard introduces the fundamental binary that enables this arch-interpretation by placing the oppositional terms "natural" and "supernatural" in quotations marks, signaling that he is at once using them and not using them. Of course, there is a very good reason why he should not want to use them and this is that, according to his theory, the very concept of "the sacred" (here, the "supernatural") does *not* exist prior to the arch-interpretation but is generated *through* that interpretation. Yet, it is their invocation here—albeit in quotation marks—that enables that very interpretation. And therein lies the auto-deconstruction of the narrative.

The story seeks to illustrate that the notion of the "outside" upon which the very idea of the sacred is premised, emerged as a result of the interpretation of the ambivalence of the original victim. But the fact is that the interpretation of that ambivalence is only enabled by the (ironic) introduction of the notion of the "beyond" and the "outside," which means that the interpretation could not have come about without assuming the very existence of the "outside," which is supposed to emerge as a result of the interpretation itself. In other words, the category of the transcendental is not created in the process of resolving the ambiguity of the original victim; rather, the victim's ambiguity is resolved with recourse to a notion of the transcendental that we now must assume to have pre-existed in the minds of the original individuals when they set out to mythologize the originary act of violence. What is supposed to emerge from the interpretation precedes the interpretation as a condition for its possibility.

One possible solution to this dilemma would consist in considering the transcendental to be *prior* to the interpretation that invokes it—perhaps as the kind of *a priori* suggested by Otto's notion of the *numinous*. But this would be contrary to the very argument advanced by Girard since the publication of *La Violence et le Sacré* (1972).

Such a deconstruction of Girard's account of the origin reveals the circularity that haunts all accounts of the origin. In fact, there is a double circularity at work here—one which echoes the contractarian circularity discussed earlier and a second that is peculiar to Girard. The contractarian echo consists in the fact that the act of creditation that resolves the ambivalent status of the original victim presupposes, as it does in the social contract narrative, the existence of a community with shared signification *of what exactly benevolence and malevolence mean* and how to express that meaning in a way that will be understood by all. In other words, what is assumed here is the pre-existence of symbolically mediated community. And this is why, earlier, I suggested that the use of the word "reconciliation" to describe the primal community's sense of peace and calm after the primordial sacrifice is problematic. In the absence of a prior community, there can be at most *unification* or *conciliation* of the primal individuals. This is their originary formation into a community. There can be no *re*-conciliation because the "re-" alludes to a pre-existing community that is being re-united or re-conciled. This cannot be the case, here.[2]

The Girardian specific version of that circularity manifests in the introduction—in quotation marks—of the terms that enable the creditation that, so the story goes, will generate those very terms. The implication of this ambivalent status of the concept of the "outside"—as that which is at once anterior and posterior to the original community—is very relevant here. I do not read it as a fundamental criticism of Girard. Rather, I see it simply as a useful way to critique the tension between the empirical and constitutive claims that haunt all accounts of the origin. Such a critique allows us to reverse the binary structure upon which his account of the origin is based and which, in this case, generates exceptions that cannot be accounted for in terms of that binary structure. It is to this reversal that I now turn.

RE-IMAGINING THE ORIGIN

The auto-deconstruction is a result of Girard's use of a binary construct that considers the brute fact of violence foundational or originary, while attributing supplementary status to the mythology of that violence, that is, to the complex creditation of the ambivalences associated with the victim. A deconstruction of that presumed relationship—one which highlights the circularities upon which it is premised—suggests that mythology, far from being supplementary to the founding, is as important to that founding as the violence it narrates. In short, that the origin itself is ambivalently split between violence and its narration, with both being equally fundamental or foundational. Let me clarify what I mean.

To deconstruct the claim that violence and violence alone is foundational does not mean that violence is not originary in the sense of being a generative principle or constitutive cause. After all, without the primal violence there can be no interpretation of that violence, no mythology of violence. What I am arguing, though, is that without the interpretation of that originary violence there will be no recollection of that violence either. The violence would not exist, and, in that sense, the mythology is as foundational or originary as the violence it commemorates. Here, the origin is dual, split between violence that is destructive in itself and violence that becomes generative because it is narrated as such. *Violence is not generative; it becomes generative when it is interpreted as generative.* In other words, violence is purely destructive until we generate a meaning through symbolic mediation, that is, through the kind of shared signification we associate with the kind of human association, however rudimentary, that remains presupposed by all accounts of the origin. Without narrative acts that credit benevolence and malevolence to the victim, there will only be forgotten brute facts; inversely, without the brute fact of violence, there will be no unifying narrative of recollection. The ambivalence Girard accredits the victim must be credited to the origin, as such, for the origin is at once destructively violent and generatively narrated as meaningful. Therein lies the ambivalence, not of the original victim but of the origin as such.

The primary function of mythologies of violence, then, consists not simply in legitimizing and instituting a difference between murder and sacrifice, between illegitimate and legitimate violence. Long before they accomplish that, and in order for them to do that, narratives of creditation act as archives of recollection that sustain the reality of the violence that happened, committing it to a memory that will, among other things, use those narratives retrospectively to confer legitimacy on the instituted difference between sacrifice and murder. Without this archival function, there can be no recollection and no founding. Narratives are foundational to memory and collective memory is foundational to the social. It makes little sense to argue that *what* is being remembered is somehow more originary than the act of remembrance.

Where does all this leave us in relation to our intuition that South Africa's transition to democracy, somehow, did not conform to the rule of the founding violence?

ORIGIN OF AN EXCEPTION

There can be little doubt that, when the former Apartheid regime entered into transitional negotiations with the African National Congress (ANC), there was wide-spread anticipation, nationally and internationally, of an imminent violent backlash from conservative sectors in the Afrikaner community. And of course, there was some violence—but nothing on the scale that was anticipated. For all intents and purposes, the peaceful transition into democracy defied expectations. In the introduction, I briefly alluded to some of the factors that may have accounted for this relatively peaceful transition. But talk of "defied expectations" does not quite add up to claims of an exception to the rule for at least two reasons. In the first instance, talk of exceptionalism takes a particularly narrow view of the extreme violence that marked both the liberation struggle and its violent repression by the Apartheid regime, at least from 1961 when the ANC officially embarked on an armed struggle. Many of the ensuing forms of collective violence conform to a classic Girardian analysis of both their scapegoating nature as well as their appropriation in terms of a retrospective mythology of founding violence.

The example of the so-called "necklace murders" in black South African townships illustrates this well. Devised as a particular form of community-based violence, individuals who were accused of subverting the ends of the liberation struggle were brutally killed by placing a car tire around their necks, dousing them with petrol and setting them alight. The accusations on the basis of which they were "convicted" exemplified the kind of accusations we associate with scapegoating in the sense that their truth could neither be verified nor contested. Accusations such as "Maki slept with a white police man" or "Maki is a police informer" could never be verified or contested for the simple reason that they would be private, unobserved acts. In other words, these accusations derived whatever legitimacy they had from the critical mass they achieved, mimetically, among the mob that needed to create the requisite solidarity among themselves necessary to oppose the Apartheid regime (Praeg 2007).

This form of violence peaked roughly in the period 1985–1992. Accurate figures are difficult to obtain but some studies have found that there were 428 necklacings in the period 1985–1990. Equally relevant here is that necklacing seemed to die down as the nationwide resistance to Apartheid withered in 1987, only to increase again from 1989 right up to the transition to democracy (Ball 1994). Not only were these classic instances of the kind of violence we associate with political transitions, they were also foundational in the very precise sense of the word. Their stated, if contradictory aim, was to bring about a new democratic order. And of course, therein lies the profound paradox or aporia we have come to associate with all forms of foundational violence, namely, that they violate exactly what they stand for in order to bring about a new order of things. In this case, the very values and principles we associate with democracy—evidential truth, due process, human rights, and so forth—were not extended to the victims that stood accused of subverting the realization of those very ideals.

The second reason why talk of exceptionalism should be treated with caution is because of the manner in which the *Truth and Reconciliation Commission* (TRC) set about to mythologize the violence that reigned right up until the formal hand-over of power. For the sake of continuity, I shall stay with the example of the necklace murders. There can be little doubt that, in the vast majority of cases, these acts of community "jungle justice" executed by "kangaroo courts" amounted to criminal acts of murder that gained whatever temporary legitimacy they may have had from an ideology of a

"People's War" in which all citizens were considered combatants in the struggle against Apartheid (see Jeffrey 2009). But, if this ideology provided a contemporaneous legitimacy to necklacing, it would be the TRC that retrospectively afforded them a spectacular foundational status that converted victims of crime onto "heroes of the struggle." One example must suffice. In his essay, "Silence in My Father's House: Memory, Nationalism, and Narratives of the Body," Robins writes how

> [t]his was graphically demonstrated in an SABC [South African Broadcasting Corporation] news broadcast of [Maki] Skosana's sister recounting to the [Truth and Reconciliation] Commission how, after her sister was burnt alive, she went to the mortuary . . . This gruesome recollection of the horror of Skosana's terrible death was interrupted by the commissioner's call for a minute of silence to salute Maki's heroism and martyrdom. This silencing of the witness sought to transform the woman who had been necklaced as an *impimpi* (informer) into a hero of the struggle, a martyr whose body had been sacrificed in the name of the new nation. (1998, 138)

I share this gruesome legacy of the anti-Apartheid struggle, here, with the sole intention of decentering the myth of a miraculously peaceful transition. Any such myth can have whatever currency it has only on the basis of a myopic view of the extreme violence that marked (and marred) the transition to a democratic order founded, in the classic Girardian sense of the word, on the successful retrospective mythologizing of that violence as sacrifice and not murder. What made these TRC-based founding myths so powerful is that, although (as the case of necklace murders clearly illustrates) they referenced forms of violence constitutive of a sacrificially constructed (predominantly) black struggle community, the mythologizing of these acts of violence allowed them to be deployed, via the TRC, as founding myths of a united, non-racial South African community.

But what does all of this have to do with the deconstruction of Girard's account of the origin, a deconstruction that, I hope, demonstrated the need to attribute equal originary status to both the brute fact of violence and its generative interpretation through acts of interpretation? That deconstruction allows me to anticipate and counter an objection to the above reading of the violent Founding of the new democratic order that goes something like this: "The claim that South Africa's transition was exceptional does not relate to the three decades of violent resistance to the anti-apartheid regime. Of course there was violence. But the transition remains exceptional because at the moment of hand-over to the new ANC-led government, there was no violent resistance. This as an exception to the rule of the founding that maintains that all new orders are sacrificially generated."

It never ceases to amaze me how people can simultaneously praise South Africa for its miraculous and peaceful transition *and* its profound discourse

on reconciliation and forgiveness. For, what are the concepts of "reconciliation" and forgiveness" other than textual archives and creditations of violence? What is "reconciliation" if not an archive of wrong-doing? What is
"forgiveness" if not, first and foremost, a recollection and creditation, an
interpretation of the violation of one human being by another? Acts of reconciliation and forgiveness are, first and foremost, acts of recollection through
which we re-member our dis-membered selves. It does not matter that there
was no excess of violence at the moment of South Africa's transition to
democracy. The absence of extreme violence *at that particular point* does
not make the transition an exception to the rule for the simple reason that
violence alone is never originary. What *is* originary, is violence *and* its
creditation, the brute fact of violation *and* the generative interpretation
through which that violence is remembered and made meaningful. That is
what it means to have had a *Truth and Reconciliation Commission*, problematic as it may have been in a great number of ways, at the founding moment. It was never a miraculous substitute or exceptional alternative *to* the
brute fact of violent civil war and retribution. Rather, it was a formalized recollection *of* violence, a generative interpretation of brute fact that was as
originary as the violence it recalled.

WHY DOES THE FASCINATION LINGER?

Much has been made of the humanism that partly informed the way the TRC
was conceived and how the victims of Apartheid conducted themselves
there. Of all the accounts of "miraculous" and unfathomable forgiveness, the
testimony of Cynthia Ngewu—whose son Christopher Piet was brutally murdered by the Apartheid security police—has perhaps become metonymic of
that humanism:

> This thing called reconciliation . . . if I am understanding it correctly . . . if it
> means this perpetrator, this man who has killed Christopher Piet, if it means he
> becomes human again, this man, so that I, so that all of us, get our humanity
> back . . . then I agree, then I support it all (discussed in Praeg 2000, 275).

I have revisited this statement many times and every time I am astounded
and fascinated all over again. And I'm not alone in this. The TRC proceedings and statements like Ms. Ngewu's fascinated people all over the world.
Much of that fascination has translated into a fascination with *uBuntu* (the
name used in South African discourse for what is generally known as African
humanism). The most well-known explanation of that humanism comes from
Mbiti (1969) who summarized it as a dictum that conveys the belief that "I
am because we are." But I am wary of our fascination with *uBuntu* because it
so easily masquerades as a contemporary instance of the West's persistent

exoticising of things African: if not the extremity of its violence, then the exceptionalism of its humanism. Anybody who is familiar with the philosophical traditions referred to as "communitarianism"—particularly of the feminist "ethics of care" variety—will recognize in the *uBuntu* claim to our interdependence something communitarians call our "constitutive attachments," that is, the idea that our selves are constituted by our attachments to others. I do not think there is a meaningful difference between *uBuntu* and these communitarian philosophies. This is not to say that there is no difference at all but rather to suggest that the difference exists at the level of praxis: *uBuntu* is a communitarian praxis while in the west communitarianism is mostly appreciated as abstract, philosophical alternative to political liberalism. The difference is one between living praxis and abstract philosophy.

What drives the fascination with the TRC and, by implication, the myth of exceptionalism is, I believe, not the extraordinary and unique humanism expressed by victims of the apartheid regime but rather the fact that so many Africans trusted communitarian praxis at a pivotal moment in South Africa's history. That praxis was the condition for the possibility of generative and founding acts of forgiveness and reconciliation—in short, the condition for a politics of grace.

REFERENCES

Ball, Joanna. 1994. "The Ritual of the Necklace." Occasional paper written for the Centre for the Study of Violence and Reconciliation. www.csvr.org.za/pubslist/pubspolt.htm.
Foucault, Michel. 1973. *The Order of Things*. New York: Vintage Books.
Girard, René. 1987. "Generative Scapegoating." Chapter 1 in *Violent Origins: Ritual Killing and Cultural Formation*, edited by Robert G. Hamerton-Kelly. Stanford: Stanford University Press.
Hampton, Jean. 1986. *Hobbes and the Social Contract Tradition.* Cambridge: Cambridge University Press.
Jeffrey, Anthea. 2009. *People's War: New Light on the Struggle for South Africa.* Johannesburg: Jonathan Ball.
Mbiti, John. 1969. *African Religions and Philosophy.* London: Heineman.
Praeg, Leonhard, *African Philosophy and the Quest for Autonomy: A Philosophical Investigation.* Amsterdam: Rodopi, 2000.
———. 2007. *The Geometry of Violence: Africa, Girard, Modernity.* Stellenbosch: SUN Press.
———. 2008 "The Aporia of Collective Violence." *Law and Critique*, Vol. 19. No. 2.
Robins, Steven. 1998. "Silence in My Father's House: Memory, Nationalism, and Narratives of the Body." Chapter 9 in *Negotiating the Past: The Making of Memory in South Africa*, edited by Sarah Nuttall and Carli Coetzee. Cape Town: Oxford University Press.

NOTES

1. A circularity that perhaps offers us a very good example of the relationship between the empirical and transcendental as analyzed by Foucault in *The Order of Things* (1973, 318) under the heading "Man and his doubles."

2. Many people criticized the South African *Truth and Reconciliation Commission* on similar grounds. Where there had never been a community but only the apartheid of various communities, it was argued, the unification of those communities for the first time into a polity cannot sensibly be called a *re*-conciliation. It should rather have been called the *Truth and Conciliation Commission.*

IV

RECONCILIATION IN CONTEXT

Chapter Twelve

Seeding Reconciliation in a Theater of War

A New Role for Military Chaplains (Mimetic Modeling the Will to Embrace)

S. K. Moore

For more than five decades, Canadian Forces (CF) chaplains have been deploying with their troops to areas of the globe still convulsing from the horrific violence that has repeatedly pitted neighbor against neighbor. Through dialogue and/or the distribution of humanitarian assistance, operational chaplains have engaged the leadership of local religious communities. Such ministry has served to ameliorate severed relationships, which may sustain continued violence or lead to entrenched estrangement. As such, ministry to divided communities is increasingly being viewed as a value added to mission mandates by Command.

Over the years, Canadian chaplains have spearheaded humanitarian assistance projects in various theaters of operations. As Brigadier General (retired) Karl McLean, former Chaplain General of the Canadian Armed Forces, was known to say, "We make peace through humanitarian assistance." His reference to "peacemaking" through humanitarian operations is demonstrative of an impulse that has stirred chaplains and troops to come to the aid of communities struggling to rebuild their lives after years of destructive conflict. Theologically, I believe this praxis to be a sometimes conscious, most often unconscious, impulse toward peacemaking beyond traditional ministry patterns in operation.

As the focus of the world's attention turned to the intra-state conflict of the former Yugoslavia in the early 1990s, so did the Government of Canada's mandates for the Canadian Forces. A noticeable shift in the complexion and complexity of missions transpired as the international community intervened within the former Yugoslavia's implosion of ethno-religious conflict. It is at this juncture that movement in the external operational ministry [1] of a number of military chaplains began to emerge—an impulse in the agency of chaplains to do ministry beyond more traditional roles. As indirect reconciliation,[2] humanitarian assistance during these years continued as a mainstay of Canadian operations. However, it was the emergence of "informal reconciliation"[3] that witnessed the strengthening of the impulse of agency. Through the building of relation among the leadership of the local ethno-religious communities, chaplains—religious leaders in their own right—began to mimetically model the will to embrace.[4] Miroslav Volf, a theologian at Yale University, describes the will to embrace as that hesitant, yet hopeful, opening of the self to the other in the arduous task of bridging the chasm of alienation and separation between the self and the other, often over against the backdrop of tremendous hurt and distrust known to conflict situations.

> The will to be in relation with the other sees the creation of a relational landscape that eclipses disfigurement. It is not that blemishes cease to exist, rather that the radiating will to embrace within the self relegates disfigurement to the shadows in the hopes of restored relationship... it is the "light" of the will to embrace that opens the mind and softens the heart to begin to see the humanity of the other; to approach the other close enough that a gesture toward reconciliation may be perceived and the restoration of relation may begin. (Moore 2013)

In conflict zones, faith group communities are often engulfed in the larger conflicts of their respective identity groups. Where religion is co-opted by leaders endeavoring "to legitimate discrimination and violence against groups of different race or language" (Appleby 2000), recurring violence often afflicts communities desperately searching for ways to stem the reciprocal tides of mimetic violence. Entrenchment and estrangement are some of the more prominent residual effects. Through the chaplains' mimetic modeling of acceptance, tolerance, and hospitality among alienated religious and community leaders, a gradual engaging of the estranged other occurs. It is in encounter—where religious leaders come together for dialogue—that one does not simply see the other from one's own perspective but begins to view oneself from the perspective of the other—one sees oneself through the eyes of the other, something Miroslav Volf calls double vision. Amplifying the role of double vision in the reframing of relation, Volf states,

> I can't simply see myself the way I see myself. I have to expose myself to hearing how I am perceived. Then, as we are seen, we can exchange perspectives. It is only though exchanging perspectives that we can gain an adequate perception both of ourselves and of the other. (Volf 1996)

During such encounters, a gradual recognition of the humanity of the other emerges.

The objective of this chapter is to explore the *mimetic* phenomenon of *modeling* in the operational ministry of military chaplains in general—specifically Canadian Forces chaplains in this instance. Documented anecdotal evidence exists in both the Bosnian and Afghan contexts. For the purposes here, the Bosnian operational ministry of Roman Catholic priest, Padre Gabriel Legault, will be consulted. His experience will serve as a lens through which to view the *mimetic modeling* of the *will to embrace*. Poignant also will be the dénouement of the *mimetic* nature of deep-rooted conflict theorized by scholar-practitioner Vern Neufeld Redekop. His concepts of open and closed relational systems will reveal the destructive dynamics prevalent among groups in conflict, discerning for the reader their provenance and manifestation. Offering balance to the deleterious nature of such overt violence, the work of Rebecca Adams will aid Redekop in depicting how the desire to be in harmonious relation with the *other* is engendered. Several schematics will be used to elucidate the *mimetic modeling* of the *will to embrace* by chaplains in theaters of operation. These diagrams will aid in illuminating how *mimesis* can precipitate the beginnings of reconciliation among estranged religious communities, still nursing the wounded memory of conflict.

The Case Study

In 2002–2003, Padre Gabriel Legault deployed to the interior of Bosnia with first battalion of the Princess Patricia Canadian Light Infantry (1PPCLI) Battle Group (1,200–1,400 personnel). As is the custom in operations, the Battle Group systematically fanned out over its assigned Area of Operations (AO), positioning company size (120 personnel) detachments in various locales. One such company was Charlie Company headquartered in Dravar, to which Padre Legault was attached. Several platoons (30–40 personnel) deployed to satellite locations, small villages of which Glamoč was one. As is the practice of *internal* operational ministry, Padre Legault visited them regularly, offering the sacrament and attending to any pastoral needs.

The platoon commander had been unsuccessful in establishing cordial relations with the local Croatian Roman Catholic priest, an influential community leader. The young lieutenant solicited the help of Padre Legault who immediately visited the priest. Upon realizing that Legault was a priest, coffee was offered and the beginnings of dialogue began extending to cordial visits over a period of months. In similar fashion, Legault was able to build relation with the local Serbian Orthodox priest as well as the resident Bosniak Imam.

Like most deployed contingents, a degree of humanitarian aid found its way to the various camps, as was the case for Glamoč. As relation with the various religious leaders strengthened, Legault soon discovered that residual estrangement from the war was most pronounced between the Serbian Orthodox community and that of the Bosniaks. He also learned of the persistent pressure these leaders felt from the people to obtain humanitarian assistance, something that was in short supply. Legault recognized an opportunity to seed reconciliation[5] between these local clerics and their respective faith communities. The idea of an *intercommunal committee* for the distribution of contingent humanitarian assistance began to crystallize in his thinking, a project to which a measure of receptivity existed despite lingering strained relations. Such was the case between the Orthodox priest and the newly arrived Imam. Having resided in Glamoč for more than two years, the Imam had yet to have a conversation with the priest.

Individually, during his visits with the various clerics, Legault delicately broached the prospect of the establishment of an *intercommunal committee* to aid in the distribution of humanitarian assistance that often arrived through the supply lines of the local Canadian contingent. His concept envisioned the initial striking of a committee comprised of the local clergy, mandated to bring forward the names of three highly regarded lay members from their respective communities for a total of nine. The concept was for this group to determine where the greatest need existed for particular items of humanitarian aid, which, in turn, would be the criteria for distribution. He believed a lay committee would be less susceptible to political polarization. The religious leaders of all three faith communities agreed. Legault's commanding officer gave his support to the initiative, cognizant of its potential long-range benefits.

A fraternal meal was shared together with the platoon commander and CIMIC[6] officer who joined the chaplain and his fellow colleagues from Glamoč. A pivotal aspect of the ministry of hospitality, the informal ritual encounter of breaking bread together, will be explored later in this chapter. Padre Legault opened the repast with a revision of the serenity prayer that he prepared for the meeting.

> Let us pray to the Creator of *mankind*, the God of all. Bless us, our families and the people to whom we minister. Bless the food we are about to receive. Grant us the serenity to accept the things we cannot change, the courage to change the things we can and the wisdom to know the difference. (Legault, 2005)

The platoon commander and CIMIC officer prayed a portion of the prayer, with Legault offering his portion in the vernacular (Serbo-Croat), itself a gesture of embrace. Of course, interpreters were always present to facilitate conversation. The age-old custom of breaking bread together bore witness to the beginning of dialogue. For the first time the local Imam and Serbian Orthodox priest shared exchanges regarding parish and mosque life in Glamoč.

Recognizing the significance and symbolic nature of the meeting, Padre Legault offered the following version of a Chinese parable,

> As the story goes, centuries ago a certain village in Asia experienced hardship. As is the case today in that part of the world, rice was the staple of their diet. An extended drought had severely reduced the rice crop and the people were beginning to starve. Fortunately, the rains returned before the end of the growing season, reviving the crop in time for a meagre but sufficient harvest. To add to their misery and due to an extended time without sufficient food, the people had developed a disease known in their region as *locked-elbow.* Their dilemma was now that they had food to eat, they could not bend their elbow to bring their chopsticks to their mouths. They were unable to feed themselves. (Legault, 2005)

Based on the above parable, Padre Legault then drew the guests' attention to the center of the table where he had prepared a plate of food. He then challenged them with the same dilemma as the Chinese, inviting them to resolve the quandary of how they would manage to eat with arms that would not bend. Legault related,

> The religious leaders began to look around the dining table and quickly determined that the only solution was to feed one another. They could put their utensils in the food and manoeuvre it to the mouth of the *other*. And I (Legault) said, "That's it. I think we are at the point now in our journey where we need to feed each other . . . where we need to help each other if we want to survive." (Legault 2005)

On that note, the meeting moved into relaxed conversation. Legault described the gathering as proactive, with all in attendance endorsing his concept for an Intercommunal Committee for the distribution of humanitarian assistance.

This gathering of the religious leaders of these formerly warring ethno-religious communities reverberated throughout Glamoč and its environs as a *symbol* of what could be *transcending* of their differences based on the greater need of the many, a sign of unity and an affirmation of the humanity of the *other*.

The Application

The catalytic nature of Padre Legault's relation among the religious leaders of Glamoč aptly exemplifies the efficacy of *mimetic modeling*. The following series of schematics are designed to illustrate this process. As indicated earlier, Redekop's notion of *open* and *closed relational systems*, and Adams's notion of intersubjectivity, will aid in articulating this operational ministry. Each schematic will build upon the previous, methodically bringing forward this operational phenomenon.

This initial schematic places us in the context of a theater of operations where Redekop's *closed relational systems* are at play. It depicts an environment, where mimetic rivalry between the *self* and the *other* is maintained in rigid exclusivity in relation, often manifested in overt violence or in protracted isolation, all of which precipitates suspicion, misunderstanding and potential reoccurrence of violence.

The uneven line portrays the unpredictability and uncertainty of life's circumstances intensified by a conflict environment. The *self* (S) and the *other* (O) are representative of either individuals or groups ensnared in a closed relational system exclusive of other groups, characterized by entrenched positions and frequently punctuated with overt violence. As indicated, *mimetic* desire manifests in the *other*, becoming an obstacle to what the *self* believes to be in their best interests. *Mimetic* rivalry exacerbates the intensity of the mounting conflict, resulting in spiralling violence that witnesses the reciprocal dynamic of victim and perpetrator continually exchanging roles in escalation. Such *mimetic* violence manifests increasing levels of

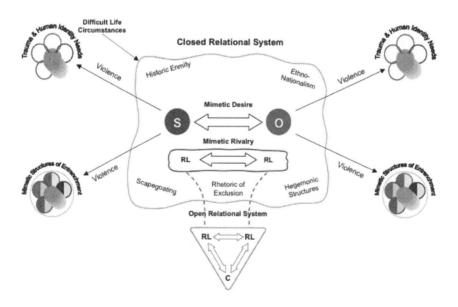

Figure 12.1. The Dynamics of Closed Relational Systems between Groups in Conflict Situations. Vern Neufeld Redekop and S. K. Moore.

hostility as "one *gives* twice as good as one gets." *Historical enmity* between groups often spans decades, if not centuries. Deep-seated resentment over past wrongs—real or perceived—is nurtured and carried forward from one generation to the next.[7] Hostilities simmer, punctuated by seasons of violence. Contributing to closed relational systems are aspirations of statehood and sentiments relating to the sacredness of land and an oft-inviolable destiny of its people. *Ethno-nationalism*, in particular, shapes identity around land *and* space—a place to live, move, and act—to becoming land *as* place. Identity becomes historically rooted in the idea of a homeland (Redekop 2001). Among other identity markers known to contribute to *ethno-nationalism*, language, religion, and culture are predominant. *Scapegoating* occurs when two or more groups are reconciled at the expense of a third party. The identified group is deemed responsible for disrupting or threatening life for the majority. Once the scapegoated are expelled or destroyed, tensions are relived, and the majority groups coalesce into a more harmonious whole (Girard 1996). Redekop adds,

> The hatred directed toward the scapegoat unites members of the community. They forget their antagonisms, and the violent emotions that they have had for one another are projected onto the surrogate victim. Everyone becomes united in desiring the same negative—the destruction of the scapegoat. (Redekop 2002)

Hegemonic structures manifest in the dialectic between the dominant (*self*) and subjugated (*other*). Few have written more passionately than Paul Farmer about oppressive socioeconomic structures. His work resonates with the topic at hand in that the conditions created by hegemonic structures invariably inflict severe socioeconomic hardship for the subjugated, something he defines as structural violence. He elucidates that structural violence is a broad rubric that includes a host of offences against human dignity, "extreme and relative poverty, social inequalities ranging from racism to gender inequality, and the more spectacular forms of violence that are uncontestably human rights abuses, some of them punishment for efforts to escape structural violence" (Farmer 2003). He further articulates that where a history exists of such domination, oppressive economically driven conditions markedly increase the probability of acts of violence. State power (the dominant) is most often responsible for human rights violations, perpetuating "social and economic inequities that determine who will be at risk for assaults and who will be shielded from them" (Farmer 2003). Rhetoric *of exclusion* is pervasive where closed relational systems have become entrenched. The *other* is deemed beyond any meaningful dialogue and the indisputable cause of the tension and conflict. This becomes the lens through which all communication is viewed. The exclusivity of closed relational systems spawns some of the more ugly aspects of deep-rooted conflict of which demonizing and dehumanizing the *other* are two. In demonizing, evil qualities repulsive to one*self* are attributed to the enemy, for the more the enemy is demonized, the purer *self* becomes, rendering *self*-criticism of no effect (Moses 1990). Dehumanization takes a further step. It is a direct attack on the humanity and dignity of the *other*. The out-group is considered to be sub-human, literally no better than animals or their behaviour is considered to be crazy and irrational (Ryan 1995). They are deemed "not worthy of being related to as presenting a likeness of ourselves, [consequently] they need not be empathized with" (Moses 1990). In closed relational systems—as indicated by the groups of circles off to the side—*human identity needs* are either threatened or unmet. These needs are meaning, connectedness, security, recognition, and action. Redekop illumines that where the relationship of *self* and *other* is entrenched, the identity need for security become heightened, leading to viewing life in black and white terms, i.e., friends become enemies. Here, there is a passionate need for validation of one's hurt and vulnerability. Where violence is a reality, people may become traumatized—the top set of circles—leaving them dissociated, unable to empathize or connect with *others*. Also, not uncommon, are the establishing of entrenched positions—the bottom set of circles—where the conflict is rigidly viewed in a black and white perspective—"us" and "them."

Pivotal to the mimetic modeling of chaplains is the building of relation with the religious other(s). John Paul Lederach speaks of the significance of relation as a means to transcend the mimetic nature of violence, releasing its victims from recurring cycles of conflict.

> . . . the centrality of relationship accrues special meaning, for it is both the context in which cycles of violence happen and the generative energy from which transcendence of those same cycles bursts forth. Time and again, where in small or large ways the shackles of violence are broken, we find a singular tap root that gives life to the moral imagination: the capacity for individuals and communities to imagine themselves in a web of relationship even with their enemies. (Lederach 2005)

This was especially true between the Serbian Orthodox priest and the Muslim Imam who had not spoken in more than two years, yet living in the same small village.

This second schematic introduces the beginnings of *mimetic modeling* by chaplains. In Glamoč, a *closed relational system* was in effect among the religious leaders, as communication was non-existent, leaving the faith communities with a negative model. This schematic cites an additional *relational system*, with the chaplain drawing them out of their *entrenched* positions, by moving the religious leaders (RL) toward an *open relational system*.[8]

Legault engendered relation with all three religious leaders, mimetically modeling the *will to embrace* via an *open relational system*, including all three communities. Explicitly or tacitly, he conveyed that their various ethno-cultural distinctions were respected and valued.

True to hospitality, trust was earned, kindness was expressed, and pain acknowledged, enabling a sense of safety to emerge that encouraged the sharing of their story.

Seen here in diagram below, the mimetic modeling that occurred between Padre Legault and the religious leaders. The solid lines represent the open relational system existing between Padre Legault and the religious leaders as they moved beyond the confines of the *self/other* dialectic to include *others*. The dotted line represents the closed relational system that continues to exist between the religious leaders, yet moving towards an inter-relational recep-tivity in the form of intercommunal committee, that is, moving away from their entrenched isolation.

Mimetic Modeling

(Movement toward a more open relational system)

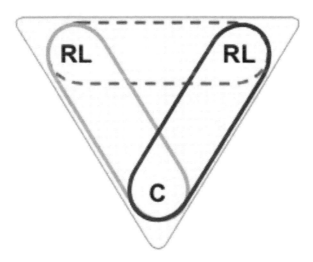

Figure 12.2.   Rehumanizing the *other* via the mimetic modeling of chaplains.
Vern Neufeld Redekop and S. K. Moore.

In nurturing an *open relational system* among the religious leaders, Legault modeled his subjectivity, i.e., "the capacity to participate fully in a loving dynamic of giving and receiving in relation to others" (Adams 2002). Legault genuinely demonstrated this loving dynamic in intersubjectivity, what Rebecca Adams defines as "the dual emphasis of both acting, yet also being acted upon; of desiring, yet also being receptive to other people's desires" (Adams in Redekop 2002). Her interdependent loving dynamic (giving and receiving in relation to the *other*), expresses itself in Redekop's *mimetic structures of blessing* as the *self* desires the well being of the *other*, with ever-expanding options oriented toward life.

Where the mimetic modeling of the will to embrace occurs, transcendence emerges. The genuine gestures of the good will of the other come into focus over and against a backdrop of tremendous hurt and wrong. In addition, the in-breaking of transcendence in Glamoč was manifested in the desired creation of the Intercommunal Committee consisting of religious lay representation from all three ethno-religious faith groups. Legault's initiation of the first multi-faith gathering of the leadership of all three faith groups in Glamoč poignantly holds significance for operations. Their "willingness" to congregate expressed the tentative, yet palpable, first yearnings of the will to embrace the other. Here, the once rigidly exclusive closed relational system between the Orthodox and Roman Catholic priests yielded to first impulses to be inclusive of former enemies, (in this case, the resident Imam, a religious and cultural leader of the local Muslim community). The mimetic modeling of an open relational system offered itself as a skylight through which rays of a different way of being could shine.

The above schematic depicts the open relational systems of the chaplain as mimetic modeling evolves to become what Adams calls the will to intersubjective creative love (Adams 2000), allowing for an interchangeability and mutuality of roles. Again, the hard lines of the closed relational system have changed to dotted more permeable lines, penetrated by the open relational system of the chaplain. Suggested are the beginnings of intersubjectivity, where *self* is enriched as a result of being in relation with the *other*. According to Adams, one could depict Padre Legault's desire for the well-being of the religious leaders as love for the other, conveying a sense of autonomy and dignity . . . not a diminishing of the *other* typical of mimetic structures of violence.

Such *mimetic modeling* promotes a movement away from the replicating of violence and actively toward an ethic of peace where human flourishing in interconnectedness is experienced as the continual creation of intersubjective relation (Adams 2000). It is in the context of such relation that "new experiences, responses, and solutions to problems between people or groups must be negotiated and created in ways that honor the reality of this fundamental intersubjectivity" (Adams 2000, 296).

Applied to such contexts, Adams's paradigm gives way to a general theory "on which we might build a common ethic, understanding of human beings, and practice of peacemaking" (Adams 2000, 298). More explicitly, mimetic modeling may be understood as *self* (Limited Subject) mimetically desiring the "enriched subjectivity" of *other* (Model), or third parties, to the degree of appropriating that subjectivity to *self*, leading to empowerment for creative change, i.e. seeing the humanity of the *other*.

Legault's desire for the well-being of the religious leaders becomes a virtual contagion. Imitating Legault's desire, they come to desire their own well-being which in turn "leads to an increase [in one's] self-esteem and self-respect, strengthen[ing] [one's] self-confidence, and lead[ing] to self-recognizance" (Adams 2002).

The hard lines of the closed relational system continue to soften (broken line), and the beginnings of dialogue and cooperation between faith group leaders and their respective communities start to emerge. A transcending of entrenchment begins to emerge as the religious leaders look to their own nongovernmental organizations (NGOs), faith groups, and militaries for a more tangible way to embrace the humanity of the *other*. Although recognizing that much mistrust and animosity has existed between them, the religious leaders look for a way to reinforce the recognition that we are all human and deserve to be treated as such. Lines of communication begin to develop and cooperation for the betterment of all becomes manifest. Albeit, Legault's initiative was embryonic, the vision is for the mimetic nature of such encounters to create a rippling effect throughout the various faith group communities.

Further reflection reveals that the informal and constructive ritual of breaking bread together in the Canadian compound holds much symbolism: the initial movement toward the mutuality of a more open relational system, the inclusivity of the *other*. The ritual of a shared meal employed a time-honoured tradition, breaking through the rigidity of the local entrenched social structures (Schirch 2005).

Relation was initiated with the religious leaders from each ethno-religious community. As such, Legault mimetically modeled the inclusion of the marginalized Imam for the Serb and Croat clergy. Politically sensitive, he selected a neutral location for the culturally traditional breaking of bread together. For the religious leaders of Glamoč, the shared meal provided a humanizing space where ossified identities could begin to soften. The meal represented an informal and constructive ritual of inversion whereby the social relations within the collective religious community of Glamoč were turned upside down, if only for the length of the ritual (Schirch 2005).

Transcendence was evident as these assembled clerics, for the first time in years, rose above their exclusivity and isolation. The *will to embrace* brought them into a new space in relation, one of mutuality and unity. In this fledgling Intercommunal Committee, they agree to choose the greater good of the need of the *other*, regardless of ethnic origin, as the guiding principle for the distribution of the much-needed humanitarian aid. Padre Legault *mimetically modeled* such mutuality and interdependence in the building of relation, thus creating a means by which the blessing of justice could emerge. Hence, the seeding of reconciliation took place.

As such, the three faith communities looked for a way to transcend the entrenchment that had robbed their people of a better way . . . wholeness and fulfillment. Padre Legault mimetically modeled for them this wholeness.

Epilogue

Ad hoc experiences of this nature are charged with possibilities and continue to occur. Sadly, as in the Legault case above, where policy and structures are not in place, it is difficult to sustain such efforts. The envisioned Lay Committee for the distribution of humanitarian aid never came to fruition. Padre Legault returned to Canada at the end of his tour, as did his Battle Group—the incoming rotation had other priorities. This is the fault of no one, simply the reality of the fluidity of Operations. However, this is not to suggest that lessons have not been learned from Padre Legault's experience and those of others, who have gone before him and served since.

Over the past decade, this author has chronicled the operational experiences of military chaplains from a number of NATO nations (and beyond) who have engaged local, regional, and in some instances, national religious leaders. In addition, the literature on peacebuilding and reconciliation has been consulted, research has been conducted, and case studies written. Due to increasing interest, senior military leadership has taken note of the potential of such operational ministry. The military in Canada and the United States, in particular, has begun to invest in what is now known as Religious Leader Engagement (RLE). As of 2013, in the Canadian Armed Forces, both RLE Policy and Doctrine now exist. Both American and Canadian Chaplain Schools are actively training chaplains in Religious Area Assessment (RAA), what might be defined as the first level of Religious Leader Engagement. With the resurgence of religion as a driver of contemporary conflict, chaplains are increasingly called upon to advise Command and to educate the troops as to the nature of the religious element within their geographical area of responsibility in a theater of operations, referred to as an Area of Operations (AO). From a strategic perspective, Commanders are desirous of all the available information about local populations in which religious communities factor significantly. In recent years, a curriculum has been developed to begin training of chaplains to be more resourceful. The following is a descriptor of RAA.

The intent of RAA in operations is to determine the basis for what people do and why they do it with respect to religion. As a capability, deploying chaplains increasingly posses the skills to accumulate and categorize information relating to the religious practices and traditions of indigenous populations within an AO. This information will be gathered from as wide a range of resources as practicably possible in the amount of time allotted prior to deployment. In a very real sense, this remains a living document once networking among local religious leaders and their communities becomes a reality.

Coupled with advanced theological training, analysis of this nature positions chaplains to better interpret the nuances of religious belief that often escape detection—something that could be very costly to a mission. In grasping something of the meaning and reality of the faith perspective, chaplains are more apt to appreciate how the belief system of the grassroots person may color their response to given mission initiatives, plans of action, troop movements, etc. The nature of command often necessitates sending troops into harms way. As such, the availability of all information pertinent to the decision-making process is critical. Advising commanders of the possible pitfalls or backlashes of given courses of action with respect to religious communities is a crucial aspect of the role of chaplains. (Moore 2013)

Further to the above, as of June 2011, Religious Leader Engagement was endorsed by the Canadian Forces Army as a new capability under development. This is inclusive of: (1) networking, whereby chaplains move among religious communities, bringing forward concerns that they may have with the view to addressing them; (2) partnering, with the focus of determining community needs, facilitating the bringing together community leaders with those who have the resources to meet those needs, and (3) actual peacebuilding, where chaplains facilitate bringing estranged religious leaders together for dialogue or collaborative activities between communities with a view to creating new narratives, where old ones have only served to create distance, misunderstanding, and, at times, hostilities. Albeit, there have been significant instances of peacebuilding, they are more rare but hold much potential, if they are managed correctly. Documented cases of RLE, in its various manifestations, have occurred with chaplains from Canada (Bosnia and Afghanistan), the United States (Iraq), France (Kosovo), Norway (Afghanistan), and New Zealand (Afghanistan) (Moore 2013). Instances have also been reported from South Africa (Burundi) and Australia (East Timor).

REFERENCES

Adams, Rebecca. 2000. "Loving Mimesis and Girard's 'Scapegoat of the Text': A Creative Reassessment of Mimetic Desire." Pp. 277–307 in *Violence Renounced: René Girard, Biblical Studies, and Peacemaking,* edited by William M. Swartley. Telford, Pennsylvania: Pandora Press, 2000.

Appleby, R. Scott. 2000. *The Ambivalence of the Sacred: Religion, Violence and Reconciliation.* Lanham, Maryland: Rowman & Littlefield Publishers.

Farmer, Paul. 2003. *Pathologies of Power: Health, Human Rights and the New War on the Poor.* Berkley and Los Angeles: University of California Press.

Girard, René. 1996. *The Girard Reader,* edited by James G. Williams. New York: Crossroad Publishing, 1996.

Lederach, John Paul. 2005. *The Moral Imagination: The Art and Soul of Building Peace.* New York: Oxford University Press, 2005.

Moore, S.K. 2013. *Military Chaplains as Agents of Peace: Religious Leader Engagement in Conflict and Post-conflict Environments.* Lanham, Maryland: Lexington Books.

Moses, M.D., Rafael. 1990. "Self, Self-View, and Identity." *The Psychodynamics of International Relationships*, Vol 1, eds. Volkan, Vamik D., Julias, Demetrios A. and Montville, Joseph V. Lexington, Toronto: Lexington Books.

Redekop, Vern Neufeld. 2001. "Deep-Rooted Conflict Theory and Pastoral Counselling: Dealing With What One Sees," *Pastoral Sciences*, Vol. 20, No.1, 9–24.

———. 2002. *From Violence to Blessing: How an Understanding of Deep-Rooted Conflict Can Open Paths to Reconciliation.* Toronto, Canada: Novalis.

———. 2008. "A Post-Genocidal Justice of Blessing as an Alternative to a Justice of Violence: The Case of Rwanda." Pp. 205-238 in *Peacebuilding in Traumatized Socities*, edited by Barry Hart. Lanham: University Press of America.

Ryan, Stephen. 1995. *Ethnic Conflict and international Relations* (Aldershot, England and Burlington. Vermont: Ashgate Publishing Group.

Schirch, Lisa. *Ritual and Symbol in Peacebuilding.* Bloomfield, CT: Kumarian Press.

Volf, Miroslav. 1996. *Exclusion and Embrace: A Theological Exploration of Identity.* Nashville: Abingdon Press.

NOTES

1. External operational ministry may be understood to be ministry "outside the wire"—among local indigenous populations. Internal operational ministry conforms more to the traditional role of providing sacramental and pastoral support for the troops.

2. Vern Neufeld Redekop uses the term indirect reconciliation to mean "joint actions toward supra ordinate goals or constructive development projects, [i.e.] reconciliation through economic development and reconciliation through joint celebration of the restoration of cultural buildings and monuments" (2008).

3. Redekop defines informal reconciliation as contributing to reconciliation "through positive interactions between people in the normal course of their everyday lives" (2008).

4. Miroslav Volf employs the theme of the *will to embrace* as a means of bridging the chasm separating exclusion from embrace . . . He speaks of the willingness of—usually the wounded party—to see the good in a gesture of the *other*, often over against a backdrop of the tremendous hurt and suffering known to conflict. Movement toward the *other* often precipitates a reciprocal reaction. The *will to embrace* is *mimetically modeled* by chaplains in their willingness to engage the *other*, most often leaders of religious communities whose respective identity groups are at odds. Exemplifying the opening of a space within one*self* to receive the *other* in a very real sense precipitates *encounter* between alienated leaders. Such incremental steps toward openness resembles accommodating the *other* within the *self's* identity boundaries, results in something of the *other* remaining within the *self* upon the conclusion of the initial *encounter*—a reflection of Volf's *double vision* . . . Rather the *will to embrace* is the hesitant yet hopeful opening of the *self* to the *other* in the arduous task of bridging the chasm of alienation and separation (1996). For "A Practical Theology of Reconciliation in Theatres of War" based on Volf's body of work, see Moore (2013, 265-287)

5. Interview with Padre Gabriel Legault, National Defence Headquarters, Ottawa, Canada, 2 June 2005.

6. CIMIC is an acronym meaning Civilian and Military Co-operation. NATO defines CIMIC as "co-ordination and co-operation in support of the mission, between the NATO Commander and civil actors, including national population and local authorities, as well as international, national and non-governmental organizations and agencies." pforum.isn.ethz.ch/

docs/747A1AFD-2ACE-4242–B87DF04c19291860.pps, accessed 25 July 2006; Sean Pollick offers a Canadian version, "CIMIC is designed to support the relation between our military and other actors in theatre, as well as including measures designed to include co-operation and co-ordination between our troops and others." http://www.cda-cdai.ca/symposia/2000/pollick.htm, accessed 25 July 2006. Significant as well are the numerous humanitarian projects initiated by CIMIC cells within local communities, a tremendous aid to the mission. Not only are local conditions improved but also much good will is generated among the people toward presence of foreign troops.

7. A recent example of *historical enmity* would be the mass demonstrations in Paris by Turkish people from across Europe protesting against the French Senate's plans to vote on a bill making it illegal to deny the 1915 mass killing of Armenians by Ottoman Turks. See http://www.youtube.com/watch?v=UkePDjhdlu4, accessed 10 Feb 2012. Accounts of the genocide are a continued source of friction between Turkey and other nations who hold to different historical versions. As reported by the *New York Times*, "Relations between France and Turkey dipped to a nadir as the French Senate approved a bill late Monday [21 Jan 2012] criminalizing the denial of officially recognized genocides, including the Armenian genocide begun in 1915." See "Genocide Bill Angers Turks as it Passes in France," http://www.nytimes.com/2012/01/24/world/europe/french-senate-passes-genocide-bill-angering-turks.html, accessed 10 Feb 2012.

8. For a discussion on *mimesis* relating to the operational roles of chaplains see Moore (2013, 113-114). Further amplification on open and closed relationships may be found in the same volume (19-45).

Chapter Thirteen

Changing Trajectory

The Role of Karma within a Framework of Reconciliation

Rupa Menon

"The best way to change these structures of violence is for sensitive people, who understand what is happening, to let people know how they can do things differently in their own spheres of influence," (Redekop 2002, 338). Those words from Redekop rang in my ears, and I hoped that through re-framing the Hindu traditional concept of *karma* we could provide the victims of longitudinal and intergenerational violent trauma the basis for constructive actions that would empower people locked in violence to be architects of a future that focuses on healing and reconciliation.

Through this new understanding of *karma*, it is envisioned that individuals would recognize that they are not destined to continue living in a passive state of acceptance, where they can only be acted upon, and, instead, become action-oriented people with the ability to create change through their own self-effort and personal accountability within the community. More specifically, with the active participation of spiritual and significant leaders, who, through their talks and teachings, could ground the concept of *karma* within a framework for reconciliation, creating a transformation of relationships between Hindus and Muslims, especially within the Asian subcontinent that includes Pakistan and India.

There are four steps to the development of this chapter. First, I will develop the concept of *karma*, drawing on the sacred texts of Hinduism. Second, I will show how *karma* could function constructively within Vern Neufeld Redekop's framework of reconciliation. Third, I will reflect on the methodology that I have used with a view to challenge those of other religions to use a hermeneutics of blessing to interpret their own texts and traditions in the interests of peace. Finally, I will look at the practical implications of my argument by inviting religious scholars, thinkers, seekers and teachers to do the same with their faiths.

THE HINDU CONCEPT OF *KARMA*

> The doctrine of Karma is a moral law, which controls existence favouring morality and discouraging immorality. Karma is an ethical force, which tends to improve the world by bringing its spiritual elements to perfection. In penalizing the wrong and rewarding the right it treats virtue as coincident with happiness. (Ramakrishna Mission Institute of Culture 1969, 296)

Karma can be understood only when we realize that three factors—the doer of action (*karta*), the instrument of action (*karma*), and the act itself (*kriya*) are necessary for gaining the fruits of action. None of them can independently produce the result. Action has no existence apart from the doer of action and no result is possible without an action being performed (Bhagwan Ramana Maharshi, quoted in Swami Tejomayananda, 1992, 6). So it is necessary to explain *karma* with reference to *vasanas*, the law of cause and effect, and the three thought textures (or *gunas*, the basic forces of life) through which the human mind functions.

Vasanas

The Hindu scriptures tell us how the *vasanas* are the impressions left in our mind when we act with selfish motives. This unconscious mass—tendencies and urges—is composed of impressions the personality has gathered from its own thoughts and actions in the past. The laws of *karma* teach us that the accumulation of *vasanas* effects our present; however, we have the capacity to eradicate these *vasanas* and transform our lives through consistent self-effort by creating a future of our choice. Swami Chinmayanda, in his *Talks*, says Sankara eloquently describes these *vasanas* as the chains that bind human beings:

> The wise have spoken of the three kinds of vasanas as iron chains shackling the feet, for him who wishes to be liberated from the prison house of this world. He who is free from them attains liberation (Chinmayanda 1989, 336, verse 272).

These three types of desire—*loka vasana* (social urges), *deha vasana* (physical urges) and *sastra vasana* (the urge to know)—bind the human being because of our constant identification with the body, mind, and intellect, preventing the real Self from emerging. Every action of ours is a fulfillment of a desire, which is the gross manifestation of a *vasana*. These *vasanas* are what result in defining our individual personality, just as the combined *vasa-*

nas of individuals become an ongoing practicing community. Likewise the combined *vasanas* function as a "social field," as Pierre Bourdieu defines it. We may even think of globally combined *vasanas*. National problems are essentially eruptions caused by the *vasanas* in all individuals in a nation put together: for example, wars, famines, natural disasters, plane crashes where many people die, etc.

Swami Chinmayanda quotes Sankara who likens the human being consumed by *vasana* to sandalwood, which when put in water and allowed to remain for a long time, emanates an obnoxious odor from the rotting wood— an image that captures the ugly side of acquisitive mimetic desire that is manifest in lateral violence. Ordinarily, sandalwood has the most heavenly fragrance (*divya vasana*) but when it remains in contact with water, for an extended period of time, it starts smelling foul. Subsequently, if the sandalwood is taken out and rubbed against the stone, the fragrance slowly emerges to waft pleasant satisfaction to all (Swami Chinmayanda 1992, 337).

Laws of Cause and Effect

The second factor according to Swami Chinmayanda to understanding *karma* is the importance and consequence of the cause-effect relationship in a human's life. Cause and effect can only occur in time. The first fact is that there can be no effect without a cause. The past is the cause and the present is the effect; and the present itself becomes the cause with reference to the future. Since we exist in the present, we are not only the effect of our past, but we are also the cause of the future (Chinmayanda 1992, 94). The laws of *karma* when properly understood, do not imply that we are helpless victims of our past actions, instead they reaffirm that we have the ability to apply our own self-effort to create our future choices. As our past efforts have combined to create our present destiny, we can create a future, which is better than our present, through our discriminating intellect and self effort to modify our future (Swami Chinmayanda 1992, 374).

The *Bhagavad Gita* in chapter 2, of the Sankhya Yoga, says the concept of rebirth or reincarnation is the consequence of the never-ending cause-effect chain, which makes it impossible for one body to express all the *vasanas* in one lifetime. Reincarnation is the need for another physical body to be born, so that the accumulated *vasanas* could move yet into another body. This transmigration of the soul is called *samsritti*. Since one can do nothing with the *vasanas* directly, the only capacity one has is to control, and redirect ones current life so as to not produce any more *vasanas*, and thereafter lead a healthier, nobler life. The idea of *karmic* causation and the concept of reincarnation and rebirth seem almost interdependent, for the soul becomes morally responsible even as it takes on different bodies to act out the *vasanas* accumulated through past lives. This would then explain why there is no meaningless suffering in the world.

The Bhagavad-Gita in chapter 2, verse 22 says:

> Just as a person casts off worn out clothes in order to don new ones,
> So the embodied Spirit discards old bodies and enters new ones.

Swami Chinmayanda in his talks quotes Sankara's philosophies and explains the secret logic of the ego's return (Chinmayanda 1989, 370). If a chance is given to the mind and its passions to express itself, there will be no end to their destructive abilities.

The *Bhagavad Gita* outlines the different aspects of action. There are three types of action: *karma, vikarma, and akarma* (Vanamali 1994, 85)—action, special action, and non-action. The common view is that it is physical action, which binds us to the wheel of *karma* and forces us to take repeated births; the truth is that even mental action can put you in bondage. A person with selfish thoughts can be forging the links of *karma*. When there is detachment in our mind, our action ceases to be action and become non-action.[1] The essence of yoga is thus the unattached action, and not inaction. Nothing is condemned, everything has its place and purpose in the evolution of life, every work, however menial, if done with the correct mental attitude, offered without the selfish intention of fulfilling a personal motive, will bring joy and happiness. Lord Krishna says "the practice of purging our *vasanas* is called *karma yoga*" (Chinmayanda 1992, 105).

The doctrine of the Karma Yoga is discussed in the third chapter of the Bhagavad-Gita (Osho 2005, 5:7).[2] There Lord Krishna replies that there are two apparently contradictory ways to salvation, one, *jnana yoga*, the yoga of knowledge and the other *karma yoga*, the yoga of action. While the former implies the renunciation of action, the latter accepts action as a means of salvation. Renunciation of action, however, does not mean that one will attain spiritual perfection, nor release from the wheel of *samsara* or the wheel of birth and death, for reality is existence full of action, and that has been decided by the Universe: "The universe is not separate from the individual. The microcosm is part of the macrocosm. In as much as there is nothing inactive in the universe, so also no individual can remain inactive" (Vanamali 1994, 72).

Gunas

The third important aspect of the laws of *karma* is the law of *gunas* (the three strands or basic forces of life), which are present in everyone's life to different degrees. It is the preponderance of one *guna* above the other two that accounts for the dissimilarities. The very meaning of the word *guna* is strand or thread; these are the three strands that bind the *jivatma* (the individual soul) and give it the semblance of bondage. So liberation is to separate oneself from identification with the three *gunas* (Vanamali 1994, 185–6). Though these *gunas* make up the physical and mental nature, they are not quantitative or physical, but qualitative and psychological in effect. They are the products of ignorance and beyond sense perception, for only their effects can be perceived (Chinmayanda 1992, 16).[3]

Vedanta[4] delineates the characteristics of these three *gunas* where *sattva* is purity—the thoughts are pure and noble. In *rajas* the thoughts are passionate and agitated. And in *tamas*, there is inertia—thoughts are dull and inactive. Even though *sattva* is considered to be the subtlest of the three *gunas*, it is still considered to be a form of bondage, since it is attached to the world of objects, emotions, and thoughts and regardless of a desire (of remaining in that state of bliss) being fulfilled, a new desire is formed almost immediately (to continue remaining in that state of bliss). If *tamas* is likened to an iron chain and *rajas* to a silver chain, then *sattva* can be called the gold chain, and a chain regardless of what material it is made up of creates the need to be liberated (Vanamali 1994, 188).

The law of *karma* cannot be understood in isolation; the most important element that determines whether an action has karmic consequences is with regard to the intent of the action, do we have a passion or desires for the object or the fruits of the action, in which case the action has karmic consequences. The ethical considerations are rooted in the laws of *karma*. The moral consequences of the action are important and whether they produce unhappiness or happiness lays the consequences to the action. Many Hindus believe that a person is born into a *guna* (caste) or acquires it by behavior, regardless of whether it is a *sattvic, rajasic*, or *tamas* state of mind, they are all still forms of bondage, and only through transcendence can one alleviate themselves (International Sivananda Yoga Centre). The consequences of events are manifested anytime later in life unlike the immediacy, which exists in the law of causation. This is why in the last Hindu rite—the *antyesti* or the funeral ceremony—the *"samaskara"*[5] or rite of passage is performed to make arrangements for the dead body, so as to give peace to the departed soul, and to enable the soul to enter the world of the *pitrs* (ancestors). (There are 16 Hindu rites of passage, which cover the life span of an individual).

Understanding the concept of *karma* within its traditional Hindu frame of reference, we hope that other religions will similarly seek the transcendence of humanity through good thoughts, action, deeds, and feelings. If the law of *karma* states that what you sow is what you reap,[6] then wouldn't it be in the interests of people from other religions to look to their own scriptures to find parallel precepts.

I will illustrate how this concept has the potential to become a symbolic first step toward reconciliation between the Hindus and Muslims in the Asian subcontinent. By putting each individual in the unique position of being consciously aware of deciding how they choose to live their life and what legacy they choose to leave behind, they might be in a position to lead people from conflict to transformation and mimetic structures of blessing as envisioned and developed by Redekop.

KARMA AND MIMETIC STRUCTURES OF BLESSING

According to René Girard, humans have a tendency to reciprocate violence with violence; conflict arises due to the mimetic desire, or the desire for what another desires. This can evoke deep feelings of envy and hatred that increase in intensity, especially when the model for desire becomes the obstacle to acquiring that desired object (Girard 1976). Mimetic, violent actions are returned mimetically through escalating cycles of revenge, which are a function of temporality, complexity, intensity of emotional involvement, and level of violence. Girard talks about how dealing with these rivalries can advance our understanding of mimetic desire (Girard 2011, 11–12).

Redekop's justice of blessing is a theoretical construct of reconciliation where the transformation of mimetic structures of violence to mimetic structures of blessing occurs. Mutually constructive mimetic effects are recognized through a number of initiatives, all moving toward mutual understanding. Mimetic theory plays a heuristic role in drawing out salient features of the dynamics between the people enveloped by violence. As Redekop says, conflict can still occur even within the existence of mimetic structures of blessing, leading to creative possibilities (Redekop 2002, 256).

The question we continually ask ourselves is what method must we use to move people enmeshed in conflict towards transcendence and healing? A change in structure and relationship is imperative. It will eventually bring on reconciliation. The diagram given by Redekop below (Redekop 2007) explains the movement toward reconciliation, keeping in mind that there is no one perfect method.

For reconciliation and justice of blessing to occur, the basic prerequisites should be met. Safety, freedom from threats, basic survival human needs are prerequisites to be met, and a clear mandate or vision and resources to work toward reconciliation should exist.

Through this discursive process, the two parties in conflict somehow connect and are open to communicating with each other, where they tell their stories of pain, loss, and suffering; express emotions, and are able to express remorse; apologize, and consciously decide to launch a new trajectory that allows the relationship to transform through time. Their openness to mercy and forgiveness, through the reframing of memory and story brought about by counseling or public education, helps people to move toward healing and a justice of blessing. Re-victimization only occurs when there is non-truth.

Reconciliation

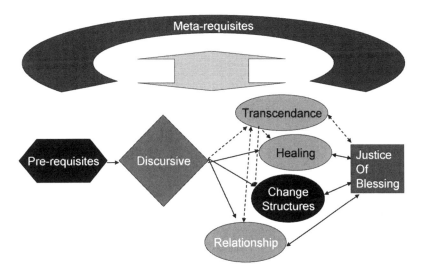

Figure 13.1.

The healing must address the necessary changes in the structure of governance and economic life, along with physical safety, needs, customs, and laws allowing for complexity and freedom, which have been missing. All of which creates a change in the relationship and an orientation toward blessing. The efficacy of this is seen through the value-laden content that drives processes and routine actions, so that the people living out these teachings become mimetic models for others.

We see a hermeneutics of blessing occurring where cultural and religious texts are read in such a way that they can be used to draw out those elements that contribute to reconciliation. In this case, the concept of *karma* is being analyzed with a hermeneutics of blessing. This enables us to generate a mimetic structure of blessing through Love of the Whole.

The idea of *karma* teaches us that no spiritual teaching, law, or theory is limited or restrictive in its application. It is the ability of the individual to effectively examine, determine, and apply these historical tools in a manner that would empower individuals, communities, and nations to transform their relational systems to something more positive and peaceful. *Karma* has the potential to be used in the reconciliation processes, where reconciliation is understood to be a transformation of the mimetic structure of violence to a mimetic structure of blessing, and where blessing is understood in terms of contributing to the mutual well-being of Self and Other. Swami Chinmaya-nanda says it is only through the individual perfection that world perfection can be achieved, for the past modified in the present is the future (Chinmay-anda 1992, 40, 100).[7]

Hindu scriptures teach us to take responsibility for the consequences of our past as well as for future actions. This locates us right in the middle of self-accountability. Besides our intuitive instinct for righteousness and toler-ance, we tend to react to violence with brutality. It is possible to address these violent issues by empowering past perpetrators with integrity by teach-ing victims how to show consideration, understanding, and forgiveness or by having perpetrators re-examine their situation so that they can arrive at rec-onciliation. We can attempt to resolve this strife by sourcing the wisdom from ancient scriptures, drawing from patent revelations in world philoso-phies teachings or through books of wisdom. Using these assets effectively is the bigger challenge today.

REFLECTIONS ON INTERPRETIVE METHODOLOGY FOR RELIGIOUS SCHOLARS AND PRACTITIONERS

Recognizing that religions have been questioning the same eternal truth through generations, we are forced to realize that the incongruence lies more often in the inability of the spiritual teacher to understand and decode these writings. Those reading world scriptures have repeatedly clung to shallow definitions of truths, as if they contained the entire truth of life. Misunder-standing such wisdom, has set the stage for misguided interpretations of sacred teachings. Interpreting works of wisdom, as if it were a "Do it your-self handbook manual" psychoanalyzed by the unqualified or interpreted by those who prattle book knowledge, is dangerous (Vanamali 1994, 19).[8]

The challenge we face is in the interpretation of religious scriptures. As people read their holy books according to a hermeneutics of blessing, it is the hope that they will begin to appreciate and understand other religions and scriptures, offering to each other their wisdom. By discovering similar con-cepts and values, they will realize that there is not much difference between the religions. This opening of commonalities would serve as an example for other faiths to imitate this interpretive practice. The validation from spiritual heads of different religions about the universality of values will create a mimetic structure of blessing and reconciliation. Religion has the potential to provide the solutions to most of the problems facing humanity, and one of the possible ways can be through an inter-faith exchange. By learning to appre-ciate the spiritual depth of each religion which has its own uniqueness and diversity, we can live relatively peacefully in a world that respects all relig-ions. Seeing the commonalities in different religions allows us the unique advantage of learning from other sacred teachings, especially recognizing that human beings are mimetic in nature and will adapt to Truth. If there is a meaning to life, that significance has to be established in this world itself. An effectual teacher would be one that models teachings through the example of an illustrious life. Setting an example (mimesis) for ideal replication needs true examples of living and walking the talk. Reconciliation, as John Paul Lederach says, has no technique; we can merely envision a framework for a process that would make room for all the elements, so that it might work (Redekop 2002, 302).

Using the concept of Gradual Reciprocated Initiatives in Tension Reduction (GRIT), where the idea is that one party makes a positive gesture toward the Other, this positive gesture is met with a positive response by the Other, the initial party is then motivated to risk another positive step, and through this slow dance of moving a step at a time, they eventually get close enough to embrace. According to the *Vedanta* the future is carved out in the present moment; tomorrow's harvest depends upon today's ploughing and sowing. Just as Action is the first step in the GRIT, sowing the seeds is necessary after ploughing. According to *Vedanta*:

> In fact, the result of an action, when understood properly is not anything different from the action itself. An action ends or fulfills itself only in its reaction, and the reaction is simply the action of the present defined in terms of a future moment. Therefore to worry about the results of our actions is to escape the present and try to live in a future that is not yet born. (Swami Chinmayanda 1992, 108)

Redekop talks about how severely traumatised people continue to suffer, long after the violent events have passed. These "*reservoirs of recollection*" (Redekop 2007) can be released by sights, sounds, and smells associated with the original violence. There is a necessity to create culturally appropriate means or rituals that will provide a visual and experiential healing of what is happening within, so as to address what the conflict was about. The process of reconciliation reduces the structures of violence by creating new opportunities for change. These symbolic acts or overtones can be acted out with several layers of meaning, where people specifically perform good, constructive actions so as to move toward healing (Redekop 2002, 299–300).

Service and charity for the betterment of all humanity is always considered to be the ideal in all religions, where the action is done with no expectation of reward or profit, and done with the sole purpose of helping others to cope with their distress and loss.

To apply GRIT to the Hindu concept of *karma*, we are aware that human beings have a discriminating intellect by which they apply self-effort to choose the paths they desire, so this choice combines with the past and creates a future better than the present, if it is done with awareness and self-effort. The future then becomes a continuity of the past, modified in the present. The law of *karma* infuses the spirit of creation into our lives by focusing our attention on the future (Swami Chinmayanda, 1992, 95). And from Redekop's concept we are making that forward movement one step at a time, the slow dance to creating a change, which in time will reach the desired point to be. Reichenbach shows how certain dispositions can have mimetic effects:

> Intentions are important in determining the moral quality not only of the action but of the agent who performed the action. A person who performs an action which results in bringing about good but which was done to bring harm is immoral because he engaged in it for that reason. In karmic actions, since the resulting disposition correlates in kind with the intentions which the agent had in performing the action, the moral quality (in form of potency) is passed on and preserved. Acts performed with the right intention lead to dispositions to perform like acts: acts performed with wrong intent produce corresponding dispositions. (Reichenbach 1988, 4)

Having looked at the key elements of reconciliation, we realize that there is no specific formula or time for reconciliation to occur. Religion and politics go hand in hand and have complementary roles to play, particularly where religion functions as a significant aspect of identity. Political resources are specifically needed to provide security, protection, and assurances so that there will be no further violence. In the next section I will show how such conscious action may not change the trial balance but do help one to transcend by forgiveness and reconciliation.

A VISION—THE PRACTICAL APPLICATION

It is said that great people often shape our impressions of a country, a place, the people, the culture, their beliefs, and how they treat others. Indian poet and Nobel Prize winner Rabindranath Tagore created a town called Shanti-niketan,[9] or "Abode of Peace" through his tireless efforts as a renowned experimental school where it would foster "an atmosphere of living aspiration" (Weiner 2012). Similarly, my intention was to find a theoretical frame within which the mimetic structure of blessing might be related to the historical concept of *karma*. Little was I prepared for the synchronicity that was already present where communities were applying these traditional concepts spontaneously in situations of conflicts within their communities. Redekop's concept of reconciliation and healing within international conflict was now a plausible, possible conceivable tool. In Redekop's opinion, "When mimetic structures of violence take over a relational system, both parties within the relationship can play the role of perpetrator and of victim" (Redekop 2007).[10]

In a world full of violence, hatred, and anger, being able to develop a new configuration of thinking around a historical concept necessitates re-education, the linking of known teachings with the actual proclamation of people, using these tools as a means to reconcile groups caught in the cycle of violence.

An obvious example is the religious, social, and political tension that exists between Hindus and Muslims, particularly in India and Pakistan since their Independence in 1947. The origin of this divide between Hindus and Muslims is old, beginning with the misinterpretation of Indian history by the British, the socio-religious cultural impact of repeated Muslim invasions in the past, and the subsequent distrust between the two countries. This animosity between the two countries has led to three wars in 1947–48, 1965, and 1971 against each other with growing tensions prevailing regarding India's rule over the Muslim dominated Kashmir. This tendency of Muslims and Hindus to treat eack other as the "Other" respectively of has resulted in unimaginable misery, human loss, enormous anger and unresolved conflict.

Initially, the roots of the conflicts between the two countries lay in the hostility between Hindus and Muslims and the disposition of self-governing princely states to map borders (Tharoor et al. 2003, 38).[11] The inhabitants of both countries share more things than what they disagree about, yet the people of Pakistan and India have had to make life choices on the basis of identity needs of safety, security, sense of belonging, and connectedness. These propelled and compelled them to make decisions and take actions that sometime necessitated moving to the country in which they felt most safe regardless of their personal preferences.

In a mimetic structure of blessing, life-oriented creativity generates new options because of the orientation towards a mutual wellbeing, which generates reciprocity and generosity (Redekop 2007). Today, more positive overtures are being made between the two countries through economic, social, cultural dialogue, and attempts to improve bilateral relationships.

Mimetic structures of blessing, like mimetic structures of violence, are diachronic. A friendly relationship that continues through time enhances the lives of all parties, from a life-long friendship at the microlevel to an international alliance or trade agreement at the macro level. Using the India-Pakistan example (earlier mentioned) and following Paul Ricoeur's concept of *ipse,* or temporal dimension of life that is constantly changing, mimetic structures, likewise, are constantly in flux (Ricoeur 1994, 3). The horizon of the past is reflected in memory, and a future horizon is expressed in imagination and anticipation. In a mimetic structure of violence, imagination and anticipation dominate. Both parties are preoccupied with the possibility that one will be harmed by the other and, therefore, with what each can do to preempt, prevent, or respond to the other's violence. In the mimetic structure of blessing, each imagines and anticipates enhancing the other's well-being.

Gandhi's cry of "Hindu-Muslim, Bhai-Bhai,"[12] was an overture toward envisioning a friendly "brotherly" relationship between India and Pakistan, pleading to both Hindu's and Muslims, who had so much in common that they should learn to see each other as brothers and sisters and attempt to get along.

When mimetic structures of violence take over a relational system, people imitate one another in being violent. Violence almost seems to take on a life of its own. Even today, there exists an underlying tension between Muslims and Hindus, regardless of the fact that India is a democratic country with the largest number of Muslims living in a non-Muslim country, second to Indonesia. Predominantly, the relational system in India does work toward the mutual well-being of one another with little regard for the distinctions; we find there are those random instigators of violence, who trigger a threat to need satisfiers of those oriented toward mimetic structures of violence. The fact that ongoing attempts[13] have been made by fundamentalists to dislodge peace efforts has only served to reinforce, between the leaders of the two countries, the necessity to keep the peace process going. Hindus and Muslims have a real capacity to use their common religious concepts as an intervention strategy to work toward Peace and Reconciliation, acknowledging that it is only by being accountable for their own actions that they can reduce the build up of tensions within themselves, as well as in the generations to come.

It is possible to open up new creative possibilities (Redekop 2002, 272) by adjusting the distance between the two so that they can learn to create a new relational system. It will be a challenging task with regard to how Hindus and Muslims look at each other in the future if Hindus collectively use this reframed concept of *karma*, and Muslims attempt to do so with their own teachings.

In addition to the Hindu-Muslim rigidity and divide, we realize what a challenge it has been for this subcontinent; besides religious tolerance, India has had to face its own subversion of the caste system, which has existed for centuries not because it was determined by ancestry or vocation but by temperament. Caste was defined as a system of segregation of people, each with a traditional occupation that was hereditary, closed, and exclusionary. This caste system encouraged the oppression of people for so long, simply by reinforcing the erroneous view that people were committed to being in the class *(guna)* ascribed to them as a result of their previous wrongdoings *(vasana)*, which they were subsequently suffering in the present for *(law of karma)*. People were labeled and got qualified for membership to certain classes, and subsequently appointed to vocations, which in turn dictated how society would treat them. The four gradations of the caste system in India have been empowered negatively because of the doctrine of *karma*.

For a Mimetic Structure of Blessing to occur within a relational system, we have to be aware that the relationship could be hegemonic, where two or more parallel relational systems could exist simultaneously. In a structure of violence where boundaries are maintained and memberships are excluded, the degree of intimacy and respect is dictated by the subtle but prevalent views held regarding religion, caste, and position. Hindu-Muslim dynamics have always been politicized and rationalized to suit the convenience and needs of the current political, economic, religious, and social beneficiaries thereby creating some of the worst differentiations, victimizations, and abuses through history. The suffering of the perpetrator, which was called for in strict justice, became one, where "the perpetrator became the model whose actions and attitudes were mimetically appropriated and the victim became like the hated one" (Redekop 2007, 4). For a structure of blessing to be accepted within the concept of *karma*, it means not holding the traditional belief that multiple incarnations is a consequence of previous wrongdoings, or that all wrongdoings in the present would be punished in the next life, justifying with one broad sweeping statement that all suffering was due to the wrongdoing of the sufferer itself (Kaufman 2005, 15–32). This new redefined approach means that we can now take responsibility, be accountable and be action-oriented in our lives instead of blaming everything that happens to events in the past.

The justice of blessing is similar to restorative justice in that the opportunity is made for the perpetrator to undertake actions that make things right by re-empowering the victim over a long period. The whole process of reconciliation thus becomes both a goal and a process, where the goal is to get out of the mimetic structure of violence and establish mimetic structures of blessing. The universal caring for all life, non-violence, compassion, love, generosity, sharing, honesty, sincerity, commitment to peace, and positive action are those that need to be encouraged and inculcated in all of humanity. And, if we are to understand that "Karma means that there is no meaningless suffering in the world," or "that all the good in life—health, wealth, happiness is due to good deeds" (Kaufman 2005, 15–32). Wouldn't it be in everybody's interest to perform good actions in this life so as to keep the law of moral responsibility as well as cause and effect in balance?

If Hindu and Muslim leaders envisioned reconciliation as an attempt to transform the debilitating conflict that has existed between them for centuries, the reconciliation process would involve taking an initial mandated action. It is envisioned that the mandated action would come from the Hindu and Muslim parties themselves or from specific leaders or people committed to the cause. *Karma* creates a need to establish a sense of belonging, without diminishing the sense of Self or Oneness. Its proper interpretation persuades people to work toward a new mandate of restoring human values because they now are aware and take responsibility for the consequences of their actions. This encourages people from all social backgrounds and religions to come together. By taking social responsibility of working towards common solutions to improve relationships, reconciliation becomes a tangible goal. Sheikh Mohammed Abdullah and Jawaharlal Nehru were two such visionary leaders who worked to improve the relationship between the Hindus and Muslims within Kashmir in Pakistan and India. Notwithstanding, time has watered down their objectives, but their viewpoint persists even today after over fifty years.

The Indian and Pakistani governments have made promises and have participated in political gestures, which ensure and guarantee safety. Working within such a secure framework, the climate may simmer down towards a semblance of harmony. However, it is necessary that physical and emotional safety be ensured for both the Hindu and Muslim parties. One of the ways to resolve such issues is through arranging safe neutral locations for the conducting of dialogues aimed at creating a new mutually agreeable (political) relationship. Within the last few decades, there have been several examples of violence that damaged relations. One was the demolition of the Babri Masjid or mosque, which was constructed by the first Mughal emperor of India, Babur in Ayodhaya in the 16th century; it was on Ramkot Hill, also known as Janmasthan (birthplace) of Rama (an incarnation of Lord Vishnu). The wonton destruction of the Masjid by Hindu activists in a riot on December 6, 1992, as with the Godhra riots in Gujarat in 2002, are examples of mindless intolerance. The potential for inciting more fear and terror for both the Muslims and the Hindus (as anniversaries approach) is real. Only by the efforts made by leaders to rationalize the need for safety, security, and confidence for all Muslims and Hindus can both countries proceed with their efforts toward reconciliation.

Redekop quotes Rafael Moses, who points out that deep-rooted conflict characterized by dehumanisation and demonization and historic enmity (Moses, quoted in Redekop 2002, 159). Sometimes, people caught in their own misery and suffering are blind to the sufferings of *Others*, the humanity of the perpetrator is almost veiled from the victim and the sufferer. Sharing, opening up, and listening to the other party, allow the victims and the perpetrators to experience and see the humanity in the other and develop an empathetic feeling where they recognize the Other has suffered equally. "It is often hard to predict what will lift the veil. Sometimes it is a story, sometimes an acknowledgment of wrongdoing. Sometimes it is a shared experience not related to the conflict" (Redekop 2002, 296). In a gathering arranged by an NGO, where Kashmiri Muslim women and Hindu women were brought together to discuss the fear and insecurity they felt with regard to their children's future, safety, and security, they suddenly realized that they were both suffering equally and feeling helpless in light of the violence that was affecting their family lives. Their common interest was the welfare of their children, concern for their safety, security, their health, the lack of basic civic amenities, their inability to educate them, and concern for their future. Regardless of where they lived in this world, these are the very same concerns that every parent has. Relating these realities to the concept of *karma* and taking responsibility *"for sowing the seeds that you reap in future,"* could remind these women that their decisions to embrace humanity as one and value the lives of the Other (as they do for their own children) would be setting an example of the futility of hate and war, or the indulgence of violence.

"Ramon Panikkar emphasises that during dialogue both parties may become intent on truly understanding one another" (Panikkar quoted in Redekop 2007d). There is the distinction as Redekop points out between *"public truth"* and *"table truth,"* the truth that is shared publicly as opposed to truths shared only with intimate close family members, for it is only at the level of table truths that true memories of past trauma and hurt are passed down, and the hurt gets entrenched to the point where blame and stereotypes get reinforced (Redekop 2002, 296). One of the unfortunate negative impacts of violent conflict is the attack on peoples' most deeply held convictions. Hindu and Muslim leaders find themselves in the unique position of having to contribute new ways to keep hope and connection alive. The various commissions that have come into existence after the major Hindu-Muslim riots in India have tried to bring to justice those who caused the violence. In some instances, because of the fear of speaking out and being subsequently targeted by the perpetrators, justice has not been served; instead, people go into hiding, preferring a life of anonymity rather than getting the justice they rightfully deserve. Yet, others have managed to move toward healing. This "co-construction of reality enables them to leave the past and envision the possibility of a shared future" (Redekop 2002, 299).

Ramon Panikkar propounds that this kind of profound transformation in orientation takes place at the philosophical, contemplative, and metapolitical levels where by rethinking identities, situations are created to enable enemies to develop "mutually tolerable" (Redekop 2002, 299) interpretations of events that normally would have been expressed violently. This change can help in the building of a new relationship and conceptualisation of a totally new perspective, where Hindus and Muslims are included together in the reframing of the narratives and will feel that they have equally worked and contributed toward reconciliation. The trauma experienced by both communities is equally recognized, where the necessary legal and economic changes are incorporated so as to avoid any future violence.

The many ways that one can improve the relationship among feuding religions are: by having a formal establishment of laws that discourage victimization where both Hindus and Muslims are given an equal voice; by reinforcing religious teachings that emphasize loving your enemies, forgiveness, charity, mercy, and selfless service; by restoring the balance to relationships through the restitution of stolen property or goods, and by acknowledging the hurt and, expressions of victimization between two communities by doing meaningful activities. It is important to recognize that victims are entitled to healing, just as the perpetrators are equally tormented with feelings of guilt. The ability to reframe any event or action allows us to take away the power of memory that entrenchment and enslavement. This reframing and structural change may involve attitude and value changes, which might need to be expressed through new teachings, laws, behavior and customs. The question we ask ourselves is: How do we start addressing this practical challenge where all the things talked about in deep rooted conflict (such as enmity, stereotyping, entrenchment, cultural, and social norms) exist?

CONCLUSION

This chapter has addressed the possibility of reframing and using traditional religious concepts as an intellectual tool to motivate people to move toward reconciliation and healing, particularly with reference to the prevailing conflict and tension that exist between different religions. We realize that religious teachings, concepts, and scriptures can contribute to a mimetic structure of blessing and healing. Visionaries who envisioned a unified world free from dogmas and narrow compartmentalization of religious thought and teachings have always propounded that our religious texts have the potential for inciting either violence or the potential to unify millions (Vanamali 1994, 14). Though the essence of most religious teachings remains the same, it is through their differences that religions contribute their unique attributes to enrich us all; for it is, and has always been, in the deconstructing of these texts that we can uncover the potentiality for violence or alternatively the tool for reconciliation. Being able to effectively bridge these differences will move us toward a hermeneutics of blessing and healing, where people will transcend to a feeling of caring and sharing.

A number of religions have started propagating different versions of the original texts, versions that suit their own political, economic, and social ideologies. Religion has subsequently become a business where the marketability of it lies in the hands of those with power, wealth, or influence. The teachings of Hinduism and Islam have many common beliefs, but, through the Brahmanism and Wahabbism of the original teachings, they have been distorted to incite people to take violent and fundamentalist stands. The necessity for the involvement of people, respected and recognized as being authority figures in their religion, or leaders who validate the universality of teachings to create an example of an act of reconciliation (or mimetic structure of blessing) can shift religion back to peaceful coexistence. In some instances, the presence of a neutral third person who is open and transparent, with the clear intention of wanting to stop the violence and abuse, opens up the possibility of addressing the conflict or victimization differently so that everyone can move into reconciliation and a mimetic structure of blessing.

As the world spirals in mimetic violence, it is heartening to know that initiatives are taken by several religious leaders, who try to influence and change fundamentalist views, so that people are inspired to move to structures of healing. By drawing attention and focus to the commonalities that all religions share, rather than the differences, peacemakers can initiate a universal change in thought, belief, and actions. It is the vulnerability in admitting that any one religion is lesser than or not equal to any other that makes people take such polarized stands, for they assume that it is only in the total destruction of the "Other" is there a chance for their own assumed survival. Drawing attention to the possibility of coexistence and collaboration among different religions opens the doors to respectful and peaceful coexistence.

Reforming Hinduism or Islam might involve reinterpretation and the creation of a new meaning and application of the *Bhagavad-Gita* or the *Qur'an*. The various existing interpretations of religious teachings, oral traditions, and philosophies clearly indicate there has been a tendency to be subjective in recognizing how historically these subjective interpretations have been used to suit the existing predominant political, economic, and social mindset. The power and potentiality for change lies in the hands of the visionary. The acceptance of a predetermined destiny, according to *Vedanta* transforms us into mere hapless actors, where the scripts of our lives have been handed out for us to perform, without questioning, and consequently we live our lives as spectators. Interpreting our thoughts, deeds, and actions from an accountable, powerful position of awareness of the consequences in the present, empowers us and ensures that we are capable of changing and creating a future that maks it possible to live a life with more authenticity.

This chapter is by no means a solution to the prevailing violent conditions that exist nor a presumed one-step remedy. It does, however, attempt to specify an area, which needs to be addressed and researched further. Religion has always been the backbone of society, where a majority of the people take their direction from the teachings and interpretations of religious scripts literally, so, in being able to use such compelling words of wisdom in a positive, creative, proactive manner, we would be moving towards bringing unity in diversity, faith, and respect for all religions and a sensitivity to the many different versions of the same truth.

REFERENCES

Allen, Paula Gunn. 2004. *The Sacred Hoop*. Boston: Beacon Press.

Andhra Café. 2007. *"Thousands of Hindus Vow to End Caste Divide."* Last modified March 10.http://www.hinduwisdom.info/Caste_System8.htm.

Bloomfield, David et al. 2003. *Reconciliation After Conflict. A Handbook.* Stockholm: International Institute for Democracy and Electoral Assistance.

Collins, Larry., and Dominique Lapierre. 1975. *Freedom at Midnight.* New York: Avon Books.

Danieli, Yael.1981a. *Differing Adaptational styles in families of survivors of the Nazi holocaust.* Children Today.

Dudley, Robert. 2000. "Evolutionary Origins of Human Alcoholism in Primate Frugivory," *The Quarterly Review of Biology* 75, no. 1.Accessed March 2000. http://links.jstor.org/sici?sici=0033–5770%28200003%2975%3A1%3C3%3AEOOHAI%3E2.0.CO%3B2–4

Gilles, Kathy. 2000. *The Golden Rule.* Toronto: Broughton's.

Girard, René.1976. *Deceit, Desire and the Novel Trans Freccero.* Baltimore: John Hopkins University Press.

Girard, René. 2011. *Sacrifice.* Translated by Matthew Pattillo and David Dawson. East Lansing: Michigan State University Press.

India Glossary, Karma, http://www.wsu.edu/~dee/GLOSSARY/KARMA.HTM (accessed March 3, 2007).

International Sivananda Yoga Centre http://www.sivananda.org/teachings/philosophy/threegunas.html (accessed March 28, 2007)

Juergensmeyer, Mark. 2001. *Terror in the Mind of God: The Global Rise of Religious Violence.* Berkeley: University of California Press.

Kaufman, Whitley R. P. 2005. "Karma, Rebirth and the Problem of Evil," *Philosophy East & West* 55, Number1 : University of Hawaii Press.

Krishnamurthi, J. 1984. *The Flame of Attention.* San Francisco: Harper & Row.

Nehru, Jawaharlal. 1946. *The Discovery of India.* Calcutta: The Signet Press.

Osho. 2005. *Inner War and Peace.* London: Watkins Publishing.

Pert, Candace B., 1997. *Molecules of Emotion.* New York: Scribner.

Portney, Charles. 2003. "Intergenerational Transmission of Trauma: An Introduction for the Clinician." *Psychiatric Times* XX, no.4.http://www.psychiatrictimes.com/showArticle.jhtml?articleId=175802427

Redekop, Vern Neufeld. 2002. *From Violence to Blessing.* Ottawa, Novalis.

——. 2007a. "Reconciling Nuers with Dinkas: A Girardian approach to conflict resolution," *Religion,* doi:10.1016/j.religion.2007.01.004.

——. 2007b. "Teachings of Blessing as an Element of Reconciliation: Intra and Inter-Religious Hermeneutical Challenges and Opportunities the Face of Violent Deep-Rooted Conflict." Pp. 129–46 in *The Next Step in Studying Religion: A Graduate's Guide,* edited by M. Courville. London: The Continuum International Publishing Group, 2002).

——. 2008. "A Post-Genocidal Justice of Blessing as an Alternative to a Justice of Violence: The Case of Rwanda." Pp. 205-238 in Peacebuilding in Traumatized Societies, ed. Barry Hart (Maryland: University Press of America).

Reichenbach, Bruce. 1988. "The Law of Karma and the Principle of Causation," in *Philosophy East and West* 38, no.4.

Ricoeur, Paul. 1992. *Oneself as Another.* Translated by Kathleen Blamey. Chicago: University of Chicago Press.

Sheldrake, Rupert. Scientific Research, "Unexplained Power of Animals." Accessed February 2007.http://www.sheldrake.org/Research/animals/

——. Biologist & Author. *The Online Staring Experiment results.* Accessed February 2007.http://www.sheldrake.org/Onlineexp/results/

——. Biologist & Author.Home page of the website of Dr. Rupert Sheldrake. Accessed on February 2007. http://www.sheldrake.org/homepage.html

Srimad Bhagavad-Gita. Chapter II, *Sankhya Yoga,* Verse 22. Accessed February 2007. http://www.bhagavad-gita.org/Gita/chapter-02.html

Swami Chinmayanda. 1989. *Talks on Sankara's Vivekachoodaman.* India: Central Chinmaya Mission Trust.

——. 1992. *Self Unfoldment.* California: Chinmaya Publications.

Swami Tejomayananda. 1992. *Upadesa Sara of Bhagavan Ramana Maharsi*. Bombay: Central Chinmaya Mission Trust.
Tharoor Shashi. 2003. *Nehru, The Invention of India*. India: Penguin Books.
The International Society for Traumatic Stress Studies. Accessed on February 2007.http://www.istss.org/resources/public.cfm
Vanamali. 1994. *Nitya Yoga*, Delhi: Vanamali Publications.
Volkan, Vamik. 1998. *Bloodlines: From Ethnic Pride to Ethnic Terrorism*. New York: Farrar, Straus and Groux.
Weiner, Eric. 2012. *Man Seeks God: My Flirtations With the Divine*. USA: Twelve.
Zehr, Howard. 1990. *Changing Lenses*. Philadelphia: Herald Press.
Zeigler, Philip, ed. 1998. *Personal Diaries of Admiral The Lord Louis Mountbatten*. London: Collins.

NOTES

1. Understanding selfless love and action without any expectation is seen in the example given by Swami Chinmayananda of a mother who does things unconditionally for her child, regardless of the discomfort and fatigue and without any expectations of the fruits of the action. Her action is no longer a burden and instead becomes an act of love. Action preceded by knowledge cannot create bondage.

2. The most famous Hindu scripture, is presented in the form of a dialogue between the enlightened Krishna and the Pandava Prince Arjuna on the eve of the Mahabharata war that occurred 5,000 years ago because of a dispute between the Pandavas and Kauravas (two branches of the royal family) with regard to who should inherit the kingdom. Arjuna is puzzled just as Osho in his book *Inner War and Peace* indicated: "When Ralph Waldo Emerson read the Bhagavad-Gita the first time, he shut the book, he was horrified . . . when Henry Thoreau came across Krishna counseling Arjuna to enter into war he too was horrified . . . Gandhi too, faced the same difficulty, he was troubled for the same reason." when Lord Krishna insists that he carry out the action of killing his relatives in the Mahabharata war. Osho, *Inner War and Peace*, (London: Watkins Publishing, 2005), 5.vii.

3. *Sattvic* thoughts can be compared to the pure calm surface of a pool of water, *rajasic* thoughts to turbulent water, and *tamasic* thoughts to dim and dirty water. Just as the sun appears dim in dirty water, so also Consciousness is practically imperceptible in a *tamasic* mind. In turbulent water, the sun's reflection is bright but unsteady, just as *rajasic* thoughts provide a bright but disturbed reflection of Consciousness. On the calm surface of a quiet pool, the sun's reflection is clear and undisturbed. So also, a *sattvic* mind is a perfect reflecting medium for Consciousness, which shines through *sattvic* thoughts clearly and steadily. Swami Chinmayanda, *Self Unfoldment* (California: Chinmaya Publications, 1992), 16.

4. Vedanta is comprised of philosophical principles underlying the Hindu religious tradition based on the essence of the Upanishads. It is one of the six classical systems of Indian philosophy created over thousand of years ago by the *rishis* (ancient masters of India.). The word hails from *veda anta*, "the end of the Vedas," and is a collection of sacred texts found at the end of each of the four vedas.

5. http://www.sanskrit.org/www/Rites%20of%20Passage/ancestors1.html (accessed March 27, 2007)

6. A similar concept is mentioned in the New Testament, Passage: Galatians 6:7 (RSV). "Do not be deceived; God is not mocked, for whatever a man sows, that he will also reap."

7. "We acknowledge that the present alone is the time when we can work, achieve, gain, gather, give, and serve. In the past, we can now do nothing, in the future, again we can now accomplish nothing. In the dead moments of the past and in the unborn moments of the future, we can never act. These living, dynamic, present moments are the only fields to be hammered at, wherein lies all the glories of life and the gains in existence. From the future, time floods over us, who are now standing in the present, and gushes out to swirl with the continuous echoes of the past. Time never stops, it is ever fleeting. The now alone is the auspicious occasion for initiating our new plans. Delays are always dangerous, useless, barren. Today is

the only day to attempt any great and worthwhile purpose." Swami Chinmayanda, *Self Unfoldment* (California: Chinmaya Publications, 1992),40, 100.

8. "A mere reading or translation will not give us the full benefit. In the study of this [*Bhagavad-Gita*] book we will have to make use of the ancient Vedic method of studying the scriptures. There are three steps, *sravan, manana, niddidhyanasana*-listening, contemplating, experiencing . . . Thus it is not a scripture which one reads every day and keeps aside reverently in the hope that the reading can bring you some spiritual benefit. The Gita has to be assimilated into the very core of your being so that one lives the Gita." Vanamali, *Nitya Yoga* (Delhi: Vanamali Publications, 1994), 19.

9. http://www.santiniketan.com/ Santiniketan is a small town near Bolpur in the Birbhum district of West Bengal, India, and approximately 180 kilometres north of Kolkata (formerly Calcutta). Nobel Laureate Rabindranath Tagore, lived here and penned many of his literary classics including "Gitanjali."

10. "Mimetic structures of violence tend to be closed, acquisitive, and death oriented and they reduce options. When mimetic structures of violence take over a relational system, both parties within the relationship can play the role of perpetrator and of victim. Victimisation means receiving violence with the understanding that the violence is unjust and undeserved. It can result in a victim mentality, in which one defines oneself as the recipient of violence and as one who is (in Ricoeur's terms) a sufferer. Violence, however, is mimesis reciprocated invariantly. Mimetic structures of violence can place great pressure on people to respond violently to one another either as individuals or groups." (Redekop 2007a)

11. Shashi Tharoor, Nehru, *The Invention of India*, (India: Penguin Books, 2003).38.

12. Meaning in Hindi for Hindu-Muslim brother-brother.

13. http://en.wikipedia.org/wiki/Terrorism_in_India.

Chapter Fourteen

There Is a Crack in Everything. . . .

New Relationships for Self and Other in Northern Ireland

Duncan Morrow

At the heart of the Rene Girard's mimetic hypothesis is a radical reaffirmation of relatedness as the defining reality of human existence (Kaptein 1995, 4–6). There is no "being human" outside of relationship. Not only does everything and everyone exist in relationships, but relationships are foundational to being rather than the other way around. Our questions about human persons and human communities are, therefore, always necessarily about the nature and quality of relationship: "with whom?" and "with what fruits?" Above all, change in human affairs is not a question of the engineering of new object-people but of a radical change in relationships within which change becomes possible for living human persons.

Among Girard's radical insights is that specifically human relationship is no longer finally determined or constrained by genetic instinct or dominance patterns (Garrels 2011, 8–30). Girard hypothesises that humanity emerges from a pattern of potentially unconstrained mimicry, reciprocity, and interaction which Girard calls "mimesis." Crucially our desires are interactive, and we learn what to desire from others. Although the concept of mimetic desire draws attention to the importance of the imitation of others, mimetic relationship in human reality is so foundational that it is more easily compared with physical processes, such as gravity or magnetism, rather than with self-conscious acts of imitation. We do not only imitate and react consciously in the face of our models—we learn what to desire from them (Girard 1976, 2–5).

Mimesis includes but is not restricted to the conscious positive "copying" of imitation but points to the possibility of bipolar patterns of attraction and repulsion (plus and minus) in which the presence and centrality of the force is separate from the valence of the response. Thus mimesis does not just create patterns of models and students but sets us in relationships as models and rivals and sets the other as an obstacle to our own desires, even as we are more frantically fascinated by them.

In the discovery that we are mimetic of each other's desires, Girard reveals both the extent and universality of our ecological inter-relationship and the risk of violent destruction that uncontrolled mimetic desire between rivals poses. The process of the mimesis of desire risks drawing us into a contagious reciprocity of the desires of others, making our models into our rivals or obstacles. It is this mimetic fascination that brings us into direct conflict. Ultimately, as rivalry escalates, the original object of desire disappears and the rivalry escalates into a potentially disastrous fascination of reciprocal revenge (Girard 1976, 137).

Mimetic relationships both define us as human and are the unstable heart of human experience (van Erp 2005, 17). For rivals, the potential for violence, especially contagious spirals of revenge, is the ultimate threat to human existence, which threatens to destroy us, unless we find mechanisms for limitation and control. For Girard, the answer, which human beings stumbled on, is known to us as religion and culture.

Girard postulates that mimetic contagion escalates to a point where it encompasses the entire group (Girard 1977, chapter 2). At a certain unpredictable point, the attention of the whole group focuses on a single target who is "clearly" different and held to be uniquely responsible. The result of mimetic unity, in the face of a single other, results in the destruction and expulsion of the scapegoat other. But this very act of expulsion also results in a miraculous peace. The mimetic unity, forged in the face of a scapegoat, both results in the expulsion and murder of the scapegoat and allows the community to experience peace and unity. Critically, the violence remains hidden to its beneficiaries and the power of violence and peace is attributed to the scapegoat other. "He" has the power of life and death over the community and must be appeased. In Girard's thinking, this is the essential core of myth: the creation story as told from the perspective of the scapegoaters (Girard 1977, 101).

The paradox at the heart of human culture is that our peace is rooted in violence, violence against a scapegoat, driven out that we can have peace. The community, aware that the miracle of peace in the midst of violence emerged from the process of eliminating the scapegoat, emerges as an entity directly from this event. The result is a division between the sacred and the profane, which is the structuring principle of all life together. Religion and culture are therefore co-identical with the act of foundation leading directly to the rituals, structures, and laws of the community together, in the form of religion. Culture and religion are the same thing, rooted in the violence of the sacred. Essentially Girard confirms Heraclitus's assertion that "violence is the father of all things" in human culture (Girard 1977, 92).

Girard's hypothesis of origins in violence and the control of violence is an unfashionable anthropological "theory of everything" for culture. It has enormous implications for our understanding of our existence as human persons and inevitably radical implications for everything touched by that human culture, for our understanding of human history, and especially our understanding of violence and the possibility of peace.

After Girard, that which we call "the self" can also only conceived of as a "being in relationship." In an age in which individuality and autonomy is our core romantic myth, the assertion of foundational and inevitable inter-relatedness is little short of a scandal. Even more radically, a relational orientation changes not only our understanding of the self but also any plausible explanation of the process of change, and no longer amenable to processes of "self-discovery" or "reconstruction." In an inter-relational universe change in personal lives and the history of communities emerges from a changed pattern of mimetic relationships through which each human reality is constituted. To seek change in the lives of each person requires a focus on relationships rather than objects. To move from violence to peace, just as is the case when the opposite movement is made, is to move into another relationship through which the possibility of peace emerges for us (Kaptein 1995, 45).

Each self is thus a specific form, each of which is always emerging from complex mimetic inter-relationship. Logically, then, the self cannot so much be reconstructed as reorientated, or "reborn," as the gospel would have it. In a world of mimetic relationship, the defining reality is "with what or with whom are we/ am I in mimesis?" In mimesis, the defining and question and locus of change is not so much "who are we" as "whose are we?" Girard establishes that the Western equivalence of freedom with the autonomy to, and of, desire is a romantic and destructive illusion. Freedom now is a question of freedom *from* mimetic desire and rivalry, and always about freedom in, rather than *from*, relationship.

Mimetic inter-relationality is not abolished by religion. Instead its potential to destroy human living together is channeled. The specific experience of modernity, however, has been the rapid erosion of the cultural nexus of structural differences. Much of this has been driven by a profound conviction of the injustice of the social order itself. Instead of containing violence, the social structure itself has become an object of conflict. At the same time, this anti-hierarchical movement toward functional equality, and the removal of distinctions on which it insists, brings with it all of the possibilities for the emergence of reciprocal violence—precisely the possibilities which cultural distinctions sought to prevent.

For Girard, the vehicle for the unveiling of culture *from within culture* has not been an accidental process but driven by the working through of specifically Judeao-Christian revelation in the west (Bailie 1995). This insistence on the centrality of the Western religious tradition has only added to the scandal surrounding his work. Girard does not, of course, postulate that historic Christianity has been unremittingly "good." Indeed, like the Hebrews before them, Christianity has been a journey between radical insight into violence and continuing dependence on and application of violence. Ultimately, however, the point is not the relative "truth" of world religions, but to trace and test the radical choice, which Girard finds in the gospels between the scapegoat and the scapegoaters, and the choices which it entails for human futures.

REVENGE OR RECONCILIATION?

The critical, and ultimately irreducible, question is whether the mimetic hypothesis not only describes and makes sense of patterns of human rivalry, but whether it also creates possibilities of human mimetic relationships free of rivalry. In this, Girard champions the specific role of the Jewish people in human history as the people shaped in their discovery of the "other side" of the scapegoat mechanism as anthropological truth. The God of Moses is different from all the other gods, because he is the God of those driven out. Violence is revealed, and Pharaoh does not have the last word. For Girard, this same revelation is clarified in the crucifixion of Jesus by the religious and political system and its consequences. In one event, both the violence at the core of human society is revealed and the word of possibility beyond revenge—forgiveness—is spoken. Reconciliation between God and humanity is possible because forgiveness is spoken by the innocent victim, exposing and bringing to an end the myth at the core of every culture, the myth of divine violence (Girard 1987, chapter 4).

In essence, Girard concludes that Jesus is mimetic with a God (father), who is entirely without violence and in contrast to the whole of culture and religion. In one revelation, both the co-identity of this God and Jesus and the possibility of release from the demands of violence as the only way of human living are visible in human history. In the light of the contrast between violence and forgiveness and between community shaped against a victim-god and a community shaped around memory of the suffering creative victim, Judeo-Christianity must necessarily refuse all equality between the world of the Egyptians and that of the slaves in the desert, between crucifiers and the crucified, between the logos of Heraclitus (violence) and the logos of John (love). The complex and troubling claim is that the universal is revealed in the particular, and that mimesis of that particular, or at least with the forgiving non-violence which it brings into the world, is the essential "way" from violence to peace (Kaptein 1995, 60).

Forgiving is always in the context of the revelation of complicity with violence. It is this revelation, which is deeply resisted by all those whose position and authority rely on its secret. The revelation of the scapegoat is always the revelation of the hypocrisy of all of us, making impossible any sustainable division of humanity into good people and bad people. Furthermore, the crucifixion does not conjoin divine violence with religious exclusivity (as it often does and has done in reality, including Christianity) but sets a suffering and non-violent god opposite a violent and bloodthirsty humanity and asks us to choose. Violence is not divine will but, instead, is the human reality from which we must now be liberated or through which we will destroy ourselves.

All of human culture, all religious and civic authority and the crowd, as participants in the human story of order, are exposed as "the children of violence." The "good conscience" of culture—scapegoating without any sense of violence—is no longer possible. But in taking away the possibility of scapegoating violence, the crucifixion also represents a profound moment of danger for human beings: we have lost the violent cultural mechanism that protected us from greater violence, only this time for good.

The "good news" inherent in this relationship is that love, not violence, is proclaimed as the parent of all things and that, as in all mimetic relationships, mimesis with love and freedom is contagious. The possibility of relationship with the scapegoat victim is now actively abroad in history. Mimesis with love in a world of mimesis with relationships whose origins lie, however deeply buried in violence, necessarily entails both discomfort and judgment. The miracle of forgiveness takes place in the context of paradox, revealing every human person as participant in violence even as it offers possibility of becoming the children of love.

After Girard, the search for peace has a different shape. Any simple presumption that peace is the absence of visible violence is unsustainable in the face of our modern knowledge. Girard is therefore radically aligned with those for whom peace in the modern context can no longer be equated with the establishment of structures of a new *pax romana*, located within the specifics of politics or the wider socio-drama, but involves the emergence of a new basis for right relationship. Indeed, modernity struggles with the reality that there can now be no new political relationship, which is not infected by the revelation that the social order itself is constituted in violence. Politics is no longer ultimate but only penultimate. Real change now depends on the possibility of finding relationship, which is after the revelation of violence.

The gospel makes peace a question of choice rather than a question of power. Far from being an esoteric "spiritual" matter this is a matter of urgent anthropological importance. From now on, scapegoats will always be visible, and culture will fail to gather around the tomb. In place of scapegoating, Jesus offers eucharist and "remember me" as a new mimetic possibility for "love" as the creative possibility for human society. Through mimetic relationship ("follow me"), the central message of the New Testament is of the possibility of freedom from the world of violence, no longer rooted in individual autonomy but in a relationship of absolute safety, given the name of *agape* or love. Problematically, it has no force and is offered in a violent world.

The challenge is finding and responding to mimetic relationship with the new reality made visible and present now in human community. The potential consequences of a world mediated by a relationship with the victim are literally revolutionary, in the sense of "turning around." From now on, we are either locked up in the mimesis of desire or we are following Jesus. Creativity, real newness in the world, is bringing lives into mimesis with this reality.

What is clear is that this analysis radically "matters" if we are to be serious about human futures. In his recent work, Girard argues powerfully that Western intellectual complacency that history converges on a Hegelian *Aufhebung* has no basis in reality. Instead, Girard sides with the Prussian military analyst von Clausewitz in his insight that war has the shape of a reciprocal duel, with a tendency not to converge but to escalate to the extremes. Victory, not convergence, is the goal, justifying ever greater violence. Violence does not take us closer to peace, except insofar as its destructive power becomes more evident; reconciliation is left not as sentimental wish fulfillment but as our only other genuine possibility. For Girard, reconciliation, the possibility for human beings to renounce violence and recognize each other, is thus not a consequence of progress but the radical alternative to apocalypse (Girard 2010, chapters 1–2).

Ultimately, the choice is radical: seek peace through driving out our rivals or find peace through stopping the scapegoating. Our knowledge of the scapegoat and scapegoating is the crack in "everything," which is now made radically new: change, creativity and blessing are dependent on the shafts of light, which that crack lets in, enabling us to find our way in a new world. Everything else is romanticism.

TRACING MIMETIC PATTERNS IN THE PREDICAMENT OF NORTHERN IRELAND

By geography and cultural orientation, Northern Ireland is deeply tied to (mimetic with) the presumptions, movements, and expectations of the Western world. Indeed, it is arguable that we live as close to the geographical center of the North Atlantic democratic community as anyone. But unlike most of Western Europe and North America, the peoples of this political borderland have lived alongside one another, without the transcendence of a common nation or state or religion.

The "being," which results from unselfconscious identity *in* and *with* these institutions in other parts of western Europe, and is the basis of the assumed order of modern western nation-states, is absent in Northern Ireland. In the place of transcendence, nationality functions to divide people into antagonistic opposites, who have developed as mortal rivals for power. The result has been endemic anxiety, the permanent fear of violence—even when there is no evidence of current threat—and pathological over-identity with the failed nations in politics and public ritual. At its worst, this has descended into rabid ethnocentric exclusion and endemic terrorism and counter-terrorism.

This historic pattern of mimetic polarization and rivalry emerged over many centuries. In many ways, the north of Ireland was collateral in the ongoing conflict within western Christendom, unleashed in the reformation and counter-reformation. In its own deep conflicts with and fears of the Catholic powers of continental Europe, the British state emerged as a project of militant Protestant liberty. Protestant domination was the transcendent principle of politics and economics, defined as freedom from authoritarian Catholic enslavement. The identity of the British state with anti-Catholicism had huge consequences in Ireland where the majority were initially unaffected by religious turmoil in England or Scotland. Religious antagonism rationalized English economic and political domination in Ireland. Unsurprisingly, within the native population, this was experienced and remembered as extreme violence and still underpins the dynamic which sets the British state, and everything associated with it, against the vast majority of the native Irish population on the basis both of religious and political identification (Wright 1993, chapter 1).

The most intimate version of this antagonism became established in the north east of Ireland. Predictable within mimetic theory, this resulted from the fact that native resistance was more intense in this part of the island than elsewhere. In order to secure the political stability of this dangerous and resistant territory, the British government extended the policy of plantation (being developed for North America) to Ulster and specifically and deliberately offered confiscated Irish land to Scottish and English Protestants who could be expected to be loyal on both theological and socioeconomic grounds. Thrust into hostile territory, however, the consequence was not a secure and self-confident settlement but a threatened and anxious frontier, especially when there was any risk that the British state might lose its willingness to defend settler interests.

Religion, politics, economics, and society were aligned behind fronts or sides in a series of binary oppositions, which overlapped sufficiently to eliminate any mechanism to separate any of the strands into separate "issues." Antagonism, rather than the reasons for it, was the only consistent reality. The violence which emerged on a sporadic but not always predictable basis had a symbolic importance for the whole population and was "remembered" and structured into the development of the limping structures of politics through the law of the land, the rituals of daily life, and the recurrent myths of the people. The settlement incubated two large, but distinct, communities infected by mutual resentment and suspicion, who also interacted in commerce and daily living (Todd and Ruane 2010, 5–25).

The domination of Ireland and its consequences confirm, beyond all doubt, that Girard's insights in relation to Judeo-Christian revelation expose in historical Christianity the deep roots of the very same cultural violence as the revelation reveals. Across Europe, the explosion of passionate violence triggered in the early fifteenth century caused political chaos. Seeking to restrict and contain the extreme contagion, the German States established a principle of territorial sovereignty and segregation at Augsburg in 1555 as *cuius regio, eius religio*. Only physical distance could reduce mimetic rivalry and limit its consequences to the anarchy of inter-state relations rather than internal politics. Eventually, after a century of catastrophic violence this led to the establishment of national sovereignty at Westphalia in 1648 (Judt 2005, 129).

In the north of Ireland the messy consequences of religious antagonism (in a context of conquest) did not establish territorial uniformity. The religious antagonism of the churches was the heart of the politics of allegiance. Thus, in this context, antagonistic versions of Christianity co-existed on different sides of a colonial expansion at close proximity. Churches were now at risk of becoming mouthpieces for ethnic identities, identifying the god of the scapegoats with their tribal predicament and the need for resistance. It is a trap that they fell into spectacularly.

Christian churches largely became ritualizers of segregation and antagonism in the north of Ireland. Whole political groups are still described in terms of denominational labels. In the absence of political security, churches were often the first available places for people to gather in security. Rival claims to authority, which are the legacy of reformation and counter-reformation, became in Ireland the fuel for community solidarity and mutual exclusion. While Protestants preached vigilance against Catholic imperialism, and turned their eyes from the impact of British (protestant) imperialism on their Catholic neighbors, Catholics preached righteous resistance without reference to the implications of Catholic power for Protestants. Worryingly for the churches, their action as ritual antidote to anxiety increased their popularity, and Northern Ireland became one of the most religiously observant parts of Western Europe. While the communities were united and calmed, and the enemy was ritually excluded, forgiveness, contrition, and reconciliation could be systematically avoided.

Through involvement in schools, churches also played a critical religious role in forming parallel communities in the modern age (Wright 1987, chapters 1–4). Understood as separate and parallel systems, the schools emphasized internal solidarity and external difference between Christian denominations, in the first instance, and later between Christians and others. In many ways the denominational schools were the midwives of the modern national selves. Separate religious instruction cemented and integrated separate understandings of history, different rituals, and different socioeconomic experiences. There are countless incidents to illustrate the complicity of organized Christianity for ritual exclusion. In general terms, Ireland has deepened the secular suspicion that Christianity is implicated in violent religious exclusion rather than freedom, forgiveness, and love.

The structuring of this division was so intense that it left northeast Ireland deeply vulnerable to ethnocentric division in later centuries. Early relationships with roots in colonialism and religious sectarianism modernized and spread as a deeply embedded antagonistic rivalry about the democratic ownership of the state. The equality of citizenship demanded under democracy simply short circuited, when equality meant equality between mimetic doubles. Thus, as Catholic democratic confidence in Ireland grew, following the formal emancipation of Catholics throughout the UK in 1829, Protestants became increasingly nervous. When Catholic emancipation evolved into modern Irish nationalism, Protestants in general became vocally antipathetic and sought closer allegiance to the globally dominant British Empire. As the rivalry deepened and modernized in the cities, so the possibility of sectarian violence also grew. The resulting violence was inevitably experienced in diametrically opposite ways, reinforcing the retreat into hopeless yet sacred violence. Yet, although shaped in increasingly similar but distinct worlds, Protestant and Catholic life in the north of Ireland was essentially constituted by and through one another with each "community" convinced that their violence was a "just" response to the threat of others. As Catholics organized, so the Catholic struggle under Protestant British rule became the founding myth of Irish nationalism. Protestants sought refuge in the historic need to resist Catholic tyranny and ritually integrated Britishness and Protestantism in politics and society (Wright 1995, 127).

World War One gave final fuel to the narrative of blood sacrifice: Protestants looked to the bloodbath at the Somme to cement Britishness as a religious cause, while modern Irish nationalism took a decisive shift toward the central importance of violence when the British government responded to an abortive uprising in Easter 1916 by executing (murdering) the rebel leadership. By war's end, national identity had become a sacred bond. In the north of Ireland, the consequence was renewed polarization.

Every attempt to "decide" rivalries depends on the transcendent authority of the decision maker. Where violence is explicitly required to enforce this decision, the transcendence of the decision maker is exposed as weak and the decider exposed not as transcendent but partisan and equivalent. This was the catastrophe of Woodrow Wilson, American president of Northern Irish origins. Seeking to promote democracy and US freedom as the antidote to failed tyrannical Empire, Wilson supported "small nations struggling to be free." Unwittingly, however, he rallied every nation into battle, with huge consequences where territory was shared. The doctrine of self-determination under conditions of rivalry was not so much an invitation to freedom from an Empire as an encouragement to conflict with neighbors. Because all change was now legitimated by winning and keeping a majority, the politics of territorial control and the suppression or expulsion of the other became logical political developments.

In the fervor of righteousness created by the cause of freedom from Empire, fear and revenge were hard to avoid. The atmosphere of violence rose everywhere, not least of course in the bitterness of the new German losers. It is the nature of rivalry that the resentment of the defeated also serves to maintain the fears of the apparent winners. It is European history that the rivalries unresolved in Czechoslovakia, Yugoslavia, and even Poland in 1920 exploded into tragedy before the twentieth century came to an end. After domination came occupation, expulsion, and murder. Europe's cultural melting pot became its theater of death.

Ireland was outside the scope of the peace conference in 1919. But Irish nationalism sought to ensure that the doctrine of self-determination applied there should apply to the British Empire. Elections in the UK in 1918 underlined divisions across the island. In an atmosphere of crisis and violence, Britain sought the line of least resistance: first, by trying to impose order by force, second, by trying to grant home rule to Northern Ireland and Southern Ireland, separately, and third, agreeing to the independence of the southern part, leaving Northern Ireland within the United Kingdom but insulated from the rest of the state and the rest of the island.

Rivalry over the very existence of Northern Ireland was thus built in from the beginning. Northern Ireland was designed to have a Protestant majority through a careful choice of territory. Nonetheless, Catholics were only a minority, if they could be successfully separated from the rest of the Catholic population on the island. Amidst considerable IRA violence, the Protestant Unionists set out to establish Northern Ireland as "a Protestant Parliament for a Protestant people" thereby deepening the despair of their own Catholic population and simultaneously defining their own project in terms of its relationships with the great Catholic other. The result was a political world dominated by fascination and the permanent possibility of mimetic escalation. The result was a world of polarization and mimetic fascination where, like an earthquake, violence was predictable, in general terms, but hard to pin down to dates and times.

When transcendence is weak or non-existent, power retreats to violence. The need to "impose" order as transcendent exposes the roots of government and its claims to a legitimacy in force as violence. Once competing claims to transcendence cannot exclude one another, there is nothing to stop their self-justifying decent into enormous violence. Religious wars are always about everything. In the post-enlightenment world, this survives as wars of ideology and nation. At the frontiers of the European Empires, both nationalism and liberal democracy found themselves exposed as murderers to all but the murderers themselves.

Instead of providing a secure identity, the nation in rivalry is exposed as a god that failed—failed to assert, failed to protect, failed to be. The political result is not security, but ever more desperate attempts by ritual means, to reassert the transcendence and security promised by the divine (autonomous) nation: the escalation to the extremes that von Clausewitz prophesied. Nationality becomes, in fact, the scene of maximum insecurity, where identity is demonstrably not taken for granted but has to be repeatedly, neurotically, and violently asserted. As violence rises, any remaining relationships free from fascination are liable to be invaded by pervading anger, fears, and mistrust, ultimately by the rising possibility of scapegoating.

For fifty years, the rest of Britain and Ireland turned their backs on Northern Ireland. A "hermetically sealed" Northern Ireland "carried away" many of those aspects of their own historically hopeless entanglement which it had not been possible to resolve. Violence was largely contained, in every sense, by and in the unplanned constitutional invention. Northern Ireland became a place apart, locked up in continuous rivalry and polarization, itself the scapegoat of more powerful forces. It was a role played well. At times Northern Ireland even enjoyed the limelight of being at the centre of such attention—there was a considerable illness bonus. Inevitably, for as long as Northern Ireland was handled as the identified patient of an otherwise functional family, the violence was concentrated but real change was elusive.

The crisis of rivalry emerged at the end of the relatively prosperous 1960s precisely when it was least expected. Although the potency of sectarian rivalry had been reduced, it had not been eliminated. It was therefore at its most dangerous.

By 1970, the extent of mimetic distance generated by the existence of Northern Ireland had allowed Britain and Ireland to treat Northern Ireland as a distinct and separate entity in which responsibility for the communal rivalry was local and specific rather than general. For the British establishment, the fifty years since the establishment of Northern Ireland had fundamentally changed the Empire. By 1970, Northern Ireland was a local difficulty not an element in the wider defense of Empire. Yet, at the same time, there was no symmetry, or approximate symmetry, between Britain and Ireland. Ireland could not engage in direct warfare with such a large neighbor without certain defeat. In Girardian terms, there were sufficient differences in both time and space to prevent an immediate crisis of reciprocity.

At the same time, democracy created ongoing obligations of history and institution, which continued to oblige both Britain and Ireland, and set them into opposed settings. Furthermore, there is no doubt that the self-conscious order of the post War West—democracy, human rights, and civic equality—and some of the inheritance of Judaeo-Christianity, especially around killing, acted to restrain violence and point toward a framework for Britain and Ireland to present change as a commitment to transformation under higher purposes rather than betrayal of previous allies.

So when violence in Northern Ireland appeared to be escalating radically out of control in 1972, the potential for contagion became urgently visible to both. Caught in this double-bind, Britain and Ireland found themselves with obligations but without interests. In practice, and unusually in international affairs, both responded by seeking to limit contagion. Attempts to stabilize the state (by the radical reliance on security policy) collapsed in 1970 in Northern Ireland, as the Unionist government went down the road of compensating for rivalry through increased homeland security with disastrous long-term consequences for all of our stated transcendences around murder, justice, and rights.

The price of driving Northern Ireland away was paid in finance and material resources, which were applied, among other things, to maintaining spatial separations and reducing the most obviously unequal elements of rivalry. The result was a remarkable conflict where Western everyday life was played out in the shadow of apocalypse, and huge resources and ingenuity were applied to manage enmity without ever transforming it.

The immediate diagnosis of culture, following Clausewitz's insight that rivalry drives an escalation to the extremes, is always to try again, only harder. But as the enemy is still present, and neither side can finally drive out the violence—cannot generate security—this deepens insecurity. National flags fly from every lamppost where violence is greatest, and aggressive, territorial marking creates a sharply segregated sense of public space. The Protestant tradition of parading through the countryside each summer acts as a lightning conductor for community tension, and self-consciously Irish sports create community solidarity for the Catholic population.

Number counting, the accepted basis for decision-making in democracies, fails in such settings, especially where an alteration in borders could clearly materially affect the outcome. Elections degenerated from ritual occasions to choose and grant authority to governments, to organized headcounts to measure the current balance in the rivalry over the state. Without an experience of mutual transcendence of making decisions together, neither the winners nor the losers of elections found any security. Instead, elections deepened the rivalry between self and other by ritually setting whole communities into rivalry, as competing and antagonistic twins, and emphasised the inadequacy of democracy as a ritual of resolving conflict.

Ritual provokes what it seeks to drive out. In practice, ritual takes on an ever more desperate character, deepening the hopelessness rather than generating release. The formal rituals continue but in bad faith. Instead of bringing peace, they deepen the rivalry and fascination between competing communities and people.

Mimetic rivalry escalated to its logical conclusion in Northern Ireland only as community-based paramilitary warfare. The surrounding states remained relatively immune to the contagion. Caught in this unusual setting of internal escalation and external distancing, both the process of escalation and the attempts at peace-building co-existed. Thousands of lives were sacrificed to the gods of self-assertion.

Violence merely deepened hopelessness. And as killing followed killing, in an ever more circular pattern, fewer and fewer could really believe that the political world was divided into the intrinsically evil and the intrinsically good. Unusually, the escalation to the extremes reached its limit as it crashed against the outside world's resolute immunity to contagion. Slowly, it has become clear that there is no way to security through repeating the old myths of our own innocence. Instead of security, desperate ritual conjures its opposite: the apocalypse. Each failed ritual recreates a radical sense of self and other, simultaneously dividing and polarizing at one level while drawing everyone into deeper fascination with one another in the violence that is generated. But just because it is obvious does not mean that the option for reconciliation is easy. In the midst of chaos, "peacemaking" emerged as a new possibility.

THAT'S HOW THE LIGHT GETS IN?

Northern Ireland is not poor or ill-educated. We speak English and have access to the global market; we have an open capitalist private ownership system, where contracts are honored and have had relatively little public corruption. We know how to vote, and we see from our neighbours how government is meant to work. In global terms we belong on average to the privileged rather than the underprivileged; and, yet, a pattern of reciprocal conflict is embedded.

In practical terms, what this suggests is that efforts to "end" conflict through the manipulation of specific social goods will always founder if they do not emerge from or with a meaningful change toward a new relationship, one in which we no longer see one another as enemies or rivals. The crisis in Northern Ireland was never a question of the distribution of goods, alone, but a question of how the distribution of goods represented the underpinning violence emerging from a relationship of desperate rivalry (Ruane and Todd 1996, chapter 1).

This is not to say that rivalry over social, political, and economic goods is not central to the lived experience and myth of conflict across the world nor that change in relationships cannot be approached in practice through practical engagements on the issues, which present as important. Indeed, change in relationships will be evidenced by the way in which we deal with social and political issues. Nonetheless, all objects remain fundamentally secondary to the relationship, which makes them a matter of envy and establishes the pattern of reciprocal mimetic desire.

The political temptation, repeated in Northern Ireland, is to believe that the objects—power, the state, jobs, housing, or whatever—are primary. Agreements over the distribution of power, institutions, and goods are not the same as the establishment of a new relationship in which distribution is done within a spirit of mutual recognition.

In practice, however, the rivalry will outlast the redistribution, and may even grow in intensity, unless the relationship of threat and desire is itself transformed in the process. We have to drop our romanticism about conflict resolution. Surface harmony can hide murderous secrets. Object-focussed approaches to peace-building are at risk, if they do not engage the driving mimetic rivalry. The sometimes critical role of third parties in contexts of violence is that through the less-rivalrous relationship with the third parties, the conflicting parties can come into new relationships with one another and with the object in dispute. Transformation in conflict is ultimately always a question of transforming relationships not of distributing goods.

After Girard, we can no longer understand "peace" as an object, which is either built or made: instead, it is a possibility in our relationships and describes a change in the mimetic rivalry underpinning conflict. Peace is a relationship that presupposes that we are no longer rivals but brothers and sisters. It is only lasting, if model-model relationships replace the previous antagonism.

Violence cannot disappear through being opposed or countered. Even where the overwhelming force of violence in structure does eliminate any rival in the short run, it always necessarily also teaches the lesson that the way to peace is through violence.

The problem of violence cannot be addressed at the level of violence but only at the level of the relationship that produces violence. Peace is always a question of contrast, of an alternative, rather than an opponent. Both violence and peace are outcomes of mimetic relationships; if we want to seek peace the task is not to "oppose" violence, but to seek a new mimetic relationship in which the rivalry over mutually desired objects, which produces violence, no longer exists.

At the same time, for as long as we live within culture, we need structures and order within which to mediate and limit our ongoing rivalries. The possibility of peacemaking in Northern Ireland in the 1990s emerged at an unusual point; instead of destroying everything, which is the predictable outcome of a cycle of mimetic reciprocity, violence was sufficiently contained that its own pointlessness became visible, and the fire of desire was increasingly exhausted. After 1993, almost the entire community began to look for alternative possibilities for relationships.

The alternative to violence and division was reconciliation. For 20 years peacebuilding in Northern Ireland developed as a dialogue between the pattern of mortal enmity inherited and deepened in 25 years of violence and the possibility, however unrealistic, of a new relationship—of reconciliation.

The language of reconciliation drew directly on the life of small groups of people who had not been drawn into the polarising bi-communalism of Northern Ireland. At their worst, these had been romantic, moralising spaces in which to establish the superiority of the "peacemakers" *vis-à-vis* their tormentors. But at their best, these were small deliberate groups of people who were not drawn into the mimetic vortex of violence that was Northern Ireland in the 1970s and 1980s. Almost all of them had roots either in the lingering worker solidarity of the trade unions or, even more, in small unofficial communities of Christians for whom following Jesus was an invitation to find follow the road of reconciliation.

To the outside world they were almost uniformly small and powerless but their crucial role was as "cradles of freedom," places where people could meet in a real sense and where the possibility of a different future could be experienced as a reality and not merely fantasized as a dream. The essential discovery of these isolated communities was that the almost universal division of people into good people and bad people was a romantic lie, which must now be set against the tragic and liberating truth that we are brothers and sisters, when it comes to the mimesis of desire.

Opportunities for experience of a new pattern of relationship, outside the mimesis of desire, do not emerge either in a single place or in a programmed form. Instead, they appear as necessarily varied and essentially opportunistic. Thus, the practical history of reconciliation was a series of stories of "appearances" in a disconnected number of settings:

- People, who left home under immediate threat of death, to find a place which was welcoming and free and offered a degree of safety and choice;
- Schools work with young people, who were encouraged and supported to reflect on their own experience, while sitting among the very people who they had learned to think of as their enemies and then return home to reflect on the troubling contrast that this experience represented to the assumed truths of their communities;
- Bereaved families of people killed by violence, living for a week together and refusing to return violence with bitterness, and instead finding a new

freedom to grieve together for the pain of loss and discover a new and
deep human solidarity across the politics of killing;
• Youth groups of people, drawn from families who had been intimidated
  from their homes less than a decade previously, meeting again and developing a joint program of youth work and looking for volunteering opportunities to together;
• Education programs that were directed to encourage people to explore
  their own experience, the way in which it related to community histories
  and myths, and the degree to which it shaped personal identities and
  emotional lives while encouraging reflection on practical, often small,
  steps that could be taken to move out of rivalry and reciprocal violence;
  and
• Church groups reflecting on the gospel imperative to love in a context
  where revenge and fear was shaping community and personal choices.

None of this was "effective" in immediate political terms. But in it, the
possibility of an alternative to the vortex of violence was seen and "believed." At heart, the survival of these small cradles of possibility depended
radically on acting and "believing" in forgiving and being forgiven in a
context where such faith seemed both misplaced and naive rather than any
possible belief that such actions could be politically effective. The critical
difference was not effectiveness but fidelity.

In the late 1980s, the language of reconciliation was adopted by the
governments of the United Kingdom and Ireland and by their supporters,
internationally, with complex results. On the one hand, this language gave
transcendence to a peace that both now knew could not be built on the
victory or suppression of any party or nation. The governments now gave
increasing protection to small groups and projects committed to reconciliation, providing money and resources to extend experimental projects in
schools, churches, and among the willing, under the label of community
relations work. At the same time, through its co-option into politics, reconciliation was now opposed to the "men of violence" deepening the illusion that
the violence of Ireland was limited to the violent rather than to the historic
relationships of rivalry, that had been used and abused by governments and
political parties across Britain and Ireland for generations.

There is no doubt that the language of reconciliation enabled the beginning of long negotiations and decisions, which were to become known as the
Northern Ireland peace process. "Reconciliation" gave shape to a series of
meetings and negotiations in which the goal was a new relationship, rather
than the definitive victory of Unionism or Nationalism. With the massive
support and engagement of international parties, each with their own interests, and drawing on the war-weariness of the ordinary people, the dynamic
of reconciliation began its slow and painful interaction with the dynamics of

mimetic rivalry and violence. In a world in need of reconciliation, Northern Ireland emerged not as a hopeless and endless disaster but as a glimpse of possibility, with all the risks of romanticization, which that entails.

The Good Friday (Belfast) Agreement of 1998 represents a high-water mark in the rhetoric of reconciliation. The institutional and political deal at its heart was prefaced by something potentially much more interesting. The Agreement speaks of a "new beginning" built on recognition that the violence of the past had left "a deep and profoundly regrettable legacy of suffering." It continues: "We must never forget those who have died or been injured, and their families. But we can best honour them through a fresh start, in which we firmly dedicate ourselves to the achievement of reconciliation, tolerance, and mutual trust, and to the protection and vindication of the human rights of all." It is within this framework that the parties agree to "partnership, equality and mutual respect as the basis of relationships within Northern Ireland, between North and South, and between these islands" and commit to a "total and absolute commitment to exclusively democratic and peaceful means of resolving differences on political issues, and our opposition to any use or threat of force by others for any political purpose" (Belfast Agreement 1998, ¶4)

The interaction of political process and reconciliation was therefore neither superficial nor malicious. However, the ways in which the search for political order—in which rivalry is managed through transcendent structures and the search for a deep reconciliation—in which a relationship of rivalry is transformed into a relationship of trust—interact have been both uncomfortable and instructive.

In spite of the commitment to seek reconciliation, negotiators agreed that any attempt to ask previous enemies to set aside their fundamental and exclusive national goals would create such a scandal that it would provoke the violence that it sought to eliminate. Thus, the agreed political structure focussed on limiting the effects of rivalry rather than seeking commitment to a shared future: violence would no longer be used, government would be a matter of forced consensus and mutual veto through a permanent and mandatory coalition, and power would be shared out on a proportional basis rather than shared by a government with an agreed program (Morrow 2007).

In effect, rivalry was capped but not eliminated. Furthermore, the Agreement was now stable because of its capacity to persuade the most anxious in both communities that the possibility of defeat had been eliminated. Thus, nationalists argued for the new deal because it was merely transitional to a new united Ireland; Unionists argued that the Agreement recognised that the Union with Great Britain was now copper-fastened. In the meantime, structures were put in place which seemed to guarantee both but delivered neither and which in practice allowed both Britain and Ireland to re-establish clear political distance between themselves and their historic catastrophe in Northern Ireland.

Even more clearly, after 30 years of almost daily violent trauma, which had the effect of normalising both the activity and the extraordinary managerial responses taken to contain the crisis in Northern Ireland, the Good Friday Agreement was essentially silent on the origins of and responsibility for violence. The unspoken understanding was that any attempt to wrestle with responsibility for violence would reignite the cycle of mutual recrimination and bitterness, making progress impossible. Furthermore, no transcendent authority could be identified who could come to final judgments on questions of guilt or innocence.

Prisoners held for paramilitary offences were released before they had completed their sentences, unless there were specific and extreme reasons not to do so, but they were released without amnesty and formally retained their criminal record. The ambiguity of guilt and innocence which this created and the confusion about whether the formal justice process had been suspended, set aside, or was still in force has probably been the most complex legacy of the peace process. Heroes remained heroes in their own camp and criminals outside, with the serious risk that the battle for memory and history was the ground on which old rivalries had permanent fuel.

Concerned not to reignite any dispute over the past, the British government adopted an extremely broad legal definition of victim, which made no distinction between victims of terrorism or the state and which allowed the relatives of those killed while placing a bomb to be put on a par with the relatives of children caught up in random events. On this basis, financial resources to address the health and social consequences of violence were also provided to all who qualified. Once more, and unusually, the safety valve was financial. Beneath the surface, and sometimes above it, deep bitterness continued among many who regarded the compromise as deeply and scandalously unjust.

The Northern Ireland peace process is an attempt to promote a new relationship, which is also a compromise with the established rivalry (Morrow 2008). In effect, it is a gamble that the requirement to work together established by the Agreement will be more desirable than the exhausted rivalry of old. Even this truth cannot be spoken for fear that it will itself reignite the fears and anxieties of conflict. What it also represents is radical political rejection of the gospel maxim that "the truth (about violence) will set you free" (John 8:32). In effect, it is founded on an implicit fear that the truth represents a sword rather than peace and a pessimistic conclusion that "truth is fine but hypocrisy saves lives" (Bell 2012). It is, to paraphrase Chou Enlai, rather too early to tell.

This exercise, in contrast, has been an extremely uncomfortable journey with still unpredictable consequences. In a world of reconciliation, our past violence returns to us as an obstacle to trust in the future. What was heroic appears as criminal. What was explained as necessary, in the face of violent opposition, now looks like violence that gave further reasons for bitterness. Above all, the revelation of our participation in a cycle of reciprocity, over so many years and in so many generations, destroys the romantic division of the world into criminals and perpetrators, the good and the bad, on which whole political careers, myths, and structures have been built, and a division that has justified so much killing. But political careers and community myths have been built on the precisely contrary notion—that each side of the division is romantically justified in its ideas and actions.

Reconciliation, it transpires, is a process of searing and relentless honesty and judgement, which can only be survived if the violence can be revealed, and those engaged in it, in this case almost all of us, are also absolved. Ultimately, what peace building in Northern Ireland also reveals again is our profound resistance both to the revelation of our own acts as violence and to the experience of forgiving and being forgiven.

The resistance to truth-telling and de-romanticisation of violence is so powerful that those asking for it are liable to be accused of undermining efforts at peace. Violence can only be stopped by a diplomatically necessary amount of blind-eye turning and denial. The bearers of a different truth—the bereaved and injured—now represent not the reason for peace but the obstacle to it. In practical terms, what they also reveal is the interest of all of us in the myth of romantic justified violence by maintaining the myth of innocence. Herein lies a new opportunity for scapegoating: driving out the truth about violence on the basis that this is itself an act of peace.

EVERY HEART TO LOVE WILL COME, BUT LIKE A REFUGEE.

The Northern Ireland peace process started from an unusual and critical insight: the impossibility of resolving problems in the modern world through violence. This was an insight, which was only reached after exhausting every other alternative, and it is still not fully accepted. It was made easier by the fact that ultimately those who had an interest in stopping the violence, the governments of Britain and Ireland and the powers in Washington and Brussels, came to a shared conclusion that putting an end to the cycle was more important than any other particular national interest. After 1993, they all pulled more or less in the same direction. For the radicalized non-state actors on the frontline in Belfast, there was now no prospect of victory against such a mighty and transcendent international coalition.

The language of reconciliation and the small practice of reconciliation came to be of critical symbolic importance in generating a contrast to reciprocal violence. Considerable financial resources and international kudos were expended on incentivising the leaders of ethnocentric movements into alternative relationships.

The consequences of this were both important and unpredictable. On the one hand, the result was indeed new relationship: ethnocentric and sectarian relationships did loosen and relax with measurable consequences. Real decisions were eventually made that changed historic patterns of engagement. The decision to stop and look for peace has created huge cracks in the edifice of ethnocentrism in Northern Ireland. On the other hand, the result was a new dependency on external financial and ethical support, and a general tendency across all of the actors, to avoid the tragic consequences of reconciliation: a reckoning with our own participation and complicity with violence, willingness to face its consequences, and a new relationship in which we set aside romantic ideas of the good and the bad. In spite of the resistance of just about every interest, the truth about our complicity with ethnocentric violence is emerging into the light. The risk is that it does not emerge to set us free but in the context of rivalry.

This hesitation, between the potential apocalypse that haunts us and the possibility of reconciliation that demands too much of us, has slowly come to define the landscape. Leonard Cohen's conclusion in the title of this section is that real love is only won in a sobering and relentless process of unveiling of our hypocrisies about violence. Like all of us, probably, Northern Ireland continues to will the end but fear the means—with good reason.

The ambivalence and hypocrisy is visible everywhere. Britain and Ireland have made peace, in part because of Northern Ireland. When Queen Elizabeth visited Ireland, the symbolism was of a deep historic rivalry being put to rest. In political terms, this is a critical symbol; what it also contains, however, is a message that the rivalries of Northern Ireland are now just that: limited to Northern Ireland alone. With a clear conscience, the emotional entanglements generated across centuries in the north are cast adrift, requiring little further change or cost in the rest of Ireland or Britain. An even harder nut to crack has been the political interests and the wish of average people in Northern Ireland. Living in a western society allowed us to participate in the trauma and thrill of battle, without too many consequences. Peace should not now require us to get involved, or to recognise any complicity in violence.

Mimetic theory illustrates that the reality is, in fact, the other way around: individual acts stem from wider mimetic desire as much as the other way around. Unsurprisingly, by focusing on the victims and immediate perpetrators and making them the only people responsible, we carry away our own responsibilities for making change and scapegoat them again.

Deeper, still, is the predicament of the churches. On a global scale, they remain committed to rivalry and separation. And in an Irish context, that rivalry has had enormously destructive consequences. No amount of assuring ourselves that we prayed for peace can take away from the fact that the Protestant churches have never been places to speak about what it means to be a people who arrived through colonial politics or that the failure to recognise the Christianity of Catholicism had the effect of sacralising religious hatred and murder. And the Catholic Church has never really spoken about how its use of the power of exclusion from communion and insistence on secular priestly authority has fuelled the same dynamic of sacred cause and made all non-Catholics feel unsafe with the church in power.

Recognising this in Ireland would have truly global consequences. There is not yet any evidence of an appetite for the humiliation, which it will entail. Having taken the step, we find ourselves in a curious place, analogous perhaps to that described by Antonio Gramsci where "The crisis consists precisely in the fact that the old is dying and the new cannot be born; in this interregnum a great variety of morbid symptoms appear" (Gramsci 1971, 275). We have seen things we cannot un-see. We know things that we cannot un-know, and true reconciliation remains ahead of us. The crisis of Northern Ireland—how we live together as our structures wane–is the crisis of the world. At its heart, our crisis illustrates Girard's contention that the dynamic of violence and revenge outlasts any sociological rationale and eventually presents itself as a deeply unpalatable choice: reconciliation or escalation to the extremes.

There is light in Northern Ireland. Icons of Irish national culture, long resisters of everything to do with police in Northern Ireland recently carried the coffin of a police officer assassinated by republican militants, while the Protestant First Minister, whose political party exists to resist Catholicism in power, broke the taboo of many generations and attended the same officer's funeral mass. Reconciliation was chosen—in the face of the potential apocalypse.

There are many other examples too. Organisations have built strong partnerships, and genuinely open places for meeting and learning are also a hallmark of Northern Ireland. Sport is no longer the centre point of hatred but has produced models of openness and change. Former paramilitaries celebrate friendship. Victims who have lost loved ones have found a way to forgiveness, not bitterness. Schools have found ways to grow as shared institutions or have built real and lasting partnerships. Young people have developed models of real leadership and broken old patterns of enmity.

Reconciliation continues to appear as a radical contrast to the world: this is precisely what makes it so dangerous. Politics belongs and always will belong to the world or religion and culture in its deepest Girardian sense. Hope in history is not just, or even mostly, chronological. It is the possibility that everything can be brought into relationship with the profound truth that we are all complicit in violence, and that we are forgiven, and that we are invited to find our way back to each other as humble imperfect and unique sisters and brothers. Sustaining hope is a task defined by faith rather than effectiveness. It is clear that change will not come from politics or in politics without the necessity and possibility of reconciliation being known more widely, and, probably, less prominently, at least in the present. We have come a long way. We have a way to go.

REFERENCES

Bailie, Gil. 1995. *Violence Unveiled: Humanity at the Crossroads*. Danvers, MA: Crossroads Publishing.

Belfast Agreement, 1998. http://cain.ulst.ac.uk/events/peace/docs/agreement.htm

Bell, Ian. 2012. "Truth is Fine—But Hypocrisy Saves Lives." *The Glasgow Herald*, 1 July.

Garrels, Scott R. 2011. *Mimesis and Science*. East Lansing: Michigan University Press.

Girard, René. 1976. *Deceit, Desire and the Novel: Self and Other in Literary Structure*. Baltimore, MD: John Hopkins University Press.

———. 1977. *Violence and the Sacred*. Baltimore, MD: John Hopkins University Press.

———. 1987. *Things Hidden since the Foundation of the World*. London: Athlone Press.

———. 2010. *Battling to the End*. East Lansing: Michigan University Press.

Gramsci, Antonio. 1971. *Prison Notebooks,* London: Lawrence and Wishart.

Judt, Tony. 2005. *Postwar*. London, UK: Penguin Books.

Kaptein, Roel and Duncan Morrow. 1995. *On the Way of Freedom*, Dublin: Columba Press.

Morrow, Duncan. 2007. "From Truce to Transformation?" Northern Ireland Community Relations Council, http://www.community-relations.org.uk/about-us/news/item/137/from-truce-to-transformation

Morrow, Duncan. 2008. "The real work begins" Northern Ireland Community Relations Council, http://www.community-relations.org.uk/about-the-council/speeches

Ruane, Joseph and Jennifer Todd. 1976. *The Dynamics of Conflict in Northern Ireland: Power, Conflict and Emancipation*. Cambridge: Cambridge University Press.

Ruane, Joseph and Jennifer Todd. 2010. *Ethnicity and Religion: Intersections and Comparisons*. London: Routledge.

Van Erp, Stefan and Andre Lascaris. 2005. *Who is Afraid of Postmodernism?* Muenster: Lit Verlag.

Wright, Frank. 1987. *Northern Ireland: A Comparative Analysis*. London and Dublin: Gill and Macmillan.

Wright Frank. 1993. *Two Lands on One Soil*. Dublin: Macmillan.

Chapter Fifteen

Reconciliation as Resistance

Martyrdom in East Timor

Joel Hodge

Religion, in particular the Roman Catholic Church, has had a deep influence on East Timorese life and culture. For example, there was a large increase in East Timorese affiliation to the Roman Catholic Church during the occupation: from approximately 25–30% of the populace as baptized Catholics in 1975 to over 90% in the 1990s. Based on original research, this chapter examines what Smythe calls "a spirituality of resistance"[1] that developed in East Timor under Indonesian occupation (Smythe 2003, 47; Hodge 2012).[2] This spiritually was based in the solidarity cultivated in the Church, especially around the martyrs, which provided a means for reconciliation and resistance. This essay particularly reflects on the importance of martyrdom in East Timor, and the prominence of the associated discourse around "the martyrs of East Timor," as providing a means to reconcile and resist based on the innocent, self-giving of Christ, which Girard identifies as central to overcoming violence.

EAST TIMOR AND THE CATHOLIC CHURCH: A HISTORICAL & CULTURAL OVERVIEW

A small, mountainous, and sparsely populated territory, East Timor is half of an island located to the east of the Indonesian islands and 400 miles off the northern coastal town of Darwin, Australia. The island of Timor was colonized by the Portuguese in the 16th century, along with many of the Indonesian islands. Later, East Timor was occupied by the Unitary Republic of Indonesia from 1975 to 1999 after Indonesia pre-empted Portugal's decoloni-

zation efforts to leave the colony after 400 years. After the Indonesian dictator, Suharto, fell from power in Indonesia, and following pressure from Portugal, Australia, the US, and the United Nations, the new president, B. J.
Habibie, gave the people of East Timor a referendum on independence,
which the UN administered. Many died directly at the hands of the state
military and militias during Indonesian occupation, including after the an-
nouncement of the result of the referendum in September 1999 in which the
East Timorese voted in favor of independence by 78.6%. The UN-sponsored
Commission on Truth and Reconciliation (CAVR) reported that at least
102,800 people, and likely even more than 183,000 people, died from unnat-
ural and conflict-related causes during the Indonesian occupation (CAVR
2005, 44 and 73).[3]

East Timor is populated by different tribal groups that follow traditional
animist practices. The Dominican religious order established missions on the
island of Timor in the 16th century, and over time, the Church established
parishes, schools, clinics, and other institutions. Nevertheless, the shift toward the Catholic Church under Indonesian occupation during the 1980s and
1990s was very large. From approximately 25–30% of the population in
1975, there was as much as 80% of the country baptized Catholic by the end
of the 1980s, and, by the end of the 1990s, this was well over 90% (Archer
1995, 127–128; Dunn 2003, 39–42). Some have attributed Timor's shift to
Catholicism to the "*pancasila*," one of the foundations for the Indonesian
state (cf. Archer 1995, 127). As part of it, the Indonesian state "is based on
the belief in the One and Only God," in which all Indonesian citizens had to
nominate one of five religions that were deemed acceptable in their belief in
"one God" (Republic of Indonesia. 2002, Article 29). These religions were
Islam, Catholicism, Protestantism, Hinduism and Buddhism. Alongside this
law, increased access to the remote areas of the Timor Island, the Church's
entrenched position in East Timor, and its separation from the state assisted
in gaining the loyalty of the people.[4]

However, the Timorese shift to the Church was not only a response to
law, but as one young Timorese remarked in my study: when there is death
all around, everywhere and constantly in your mind, the Catholic Church was
a place to find hope; otherwise, there was just death. In other words, the
fervent Catholic practice of the people and the internalization of Catholic
beliefs seem to point to a deeper need and change within Timorese culture.
Suffering and death were confronted daily and pervaded every aspect of East
Timorese life: "An ever-increasing war rages in Timor. The group of villages
in which I lived has been completely destroyed. There is not one soul
there . . . there are very few Timorese for the majority is either in the forest,
dead or in jail. The luck of the Timorese is to be born in tears, to live in tears,
and to die in tears" (Dunn 2003, 270–271).[5] Death profoundly and deeply
affected Timorese culture and life. In this context, there seemed to have been

some intrinsic qualities in Christianity that appealed to the Timorese in their experience of violence and oppression.

"A SPIRITUALITY OF RESISTANCE"

The Church helped to provide discursive, liturgical, pastoral, ideological, and spiritual means by which to confront the experience of oppression, violence, and loss, and develop resistance to Indonesian occupation.[6] The Church provided practical assistance to the resistance, such as by sharing information and resources, providing sanctuary and advocacy for political prisoners, protecting resistance and clandestine fighters, providing a political space for free speech and assembly, informing the outside world of events inside Timor, and ministering to the resistance fighters. The Church also established Tetum as the primary liturgical language, which gave implicit support and encouragement to the local culture in opposition to the Indonesian occupation and language. Combined with these practical forms was a framework for understanding and resisting oppression. The nature of the Timorese experience under Indonesian occupation seemed to be given meaning and sense within a Christian context, which could provide cultural resources for hope and "a spirituality of resistance."

Patrick Smythe, who studied the different responses of the Catholic Church to the East Timor situation during Indonesian occupation, analyzed the Church's role and Timor's shift to Catholicism in terms of the experience of oppression and the contribution of Christianity to Timorese resistance, identity, and survival (Smythe 2003, 47–8).[7] According to Smythe, the Church remained the only independent institution that was loyal to Timorese culture, which assisted the people in their suffering and spoke for the people (Smythe 2003, 47). He identified how the Church gave "fresh hope to those in despair" and generated a "spirituality of resistance" through Gospel preaching that emphasized God's justice and freedom in the midst of oppression. Similarly, Lundry speaks of the important contribution the Church made to the East Timorese sense of national identity through the provision of material, organizational, and ideological resources for collective action (Lundry 2000; see also Deakin 1998; Dunn, 2003, 39–44 and 134–135; Durand 2004). Lyon describes the Church as a resource for the Timorese as it provided hope for living and resisting, and a bridge to the outside world, which included connecting to the international solidarity movement and even resulted in the Pope visiting East Timor (Lyon 2006, 143–144).

In the context of the Church's advocacy for and support of the Timorese, Carey speaks of the deep bonds that were forged between the Church and the resistance during the Indonesian period such that the resistance leader, Xanana Gusmão, described the Church "as the very 'backbone of the resistance'"

(Carey 1999, 82). These bonds involved practical, spiritual, and ideological support, including the sharing of information and resources, moral and spiritual assistance, and care for the families of the resistance (Carey 1999, 82). Both the political resistance and the Church hierarchy were transformed by this experience, which brought them closer together and closer to the people.

The Church provided a framework to address and transform the experience of suffering and victimization on a personal and social level, which itself renewed the Church: "Suffering, for the people of East Timor, is not distinct from their vision of God. It is, in fact, integral to their identity as Timorese. Challenged as deeply by the same experience of suffering, the Timorese clergy have remade their Church, once steeped in the experience of colonialism, into a church of service" (Archer 1995, 120). This framework seemed to challenge the widespread violence perpetrated by the regime, which was used as a means to re-create East Timorese society by dominating the physical and social lives of the people. During the occupation, violence was institutionalized in the main organs of the Indonesian state: the military, police, and local government. The Indonesian regime, led particularly by the military, gathered and enforced support by targeting specific people or groups, such as the local resistance and the Church, as part of its violent campaigns. The violent tools of the state included torture, rape, arbitrary imprisonment, disappearances, killings, massacres, mutilation, and mass displacement and relocation of peoples. The discourse of the state was based on the singling out of people as enemies (such as communists, dissidents, or seditionists), which sought to ensure the state's sole control over and use of the means of violence. In addition to the use of torture, which involves the conscious targeting of violence against a victim, there were regular and generalised campaigns of massacres and mob violence perpetuated by the Indonesian military and government in East Timor. Like torture, the violent campaigns led by the military and their auxiliary militias were an effective means to create and destroy enemies and, so, enforce the discipline and power of the "omnipotent" state on the victims and the general populace.

By targeting enemies, the Indonesian state sought to inculcate a particular belief in its East Timorese citizenry through the institution of a particular form of violent transcendence that filled the consciousness and structured the relationships of the people. The production of enemies who pollute and defile the social body is, according to René Girard, a common way to create and manufacture cultural unity founded in scapegoating (Girard 1977; Girard 1987). Targeting scapegoats was an effective way for the regime to maintain unity, firstly, amongst the state actors, and secondly, to extend that unity to the conquered populace through capturing them within cycles of violence, especially through fear, envy, and acquiescence, in which the people were terrorized into disassociating themselves from the victims and their families. Drawing on Tilly's work concerning the monopolization of violence by the nation-state, Cavanaugh argues that the ". . . assent of the governed *followed*, and is to a large extent *produced by*, state monopoly on the means of violence within its borders . . .," particularly the legitimization of forms of victimization by the nation-state to bolster its power and ensure unity around it (Cavanaugh 2002, 76). Like the violent sacred that Girard identifies in archaic cultures, the Indonesian regime held out the threat that anyone could be punished or saved through state-sanctioned violence. In particular, anyone could become an enemy if they did not follow the state's dictates, which are established under mob-like conditions.[8]

THE "SPIRITUALITY OF RESISTANCE" IN THE MARTYRS OF EAST TIMOR

The proclamation of the innocent persecution of East Timorese people was crucial to the aims and success of the East Timorese resistance, which was given important support by the discourse and practices of the Church, particularly around martyrdom. Those who were innocently and unjustly persecuted by the regime and who were regarded as giving their lives for others or the faith were generally called the "martyrs of East Timor." Particularly through this discourse of martyrdom, the Church provided an alternative to the violent regime—one that could make sense of suffering and form solidarity in the self-giving victimhood of Jesus—which seemed to pose a real threat to the regime. The regime became increasingly concerned about the Church, which resulted in the targeting of Church personnel and property. For example, in 1999, the Church was targeted in all parts of the country, such as in the massacres at Lautem, Dili, Liquiçá, and Suai[9], for supporting independence and threatening the Indonesian regime (Dunn 2003, 354–358; Robinson 2003). Robinson comments that the targeting of the Church was "one of the most shocking aspects of the pro-autonomy strategy" in 1999 (Robinson 2003, 255).[10]

Fernandes gives an account of how the Indonesian authorities deliberately fomented violence between pro- and anti-Indonesian groups in 1999, which included targeting the Church as supposedly enemy of the regime (Fernandes 2004, 47–85). They did this in order to make it appear that East Timor had descended into civil war as a result of what the Indonesians called an "illegitimate" referendum vote administered by the United Nations. However, it was clear to those inside and outside East Timor that the Indonesian military and state officials were deliberately causing violence to construct a false situation in which Indonesia supposedly needed to stay in East Timor. This constructed story, which was meant to ensure Indonesia's continued presence in East Timor, was revealed to be a lie; and the most striking witnesses to the falsity of this story were the martyrs who died innocently at the hands of the Indonesian military and militias.

One well-known group of martyrs who were killed by a militia during the violence of September 1999 was a group of Catholic charity workers administering aid to displaced persons. The pro-Indonesian militia, whose members were Timorese, killed eight people on the road from Los Palos to Baucau, on the eastern side of East Timor.[11] The eight people killed—including two Catholic nuns (one Italian and the other East Timorese), three seminarians (who were to become priests), a journalist, and two lay people (including a nurse) working with the Catholic Diocese under its charitable arm of Caritas—were delivering aid to a refugee camp in Com, near the eastern tip of East Timor.

The refugee camp to which the group was delivering aid was isolated and cut off by the Indonesian military and militias. The group had traveled from the biggest town in that part of the territory (Baucau) to a more remote area near the eastern tip of the island. They had previously negotiated with the militia to deliver much-needed food and medical supplies to the refugees. When they heard of this arrangement, another group led by the parish priest of Los Palos accompanied the Baucau group. On their way back after delivering the aid, the combined group did not meet the militia at its normal road-block, and so they surmised that something was amiss. At this point, the groups separated as Baucau lay to the north and Los Palos to the south. Following this, the group going to Baucau was ambushed by the militia known as "Team Alpha" (under instruction from the Indonesian military) (Belo 2007). The militia shot the car down and killed some of the group immediately (Cf. Robinson 2003, 246). The driver and the Timorese Sister were amongst those first killed. Two of the seminarians, one of whom was the director of Caritas for the Diocese of Baucau and had seen the militia before, and knew of their loss of conscience, tried to negotiate with the militia, but they were killed.[12] The others tried to escape but were hunted down. Dunn (2003, 357) and Robinson (2003, 246; see also ZENIT 1999) report that an Indonesian journalist was also killed and mutilated. Some of the group were even set on fire.

The last to be killed was the Italian Canossian Sister, Erminia. She was reported to have knelt down beside the car and prayed to God. As her attacker came toward her, she finished her prayer and offered her rosary beads to her attacker (Robinson 2003, 246).[13] As the militia approached her, she talked with them and asked for mercy, while praying for them. Despite the protests of one militiaman, the Sister was beheaded by one of the militia members, goaded by his militia leader. The militia dumped the car and bodies into a nearby river so that they could not be discovered. The militia leader then threw a grenade into the river. However, because of a young male eyewitness, the bodies were recovered (Robinson 2003, 245–247).

The killing occurred in the area of Apikuru-Lautem, a town on the eastern side of East Timor. The villagers originally found the dead bodies of the group, which were mutilated. Upon their discovery, the villagers were shocked and frightened because of the gravity of the crime committed. The village recognized and felt the grim nature of killing innocent people, especially nuns and seminarians. The village gathered and immediately knelt and prayed for forgiveness because such a terrible tragedy had occurred in their land. Later, Roman Catholic funeral (or requiem) masses were held in Los Palos and Baucau, which people from all over East Timor attended. These masses were special remembrances for those killed. Masses are not always celebrated on the death of East Timorese as traditional burial rites are usually performed. Yet, in this case, mass became the central point for Timorese to remember those who had been martyred.

The targeting of the Church, the resistance, and certain members of the populace during the Indonesian occupation resulted in a widespread discourse about the "martyr," which was seemingly influenced by a framework of Catholic beliefs.[14] The example of a self-sacrificial life (and death) such as Jesus's made sense in the Timorese context as a way to expose unjust violence and resist. This example was most clearly enacted in the lives of the so-called "martyrs of East Timor." Influenced by the appropriation of Christian beliefs and terms, the discourse of martyrdom became central to the identity of Timorese resistance and the understanding of sacrifice, violence, and death.[15] Martyr means "witness" (Cf. Cavanaugh 1998; Kirwan 1998; *Catechism* #2471–2474). To the Christian, martyrdom witnesses simply to the death and resurrection of Jesus Christ—to the victimized Christ who breaks through violence and death through loving relationship with God (the Father) for the good of others. In the midst of a regime trying to impose its will through death and violence, one can see how this Christian belief appealed to the East Timorese: It made sense of brutal violence through the discourse of sacrifice that transformed external dominance and empowered the victims and the populace who were in solidarity with them. The discourse was not suicidal, in tone, but identified the act of unavoidably having to give one's life for the good of the people and nation with a loving God who gave his life for the good of humanity in the midst of unjust violence. The martyr represented someone who had lived their faith in Christ for others, even to the point of becoming a self-giving victim like him.

This understanding of martyrdom transformed the violence of the regime: violence and death went from being seen as destructive tools of the regime to a positive sacrifice made for others that resisted the regime. The "martyrs of Lautem" are a particularly well-known and venerated group. In particular, the Italian Sister, Erminia, who was the last to be killed, was remembered for kneeling before her killers, peacefully praying and offering her rosary beads to her killer as a sign of peace and reconciliation. Her death and the deaths of the others in the group became a powerful witness and sign in the East Timorese community. Despite being killed, their witness was not forgotten, particularly in large-scale funeral liturgies and a site of remembrance. In fact, their deaths provided the space for the community to *remember*—to have a memory of the group as self-giving victims like Christ, not as guilty criminals or enemies (which the regime accused them of being), or even as people to be avenged.

Girard's anthropological perspective seems to shed light on why Christianity may be efficacious in these circumstances.[16] Girard argues that the proper memory of the victim as innocent is central to Christianity (Girard 1986, 109, and 198–199):

> The essential factor . . . is that the persecutors' perception of their persecution is finally defeated. In order to achieve the greatest effect that defeat must take place under the most difficult circumstances, in a situation that is the least conducive to truth and the most likely to produce mythology. This is why the Gospel text constantly insists on the irrationality ("without a cause") of the sentence passed against the just and at the same time on the absolute unity of the persecutors, of all those who believe or appear to believe in the existence and validity of the cause, the *ad causam*, the accusation, and who try to impose that belief on everyone. (Girard 1986, 109)

The militias wanted the Church group remembered as interfering criminals who had helped to undermine the national referendum on integration with Indonesia. Instead, in funerals, shrines, and the popular imagination, they were remembered as innocent and self-giving victims like Christ, who could even forgive their enemies. The deaths of these martyrs, and others like them, became powerful witnesses in the East Timorese community to the efficacy of self-giving sacrifice that challenged the belief of the regime and its supporting mobs. The lens of innocent and self-giving sacrifice provided by the Church helped the Timorese to see the real nature of the martyrs' deaths. Thus, through the example of the martyrs, the Timorese community found new meaning in death. In loving sacrifice, modelled by God himself, violence and death can be overcome, thereby exposing the injustice of the regime. The struggle of the East Timorese for twenty-four years under Indonesian rule was to resist the power of the dominant discourse established by those wielding violence against supposed "enemies of the state." In funerals, shrines, and burials, the Timorese community came to publicly acknowledge the innocence and sacrifice of the martyrs, particularly in the light of Jesus himself, which became a source of resistance.

In demonstration of the particular witness of the Church and the martyrs, the Constitution that was written for the independent East Timor in 2002 has in its preamble an explicit recognition of both (in consecutive order):

In its cultural and humane perspective, the Catholic Church in East Timor has always been able to take on the suffering of all the People with dignity, placing itself on their side in the defence of their most fundamental rights.

Ultimately, the present Constitution represents a heart-felt tribute to all martyrs of the Motherland. (República Democrátic 2002, The Preamble)

In this statement, the Church is recognized as taking on the suffering of the people and defending their rights—a stance that the Church herself professes to seek and one that is publicly on display in the martyr. In the Indonesian period, the Church recognised the injustice of the violence being done to the people and stood with the victims—even to the point where priests, religious, and laity gave their lives, as the Lautem martyrs did. In being willing to stand with the oppressed in their suffering, even to the point of death, the Church is said to have given dignity, hope, and voice to the victims in particular solidarity with them, which enabled the Church to defend their "fundamental rights." Bishop Belo, the leader of the Catholic Church during most of the Indonesian occupation and Nobel Peace Prize winner in 1996, points to something intrinsic to the Christian faith that may help answer this question. He says that the clergy and religious witnessed to the "...self-sacrificing love for Jesus and for His brothers and sisters who were suffering and helpless" (Singh 1995, 235). For example, the Mother Superior of the Canossian Sisters in East Timor and Indonesia described the martyrdom of one of the Sisters at Lautem in this way: "She gave her life to be with the people" (ZENIT 1999). This example, and the associated discourse of sacrifice were important for the spirit and hope of Timorese resistance. Through the influence of the Church, real sacrifice was no longer regarded as a bloody and transcendent reckoning for the regime or "for God's justice" but, instead, became the offering of the self for others and God.

As the Constitution shows, the discourse of sacrifice and martyrdom became very important to the Timorese sense of nationhood. The martyrs to the nation became those who resisted until death and who opened a space to imagine a nation—a body of people—living beyond the violence and death inflicted upon it. This imagined space drew on Christian belief and practice. The remembering of the martyrs by the Timorese community, particularly through Catholic funeral masses, opened a space to challenge the violent actions and justifications of the regime through a holistic vision and practice that sought to collapse the artificial barrier made by the state-sanctioned mob against the victims ("enemies") by *remembering* them as innocent and self-giving victims with Christ. The Catholic Church in East Timor popularized the word for those they regarded as witnessing to Jesus Christ's self-giving death and resurrection in service to the Church and world in liberating people from the power of violence and death.[17] For the Timorese, reconciliation around the body of the martyr, celebrated through the Church, gave grounds for resistance.

William Cavanaugh shows that in various countries in South America during the oppression of military dictatorships the Christian discourse of martyrdom (in pacifically giving of one's life for faith, justice and the common good) was used to understand and remember the sacrifice of many of those who died unjustly (Cavanaugh 1998, 59–70). In a similar way, martyrdom was a communal way of remembering the sacrifice of ordinary people in East Timor. Yet, some of those who were killed or disappeared by the state and who were called martyrs in East Timor (and in South America) did not specifically die for their faith. According to Cavanaugh, the South American liberation theologians, Jon Sobrino and Leonardo Boff, try to explain why various people in South America are regarded as martyrs by arguing that the martyr is not just dying for Christ but for Christ's cause in constructing an order of love and justice in the world (Cavanaugh 1998, 60–61). Based on his own extensive study of state-sanctioned violence and the non-violent resistance of the Catholic Church in Chile, Cavanaugh finds this an unsatisfactory answer because it replaces the effect and form of the sacrifice, which is modeled on Christ, with abstract principles (Cavanaugh 1998, 60–65). Cavanaugh argues that rather than focusing on the intention of the martyr, the most important factor in the discourse of martyrdom is the community's remembrance of the victim (Cavanaugh 1998, 62–63). This remembrance attempts to identify the true nature of the martyr's sacrifice as participating in Christ's victory over death and violence by suffering unjust persecution on behalf of their community.

Cavanaugh's analysis of martyrdom in Chile seems to accord with the situation in East Timor. For example, in the Roman Catholic funeral masses and burial rites for the martyrs of Lautem, the Christ-like dimensions of the martyrs' sacrifice were a distinctive and central part of the remembrance that emphasised their imitation of Christ and their sharing in his victory over death. The ability of the Christian community in East Timor to see the martyr's non-violent resistance and self-sacrifice as a virtue modelled by God, and to remember this sacrifice as a victory rather than a defeat, was directly related by them to Christ's own sacrifice. This understanding was emphasised as the oppressed communities (like those who remembered the martyrs of Lautem) took ownership of the victims' bodies and remember the deceased through the (Roman Catholic practice of) Eucharist (or mass) (Cavanaugh 1998, 60–68).

Cavanaugh remarks that taking ownership of the bodies of the martyrs is very important as it undermines the state's attempts to mutilate and hide the bodies as a sign of their dominance (Cavanaugh 1998, 66–68). Instead, the Timorese people brought the bodies of the Lautem martyrs into the Eucharistic liturgy in which Christ's Body is believed to be made present. A profound unity was being suggested by the Timorese community—the body of the martyr was united to the Body of Christ; the presence of Christ in the martyr's death was united to Christ's presence in the Eucharist (which literally means "thanksgiving")—that undermined the state's story that these martyrs were enemies and threats, who deserved their deaths. The martyr was seen to act out and make present Christ's pacific and sacrificial way of being put to death—a way of being recognized, made intelligible and celebrated by the Christian Church. In this way, God himself is identified in the martyrs' deaths—*not* in the violence of the mob, which tries to establish the state's claims and powers as absolute, but in the innocent, self-giving of the oppressed and victimized. Thus, the violent transcendence of the state, which tries to establish itself as absolute through violence, is undermined by a pacific form of transcendence grounded in the absolute self-giving love of God in Christ.

STATE-SANCTIONED VIOLENCE AND ECCLESIAL SOLIDARITY

In Christian faith and solidarity, the East Timorese seemed to find an enacted narrative that resisted the aims of the regime's violence and assisted them to re-constitute their unity and identity in consistency with their own culture and experience. In particular, one of the distinctive characteristics of the Christian influence in East Timor was how the experience of suffering and victimization merged with identification and faith in Christ, particularly as innocent, suffering, and self-giving victim:

> The undermining of mythical beliefs begins with the acts of violence against those the Christians call *martyrs*. We see them as innocent people who are persecuted. This truth has been transmitted by history, and the perspective of the persecutors has not prevailed. The victim would have to be glorified as a result of the persecution in order to have sacredness in the mythological sense. The crimes imagined by the persecutors would have to be accepted as real. . . . The innocence of the martyr is never in doubt. "They hated me [without a cause]." The Christian passion produces its first fruits. The spirit of vengeance leads vigorous rear-guard actions, but the martyrs nonetheless pray for their executioners: "Father, forgive them, they know not what they do." (Girard 1987, 198–199)

As seen in the case of the Lautem martyrs, suffering and violence were undermined and transformed by an alternative form of mimetic solidarity enacted in the place where the state builds and imposes itself. The ability for the martyr to be remembered and re-integrated into a communion based around the self-giving victimhood of Christ resulted in state-sanctioned losing its effectiveness to force the people into submissive support of the regime. The solidarity with a victimized God seemed to help build solidarity among the people, themselves, particularly in the spirit of self-sacrifice (which was exemplified by the so-called martyrs). This solidarity in sacrifice was modeled by the main liturgical practice of the Church, the Eucharist, where Jesus gives of his Body and Blood. This liturgical practice grew in importance during the Indonesian period. [18] Thus, at the heart of what Smythe calls the "spirituality of resistance" seems to be the God who shared the sufferings of the Timorese people as victim out of loving forgiveness, enabling resistance to the violence of the regime that targeted people as guilty enemies.

The resistance to victimization, advocacy for the victimized and the desire of the East Timorese to bring the truth of their persecution to the attention of the world was vital to their success in gaining independence. The rare nature of the victory of the East Timorese to gain independence from an overwhelming military force [19] involved overturning the dominance of the "persecutor's perception" locally and internationally (Girard 1986, 109). There was a belief in East Timor that, once the truth of their persecution was told and recognised, amidst all the lies of the Indonesian military and their allies (including Australia), they could be saved. Though the Indonesian state tried to create a story to the contrary, the East Timorese plight as victims eventually became accepted, as fact, and affected the consciences of those in neighboring countries and in multilateral institutions, such as the United Nations where the Indonesian invasion of East Timor had never been recognized. The Timorese harnessed this support by directly resisting the central element of the Indonesian state's attempts to legitimate itself, which was to create enemies/victims and appropriate the victim's story in support of the Indonesian regime. The perception of the good order of the Indonesian state and its benign intentions was undermined by the Catholic Church, the local resistance and international solidarity network by presenting the *victims* of the Indonesian state to the East Timorese, Indonesian, and international communities. Despite lacking support, even among some in the Church, the Timorese bishops, priests and religious were integral in telling the Timorese story to the world and sheltering those undergoing persecution. [20]

These combined actions helped eventually to erode the claims of the Indonesian state by showing the truth of what was occurring in East Timor, the violence of which had little to do with the regime's claim to protect the people and state from "enemies." In particular, the filming of the Dili massacre in 1991, when hundreds of mourners at a funeral procession were shot by the Indonesian army, in particular, was a major turning point for the international community to recognize what was occurring in East Timor. Max Stahl, the film-maker who witnessed and filmed the Santa Cruz massacre, commented that it was a special occurrence that the sacrifice of ordinary people in East Timor on a large scale overturned the "logic of force" (what Girard would identify with victimization) (Adams 2007). This sacrifice, he says, made a significant impact not only on the East Timorese people but on the international community. As discussed, the example, understanding, and practice of sacrifice was informed by Christian belief and practice, most particularly in the example of Jesus's own life and in the Eucharistic liturgy of the Church. In particular, this sacrifice (as Girard argues) highlights the innocence of the victimized, which is at the heart of the Christian message and is what the Church and resistance sought to expose to the world about the Timorese condition. Showing the innocence of the victims in East Timor (at the hands of the violent Indonesian state) was central to the appeal of the East Timorese to the conscience of the international community; this appeal made on the basis of self-giving sacrifice, and the ecclesial solidarity that emerged from it, eventually overcame the "logic of force."

REFERENCES

Adams, Philip. 2007. "Ex-Pats with Deep Roots: *Late Night Live* in Timor-Leste" (radio interview). December 17. ABC Radio National. http://www.abc.net.au/rn/latenightlive/features/timor/episode10.htm.

Archer, Robert. 1995. "The Catholic Church in East Timor." In *East Timor at the Crossroads: The Forging of a Nation*, edited by Peter Carey & G. Carter Bentley. Honolulu: University of Hawaii Press.

Belo, T. 2007. "E.Timor Ex-militia Chief Blames Indonesia for 1999 Mayhem." *Reuters*, September 26, http://www.reuters.com/article/latestCrisis/idUSJAK220404.

Carey, Peter. 1999. "The Catholic Church, Religious Revival, and the Nationalist Movement in East Timor, 1975–98." *Indonesia and the Malay World* 27 (78): 77–95.

Catechism of the Catholic Church. 1993. Vatican City, VA: Libreria Editrice Vaticana.

Cavanaugh, William T. 1998. *Torture and Eucharist: Theology, Politics, and the Body of Christ.* Oxford: Blackwell.

Cavanaugh, William T. 2002. *Theopolitical Imagination: Discovering the Liturgy as a Political Act in an Age of Global Consumerism.* New York, NY and London, UK: T & T Clark.

Commission for Reception, Truth, and Reconciliation East Timor (CAVR). 2005. *Chega! The Report of the Commission for Reception, Truth, and Reconciliation East Timor (CAVR).* Dili, Timor-Leste: CAVR. http://www.cavr-timorleste.org/en/chegaReport.htm.

Deakin, Hilton. 1998. "East Timor and the Catholic Church." In *Free East Timor: Australia's Culpability in East Timor's Genocide*, edited by Jim Aubrey. Milsons Point, Aus: Random House.

Dunn, James. 2003. *East Timor: A Rough Passage to Independence.* Double Bay, Aus: Longueville Books.

Durand, Frederic. 2004. *Catholicisme et protestantisme dans l'ile de Timor: 1556 – 2003 — Construction d'une identite chretienne et engagement politique contemporain.* Toulouse, France & Bangkok, Thailand: Editions Arkuirus-IRASEC.

Fernandes, Clinton. 2004. *Reluctant Saviour: Australia, Indonesia, and the Independence of East Timor.* Melbourne, Aus: Scribe.

Girard, René. 1977. *Violence and the Sacred*, translated by Patrick Gregory. Baltimore, MD: Johns Hopkins University Press.

Girard, René. 1986. *The Scapegoat*, translated by Y. Freccero. Baltimore, MD: Johns Hopkins University Press.

Girard, René, with Jean-Michel Oughourlian and Guy Lefort. 1987. *Things Hidden since the Foundation of the World*, translated by Stephen Bann and Michael Metteer. Stanford, CA: Stanford University Press.

Hodge, Joel. 2012. *Resisting Violence and Victimisation: Christian Faith and Solidarity in East Timor.* Farnham, UK: Ashgate.

Hodge, Joel. 2010. "Overcoming Violence and Death in East Timor: The foundations for a new nation." *Australian E-Journal of Theology* 16 (August). http://www.acu.edu.au/__data/assets/pdf_file/0015/272004/AEJT16_Hodge_East_Timor.pdf.

Hodge, Joel. 2011. "Violence, Resistance & Reconciliation: A mimetic analysis of East Timorese story-telling." *Contagion: Journal of Violence, Mimesis, and Culture* 18: 71–92.

Jolliffe, Jill. 2009. *Balibo.* Melbourne, Aus: Scribe.

Kirwan, Michael J. 1998. "Friday's Children: An Examination of Theologies of Martyrdom in the Light of the Mimetic Theory of René Girard." PhD diss., Heythrop College, University of London.

Kohen, Arnold S. 1999. *From the Place of the Dead: Bishop Belo and the Struggle for East Timor.* Oxford: Lion Publishing.

Lennox, Rowena. 2000. *Fighting Spirit of East Timor: The Life of Martinho Da Costa Lopes.* Annandale, Aus: Pluto Press.

Lundry, Chris. 2000. "From Passivity to Political Resource: The Catholic Church and Nationalism in East Timor (abridged version)." Brooklyn, NY: East Timor Action Network. http://www.etan.org/etreligious/2001a/polresrce.htm.

Lyon, A.J. 2006. "The East Timorese Church: From Oppression to Liberation." In *The Catholic Church and the Nation-State: Comparative Perspectives,* edited by P.C. Manuel, L.C. Reardon and C. Wilcox. Washington, D.C.: Georgetown University Press.

Neaves, Kyle, Thomas, Peter and Downey, Chris. 2000. "The Martyrs of East Timor" (documentary). Melbourne, Aus: Albert Street Productions.

Republic of Indonesia. 2002. *Constitution of the Republic of Indonesia (unofficial translation),* Washington, D.C.: Embassy of the Republic of Indonesia. http://www.embassyofindonesia.org/about/pdf/IndonesianConstitution.pdf (or http://en.wikisource.org/wiki/Constitution_of_the_Republic_of_Indonesia#Section_XI_:_Religion or www.usig.org/countryinfo/laws/indonesia/constitutionindonesia.doc).

República Democrátic de Timor-Leste. 2002. *Constitution of the Democratic Republic of East Timor.* http://www.constitution.org/cons/east_timor/constitution-eng.htm.

República Democrátic de Timor-Leste. 2008. "Solemn Public Homage Ceremonies for Combatants and Martyrs of National Liberation." Office of Prime Minister, Commission of Tribute, Supervision of Registration and Appeals. 16 December. http://www.easttimorlegalinformation.org/Miscellaneous/martyrs_pubic_homage_ceremonies_portuguese_text.html.

Robinson, Geoffrey. 2003. "East Timor 1999 Crimes Against Humanity: A Report Commissioned by the United Nations Office of the High Commissioner for Human Rights (OHCHR)." Geneva: OHCHR. www.etan.org/etanpdf/2006/CAVR/12–Annexe1–East-Timor-1999–GeoffreyRobinson.pdf.

Scott, David, 2005. *Last Flight out of Dili: Memoirs of an Accidental Activist in the Triumph of East Timor.* North Melbourne, Aus: Pluto Press.

Singh, Bilveer, 1995. *East Timor, Indonesia and the World: Myths and Realities,* rev. ed. Kuala Lumpur: ADPR Consult (M) Sdn. Bhd.

Smythe, Patrick A. 2003. *'The Heaviest Blow': The Catholic Church and the East Timor Issue.* Munster, Ger: Lit Verlag.

ZENIT. 1999. "Bishop Do Nascimento Speaks at Funeral of Religious Killed in Timor," September 29. http://www.catholic-church.org/canossians-sg/the%20Canossians/holy%20women/HolyWomen1.htm.

NOTES

1. The stories and examples in this chapter come from my qualitative research into the Catholic Church and faith in East Timor. Interviews, participant observation, and historical research were conducted from 2004.

2. Timor-Leste is the official Portuguese title of the country. East Timor is the English equivalent.

3. This total came from a population of approximately 700,000 when the Indonesians invaded.

4. However, while the Timorese were seemingly inclined to become Catholic, there was pressure from the Indonesian regime to convert to Islam through coercion and incentives of food, money, employment, and status. While some did accept this offer, the majority resisted because of their religious and political beliefs and familial obligations.

5. These are quotes from an early series of reports from the Catholic Church.

6. When speaking of the Church in this chapter, I am speaking of the whole Church—bishops, clergy, religious, and laity, not just the Church hierarchy. When speaking of the Church hierarchy, I am referring to the ordained ministers, i.e., bishops, priests, and deacons. The Church is divided into dioceses led by bishops. In each diocese, the Church is fully present with the bishop as the vicar and representative of Christ, who is head of the Church. East Timor originally had only one diocese, the Diocese of Dili. In 1996, another diocese was erected, the Diocese of Baucau, covering the east of the country.

7. The Vatican assisted the local Church in fulfilling this role, such as by placing the Diocese of Dili under its direct auspice, free from the influence and control of the Indonesian bishops and state (Dunn 2003, 287).

8. This threat of violence also acted as a way to draw people into the state's own practices of violence, which attracted disaffected young people and manipulated tribal leaders and groups. The government and military used tribal and family rivalries and allegiances, and rewards of money, food, alcohol, drugs, and status, to garner support from local leaders, form militias, and control local populations and villages.

9. A massacre of local people and their priest taking refuge in the Catholic Church in Liquiçá occurred in early 1999. In September 1999, other areas, such as the Bishop's residence in Dili, which was sheltering many refugees, was targeted.

10. In fact, the then Indonesian-appointed governor of East Timor, Abilio Soares, explicitly told militia leaders and Indonesian supporters that the Church needed to be targeted: "We have to kill the priests and nuns because they have done a lot to help the people of Falintil and the civilian underground" (Jolliffe 2009, 254). As Dunn says, this statement by the governor was a major departure from the previous policy to respect the Church (Dunn 2003, 346). This shift showed an increasing desperation to target perceived enemies of the state, especially the Church.

11. This story is based on interviews conducted in 2005–2006, available documentation, visitations of the site of the massacre, and other sources such as Robinson (2003); and the documentary: Neaves, Thomas, and Downey (2000). Some of the events were originally reported by a young male, who was an eyewitness.

12. Some of this information appears at the monument to this group of martyrs.

13. Robinson (2003, 246) reports: "One of the nuns, Sister Erminia, got out of the vehicle and knelt down by the roadside to pray. As she prayed, a militiaman (Horacio) slashed her with a machete. Another militiamen (Pedro da Costa) testified that he had yelled 'Don't kill a Sister!' but that Joni Marques had replied 'Kill them all! They are all CNRT!' A militiaman then picked up Sister Erminia and threw her in the river, before shooting her twice. At the trial, a witness testified: '*I noticed a nun sitting beside a [ditch]. There was a body beside the nun. I noticed the cap of the nun was on her shoulder. The nun talked to me in Tetum. I cannot remember all the words, but I remember she was saying "Oh! God!"*' [Based on testimony from the trial]. At about this time, Joni Marques ordered his men to push the clergy's vehicle into the river. Several witnesses testified that he shouted: 'Come here and push the car, you mother fuckers!' The men did so, though one person was still inside the vehicle. When the person got out of the car, he was shot and killed."

14. Judaism and Christianity developed a distinctive idea of martyrdom, which was not present in the same form in the local Timorese culture (as is denoted by the use of a Portuguese loanword in Timor to describe the martyrs).

15. See "The Preamble" in the *República Democrátic de Timor-Leste 2002; República Democrátic de Timor-Leste 2008*.

16. It is important to note that Girard's insights were not developed as an apologetic for Christianity but were discovered and tested as he studied ancient and modern literature and anthropological studies.

17. Martyrdom is used in other religious and cultural contexts but it is not used in the same way as in Christianity.

18. For example, in the remembrance of the martyrs of Suai in Christmas 1999, the whole community gathered after returning from refuge in the surrounding countryside and began their remembrance with the Eucharistic liturgy (or mass). See Hodge 2012.

19. This victory has been commented on by various authors (Fernandes 2004, 1–3; Scott 2005, 5–11).

20. See the story of Msgr. Lopes (Lennox 2000) or Bishop Belo (Kohen 1999). For an account of the difficulties that the Catholic Church in East Timor faced inside the universal Church, see Smythe 2003.

Chapter Sixteen

Mimesis, Residential Schools, and Reconciliation[1]

Cynthia D. Stirbys

In Canada, throughout most of the twentieth century, approximately 150,000 Indigenous children were forced to attend over 130 residential schools. This chapter explores the dissimilarities in the memories (or stories) of Aboriginal people and Canadians (colonist society) about the history, the impact, and the meaning of the Indian Residential School[2] experience, and the politics of forgiveness in Canada. René Girard's theory of mimesis will be applied to the discussion of the impact of residential schools and the deep-rooted conflict that emerged and continue to affect what Redekop calls the "identity need satisfiers" of Aboriginal peoples (2002).

Redekop's (2002) five identity needs—Meaning, Connectedness, Security, Recognition, and Action—will illustrate how mimesis (or lack of positive mimesis) has fueled both the inner-conflict of Aboriginal people and the deep-rooted conflict that remains between Aboriginals and Canadians, today. Shackled to one another in mimetic cultural conflict and political struggle, Aboriginal people and members of Canadian colonist society live different social realities, in part because they have different national memories and live by different stories. Two models for reconciling instances of abuse of Indigenous peoples, whether institutional or societal, will be outlined, illustrating an approach that encourages the reclamation of cultural practices as a way to promote healing and self-love. And in healing, Aboriginal people will gain a fuller capacity to reconcile the conflict within themselves and their conflict with the colonist society.

MIMESIS AND RESIDENTIAL SCHOOLS

From the Girardian perspective, Indian residential schools are a marker of colonial control and historical silence in Canada. They are an indicator of a mimetic structure—a pattern of orientation, attitudes, and behaviors—that persists through time. By "silence" we mean, the colonist society's silent refusal to recognize the rights of the Indigenous people and also, the silence of the residential school survivors. Colonists silently viewed their rights as superseding the rights of all others. For example, they received certificates of parcel without regard for existing use of the land by Aboriginal peoples. And for many years, residential school survivors silently acted out a legacy of guilt and shame through several generations. Residential schools were, in fact, an extension of the silence and of the structural violence of hegemony that was representative of many of the federal policies developed for Aboriginal people.

But these "draconian policies were not *meant* to hinder" Aboriginal peoples (Stirbys 2004, 15). They were, after all, *allowed* to join in the new Dominion in one of two ways: by becoming absorbed into a homogenous white Christian colonist society or by becoming extinct as part of the process of the evolution of that society. But, either way, the new nation had access to Aboriginal lands and all their resources (Stirbys 2004, 15). And who would not be moved to a feeling of pride in being a member of an emerging nation with such potential for prosperity and future development?

For Aboriginal people, however, memories of the formation of the new nation of Canada include the forced occupation of land, confiscation of resources, destruction of cultures, and the repression of sovereign Indigenous nations. In the social imaginaries and public narratives that emerged in popular culture, the lived realities and personal memories of Aboriginal people became cloaked in stereotypes or concealed in silence.

In his book entitled, *How Societies Remember*, Paul Connerton (1989, 3) writes, "Our images of the past commonly serve to legitimate a present social order." For 500 years, the conflicting social imaginaries of the primitive or noble, nomadic Indian and the civilized, or Christianized, pioneering white man have traveled together on distinct historical journeys. In this long colonial gaze, Aboriginal people have been misrepresented by "Others" in proclamations, policies, and studies and stories. During the years when Aboriginal voices "were silenced by commission or omission," their legacy was claimed and written by non-Native politicians and colonists, anthropologists, and historians, photographers and novelists, promoting inaccuracies in history and stories of a savage but conquered people (Valaskakis 2005, 2).

Until 1992, the unwritten memories of nearly 107,000 Aboriginal people, who attended residential schools, were ignored in the social and political history of the nation-state (Aboriginal Peoples' Survey conducted by Statistic's Canada in 1991). Early in the 21st century, survivors, who were numbered at approximately 93,000, recall the despair of losing connections to their families, communities, cultures, and languages, and for some, enduring the pain of physical and sexual abuse (Aboriginal Healing Foundation 2002, 2). Their experiences of isolation, subordination, and abuse have effected generations of Aboriginal children, adding to the current tensions between Aboriginal people and Canadians.

MEMORY AND HISTORIC TRAUMA

N. Scott Momaday (1976, 22) writes about the stories he shares in common with his people: "Some of my mother's memories have become my own. That is the real burden of the blood." Linda Hogan (1987, 235) also says of her grandfather, "All his people are walking through my veins without speech." The assertions of "blood memory" (Van Winkle in Strong and Van Winkle 1996, 560) expressed by Momaday, Hogan, and other Aboriginal writers may be inaccurate and incongruous, but they are powerful expressions of shared heritage. For Aboriginal people, "cultural bloodism" represents the pain and joy of a memoried past, a lived heritage that is both collective and personal. In this transposition of the knowledge and relationships that are encoded in oral tradition, Indian stories that travel through time, "are experienced as transformations of a familiar pattern" (Ridington 1990a, 138).

Sharing stories is not simply about retrieving recollections. It is a process of reframing memory. Memoried relationships with "grandfathers" and "grandmothers," with the experience and understanding of those who walked before us, our Elders, forge the imaginative basis for stories, including the contemporary narratives of dominance and survival that are lived, reframed, imagined and transformed. For outsiders, the articulation of blood and culture, experience and ancestry—formed in Aboriginal heritage and fixed in colonial policy—is wrapped in a naturalized perspective that is essentialist and racist (Van Winkle in Strong and Van Winkle 1996, 562). But for Aboriginal people, "memory in the blood" represents an affective, cultural bond to the past, expressing collective and personal experiences, including the traumatic memories of residential schools.

Since the 1990s, the trauma experienced by Canadian Aboriginal people who attended residential school has been well documented. Books such as *A National Crime* (Milloy 1999) and *Shingwauk's Vision* (Miller 1996) join personal accounts, research reports, court cases, and mediation files to support the storied memories of survivors:

> Scores of First Nations children died from disease while in the care of residential schools; others were emotionally and spiritually destroyed by the harsh

discipline and living conditions. Confinement, humiliations, lack of privacy, physical, sexual and psychological abuses resulted in dislocation, loss of pride and self-respect, and loss of identity within the family, community and nation. (*Residential School Update*, Assembly of First Nations 1998, 5)

The effects of residential school trauma that have been documented among residential school survivors include depression, domestic violence, and addictions (Corrado and Cohen 2003). However, in recent years, American academics such as Eduardo and Bonnie Duran and Maria Brave Heart have recognized historical trauma as a form of "psychic wounding" caused by the intergenerational memories of Aboriginal people (Duran, et. al. 1998, 342). They argue that the impact of death, disease, relocation, deprivation and systematic cultural genocide, which some call an "American Indian holocaust," has meant Aboriginal people experience "intergenerational post-traumatic stress disorder." (1998, 341), an Aboriginal "Soul Wound" caused by unresolved trauma that is multigenerational and cumulative over time (Duran, et. al. 1998, 341).

In Canada, Cynthia Wesley-Esquimaux and Magdelena Smolewski (2004, 66) agree that residential schools are experiences among the burden of memories that contribute to what they call "historic trauma transmission," which they define as ". . . the cumulative waves of trauma and grief that have not been resolved within the Aboriginal psyche and have become deeply embedded in the collective memory of Aboriginal people" (2004, iii). From their perspective, "Hidden collective memories of this trauma, or a collective non-remembering, is passed from generation to generation, just as the maladaptive social and behaviourial patterns, are the symptoms of many different social disorders caused by the historic trauma" (2004, 66). The result is not a single historical trauma response, but ". . . different social disorders with respective clusters of symptoms" (Wesley-Esquimaux and Smolewski 2004, 65).

In a relentless process, the clusters of symptoms of historic trauma, such as family violence and sexual abuse, are passed on to and internalized by Aboriginal children. As a result, Wesley-Esquimaux and Smolewski point out that socially learned behaviors associated with historic trauma cause "deep breakdowns in social functioning that may last for many years, decades or even generations" (2004, 65). They build upon the work of Arthur Neal (1998), who suggests that "with time, boundaries around traumatic events become blurred, stereotyped and selectively distorted and, as such, they enter the collective image of the past that people pass from generation to generation" (2004, 71).

STORIES AND MIMESIS

Although Girard's *mimesis* reflects *imitation*, which "connotes copying what is clearly observable," it is through mimesis and the "copying of interiority" (tacit knowledge) that all culture is passed along (Redekop 2002, 65). It is through mimesis that we "learn language, values, and patterns of behavior by imitating our parents, members of the community, and peers" (*ibid.*). It is through mimesis that the "clues that come from the interaction between knowledge of ourselves" and our actions in "relation to our desires, and discerning similar patterns with the Other" are used to build a narrative. The narrative is then verified "'through dialogue and testing" in forming one's identity (*ibid.*).

Robin Ridington writes that Aboriginal people tend to live "storied lives," lives that are forged and intertwined in spoken narratives (1990b, 277). Likened to the process of mimesis, narratives emerge from personal experience as well as from the experience of others; as Ridington tells us: "storied speech makes subtle and esoteric references to common history, common knowledge, common myth" (1990b, 278). Aboriginal people have always known about the importance of stories. Speaking as the first Aboriginal person to give Canada's prestigious Massey Lecture, Thomas King (2003, 2) tells us, "The truth about stories is that that's all we are." N. Scott Momaday (in Swann and Krupat 1987, 566) says, "We are what we imagine." And Lenore Keeshing-Tobias (in Slapin and Seale 1992, 98–99), writes, "Stories are not just entertainment. Stories are power. They reflect the deepest, the most intimate perceptions, relationships and attitudes of a people. Stories show how a people, a culture thinks."

Academics have long recognized narratives expressing memory and experience as a window on who we are, what we experience, and how we understand ourselves and others. But resonating with the words of Thomas King, more recent writings reveal a more complex relationship between oral, written, or visual narratives and the formations of identity, community, and the alliances and relations of power that construct our social lives. In particular, writings in cultural studies suggest that we actually construct who we are through a process that involves an individual's identification with the cultural images and narratives that dominate our ways of seeing and representing the social worlds in which we live.

Similarly, the dominant narrative shown in Eurocentric educational curricula has had a lasting impact on the lived experiences of Aboriginal Peoples. Duncan Campbell Scott, who was once the most powerful man at Indian and Northern Affairs in the early part of the 20th century, committed to "end the Indian problem" through the policy of education (Stirbys 2004, 3). Any method, he deemed necessary, would be applied through curricula that would destroy the tribal identity and ultimately lead to the Indian's disappearance. This policy, according to Scott, "might be frustrated by the gradual extinction of the race while in the tutelary stage, but that is hardly to be feared" (Stirbys 2004, 3–4). Assimilation of Aboriginal children into Canadian mainstream society began by removing them from the influence of their families and communities, placing them in centrally located schools, and punishing them for engaging their cultural norms. To accomplish full assimilation, the government appealed to the churches, who sought "the development of a child's character in accordance with the concepts of Christian education" (Haig-Brown 1988, 57).

MIMETIC PATTERN AND BEHAVIOR DEVELOPMENT

The question asked is, "How does a child in residential school form their character in accordance with their culture when policy dictates otherwise?" Egerton Ryerson of Indian Affairs (1847) wrote a report concluding that education for Indians must include "a weaning of habits and feelings of their ancestors, and the acquirements of the language, arts and customs of civilized life" (Ray 1996, 238). Children who started school (at approximately five years of age) were not allowed to see their parents for "several years at a time; the department discouraged students from visiting home, fearing they would be exposed to 'undesirable influences'" (Ray 1996, 241).

Therefore, if Indian children were not allowed to know the *feelings of their ancestors* (that includes memories and stories) and were not allowed to return home, their security and connection to family would be broken. For example, native children were seen as "less than human, [and] authorities at all levels within the system failed to give them the care and protection to which they were entitled" (Legacy 2003, 58). And, when a child's basic human needs (ontological needs) are not met and their culture, spirituality, relationships, and history thwarted, everything about their Identity has been marred.

Because they were notable to solidify their Aboriginal roots and identities, children were not often able to experience what Redekop (2002) refers to as "mimetic structures of blessing" (positive mimesis) by solidifying their Aboriginal roots and identities. Having suffered years of neglect and other atrocities, these children did not have a chance to satisfy core identity needs: a young Aboriginal child's *sense of meaning* does not develop when they are unable to role model their parents and experience parental nurturing. Children begin to question their place in the world and, not experiencing *recognition* for their basic and cultural needs, become angry and eventually feel shame. Depression eventually sets in as self-esteem is diminished, through beatings for speaking in their native tongue, for example. Over time, children learn they can never take *action*. On average, children remained in residential school for 10–15 years (as told by a residential school survivor). Without visitors and sufficient time with family and community, a child could not maintain the *connectedness* that would lead to self-respect. The result was a very sad existence. Without the comfort and protection of loved ones, many Aboriginal children's *security* was destroyed and self-confidence could not grow. Children lived in fear because of the abuse they endured. Yet, we know that many children did survive this kind of trauma. The *Human Identity Needs Through Time* diagram (Redekop 2002, 50) has been helpful in understanding how such young children survived atrocities done to them.

The need for memory, story, and coherence illuminates what Paul Ricoeur calls the *ipse*, or temporal, dimension of Self. A person needs (from the past) will gradually change through time into the future. As our memories, and stories develop and we receive validation, coherence increases—that is, once we make sense of our emotions that emerge from these memories and stories, coherence allows us to move fluidly into the future to create more memories and stories to build who we will become. But for a young child who is not allowed to see their family, and thereby experiences an emotional

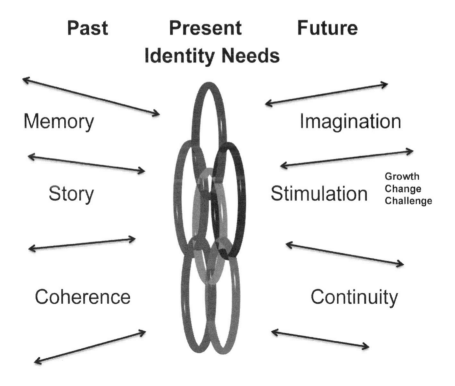

Figure 16.1.

disconnect, those past memories of family and traditions will fade over time. Not having contact with family means not hearing the life stories of their Elders, not learning the values through their own kinship ties and culture and how they fit in with the family story. When children do not know how they belong, how can they fill their coherence need and make sense of their emotional disconnection away from the familial stories that are never allowed to fully develop? For those children, validation will never come from family or from the authorities (often ministers or nuns) who ran the school.

Recall Ricoeur's *ipse* dimension mentioned earlier. It not only includes the past but also future needs for stimulation, continuity and imagination. A child in residential school did not have their need for stimulation met in terms of positive change, growth, or challenge in most cases, since "barely two hours a day were devoted to scholarly activities" (Ray 1996, 240) and the rest of the time they did hard labor (Legacy 2004, 33–34). However, a person will innately try to stay physiologically and psychologically alive when faced with danger; and it is the *will* that most likely sustained children's need for continuity. The third need (and the one that may have been the saving grace for many children) is *imagination*. Redekop states that with imagination, "we can see ourselves being and acting in another place and time" (2002, 51). Even if a child's past memory has faded, it is the ability to imagine a future away from residential school that enables a child to survive a trauma. Children may be stripped of their cultural identity and made to feel shame for their heritage but it takes much more to drive out imagination. Since the *ipse* dimension of the Self greatly impacts on the *idem* need categories of *Meaning, Connection, Security, Recognition,* and *Action*, a child may be able to use their imagination as a means to wellness within the chaos of their environment, and human identity satisfaction.

Stories, then, are not just the cultural glue that holds social or political collectivities together or transmits them over time. Stories express the dynamic cultural ground in which identities and collectivities are formed through a continual process of adopting allied or conflicting representations and the ideological messages they signify. In Aboriginal communities, stories of residential schools that were entrenched in the experience of Aboriginal people for a hundred and fifty years are embodied in memories and the behaviors that emerge in fragments and are passed on in the discursive exchange of oral tradition and parenting or lack thereof.

In the webs of meaning we spin to orient our lives, we engage and express, enact, and act upon, collective and individual memories. For Aboriginal people, the memories they reveal, retell, or imagine are often traumatic. These memories are then passed from generation to generation through the narratives that emerge and circulate in stories, verbal or visual, internalized or enacted. In contrast to the public disregard that has surrounded the lived experience of Aboriginal people with respect to residential schools, Aboriginal people remember. They remember the trauma of their experiences and memories engender individual and intergenerational impact that is also mimetic in nature. The maladaptive behaviors repeat, when there is no alternative. *The only time you can change the mimetic structures of trauma to a positive model is when you recognize that there are other ways of being, of acting, and of engaging that you have NOT learned but that you want to imitate.*

HEALING AND RECONCILIATION: A CULTURALLY AFFIRMING APPROACH

From an Aboriginal perspective, healing is generally understood as a restoration of "wholeness," or the health of the body, mind, and spirit. One way in which Aboriginal people can achieve wholeness is through a return to their culture. Maria Yellow Horse Brave Heart discusses the Takini (Survivor) Network of the Lakota, which implements a model called the *Historical Trauma and Unresolved Grief Intervention* (HTUG), developed for Indigenous survivors' healing efforts to overcome the effects of the residential school experience and other aspects of historical trauma (HT), historical unresolved grief, and historical trauma response (HTR) (Brave Heart 2003). Brave Heart's theory is based on more than 20 years of clinical practice and "describes the massive cumulative trauma across generations rather than the more limited diagnosis of post-traumatic stress disorder (PTSD), which is inadequate in capturing the influence and attributes of Native trauma" (2003, 7–8). The four major components of historical trauma intervention programming include: Confronting, Understanding, Releasing, and Transcending trauma (Brave Heart n.d.). The focus is on collective communal healing as well as individual healing; methods based on Lakota spirituality, traditional cultural practices, combined with trauma theory. There have been positive outcomes of historical trauma intervention such as the regulation of emotion (i.e., reduction of hopelessness, sadness, grief) and an increase in hope and pride among the Lakota Peoples enabling them to live their Indigenous values and to strengthen their familial relationships (Brave Heart 2003).

Today, Aboriginal self-determination and cultural continuity are intertwined in a movement toward wholeness or healing. Healing is an iterative process, an incremental movement of change in the realities and perceptions of individuals, communities, and nations. And while there is a difference between individual and collective healing, the different processes are related, and they share a common goal: reconciliation. It is, therefore, generally agreed that reconciliation is both a process and a goal. There is a distinction in the literature between instrumental reconciliation that involves people working together toward a shared end and socio-emotional reconciliation that touches on the deeper elements of hurt, trauma, and victimization. But as a process, reconciliation is meant to move us towards eliminating violence to eventually reach the end goal of making peace with oneself and with others. Reconciliation involves the recall and expression of memory, or "telling one's story." The legitimization, or "naming" of the abuse and the mutual raising of consciousness that can occur in personal or public dialogue can help to achieve resolution, restoration, or reparation.

At the 2006 COV&R Conference, René Girard asked, "How can mimetic theory make a contribution to the reduction of violence?" In the case of residential schools, we first have to recognize how we all unconsciously contribute to the violence and on-going conflict. For example, do we add to the continuing stereotypes or derogatory labels used against Aboriginal people? Aboriginal survivors of residential schools are beginning to end the cycle of their own trauma by breaking their silence and speaking up for their rights, which is healing for not only the individual but also for the whole of the community. This healing process includes reclamation of cultural ways, while at the same time addressing the traumas they have survived.

In the latter part of 2012, four First Nations women from Saskatchewan began the "Idle No More" (INM) movement at the same time Chief Spence of Attawapiskat began her sacred fast in order to bring attention to the injustices Aboriginal Peoples continue to experience in Canada. These grassroots movements were undertaken to bring attention to Treaty Rights agreements between First Nations and the Government of Canada, which have been largely ignored. In addition, the Omnibus Bills C-45 and C-38 that once passed, threaten environmental degradation of our rivers and lakes, our land and Canadians' democratic right to carefully consider, scrutinize, and debate such important issues. The INM movement and Chief Spence have remained true to their cultural roots and the Treaty Protocols by taking action to protect their inherent Treaty rights as well as the environment for the benefit of the next seven generations.

Historically, First Nations' culture has proven to be healing because it provides grounding for individuals as a consequence of the accountability mechanisms and conflict resolution processes built into their traditional governance structures. For example, within the Iroquois Confederacy, the Iroquois have lived by their Great Law of Peace, which is still reflected within the traditional values of the Akwesasne community. The Akwesasne Community Peacemaking Process (ACPP) established in the early 1990s is rooted in these traditional values as well as modern alternative dispute resolution (ADR) methodologies. The ACPP was created to address the on-going conflicts between members within this divided community. The conflict resolution process developed was intended to draw families together so that as a community they could speak as "one people–one voice."[3] The ACPP showed great success, in their approach of inclusivity, by hearing the concerns of all community members, while developing different processes for different types of conflicts. Some of the processes developed were: fact finding, rumor control process development, mediation training, and conflict management (from negotiation to arbitration), and family reconciliation. The latter succeeded despite all odds.

Today, few people realize that the Iroquois Confederacy's *Great Law of Peace* was the foundation for the development of community-based conflict resolution (CBCR) procedures currently taught by the Canadian Institute of Conflict Resolution/Institut canadien pour la resolution des conflits (CICR/ICRC) housed at Saint Paul University in Ottawa, Ontario.[4] Over the years, these CBCR procedures have been successfully used to help resolve deep-rooted conflicts nationally and internationally (ie. The Bosnia-Herzegovina conflict).

To date, the Government of Canada has yet to break their silence in recognizing the value of Aboriginal Peoples as contributing members of the Canadian blended society.[5] In 2008, the Prime Minister of Canada delivered an apology on behalf of the Canadian Government for the harms done to Aboriginal children and their communities, flowing from the implementation of the Indian Residential School Policy. But many still wonder what form of reconciliation could bridge the divide between Aboriginal People and the rest of Canada and heal the legacy of mistrust. As a starting point, many residential school survivors and their families speak about how the IRS experience left them grieving for the loss of their languages. A reconciliatory effort can be found by expanding Canada's *Official Languages Act* to include the original languages of Algonquian, Ojibway, Cree, Iroquoian, Mohawk, and Inuktitut for example, along with the English and the French languages.[6] In this way, true multiculturalism is born when all Canadians recognize this country could not have been built without the efforts and cooperation of Aboriginal Peoples alongside the English and the French. In expanding the language base, Canada has a real opportunity to demonstrate gratitude for the contributions made by the original Peoples and for many Aboriginal People, this one act alone can carry the reconciliation seed forward for many generations to come.

At the 2006 Conference Duncan Morrow asked the question "how do we come back to humanity?" We are dependent on our victims (survivors) to help bring us back! This begs the question, "How can this be achieved?" The answer is to be found by revealing the reality of Aboriginal Peoples' circumstances and the illegitimate ways in which the Canadian Government creates legislation that undermines the human rights and aspirations of Aboriginal Peoples (and by extension, all other Canadians). Becoming allies with Aboriginal Peoples, Canadians can assist in the healing process. Collectively, we can no longer remain silent; we must work together for the human rights of all. Taking the time to learn the stories, concerns, and even supporting the revival of Indigenous languages of First Nations, Inuit, and Métis Peoples will do much to promote healing and reconciliation within our country and develop those authentic peaceful relationships we are all so desperately seeking.

REFERENCES

Aboriginal Healing Foundation. May, 2002. *The Healing Has Begun: An Operational Update.*

Brave Heart, Maria Yellow Horse. 2003. "The Historical Trauma Response Among Natives and Its Relationship with Substance Abuse: A Lakota Illustration." *Journal of Psychoactive Drugs*, 35:1, 7–13.

———. (n.d.). "Historical Trauma, Boarding School Trauma." Power-point presentation prepared on behalf of the Takini Network.

Connerton, Paul. 1989. *How Societies Remember.* Cambridge, UK: Cambridge University Press.

Corrado, Raymond R. and Irwin M. Cohen. 2003. *Mental Health Profiles for a Sample of British Columbia's Aboriginal Survivors of the Canadian Residential School System.* Prepared for The Aboriginal Healing Foundation. Ottawa, ON: Aboriginal Healing Foundation.

Duran, Eduardo, Bonnie Duran, Maria Yellow Horse Brave Heart and Susan Yellow Horse-Davis. 1998. "Healing the American Indian Soul Wound." In *International Handbook of Multigenerational Legacies of Trauma,* edited by Yael Danieli. New York: Pienum.

Haig-Brown, Celia. 1988. *Resistance and Renewal: Surviving the Indian Residential Schools.* Secwepeme Cultural Society/Tillacrum Library.

Hogan, Linda. 1987. "The Two Lives." In Brian Swann and Arnold Krupat, eds., *I Tell You Now: Autobiographical Essays by Native American Writers.* Lincoln: University of Nebraska Press.

King, Thomas. 2003. *The Truth About Stories: A Native Narrative.* Toronto, ON: Anansi.

Legacy of Hope Foundation. 2003. *Where Are the Children? Healing the Legacy of Residential Schools.* Ottawa, ON: Legacy of Hope Foundation.

Miller, J. R. 1996. *Shingwauk's Vision.* Toronto, ON: University of Toronto Press.

Milloy, John. 1999. *A National Crime.* Winnipeg, MB: University of Manitoba Press.

Momaday, N. Scott. 1976. *The Names.* New York: Harper and Row.

Ray, Arthur, J. 1996. *I Have Lived Here Since The World Began. An Illustrated History of Canada's Native People.* Toronto, ON: Lester.

Redekop, Vern Neufeld. 2002. *From Violence to Blessing. How an understanding of Deep-Rooted Conflict Can Open Paths to Reconciliation.* Ottawa, ON: Novalis.

Residential School Update. 1998. Ottawa: Assembly of First Nations.

Ridington, Robin. 1990a. *Little Bit Know Something: Stories in a Language of Anthropology.* Vancouver, BC: Douglas and McIntyre.

———. 1990b. "Cultures in Conflict: The Problem of Discourse." In W. H. New (Ed.) *Native Writers and Canadian Writing.* Vancouver: UBC Press.

Slapin, Beverly and Doris Seale, eds. 1992. *Through Indian Eyes: The Native Experience in Stories for Children* Gabriola Island, BC: New Society Publishers.

Statistics Canada. (2006, 05, 04). Aboriginal People's Survey 1991. Retrieved from: http://www23.statcan.gc.ca/imdb/p2SV.pl?Function=getSurvey&SurvId=3250&SurvVer=1&InstaId=16692&InstaVer=1&SDDS=3250&lang=en&db=imdb&adm=8&dis=2.

Stirbys, Cynthia. 2004. The Policy of Hegemonic Structures in Aboriginal Country & The Paradox of Altruism and Fear. Paper written as an MA Candidate in Conflict Studies, Saint Paul University, Ottawa, ON.

Strong, Pauline Turner and Barrik Van Winkle. 1996. "'Indian Blood': Reflections on the Reckoning and Refiguring of Native North American Identity." *Cultural Anthropology* 11, no. 4: 547–576.

Swann, Brian and Arnold Krupat, eds., *I Tell You Now: Autobiographical Essays by Native American Writers.* Lincoln: University of Nebraska Press.

Valaskakis, Gail Gutherie. 2005. "Introduction: Approaching Indian Country." *Indian Country: Essays on Contemporary Native Culture*. Waterloo, ON: Wilfred Laurier University Press: 1–8.

Wesley-Esquimaux, Cynthia, and Magdelena Smolewski. 2004. *Historic Trauma and Aboriginal Healing*. Ottawa: Aboriginal Healing Foundation.

NOTES

1. This chapter was developed in collaboration with the former Research Director of the Aboriginal Healing Foundation, Gail Guthrie Valaskakis. It was originally delivered at Saint Paul University's *Colloquium on Violence and Religion* in June 2006. It was an honor and a privilege to present the topic of Mimesis, Residential Schools, and Reconciliation between Aboriginal Peoples and Canadian society on both mine and Ms. Valaskakis behalf. I would therefore, like to dedicate this newer version of our work to her memory. This article is based on the original presentation of the same name and has been revised and updated for purposes of this publication.

2. Please note that in Canada Indigenous peoples are referred to as "Aboriginal," which includes the Métis, the Inuit, and the First Nations people, who are sometimes called "Indian." Residential schools in Canada were attended by all three of these groups; however, the schools were known as Indian Residential Schools.

3. This quote is taken from a confidential document written about the ACCP that was given to me so that I had the full background story and understanding of the ACCP.

4. As told in conversation with the first executive director of the CICR (February, 2013).

5. The Treaty Agreements were originally made with the Crown, and during the patriation of Canada's Constitution (1982) this responsibility was passed onto the Federal Government of Canada. However, Canada has consistently breached these obligations. See "The Substance of Great Britain's Obligations to the Indian Nations": http://constitution.ubcic.bc.ca/sites/constitution.ubcic.bc.ca/files/OCRrussell2optimized.pdf.

6. After all, why should the First Nations, Inuit, and Métis Peoples of Canada, who have been constitutionally recognized since 1982, not have their languages recognized as well? Around the world, there are models to illustrate that this is indeed possible, such as India, which is not just multilingual but in fact has 23 constitutionally recognized languages.

Chapter Seventeen

Bosnia's Children Born of War

A Girardian Case Study

Angela Kiraly

In 2010, fifteen-year-old Bosniak Zerina (name changed) told researchers, "I see myself as a scapegoat because I have a Serbian blood, and in this way, I am kind of . . . available for everyone to hate me. I am a channel for their sadness . . . I am guilty for their pain. I am guilty for their misery; that lives on. And no one likes me, everyone avoids me, everyone hates me" (Erjavec and Volcic 2010a, 367). This disheartening statement is a clear and potent example of what is experienced endemically by the children conceived as a result of wartime rapes in the former Yugoslavia. Similar scapegoating language was employed in self-descriptive narratives by a majority of interviewed adolescent girls born of war rape in Bosnia.

The systematic war rapes of the Bosnian war were considered unprecedented at the time and are the first time that rape was considered a war crime, in itself, rather than a bi-product of war (Carpenter 2009, 24). Between 1991 and 1995, it is estimated that between 20,000 (by a delegation from the European Community) and 50,000 (figures from the Bosnian Ministry of the Interior) officially sanctioned rapes occurred (Niarchos 1995, 654).[1] These rapes have also been considered acts of genocide, since the attacks were specifically intended to alienate women from their ethnic group, humiliate, destroy the ethnic identity of the women, demoralize and "to persuade and prepare victims to hate and eventually destroy their own children" (Slapsak 2000, 55). The Serbian logic being that the offspring created would "be 'Chetnik babies' that would grow to kill Muslims" (Daniel-Wrabetz 2007, 23). Catherine Niarchos suggests that the rapes and the children conceived would be the ultimate reminder of Serb dominance: "The body of a raped women becomes a ceremonial battlefield, a parade ground for the victor's

319

colors. The act that is played out upon her is a message passed between men—vivid proof of victory for one and defeat for the other" (Niarchos 1995, 661). Ingrid Skjelsbaek explains that, traditionally, women maintain the home during war time and represent stability and future prospects and peace; these officially sanctioned rapes were intended to undermine the security women represent (2006).

Locally, and in western media, the "patriarchal ethnicity" myth, stating that children always receive the ethnicity and identity of their father, has been largely accepted. Consequently, the children's communities primarily associate the children born of war with their fathers, rather than with their mothers' and community's ethnicity.

The Bosnian government estimates that 35,000 women, primarily Bosniak but also Croat and Serb, became pregnant from rape (Daniel-Wrabetz 2007, 23); many pregnancies were terminated, but in many instances a child was raised by the biological mother. Scholarly work on the subject has tended to focus on the mothers. These women have been presented in the media as passive and powerless victims, despite many instances in which survivors bravely testified at the International Criminal Tribunal for the Former Yugoslavia and/or took up arms to defend themselves and their people (Carpenter 2009). This perception does a serious disservice to the self-narrative of the women and children involved, since the self-understanding of the mother as survivor or victim is critical to the process of reconciliation and social integration for these children. Skjelsbaek's theory of narrative shows that an individual attributes agency, in their self-narrative, by placing themselves and others along the plot line (Skjelsbaek 2006, 375). This plot is developed jointly by the individual and those around them. When the media and local community use "victim" language, they actively attribute to that woman's self-narrative a sense of being powerless. A mother's self-narrative plays a significant role in determining the self-narrative of their children, and whether their relationship with the community is marked by conflict or flourishing.

The children conceived by means of these war rapes are evidence of the mimetic and scapegoating processes identified by René Girard. This chapter relates the reported life experiences of the children born or war to Girard's scapegoating and mimetic theory, based on the findings of nineteen interviews of Bosniak adolescents (all of whom are female), conducted by Karmen Erjavec and Zala Volcic (Erjavec and Volcic, 2010a and 2010b). The interviews show, following the scapegoating pattern identified by Girard, that a crisis led to the community selecting members with specific characteristics (described below) to serve as scapegoats and that the scapegoats accepted their role passively due to mimetic doubling. While these interviews demonstrate that many of the interviewees report being victims of scapegoating violence, there is a minority of girls who describe a positive self-narrative related to a loving, up-building mimetic relationship with their mother. These relationships follow an alternative mimetic pattern of mutual admiration, love, and care based on truth, which produces creativity rather than conflict and destruction.

RENÉ GIRARD: MIMESIS AND SCAPEGOATING

The mimetic theory, originally outlined by Girard in the 1960s, is much more complex than the simple mimicry of children's games. He asserts that human beings learn desire and what is desirable by mimicking those around them. This mimicry includes the emotions, mental states, and desired possessions of the models surrounding the subject. He writes, "To say that our desires are imitative or mimetic is to root them neither in their objects nor in ourselves, but in a third party, the *model* or mediator, whose desire we imitate in the hope of resembling him or her, in the hope that our two beings will be 'fused' . . ." (Girard 2008, 246). Individuals choose models and learn from them what will satisfy the need for meaning, action, connectedness, security, and recognition (Redekop 2002). The model and the subject have variable and flexible roles in the process of mimetic doubling. Once the subject has succeeded in obtaining the mutually desired thing, the subject may then become a model to his or her model. In such cases, a mimetic rivalry will develop. Girard explains that, "No one fans my desires as effectively as the one who inspires it by desiring it for himself, diabolically it seems, an object I believe I desire independently of his influence" (Girard 2011, 19). In situations where a subject is influenced by many models at a single time, it is unlikely that an intense rivalry will develop. The multiplicity of influences diffuses the concentration of desire for the possessions of any single model. Girard also explains that, in particularly intense rivalries, the desired object may actually be forgotten as the rivals lay hold of another (Girard, 2011). On the other hand, in closed systems where there are few outside influences, the rivalries are direct and are inclined toward extremes. The more intensely the model desires the object, the more intensely the subject will also desire the object.

Mimetic theory does not condemn people to living a competitive and violent life. The mimetic process can alternately work for the benefit and mutual gain of the subject and model (Adams, 2000). It is mimesis, not violence itself, which underlies Girard's theories. The capacity for violence and the ability for reconciliation both lie in the mimetic nature of humans. Under positive circumstances, there is the potential to participate fully in caring for another. Individuals become capable of loving, giving, and receiving in relationships in a way that is dynamic and produces real positive change in the individuals involved on a core level. It helps the individual develop the inner resources necessary to become fully autonomous and to act in their community in a way that is life-enhancing rather than destructive. Adams asserts that loving a person confers dignity and autonomy. In short, when a model desires the freedom and autonomy of the subject, they contribute to that freedom.

This mimetic phenomenon is a structure of blessing, in contrast to hegemonic structures and structures of conflict in which a dominant party desires the subjugation and enslavement of another party (Redekop 2002). Structures of blessing are marked by a number of characteristics, including openness to diversity and life, generosity, gratitude, receptiveness, creativity, and peacefulness. These structures are, moreover, fed by justice and truth.

The mimetic process often results in scapegoating, which gets its name from ancient ceremonies in which the perceived tensions and guilt of a group's members were ritually transferred to a goat that would be banished, or killed. This would free everyone who participated in the ritual from blame, releasing the pressures and stress felt by group members (Girard 2011; 2008). In modern societies, this still occurs in group interaction at all social levels. Instead of a ritual victim, a member of the community who is convenient to blame for group tension is unconsciously selected. The other members of the group will begin to truly believe that, if that person were no longer part of the group, all conflicts, crisis, and tension would be alleviated. The unlucky scapegoat is then harassed and attacked. The group is united by their rejection of the scapegoat, and when the scapegoat is driven out, leaves voluntarily, or is killed (in very extreme cases), the group feels a deep sense of relief. As tension builds again, the group will unconsciously begin the process of selecting and ostracising another individual. The unconscious belief that the removal of a single party can alleviate tension and crisis is make-believe. In order for real change to occur, every member of the community must change, not only the scapegoat victim (Gemmill 1989, 407). The scapegoating process is full of illusory thinking, self-deception of the participants, and invalid logic. According to Girard, the community must believe that the scapegoat has no redeeming qualities or consensus on the rejection would not be reached and could not reconcile the group (Girard 2011).

CHILDREN OF WAR: IDEAL SCAPEGOATS

The children born of war have been formally identified internationally as secondary rape victims, who are at risk and require special protection (Daniel-Wrabetz 2007). Yet, within their own communities and especially within their peer group, they describe being rejected and subjected to daily social exclusion, maltreatment, and harassment (Erjavec and Volcic 2010a, 2010b).

Girardian theory suggests that this is because they have been made into scapegoats for the pain felt by Bosniak communities and for their mothers.

The scapegoat function is usually preceded by a community crisis. In some cases, it can be the conglomeration of many private frustrations, like denied needs. More commonly, however, the crisis arises from a major upheaval that challenges the society as a whole. Usually, it occurs when mimetic rivalries are inflamed by threat to a group's distinctiveness or existence. A process of mimetic doubling is initiated, as the group sees other groups whom appear secure and powerful. The group becomes fixated on obtaining the same security as the other group and begins searching for a way to achieve this ends. The Bosnian community, as a whole, continues to suffer as a result of the war, although it was officially ended by the Dayton Agreement in 1995. Speaking generally, Girard explains this phenomena thusly: ". . . it is not because the conflict is poorly extinguished, but because there are always new objects kindling new desires and these new desires kindle new rivalries, which are cooled each time by new sacrificial interventions" (Girard 2011, 18). For instance, economic inequality amongst ethnic groups, poverty, unemployment, and animosity, as well as depression and grief from lost loved ones are common experiences (Layne et al. 2001). Furthermore, the Bosnian war was ethnic and nationalist in nature, meaning that there was a clear and present threat to the communal and ethnic identity of the Bosniaks.

Given that the scapegoating process augments the interrelations of a group at the expense of a third party, rejection of that individual by the group serves as a point of convergence and brings the suffering group together. This process requires the scapegoat to possess a few key attributes. The scapegoats are usually a party that could be deemed responsible for the group's entire suffering. While it is clear, rationally, that the children born of war are not the cause of the suffering, they do serve as a persisting and painful reminder to the Bosniak community that their military forces could not protect the most vulnerable members of their community. The use of rape as a war tactic did more than deeply traumatize and shame the women involved; it served to shame the entire community; it was destructive of the self-image of the entire society and culture. Lejla (name changed) told interviewers, "I'm also unwanted by all—since I remind everyone that the war is going on here . . . the war has not ended. We haven't reconciled, and some haven't paid for their sins" (Erjavec and Volcic 2010a, 366–367). The scapegoating function is a response to the lasting feeling of threatened identity. It makes the community feel a sense of relief and renewed cohesiveness within the group to reject the children born of war.

Furthermore, the children born of war possess a number of other attributes that make them convenient scapegoats. For instance, their identification with the rest of the community is strong, since the children are genetically, culturally, and linguistically Bosniak through their mothers and their upbringing. In Girardian theory, the more the subject identifies with the model, the more he or she will be prone to enter into a mimetic rivalry. Subjects tend to choose models from similar a demographic to their own. It follows that the more similarities there are, the more intense the mimetic effect. The Bosniak community identifies strongly with the children, yet the children born of war are also enemy outsiders, since their Serbian parentage makes them different from the rest of the community and associates them directly with the foreign forces. The very existence of mixed babies is taken as a strong message of Serb ethnic dominance, and the children themselves are held responsible for the suffering inflicted by their fathers.

Scapegoats are vulnerable; they cannot fight back and protect themselves. The community consciously knows that it was Serbian forces that were responsible for the trauma they experienced. However, aggression and the venting of frustrations against the Serbians would result in an increase in conflict, since the Serbian forces would defend and counter those acts. The ultimate goal of scapegoating is to reduce violence and tension; were there to be reprisal attacks, the scapegoating process would be a failure. Jasenka (name changed) understands this. She told researchers, "My classmates . . . they constantly attack me, since in a way I am the only one who could be used for their frustration and anger [. . .] they are cowardly enemies, because they shoot at me but they don't shoot at the real enemies . . . who really cause their suffering. It is not my fault that they lost their fathers or their mothers" (Erjavec and Volcic 2010b, 532–533). Elsewhere, she told them, "I have nothing to do with the Serbs; I hate them too, but everyone sees a little Chetnik in me" (Erjavec and Volcic 2010a, 369). This young girl has accurately identified herself as the most accessible scapegoat. She understands that her classmates reject her, because she is a convenient and safe outlet for their otherwise impotent rage. Usually, a person or group is selected as a scapegoat because they threaten the social order and threaten the group's feeling of distinctiveness (Redekop 2002, 90). The usual emotional response to this threat is anger (Redekop 2002, 92).

Scapegoats usually lack the social ties and connections that other members have; yet they have the power to disrupt the community. They are almost always outsiders, marginalized, or distinct from the rest of the group members for some reason, while having some significance that makes it possible for the community to truly believe expulsion will alleviate tension. Often, the turmoil created by violating a culture-specific taboo is sufficient reason for a scapegoat to be selected. This is a very potent form of power that even the lowest members of society can hold. The Bosnian children of war are a vulnerable group in many ways. Most are poor, young, forgotten by the international community, making them essentially voiceless. Seventeen out of the nineteen interviewed by Erjavec and Volcic (Erjavec and Volcic, 2010a, 2010b) are from low-income families or are living in an institution.

They forcefully and unintentionally disrupt the social order within Bosnia, since they defy classification according to strict traditional ethnic categories. They force the Bosniak community to reconsider their uniqueness and difference from the Serbians. In this way, these children are in fact powerful, despite having little influence.

The gender-based violence, forced impregnation, followed by displacement and disruption of the mother's previous family, generate a situation of intense crisis for the mothers. The mothers project their frustrations onto their children. Those frustrations and negative feelings are compounded by the negative feelings of her immediate family (there are instances in which the woman and child were rejected by husbands and parents because of the pregnancy) and those of the entire society. While scapegoating technically involves two or more parties, who are united through a common act of projecting their violence onto a third party, the relationships between mother and child have many characteristics similar to scapegoating and many of the same negative results for the self-narrative of the children involved.

Scapegoating within the family is further explained by Robertson and Duckett (2007), who report that many wartime mothers have difficulty identifying that their child (or children) has (have) problems with postwar adjustment or grief. This suggests that mothers in war zones have distanced themselves from the experiences of their children, producing a "self-other" dichotomy. This has a marginalizing effect on the children within their own family unit. This distance allows the scapegoating action to occur even within mother/child relationships, which are normally very intimate. Garrells writes:

> The attunement and responsiveness that psychologists associate with healthy parenting is based on an active state of imitative reciprocity. Parent-child interactions must be imitative in nature to produce the interpersonal connectedness and rich affective experience necessary for stimulating further development, not only psychologically, but also biologically via experience-dependent neural growth. (Garrells 2006, 61)

Many of the war child mothers have been unable to consistently participate in the process of physically (smiles and waves in infancy) or emotionally imitating their children and being imitated by them. Imitation between parent and child is also important for developing self-other recognition and differentiation, which Garrells calls, "the foundation for human relational motivations and attachments" (2006, 61). The tension between mother and child disrupts this learning process and is highly likely to have lasting effects on the social skills of the children as adults (Garrells 2006, 51). This is evidenced by the extreme difficulty the adolescent children born of war had with friendships and relationships, generally. Most of the girls reported having no meaningful relationships, beyond their mother, and no strong social bonds in the community (Erjavec and Volcic 2010a, 2010b). For the majority of girls, their relationship with their mother is particularly difficult and complicated; the girls report both intense conflict with and alienation from their mother and simultaneous dependence, admiration, and identification with her. This is a clear example of the fusion of model and subject that Girard discusses; one girl went so far as to say, "I am one with my mother" (Erjavec and Volcic 2010a, 372), meaning that she and her mother experience the same desires, fears, and pain.

Many of the girls report being an outlet for their mother's frustrations. Samra (name changed) said, "The worst is when my mother attacks me as well . . . she would scream at me . . . and also . . . beat me up. She is a traitor. I hate her . . . [Cries] Do you understand me; I am a shooting target for everyone, including my own mother" (Erjavec and Volcic 2010b, 533). Not all mothers of war children have this difficulty. Three of the interviewed girls reported that their mothers have been exceptionally supportive. However, in the majority of cases, mothers alternated between caring tenderly for their child and unexpected angry outbursts. Mothering a child conceived in violence is never an easy thing. Limited financial resources, limited access to psychological care, and intense stigma related to having a war child have increased the difficulty of mothering exponentially for these women.

The victim is progressively dehumanized by the increasing blame attributed to them. The group is unable to see the suffering of the scapegoat. The group stops relating to the scapegoat and believes the scapegoat deserves the treatment he, she, or they receive. The entire process is considered legitimate by the community. For this reason, Redekop (2002) calls scapegoating a hidden process. No one actively chooses the scapegoating path, and participants are unaware that they have become aggressors against what is likely an innocent victim or a victim, who is only partially at fault for the tension. When a person is socialized over a long period to be a scapegoat, and is regularly excluded for a prolonged period of time, they begin to believe themselves to be guilty of what they are accused. This follows from the mimetic process; the children are miming the negative feelings of their community. This directly affects the self-narratives of the children born of war, since they have been treated as scapegoats within their families and within their communities for their entire lives.

Erjavec and Volcic (2010a, 2010b) found that the adolescent war babies believed that they were abnormal. They have been conditioned by years of social exclusion, including physical violence, name calling, and staring by strangers. Others do not treat them with the respect cultural norms demand for interpersonal interaction. The majority of these girls are treated by their communities as if normal values, courtesy, rules, and fairness did not apply (Erjavec and Volcic, 2010a). Being denied basic human respects is indicative of the dehumanization and internalization process that accompanies the scapegoat mechanism. Erjavec and Volcic explain that, "Due to a sense of internalized guilt and feelings of abnormality, the girls isolate themselves from society and close themselves off from others. They reproduced the ostracization that has been visited upon them by 'othering' themselves" (Erjavec and Volcic 2010b, 536). Many of the girls go so far as to believe deep friendships are not possible for them, because they do not believe they are deserving of love and connection

The majority of the girls described themselves as "different," "dirty," and destructive (Erjavec and Volcic, 2010a). They feel deep self-loathing. While describing herself, one girl said, "I think I am kind of a destructive force . . . a negative character, who typically ruins other people's lives" (Erjavec and Volcic 2010a, 371). Almost all the girls consider the day they found out about their father as the most traumatic event of their lives. The dark discovery destroyed their coherent self-narrative. Erjavec and Volcic explain, ". . . the girls' representations of their identity in trauma are characterized by a fundamental lack of unity and cohesion in the narrative devices that usually work toward the construction and maintenance of a character's identity" (Erjavec and Volcic 2010a, 373). The feelings of difference, guilt, and self-loathing have caused the girls to withdraw from their communities. The girls have come to prefer isolation, because they fully believe they deserve to be alone. Redekop sums up the process, "as hegemonic structures are established, they are interiorized by the Subjected who assume the identity projected onto them by the Dominant" (Redekop 2002, 168). As such, most scapegoats believe their failings to be personal attributes, rather than failings of the entire social system.

A number of interviewed girls repeatedly referred to themselves as a "destroyer" or "destructive force" in their personal relationships. Specifically, this applies to their relationships with their mothers, for whom they believe they are, "a live reminder of rape" (Erjavec and Volcic 2010a, 372). They believe they are specifically guilty for the suffering of their mothers. Since the mothers are the primary models for their daughters, one girl even said, "I am one with my mother" (Erjavec and Volcic 2010a, 372). The girls have doubled the pain and anger of their mothers—the mothers are first humiliated and scapegoated for having been sullied through the rape by an enemy man and second by having a child that is born out of wedlock and fathered by an enemy of the community. It is significant that many of the interviewed girls used passive metaphors to describe themselves in the scapegoat role. The frequently used term "a shooting target," for instance, implies that the abuse they suffer is being inflicted on them, and that they cannot change this.

CHILDREN BORN OF WAR: IDEAL PEACEMAKERS

Mimetic structures of blessing (see chapter 4 for a definition) exist in small, but significant, pockets in Bosnia. One of the interviewed girls, Seada (name changed), describes herself and her life as following a very different pattern. What makes her different from the other seventeen girls is the example set by her mother. She has experienced mimetic doubling positively, because her mother desired justice and truth and loved her daughter and desires Seada's full agency, despite the circumstances surrounding Seada's conception, where the other girls doubled feelings of guilt, dirtiness, and difference, and they have become participants in a system of violence that alienates them.

Truth plays a major part in Seada's healthy self-narrative. It is significant that her mother testified at the Hague about her rape; she spoke the truth about her attack, publically. In so doing, she worked toward showing her community that the stigma associated with being raped is undeserved. Seada told researchers that her mother, "stands for courage and empowerment to all women in similar situations around the world" (Erjavec and Volcic 2010a, 379). Testifying gave her the opportunity to heal, emotionally, in a more thorough way. Seada explain that, "My mother decided to go public with her story—not just witnessing at The Hague, but also to tell her story to the wider community here in Bosnia. I also decided not to be ashamed of it—and I started to talk about it to my friends in my school . . . We all have to make sure this does not happen again" (Erjavec and Volcic, 2010a, 379). This demonstrates that her mother's self-narrative and beliefs about her attack are mirrored in her daughter's feelings about herself and her paternity.

Seada was also told the truth about her father fairly early on. Consequently, Seada never had the traumatic experience of having her identity and self-narrative destroyed by the discovery. She describes learning about her father as a shift that gave her "the meaning of life" (Erjavec and Volcic, 2010a, 379), suggesting that she saw life itself, and her life in particular as something that transcended human boundaries and divisions. The positive effect the truth has had in Seada's life stands as a lesson that can be applied to future children born of war.

Seada is an active participant in this structure of blessing. Seada and one other interviewed girl view themselves as being endowed with a special mission of healing. They identify themselves as uniquely suited to help reconcile Bosniaks and Serbians because of their mixed blood lines. Seada in particular uses the self-designations: "rescuer," "fighter for peace," and "bridge-builder" (Erjavec and Volcic, 2010b, 536). Erjavec and Volcic describe Seada as feeling compelled to speak out about injustices (rather than passively accept them, as her counterparts did). Seada also exhibits openness to diversity in her decision to identify herself with both racial categories, rather than neither. She spoke to interviewers about the Sarajevo community (and her friends), which includes people of all ethnic backgrounds. Her narrative does not have a villain it. She also believes it is her "duty" to get people openly talking to one another and reconciling in a more meaningful way. Seada also exhibits the blessing-based characteristic of creativity. She actively participates in bridge-building by opening up the door for dialogue that develops relationships rather than destroys them. She views the two groups as mutually responsible for the care of one another. She told researchers, ". . . I want to explain to my classmates that it is important to collaborate and to get to understand or get to know each other better. We should not be divided into different ethnic groups" (Erjavec and Volcic 2010a, 377). Her ability to create has spilled over into artistic endeavours as well. She is part of her school's pop rock band. She describes the band as "mixed" since the drummer is a Muslim and the guitarist is a Serb. She even notes that the combining of racial backgrounds is beneficial to her band's creative energy. The music they produce usually focuses on themes related to love, and non-violence. Seada's life is also marked by an openness to life and thankfulness. She is grateful for her mother and her family. She believes that her community, which is not limited to Bosniaks, is capable of meaningful and deep reconciliation. She desires a peace which will be mutually beneficial, rather than the absence of armed conflict, because one party has completely subjugated another. She has successfully reframed what has been viewed as a zero-sum conflict into a situation that could be win-win. She told researchers, "I can work towards a better future of Sarajevo—it is here that we could all live together, without anger or hate" (Erjavec and Volcic 2010a, 378). Saeda also understands that lasting and self-sustaining reconciliation cannot occur without justice. She does not believe any person or group should be denied justice. Rather, peace will come from justice being executed.

CONCLUSION

The Bosnian war saw a great number of atrocities. It was particularly gruesome for the women who were held in rape camps and impregnated. Many of the children produced from these rape camps are now being re-victimized daily as scapegoats for their community's pain. The Bosniak community is seeking an outlet for their frustrations and unmet needs for a unique identity and for security. By means of a self-deceptive, hidden, mimetic process described in Girard's mimetic theory, the children conceived in war have been selected as scapegoats. As mixed children, the war babies violate a taboo by existing and reminding their mothers and communities that they failed during the war and that the Serbs succeeded (at least partially) in tainting Bosniak blood. Many of the children have been socialized to agree with the paternal ethnicity myth. They have become entrenched in the belief that they deserve the treatment they receive and that they are destructive and undeserving of love. This has resulted in a highly disrupted self-narrative. The war babies are seen as less than human and are harassed, mistreated, and denied basic respect consistently. There is cause for hope in what appear to be very dismal circumstances. Some of the rape survivors have chosen a path of truth, justice, and openness about their rape, rather than accepting undeserved guilt. One such mother raised Seada to be a well-adjusted youth, who has chosen a clear purpose for her life. Because her mother chose to tell the truth publically about her war-time experiences as a way of reclaiming her identity, autonomy, and self-sufficiency, Seada has the inner resources to love her daughter and desires that she become a full subject, capable of acting in the world in creative rather than destructive ways. Seada is devoted to promoting truth-telling in her community for the sake of justice, not blaming. She is creative, grateful, and open to life. She participates in a mimetic structure of blessing in which she has doubled her mother's strong self-image. The evidence from her experience demonstrates that while the structures of blessing are difficult and rare for the individuals involved, they are not impossible.

REFERENCES

Adams, Rebecca. 2000. "Loving Mimesis and Girard's 'Scapegoat of the Text' : A Creative Reassessment of Mimetic Desire." Pp. 277–307 in Willard Swartley (ed.). *Violence Renounced : René Girard, Biblical Studies and Peacemaking*. Telford: Pandora.
Carpenter, Robyn Charli. 2009. "A Fresh Crop of Human Misery: Representations of Bosnian 'War Babies' in the Global Print Media, 1991–2006." *Millennium Journal of International Studies*.38 (1), 25–54.
Daniel-Wrabetz, Johane. 2007. "Children Born of War Rape in Bosnia-Herzegovina and the Convention on the Rights of the Child." Pp. 21–39, in *Born of War, Protecting Children of Sexual Violence Survivors in Conflict Zones,* edited by Robyn Charli Carpenter. Connecticut, USA: Kumerian Press.
Ejavec, Karmen and ZalaVolcic. 2010a. "Living with the Sins of Their Fathers: An Analysis of Self- Representation of Adolescents Born of War Rape." *Journal of Adolescent Research*. 25 (3), 359–386.
———. 2010b. "'Target,' 'cancer,' and 'warrior': exploring painful metaphors of self-representation used by girls born of war rape." *Discourse and Society*. 21 (5), 524–542.
Garrells, Scott R. 2006. "Imitation, Mirror Neurons, and Mimetic Desire: Convergence Between Mimetic Theory of René Girard and Empirical Research on Imitation." *Contagion: Journal of Violence, Mimesis and Culture*. 12–13, 47–86.
Girard, René. 2011. *Sacrifice*. Translated by Matthew Pattillo and David Dawson. Michigan: Michigan State University Press.
———. 2008. *Mimesis & Theory*. Edited by Robert Doran. Stanford, California: Stanford University Press.
Gemmill, Gary. 1989. "The Dynamics of Scapegoating in Small Groups." *Small Group Behaviour*. 20 (4), 406–418.
Kearney, Richard. 1995. "Myths and Scapegoats: The Case of René Girard." *Theory, Culture and Society*. 12, 1–14.
Lanye, Christopher, Pynoos, Robert, Saltzman, William, Arslangic, Bernina, Black, Mary, Savjak, Nadezda, Popović, Tatjana, Durakivić, Elvira, Mušić, Mirjana, Ćampara, Nihada,

Djapo, Nermin and Houston, Ryan. 2001. "Trauma/Grief-Focused Group Psychotherapy: School-Based Postwar Intervention With Traumatized Bosnian Adolescents." *Group Dynamics: Theory, Research and Practice*. 5(4), 277–290.

Redekop, Vern Neufeld. 2002. *From Violence to Blessing: How an Understanding of Deep-Rooted Conflict Opens Paths to Reconciliation.* Ottawa: Novalis.

Niarchos, Catherine. 1995. "Women, War and Rape: Challenges Facing the International Tribunal for the Former Yugoslavia." *Human Rights Quarterly.* 17(4), 649–690.

Robertson, Cheryl and Laura Duckett.2007. "Mothering During War and Postwar in Bosnia." *Journal of Family Nursing. University of Minnesota*. 14 (4), 463–483.

Skjelsbaek, Ingrid (2006). "Victim and Survivor: Narrated Social Identities of Women who Experienced Rape During the War in Bosnia-Herzegovina." *Feminism and Psychology*,16 (4), 373–402.

Slapsak, Svetlana. 2000. "Yugoslav War: A Case of/for Gendered History." Pp. 17–68 in *War Discourse, Women's Discourse,* edited by S. Slapsak. Ljublijana, Slovenia: IHS.

NOTE

1. Several features of the campaign waged by the Serbian forces suggest that the gender-based violence committed against primarily Bosniak women was systemic. This includes what the United Nations Final Report of the Commission of Experts referred to as "so called rape camps," and survivor testimony that the soldiers committing the attacks claimed they were "following their president's orders" (Daniel-Wrabetz 2007, 23).

Chapter Eighteen

"We Forgive and Ask Forgiveness"

*The Papal Prayers for Forgiveness in Mimetic
Perspective — With an Afterthought on Recent Cases of
Sexual Abuse of Minors by Church Officials*

Nikolaus Wandinger[1]

The creed professes the Church to be holy. For that reason, popes, and bishops normally do not speak of the sins of the Church. On the other hand, the Church is the Church of sinners. For that reason, St. Ambrose called the Church a *casta meretrix* (Balthasar 1961, 289), a chaste harlot. She is chaste by virtue of the God-given holiness she possesses, yet she is a harlot because of her human sinfulness. The Second Vatican Council explicitly stated: "the Church, embracing in its bosom sinners, at the same time holy and always in need of being purified, always follows the way of penance and renewal" (Second Vatican Council 1964/LG, no. 8), which means that the sins of her sons and daughters really defile the Church herself; those sins are not merely marginal to her but do real harm to her, although they do not extinguish her essential, God-given holiness. Still, she is not only the holy Church, she is also the Church of sinners. This seems to apply even more to those sins that were committed in the Church's name and by her highest representatives: popes, bishops, and councils.

In the holy year of 2000, Pope John Paul II inserted a special part into the liturgy of the First Sunday of Lent: prayers of forgiveness for those sins. They were spoken by the pope and those cardinals who were then responsible for the areas of conduct in which the sins had been committed. His successor, Benedict XVI, headed the Congregation for the Doctrine of the Faith at the time, so it was his task to confess that "men of the Church, in the name of faith and morals, have sometimes used methods not in keeping with the Gospel in the solemn duty of defending the truth" (John Paul II 2000b).

These prayers were met with praise but also criticism, and the criticism came from two opposing sides. Conservative Catholics decried that the pope had acknowledged sinful behavior by the Church at all, while liberals— Catholics or other—complained that the pope had not named any culprits, that he had not spoken of sins *of* the Church, that the missteps were named only reluctantly and euphemistically. And, finally, they complained that he had not apologized to the people who were hurt but only prayed to God for forgiveness.

Briefly, I want to shed some light on these prayers from the point of view of mimetic theory[2] in order to evaluate some of the criticism and, then, to attend to pressing further questions.

ESCALATING REVENGE VS. ESCALATING FORGIVENESS—A BIBLICAL PRELUDE

To begin with, it should be noted that the Bible portrays forgiveness and retribution as two possible opposite reactions to injustice—moreover, as two reactions that tend to exert a mimetic pull by which they escalate easily. *Genesis* 4 portrays God very anthropomorphically, as someone who tries to deter human violence by the threat of escalating retribution. After Cain has murdered his brother and was punished by God for that, he fears that other people might feel emboldened to kill him, copying his very own deed. God reacts by declaring: "Not so! Whoever kills Cain will suffer a sevenfold vengeance" (Genesis 4:15). Thus, in order to prevent Cain from becoming the victim of someone who emulates him, God decides to emulate him instead, yet in an escalating manner. The threat of violence has to be increased to have any deterring effect. Limiting violence by violence thus easily leads not only to reciprocal violence but to a disproportionate increase in violence.

On first sight, it seems to have succeeded, though, for the Bible records nothing about Cain being murdered; it actually says nothing at all about his death. Yet, the logic of escalating revenge soon bears poisonous fruit. Only 9 verses later, after six generations, we encounter an offspring of Cain by the name of Lamech, who was obviously well reared in a whole family tradition of escalating revenge. He brags to his two wives: "I have killed a man for wounding me, a young man for striking me. If Cain is avenged sevenfold, truly Lamech seventy-sevenfold" (Genesis 4:23–24).

Against this escalation of revenge, Jesus counter-poses an escalation of forgiveness. When Peter approaches him with the question of how often he should forgive his brother and suggests himself that seven times would be a good measure (cf. Matthew 18:21), we may assume that Peter had already chosen a suggestion that seemed quite generous to him (even if we leave out the highly symbolic character of the number seven). Jesus, however, in a reverse emulation of Lamech's logic, challenges Peter to forgive "not seven times, but, I tell you, seventy-seven times" (Matthew 18:22).

The multiplication of retribution that occurs in the six generations from Cain to Lamech emphasizes how dangerous an instrument vengeful justice and the deterrence based upon it is. What is meant to limit violence can easily be transformed—by a kind of mimetic exaggeration—into a disseminator for violence. Jesus clearly wants to reverse that with a mimetic pull toward the opposite: a multiplication and escalation of forgiveness, which, however, does not provide the function of deterrence at the same time. This is clearly illustrated by the parable after the challenge to Peter, in which a king forgives his servant an enormous debt, for which there was no way of paying it back—and he expected the servant to forgive his fellow servant a much smaller amount, namely one-hundred days' wages.[3] When the king hears that the servant fails to do so, he reverses his decision and hands him over to be tortured, until he settles his debt. And the king explicitly grounds that on the servant's failure to emulate him: "Should you not have had mercy on your fellow slave, as I had mercy on you?" (Matthew 18:33). When the servant fails to emulate the king, the king reverses his judgment and instead emulates the servant and thus returns to the logic of deterrence, which is also a logic of violence. This is the same reversal of model and imitator that happened in the Cain story. But Jesus tries to correct the image of God. If God is perceived as avenger, emulating him leads to more violence, as shown in the figure of Lamech. If God is perceived like a generous king, as in the beginning of Jesus's parable, then imitating him means a reversal of the process of escalating revenge in favor of escalating forgiveness, as R. Schwager explains:

> Wherever people are ready to forgive and to receive there they will be given more, and they will become ever more able to give themselves. Wherever they are not ready to receive, and remain trapped in the norms of payment and repayment, there they will lose again even what they have received, and they hand themselves over to a process of judgment, based on repayment and payment down to the last penny. As each of us is a debtor, no one can endure this process; the demand for repayment becomes ever greater and the end of this escalating process can only be hell. (Schwager 1999, 67)

This escalation actually materialized with Jesus's way to the cross. However, his misguided opponents actually did not bring judgment against themselves for the simple reason that Christ bore it in their place. While they followed their escalation of judgment, Jesus followed his own recommendation of an escalation of forgiveness. He even prayed for forgiveness for his actual killers, while he still was in the process of being killed. This escalation of forgiveness even surpasses by far what Jesus had taught in the Sermon of the Mount, because the possibility of having to face one's being put to death is not yet thematized there (cf. Schwager 1999, 79; 93–94).

This short look at a New Testament gloss on an Old Testament story reminds us how strong the emphasis on forgiveness is in biblical writings, and it clearly indicates that forgiveness as well as revenge are not just measures in themselves, but they have an outward effect through mimesis. I think it is important to keep this in mind, when attending to the papal payers for forgiveness.

PENANCE IN CIVIL RELIGION

Another matter to keep in mind is that the pope's action was not unique: In recent years, other Church and political leaders have publicly asked for forgiveness for sins that the institutions they headed had committed in the past.[4]

The political scientist H. Lübbe explains that these almost ritualistic ceremonies have become an element of civil religion. In this, they differ from the papal prayers for forgiveness: The papal prayers were not an act of civil, but of ecclesial religion, and they were not directed at the descendants of victims, but at God. Yet, in some measure, the two can be compared. The most interesting points of similarity between the two are, as follows:

> A public plea for forgiveness should not be confused with a guilty plea in court, which would, in case of a conviction for capital offenses, lead to heavy penalties, removal from office, in case of collective responsibility to the liquidation of the incriminated institution. In the case of both the papal prayers and the prominent civil penitents, they did not refer to sins or crimes that could still be brought before a court. Whoever wanted to see the severe crimes of humanity tried in court would have to wait until the Last Judgment. (Lübbe 2001, 39–40, my translation)

Therefore, reconciliation is only possible through forgiveness, not through retribution. The parable's peculiarity that the debt to the king, who of course stood for God, can never be properly repaid because of its sheer size, finds its human parallel here. Even between humans, there are instances of debt that can never be repaid.

> Oftentimes, these deeds were crimes whose criminal character could easily be denied or suppressed by its perpetrators, though they were clearly experienced by the victims. (cf. Lübbe 2001, 41–42, my translation)

This property is typical for crimes committed within a mimetic contagion, where the perpetrators think they are doing nothing but justice, but only victims can feel that they are unjustly condemned. At least, this is true when the scapegoat mechanism has already been somewhat weakened, which is the case with the great crimes of humanity that happened in cultures that were influenced by biblical revelation.

> The lasting merit of the papal, as well as the political-civil-penitential, com-
> memoration of these atrocities seems to be the effective institution of the
> prohibition to legitimize these atrocities in retrospect by appealing to their
> purported higher purposes. (Lübbe 2001, 40, my translation)

This means that the aim of this public penance is not to announce the willingness to pay retribution but to re-evaluate these deeds in retrospect, publicly declare their wrongness, delegitimize them for the future, and pro-scribe their being justified by purportedly higher ideals.

And finally:

> By acknowledging the victim status of a group, an important factor in the
> identity of that group is taken account of. (cf. Lübbe 2001, 61–68, my transla-
> tion)

This fourth aspect is certainly not unproblematic, because, in our times, victim status has become a coveted asset for some and a bothersome burden for other persons—often members of the same group. The acknowledgment of the victim status of others—and thereby of one's own group's victimizer status—can only be fruitful, if it goes hand in hand with the recognition of one's own group's victimization. The importance of a mutual recognition of the roles of victim and victimizer that Raymund Schwager emphasized for the Israeli-Palestinian conflict (cf. Schwager 2005) must in a certain sense be upheld for any process of overcoming enmity and moving toward peace.

This can be seen as another instance of a reversed mimetic reciprocity. The usual reciprocity of mutual accusation is reversed by a mutual acknowl-edgement of one's own sins, ideally accompanied by the other's forgiveness for these sins. But, of course, asking for that kind of reciprocity is not appli-cable to many instances of the great crimes of humanity. While it may seem reasonable that Israelis and Palestinians recognize the victimization of the other party, it would be outrageous to say the same about Jews and Germans with respect to the Nazi era, or of Americans and Ugandans with respect to slavery for that matter.

This might lead one to dismiss the idea of mutual reciprocity in forgiving. On the other hand, however, it might be taken as a clear sign that civil religion has its limitations, and this provides us with an impetus to look beyond these limitations to the peculiarities of the papal prayers for forgive-ness as prayers of ecclesial religion.

PECULIARITIES WITH RESPECT TO THE CHURCH

When the Church is seen as subject of these prayers, all the points mentioned above are still valid; they are part of a correct understanding of the papal prayers. Yet, there is more to them and that can only be understood with some knowledge about the Church's self-perception.

CHURCH—SIGN AND INSTRUMENT OF UNITY IN CHRIST

According to the Second Vatican Council's Dogmatic Constitution on the Church, the Church is "a sign and instrument both of a very closely knit union with God and of the unity of the whole human race" (Second Vatican Council 1964/LG, no. 1). Her mission and purpose are to signify this unity, and *by signifying* it to be an instrument of realizing it.

The Church can only be this efficacious sign because Christ has already accomplished the unity of humanity with God in his person, and he has laid the foundation for the unity of the whole of humanity by identifying with all humans. This universal identification was initiated in his taking on human nature (cf. Second Vatican Council 1965/GS, no. 22) and found its irrevocable affirmation, when Christ again identified with all of humanity on the cross. R. Schwager explains, however, that this universal identification on the cross was qualified. It pertained to all humans in as far as they are *victims* of sin. He then argues, however, that the passion of Christ actually reveals that sinners become themselves the victims of their own sins in the very act of sinning. Therefore all sinners are necessarily also victims of sin. The cross and Jesus's identification with humans on the cross thus reveal that the frontier between victims and perpetrators of sin is not one *between* people; it is a distinction *within* people, thus showing that everybody is victim *and* perpetrator of sin (cf. Schwager 1999, 192–193), although that might be in different measure and with respect to different sins.

Because of the unity that the Church signifies, her identity not only transcends her individual members, it is synchronic as well as diachronic: the whole Church is not just her currently living members but all those who lived in her during the ages. Christ's strong identification with the Church has been expressed since the time of St. Paul's writings by the image of the Church as Christ's body, with Christ being her head. Catholic ecclesiology always stands in the tension of seeing the Church, on the one hand, as this transcending, universal mystical body of Christ, while, on the other hand, acknowledging that she is also a worldly institution with social boundaries, laws, and human executives. The Second Vatican Council tried to bridge these two views by the metaphor of the Church as the people of God, which is, of course, inspired by the Old Testament and Jewish self-understanding. All this has immediate consequences for the interpretation of the papal prayers.

ANOTHER KIND OF RECIPROCITY

The first of these consequences is that the reciprocity of acknowledging the other's victim status can be universal. Since everybody is victim of sin in some respect and some instance, everyone's being a victim can be acknowledged; since everyone is also a perpetrator of sin—again in some respect and some instance— all are in need of forgiveness as well. In the papal prayers, the Church especially thematizes those instances where (leading) members of the Church have become perpetrators of evil, yet she also remembers where her members became victims of sin. But she does not do so in order to offset her crimes with her sufferings. She does so to signify that all of humanity stands before that problem. We have committed sins and have been hurt by sins, we have victimized and have been victimized. Instead of a reciprocity of accusation that could lead to escalating revenge, Pope John Paul II resorted to a reciprocity of forgiveness, in the hope to kindle a process of reconciliation. In his sermon he proclaimed:

> Today [. . .] seemed to me the right occasion for the Church, gathered spiritually round the Successor of Peter, to implore divine forgiveness for the sins of all believers. *[. . . We] forgive and ask forgiveness!* While we praise God who, in his merciful love, has produced in the Church a wonderful harvest [. . .], we cannot fail to recognize *the infidelities to the Gospel committed by some of our brethren,* especially during the second millennium. Let us ask pardon for the divisions which have occurred among Christians, for the violence some have used in the service of the truth and for the distrustful and hostile attitudes sometimes taken towards the followers of other religions. [. . .] At the same time, as we confess our sins, *[. . . we] forgive the sins committed by others against us.* [. . .] Countless times in the course of history Christians have suffered hardship, oppression and persecution because of their faith. Just as the victims of such abuses forgave them, so let us forgive as well. The Church today feels and has always felt obliged to *purify her memory* of those sad events from every feeling of rancour or revenge. In this way the Jubilee becomes for everyone a favourable opportunity for a profound conversion to the Gospel. The acceptance of God's forgiveness leads to the commitment to forgive our brothers and sisters and to be reconciled with them. (John Paul II 2000a, no. 3–4, for translation issues see endnote 5)

The expression "purify her memory" might be construed to mean an erasing from memory. This, however, would be a misunderstanding. Read as a whole, the sentence makes it very clear that what is meant is to hold the sufferings in memory but to purify that memory from the emotions of resentment, hatred, and the urge for revenge.

The central phrase "Let us forgive and ask forgiveness"[5] has an interesting history. Pope Paul VI introduced the theme, when he apologized to the non-Catholic Christian communities at the beginning of the second session of the Second Vatican Council in 1963 (cf. Accattoli 1999, 30). The formulation was taken up two years later in a letter sent by the Polish bishops' conference to its German counterpart (Polish Bishops' Conferece 1978).[6] Karol Woityla, who later became Pope John Paul II, attended the council from its beginning in 1962 as auxiliary bishop of Krakow and became archbishop of that diocese in 1964 (cf. Weigel 2005, 145), so that he was one of the signatories of the letter to the German bishops' conference. The choice of his wording in 2000 therefore is hardly accidental. The pope wanted to take up a thread of quite recent Church history and to forge a tradition by doing so.

With this formulation, the pope tried to transcend the lop-sided view of one side as victims and the others as culprits and acknowledged both sides' status as victims, while at the same time recognizing both sides' involvement with guilt. This might also be one reason why the prayers are rather vague and cautious in naming the sins committed and why they refrain completely from naming the culprits—either by name or by office. The important fact is that they were sinful human beings, and inasmuch as they committed their sins especially as members of the Church and in her name, it is her special mandate to pray for forgiveness.

It is also noteworthy that the pope presupposes that Christian victims of persecution have forgiven their persecutors. This can hardly be accepted as a general statement of historical fact. It is a statement of fact with normative character, however. Those that really reacted to their persecution in a Christian spirit, in the discipleship and in emulation of Christ, did forgive. The pope's significant aside should be seen in connection with his adjustment of the criteria for the Church's decision to recognize someone as a martyr and the many canonizations of martyrs of the 20th century that he advanced (for that see: Niewiadomski 2008, 2011; Siebenrock 2009, 2011).

ANOTHER KIND OF IDENTITY

As a consequence of the diachronic identity of the Church, the sins of the past are not mere historical facts. They have a real effect on the Church and her members today. Therefore the pope wrote in his Bulletin *Incarnationis Mysterium*, which proclaimed the year 2000 as the great jubilee year:

> Because of the bond which unites us to one another in the Mystical Body, all
> of us, though not personally responsible [. . .], bear the burden of the errors and
> faults of those who have gone before us. Yet we too, sons and daughters of the
> Church, have sinned [. . .]. Our sin has impeded the Spirit's working in the

hearts of many people. Our meagre faith has meant that many have lapsed into apathy and been driven away from a true encounter with Christ. As the Successor of Peter, I ask that in this year of mercy the Church, strong in the holiness which she receives from her Lord, should kneel before God and implore forgiveness for the past and present sins of her sons and daughters. All have sinned and none can claim righteousness before God (cf. *1 Kgs* 8:46). Let it be said once more without fear: "We have sinned" (*Jer* 3:25), but let us keep alive the certainty that "where sin increased, grace abounded even more" (*Rom* 5:20) (John Paul II 1998, no. 11).

What the pope advocates here, is nothing less than a universal solidarity of sinners—not a solidarity in sinning, but a solidarity in confessing one's sins and asking for forgiveness, a process in which every person and every group is challenged to direct its attention foremost to its own faults, while at the same time being aware of its own status of victimhood, without any need to downplay or suppress it. And John Paul emphasizes that the strength to do so comes from the Church's holiness, which is not her merit but the pure gift of Christ. Being able to confess one's sins is a sign of that strength which comes from a Christ-given holiness.

It is noteworthy that John Paul's successor, Benedict XVI, has taken up this tradition at least once, namely on his visit to Poland. Addressing priests in the cathedral of Warsaw, he said:

On the occasion of the Great Jubilee, Pope John Paul II frequently exhorted Christians to do penance for infidelities of the past. We believe that the Church is holy, but that there are sinners among her members. We need to reject the desire to identify only with those who are sinless. How could the Church have excluded sinners from her ranks? It is for their salvation that Jesus took flesh, died and rose again. We must therefore learn to live Christian penance with sincerity. By practising it, we confess individual sins in union with others, before them and before God. Yet we must guard against the arrogant claim of setting ourselves up to judge earlier generations, who lived in different times and different circumstances. Humble sincerity is needed in order not to deny the sins of the past, and at the same time not to indulge in facile accusations in the absence of real evidence or without regard for the different preconceptions of the time. (Benedict XVI 2006).

The warning against being presumptuous against the past, which—as R. Girard has repeatedly mentioned—amounts to a form of scapegoating the past, had been present as well in John Paul's considerations about the Church asking for forgiveness.

SIN AS COUNTER-WITNESS

Finally, there is a special significance to those sins committed in the Church that contribute to a split in the Church or within humanity. If the Church is to promote the unity of all of humanity by signifying that unity, schisms within the Church directly counteract this purpose. They are counter-signs constituting a counter-witness to the Church's mission. Here the Church stands under Christ's verdict: "[. . .] whoever does not gather with me scatters" (Matthew 12:30).

John Paul especially mentioned:

> Among the sins which require a greater commitment to repentance and conversion should certainly be counted those which *have been detrimental to the unity willed by God for his People.* In the course of the thousand years now drawing to a close, even more than in the first millennium, ecclesial communion has been painfully wounded, a fact "for which, at times, men of both sides were to blame." Such wounds openly contradict the will of Christ and are a cause of scandal to the world. These sins of the past unfortunately still burden us and remain ever present temptations. It is necessary to make amends for them, and earnestly to beseech Christ's forgiveness. (John Paul II 1994, no. 34 with reference to Second Vatican Council 1964/UR, nos. 3 and 1)

> Another painful chapter of history to which the sons and daughters of the Church must return with a spirit of repentance is that of the acquiescence given, especially in certain centuries, to *intolerance and even the use of violence* in the service of truth. It is true that an accurate historical judgment cannot prescind from careful study of the cultural conditioning of the times [. . .]. Many factors frequently converged to create assumptions which justified intolerance and fostered an emotional climate from which only great spirits, truly free and filled with God, were in some way able to break free. Yet the consideration of mitigating factors does not exonerate the Church from the obligation to express profound regret for the weaknesses of so many of her sons and daughters who sullied her face, preventing her from fully mirroring the image of her crucified Lord, the supreme witness of patient love and of humble meekness. From these painful moments of the past a lesson can be drawn for the future, leading all Christians to adhere fully to the sublime principle stated by the Council: "The truth cannot impose itself except by virtue of its own truth, as it wins over the mind with both gentleness and power." (John Paul II 1994, no. 35, quoting Second Vatican Council 1965/ DiHu, no. 1)

What might give the impression of belittling the misdeeds committed, namely the mentioning of an emotional climate that somehow held people captive, could also be seen as an acknowledgment of social interwovenness, of structural sin and—in our terminology—of mimetic contagion.[7] If mimetism creates an emotional climate that drives a group to build its identity by scapegoating dissenters, it is true indeed that "only great spirits, truly free and filled with God" can escape the mimetic pull and truly follow Christ's example, which means in these circumstances to mirror the image of the crucified Lord, rather than mirroring the image of his persecutors. One can hardly think of a clearer example of the Church giving a counter-witness, opposed to its real mission.

There is, however, a real instance of understatement in the quoted passage: men and women of the Church did not only "acquiesce" to those means, they perpetrated and promoted them. For reasons of the power structure within Church and state, one also has to say that it was mostly men who were able to do so because most women lacked the means of power to act in that way—which does not make them better persons as such; they probably would have contributed as well, if these inequalities had not existed. Still, it is part of the historical truth that they were more often than not victims and not perpetrators.

ON SOME CRITICAL OBJECTIONS

Finally, I want to attend to some of the criticisms mentioned in the reception of the papal prayers, and then voice some considerations of my own.

Some critics were unhappy about those prayers because they were only that—prayers to God and not apologies to the victims or their descendants. This objection, however, does not seem fair. It overlooks the setting of these prayers and Pope John Paul's efforts for reconciliation on his manifold pastoral visits. The liturgy is the place to ask God for forgiveness; it is not the setting to apologize to fellow human beings. This, however, does not mean that asking God for forgiveness in liturgy dispenses one from apologizing to the victims of one's sinful conduct. On the contrary: It demands an attempt at human reconciliation, if that seems at all viable.

This is true for the individual believer who attends Mass or receives the Sacrament of Reconciliation. It also pertains to the Church as a social body. Consequently, the pope did not apologize to human victims of ecclesial sins in the liturgy on the First Sunday of Lent in 2000, but he did so repeatedly on his journeys and especially at ecumenical meetings or on his visit to Israel. The Italian journalist Luigi Accattoli enumerates 94 instances where John Paul II asked for human forgiveness during his travels, and he explains that this theme runs like a thread through his pontificate.[8]

Still, the pope never spoke of the sins *of* the Church, not even of her representatives, but only of sins committed by the sons and daughters of the Church. To many this seemed a very euphemistic approach. One reason why the pope never spoke of the Church as subject of sins might be the theology of the Church as body of Christ with Christ as her head. Speaking of the

Church's sins might be misunderstood as saying that Christ was sinful. Yet, here the memory of St. Ambrose's courage to call the Church a "chaste harlot," and then to distinguish clearly between the origin of her chastity that of her whoring, would allow for more courage today as well. Also, a more open admission that many sins were not committed indiscriminately by sons and daughters of the Church but by those sons who are called Fathers or even Holy Fathers, need not necessarily lead to a scapegoating of these. His formulations clearly show that he did not want to exempt popes or bishops. Yet, a more candid expression of that would certainly have done no harm but would have accounted for the reality of social and structural sin, which also nested itself into the Church and her leadership.

This, however, brings a different problematic to the fore: judged from the gospel, it is absolutely correct to address popes and bishops as brothers rather than as fathers in the Church (cf. Matthew 23:8–10). Jesus's warning against calling someone on earth one's father certainly does not preclude one from addressing one's male parent in the usual way. Yet, it contains an important psychological and mimetic insight: After we have outgrown childhood, it is not healthy to follow someone on earth in a childlike mimetic dependence; this childlike trustful abandoning of oneself is only appropriate then towards God, the heavenly Father. So, Pope John Paul is certainly right in not calling popes and bishops fathers of or in the Church. They are brothers. The problem is that outside these prayers for forgiveness, they are addressed as Fathers (in many languages, as in English, all priests are addressed in that way), and what makes it really problematic is that this is not only a figure of speech but the mimetic, psychological dependence expressed in these words really exists in many places, where docile subservience is demanded and rendered, but also where rebellious protest takes over. Both are different forms of an unhealthy structure that the gospel of Matthew wanted to avoid within the Church. So, in my view, these prayers are not to be criticized for refraining from mentioning "fathers," instead of brothers; the criticism should be directed at the exceptionality of this terminology.

AFTERTHOUGHT ON RECENT CASES OF SEXUAL ABUSE OF MINORS BY CHURCH OFFICIALS

This brings me to more recent events in the Church that should be addressed in the context of the Church asking for forgiveness. For the Church in Europe, especially in Germany and Austria, 2010 was a year of special significance, because a storm of accusations against Church officials about the sexual abuse of children and youngsters showed another aspect of the Church giving counter-witness to its mission. When clergy and lay employees of the Church gravely abuse the trust they enjoy because of their ecclesial standing, this certainly amounts to sin that harms the very core of the Church's mission, which is witnessing to the salvation in Christ. When clergy harm young people in this way, they destroy more than other offenders. In addition to the pain that any sexual misconduct causes in the victim, it also destroys trust in Christ's Church. These sins are also sins by which "ecclesial communion has been painfully wounded [. . .]. Such wounds openly contradict the will of Christ and are a cause of scandal to the world" (John Paul II 1994, no. 34).

These sins, however, lie not far in the past, especially their uncovering still happens in the present, and so remarks might be made, as to how the Church might react constructively, in a way consistent with the meaning of the prayers for forgiveness presented here but also with her obligation to protect minors and to prevent future crimes of that type.

The recentness of the crimes mentioned distinguishes them from those mentioned in the prayers for forgiveness in 2000. This has several consequences: one has shown infamously in Church authorities' reaction: denying and covering up crimes is an all-too-human reflex to accusations. The Church as an institution underlies the same mimetic mechanisms as other institutions. As Christ's Church, however, she should find the power to withstand them. Reality shows that she fails all too often in this and that even now it is "only great spirits, truly free and filled with God [. . . who are] in some way able to break free" (John Paul II 1994, 35). The first lesson gained from the papal prayers for forgiveness is that naming these sins, not hiding them, is the Christian way of dealing with them.

Then, of course, the legal situation is different. The crimes committed are subject to the legal prosecution by the state; the Church, its members and officials are subject to the criminal jurisdiction of the state, and they should cooperate with the legal authorities.[9] Some might wonder, however, whether this violates the idea of forgiveness that we espoused in this article. One could even argue that it was real concern for the offenders as sinners that led Church officials to false reactions to the problem, namely to transferring priests who had been accused—and thus enabling them to continue their sexual abuse of minors, sometimes for decades—because each time when complaints were raised, the accused were transferred and could start anew. This practice needed to be stopped. But then, how is it compatible with the message of forgiveness that the Church is also called to stand for?

Catholic canon law distinguishes between a *forum internum* and a *forum externum*. Somewhat simplified, the exterior forum deals with public matters and also has public interest in the foreground; the internal forum deals with personal matters and emphasizes the concern for the individual person (cf. May 1995). Applied to our question, this would mean: in the *forum externum*, the Church must deal with offenders in her own ranks as the public interest—in a two-fold sense—demands. The public interest of society at large clearly demands in the case of sexual abuse of minors a judicial process according to criminal law and the punishment accorded in this process. The public interest of the Church herself demands that her function as a sign of unity in the world should not be counteracted; therefore, her own interest also demands significant disciplinary measures against the culprits. This, however, does not preclude the Church from fulfilling her mission even to the convicted offender. This mission is to attend to his salvation as well and to also offer him God's forgiveness, which can only be accepted if and when genuine remorse occurs.

It appears that two extreme and opposed reactions to these offenses are but two sides of the same coin, because both are ways of behavior directed by mimetic contagion: One is the covering up and playing down of the offenses for the sake of the image of the Church and its officials. This is merely an attempt to close ranks and view the accusations as inimical to the Church as such. It is an us-against-them mentality that in no way is proper conduct for the Church but is even more harmful where it tramples on the feelings of people who have already been victimized. And, of course, it causes the opposite of what it purports to do: It will cast doubt on the trustworthiness of the Church and will foster the very enmity it claims to avert.

The opposite trap, however, is the scandalized outcry about these crimes that portrays the offenders as non-human and wants to ostracize them from human society. Some champions of public opinion are specialists in this discipline, and in some instances, the search for pedophile priests has similarities to the witch hunts of earlier centuries. Once again, this approach is not appropriate and it is also counter-productive. It is not appropriate because it will not help prevent further offenses by the same offender. The offender, who must be certain that he will be ostracized, if discovered, has no motivation to face his guilt and seek help. Where there is not even the slightest hope for forgiveness, it cannot be asked for. (On the other hand, where forgiveness is demanded as a right, the offender still has not realized what harm he has done, and that forgiveness is always a gift, never an obligation.) It is counter-productive because the sensationalist scandalization of sexual abuse creates further interest in the phenomenon and maybe even engenders mimetic desire to acquire what these offenders already had acquired; it might thus provide additional incentive to break one of the last remaining taboos of modern society. The proper way would be to convert the taboo into a heeded prohibition. That means that open public discussion, avoiding scandalization and sensationalism, is necessary; and for that—and to counteract the inappropriate reflexes of covering up the offenses—a free and critical media is indispensable.

Thus, it seems, the path indicated by Pope John Paul II on the first Sunday of Lent 2000 is instructive also for dealing with these problems. The Church should here follow the example of the pope whom she beatified (on May 1, 2011). Yet, the necessary modifications must be made.

Beyond those already mentioned—namely close consideration of the danger of cover-ups because of the closeness of these events, the duty to cooperate with legal institutions, because the crimes are still subject to prosecution—these following responses are called for.

Since the victims and most offenders are still alive, the juridical procedures must be followed and compensation must be given. This should be done, however, not in a vengeful spirit. Society should realize that it is in the service of an eventual healing for the victims that the offender is not dehumanized and ostracized (a prison term does not mean ostracism; the latter is a social phenomenon that is not connected to any particular judicial sentence). Because of their nature, these crimes can never really be compensated for. This does not mean that no compensation can be given. It should neither mean that the highest possible compensation must be demanded. No matter how high any sum of money would be, it could not compensate properly. So, in fact, the compensation awarded is always symbolic; as such, however, it can be an indicator of the severity of the crime and the needs caused by it in the victim but also of the attitude of society toward the offenders. If it is directed at the offender's complete economic destruction, or even "the liquidation of the incriminated institution" (Lübbe 2001, 39), it shows that it does not want to leave room for a future reconciliation. It should, however, leave room for reconciliation, no matter how impossible or remote this possibility might seem at the moment.

Offenders should be helped to realize and acknowledge the gravity of their guilt. To this end, clear sanctions in the public realm but also empathic guidance, pastoral and psychological care in the internal realm are necessary. It is obvious that, in the first place, this care must be given to the victims; but leaving out offenders from care will not be sufficient.

In the painful healing processes for the victims, the point might eventually come when the question arises of also viewing the offenders as victims of sin and of granting them forgiveness. Under no circumstances can this be urged or demanded, but eventual healing and closure might only be possible when this is also done. For a deeper Christian understanding, as we have seen, every human person is also a victim of sin—his/her own sins, but also the sins of others. Often sexual offenders have been victims of sexual abuse in their own childhood. This cannot be utilized to downplay or excuse their crimes, but a truthful reckoning will have to take this into account.

Because of the special unity of the Church, all its members "though not personally responsible [. . .], bear the burden of the errors and faults of those who have gone before us" (John Paul II 1998, no. 11) or those that sinned beside us, even more so when negligence and turning a blind eye contributed to the sins in question. Can there be a universal solidarity of sinners in confessing one's sins and asking for forgiveness even with child molesters? Since this is the very opposite of condoning the deed but of supporting the process of conversion, it seems not only possible but advisable and a challenge that the gospel poses to the Church—to her leaders and all her members. It requires the strength of the holiness that the Church has been given by Christ and which remains in spite of all sins. It serves the purpose of not dehumanizing and ostracizing the offenders and thus supports them in acknowledging the severity of their sin and crime. The Church should be different from those media who treat the topic in a merely sensationalist manner and from secular society, especially in this respect. One might even ask whether the Church might be able to help society at large find a better way of adequately dealing with these crimes. When they happen in the Church, special attention is aroused, and the pain caused is excessive, as was already stated. Still, the Church is not the only environment or institution in which these things happen. As terrible as the Church's involvement in these crimes is, it might enable her to offer her experiences about coming to terms with them to society at large and to help it in this painful process.

Finally, a public prayer for forgiveness to God that is imbued with the spirit of the papal prayers of 2000 could support these processes within the Church. There were few instances of this. But one very notable exception occurred in the Cathedral of Vienna on Ash Wednesday, February 17, 2010. There, Cardinal Schönborn in his sermon expressed the deep regret at the counter-witness that so many clergy had given:

> The persons who are supposed to bring the closeness and the name of God become destructors of the relationship to God. [. . .] As long as the Church does look away and does not listen, she will only obstruct the liberating and saving God, she will not only refuse to proclaim the message of the God of liberation from slavery, she will also worsen that slavery. This is a painful experience for the Church. But what is that pain compared to the victims' pain that we have overlooked and overheard for such a long time! Now that the victims speak, God speaks to us, to His Church, to shake her up, to purify her; now God speaks to us through the victims [. . .]. (Schönborn 2010, my translation)

Here, we are very close again to the God of victims that Girard discovered successively in the Biblical writings. The subsequent prayers for forgiveness in Vienna followed Pope John Paul's example in many ways and were even clearer and more outspoken in others. If only there were more to emulate that! And if only the practical consequences in the outer realm would be drawn everywhere!

REFERENCES

Accattoli, Luigi. 1999. *Wenn der Papst um Vergebung bittet. Alle "mea culpa" Johannes Pauls II. an der Wende zum dritten Jahrtausend*. Translated by P. F. Ruelius. Innsbruck: Tyrolia.

Balthasar, Hans Urs von. 1961. "Casta meretrix". Pp. 203–305 in *Sponsa verbi. Skizzen zur Theologie 2*. Einsiedeln: Johannes Verl.

Benedict XVI, Pope. 2006. *Address by the Holy Father. Meeting with the Clergy. Warsaw Cathedral 25 May, 2006*. The Holy See [cited 08/01 2011]. Available from http:// www.vatican.va/holy_father/benedict_xvi/speeches/2006/may/documents/hf_ben-xvi_spe_20060525_poland-clergy_en.html.

Girard, René. 1986. *The Scapegoat*. Translated by Y. Freccero. Baltimore: The Johns Hopkins University Press.

———. 1987a. *Job. The victim of his people*. Translated by Y. Freccero. London: Athlone.

———. 1987b. *Things Hidden since the Foundation of the World: Research undertaken in collaboration with J.-M. Oughourlian and G. Lefort*. Translated by S. Bann and M. Metteer. Stanford: Stanford University Press.

———. 2001. *I See Satan Fall Like Lightning*. Translated by J. G. Williams. Maryknoll, NY: Orbis Books.

Gnilka, Joachim. 1988. *Das Matthäusevangelium, 2. Teil: Kommentar zu Kap. 14,1–28,20 und Einleitungsfragen, Herders theologischer Kommentar zum Neuen Testament I/2*. Freiburg: Herder.

John Paul II, Pope. 1994. *Apostolic Letter "Tertio Millennio Adveniente."* The Holy See [cited 08/26 2008]. Available from http://www.vatican.va/holy_father/john_paul_ii/apost_letters/ documents/hf_jp-ii_apl_10111994_tertio-millennio-adveniente_en.html.

———. 1998. *Bull of Indiction of the Great Jubilee Year 2000: Incarnationis Mysterium*. The Holy See [cited 08/01 2011]. Available from http://www.vatican.va/jubilee_2000/docs/doc-uments/hf_jp-ii_doc_30111998_bolla-jubilee_en.html.

———. 2000a. *Day of Pardon. Homily of the Holy Father*. The Holy See [cited 08/01 2011]. Available from http://www.vatican.va/holy_father/john_paul_ii/homilies/2000/documents/ hf_jp-ii_hom_20000312_pardon_en.html.

———. 2000b. *Universal Prayer: Confession of Sins and Asking for Forgiveness*. The Holy See [cited 08/01 2011]. Available from http://www.vatican.va/news_services/liturgy/docu-ments/ns_lit_doc_20000312_prayer-day-pardon_en.html.

Lübbe, Hermann. 2001. *"Ich entschuldige mich." Das neue politische Bußritual*. Berlin: Siedler.

May, Georg. 1995. Forum. In *Lexikon für Theologie und Kirche*, edited by W. u. a. Kasper. Freiburg: Herder.

Niewiadomski, Józef. 2008. "Victima versus sacrificium. Nuancen der spannungsreichen Beziehung zwischen Liebe und Opfer." Pp. 176–209 in *Lieben. Provokationen. Salzburger Hochschulwochen 2008*, edited by G. M. Hoff, *Wissenschaft in Bewegung*. Innsbruck: Tyrolia.

Niewiadomski, Józef. 2011. "Märtyrer, Selbstopfer, Selbstmordattentäter". Pp. 275–291 in *Opfer – Helden – Märtyrer. Das Martyrium als religionspolitologische Herausforderung*, edited by J. Niewiadomski and R. A. Siebenrock, *Innsbrucker theologische Studien 83*. Innsbruck: Tyrolia.

Polish Bishops' Conferece. 1978. "Wir gewähren Vergebung. Wir erbitten Vergebung. Die Botschaft der polnischen Bischöfe an die deutschen Bischöfe vom 18. November 1965". Pp. 76–87 in *Begegnung der Konferenz des polnischen Episkopats mit der deutschen Bischofs-konferenz in Deutschland im September 1978, Stimmen der Weltkirche 4*. Bonn: Sekretariat der deutschen Bischofskonferenz.

Schönborn, Christoph Kardinal. 2010. *Wenn die Opfer sprechen, spricht Gott zu uns. Predigt beim Klage- und Bußgottesdienst*. Medienreferat der Österreichischen Bischofskonferenz [cited 08/03 2011]. Available from http://www.katholisch.at/content/site/minidossiers/arti-cle/53660.html.

Schwager, Raymund. 1999. *Jesus in the Drama of Salvation: Toward a Biblical Doctrine of Redemption*. Translated by J. G. Williams and P. Haddon. New York: The Crossroad Publishing Company.

———. 2005. "The Innsbruck Research Project and the Israeli-Palestinian Conflict." Pp. 295–305 in *Passions in Economy, Politics, and the Media. In Discussion with Christian*

Theology, edited by W. Palaver and P. Steinmair-Pösel, *Beiträge zur mimetischen Theorie 17*. Wien: LIT.

Second Vatican Council. 1964/UR. *Decree on Ecumenism: Unitatis Redintegratio*. The Holy See [cited 08/01 2011]. Available from http://www.vatican.va/archive/hist_councils/ ii_vatican_council/documents/vat-ii_decree_19641121_unitatis-redintegratio_en.html.

———. 1964/LG. *Dogmatic Consitution on the Church, Lumen Gentium*. The Holy See [cited 08/01 2011]. Available from http://www.vatican.va/archive/hist_councils/ ii_vatican_council/documents/vat-ii_const_19641121_lumen-gentium_en.html.

———. 1965/DiHu. *Declaration on Religious Freedom, Dignitatis Humanae*. The Holy See [cited 08/01 2011]. Available from http://www.vatican.va/archive/hist_councils/ ii_vatican_council/documents/vat-ii_decl_19651207_dignitatis-humanae_en.html.

———. 1965/GS. *Pastoral Consitution on the Church in the Modern World, Gaudium et Spes*. The Holy See [cited 08/01 2011]. Available from http://www.vatican.va/archive/ hist_councils/ii_vatican_council/documents/vat-ii_const_19651207_gaudium-et-spes_en.html.

Siebenrock, Roman A. 2009. *Christliches Martyrium. Worum es geht, topos taschenbücher 662*. Innsbruck: Tyrolia.

Siebenrock, Roman A. 2010. "Geheiligte Kirche der Sünder – oder: vom Risiko Gottes mit uns Menschen." Pp. 159–182 in *Heilige Kirche–Sündige Kirche / Chiesa santa–Chiesa di peccatori*, edited by J. Ernesti, U. Fistill and M. M. Lintner, *Brixner Theologisches Jahrbuch / Annuario Teologico Bressanone 2010*. Innsbruck–Wien: Tyrolia.

———. 2011. "Zeichen der Erlösung in einer Welt der Gewalt. Eine systematisch-theologische Kriteriologie des christlichen Martyriums." Pp. 153–172 in *Opfer – Helden – Märtyrer. Das Martyrium als religionspolitologische Herausforderung*, edited by J. Niewiadomski and R. A. Siebenrock, *Innsbrucker theologische Studien 83*. Innsbruck: Tyrolia.

Wandinger, Nikolaus. 2003. "'Wir vergeben und bitten um Vergebung'. Kommentar zu den kirchlichen Schuldbekenntnissen und Vergebungsbitten des Ersten Fastensonntags 2000." Pp. 143–179 in *Religion erzeugt Gewalt – Einspruch! Innsbrucker Forschungsprojekt ‚Religion – Gewalt – Kommunikation – Weltordnung'*, edited by R. Schwager and J. Niewiadomski, *Beiträge zur mimetischen Theorie 15*. Münster: LIT.

Weigel, George. 2005. *Witness of Hope. The Biography of Pope John Paul II. 1920–2005*. New York: Harper Collins.

NOTES

1. As readers will easily realize, I am writing as a Roman Catholic theologian. Still I think much of what is said here applies to the Church as a whole, not only the Roman Catholic Church. A more elaborate analysis of the papal prayers of forgiveness—yet with less consideration of the mimetic theory and of recent developments—can be found in German: Wandinger 2003. I am grateful for advice and suggestions to my colleague Roman Siebenrock, especially concerning section 4. For the topic, also compare Siebenrock 2010.

2. Because the readers of this chapter are very likely to be familiar with this theory and René Girard's writings, I will not provide detailed references to his works. The most important works that are in the background of this analysis are: Girard 1986, 1987a, 1987b, 2001.

3. Exegetes tell us that the debt amounted to more than 190,000 years' (!) salaries. Gnilka (1988, 145–146) calls 10,000 talents the largest conceivable sum of money. A *talent* was the highest coin, its worth is estimated at between 6,000 and 10,000 *denarii*. A *denarius* was a day's wage. 10,000 talents thus are at least 60 million, at most 100 million days' wages. Calculated for a six-day work-week that amounts to at least 192,307, at most 320,512 years' salaries.

4. Among the most prominent were German Chancellor Willy Brandt kneeling (1970) before the memorial for the victims in the Jewish ghetto in Warsaw during Nazi-German occupation; German President Johannes Rau asking for forgiveness in the Knesset in Jerusalem (2000); US President Bill Clinton apologizing for the deportation of slaves in Uganda (1998); Japanese Prime Ministers Obuchi apologizing for Japan's colonial rule over Korea in Seoul

(1998) and Kuizumi in Pyonyang (2002). Lübbe also notes that the Canadian government apologized in 1998 to its indigenous people for the hardship they endured.

5. I give here the official English translation "let us forgive and ask forgiveness." However, the original version was an indicative form ("we forgive and ask forgiveness"), which is grammatically not an exhortation, but a statement of fact; yet it is a fact that has to be put into practice by more and more of the faithful; therefore the statement does have a strong exhortative function as well.

6. This is very significant in itself. It constitutes a proactive offer by the Polish bishops that was very controversial at the time because it acknowledged a kind of reciprocity of the need for forgiveness between Germans and Poles. If one considers only the history of WWII, this cannot stand, Germany bearing the sole responsibility for starting this war and committing so many crimes in its course. This offer of reciprocity by the Polish bishops thus can only be interpreted in the larger context that we have tried to open up here.

7. It is noteworthy that this social aspect is absent from the earlier quotation from Pope Benedict's speech in Warsaw.

8. Cf. Accattoli 1999, 11. Accattoli mentions among others: speech at the Ecumenical Council of Churches in Geneva in 1984 (77), the speech to the representatives of academia and university research in Madrid in 1982 (88), the speech to the Parliamentary Assembly of the Council of Europe 1988 (89), the Memorial service for Albert Einstein in the Apostolic Palace in 1979 (91–92), the Speech to the Papal Academy of Sciences in 1992 (98–101), the Speech during the pope's visit to the Synagogue of Rome in 1986 (105–106), the Speech at the encounter of Muslim youths in Casablanca in 1985 (114), Ecumenical Encounter in Paris in 1980 (120), Speech to the representatives of the Association of Christian Churches in the Federal Republic of Germany and West Berlin in Mainz in 1980 (120–121), the Speech to the representatives of Christian Churches in the Arch-episcopal Residence in Vienna in 1983 (121), the Opening Ceremony of the European Synod in Rome in 1991 (121), the Ecumenical celebration at the conclusion of the European Synod in Rome in 1991 (122), the Canonization of the martyr priest Jan Sarkander in Olomouc (Czech Republic) in 1995 (127–128), the visit of the pope at a memorial for Calvinist martyrs who had been killed by Catholics in Prešov in 1995 (128–129), the Speech at an ecumenical liturgy in Salzburg in 1988 (130), the sermon at an ecumenical service in Paderborn in 1996 (132–133), the Speech at an encounter with representatives of the Evangelical Church in Germany in Mainz in 1980 (135), the Message to representatives of the indigenous people in Santo Domingo in 1992, which the pope, back in Rome, interpreted in his general audience on October 21, 1992 (186–187).

9. One exception might be made to this. In many countries the Church is still under persecution; many of the same countries do not have a reliable judiciary. In these circumstances, it is understandable that Church leaders are reluctant to cooperate with state authorities. This, however, does not dispense them from doing everything in their power and using all provisions of canon law and other Church regulations to effectively stop offenders and show them that their conduct is unacceptable and to attend to the needs of the victims. It is also evident that the untruthful accusation of child molestation is more than suitable for scapegoating the Church or Church officials. Therefore, legal procedure has to be followed meticulously and the rights of the accused safeguarded, so as to test the validity of the accusation. However, when Church officials in democratic states under the rule of law imagine conspiracy theories against the Church, they display a complete misunderstanding of the situation—to say the least.

Chapter Nineteen

From Fracturing Resemblances to Restorative Differences

Identity, Conflict, and Mimetic Desire among the Maya Chamula Tzotzil of Chiapas, Mexico

Fr. Miguel B. de Las Casas Rolland, OP

It is a strange paradox that reconciliation is sometimes more difficult among people who know each other very well, than if it occurs among those who barely know each other because of notable or attributable differences. René Girard (1997) argues that the denial of resemblance fuels conflict and fans the fires of rival passions. He often refers to this denial as misrecognition (*méconnaissance*). I argue that if *misrecognition* is the problem, then *recognition* is the likely solution to conflict. Recognition suggests a more edifying form of imitation and means learning to draw new lines based on new understandings of real relationships, however once fractured. By constructing flexible or porous boundaries based upon *recognition* rather than *mis-recognition*, community members enable one another to appreciate semblance *as well as* difference. Recognition, then, serves to reshape boundaries that are salubrious for all.

Although not necessarily a conscious or deliberate and rational process, recognition is preferable to the negative alternative of violent differentiations that escalate conflict. Using a few ethnographic examples, I wish to show how a particular community of Maya Indians experienced a propitious form of imitation that led to a creative approach to reconciliation.

IMITATIVE DESIRE

The speculations I present are not about specific *techniques* for conflict resolution but rather emphasize a dynamic of mutual *resolve* driven by imitative
desire (Girard 1965, 1979). Imitating the *desires* of others, whether positive
or negative, is a hazardous dynamic that affects multiple interactions, that is,
it affects what another person or group appears to seek, do, or act, or appear
to represent (Girard and Doran 2008). At the same time, such desire can
present propitious opportunities, depending on the model(s) or mediators for
imitation.

Anthropologist Simon Harrison links Girard's understanding of mimesis
to views from Sax (1998) and Barth (1969) on how identity construction is at
heart a boundary formation process:

> To understand how identities are created and maintained is to understand the
> ways that separations between the Self and Other, between the in-group and
> the out-group, between Us and Them, are posited, contested, defended, ef-
> faced, and so forth. In short, identities are defined at, or by, their boundaries.
> [And] in the context of ethnicity and nationalism, cultural differences are not
> mere ethnological dissimilarities . . . they are distinctions conceived, valorized
> and communicated by people interacting with one another, as ways of structur-
> ing their interactions. (2006, 63)

Applying Barth's anthropological view to the way groups copy one another, Harrison sees "cultural difference" as a particular idiom of sociality
where ethnic (and national) *differences* have fractured aspects. These situations, he says (2006, 63) are "much better conceptualized as broken resemblances (muted similarities) which are configured as either inferior relations,
superior relations, or some degree of equality to the 'Self.'"[1]

Because copying tends toward similarity, imitative semblance is *a priori*
to identity differentiation. Girard's mimetic theory proposes the paradox that
the more rivals seek to differentiate, the more they will resemble each other's
forms of competition. Identities form through arbitrary divisions rooted in
competition. The ability to perceive the implications of imitative desire
means that one has become aware of what acquisitive or appropriative desire
does and how it operates psycho-socially to generate conflict (Hurley and
Chater 2005).

Increased awareness of mimetic dynamics through *recognition* is a socially useful mechanism for holding back situational passions of *misrecognition*
that often prevent actors from discovering and then following model alternatives to conflict. One such alternative is how recognition leads to meaningful
forms of reconciliation through a *restoration of differences* (or what is the
social re-construction of inter-subjective boundaries through positive forms
of imitation).

In recent decades, as the anthropology of conflict and violence has become a more established area of study (see Krohn Hansen 1997; Riches 1986; Schmidt and Schroder 2001; Stewart and Strathern 2002), the phenomenon of imitative desire is noticeably missing as a research agenda item. Eller (2006) only briefly mentions Girard's theory of mimetic violence in the context of several other theories of social conflict. Filling the gap somewhat, Harrison (2006) uses Girard's understanding of mimesis in a critical fashion to juxtapose the notion of *imitative desire* with several classical views of social conflict from sociology. Harrison discusses distinctive views regarding how destructive forms of antagonism very often occur in close rather than distant relationships:

> Simmel argued that the more completely and intimately people are involved with one another—the more their ties encompass what he called the totality of their being—so their conflicts too, when they arise, tend to be all the more total and all-consuming. And to people who are very much alike, the smallest differences can appear major and seriously divisive. Hence, for instance, the bitterest and most violent controversies in religion have tended to occur between confessions whose doctrines were most similar. (2006, 1; cf. Simmel 1955, 43; see also Enloe 1996)

Additionally, Harrison employs Freud to explain how people intimate in common cultural terms are inevitably hostile to one another.[2]

Harrison (2006, 2) returns to a minority view in sociology concerned with what happens when people are insufficiently distinct from one another and with why some groups living in close proximity tend to exaggerate their distinctiveness. He presents Girard's ideas about imitative rivalry (acquisitive or appropriative mimesis) in this scholarly context, attempting to integrate previous explanations for how reciprocal copying influences aggression, competition, and rivalry. Girard claims that his views of imitative desire are not easy for researchers, because, since the time of Plato, most scholars have missed noticing the very dangerous implications of *mimesis* as representation.[3]

Harrison finds support for Girard's ideas in Bateson's theory of *schizmogenesis* (1958, 175–97). He sums up Bateson's challenge to the prevailing views of his time:

> Schizmogenesis is a process in which two or more protagonists react to one another, and react to one another's reactions, in a circular, escalating pattern. Bateson envisaged schizmogenesis as taking two alternative forms. In one, the actors' mutually reinforcing behavior patterns are the complements of each other: for instance, the assertiveness of one pattern in a relationship may evoke, and be evoked by, submissiveness on the part of the other. In the second pattern, which Bateson called symmetrical schizmogenesis, the escalating behavior patterns are identical, as happens when two rival states, for in-

stance, elicit mutually intensifying hostility from one another in an arms race. (2006, 3)

For Harrison, both ideas explain why opponents easily lock themselves into rivalry:

> a rivalry generating further reciprocal imitation—and escalating rivalry. To Bateson and Girard alike, this is a relation of interdependence as well as competition, in which the identities of the antagonists are, to some extent at least, shaped by the very rivalry itself and owe continued existence to it. (2006, 3)

Harrison's integrative view probes generative factors of violence for most Western societies and argues that the notion of imitative desire integrates similar theories of conflict, thus accounting for multiple dynamics of rivalry and group violence. Harrison insists, therefore, that it is not the mere lack of differentiation that attracts formations of difference but how "conflict itself is an inherently imitative process, tending to generate similarities at the same time as it is generated by them" (2006, 3). Together, these notions make it possible to recognize the somewhat hidden motivating factors that fuel inter-subjective strife.

RECOGNIZING THE HIDDEN NATURE OF MIMETIC CONFLICT

According to Harrison, *collective identities* (ethnicity) "are conceptualized as arising from relationships, not of difference or perceived difference, but of denied or disguised resemblance" (2006, 13). These identities emerge through processes in which certain kinds of felt similarities, and other shared features of identity are disavowed, censored or systematically forgotten. Underlying processes bring about extreme and even violent forms of ethnic "othering" and as such, he observes (2006, 13), they "are more likely to occur within relationships that are in some sense close, rather than in distant ones." Moreover, Harrison emphasizes how some scholars see social identity as created by constraints on imitation and resemblance. Resemblance and imitation are ontologically primary and "differences" are secondary effects produced by the control or denial of similarities (Harrison 2006, 13).

Harrison's observations seem to apply to ethnic conflicts beyond Melanesia, such as those I have observed among Maya Tzotzil Chamula groups in Chiapas, Mexico. These regions are clearly affected by the greater world around them, not least of which are questions about how imitation, representation, and reproduction (mimesis) affect the historical forces of globalization and capitalist modes of development. A major aspect of such forces is how acting subjects are habitually motivated by models who desire certain objects (Xenos 1989). Whether among the peoples of Melanesia or the indigenous of Chiapas, cultural and social objects of worth (material or psychosocial "things") have significance because their ascribed value emerges in a dialectical fashion. For most peoples, it seems, the interactive process of constructing meanings (values) is never a one-way process of acculturation (cf. Pitt-Rivers 1967).

The same is true for social interactions that constitute the process of *reconciliation*. If desire is truly mimetic, then reciprocal violence is highly mimetic. Like a contagion, it advances through vengeance. Stopping so dangerous a progression calls for a mutual recognition, one that discourages actors from escalating the patterns of negative imitations. If opponents have the chance to see, that is, recognize the elements of a common or communal problem, they can recognize the traps of imitative reciprocity (what Harrison calls the *mimetic misrecognition of mimesis*). It may take awhile, but actors can learn to avoid reacting to each other's reactions.

Reconciliation has a lot to do with pulling back "psychological projections"—postures that tend to scapegoat others because of one's own unconscious anxieties. The key to reconciliation would seem to be learning how to welcome rather than fear *similarity*. If we think about reconciliation as an emotional learning process, then we can see ways for actors to respect differences (real or imaginary). A propitious or positive mimesis suggests creating a critical form of awareness that respects not just differences but the fearsome fact of familiarity (sameness in the sense of identity). I am arguing that an authentic experience of *reconciliation* depends upon seeing a particular social reality in a *refracting* rather than fracturing light. This would mean viewing life *as it is* (social reality) but from a full spectrum perspective of diversity. This posture suggests opponents can find common features and shared characteristics without a sense of threat or competition and rivalry. This may seem sensible enough, but social practices often tend to emphasize difference and deny familiarity.

RE-*COGNITION* AND THE RESTORATION OF DIFFERENCE(S)

Social imitation is not always bad or threatening. It can provide for a propitious or good sort of interaction because it offers a vital perspective on how social relationships take shape. Positive imitations, like following an ideal or persons who embody that ideal, represent an alternative to the kinds of narrow categories by which people will follow a crowd mentality that produces (or reproduces) blindness (the denial of semblance) and *misrecognition*. Thus, a disposition of *recognition* (to re-*cognize*, to think twice) functions as a kind of beneficial seeing mechanism. To perceive the precarious nature of imitative behavior is a great advantage in human affairs. Peace is possible when would-be contraries can unveil and thus actually perceive their own appropriative desire at work, seeing what it does in cultural practice. This new consciousness comes, when interacting subjects can critically assess their own mutual influence over the negative ways imitation leads them to want, do, or attempt to represent.

Recognition is thus a compassionate perspective that can heal the fracturing effects of negative imitations gone awry. It affects even unconscious misrecognitions such as racism and prejudice. When recognition becomes an acquired or customary skill, it provides a means to reconcile people who might otherwise construct a felt-sense of identity from an imitated sense of bounded difference and exclusion. As Harrison observes:

> Difference, or felt difference, is widely understood to lie at the heart of social identity. The important insight that all perspectives of this kind share is that human collectivities exist only by having outsiders, and by having boundaries to keep them out. In this, albeit perverse, respect groups rely on one another for their existence. Each can sustain a sense of separate identity only in the context of relationships with others, however much these relationships may be conflict-ridden and unequal.[4] (2006, 8)

To move away from "fractured resemblances" produced by interactions of mimetic rivalry and thus begin to more move toward a sense of *restored differences* (respectful boundaries) depends upon interdividual circumstances rather than any individual rational choices. A wise acceptance and appreciation for difference(s) can open up identity formations and develop some kind of hierarchy. Structuring efforts—including police actions—reflect practical attempts to contain rivalrous actions rooted in the triangular mimesis of desire between Models and Subjects, and the Object(s) they compete to obtain or appropriate (Girard 1978).

MAYA TZOTZIL CHAMULA ETHNOGRAPHIC EXAMPLES

As mentioned earlier, Harrison (2006) refers to "fractures" of ethnic semblance due to an excessive degree of too much *sameness*. Such situations are problematic because they often lead to severe forms of conflict. Situations of this kind among the Maya Tzotzil Chamula of Chiapas, Mexico suggest how familiarity can breed a sense of contempt. Excessive conformity seems to precipitate violent attempts at differentiation as otherwise loyal community members contend over the "same" prizes (e.g., power, prestige, pecuniary privileges). This kind of internal struggle suggests the need for reconciliation, especially when Chamula consciously try to recognize how much imitation often leads to problems within and between their communities.

Many of the conflicts I will discuss have been well documented and in large part have to do with competing claims to certain religious values.[5] Incidents of violent conflict in a Chamula community often overlap other claims to identity rooted in political, economic, and religious interests that combine to inform Tzotzil ethnicity. Issues of identity are complex as members negotiate their pertinence to a particular group, party, organization, or hamlet in the region.[6]

CHAMULA RELIGIOUS CONFLICTS AND MIMETIC DESIRE

During the 1990s, numerous situations of severe religious conflict took place within the large ethnic township or *municipio* known as San Juan Chamula, located only a few kilometers from the highland city of San Cristóbal de Las Casas in Mexico's southern most state of Chiapas. My observations focus on internal rather than external examples of ethnic strife, highlighting *intra*-ethnic aspects of political and religious strife at the level of community.[7]

Intra-ethnic conflict between groups of the Maya Tzotzil Chamula themselves (in contrast to inter-ethnic conflicts with Ladinos) is a phenomenon attributable in part to exterior pressures. The hamlet of Ch'ul Vo' provides some empirical indication of how intra-ethnic conflicts emerge out of mimetic rivalry.[8] The history of suffering for this particular hamlet is representative of similar conflicts in the area. External factors for conflict include socio-economic stress,many Traditionalist Catholics involved in perpetuating violence such as rapid population growth and density.[9] Other factors include retrograde national "Indian" policies, ambiguous church relations, and inequitable land acquisition politics. Whatever the influence of external pressures, it is interesting how such factors become "objects of desire" in the first place, that is to say, fodder for mimetic exchanges.

TWO KINDS OF CATHOLICS

In the hamlet of Ch'ul Vo' there are two kinds of "Catholics." One group vehemently identifies itself as *Catholic* but not in terms of Christian belief and doctrine. For this group, being "Catholic" is almost a code term for guardians of local *tradition*—the particular sacred life-ways presumably set forth by leaders in previous generations. "Traditionalists" abide by customary ways not so much because of hard and fast religious tenets, but because tradition means belonging, and thus a felt sense of adherence regarding spiritual practices, cultural expressions, performances—in a word, identity. Observers generally refer to Chamula customary praxis as *costumbre*, a religious expression of syncretistic developments from many years of borrowing and re-interpreting colonial Catholic imaginaries. It is interesting to note that what is often thought to be traditionally exclusive to Chamula followers of *costumbre* are actually common popular religious practices found among most Indian as well as non-indigenous rural peoples throughout Mexico (e.g., "the day of the dead" or all Souls/all Saints day, or the healer's diagnostic derived from "listening" to a person's pulse).[10] Nevertheless, it is important to note that *costumbre* religion has become a somewhat fixed marker of Chamula historical identity (Gómez Sántiz 2005; Pérez López 1990). This aspect of identity has become so strong that Chamula who do not follow *costumbre* are easily accused of being inauthentic, that is to say, condemned for not being or acting as true or original (*batz'i*) Chamula.

There is another kind of Catholic, however, known as "Word of God" or biblical Catholics (cf. Kovic 2005; Chojnacki 2010). A minority group, these Chamula try to reshape their life-ways according to biblical precepts, especially the four Christian Gospels. Within the township of San Juan Chamula, *Word of God* Catholics choose to identify with the Roman Catholic diocese of San Cristóbal de Las Casas. They generally adhere to the Church's reforms developed since the Second Vatican Council [1962–1965].

Although both groups claim to be *Catholics* (Traditionalist Catholics vs. Word of God [or Roman] Catholics) and live within the same ethnic *municipio* (the township of San Juan Chamula) both are generally very poor; they are also very much alike—at least in basic life-ways, language, and occupation (such as farmers, bricklayers, carpenters, merchants). Until recently, each group thought of itself in perpetual contention with the other due to distinctions that reflect differences of religious belief and practice (Rivera Farán 2000), not to mention distinct partisan political and economic dispositions (Robledo Hernández 1997). Both groups of Chamula Catholics who live in Ch'ul Vo' hamlet seem to know things about each other. This means that conflicts seem more intense because strife often impacts upon natural kinship (parents, siblings) as well as fictional relations (godparents). Members of both Catholic groups are constantly crossing each other's paths on the local roads, especially during market days, or when walking or working in proximity to each other's *milpas* (corn fields), or using the same taxi transports. Even though traditional in many respects, the *Word of God* Catholics try hard to limit certain aspects of local *costumbre* such as the way certain drinking customs impact negatively upon family and community relationships.

The story of strife within the community of Ch'ul Vo' is not unlike many others in the municipality of San Juan Chamula, after several decades of religious and economic persecution against non-conformists—those who reject the supposedly traditional ways of *costumbre*. Years of anguish have left many Chamula scarred emotionally by fear, regrets, resentments, anger.[11] In Ch'ul Vo', there are other religious groups of Chamula who follow Evangelical styles of Christianity (Pentecostal, Presbyterian), but space does not allow for an adequate description of how these groups have also suffered.[12] One way, perhaps, to understand the history of internecine violence among some (not all) Chamula groups and communities is to look carefully at the dynamic of rivalry and how internal differences may have arisen in the first place.

PRACTICES AND "PROPRIETARY IDENTITIES"

As opposed groups, each is anxious to protect their particular forms of religious practices (e.g., Baptismal ritual). Both Traditionalists (of the *costumbre* religious expression) and the Roman Catholics (Word of God) insist that their rivals are inauthentic or false Catholics and therefore not Chamula. Typical identity markers for both groups include participating in proper forms of prayer, ritual respect for images of Saints, practicing ancestral ways, speaking the true language (batz'i k'op), and belonging to the correct political party. The collective identities of being a Mexican, or a Chiapaneco, further complicate the sense of Chamula identity or "peoplehood."[13]

Besides competing claims over what "Catholic" signifies, both groups also claim to be guardians of tradition. Here "traditional" refers to ways of doing things (or ways of thinking) handed down through generations. *Tradere* (Latin) in this sense suggests unchanged ways of life, when in fact they only reflect controlling change long enough (or slowly enough) to provide a felt-sense of continuity. For both groups of Catholics, however, traditional forms of religious expression, while similar in appearance, are in many ways radically distinct in terms of actual content and symbolic meanings.[14]

One important example of this difference is the tradition of the Eucharistic sacrifice or "Mass." For Chamula Roman Catholics (*Word of God* Catholics), the Eucharist signifies engaging a communal "mystery" (*sacramentum*) whereby believers praise and thank God for His sacrifice and the gift of salvation. These Roman Catholic Chamula see the mass as a celebration representing the suffering, death, and resurrection of Jesus, *the Christ* (Anointed Messiah), or what is the Paschal mystery, and the lives of the Saints who participate in that mystery. In contrast, for the Traditionalists of *costumbre* religion, the Catholic mass is not about giving thanks, but is rather a means by which to acquire some benefit of self-interest.

What these examples indicate is that Chamula feel strongly about certain objects. These "things" are culturally constituted, and Chamula collectively possess them as one possesses property. Harrison (2006) argues that these kinds of possessions amount to a "proprietary identity" and are related to the imitation of desire Girard calls acquisitive or appropriative mimesis. In my view, the fact of at least doubles or two kinds of Chamula Catholics is due in part to competition over "proprietary identities." Harrison sees such cultural constructions of ownership as a deeply socialized sense of trademark: "By this term I refer to social identities whose outward symbols or markers are treated as property, and may be disputed as property. In conflicts of this sort, the opponents' perceptions of each other are not so much those of difference or otherness, but of mutually hostile resemblance" (2006, 4). The idea that cultural practices (specific religious rituals, for example) are "things" and thus available as objects of competing desire helps explain why Chamula import many aspects of their "traditional" culture, in other words, acquired, borrowed, or simply purloined from other persons or groups. Once obtained, these "objects of desire" serve to mark a new or rearranged sense of an authentic collective identity for groups or communities. Once a group acquires or incorporates another's things, ideations, or practices, they can then be used to demarcate boundaries vis-à-vis "others" who may or may not have similar stuff.

In most Chamula hamlets today, intangible goods (e.g., spiritual beliefs) as well as concrete religious paraphernalia (images, incense, etc.) seem to constitute protected precious commodities. Acquisitions from "outsiders" or insiders occur, but in ways that are so slow or at an almost imperceptible pace that it is not always easy to detect changes to tradition within a single generation. As mentioned earlier, most of today's "traditional" practices that constitute Chamula *costumbre* religion come from late 18th century practices of European Catholicism.

One important example of "proprietary identities" is the emotional connection a majority of Chamulas have long felt with Mexico's historically hegemonic political party known as the *Partido Revolucionario Institucional*, or the PRI. After some eight decades, this party still dominates many important aspects of Chamula life, even after the year 2000, when other political parties gained ground in Mexico and in Chiapas. To be a member of the PRI carries an important sense of belonging. The identification is not about "ideas" or political platforms but rather access to resources (objects of desire), including ethnicity as a resource. Belonging, in this way, suggests a sense of shared risk and thus protection and solidarity with friends, family, and fellow Chamula neighbors. Since the 1930s, and despite changes in recent years, the *PRIista* identification works as an important signifier of group belonging (perhaps even more than the useful identity of being Catholic). Being both *PRIista* and *Católico* together constitutes a popular Chamula "trademark" and any competing threat against it is sure to invite conflict.

On the level of religious identity, it is interesting to see how the Roman Catholic mass (or liturgy of the Eucharist) has also become a very important "thing" to possess. Ostensibly, this ritual possession seems important mostly because it feeds or nourishes the local Chamula god, San Juan, whose image presides high above the main altar in the apse of the Traditionalist church of San Juan Chamula. Mass is not something a Chamula person participates in for his or her self, let alone any regular basis such as attending mass on

Sundays. The mass exists for the pleasure of San Juan (John the Baptist), who desires it. The performance of the liturgy, however, requires an ordained priest from the local diocese. The priest is co-opted to act as producer and minister of the sacrificial food (communion host, incense, candles, prayers). However, because the mass means something different to Traditionalists than it means to *Word of God* Catholics, this particular "proprietary identity" presents a daunting difficulty to reconcile.

However, when Chamula attempt to "dis-identify" with a long-standing customary disposition or, as Bourdieu might argue, their *habitus* of being both PRI and *católico*, it is because a double identity represents a threat. Because Chamula Traditionalists, in ways similar to the *Word of God* Catholics and many Evangelical Protestants, treat their respective customs and traditions very much like property and thus jealously guard what is rightfully theirs (however much borrowed or imported originally). They will fight to keep their "properties" free from the appropriative desires of "outsiders"—a posture which may explain very strict rules for tourists visiting the main Chamula church in the central plaza.

Chamula "Roman Catholics," who self-identify in an antithetical fashion, do so in favor of a new, perhaps more prestigious "marker" of identity. They thus *dis*-identify with being a "typical" Chamula, making it a point to avoid the everyday practices of those who practice *costumbre*. As counter-cultural agents or "dissidents," these Chamula self-ascribe by what they reject, by what they are not (though perhaps, unconsciously, longing for the very things they deny, such as access to power, prestige, or pecuniary privileges). These Chamula opt instead for what seems presumably new and perhaps better or superior. Like the Traditionalists, the mimetic desire of "dissidents" revolves around models, who incarnate and thus mediate desire. If reconciliation is likely to proceed in ways that allow competing or rival Chamula to come together in dialogue or cooperation, then much depends upon how actors' attitudes and actions creatively develop reconfigurations of their "proprietary identities."

THE SOCIAL IDIOM OF IMAGES

Because the beliefs, postures, and practices of both Catholic groups are very similar in form, the media and other observers have often confused them in contradistinction to Protestants. The press often report Chamula religious conflicts as a chronic problem of religious intolerance—as if a clear matter of irreconcilable differences. Although both groups of Catholics are very much aware of their minor but highly significant differences in religious expressions, to many outside observers both groups look the same. In the early 1990s, many Traditionalist Catholics involved with perpetuating violence against Protestant Evangelical Christians groups were often held suspect and accused but seldom found responsible for crimes (cf. CDHFBLC 2005). Less known, however, was the fact that Traditionalists Catholics were persecuting *Word of God* or Roman Catholics as well as Protestants.

In Ch'ul Vo' the attempt to craft meaningful "differences" over several decades has resulted in a great deal of religiously motivated violence.[15] For instance, in the late 1990s, both the municipal government and the state collaborated to accuse church members in Ch'ul Vo' of being "evangelicals" and also responsable for fomenting disorder.[16]

With warrants issued for their arrests, the Word of God Catholic and lay-deacon Romín, along with his wife, Catalina (then the principal pastoral leaders of Ch'ul Vo'), spent many years in virtual exile hiding from state and federal authorities. In addition, four other church members spent five years in jail falsely accused of having murdered several foot soldiers of a local boss. The Catholic Traditionalist bosses have several times destroyed the church building of the Ch'ul Vo' Word of God Catholics.

The violence from within the community of Ch'ul Vo' relates to an earlier event of violence in another Chamula community. In the fall of 1995, Traditionalist Catholics of the *costumbre* religion attempted unsuccessfully to massacre Presbyterian Christians in Arbenza, a small hamlet not far from the central plaza of San Juan Chamula township. The Traditionalists were surprised to find the Presbyterians armed and ready to fight back.

The Presbyterians of Arbenza managed to kill scores of Traditionalists who had arrived firing automatic weapons, mimetically responding with the same kind of violence they had suffered for years. This violent clash suddenly created a new sense of boundary. In turning-the-*Other's*-cheek, the victims were now fighting back—a novelty in Chamula territory. The press attributed this "pay back" to Chamulas who were likely following (imitating) the then recent regional example of rebellion from the mostly indigenous EZLN, or Zapatista Army of National Liberation.[17]

However, it is just as important to note that this reciprocal violence mimetically mirrored the violence of local political bosses (called *caciques* or chiefs). When the Christians of Arbenza decided to respond *in kind* to the violence expressed by their persecutors, their actions very quickly reconfigured the moral landscape for many indigenous organizations including many Catholic (Word of God) and Protestant (Evangelical) associations in highland Chiapas (Morquecho 1997). It was generally thought that, this justified violent response would finally bring equilibrium, if not an end, to decades of fear, insecurity, and suffering. After 1995, Chamula bosses took extra precautions before attacking any nonconformists.

IDENTITY POLITICS, DIFFERENTIATION, AND THE SEARCH
FOR ALTERNATIVES

Costumbre Catholics are by far the majority of the population within the municipality of San Juan Chamula. Historically, however, the perceived threat of nonconformity has less to do with differing specific beliefs and much more to do with long-standing issues of "identity politics" (Robledo Hernández 1997; Rus 2005). In other words, it touches on sensitive issues of status and class. Though these issues are largely hidden, muted, or denied, they reveal economic and power relations pervasive throughout the municipality of San Juan Chamula. Problems of social position link to regional struggles over power, including access to resources associated with rural assistance programs of the Mexican state (Rus 1994, 1995, 2005). For decades, a relatively small oligarchy of powerful Chamula families successfully governed their supposedly "closed" municipality. Until Protestants took up arms in their own defense during the 1990s (e.g., Arbenza), these few traditionalist families had managed to govern with relative impunity (López Meza 2002). After suffering decades of corruption, and because of many rural-to-urban transformations, many of the older "traditional" ways of accomplishing social, political, or economic control through state-sponsored protection largely disappeared. Recent shifts in national and state politics further impeded open violent reprisals, though there were sporadic incidents. Bosses have lost much of their ability to openly threaten non-conformists or "dissidents" with expulsion (Rus 1994, 2005; Robledo Hernández 1997).

No longer controlled by a few wealthy families, the municipality of San Juan Chamula has become a complex and economically stratified entity divided by multiple hierarchies. Issues revolve around ritual or cultural status as usual, but these are increasingly tied to desires for wealth and class difference.[18] Far from monolithic, the town is adjusting to multiple religious and political affiliations, where a variety of groups constantly organize and interact in search of power and advantageous positions. Nevertheless, some traditional power-broker groups still exist who still hold significant political and economic influence as to what constitutes "normative" life within certain hamlets (cf. Burguete Cal y Mayor 2000). Christian dissidents—both Roman Catholic and Protestant Evangelical—continue to refer to bosses and their gangs in a pejorative manner. They refuse to call them "authorities" or acknowledge them as leaders, referring to them instead as "those that give orders."[19] In the hamlet of Ch'ul Vo', however, because of the diversity of beliefs that exist, members are finding alternatives for dealing with threats once rooted in a politics of exclusion.

MEDIATORS, SUBJECTS, AND THEIR "OBJECTS OF DESIRE"

Since the 1930s, if not before, younger generations of Chamula have sought ways to rival the more established generation (Rus 1994). They often imitate the astute methods of available role models in local commerce, ritual ways, and other interests. Some eventually learn to surpass their elders, including established local bosses, having learned well how to move in networks inside and outside the community. Examples include monopolizing local distribution for Coca-Cola, as well as all sales of beer and cane liquor (*posh*), the production, and resale of candle wax (used in religious rites), the control of tourism and even limiting local access to traditional water holes.[20] Another important economic monopoly pertains to taxing local systems of transport for people and materials moving through the town. In addition, the *Templo* or Chamula church represents a sacred and ritualized dwelling place for the patron saint, San Juan, but it also represents a lucrative operation of material and symbolic capital over which the local Roman Catholic diocese has no control.

Much of this kind of power mediates through all levels of local government (cf. Rus 2005) as well as through other non-state entities such as labor cooperatives, political parties, and churches (Morquecho 1992). Although constrained somewhat by local customary expectations, many traditionalist bosses circumvent their rivals (young or old) by finding ways to become "extra-traditional" or "extra-judicial," thus moving beyond mere custom and law. Youth, who aspire to become traditionalist bosses, desire to become like powerful Chamula who model how to be effective commercial entrepreneurs, state legislators, or similar agents of change capable of gaining wealth and social advantages. Ambition moves young subjects to become just like their older models, eventually establishing their own "traditions" within the township, while procuring luxurious houses, ranches, and other objects of conspicuous consumption. These actions are semiotic and serve to communicate unmistakable signs of material and psychosocial power.

Since 1975, both Evangelical as well as Roman Catholic *Word of God* Christians have been scapegoat targets of ambitious bosses eager for political gain.[21] Although obviously "100% Chamula" in ethnic terms, these victims were made the focus for anything that seemed wrong. Although corrupt and often not in conformity with actual age-old traditions, Chamula bosses have often escaped legal scrutiny by blaming dissidents as the source of community problems. Catholics and Protestants are no less ambitious than their Traditionalist neighbors, even though they have a history of opposition to the corrupt practices of the political bosses. Interestingly enough, some of the opponents have become mimetic "victims," that is to say, they have come to resemble the very people they opposed, becoming bosses themselves under the pressure of power, privilege, and pecuniary predicaments.

INTERPRETATION: SIMILARITY DENIED

The case of Ch'ul Vo' as presented in the above examples (along with other elements not discussed), amount to a denial of intra-ethnic *similarity*. I see it as a case of *misrecognition*; more than a question of perceived differences about religious beliefs, it is an ontological problem as in *the meaning of being*, i.e., of "being Chamula." It is remarkable how in Ch'ul Vo' and other similar communities, conflict happens between people with very similar life-ways and familiar aspects/markers of identity (language, location, life ways, forms of labor, religious feelings, and so forth).

Interestingly, the persecuted Catholics have often fueled the fires of "Othering" as much or more as their persecutors have sought their alienation. Hardly innocent in their roles as victims, they have sometimes exacerbated the ire of their enemies (neighbors and relatives) in an attempt to feel right-eous or morally superior. Sadly, although each group of Chamula may have much in common historically and culturally, mutual insistence upon "us/them" differentiations has too often led to intractable polarizations that then only generated more violence. However, as a means to differentiation from too much sameness, violence seems not only counter-productive but also counter-intuitive, since it prevents groups in opposition from learning to cooperate for common purposes and joint advantages.

Historically, the Chamula Tzotzil frequently divide over political party affiliation, land tenure, water rights, and other socio-economic woes.[22] In the face of rivalry over material as well as ideational objects of desire, the Cha-mula have to negotiate between home-grown expressions and what amounts to acquired notions about themselves, including neo-essentialist views about who the Chamula are supposed to be.[23] Such assumptions can impede recon-ciliation between Chamula groups because of a refusal to recognize sem-blance.

Tensions can escalate as members seek to differentiate themselves by assuming definitions over *what they are not*, as opposed to who they "are," ontologically. Publically, this drama of individualism can mean aligning one's self to collective interests: the political and economic desires of other Chamula as well as those of non-indigenous society and the Mexican nation. Historically, Chamula people have frequently been manipulated, collectively, as an object of desire—paraded in media as a kind of "showcase" group of Indians for Mexico's *Indianist* policies. This cooptation is sometimes mutual however, as when the state Governor and/or the national President arrives, mimetically dressed head to toe as a Traditional Chamula in order to speak in the town center of San Juan Chamula.

In Chamula society, strong men (*caciques*) maintain order through a coer-cive application of "tradition" that guarantee patron/client services to their "gente" (followers). Church people also have their "strong men" and thus their *gente*. There is the famous example of a Chamula Protestant pastor, Miguel Caxlan. The Chamula leader came to a violent end once he began to congregate power, influence, and above all, a large following of fellow Chamula (see Martínez García 2008). What happened to Caxlan and other victims relates to Girard's theory that accusers obtain a temporary social peace by sacrificing a surrogate victim. Like the black chickens ritually killed by a *curandero/a* in the Temple of San Juan, a scapegoat goes a long way to quell chaos by absorbing the vexing anger caused by strange "others."

TEOLOGÍA INDIA AND NEW PATHS TO RECONCILIATION

In Ch'ul Vo' there exists a nascent reconciliation movement called *Teologia India*, or Indian Theology (TI for short). This grass-roots movement introduces a dialogue of ideas from both Word of God Catholics and Evangelical Christian churches regarding their historical and actual participation with indigenous communities. The movement was initiated in the 1980s as a dialogue process, one that especially embraces non-Christian indigenous people and their ritual practitioners from the Maya region of Mexico and Guatemala. The TI movement organizes reflections in order not to change the past but to try healing it.

TI gatherings or congresses bring together several hundred participants to study themes chosen ahead of time by a coordinating committee. Topics range from ethnic pride and dignity, to learning how to interpret historical documents, anthropological findings, comparisons of ancient and modern cosmology, theological discourse new and old, and much more. Major goals include how to better understand each other's native traditions or concept of the divine. Criticisms of the movement range from accusations of "heresy" to preoccupations with so-called "new age" discourse and a reductive or romantic view of indigeneity.

TI conferences and workshops promote an attitude of respect towards ancient and contemporary socio-cultural practices. Each gathering considers current problems, especially those rooted in political oppression, religious prejudice, and more.[24] Participants seek to share their interest in concepts putatively ancestral and/or expressions successfully adopted and adapted by the "past ones" (*antepasados* in Spanish). This means cherishing sacred and wise words from the "grandfathers and grandmothers" of previous times. The past, in this sense, has more authoritative resonance for change than any idealized future or utopian political agenda. The past provides meaning and orientation for those now alive. Cognizant of past injuries and oppressive practices perpetuated since even before the European Conquest, but above all lamenting the tragic devastation for indigenous people everywhere through the legacies of colonialism, these dialogues try to avoid discourse that imposes any *a priori* sets of ideas (ideology).

TI participants recognize and use other kinds of "scriptures." For example, in addition to celebrating passages from the Judeo-Christian tradition, participants will frequently promote the use of autochthonous historical documents such as the *Popol Wu* (of the K'ich'e Maya in Guatemala) or the books of *Chilam Balam* (the Chumayel books from the Maya of Yucatan, Mexico, XVI and XVII centuries). Participants show reverence toward these documents, often employing a kind of mimetic response to the way Christians regard their sacred books. Readings from these writings, along side similar themes from the Christian scriptures, support elaborate ritual moments during workshops, retreats, or courses.

By recognizing rather than denying the past, and by engaging the present, the TI movement attempts to project an imaginative future. Aware of how much indigenous people have in common historically, the TI gatherings motivate many to build anew the precious old things that seem to make life meaningful. One major example of this appreciation is the desire to see (*recognize*) everyone (all creatures) as the children of the living God, i.e., the one inter-connected sense of the Divine that represents God [or the gods] as the source of all life and being. For many Chamula, this sense of the divine often refers to the image of God and god-like people as *jtotikmeil*, "our father-mother." God is both father and mother—a theological construct that reflects something of the cosmological duality of ancestral beliefs before the Conquest.

RECOGNITION AND RECONCILIATION

In Indian Theology, "reconciliation" means learning to *recognize* that we are all related yet not without distinction and variety. When it comes to seeking the meaning of the divine, adherents contend that human creatures are in many ways all similar. TI dialogues stress cultivating mutual respect in order to effectively recognize and appreciate differences, without having to destroy them or fear them as a threat to one's very existence. Instead, respect reminds people just how curious, creative, and comforting differences are. Respect thus *re*-minds acting subjects to *re-cognize* the fundamental fact (experience) of just how inter-connected and "sacred" everything is for human beings. In the context of indigenous theology, reconciliation is about cooperation and remembering rather than any simplistic redress of wrongs or amendment of transgressions. In this broader sense, reconciliation means "adding on" instead of subtracting; it is about bringing together instead of taking away or forgetting.

As observed earlier, many problems arise within Chamula communities when religious beliefs and practices are treated as proprietary "brands"—fetishizing spiritual ideas or practices as though possessable objects. For many Chamula, the "peaceful" solution to escalating conflict due to acquisitive mimesis has been to destroy or to expel the problem-makers. Quelling instigators by force were attempts to make "dissidents" disappear.

In contrast to this negative mimesis, *teología india* offers a positive or propitious approach to imitation. After a few members attended some TI conferences, the Chamula Catholic Christians of Ch'ul Vo' (Word of God Catholics) began to explore creative new ways to form their church as an *ecclesia* or community. As subjects look to models, the exemplars tend to mediate value from the past or present—whether real, imagined, or reconstructed—demonstrating how the process of mutual interactions is always imitative (mimetic).

CONFLICT AND VIOLENCE IN PERSPECTIVE

In an attempt to revalorize custom and tradition as a positive *mimesis* of respect for differences, the new model promoted by the *teologia india* movement has helped Chamula Roman Catholics to appreciate the importance of seeking *autochthonous* or "home grown" alternatives to their problems. This path resists state-influenced efforts to reproduce romantic images of indigenous community that reduce complex exchanges to limited, bounded, and discrete traits. It remains problematic that folkloric images promoted by the Mexican state too easily draw national and foreign tourists to the so-called *Ruta Maya* of highland Chiapas (the archaeological sites of exotic Maya pyramids). Federal and local state agencies for tourism are quick to promote "Maya ruins" as objects of curiosity without addressing the historical issues of the living, ruined Mayas who continue their struggles for respect (human rights).

As a way to model a more positive *mimesis*, Indian theology offers an alternative to the destructive aspects of appropriative desire. Instead of stealing from natives, or producing illicit copies or imitations of this or that custom, TI promotes a positive but non-coercive form of appropriation based on meaningful models or exemplars. It promotes imitations of those who demonstrate compassion, identification with the other, or love of neighbor. To accomplish this alternative, ritual and customary life become essential features.

What TI methods mean for Ch'ul Vo' residents is that *Word of God* Catholics look for ways to be more like the former enemies, the Traditionalists, i.e., to be more recognizable to them and thus less "strange," or unacceptable. In this way, Catholics can show their typical enemies just how much they actually do care about traditional or customary life-ways. The challenge for *Word of God* Catholics is to express "kindness"—in other words, *to act like or to be like* the very people they often deny because of fear of similarity (denied resemblances). From the TI perspective, it is good *to be like* one's opponent—to respect them, despite past hurts. Such an understanding seems counter-intuitive in the full context of Chamula life, where much depends upon structures of exchange that imply loyalty to powerful men and conformity to socio-cultural sameness.

NEW STRATEGIES

Having survived *cacique*-inspired violence, the Chamula Catholics in Ch'ul Vo' have developed a variety of reconciliation strategies. Their primary strategy is a "both/and" style of participation with the traditional *costumbre* religion. This strategy aims to ensure that the religious practices they "possess" as Christians will resemble what other Chamula can recognize or find familiar. They agree that their public conduct should try to be a conscientious effort to look "normal"—that is, visibly practicing traditions much as their fellow Chamula. For example, instead of avoiding customary clothing, they make it a point to wear it proudly; or instead of avoiding the simple dances at customary prayer events, they make it a point to enjoy them as an embodied form of prayer. On the feast of San Juan Bautista (June 24), the small community of believers decided, bravely, to go together to the great Church in the central plaza and offer flowers to the patron Saint, an act Traditionalists found surprising and thus difficult to fault or accuse as dissident.

In any case, the apparent goal of this cultural identity strategy is, on one level, to enact a form of protection (making it harder to accuse Chamula Roman Catholics of refusing traditional ways); on another level, however, the strategy exposes the dubious nature of *cacique*-led justifications for violence "in the name of tradition" (Hess chapter 7). Here we have a social paradox: Traditionalists are not traditional while the non-Traditionalists are the keepers of tradition. This new strategy unveils the hidden agenda behind violations of religious and cultural rights. Even so, drinking rituals remain the most difficult for many Chamula Roman Catholics who want to insist that the Word of God discourages drunkenness as sinful behavior. While some might argue for moderation, most Chamula relate to the Evangelicals, who have experienced strong conversions related to sobriety, a point of irritation for Chamula bosses who have long controlled the local concessions on beer and liquor distribution (cf. Eber 2000).

The elders or *Principales* of Ch'ul Vo' felt emotionally satisfied with this mirroring strategy on the part of the "other" Catholics, even though they were all still suspected of being rebels or non-conformists. The elders, at least, appreciated an alternative to the "all or nothing" stance that a number of Evangelical Christians prefer, always at the risk of more violence. However, evangelical Chamulas worry that anything less means compromising fidelity to the gospel (orthodoxy); it renders their moral convictions meaningless.

Word of God Catholics in Ch'ul Vo' have a different perspective. Rather than reject or try to ignore the life-ways of fellow Chamula who are *costumbristas*, they attempt to identify and relate by expressing love and respect. Inspired by anthropological orientations from the *teologia india* movement mentioned earlier, the new approach promotes *recognition* as a way to distinguish acceptable and unacceptable customs and thus avoid an across the board rejection of all Chamula traditions. Drinking alcohol, because of its adverse effects, is still discouraged, but this is a secondary or tertiary concern. Looking at core values, Catholic Christians are able to reintroduce into their own faith communities a number of important symbols from traditional (*costumbre*) Chamula life-ways and religious praxis. Recovered practices include, for example, traditional dancing with seed rattles, the revered use of Chamula style crosses, visiting images of Saints with flowers, incense, and burning simple wax candles as prayer offerings. By using these things, Catholics promote *connection* rather than *disconnection* with Chamula *Traditionalistas*.

Recalling Girard's mimetic theory and Harrison's notion of "fractured resemblances," the return to traditional modes suggests a risky strategy. The more that Roman Catholics resemble their Traditionalist neighbors, the greater the possibility of undifferentiation and the possible threat of a loss of identity through too much sameness. However unwittingly, the strategy to narrow differences could intensify rather than prevent conflict. As Harrison (2006) has pointed out, the danger that characterizes ethnic conflict is a "mimetic misrecognition of mimesis" or a failure to see and thus recognize the need for differences that, once respected, can open up new kinds of emotional space where diversity produces a measure of peace.

In the hamlet of Ch'ul Vo' this strategy of accepting rather than rejecting customs has thus far (since 2003 at least) had mixed results. Despite occasional turmoil, it is interesting to note how once able to recognize themselves in the people they attack, many Traditionalist who once were persecutors now find their victim's way of life attractive or desirable; some join the very church community their former bosses once ordered them to attack. By reaffirming traditional life-ways, *Word of God* Catholics and Traditionalists of *costumbre* alike can better see their fellow Chamula as they are: people worth imitating, copying, appropriating—at least to a point. Because the *Word of God* Catholics, as Christians, insist upon looking, acting, and generally participating in customary life, there eventually emerges a "live and let live" policy for all groups in the hamlet of Ch'ul Vo'. Thus do they mutually generate public modes of cooperation that lead to security and peace within the hamlet.

THEOLOGICAL REFLECTIONS

Considering the complex context of strife within Maya communities, what does the reconciliation of *differences* ultimately mean? From what I have observed among the Chamula, reconciliation can sometimes happen when contending parties acknowledge "kindness"—that is to say, when they can see they are the same *kind*—human kind (*batz'i vinik* or "authentically human"). If such "kindness" is possible for some, then other Chamula groups might also be able to accept one another if disposed to a deeper level of recognition and understanding. When human beings see each other as they truly *are* (however constructed, imagined, or "essentialized" by myth, prejudice, revelation, and so forth), they no longer need to see one another as strangely "other." Looking at potential reconciliation in these terms, I believe Chamula, like any other group of people, are quite able to recognize and live with their limitations.

Looking at people superficially, in terms of mere "cultural features" is not the same as imagining them as distinct beings in an ontological sense (in this case, both groups claiming to be true or authentic *Catholics*). The spiritual notion of *recognition*, however, sets-up a framework that allows for important differences to exist, but in ways that are more meaningful than mere tolerance. Chamula no longer need to imagine themselves in ways that deny "sameness"—that is to say, as non-Catholic, non-PRI, and so forth. Profound experiences of recognition-as-reconciliation come, I theorize, when one or both sides in a conflict actually move to accept (rather than reject) their similarity. This allows them to courageously embrace rather than deny one another's differences or claims to difference.

In terms of Girard's notion of "acquisitive desire" (desiring according to the desire of another), *recognition* ultimately means cooperation. Mutual assistance, rather than rivalry, allows acting subjects to reach out for the same object cooperatively, finding ways to share it. Reconciliation follows when acquisitive desire becomes *cooperative desire*, desiring in favor of the other. Reconciliation happens not by force, therefore, but by the highly significant experience that is the *recognition of kindness*. This means developing a broader, more comprehensive view of sameness, one that promotes "both/and" cognition rather than a polarizing "either/or" mentality of imputed differences based on a denial of similarity or alikeness (Harrison 2006, 63–64).

By "restoring" a true but transformed sense of a once fractured identity, acting subjects can dare a second look (*respectar, re + specto*) at socially constructed difference(s). Reconciliation is best understood as a process that works to slow down competing desires that so easily fracture otherwise cooperative relations. As such, recognition-as-reconciliation alleviates anxieties generated from perceptions of too much (competing) semblance.

Without shadow or contrasts, it is nearly impossible to actually see *others*. Contrasts, however, if sharp enough, allow interacting subjects to see other people distinctly, and thus who they really are, even from within the givens of culturally constrained categories. The preacher and apostle Saint Paul, preaching among the non-Jews, seems to have understood the challenge of contrast: *At present, we see indistinctly, as in a mirror, but then face to face. At present, I know partially; then I shall know fully, as I am fully known.*[25] Here the apostle Paul seems to suggest that we all have a need to share the available light, if we even hope to see anything or anyone (even God).

USEFUL SCANDAL ON THE PATH TO RECONCILIATION

From a Christian perspective, reconciliation involves a positive mimetic reproduction of Christ-like *pathos* (suffering). The following of Christ implies an imitation of His *kenosis* (emptying) or giving up claims to exclusive difference, status, regard, etc. The subsequent moral action that this imitation sets in motion is one of liberation: a way out of dualisms and thus beyond conflict and violent forms of differentiation supporting "us vs. them" scenarios.

The first step beyond dualism is the recognition rather than the denial of differences. This is not an easy step, and for many amounts to something of a "stumbling block" (what the Christian scriptures refer to as a *skandelon*); yet until one trips up (or down), it remains difficult to evaluate the path ahead, let alone find the crossroads. Learning to fall down is a first requirement for those who would dare to stand upright, or who would seek to walk humbly in the "way, truth, and life" that is the Christ.

Human eyes seldom open wide, however, without a "scandal"; i.e., when reality confronts you from an unexpected perspective. In order for acting subjects to truly open their eyes (even if escaping a figurative blindness), *recognition* requires that agents reach out interactively, feel for, and somehow embrace the meaning of differences, where they come from, what their meaning might be, and so forth.

Scandal is somewhat paradoxical. How can "falling down" help someone to "stand up" or enable them to see a different path than the one previously traveled? If we consider how the Greek term *skandalon* connotes "tripping upon something substantial,"[26] it is possible to imagine how a positive opportunity can present itself from seemingly disadvantageous circumstances.

Scandal, in other words, potentially reconfigures assumptions about what constitutes social balance; however idealized, assumptions undergo modification. In contrast, by refusing to learn from the scandals of one's life or those of the real world, one can avoid an honest conversion or *catharsis*, making reconciliation all the more difficult.

Recognition, then, is the very first step. The recognition that differences not only exist, but are also meaningful is an important speed bump (*skandelon*) on the road to a more propitious identity formation. If aggression is slowed down long enough in this way, it will give pause for thought and a chance to see things distinctly. Such a pause can lead to realistic thinking. Slowing down is especially helpful for those caught-up in the mimetic frenzy of violent desire, allowing them to actually comprehend the importance of limitation step by step as boundaries form.

TURNING AROUND BEGINNING AGAIN

The traditional Christian term for this new kind of seeing is *metanoia* or "conversion." The notion means at least two things in the context of "restored differences": 1) it conveys a literal "turning around" so as to actually see things quite differently than before, but 2) it also means a paradox: where constraint (boundary, difference) implies an ample measure of freedom. As a fresh way of seeing, *recognizing* limitations and boundaries (instead of ignoring them) implies a fresh opportunity for change and renewal. It suggests that it is indeed possible to have a second, more realistic chance of life with "others"—i.e., those who can actually see one another instead of pretending not to (Girard's notion of *misrecognition* or the denial of semblance).

The possibility of bringing opposites or contraries together also means that violent forms of differentiation are not some "innate" or predetermined disposition from birth. To frame the problem in humanistic terms, learning about differences and reconciliation promotes a kind of re-socialization process where groups can literally learn from their *mis*takes. Once the stumbling begins, those who trip over Christ as the *skandelon* begin to see what they could not or would not see before. In this way, groups otherwise prone to violent boundary making can find ways to resist its alluring aspects of overly defined identity (non-ambiguous and powerful). They gain ability to embrace rather than *mis*take and deny the power of mimetic desire in human relations (here-to-fore hidden *from the foundations of the world . . .* Girard 1987; cf. Matthew 13, 35).

For the Chamula of Ch'ul Vo', reconciliation has been a slow and unsure process of coming to an awareness through *re*-cognition with all the setbacks and inconsistencies such a process entails over time. To further illustrate this thesis of *restorative difference as a propitious mimesis*, images from the Christian scriptures may help.

WE ARE HEALED BY HIS FRACTURED RESEMBLANCE

It is curious that Jesus the Christ, the Risen One, who makes all things "one in Him" and "all things new" and so forth, makes a specific point of showing to doubters his (by now, old) wounds. The strange image and presence of a fractured Jesus would seem to indicate that nothing has changed. Violence wins again, as it always seems to do. Yet, mysteriously (sacramentally), after passing twice through the *separating reality* of a locked door to a room closed by the lingering fears and anxieties of the Apostles (John 20, 19–23), but passing through without destroying the portal of *liminality*, Christ eventually invites the astonished apostle Thomas to probe the fractured reality of his visible wounds. Likewise, the Risen Christ appears elsewhere where He invites others to see Him in astonishing new ways. The outstanding example, of course, is the way He does this with the two companion disciples traveling fast away on the road to Emmaus. Perhaps in a panic, these two followers of Jesus separate themselves from those they know, differentiated or disassociated and increasingly far away from the familiar and central sphere of Jerusalem, the two disciples become "Others." As they gain distance they also increase plausible deniability regarding any semblance with the scandalous Jesus and his inglorious demise. As Jesus re-appears, and the intimacy of breaking bread closes any gap, a new relationship begins.

Evidently, the Risen One does not insist upon the removal of scandalous wounds. He does not even insist upon removing the scars which seem to so define him as the man of sorrows, the scapegoat, and the publically blameworthy of all that has gone wrong. These scars are the bodily reminder of his rejection from humankind—rejected, perhaps, for being too much like them. But it remains curious that upon resurrection the markings of scandal and separation do not disappear. Instead, these now non-painful wounds remain open, a profound semiotic reminder of how God loves into wholeness even the most fractured human reality. The image of the wounded Christ provokes an *anamnesis* (remembering) of the great Mystery: God reconciling the world to Himself, making all things new again, even after the flood of disaster.

Recognition is a key factor in these resurrection stories of God's restoring love. On the level of human semblance, nothing much has changed since human flesh is as frail and fractured as ever; yet, on a transcendent level, everything is now mysteriously different. The Christ, in resurrection, presents a powerful image of "restorative difference." The differentiation, understood within an entirely new frame (a *revealed* perspective), not only gives us pause, it draws us toward a deeper reality. It attracts human desiring to something beyond itself.

This new kind of differentiation that only a God of love can provide invites seekers into the unfathomable mystery of God's semblance with humanity. This happens through the unlikely pathway of wounds, the very marks of difference. The anthropologist Victor Turner (1969) once observed that for some tribes of Africa their boys learn to become adults when they can learn to pass through a *liminal* space; that is to say, they come to see distinctly when they cross over from one level of awareness to another. Rites of initiation are often about the rough and painful stages of real life. Mimetic ritual touches upon profound issues of separation and difference, that is to say, learning to leave one's presumed identity and daring to embrace the true Self that exists "betwixt and between"—between life as it is and life as it should be.

LEARNING THE PATTERN OF THE PASSION

In the paradoxical mystery of vulnerability, the followers of Christ eventually recognize how "by his stripes" there is strength, healing, salvation, and liberation. Christians are often in the position of identifying with the doubting apostle Thomas—one who is so close to Christ he cannot see Him, nor even the truth of his wounds. Christians are in many ways like the apostle Thomas, called simultaneously into and beyond semblance by learning to touch the marks of difference. Recognizing this truth, Thomas begins to see; he begins to recognize with sudden alarm that new life is possible not only in Christ's visible wounds, but through his own as well. The Apostle cries out in recognition of a *restored difference*: "My Lord and my God!"

The notion of a "restorative difference" means that Christians accept the fact that they are not God, however much they are like God. Divine action does not destroy but restores the felt-sense of boundary that becomes a transformative relationship, a new way of being. It is not a hard and fast boundary (exclusive); through Christ the Lord, "boundaries" become porous and purifying (inclusive). Here, then, is a truly propitious mimesis, a positive or good imitation of the way God in Christ restores all things to Himself. By His passion, He motivates others to "act like him, be like him" thus ending the separation between human and divine, while creating a new heaven and a new earth (Rev 21, 1–5; 2 Pt 3,13) and a "universal restoration" (Acts 3, 21).

In this theological sense of ending separations and reconciling differences, the experience of "boundary" is vital. A possible image of this liminal space reveals itself in the Gospel story of the wealthy man who, suddenly conscious of his negative fate, cries out to Abraham across the eternal divide. The patriarch is holding the poor man Lazarus in his bosom, the victim *par excellent.* This scene suggests the wounds of Christ, i.e., the "victim" who reveals the boundaries of the all too familiar "other side" (the reality people often flee from in fear and apprehension rather than bravely try to face or embrace). Without such a boundary or distinction, however, it is arguably more difficult to see what really matters. Death itself represents the great abyss—the lasting separation, or divide. The reality of the "in-between" (symbolized by Lazarus as a fractured, poor person, but redeemed) is worth paying attention to. To follow the pattern of the Passion, however, suggests a way to cross over and thus to embrace differences rather than to deny them, just as the rich man might have seen Lazarus when he had the chance to open his eyes through an awareness that could only have come from recognition.

CHAMULA RESTORATION

Among the Chamula Tzotzil, there is some evidence that communities have begun to focus upon their own wounds as they recognize the wounds of Christ. As hope grows, they desire a true reconciliation of differences in a new kind of sameness or solidarity, the human semblance of kindness. This hope promises redeemed or repaired fractures that would comprise a new kind of common unity. Even though the wounds or scars would still be visible, a *restorative difference* would not only be difficult to deny but impossible to fracture anew.

If this understanding is correct, it is arguably true that authentic reconciliation in society does not come from removing fences. Nor will reconciliation ever likely come from establishing yet wider fields of unmitigated or liberal imitation (as in democratic or egalitarian sameness where everyone supposedly shares alike without hindrance). A lasting resolution of conflicts is not likely from merely blending or blurring extant differences and so have them disappear altogether. On the contrary, an efficacious reconciliation does not destroy fences or those who make them, but *mends* or restores the fences of meaningful demarcations. In colloquial parlance, *good fences make good neighbors.* This does not mean literal "fences" but rather a true sense of limit or differentiation—a process of understanding through distinctions and contrasts.

Indeed, when it comes to the complexity of human interaction, it is better to have some boundary markers than none at all. Boundaries (the edge of one thing and the beginning of another) are often counter-productive when they are hard and impervious. The Risen Christ invites the Apostle Thomas to *probe* his glorious wounds, i.e., the transfigured marks originally meant to shame and alienate. Similarly, the role of the Magdalene in this resurrection story (John 20, 11–18) seems to close the gap of previous boundaries of difference and separation. In spite of the instruction "not to touch" the Magdalene finds herself suddenly a co-equal "apostle"—one sent to proclaim the *Risen* Christ as Good News. Her new role begins, however, in a liminal place "here" and a transcendent other place "there." "Where I am going, you cannot come," (John 8, 21), is a clear statement, perhaps, of a healthy boundary formation, and the profound need to first suffer the transformation/conversion process that leads to reconciliation.

TRANSFIGURING RATHER THAN ELIMINATING DIFFERENCES

Good fences and healthy boundaries appear to be part of the Divine plan. Yet, Christians often miss the point by trying too hard to become like God (or gods) instead of allowing the Incarnate mystery to unfold. Perhaps this tendency explains Simon Peter's misperception at the Transfiguration on Mount Tabor (Mt 17, 1). Amazed, Peter elects to elaborate clear distinctions, making separations for Moses, Elijah, and for Christ that only avoid the mystery of the "beloved Son." This misperception seems representative of many religions, founded as they are through discrimination rather than transformation.

For the Chamula the slow and delicate process that is recognition-as-reconciliation entails a new *imitatio* for their everyday lives. It means striving to emulate Christ's refusal to blame his captors, or His refusal to create scapegoats and victims through fear, revenge, resentment. Instead of replicating the way others *refuse* to see the dangers of copying, (the mimetic misrecognition of mimesis), actual *reconciliation* is about doing just the opposite; it is a refusing to refuse recognizing others. *Scandal*, and the subsequent experience of changing one's mind, can teach would-be antagonists how to *recognize* the pattern of their traps. The most important trap to recognize is how imitative rivalries arise in the first place, thus pausing long enough to reconsider a situation. Once the parties to conflict are aware of mimetic desire, they can see the importance and meaning of boundaries, the redeeming significance of differences. *Reconciliation* happens not by getting rid of differences but by learning to honor their purpose or meaning.

As I infer through the ethnographic examples, restorative difference is not about advocating divisiveness, discrimination, or new elite forms of separatism. On the contrary, it is about seeing existing demarcations as wounds currently bleeding, but viewing them in a new, redeeming way. This means that what was a once a fractured or disconnected semblance has become, in Christ, a *re*-semblance, and thus a restorative difference. Denied similarities (with God, with neighbor) and the pieces of a fractured human-divine reality begin to fit together again, however imperfectly. By looking closely, keen observers can *recognize* their own image in the mystery of Christ's wounds and through the unifying love that only reconciled fractures can inspire.

Reconciled to live with porous rather than solid boundaries, it is possible now for the Chamula of Ch'ul Vo' to pass from one level of understanding (separation) to another (the recognition of community). Like human beings everywhere, the journey that both Catholic groups now share is a life-long sojourn of learning respect, recognition, and hopefully, liberation.

REFERENCES

"Fray Bartolomé de Las Casas," Center For Human Rights. 2001. *Donde Muere El Agua: Expulsiones y derechos humanos en San Juan Chamula*. San Cristóbal de Las Casas, México: Fray Bartolomé de Las Casas Center for Human Rights (Centro de Derechos Humanos Fray Bartolomé de Las Casas).

Barth, Fredrik, and Universitetet i Bergen, eds. 1969. Ethnic groups and boundaries. The social organization of culture difference. (Results of a symposium held at the University of Bergen, 23rd to 26th February 1967). Boston: Little.

———. 1958. *Naven, a survey of the problems suggested by a composite picture of the culture of a New Guinea tribe drawn from three points of view*. Stanford, CA: Stanford University Press.

Burguete Cal y Mayor, Aracely. 2000. *Agua que nace y muere: sistemas normativos indígenas y disputas por el agua en Chamula y Zinacantán*. México: Programa sobre Investigaciones Multidisciplinarias sobre Mesoamérica y el Sureste, UNAM.

Chance, John K and William B. Taylor. 1985. "Confradías and Cargos: An Historical Perspective on the Mesoamerican Civil-Religious Hierarchy." *American Ethnologist* 12:1–26.

Chance, John K. 1990. "Changes in Twentieth-Century Mesoamerican Cargo Systems." In "Class, Politics, and Popular Religion in Mexico and Central America." Edited by L.S.a.J. Dow. Pp. 27–42. Washington, DC: American Anthropological Association.

Cleary, Edward L. 1997. "Birth of Latin American Indigenous Theology." In *Crosscurrents in Indigenous Spirituality*. Edited by G. Cook. Leiden, New York, Koln: E. J. Brill.

Cleary, Edward L., and Timothy J. Steigenga. 2004. *Resurgent voices in Latin America: indigenous peoples, political mobilization, and religious change*. New Brunswick, N.J.: Rutgers University Press.

Collier, George A. 1994. The New Politics of Exclusion: Antecedents to the Rebellion in Mexico. *Dialectical Anthropology* 19(1):1–44.

Collier, George Allen, and Elizabeth Lowery Quaratiello. 2005. *Basta!: land and the Zapatista rebellion in Chiapas*. Oakland, CA: Food First Books.

Collier, M. J., ed. 2000. *Constituting Cultural Difference through Discourse*. London: Sage.

Cook, G., ed. 1997. *Crosscurrents in Indigenous Spirituality*. Leiden, New York, Koln: E. J. Brill.

Early, John D. 2006. *The Maya and Catholicism: an encounter of worldviews*. Gainesville, FL: University Press of Florida.

Eber, Christine Engla. 2000. *Women & alcohol in a highland Maya town: water of hope, water of sorrow*. Austin: University of Texas Press.

Eller, Jack David. 2006. *Violence and Culture: A Cross-Cultural and Interdisciplinary Approach*. Wadsworth Publishing.

Enloe, Cynthia. 1996. "Religion and Ethnicity." Pp. 197–201 in *Ethnicity*. Edited by J. Hutchinson and A.D. Smith. Oxford ; New York: Oxford University Press.

Estrada Martínez, Rosa Isabel. 1995. *El problema de las expulsiones en las comunidades indígenas de los altos de Chiapas y los derechos humanos: segundo informe*. México, D.F.: Comisión Nacional de Derechos Humanos.

Fischer, Edward F. 2001. *Cultural logics and global economies: Maya identity in thought and practice*. 1st ed. Austin: University of Texas Press.

Fischer, Edward F., and R. McKenna Brown. 1996. *Maya Cultural Activism in Guatemala*. 1st ed, Critical reflections on Latin America series. Austin: University of Texas Press/Institute of Latin American Studies.

Freud, Sigmund. 1945 [1921] . *Group Psychology and the Analysis of the Ego*. London: Hogarth Press - for the Institute of Psycho-Analysis.

Freud, Sigmund, and Joan Riviere. 1930. *Civilization and its discontents*. London: L. & Virginia Woolf at the Hogarth press.

García Méndez, José Andrés. 2008. *Chiapas Para Cristo - Diversidad Doctrinal y Cambio Político en el Campo Religioso Chiapaneco*. DF, Mexico: MC Editores.

Girard, René. 1965. *Deceit, desire, and the novel; self and other in literary structure*. Baltimore: Johns Hopkins Press.

———. 1977. *Violence and the sacred*. Translated by Patrick Gregory. Baltimore: Johns Hopkins University Press.

———. 1978. *"To double business bound": Essays on Literature, Mimesis, and Anthropology*. Baltimore: Johns Hopkins University Press.

———. 1979. "Interdividual Psychology." *Denver Quarterly* 14:3–19.

———. 1987. *Things hidden since the foundation of the world*. London: Athlone.

———. 1991. *A theater of envy: William Shakespeare*. New York: Oxford University Press.

Girard, René, and Robert Doran, eds. 2008. Mimesis and Theory: Essays on Literature and Criticism, 1953–2005. Stanford, CA: Stanford University Press.

Gómez Sántiz, María Magdalena, and Centro Estatal de Lenguas Arte y Literatura Indígenas (Chiapas Mexico). 2005. *J-Iloletik: médicos tradicionales de los altos de Chiapas*. Tuxtla Gutiérrez, Chiapas: Centro Estatal de Lenguas, Arte y Literatura Indígenas, Gobierno del Estado de Chiapas.

Gossen, Gary H. 1983. "A Modern Maya Diaspora: Out-migration and the Cultural Persistence of San Juan Chamula, Chiapas." *Mesoamérica* 5(June):253–276.

———. 1999. *Telling Maya tales: Tzotzil identities in modern Mexico*. New York: Routledge.

Gossen, Gary H., and Miguel León Portilla. 1993. *South and Meso-American Native Spirituality: From the Cult of the Feathered Serpent to the Theology of Liberation*. New York: Crossroad.

Harrison, Simon. 2006. *Fracturing Resemblances: Identity and Mimetic Conflict in Melanesia and the West*. New York: Berghahn Books.

Hurley, Susan, and Nick Chater. 2005. *Perspectives on Imitation: From Neuroscience to Social Science*. Volume 1. Cambridge, MA: MIT Press.

INEGI. 2005. II Conteo de Población y Vivienda.

Irribarren Pascal, o.p., Pablo. 2002 [1980]. *Misión Chamula-Experiencia de trabajo pastoral de los años 1966-1977 en Chamula*. Pp. 55. San Cristóbal de Las Casas, Chiapas, México: Archivo Diocesano, Diócesis de San Cristobal de Las Casas.

Knight, Alan, and W. G. Pansters. 2005. *Caciquismo in Twentieth-Century Mexico*. London: Institute for the Study of the Americas.

Kovic, Christine Marie. 2005. *Mayan Voices for Human Rights: Displaced Catholics in Highland Chiapas*. Austin: University of Texas Press.

Krohn-Hansen, Christian. 1997. "The Anthropology and Ethnography of Political Violence." *Journal of Peace Research* 34(2):233–240.

López Hernández, Eleazar. 2000. *Teología India: Antología*. Cochabamba, Bolivia; Buenos Aires, Ar.: Editorial Verbo Divino: Universidad Católica Boliviana, Instituto Superior de Estudios Teológicos; Editorial Guadalupe.

López Meza, Antonio. 2002. *Sistema religioso-político y las expulsiones en Chamula*. Tuxtla Gutiérrez, Chiapas: Consejo Estatal para la Cultura y las Artes de Chiapas, Polyfórum Mesoamericano, Gobierno del Estado de Chiapas.

Marcus, George E., and Michael M. J. Fischer. 1986. *Anthropology as Cultural Critique: An Experimental Moment in the Human Sciences*. Chicago: University of Chicago Press.

Martínez García, Carlos. 2008. *El Martirio del Miguel Caxlán—vida, muerte y legado de un líder chamula protestante*. Puebla, Mexico: Editorial Cajica.

Morquecho, Gaspar. 1992. Los indios en un proceso de organización. La Organización Indígena de los Altos de Chiapas, 1981–1991, Antropología Social, UNACH, Universidad Autónoma de Chiapas.

Morquecho, Gaspar y Dolores Aramoni. 1997. "La otra mejilla ...pero armada. el recurso de las armas en manos de los expulsados de San Juan Chamula" In *Chiapas: el factor religioso*. Pp. 235–292. Bosques de Echegaray, Edo de México: Revista Académico para el Estudio Estudio Científico de las Religiones.

Moscoso Pastrana, Prudencio. 1972. *Jacinto Pérez, "Pajarito," el último líder chamula*. Tuxtla Gutiérrez: Gobierno del Estado de Chiapas.

Nash, June C. 2001. *Mayan Visions: The Quest for Autonomy in an Age of Globalization*. New York ; London: Routledge.

———. 2007. "Consuming Interests: Water, Rum, and Coca-Cola from Ritual Propitiation to Corporate Expropriation in Highland Chiapas." *Cultural Anthropology* 22(4):621–639.

Pérez López, Enrique. 1997. *Chamula: un pueblo tzotzil*. San Cristóbal de Las Casas, Chiapas: Gobierno del Estado de Chiapas, Consejo Estatal para la Cultura y las Artes de Chiapas, Centro Estatal de Lenguas, Arte y Literatura Indígenas.

Pitt-Rivers, Julian. 1967. "Words and Deeds: The Ladinos of Chiapas." Man 2(1):71–86.

Pozas, Ricardo. 1977. Chamula. 2 vols. México: Instituto Nacional Indigenista.

Riches, David, ed. 1986. *The Anthropology of Violence*. Oxford, UK ; New York, NY, USA: Blackwell.

Rivera Farfán, C. 2000. "Expressiones del Cristianismo en Chiapas." In *Revista* "Pueblos y Fronteras," Vol. 1.

Robledo Hernández, Gabriela. 1997. *Disidencia y religión: los expulsados de San Juan Chamula*. San Cristóbal de Las Casas, Chiapas: Universidad Autónoma de Chiapas Facultad de Ciencias Sociales: Asociación Mexicana de Población.

Ruiz García, Bishop Samuel. 1990. "Ponencia - La Sabiduría Indígena." In *Teología India -- Primer encuentro Taller Latinoamericano*. CENAMI (El Centro Nacional de Ayuda a las Misiones Indígenas, México, D.F.).

Rus, Jan. 1983. "Whose Caste War? Indians, Ladinos, and the 'Caste War.'" Pp. 127–168 in *Spaniards and Indians in Southeastern Mesoamerica: Essays on the History of Ethnic Relations*. Edited by M.J.M.a.R. Wasserstrom. Latin American studies series. Lincoln: University of Nebraska Press.

———. 1994. "The 'Comunidad Revolucionaria Institucional': The Subversion of Native Government in Chiapas, 1936–1968." Pp. 265–300 in *Everyday Forms of State Formation: Revolution and the Negotiation of Rule in Modern Mexico*. Edited by G.M.J.a.D. Nugent. Durham, NC: Duke University Press.

———. 1995. "Local Adaptation to Global Change: The Reordering of Native Society in Highland Chiapas, Mexico, 1974–1994." In *European Review of Latin American and Caribbean Studies* 58(June):71–78.

———. 2005. "The Struggle against Indigenous Caciques in Highland Chiapas: Dissent, Religion and Exile in Chamula, 1965–1977." Pp. 169–200 in *Caciquismo in Twentieth Century Mexico*. Edited by A.K.a.W. Pansters. London: Institute for the Study of the Americas.

Rus, Jan and George Allen Collier. 2003. "A Generation of Crisis in the Central Highlands of Chiapas: The Cases of Chamula and Zinacantan, 1974–2000." Pp. 27–61 in *Mayan lives, Mayan Utopias: The Indigenous Peoples of Chiapas and the Zapatista Rebellion*. Edited by J. Rus, R.A. Hernández Castillo, and S.L. Mattiace. Lanham, Md.; Oxford: Rowman & Littlefield.

Rus, Jan, Rosalva Aída Hernández Castillo, and Shannan L. Mattiace. 2003. *Mayan Lives, Mayan Utopias: The Indigenous Peoples of Chiapas and the Zapatista Rebellion*. Lanham, Md. ; Oxford: Rowman & Littlefield.

Rus, Jan, and Robert Wasserstrom. 1980. "Civil-Religious Hierarchies in Central Chiapas: A Critical Perspective." *American Ethnologist* 7(3):466–478.

Sax, William S. 1998. "The Hall of Mirrors: Orientalism, Anthropology, and the Other." *American Anthropologist* 100(2):292–301.

Schmidt, Bettina E., and Ingo W. Schroder, eds. 2001. *Anthropology of Violence and Conflict*. London and New York: Routledge.

Schreuder, Alan John. 2001. *A History of the Rise of the Chamula Church*. School of World Mission, Fuller Theological Seminary.
Simmel, Georg. 1955. *Conflict-The Web of Group-Affiliations*. Glencoe, IL: Free Press.
Sterk, Vernon Jay. 1992. *The Dynamics of Persecution*. School of World Mission. Fuller Theological Seminary.
Stewart, Pamela J., and Andrew Strathern. 2002. *Violence: Theory and Ethnography*. London ; New York: Continuum.
StudyLight.org. 2013. *The New Testament Greek Lexicon*. http:// www.studylight.org/lex/grk/view.cgi?number=46).
Turner, Victor 1969. *The Ritual Process: Structure and Anti-structure*. Chicago: Aldine Pub. CO.
Warren, Kay B. 1989. *The Symbolism of Subordination: Indian Identity in a Guatemalan town*. Austin: University of Texas Press.
———. 1998. Indigenous Movements and their Critics: Pan-Maya activism in Guatemala. Princeton, NJ: Princeton University Press.
———. 2001. "Rethinking Bi-Polar Constructions of Ethnicity." *Journal of Latin American Anthropology* 6 (2):90–105.
Wasserstrom, Robert. 1983. *Class and Society in Central Chiapas*. Berkeley: University of California Press.
Watanabe, John M. 1995. "Unimagining the Maya: Anthropologists, Others, and the Inescapable Hubris of Authorship." *Bulletin of Latin American Research* 14 (1):25–45.
Wolf, Eric R. 1982. *Europe and the People without History*. Berkeley: University of California Press.
Wolf, Eric R., et al. 1994. "Perilous Ideas: Race, Culture, People [and Comments and Reply]." *Current Anthropology* 35(1):1–12.
Xenos, Nicholas. 1989. *Scarcity and Modernity*. London & New York: Routledge.

NOTES

1. Harrison (2006, 63–64) elaborates three configurations of Self /Other social relations: (1) "Difference-as-inferiority," where the cultural Other is made to represent censored and disclaimed attributes of the Self, a kind of "anti-mimesis" or process of projection of everything the Self disowns or rejects; an anti-Model. (2) "Difference-as-superiority," where the cultural Other is part of a cultural pattern of emulation of another's ethnic identity, valorized in a positive or idealistic way as a Model. (3) "Difference-as-equality," where the Other is conceived as essentially similar culturally to the Self, sharing common features of identity at some inclusive level. As Harrison points out (2006, 63–64), It is this latter which corresponds to Freud's portrayal of the narcissism of minor differences, in which groups differentiate themselves with whom they are also closely identified, doing so by negating or diminishing these commonalities in some way.

2. Freud observes that this is especially true, when people come to see that what they have in common with others serves as a threat to their particular sense of identity. Using a basic idea from Freud (cf. 1945, 101; 1930, 114) Harrison (2006:2) emphasizes a fundamental phenomenon within conflict relations, i.e., the *narcissism of minor differences.*

3. For a fuller understanding of Girard's ideas on mimetic rivalry as a source of conflict, see Girard 1965, 1977 1978, 1987, 1991.

4. On this point, Harrison (2006, 8) notes similar perspectives from a number of scholars, including Collier 2000; Marcus and Fischer 1986; and Wolf 1982.

5. See for examples, the published work of CDHFBLC 2001; García Méndez 2008; López Meza 2002; Martinez García 2008; Morquecho 1997; Rus 2005; Schreuder 2001; Sterk 1992.

6. See, for example, Gossen 1993; 1999; Irribarren 1980; López Meza 2002; Moscoso Pastrana 1972; Pérez López 1990; Pozas 1962.

7. For some important "external" aspects of strife involving Chamula, see the story of the leader known as "Pajarito" in Moscoso Pastrana (1972). For similar conflicts, see also Gossen

(1993) on Chamula perceptions of the "Other" and Rus (1983) on the so-called 'Caste War" of 1869.

8. Given the public nature of many conflicts that local people know from human rights reports, newspaper articles, or government documents, I have collapsed two hamlets into one, and have changed the names of people and places. My precaution reflects both ethnographic ethics and pastoral concern for confidentiality and what remains an ongoing, if vulnerable process of reconciliation within communities.

9. According to recent census data from México (INEGI 2010), there are 76,941 Chamula living in the municipality of San Juan Chamula, up from 67,085 in 2005. The entire municipality is comprised of 145 official hamlets and villages. These numbers do not include large populations of displaced Chamula and their growing families, nor does it count those who have migrated beyond the highlands, Gossen's so-called "Diasporas" (see Gossen 1983, 1999). In any case, the Chamula, estimated at more than 100,000 population, constitute the largest single ethnic grouping among the Maya Tzotzil speaking peoples of Chiapas, México.

10. For a comparative perspective on approaches to form and content in religious expressions among Maya peoples, see John D. Early (2006).

11. See Christine Kovic's book, *Mayan Voices for Human Rights – Displaced Catholics in Highland Chiapas*. Austin: University of Texas Press; 2005. For an additional contextual view of conflicts among the Tzotzil, see the work of Jan Rus and George Collier: "A Generation of Crisis in the Central Highlands of Chiapas: The Cases of Chamula and Zinacantan, 1974–2000, " in Rus *et al.* 2003.

12. Additionally, there are some non-Christian groups such as Seventh Day Adventists, Jehovah's Witnesses, and the Mormons. From the point of view of the *costumbre* religious expression, these groups are all the same, known as "Evangélicos," which includes the Roman Catholic practitioners since they all reflect a connection to the Word of God or Bible. According to the 2010 census for Chiapas, only 58% self-identify themselves as *Catholics*. See http:// cuentame.inegi.gob.mx/monografias/informacion/chis/poblacion/diversidad.aspx?tema=me& e=07

13. "Peoplehood" is Eric Wolf's alternative term for "ethnicity." See Wolf *et al* (1994).

14. There is confusion around the meaning of "usos y costumbres" (local uses and customary traditions). Arguments about what constitutes tradition revolve around particular organizing mechanisms such as the "cófradia" (ritual brotherhoods) and "cargo" (burden/responsibility) system of civil and/or religious obligations (office). People with *cargos* serve the *templo* (church) and *la comunidad* (municipal and state authority) or *jteclum*. However, what was once thought essentially unchanged since pre-Colonial times is actually a constantly evolving response to the circumstances of political economy and prevailing discourses of power and authority. For a revisionist view, see Chance 1990; Chance and Taylor 1985; Rus and Wasserstrom 1980.

15. See Gabriela Robledo Hernández, 1997. For an official government perspective, see Estrada Martinez 1995.

16. Many such incidents are documented by the local human rights organization, Centro de Derechos Humanos, "Fray Bartolomé de Las Casas." (CDHFBLC). For more information on these and other similar violations, see the Center's report "Donde Muere El Agua" (tr: *Where the water dies*) that discusses the historical, political, economic, and juridical contexts of violations in the municipality of San Juan Chamula; consult the link at http:// www.laneta.apc.org/cdhbcasas/index.htm.

17. See Freddy López, correspondent (1995) *Cuatro Poder*. San Juan Chamula. The double headline reads "San Juan Chamula—Vieron que su estrategia de resistencia pacifica no había dado resultados. Evangélicos imitaron al EZLN tomando las armas."

18. For an historical perspective on the development of class and society in San Juan Chamula, see Wasserstrom 1983.

19. For background on the development of political bossism in Mexico, see Knight and Pansters 2005; for Chamula, see Rus 1994, 2005; Rus and Collier 2003.

20. On the formation of monopolies and competitive interests among elite Chamula families, see López Meza 2002: 165–173; see also Nash 2007.

21. For a similar development in the neighboring indigenous municipality of Zinacantán, see Collier 1994.

22. For an in-depth perspective on the socio-economic challenges facing the Chamula and other indigenous peoples of the region, see Burguete Cal y Mayor 2000; Collier and Quaratiello 2005; Rus and Collier 2003; Nash 2001; and Rus et al. 2003.

23. For a larger discussion on ethnic identity formations in Mesoamerica, see Castañeda 2004; Fischer and Brown 1996; Fischer 2001; Gossen 1999; Warren 1989, 1998, 2001; Watanabe 1995.

24. I have participated in a number of these conferences since 1995. For examples of literature from what is largely a grass-roots movement, see Lopez Hernández 2000. See also the series on *Teologia India* conferences 1991, 1993, and 1994 and the *Ponencia* by Bishop Samuel Ruiz Garcia 1990. For analysis of the movement in the larger context of Latin America, see Cleary 1997, Cook 1997, as well as the essays edited by Cleary and Steigenga 2004.

25. 1 Cor 13, 12. Cited from online version of the *New American Bible* 1991 [1986, 1970]. Confraternity of Christian Doctrine, Inc., Washington, DC. [http://www.usccb.org/nab/bible/1corinthians/1corinthians13.htm].

26. *Skandalon*, as defined by The New Testament Greek Lexicon at StudyLight.org. (http://www.studylight.org/lex/grk/view.cgi?number=46).

Conclusion

Vern Neufeld Redekop and Thomas Ryba

In the Introduction, we stated that a new conceptual *Gestalt* emerges in these chapters, one not fully integrated in a formal way but showing a clear understanding of some of the challenges and possibilities for dealing with the deep divisions, enmity, hatred, and other effects of violence.

We are now in a position to explore some aspects of this "conceptual *Gestalt*" with greater clarity. We will look at the following intertwined concepts in the light of the contributions of this volume: truth-telling, hermeneutics, orientation of blessing, response to oppression, deliberate mimetic modeling, hospitality, role of religion, and complexity.

TRUTH-TELLING

Given the horrors of the violence and the many aspects of woundedness and loss suffered by the victims, making the truth public is of vital significance. Victims want the truth acknowledged and never forgotten so that the same things will not happen again. Perpetrators of violence can be extremely reluctant to own up to the truth. This may be because of an ongoing hermeneutics of justification—they think that what they did was warranted—or because of the potential shame and guilt that are implied. One can almost feel the agony around telling the truth in the chapters by Morrow (ch. 14) and Wandinger (ch. 18). In Northern Ireland, for victims to tell the truth is uncomfortable, because the implication is that someone did something terribly wrong. Where there is a tacit denial of wrong-doing, truth becomes a difficult truth. Truth about sexual abuse of children by leaders in the Church is the difficult truth that popes and other leaders have struggled with—not always successfully as Wandinger points out. Alluding to this difficult truth in prayers for forgiveness and public apologies has been a complicated matter; the factors that Wandinger alludes to could well resonate in many other instances because there are vested interests who do not wish to own up to these truths. But yet we see from the chapter by Stirbys (ch. 16) that the expression and acknowledgment of the difficult truths about the horrific experience of residential school survivors is very important for victims. Thus, telling the truth and framing it constructively can function redemptively for victims as was the case for Seada, whose mother told her the truth about command rape during the war (ch. 17).

HERMENEUTICS

A theme which winds through many of the chapters is that how we interpret events, communications, roles, and value-laden texts has a significant role, perhaps even a central role, to play in reconciliation processes. The more we become conscious of this, the more we have choices as to how to interpret what is happening. Truth has levels to it. There are raw data of the event. There is the connection of the data with what happened before and after—the initial meaning that is located within narrative. Finally, there is the meaning ascribed to or derived from what happened (cf. Ricoeur 1984; Redekop 2002, ch. 9). Weaving these together with whatever coherence is warranted, while respecting the complex paradoxes and limitations, is the stuff of hermeneutics. The hermeneutical enterprise can either be oriented toward justifying violence or contributing toward mimetic structures of blessing, as Redekop describes it (ch. 4).

For a concrete example, let us turn to the final case described by Kiraly (ch. 17); namely, that of a child of command rape by men of the enemy identity group. In this instance, the mother chose to start early on with a proclamation of her truth. Alongside that truth-telling was the valence of blessing she passed on to the daughter. What emerged was a re-interpretation of the significance of that event such that the daughter could frame her identity as a bridge-builder, based on her very DNA, as being composite of two antagonistic identity groups.

Our communal identity as hermeneutical creatures is central to the argument of Richardson and Frost (ch. 10). The value-added sense that they bring is that hermeneutics takes place in the context of our relational ontology. That means that how we interpret what is going on is always influencing and being influenced by those with whom we are in relation. Even within the context of the scapegoat-based reconciliation described by Girard, Praeg argues persuasively that it is how the event is interpreted and narrated that makes all the difference (ch. 11). The sense of peace following the scapegoat act comes about as people acknowledge a sense of awe and togetherness and *interpret* this as being associated with the action taken against the scapegoat, who, in time, is re-interpreted as being the hero or god associated with the emergence of a peaceful reality. Praeg illustrates these dynamics by showing how (in the South African context), the victims of the "necklace" killings are now framed as hero-martyrs (ch. 11).

There are also some rather surprising hermeneutical twists and turns exemplifying the potential of hermeneutical creativity in a relational context. First, Webb turns to Hinduism and Buddhism to delve into what a metaphorical concept of sacrifice might mean in the Christian letter to the Hebrews (ch. 9). Through the image of fire, and reference to a fire god, he finds new meaning: associating the "sacrifice" of Jesus as letting go of acquisitive mimetic desires. Second, Menon, a Hindu in conversation with the discourse of reconciliation finds a new, life-giving interpretation of *karma* (ch. 13). Often *karma* is associated with a type of fatalism that suggests that because of what has gone before—the build up of *vasanas*, and the binding force of *gunas*, basic forces of life—what happens is inevitable. In her reinterpretation, *karma* entails a capacity to change the trajectory of one's life path. Every moment becomes a time for potential change of orientation, intentions, and actions. This resonates with Thomson's (ch. 1) concept of *metanoia*—change, transformation, or repentance (see Newman 2010 for *teshuvah*, a Hebrew conceptual equivalent).

Hodge (ch.15) emphasizes how pivotal hermeneutics, and with it the public framing of truth, can be. By interpreting the death of religious figures in East Timor as martyrdom, as witnessing to a truth, the Church of that country was able to channel the impact of these killings toward resistance to an oppressive regime.

Rolland (ch. 19) shows how a true recognition of the situation of one's Other can lead to a mutual respect of differences and the reconciliation of identity-based conflict. This kind of recognition is part of the hermeneutical enterprise.

ORIENTATION OF BLESSING

Following Redekop (ch. 4), an orientation of blessing is one aspect of a mimetic structure of blessing in which parties contribute to the mutual well-being of one another. Obviously, the willingness to listen in the interest of reconciliation requires that one is oriented toward wanting reconciliation. There is a mutually reinforcing dialectic that occurs between a hermeneutics of blessing and an orientation of blessing. One can start with an orientation of blessing which leads one to interpret texts and events in a blessing-conducive way. On the other hand, the use of a hermeneutics of blessing leads one to teachings of blessing, which in turn inspire and strengthen an orientation of blessing. Chapters by most of the contributors could be framed as teachings of blessing, in that they provide a basis for attitudes and actions that contribute to reconciliation. They provide a social imaginary for constructive relations in that they first foreground relationships as being central to human ontology and suggest ways in which those relationships can be transformed to enhance life. For instance, the sustained argument of Thomson (ch. 1) for *aphetic* mimesis as an essential part of our humanity, from hominization onwards, provides a new insight—we can learn to let go of negative feelings, desires, and attitudes. Webb (ch. 9) associates the holding on to acquisitive desires with the creation of a "false self." Putting these together suggests that we have a choice and, hence, a capacity to release ourselves from mimetic rivalries and obsessions that can make our lives miserable and can prompt us to violence. This is corroborated by the sense of choice Menon (ch. 13) opens up, so we can decide to let go of the sources of resentment, jealousy, and impotent hatred that Girard unmasks in his study of literature (1976).

NON-VIOLENT RESPONSE TO OPPRESSION

One context in which it is difficult to begin to think about reconciliation, or any of the related topics such as forgiveness or love, is that of ongoing domination and oppression. Such was the context of Jesus—the Jewish nation had been overrun by the Roman Empire and the domination system was kept intact through violence. As Walter Wink points out (see Hess, ch. 7), Jesus advocated a creative response which would maintain the dignity and agency of the victim and at the same time draw attention to the injustice, often in a symbolic way. Smith builds on this idea (ch. 8), saying that this approach can become an ongoing improvisational process. Kiraly's example of the victim of rape (ch. 17) exemplifies how her own telling of the truth and giving a sense of pride to her daughter bolstered her own dignity and drew attention to the injustice of what had happened. Hodge's example of an oppressive event framed as martyrdom, with all the attendant meaning attached to it, has the characteristic of showing up the injustices of an oppressive system. To have a capacity for a creative response to injustice addresses the key need to achieve a sense of justice.

DELIBERATE MIMETIC MODELING

Moore introduces the term "mimetic modeling". It is an essential concept in his framework for Religious Leader Engagement on the part of military chaplains. As they model openness and respect for religious leaders from different camps, these leaders start contagiously respecting and listening to one another. This is but one form of "loving mimesis"—desiring the full subjectivity of the other (Adams 2000). Once mimetic modeling as a concept is introduced, it raises the possibility that all of us can become conscious of the way in which we become models for one another. The various chapters can be seen as tools to make us conscious of how we can deliberately take steps that enhance the potential for reconciliation by modeling attitudes, orientations, and behaviors that could inspire a positive contagion.

HOSPITALITY

Goodhart, drawing on Levinas, shows how a basic, almost primal, sense of hospitality is an essential part of our responsibility to our Other (ch. 2). For him, this hospitality is an opening up of ourselves to the Other—to let the Other become part of our lives. Moore interprets this in a more concrete fashion when he describes how military chaplains can seed reconciliation among religious leaders of antagonistic identity groups through a ministry of reconciliation (ch. 12). Concrete hospitality—in the traditional sense of breaking bread together—has its own symbolic importance. And in the *doing* of the hospitality there is concomitant modeling of the kind of ontological hospitality that Goodhart describes. Delicata offers yet another take on hospitality, putting it in the context of the global village and our electronic interconnectedness (ch. 5). She helps us conceive of a virtual hospitality modeled on the concrete practice, yet having ontological overtones.

RELIGION

Though religion is not a theme of these chapters, *per se*, it is a significant sub-text. As such, it provides a particular context for the work of reconciliation, as conceptual source to understand aspects of reconciliation, and a source of teachings that motivate initiatives of reconciliation.

Religion as a context includes people as members of religious bodies who are victims, perpetrators, or third party interveners. In Hodges's Timor Leste, Catholics were clearly victims (ch. 15). Wandinger focuses on religious perpetrators of sexual abuse (ch. 18). In Rolland's analysis there were two Catholic groups with "fractured resemblances" who were reconciled to "restorative differences" (ch. 19). Moore develops the role of chaplains who are third parties working with religious leaders representing groups in conflict (ch. 12). There are religious overtones to the conflict between India and Pakistan (Menon, ch. 13) and in the tragic use of church-run residential schools (Stirbys, ch. 16).

Behind Levinas's is concept of the face to which Goodhart refers, is the theme of *panim*, or face, within the Hebrew Bible (ch. 2). Behind Thomson's development of *aphetic* mimesis is the New Testament concept of *aphesis* as forgiveness (ch. 1). Redekop likewise draws inspiration from the Hebrew *berakah*, the word for blessing (ch. 4). Delicata grounds friendship and hospitality in theological categories and Pahl find hope for a more peaceful world in the irenic orientation of the majority of adherents world religions (ch. 6). Webb grounds his analysis of sacrifice in religious texts (ch. 9).

Charting a bold path toward a justice-seeking response to violent structures, Hess (ch. 7), via Wink, and Smith (ch. 8) outline a creative, nonviolent approach to peace based on teachings of Jesus. Wandinger explores the complex and agonizing path toward forgiveness, based on normative understandings of Christianity (ch. 18). Menon finds the impetus for transformative change through a reinterpretation of Hindu texts and teachings (ch. 13).

COMPLEXITY

An overall observation about the grand corpus of Girard's work is that, under the rubrics of mimetic desire and the scapegoat/sacrificial mechanisms, there are a complex array of dynamics whereby passions that fuel violence are generated, diffused, hidden, and revealed. In like manner, this volume, which looks at ways of reconciling, nonviolent ways that do not involve scapegoating, presents as a metamessage that reconciliation is a complex phenomenon. There are no formulas or shortcuts to reconciliation in the wake of deep hurts and trauma. The strands of injustice, trauma, woundedness, abuse of power, and systemic violence—all must be attended to. Just as, from a scientific point of view, bumblebees should not be able to fly (too heavy), so from a material/realistic point of view, reconciliation should not be possible. Yet both take place. Limits, challenges, and obstacles are transcended. The various chapters of this book point to animating factors that put wind under the wings of those who wish to attempt the apparently impossible. Each instance of reconciliation can be framed as an instance of emergent creativity, a phenomenon attributed to complex adaptive systems (Kauffman 2008). This means that when the circumstances are right—when the various elements of reconciliation are present and there is an openness to proceed—those caught up in violent conflict can find themselves mimetically changing; that is, change happens within themselves and in the relationship. This change is an emerging phenomenon that can be encouraged but cannot be forced. The opening up of ourselves, as individual and collective entities, to the potential of reconciliation in trying circumstances constitutes hope. This is a hope grounded empirically in the fact that reconciliation happens and theoretically in the conceptual base that is itself creatively emerging. The chapters in this book support to a new conceptual *Gestalt* that is becoming increasingly influential.

REFERENCES

Adams, Rebecca. 2000. "Loving Mimesis and Girard's 'Scapegoat of the Text': A Creative Reassessment of Mimetic Desire." Pp. 277–307 in *Violence Renounced: René Girard, Biblical Studies, and Peacemaking*, edited by Willard M. Swartley. Telford, PA: Pandora Press.

Girard, René. 1976. *Deceit, Desire, and the Novel: Self and Other in Literary Structure.* Translated by Y. Freccero. Baltimore: Johns Hopkins University Press.

Kauffman, Stuart A. 2008. *Reinventing the Sacred: A New View of Science, Reason, and Religion.* New York: Basic Books.

Newman, Louise. 2010. *Repentance: The Meaning & Practice of Teshuvah.* Woodstock, VT: Jewish Lights.

Ricoeur, Paul. 1984. *Time and Narrative,* Volume 1. Translated by Kathleen McLaughlin and David Pellauer. Chicago: University of Chicago Press.

Index

About the Contributors

Nadia Delicata is lecturer in fundamental moral theology and Christianity and culture, Faculty of Theology, University of Malta. Interested in the theology of the Christian life in the digital age through the cultural hermeneutic of media ecology and Girard's mimetic theory, she authored "Marshall McLuhan: Media Ecologist and Educator," special edition *Extraordinary Canadian Thinkers*, *Journal of Ultimate Reality and Meaning* (2012).

Kathy Frost teaches social psychology at St. Joseph's College, Long Island, New York. A Fulbright Scholar to Romania (1998–2000; 2004–2005), she is now using mimetic theory to reinterpret studies of intergroup conflict in the field of social psychology, highlighting the interdividual nature of human existence and its implications for agency. Her article "Hate, Individualism and Dialogue," was published in *Humanity and Society*.

Sandor Goodhart is a professor of English and Jewish studies at Purdue University. A former President of the Colloquium on Violence and Religion, he is a leading scholar on the links between Girard and Levinas. His books include *Sacrificing Commentary: Reading the End of Literature* and (forthcoming) *The Prophetic Law: Essays in Judaism, Girardianism, Literary Studies, and the Ethical.*

Sue-Anne Hess is a recent graduate of the MA (Conflict Studies, Saint Paul University, Ottawa) program and is keenly interested in the place of creativity as a means to resolve and heal conflict. As a seasoned public speaker, she is passionate about stimulating dialogue and creating opportunities for new directions of thought.

Joel Hodge is lecturer in the School of Theology at the Australian Catholic University (St. Patrick's Campus, Melbourne). Author of *Resisting Violence and Victimisation: Christian Faith and Solidarity in East Timor* (Ashgate, 2012) and co-editor of *Violence, Desire, and the Sacred: Girard's Mimetic Theory Across the Disciplines* (Continuum, 2012), he is also founding treasurer and Secretary of the Australian Girard Seminar.

Angela Kiraly is completing an MA in Conflict Studies, Saint Paul University, Ottawa, Canada. Her thesis is on post-conflict reconciliation and reconstruction programming, with a focus on the conflict in the former Yugoslavia. She has engaged in youth outreach work in Ireland in 2008–2009, and held a position at the United Nations Development Program Interagency Framework Team for Preventative Action in 2013.

Rupa Menon, with an MA in Conflict Studies, Saint Paul University, Ottawa, an MA in Psychology, and further training in counseling, facilitation, and coaching, has been providing coaching to new immigrants and Canadian public servants, particularly in Health Canada.

Steve Moore, director of Development, Integrative Peacebuilding, Saint Paul University, served for 22 years as a padre in the Canadian Forces (CF), including Bosnia (1993) and Afghanistan (research). Based on his work, the CF Army Capabilities Development Board endorsed Religious Leader Engagement (RLE). His recent book is *Military Chaplains as Agents of Peace: Religious Leader Engagement in Conflict and Post-conflict Environments*.

Duncan Morrow, lecturer in politics and director of Community Engagement, University of Ulster, Northern Ireland (NI), is former chief executive, NI Community Relations Council. For over 20 years, he has worked toward reconciliation in community processes, research, policy development, and work with victims and survivors of conflict. He was the sentence review commissioner responsible for the early release of prisoners, following the 1988 Good Friday Peace Agreement.

Jon Pahl, Peter Paul and Elizabeth Hagan Professor of History, Lutheran Theological Seminary, Philadelphia, is the author of six books, including *Empire of Sacrifice: The Religious Origins of American Violence* and *Shopping Malls and Other Sacred Spaces: Putting God in Place*. Nearing completion is *A Coming Religious Peace*.

Leonhard Praeg is associate professor in Political and International Studies at Rhodes University, South Africa. He has published books and articles on African philosophy and violence in postcolonial Africa. His current research focus is African humanism and his book, *A Report on Ubuntu*, will appear in 2014 (UKZN Press).

Vern Neufeld Redekop is Professor of conflict studies at Saint Paul University, Ottawa. His involvement in training and program development has taken him to Indigenous communities in Canada as well as to Bosnia and Herzegovina, Sudan, Taiwan, and other countries. His theoretical and practical insights found expression in his book, *From Violence to Blessing: How an Understanding of Deep-Rooted Conflict Can Open Paths to Reconciliation* (2002). Most recently, Oxford University Press has published *Introduction to Conflict Studies: Empirical, Theoretical, and Ethical Dimensions* (2012), a textbook which he co-authored with Jean-Francois Rioux. Current research focuses on Spirituality, Emergent Creativity and Reconciliation, for which he received a Templeton grant, and social reconciliation and its links to economic development.

Frank C. Richardson is professor of educational psychology (emeritus), University of Texas, Austin. His research interests include the philosophy of social science, theoretical psychology, and topics in psychology and religion. He is the author of several books and many chapters and articles in these fields. The title of one of his latest articles is "On Psychology and Virtue Ethics."

Miguel de Las Casas Rolland, OP, is a Dominican friar and the current pastor of Santa Maria de Guadalupe mission parish in Mexicali, Baja California, Mexico. He earned his PhD in socio-cultural anthropology from Arizona State University (2012). His research focus is understanding inter-subjective aspects of mimetic desire from an ethnographic perspective, especially among the Maya Tzotzil Chamula of Chiapas, Mexico.

Thomas Ryba is Notre Dame Theologian-in-Residence at the Saint Thomas Aquinas Catholic Center lecturer in philosophy and religious studies and Adjunct Professor of Jewish studies at Purdue University. His primary interests are systematic theology, the history of ideas, and the historical relations between theology, religion, philosophy, science, and ideology. Author of *The Essence of Phenomenology and Its Meaning for the Scientific Study of Religion* (1991) and over fifty articles on theology, philosophical theology, and theories of religion, Ryba is principal editor of *The Comity and Grace of Method* (2004), contributed to *Revelation: Catholic and Muslim Perspectives* (2006) and *The Blackwell Companion to the Study of Religion* (2006), and is co-editor with Sandor Goodhart of *For René Girard: Essays in Friendship and in Truth* (2008).

Peter Smith is assistant professor of peacemaking & conflict studies at Fresno Pacific University. Prior to this appointment, he served for several years as a peace educator in Zambia as part of Mennonite Central Committee. His research interests lie in the varied intersections of peacemaking and theology, cultural understandings of peace, and in mimetic theory and conflict transformation.

Cynthia Stirbys is Saulteaux-Cree from the Cowessess First Nation in Saskatchewan. She holds a Master's of Arts degree in Conflict Studies and is completing her PhD at the University of Ottawa. Using the classic grounded theory methodology, her focus in research is the Indian residential school experience. Her research motivation is to optimally advance Indigenous peoples' well-being.

Cameron Thomson, PhD, University of Toronto, works in the areas of moral philosophy and philosophy of religion. His research puts Girard's mimetic theory into conversation with such figures as Kant, Hume, Freud, Adorno, Habermas, Agamben, and Derrida, and centers upon the topics of mimesis, freedom, moral accountability and especially, crime and punishment—in both the latters' political and eschatological registers.

Nikolaus Wandinger, associate professor, dogmatic theology, University of Innsbruck, Austria, studies in philosophy and Catholic theology in Innsbruck, San Francisco and Berkeley, California. Main fields of research are theology of the human person (sin and grace), Christology, dramatic theology, theology in pop culture.

Eugene Webb is professor emeritus in the Henry M. Jackson School of International Studies at the University of Washington, where he organized and chaired both the Comparative Religion Program and the European Studies Program. His most recent books are *World View and Mind: Religious Thought and Psychological Development* (2009) and *In Search of the Triune God: The Christian Paths of East and West* (2013).